THE LONGMAN STANDARD HISTORY OF MODERN PHILOSOPHY

THE LONGMAN
STANDARD HISTORY
OF MODERN
PHILOSOPHY

DANIEL KOLAK

William Paterson University of New Jersey

GARRETT THOMSON

College of Wooster

PEARSON

Longman

New York   San Francisco   Boston
London   Toronto   Sydney   Tokyo   Singapore   Madrid
Mexico City   Munich   Paris   Cape Town   Hong Kong   Montreal

Publisher: Priscilla McGeehon
Executive Marketing Manager: Ann Stypuloski
Supplements Editor: Kristi Olsoh
Production Manager: Denise Phillip
Project Coordination, Text Design, and Electronic Page Makeup: WestWords, Inc.
Senior Cover Designer/Manager: Nancy Danahy
Cover Photo: © Corbis/Sygma. England, Oxfordshire, Woodstock, Blenheim Palace.
   Photographer: Sandro Vannirii
Senior Manufacturing Buyer: Dennis J. Para
Printer and Binder: Courier Corporation
Cover Printer: Courier Corporation

Library of Congress Cataloging-in-Publication Data

Kolak, Daniel.
  The Longman standard history of philosophy / Daniel Kolak, Garrett Thomson.
     p. cm.
  Includes bibliographical references and index.
  ISBN 0-321-23511-8 (volume 6 (comprehensive) : alk. paper)—ISBN 0-321-23513-4
(volume 1 (ancient) : alk. paper)—ISBN 0-321-23512-6 (volume 3 (modern) : alk. paper)—
ISBN 0-321-23510-X (volume 5 (20th century) : alk. paper)
  1. Philosophy—History. I. Title: Standard history of philosophy. II. Thomson, Garrett. III. Title.
  B72.K635 2006
  190—dc22

                                                              2005010370

Please visit our website at http://www.ablongman.com

ISBN 0-321-23512-6

1 2 3 4 5 6 7 8 9 10—CRS—08 07 06 05

◆ CONTENTS ◆

III: THE EMPIRICISTS   179

❖ PREFACE. ❖

Philosophy may not be the oldest profession but it is the oldest discipline, the source of our views about reality, knowledge, and morality. To understand the revolutionary nature of the evolution of philosophy is to understand ourselves and our world anew. Inspired by the intellectual intimacy that philosophy affords, the mind is broadened and refreshed. In that sense philosophy is always anything but old: awash with new possibilities of inquiry and understanding, the illuminating questions of philosophy liberate us from the blinding obviousness of accepted answers, the blinders of our individual and collective biases.

Though philosophers build upon the work of their predecessors, they continually revise and often overthrow the views of their predecessors—sometimes, even those of their own teachers. One of the most famous examples is the sequence from Socrates to Plato to Aristotle. And yet throughout the evolution of thought that philosophy heralds much remains the same: the call to wonder, to dispute, to question, to liberate, to ponder, to inquire, to understand everything one can about the whole of our being—reality, knowledge, and morality—without becoming ourselves closed off. To behold the whole without being conquered by the wholeness of the vision, that is the sum and substance of the western intellectual tradition made possible by philosophy. To see new wisdom in the old and old wisdom in the new is to be not just learned but wise. And to not just tolerate such expansive openness but to love it now and then is what it means to be a philosopher, then and now. This book may not make you a philosopher. But it will provide you with everything you need to become one. A big claim and, therefore, a big book: with 28 of the greatest works by 16 of the most important western philosophers from the modern period, this volume assembles into one book some of the most profound and edifying ideas in the history of human thought. In addition to the metaphysical and epistemological classics of the period, this volume contains some of the major ethical and political works of modern thought such as those of Hobbes, Locke, Rousseau and Kant. It also includes selections from major scientific thinkers such as Copernicus, Kepler, Galileo and Newton.

Suitable for a one-semester introduction to modern philosophy, history of philosophy, history of ideas, or western intellectual history, this book is a covert assembly with a covert purpose, to bring philosophy to you but even more importantly: to bring you to philosophy.

We have structured the book to make this possible. The volume as a whole is divided into four standard divisions: "Section I, the Philosophers of Nature," "Section II, the Rationalists," "Section III, the Empiricists," and "Section IV, the Enlightenment Philosophers." Each Part opens with a "Prologue", offering a context for specific philosophers, such as "Prologue to Locke," or to key schools of thought, such as "Prologue to Rationalism." These are designed to let you in on what has come before, so that you don't enter the conversation in the middle. Individual "Biographical Histories" give pertinent details about the life and times of each philosopher, such as "Leibniz: A Biographical History." The pur-pose is to show you that philosophers are neither divine demigods nor depersonalized thinking machines but individual human beings with a penchant for grappling with the perennial big questions. The purpose of the "Philosophical Overviews" to each philosopher is two-fold: first, to show how that philosopher's thinking about reality, knowledge and morality integrate into a coherent view; second, to integrate each particular philosopher into a broader philosophical context. Each reading selection comes with its own concise introduction designed to quicken your entry into the issues and prepare you for what is to come. The selections themselves have been chosen for their profundity and edited to high-light the central importance, while leaving in the all-important methods, processes, and development of the views expressed therein. Where translations are involved, we have in each case selected the most lucid. The "Study Questions" at the end of each chapter, such as "Study Questions for Kant's Critique of Pure Reason," provide comprehension questions as well as wider discussion questions; these are for you, to test yourself, to see how well you have understood what you have read. "The Philosophical Bridges" at the end of each chap-ter, such as "The Influence of Hume," summarizes the influence of each thinker on later generations in order that you can appreciate the threads connecting different periods and see how philosophy's perennial questions lead to ever more evolving views.

For those readers who would prefer a historical structure, please use the following order:

Copernicus, *On the Revolutions of Celestial Orbs* (1543) 1, p. 7
Galileo, *The Sidereal Messenger* (1610) 3, p. 19
Bacon, *Novum Organum* (1620) 9, p. 182
Descartes, *Meditations On the First Philosophy* (1641) 5, p. 42
Hobbes, *Leviathan* (1651) 10, p. 205
Pascal, *Pensées* (1659) 6, p. 102
Spinoza, *The Ethics* (1677) 7, p. 109
Newton, *Principia* (1687) 4, p. 30
Locke, *An Essay Concerning Human Understanding* (1690) 11, p. 224
Berkeley, *A Treatise Concerning the Principles of Human Knowledge* (1710) 12, p. 281
Leibniz, *Monadology* (1714) 8, p. 168
Hume, *A Treatise of Human Nature* (1740) 13, p. 358
An Enquiry Concerning Human Understanding (1748) 13, p. 324
Rousseau, *The Social Contract* (1762) 15, p. 380
Voltaire, *Dictionary of Philosophy* (1764) 14, p. 375
Kant, *Critique of Pure Reason* (1781) 16, p. 392

The numbers on the right indicate the existing sections of the volume.

Special thanks to each of the following reviewers, whose comments about one or more of the volumes in the "Longman Standard History of Philosophy" series helped to enhance each book.

Michael L. Anderson, University of Maryland
Marina P. Banchetti-Robino, Florida Atlantic University
David Boersema, Pacific University
Stephen Braude, University of Maryland Baltimore County
Cynthia K. Brown, Catholic University of America

Richard J. Burke, Oakland University
Marina Bykova, North Carolina State University
Jeffrey Carr, Christopher Newport University
James P. Cooney, Montgomery County Community College
Elmer H. Duncan, Baylor University
Christian Early, Eastern Mennonite University
Emma L. Easteppe, Boise State University
James E. Falcouner, Brigham Young University
Chris L. Firestone, Trinity International University
Merigala Gabriel, Georgia Southern University
Bruce Hauptli, Florida International University
Larry Hauser, Alma College
David J. Hilditch, Webster University
Mary Beth Ingham, Loyola Marymount University
Betty Kiehl, Palomar College
John H. Kulten, Jr., University of Missouri
Nelson P. Lande, University of Massachusetts
Dorothea Lotter, Wake Forest University
Charles S. MacKenzie, Reformed Theological Seminary
Thomas J. Martin, University of North Carolina Charlotte
D. A. Masolo, University of Louisville
Leemon B. McHenry, California State University, Northridge
John T. Meadors, Mississippi College
Glenn Melancon, Southeastern Oklahoma State University
Mark Michael, Austin Peay State University
Thomas Osborne, University of Nevada, Las Vegas
Walter Ott, East Tennessee State University
Anna Christina Ribeiro, University of Maryland
Stefanie Rocknak, Hartwick College
George Rudebusch, Northern Arizona University
Ari Santas, Valdosta State University
Candice Shelby, University of Colorado-Denver
Daniel Silber, Florida Southern College
Allan Silverman, Ohio State University
James K. Swindler, Illinois State University
David B. Twetten, Marquette University
Thomas Upton, Gannon University
Barry F. Vaughan, Mesa Community College
Daniel R. White, Florida Atlantic University
David M. Wisdo, Columbus State University
Evelyn Wortsman Deluty, Nassau Community College

We would like to thank the following people for their help. Brandon West of the College of Wooster for his sterling work as a student research assistant. Amy Erickson and Patrice Reeder of the College of Wooster for their unfailing secretarial help. Professors Martin Gunderson, Ron Hustwit, Henry Kreuzman, Adrian Moore, Elizabeth Schiltz, and Philip Turetzsky for their useful comments. Everyone at Longman Publishers for their very professional work, especially Priscilla McGeehon, who has supported the project with tireless energy and enthusiasm. Our wives, Wendy and Helena, for their help and understanding. Finally, we would like to dedicate this volume to our children: Julia, Sophia, Dylan, and Andre Kolak; and to Andrew, Frances, Verena, Susana, and Robert Thomson.

One can view the modern period as an extraordinary drama, an intense struggle between two worldviews: medieval Scholastic thought and the emerging modern science. This struggle led eventually to the Enlightenment. Such a view simplifies the intellectual history of the medieval period by ignoring the wealth and diversity of its thought; nevertheless, the following sketch captures a relevant aspect of history.

During the medieval period, a tiny minority of people had access to learning, and almost exclusively through the Church, which controlled dogma. The general medieval picture of the universe was inherited from the ancient philosophers. The earth was seen as the center of the universe, around which there are seven spheres, or domes. The universe was composed of the four elements: earth, water, air, and fire. Philosophical disputes were settled often by appeal to two authorities, scripture and Aristotle. This simplified picture does not apply to the great philosophers of the medieval period such as William of Ockham and Thomas Aquinas.

In the thirteenth century, Aquinas tried to reconcile the revelations of Christianity with the earthly knowledge of Aristotle, and attempted to show that theological claims are consistent with the demands of reason. His *Summa Theologica* became the main textbook for instruction in theology. Thomas' version of Aristotle became Scholastic dogma. The Church, worried about any deviations from authorized belief, actively discouraged free learning. For example, as late as 1586, the Jesuits issued the following doctrine: 'In logic, natural philosophy, ethics and metaphysics, Aristotle's doctrine is to be followed.'

The revolution that changed all this was political, scientific, and conceptual. There are some important landmarks in the political and social revolution. The first was the invention of the printing press in 1455. As more and cheaper books became available, more people outside church institutions became interested in learning, and there emerged a European community of freethinkers. The second landmark occurred in 1517, when Martin Luther rebelled against the Catholic Church in Germany. Scandalized by the indulgences being sold by the Church, he campaigned publicly for its reform. Finally, Luther established a new church, which led to the proliferation of Protestant sects around Europe. The third milestone was the greater separation of the state from the Church, especially in northern Europe. During the medieval period, the Church was the most powerful and wealthy institution in Europe. The pope appointed and dismissed kings and emperors, while the Church taxed nations for the Crusades and for its buildings and administration. After Luther, many northern European states became independent of the Roman Church, and the new Protestant churches were in a subordinate position to the state. For example, in 1531, Henry VIII established the Church of England. Just as Johannes Gutenberg's printing press made Luther possible, Luther made Henry VIII possible.

Throughout the fifteenth and sixteenth centuries, learning became gradually more independent of Christianity. Philosophy separated itself slowly from theology. As Europe became wealthier, a new middle class developed, which included professionals devoted to learning outside ecclesiastical institutions. Furthermore, the Renaissance in Italy caused a huge increase in translations of classical pagan works, including those of Plato and the atomist Lucretius. The arts and humanism flourished. There was a fresh confidence in the air and a new desire for learning. By the end of the sixteenth century, the conditions were ripe for a revolutionary change. The modern era was about to be born. Modern science and philosophy began to replace Aristotelian Scholasticism. Probably, the three people most important in causing these changes were Galileo Galilei, Francis Bacon, and René Descartes.

The Birth of Science

Philosophically, the modern challenge to the Scholastic tradition was a dispute about the nature of evidence and explanation.

1. Evidence: up to the late sixteenth century, an investigation consisted in studying authoritative texts such as those of Aquinas and the Bible, and debate comprised citing and making deductions from them. However, the emerging new sciences, such as astronomy, had no place for arguments from authority. They relied on observation and reasoning. The English philosopher Francis Bacon strongly attacked authoritarian arguments on the grounds that the new sciences required freedom from the old traditions to investigate the universe without prejudice and superstition.

2. Explanation: traditionally, medieval thinkers tried to explain natural events, such as the motion of planets, in terms of natural and divine purposes. Viewed in this way, nature becomes the handiwork of God. Early modern philosophers, such as Descartes and Bacon, argued that final causes could not be used in the scientific study of matter. They replaced explanation by purposes with mechanistic explanation employing physical causal laws. Additionally, medieval tradition conceived the universe as a hierarchical whole, with different levels of being. Between the macrocosmic universe and the microcosm man, there existed affinities which were used in explanation.

In sharp contrast, according to Galileo and Descartes, the study of nature should concern itself only with the measurable properties of matter, such as size, shape, and motion. This puts all natural things on the same level, subject to the same mathematical, physical laws, and it means that natural objects differ only in quantitative ways. This, in turn, implies the rejection of Aristotle's four elements, earth, water, air, and fire, and the denial of his distinction between the lower earthly and the higher celestial levels.

At stake in this conflict was the nature of the universe and human life. According to the medieval view, the universe was a quasi-organic piece of handiwork created by God, full of omens and signs. Modern science seemed to portray the universe as completely material, and all changes as mechanical, leaving no place for the soul or for God and, thus, threatening to make religion redundant. On the other hand, the optimism of the new science promised progress and freedom.

Descartes framed the fundamental questions of this age of transformation. How could the new sciences be reconciled with religion? Descartes pioneered this philosophical reflection. He saw the need to reevaluate the basis of knowledge in order to reconcile the new science with religion. He wrote: 'No more useful inquiry can be proposed than that which seeks to determine the nature and scope of human knowledge' (AT X 397).

The Rise and Conflicts of Modern Philosophy

The changes of the modern period occurred gradually. Furthermore, despite the radical break with the past, the science of Descartes' time was not like that of today. What we today call the scientific method was very much a work in progress. Therefore, the modern philosophers were struggling not only with the broad philosophical implications of the new science, but also with its important details. As a result, the modern period contains an extraordinary burst of philosophical activity and a proliferation of different metaphysical views about the nature of the universe.

The development of science implicitly contained two models of knowledge. The first is typified by insistence on the importance of experimentation and sense experience, on the idea that hypotheses based on carefully made observations are less susceptible to error. The second model is based on the example of mathematics, on the idea that reasoning logically from self-evident truths yields error-free conclusions. Based on these two models, we can give a simplified portrait of modern philosophy by distinguishing two currents of thought about knowledge: Empiricism and Rationalism. Whereas Empiricists emphasize the empirical source of knowledge, the Rationalists stress its rational nature.

Furthermore, to extend this picture, although the early Empiricists stated the principles of Empiricism, they did not realize their full implications, and George Berkeley and David Hume progressively took these Empiricist principles to their logical conclusion. Similarly, although Descartes articulated the fundamental principles of Rationalism, he did not apply them consistently, and Baruch de Spinoza and Gottfried Leibniz took Rationalism to its logical conclusion.

Finally, Immanuel Kant tried to transcend these two major currents of thought. He argued against the extreme positions of both Hume and Leibniz by giving a nonempiricist critique of Rationalism, and thereby forging a new vision of the world and humanity's place in it, which emphasized the importance of human freedom. In this way, Kant represents the final step in the huge change from the Scholastic medieval worldview to that of the Enlightenment.

Of course, this picture of the development of modern philosophy from Galileo to Kant is an oversimplification. The thinkers of the period did not see themselves as members of any philosophical school; the Empiricist/Rationalist distinction was invented after the fact. Furthermore, often the similarities between a so-called Empiricist and a so-called Rationalist are more striking than their differences. For instance, one could classify Thomas Hobbes as both and Blaise Pascal as neither. Also, the picture ignores many other important thinkers of the time, such as Pierre Gassendi, Nicolas Malebranche, Thomas Reid, Christian Wolff, and Mary Wollstonecraft. Nevertheless, this rough classification helps make initial sense of the modern era, and the great philosophers of the period can be divided provisionally according to the table of contents of this volume.

Toward the Enlightenment

The modern period also saw a dramatic revolution in thinking about morality, politics, and human values. The medieval conception of values was based largely on the authority of God, both in politics and ethics. In contrast, Descartes, Bacon, and Hobbes optimistically stressed the practical potential of science to improve the material lives of people, and the dominant conception of morality became based increasingly on reason (or, in the case of Hume, human feeling), rather than God's commands. At the same time, the conception of the state altered. Hobbes and John Locke tried to apply the principles of reason to political thought. They initiated a process that replaced the old concept of divinely appointed kings or rulers with the idea of a social contract that guaranteed certain freedoms and rights for the citizen. This new political philosophy went hand in glove with changes in the power structures governing society, especially in England, where the elected Parliament gradually gained ascendancy over the king.

In this, Locke was the pioneer. His philosophy was directed against authoritarianism, dogma, and the repression of individual free thought. He developed a conception of political power based not on command, but on consent. He advanced a view of knowledge founded on individual experience instead of dogma and authority, and an understanding of religion that embraced tolerance. This led the way to the French Enlightenment of Voltaire, to the French Revolution, and, finally, to the ideals enshrined in the Constitution of the United States of America.

SECTION I

◇ THE PHILOSOPHERS ◇

OF NATURE

PROLOGUE

Nothing quite captures the revolutionary spirit of the modern period as the rapid development of science. There are only about 120 years between Nicholas Copernicus' main publication in 1540 and 1666, the year during which Newton made many of his discoveries. Copernicus' claim that the earth orbits the sun is regarded as a historical watershed because his view challenged decisively the authority of the church, and also because it was the first in a series of astronomical discoveries that led finally to Newton's theory of motion and gravity.

When Copernicus first advanced his heretical claim, science as such hardly existed. There was no accepted idea of inert matter, and no conception of mathematical causal laws that explain mechanically all natural phenomena. The concept of rigorous experimentation was not established. In fact, Copernicus himself had no direct evidence for his bold hypothesis. In short, physics as we know it did not exist; there were quietly emerging but unconnected areas of physical investigation, such as magnetism, mechanics, and astronomy, but there was no idea how these might be unified under one single branch of knowledge, namely, physics as the scientific study of matter in motion. Insofar as the discipline of physics existed at this time, it consisted solely in the authority of Aristotle's teleological physics, which was taught at the universities.

After Copernicus, the situation changed with four parallel fundamental developments. First, there was the groundbreaking astronomical work of Tycho Brahe and Johannes Kepler. Brahe's patient years of detailed observation of planetary movements permitted Kepler to formulate finally three simple laws that describe all planetary motion. Surprisingly, the planets orbited around the sun in ellipses and not circles as had been assumed. Second, Galileo made a huge leap forward in the development of mechanics by postulating the law of inertia, namely, that a body will continue in uniform motion in a straight line unless acted on by some external force. This further undermined Aristotle's physics. Third, Galileo also began to formulate the notion of matter as an inert substance governed by mechanical laws, thereby jettisoning the ancient idea of the four elements and Aristotle's conception of natural purposes. Descartes extended this conception of matter and, from it, built the idea of physics as a way of explaining all physical phenomena, thereby unifying the otherwise disjointed studies mentioned earlier. Fourth, the work of all these and other investigators contributed toward an increasingly explicit formulation of a new scientific method based on mathematically precise observations under experimental conditions and on deductions from those results.

These four streams of development converged in the genius of Isaac Newton, whose work can be regarded as the pinnacle of modern science at least until the 1800s. Regarding the first two streams, Newton's laws of motion and his theory of gravity unified Galileo's mechanics with Kepler's laws of planetary motion. Concerning the third stream, Newton's laws seemed to underlie all instances of matter in motion and, thereby, constitute the fundamental physical theory. Finally, Newton introduced explicitly a new level of rigor into the scientific method by emphatically rejecting speculation and imprecision.

NICOLAUS COPERNICUS (1473–1543)

Biographical History

Nicolaus Copernicus was born in Torun in a part of Poland that had previously been Prussia; his mother was Prussian and his father was Polish. After the death of his father in 1483, he came under the charge of his uncle, the prince bishop of Ermland. At the age of 18, Copernicus was dispatched to the University of Cracow to study for the priesthood. He convinced his uncle to allow him to move to the University of Bologna in Italy, where he studied astronomy and mathematics, becoming fascinated by the radical idea that the earth orbited the sun. Meanwhile, his uncle had appointed him a canon in the cathedral of Frauenburg in Polish Prussia. In 1500, Copernicus returned to Italy to study law and medicine. He gained a degree in law in 1503, after which he worked for the Church back in Poland. During this time, Copernicus worked on trying to prove the hypothesis that the earth orbited the sun. Finally, around 1514, he wrote his findings in a pamphlet called the *Little Commentary*, which he circulated. Pope Leo X expressed interest in the theory, and Luther scorned it, but Copernicus' work attracted little attention among scientists until 1539, when a young German mathematician, Georg Rheticus, expressed enthusiastic support of Copernicus' findings. Meahwhile, Copernicus had completed his main work, *On the Revolutions of Celestial Orbs*, and Rheticus finally convinced him to publish the work in 1542. It was published a few weeks before Copernicus' death, with a dedication to Pope Paul III. Copernicus was handed a copy of his work on the day of his death.

Philosophical Overview

The ancient cosmology of Ptolemy assumed that the earth was still and the planets and sun revolved around it. To make this theory fit new observations, Ptolemy's successors had had to postulate increasingly complex epicycles. When the movement of a planet was not a perfect circle, another smaller circle, called an epicycle, was postulated. By the time of the Renaissance, Ptolemy's original theory had become very complex and inelegant.

Copernicus first heard of the hypothesis that the earth orbited around the sun while he was studying in Bologna. The idea had been proposed by a few ancient astronomers and also by a few more recent writers such as Nicolaus de Cusa (1401–1464). Copernicus' investigations led him to the conclusion that further reform of the Ptolemic system was impractical. Because of his neo-Platonic background, Copernicus was convinced that a few simple mathematical laws must govern the universe and so he took the bold step of working out the detailed implications of this heliocentric hypothesis. He did not have the equipment to make many new astronomical observations, but in general, he worked with already existing data. In fact, the data that he had do not clearly support his theory. Indeed, Copernicus had to postulate that the sun was not quite the center of the solar system. Despite the fact that Copernicus' theory was not very well supported by the evidence, his theory paved the way to those of Kepler and Galileo, and, for reasons explained in the Philosophical Bridges after the reading, it caused a revolution.

ON THE REVOLUTIONS OF CELESTIAL ORBS

Notice that Copernicus advances his thesis as a hypothesis rather than as a true theory. He argues that the planets revolved around the sun in the sequence of Mercury, Venus, Earth, Mars, Jupiter, and Saturn. He starts his argument from the claim that Venus and Mercury revolve around the sun. On this basis, he argues that Mars, Jupiter, and Saturn also have the sun as the center of their orbit in ever-increasing spheres. He argues that there is a space for a sphere or orbit in between those of Venus and Mars, whose solar orbits would take respectively 9 months and 2 years. He then tries to explain the perceived reversals of direction in the planets as caused by the movement of the earth. Finally, he postulates a threefold motion of the earth.

TO HIS HOLINESS, POPE PAUL III, NICOLAUS COPERNICUS' PREFACE TO HIS BOOKS ON THE REVOLUTIONS

I can readily imagine, Holy Father, that as soon
5 as some people hear that in this volume, which I have written about the revolutions of the spheres of the universe, I ascribe certain motions to the terrestrial globe, they will shout that I must be immediately repudiated together with this belief. For I am not so enamored of my own opinions that I disregard what others may think of them. I am aware that a philosopher's ideas are not subject to the judgement of ordinary persons,
10 because it is his endeavor to seek the truth in all things, to the extent permitted to human reason by God. Yet I hold that completely erroneous

views should be shunned. Those who know that the consensus of many centuries has sanctioned the conception that the earth remains at rest in the middle of the heaven as its center would, I reflected, regard it as an insane pronouncement
15 if I made the opposite assertion that the earth moves. Therefore I debated with myself for a long time whether to publish the volume which I wrote to prove the earth's motion or rather to follow the example of the Pythagoreans and certain others, who used to transmit philosophy's secrets only to kinsmen and friends, not in writing but by word of mouth, as is shown by Lysis' letter to
20 Hipparchus. And they did so, it seems to me, not, as some suppose, because they were in some way jealous about their teachings, which would be

Nicolaus Copernicus, translation and commentary by Edward Rosen, from *On the Revolutions: Nicolaus Copernicus' Complete Works*, pp. 3, 4–5, 7–8, 20–23. Copyright © 1978 Edward Rosen. Introduction © 1992 Johns Hopkins University Press. Reprinted by permission of Johns Hopkins University Press.

spread around; on the contrary, they wanted the very beautiful thoughts attained by great men of deep devotion not to be ridiculed by those who are reluctant to exert themselves vigorously in any literary pursuit unless it is lucrative; or if they
25 are stimulated to the non-acquisitive study of philosophy by the exhortation and example of others, yet because of their dullness of mind they play the same part among philosophers as drones among bees. When I weighed these considerations, the scorn which I had reason to fear on account of the novelty and unconventionality of my opinion almost induced me to abandon completely the work which I had undertaken.

30   But while I hesitated for a long time and even resisted, my friends drew me back. . . .

They exhorted me no longer to refuse, on
40 account of the fear which I felt, to make my work available for the general use of students of astronomy. The crazier my doctrine of the earth's motion now appeared to most people, the argument ran, so much the more admiration and thanks would it gain after they saw the publication of my writings dispel the fog of absurdity by most luminous proofs. Influenced therefore by these persuasive men and by this hope, in the end
45 I allowed my friends to bring out an edition of the volume, as they had long besought me to do.

However, Your Holiness will perhaps not be greatly surprised that I have dared to publish my studies after devoting so much effort to working them out that I did not hesitate to put down my thoughts about the earth's motion in written form too. But you are rather waiting to hear from me how it occurred to me to venture to conceive any motion of the earth, against the traditional opin-
5 ion of astronomers and almost against common sense. I have accordingly no desire to conceal from Your Holiness that I was impelled to consider a different system of deducing the motions of the universe's spheres for no other reason than the realization that astronomers do not agree among themselves in their investigations of this subject. For, in the first place, they are so uncer-
10 tain about the motion of the sun and moon that they cannot establish and observe a constant length even for the tropical year. Secondly, in determining the motions not only of these bodies

but also of the other five planets, they do not use the same principles, assumptions, and explanations of the apparent revolutions and motions. For while some employ only homocentrics, others
15 utilize eccentrics and epicycles, and yet they do not quite reach their goal. For although those who put their faith in homocentrics showed that some nonuniform motions could be compounded in this way, nevertheless by this means they were unable to obtain any incontrovertible result in absolute agreement with the phenomena. On the other hand, those who devised the eccentrics seem thereby in large measure to have solved the
20 problem of the apparent motions with appropriate calculations. But meanwhile they introduced a good many ideas which apparently contradict the first principles of uniform motion. Nor could they elicit or deduce from the eccentrics the principal consideration, that is, the structure of the universe and the true symmetry of its parts. On the contrary, their experience was just like some
25 one taking from various places hands, feet, a head, and other pieces, very well depicted, it may be, but not for the representation of a single person; since these fragments would not belong to one another at all, a monster rather than a man would be put together from them. Hence in the process of demonstration or "method", as it is called, those who employed eccentrics are found
30 either to have omitted something essential or to have admitted something extraneous and wholly irrelevant. This would not have happened to them, had they followed sound principles. For if the hypotheses assumed by them were not false, everything which follows from their hypotheses would be confirmed beyond any doubt. Even though what I am now saying may be obscure,
35 it will nevertheless become clearer in the proper place.

For a long time, then, I reflected on this confusion in the astronomical traditions concerning the derivation of the motions of the universe's spheres. I began to be annoyed that the movements of the world machine, created for our sake by the best and most systematic Artisan of all,
40 were not understood with greater certainty by the philosophers, who otherwise examined so precisely the most insignificant trifles of this world.

For this reason I undertook the task of rereading the works of all the philosophers which I could obtain to learn whether anyone had ever proposed other motions of the universe's spheres than those expounded by the teachers of astronomy in the schools. And in fact first I found in 45 Cicero that Hicetas supposed the earth to move. Later I also discovered in Plutarch that certain others were of this opinion. I have decided to set his words down here, so that they may be available to everybody:

Some think that the earth remains at rest. But Philolaus the Pythagorean believes that, like the sun and moon, it revolves around the fire in an oblique circle. Heraclides of Pontus and Ecphantus the Pythagorean make the earth move, not in a progressive motion, but like a wheel in a rotation from west to east about its 5 own center.

Therefore, having obtained the opportunity from these sources, I too began to consider the mobility of the earth. And even though the idea seemed absurd, nevertheless I knew that others before me had been granted the freedom to imagine any circles whatever for the purpose of 10 explaining the heavenly phenomena. Hence I thought that I too would be readily permitted to ascertain whether explanations sounder than those of my predecessors could be found for the revolution of the celestial spheres on the assumption of some motion of the earth.

Having thus assumed the motions which I ascribe to the earth later on in the volume, by long and intense study I finally found that if the 15 motions of the other planets are correlated with the orbiting of the earth, and are computed for the revolution of each planet, not only do their phenomena follow therefrom but also the order and size of all the planets and spheres, and heaven itself is so linked together that in no portion of it can anything be shifted without disrupting the remaining parts and the universe as a 20 whole. Accordingly in the arrangement of the volume too I have adopted the following order. In the first book I set forth the entire distribution of the spheres together with the motions which I attribute to the earth, so that this book contains, as it were, the general structure of the universe.

Then in the remaining books I correlate the motions of the other planets and of all the spheres with the movement of the earth so that 25 I may thereby determine to what extent the motions and appearances of the other planets and spheres can be saved if they are correlated with the earth's motions. I have no doubt that acute and learned astronomers will agree with me if, as this discipline especially requires, they are willing to examine and consider, not superficially but thoroughly, what I adduce in this volume in proof of these matters.

BOOK ONE

Introduction

Among the many various literary and artistic pursuits which invigorate men's minds, the strongest affection and utmost zeal should, I think, promote the studies concerned with the most beautiful objects, most deserving to be known. This is the nature of the discipline which deals with the universe's divine revolutions, the asters' motions, sizes, distances, risings and settings, as well as the causes of the other phenomena in the sky, and 10 which, in short, explains its whole appearance. What indeed is more beautiful than heaven, which of course contains all things of beauty?

However, this divine rather than human science, which investigates the loftiest subjects, is 40 not free from perplexities. The main reason is that its principles and assumptions, called "hypotheses" by the Greeks, have been a source of disagreement, as we see, among most of those who undertook to deal with this subject, and so they did not rely on the same ideas.

Chapter 10

5 In my judgement, [therefore] we should not in the least disregard what was familiar to Martianus Capella, the author of an encyclopedia, and to certain other Latin writers. For according to them, Venus and Mercury revolve around the sun as their center. This is the reason, in their opinion, why these planets diverge no farther from the sun than is permitted by the curvature of their revolutions. For they do not encircle the earth,

10 like the other planets, but "have opposite circles".
Then what else do these authors mean but that
the center of their spheres is near the sun? Thus
Mercury's sphere will surely be enclosed within
Venus', which by common consent is more than
twice as big, and inside that wide region it will
occupy a space adequate for itself. If anyone seizes
this opportunity to link Saturn, Jupiter, and Mars
15 also to that center, provided he understands their
spheres to be so large that together with Venus
and Mercury the earth too is enclosed inside and
encircled, he will not be mistaken, as is shown by
the regular pattern of their motions.

For [these outer planets] are always closest to
the earth, as is well known, about the time of
their evening rising, that is, when they are in
20 opposition to the sun, with the earth between
them and the sun. On the other hand, they are at
their farthest from the earth at the time of their
evening setting, when they become invisible in
the vicinity of the sun, namely, when we have
the sun between them and the earth. These facts
are enough to show that their center belongs
more to the sun, and is identical with the center
25 around which Venus and Mercury likewise execute their revolutions.

But since all these planets are related to a
single center, the space remaining between
Venus' convex sphere and Mars' concave sphere
must be set apart as also a sphere or spherical
shell, both of whose surfaces are concentric with
those spheres. This [intercalated sphere] receives
30 the earth together with its attendant, the moon,
and whatever is contained within the moon's
sphere. Mainly for the reason that in this space
we find quite an appropriate and adequate place
for the moon, we can by no means detach it from
the earth, since it is incontrovertibly nearest to
the earth.

Hence I feel no shame in asserting that this
35 whole region engirdled by the moon, and the
center of the earth, traverse this grand circle
amid the rest of the planets in an annual revolution around the sun. Near the sun is the center of
the universe. Moreover, since the sun remains
stationary, whatever appears as a motion of the
sun is really due rather to the motion of the
earth. In comparison with any other spheres of

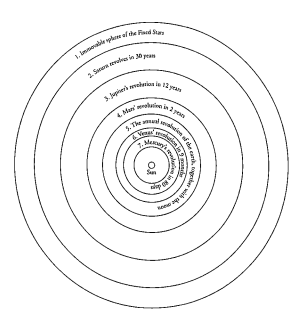

the planets, the distance from the earth to the
40 sun has a magnitude which is quite appreciable
in proportion to those dimensions. But the size of
the universe is so great that the distance earth-
sun is imperceptible in relation to the sphere of
the fixed stars. This should be admitted, I
believe, in preference to perplexing the mind
with an almost infinite multitude of spheres, as
must be done by those who kept the earth in
45 the middle of the universe. On the contrary, we
should rather heed the wisdom of nature. Just as
it especially avoids producing anything superfluous or useless, so it frequently prefers to endow a
single thing with many effects.

All these statements are difficult and almost inconceivable, being of course opposed to
the beliefs of many people. Yet, as we proceed,
with God's help I shall make them clearer than
sunlight, at any rate to those who are not unac-
quainted with the science of astronomy. Conse-
5 quently, with the first principle remaining intact,
for nobody will propound a more suitable principle than that the size of the spheres is measured by the length of the time, the order of
the spheres is the following, beginning with the
highest.

The first and the highest of all is the sphere
of the fixed stars, which contains itself and every-

thing, and is therefore immovable. It is unquestionably the place of the universe, to which the
motion and position of all the other heavenly
bodies are compared. Some people think that it
also shifts in some way. A different explanation
of why this appears to be so will be adduced in
my discussion of the earth's motion [I, 11].

[The sphere of the fixed stars] is followed by
the first of the planets, Saturn, which completes
its circuit in 30 years. After Saturn, Jupiter
accomplishes its revolution in 12 years. Then
Mars revolves in 2 years. The annual revolution
takes the series' fourth place, which contains the
earth, as I said [earlier in I, 10], together with
the lunar sphere as an epicycle. In the fifth place
Venus returns in 9 months. Lastly, the sixth
place is held by Mercury, which revolves in a
period of 80 days.

At rest, however, in the middle of everything is the sun. For in this most beautiful temple, who would place this lamp in another or
better position than that from which it can light
up the whole thing at the same time? For, the sun
is not inappropriately called by some people the
lantern of the universe, its mind by others, and
its ruler by still others. [Hermes] the Thrice
Greatest labels it a visible god, and Sophocles'
Electra, the all-seeing. Thus indeed, as though
seated on a royal throne, the sun governs the
family of planets revolving around it. Moreover,
the earth is not deprived of the moon's atten-
dance. On the contrary, as Aristotle says in a
work on animals, the moon has the closest kin-
ship with the earth. Meanwhile the earth has
intercourse with the sun, and is impregnated for
its yearly parturition.

In this arrangement, therefore, we discover a
marvelous symmetry of the universe, and an
established harmonious linkage between the
motion of the spheres and their size, such as can
be found in no other way. For this permits a not
inattentive student to perceive why the forward
and backward arcs appear greater in Jupiter than
in Saturn and smaller than in Mars, and on the
other hand greater in Venus than in Mercury.
This reversal in direction appears more frequently in Saturn than in Jupiter, and also more
rarely in Mars and Venus than in Mercury. More-

over, when Saturn, Jupiter, and Mars rise at sun-
set, they are nearer to the earth than when they
set in the evening or appear at a later hour. But
Mars in particular, when it shines all night, seems
to equal Jupiter in size, being distinguished only
by its reddish color. Yet in the other configurations it is found barely among the stars of the second magnitude, being recognized by those who
track it with assiduous observations. All these
phenomena proceed from the same cause, which
is in the earth's motion.

Yet none of these phenomena appears in the
fixed stars. This proves their immense height,
which makes even the sphere of the annual
motion, or its reflection, vanish from before our
eyes. For, every visible object has some measure
of distance beyond which it is no longer seen, as
is demonstrated in optics. From Saturn, the
highest of the planets, to the sphere of the fixed
stars there is an additional gap of the largest size.
This is shown by the twinkling lights of the
stars. By this token in particular they are distinguished from the planets, for there had to be a
very great difference between what moves and
what does not move. So vast, without any question, is the divine handiwork of the most excellent Almighty.

Proof of the Earth's Triple Motion

Chapter 11

In so many and such important ways, then, do
the planets bear witness to the earth's mobility. I
shall now give a summary of this motion, insofar
as the phenomena are explained by it as a principle. As a whole, it must be admitted to be a
threefold motion.

The first motion, named *nuchthemeron* by
the Greeks, as I said [I, 4], is the rotation which is
the characteristic of a day plus a night. This turns
around the earth's axis from west to east, just as
the universe is deemed to be carried in the opposite direction. It describes the equator, which
some people call the "circle of equal days", in
imitation of the designation used by the Greeks,
whose term for it is *isemerinos*.

The second is the yearly motion of the center, which traces the ecliptic around the sun. Its

5 direction is likewise from west to east, that is, in the order of the zodiacal signs. It travels between Venus and Mars, as I mentioned [I, 10], together with its associates. Because of it, the sun seems to move through the zodiac in a similar motion. Thus, for example, when the earth's center is passing through the Goat, the sun appears to be traversing the Crab; with the earth in the Water Bearer, the sun seems to be in the Lion, and so on, as I remarked.

10 To this circle, which goes through the middle of the signs, and to its plane, the equator and the earth's axis must be understood to have a variable inclination. For if they stayed at a constant angle, and were affected exclusively by the motion of the center, no inequality of days and nights would be observed. On the contrary, it would always be either the longest or shortest 15 day or the day of equal daylight and darkness,

or summer or winter, or whatever the character of the season, it would remain identical and unchanged.

The third motion in inclination is consequently required. This also is a yearly revolution, but it occurs in the reverse order of the signs, that is, in the direction opposite to that of the motion of the center. These two motions are 20 opposite in direction and nearly equal in period. The result is that the earth's axis and equator, the largest of the parallels of latitude on it, face almost the same portion of the heavens, just as if they remained motionless. Meanwhile the sun seems to move through the obliquity of the ecliptic with the motion of the earth's center, as though this were the center of the universe. Only remember that, in relation to the sphere of the 25 fixed stars, the distance between the sun and the earth vanishes from our sight forthwith.

STUDY QUESTIONS: COPERNICUS, *ON THE REVOLUTIONS OF CELESTIAL ORBS*

1. What are ways in which, according to Copernicus, astronomers do not agree among themselves?
2. Reflecting on this confusion, Copernicus became annoyed by what? Why should this annoy him?
3. What did Copernicus discover finally about the other planets and the orbit of the earth 'by long and intense study'?
4. How does Copernicus argue for the claim that the planets, including the earth, revolve around the sun?
5. How does Copernicus try to justify the claim that the sun is still?
6. What is the triple motion of the earth?

Philosophical Bridges: The Influence of Copernicus

Copernicus' theory was a first step in an intellectual revolution. There are four revolutionary aspects to his claim. First, the idea that the earth is not the still center of the solar system and universe is a powerful image that upsets the medieval conception of human life and its meaning. Literally and symbolically, we are no longer the center of the universe. Instead of inhabiting God's special garden, which is at the center of God's magnificent creation, we must conceive of ourselves as living on a ball of stone that revolves around the sun. With Copernicus, science has begun the process of teaching us not to be provincial and anthropocentric.

Second, Copernicus' claim contradicts the authority of the Bible. For example, Psalm 93 states; 'The world also is stabilized that it cannot be moved.' The emerging Protestant churches realized that the theory was a fundamental challenge to the authority of scripture, even though the Catholic Church was not hostile initially to Copernicus' work. However, as time progressed, the dangerous implications of the theory became more apparent and the Catholic Church began to perceive Copernicus' theory as a more fundamental threat than even Luther and John Calvin. In 1616, his book was placed on the list of forbidden works. It initiated the sharp division between science and philosophy on the one hand, and revealed religion on the other.

Third, Copernicus' claim appears to be an insult to common sense as well as to tradition. The earth does not appear to be moving. Yet, Copernicus tries to explain this. Copernicus' theory highlights the ability of scientific explanation to explain appearances in a way that contradicts common sense. This point becomes important later when the orbiting of the earth is more firmly established.

Finally, Copernicus' hypothesis initiated a more scientific approach to astronomy, which resulted in the work of Kepler and Newton. Copernicus' revolution unleashed a series of other early scientific discoveries that also threatened the established order. For instance, in 1543, Andreas Vesalius' anatomy supplanted that of the ancient Greek Galen (130–200 A.D.), and paved the way for William Harvey's (1578–1657) later theory of the circulation of the blood, as well as Paracelsus' chemically based theory of medicine. It was the first step in a process that altered radically our view of the universe and ourselves.

Johannes Kepler (1571–1630)

Biographical History

Johannes Kepler was born near Stuttgart in Germany. As a young boy, he worked in his father's inn. However, a local duke sponsored the boy's education, and after completing his degree, Kepler became a schoolteacher at Graz. In 1596, he published a pamphlet advocating the Copernican system, which he sent Brahe and Galileo. Tycho Brahe (1546–1601) was the astrologer of Emperor Rudolf II. During this time, many astronomers earned their living as astrologers. Brahe had built an observatory near Prague and was amassing a huge amount of carefully observed mathematical data of the movement of the sun, stars, and moon. In 1600, he invited Kepler to work as his assistant. When Brahe died, Kepler inherited his mathematical observations. Instead of trying to compile yet more data, Kepler studied Brahe's figures in great detail in order to make sense of them. Finally, in 1604, he was able to frame the hypothesis that the planets revolve around the sun in elliptical orbits, which he published in the *New Astronomy* in 1609. In 1612, Kepler moved to Linz, where he returned to working as a schoolteacher. He continued to ponder the relationship between the speed of the planets and the size of their orbits. Finally, around 1618, he was able to frame his third law, and he published his results in *The Harmony of the World* in 1619. In his last years, after having worked as an imperial astronomer, Kepler earned his keep as an astrologer, a profession that was not separated clearly from astronomy at the time.

Philosophical Overview

In 1604, after many false starts, Kepler framed the bold hypothesis that Mars orbits around the sun elliptically, rather than in circles. Once he found that this hypothesis fitted the data, he generalized it for the other planets, and formulated his first law: that the planets orbit the sun in ellipses. His second law affirms that each planet moves more rapidly when it is closer to the sun.

Kepler did not discover his third law until around 1618. The third law states that the square of the time of the orbit of a planet around the sun is proportional to the cube root of its mean distance from the sun. This was published in *The Harmony of the World* (1619). Kepler gave his work a Pythagorean title because he believed that his laws described a celestial harmony akin to music. This new theory matched precisely the available observational evidence. All the planetary motions could be accurately described and predicted with three simple and precise mathematical laws.

Kepler's work supported decisively the Copernican claim that the earth revolves around the sun, and in his treatise *The Epitome of the Copernican System* (1620), Kepler argued that the Copernican claim, once suitably amended, had been proved.

NEW ASTRONOMY

This was Kepler's 1609 book in which he explained the breakthrough discovery that Mars and hence the other planets revolve around the sun in elliptical orbits. In his introduction, Kepler describes the process of reasoning by which he arrived at this conclusion.

Kepler realized that his theory did not explain why the orbit of the planets was in an ellipse. Influenced by William Gilbert's (1544–1603) work on magnetism and his idea of the earth as a giant magnet, Kepler argued that the planets moved elliptically through the action of a purely mechanical force. This was an informal explanation that was replaced by Newton's theory of gravity.

INTRODUCTION

It is extremely hard these days to write mathematical books, especially astronomical ones. For unless one maintains the truly rigorous sequence of proposition, construction, demonstration, and conclusion, the book will not be mathematical; but maintaining that sequence makes the reading most tiresome. . . .

The reader should be aware that there are two schools of thought among astronomers, one distinguished by its chief, Ptolemy, and by the assent of the large majority of the ancients, and the other attributed to more recent proponents, although it is the most ancient. The former treats the individual planets separately and assigns causes to the motions of each in its own orb, while the latter relates the planets to one another, and deduces from a single common cause those characteristics which are found to be common to their motions. The latter school is again subdivided. Copernicus, with Aristarchus of remotest antiquity, ascribes to the translational motion of our home the earth the cause of the planets' appearing stationary and retrograde. Tycho Brahe, on the other hand, ascribes this cause to the sun, in whose vicinity he says the eccentric circles of all five planets are connected as if by a kind of knot (not physical, of course, but only quantitative). Further, he says that this knot, as it were, revolves about the motionless earth, along with the solar body.

My aim in the present work is chiefly to reform astronomical theory (especially of the motion of Mars) in all three forms of hypotheses, so that our computations from the tables correspond to the celestial phenomena. Hitherto, it has not been possible to do this with sufficient certainty. In fact, in August of 1608, Mars was a little less than four degrees beyond the position given by calculation from the Prutenic tables. In August and September of 1593 this error was a little less than five degrees,

---

From the Introduction to Kepler, *New Astronomy* translated by W. H. Donahue.

while in my new calculation the error is entirely suppressed.

Meanwhile, although I place this goal first and pursue it cheerfully, I also make an excursion into Aristotle's *Metaphysics*, or rather, I inquire into celestial physics and the natural causes of the motions. The eventual result of this consideration is the formulation of very clear arguments showing that only Copernicus's opinion concerning the world (with a few small changes) is true, that the other two are false, and so on.

Now my first step in investigating the physical causes of the motions was to demonstrate that [the planes of] all the eccentrics intersect in no other place than the very centre of the solar body (not some nearby point), contrary to what Copernicus and Brahe thought. . . .

In the second part of the work I take up the main subject, and describe the positions of Mars at apparent opposition to the sun, not worse, but indeed much better, with my method than they expressed the positions of Mars at mean opposition to the sun with the old method.

Meanwhile, throughout the entire second part (as far as concerns geometrical demonstrations from the observations) I leave in suspense the question of whose procedure is better, theirs or mine, seeing that we both match a number of observations (this is, indeed, a basic requirement for our theorizing). However, my method is in agreement with physical causes, and their old one is in disagreement, as I have partly shown in the first part, especially chapter 6.

But finally in the fourth part of the work, in chapter 52, I consider certain other observations, no less trustworthy than the previous ones were, which their old method could not match, but which mine matches most beautifully. I thereby demonstrate most soundly that Mars's eccentric is so situated that the centre of the solar body lies upon its line of apsides, and not any nearby point, and hence, that all the [planes of the] eccentrics intersect in the sun itself.

This should, however, hold not just for the longitude, but for the latitude as well. Therefore, in the fifth part I have demonstrated the same from the observed latitudes, in chapter 67.

For whether it is the earth or the sun that is moved, it has certainly been demonstrated that the body that is moved is moved in a nonuniform manner, that is, slowly when it is farther from the body at rest, and more swiftly when it has approached this body. . . .

For if the earth is moved, it has been demonstrated that the increases and decreases of its velocity are governed by its approaching towards and receding from the sun. And in fact the same happens with the rest of the planets: they are urged on or held back according to the approach toward or recession from the sun. So far, the demonstration is geometrical.

And now, from this very reliable demonstration, the conclusion is drawn, using a physical conjecture, that the source of the five planets' motion is in the sun itself. It is therefore very likely that the source of the earth's motion is in the same place as the source of the other five planets' motion, namely, in the sun as well. It is therefore likely that the earth is moved, since a likely cause of its motion is apparent.

That, on the other hand, the sun remains in place in the centre of the world, is most probably shown by (among other things) its being the source of motion for at least five planets. For whether you follow Copernicus or Brahe, the source of motion for five of the planets is in the sun, and in Copernicus, for a sixth as well, namely, the earth. And it is more likely that the source of all motion should remain in place rather than move.

But if we follow Brahe's theory and say that the sun moves, this first conclusion still remains valid, that the sun moves slowly when it is more distant from the earth and swiftly when it approaches, and this not only in appearance, but in fact. For this is the effect of the circle of the equant, which, by an inescapable demonstration, I have introduced into the theory of the sun.

Upon this most valid conclusion, making use of the physical conjecture introduced above, might be based the following theorem of natural philosophy: the sun, and with it the whole huge burden (to speak coarsely) of the five eccentrics, is moved by the earth; or the source of the motion of the sun and the five eccentrics attached to the sun is in the earth.

Now let us consider the bodies of the sun and the earth, and decide which is better suited to being the source of motion for the other body. Does the sun, which moves the rest of the planets, move the earth, or does the earth move the sun, which moves the rest, and which is so many times greater? Unless we are to be forced to admit the absurd conclusion that the sun is moved by the earth, we must allow the sun to be fixed and the earth to move.

What shall I say of the motion's periodic time of 365 days, intermediate in quantity between the periodic time of Mars of 687 days and that of Venus of 225 days? Does not the nature of things cry out with a great voice that the circuit in which these 365 days are used up also occupies a place intermediate between those of Mars and Venus about the sun, and thus itself also encircles the sun, and hence, that this circuit is a circuit of the earth about the sun, and not of the sun about the earth? These points are, however, more appropriate to my *Mysterium cosmographicum*, and arguments that are not going to be repeated in this work should not be introduced here.

I, too, implore my reader, when he departs from the temple and enters astronomical studies, not to forget the divine goodness conferred upon men, to the consideration of which the psalmodist chiefly invites. I hope that, with me, he will praise and celebrate the Creator's wisdom and greatness, which I unfold for him in the more perspicacious explanation of the world's form, the investigation of causes, and the detection of errors of vision.

But whoever is too stupid to understand astronomical science, or too weak to believe Copernicus without affecting his faith, I would advise him that, having dismissed astronomical studies and having damned whatever philosophical opinions he pleases, he mind his own business and betake himself home to scratch in his own dirt patch, abandoning this wandering about the world. He should raise his eyes (his only means of vision) to this visible heaven and with his whole heart burst forth in giving thanks and praising God the Creator. He can be sure that he worships God no less than the astronomer, to whom God has granted the more penetrating vision of the mind's eye, and an ability and desire to celebrate his God above those things he has discovered.

But enough about the truth of the Copernican hypothesis. Let us return to the plan I proposed at the beginning of this introduction.

I had begun to say that in this work I treat all of astronomy by means of physical causes rather than fictitious hypotheses, and that I had taken two steps in my effort to reach this central goal: first, that I had discovered that the planetary eccentrics all intersect

in the body of the sun, and second, that I had understood that in the theory of the earth there is an equant circle, and that its eccentricity is to be bisected.

Now we come to the third step, namely, that it has been demonstrated with certainty, by a comparison of the conclusions of parts 2 and 4, that the eccentricity of Mars's equant is also to be precisely bisected, a fact long held in doubt by Brahe and Copernicus.

Therefore, by induction extending to all the planets (carried out in part 3 by way of anticipation), since there are (of course) no solid orbs, as Brahe demonstrated from the paths of comets, the body of the sun is the source of the power that drives all the planets around. Moreover, I have specified the manner [in which this occurs] as follows: that the sun, although it stays in one place, rotates as if on a lathe, and out of itself sends into the space of the world an immaterial *species* of its body, analogous to the immaterial *species* of its light. This *species* itself, as a consequence of the rotation of the solar body, also rotates like a very rapid whirlpool throughout the whole breadth of the world, and carries the bodies of the planets along with itself in a gyre, its grasp stronger or weaker according to the greater density or rarity it acquires through the law governing its diffusion.

Once this common power was proposed, by which all the planets, each in its own circle, are driven around the sun, the next step in my argument was to give each of the planets its own mover, seated in the planet's globe (you will recall that, following Brahe's opinion, I had already rejected solid orbs). And this, too, I have accomplished in part 3.

But my exhausting task was not complete: I had a fourth step yet to make towards the physical hypotheses. By most labourious proofs and by computations on a very large number of observations, I discovered that the course of a planet in the heavens is not a circle, but an oval path, perfectly elliptical.

Geometry gave assent to this, and taught that such a path will result if we assign to the planet's own movers the task of making the planet's body reciprocate along a straight line extended towards the sun. Not only this, but also the correct eccentric equations, agreeing with the observations, resulted from such a reciprocation.

Finally, the pediment was added to the structure, and proven geometrically: that it is in the order of things for such a reciprocation to be the result of a magnetic corporeal faculty. Consequently, these movers belonging to the planets individually are shown with great probability to be nothing but properties of the planetary bodies themselves, like the magnet's property of seeking the pole and catching up iron. As a result, every detail of the celestial motions is caused and regulated by faculties of a purely corporeal nature, that is, magnetic, with the sole exception of the whirling of the solar body as it remains fixed in its space. For this, a vital faculty seems required.

Next, in part 5, it was demonstrated that the physical hypotheses we just introduced also give a satisfactory account of the latitudes.

STUDY QUESTIONS: KEPLER, *NEW ASTRONOMY*

1. What are the three astronomical theories that Kepler disputes?
2. What are the data that are not adequately explained by these three theories?
3. How does Kepler describe the nonuniform movement of the earth or sun? Why does this motion indicate that it is the other planets that move rather than the sun?
4. How does Kepler deduce that the earth is moved by the sun?
5. What was Kepler's fourth step in arriving at his conclusion?

Philosophical Bridges: Kepler's Influence

The work of Kepler was for the time a model of scientific discovery. First, his work showed how scientific projects could cross generations. Without Brahe's observations, Kepler's discovery would be impossible, but without Kepler's theorizing, the detailed observations amassed by Brahe would have been without significance. The findings of one generation can become the starting point for the investigations of the next generation; this apparently shows how the physical sciences can steadily accumulate knowledge. Einstein once claimed that his work was possible only because he stood on the shoulders of giants. Newton stood on the shoulders of Kepler.

Second, the work of Kepler and Brahe appears to be an epistemological model of the process of discovery: a theory built carefully on a mass of mathematically precise data. Kepler spent years testing different hypotheses against Brahe's data. The development of physics revolutionized society in part because it required epistemological attitudes quite distinct from those inculcated by medieval Scholasticism. Kepler's work exemplified this.

Third, Kepler's laws are a paradigm of descriptive simplicity: three simple and precise laws that can be stated mathematically, which describe all the planetary motions and can be used to make accurate predictions. The natural philosophers of the modern period developed bit by bit the scientific method and showed how its application might lead to knowledge of the principles that govern the workings of the universe. Kepler's work was a big step in that direction.

GALILEO GALILEI (1564–1642)

Biographical History

Galileo was born in Pisa, during the Italian Renaissance, on the same day that Michelangelo died. As a young man, he studied mechanics and mathematics with passion, and at the age of 25, he was appointed chair of mathematics at the University of Pisa. In 1592, he moved to the University of Padua and, in 1610, to Florence. Galileo's life work was to

PAOLO C. BIONDI

understand the physical world through careful experimentation. To this end, he opposed the Scholastic Aristotelian physics that dominated Europe. The first confrontation occurred after Galileo had indicated that the Copernican hypothesis was proven. In 1616, the Church initiated an inquisition of the astronomer and issued a decree forbidding Galileo from defending the Copernican theory on pain of imprisonment. In 1622, he published the *Assayer* rejecting the idea that authority has a role in science. The new pope, Urban VIII, sanctioned the publication of this work. Heartened, Galileo worked on his manuscript, the *Dialogue Concerning the Two Great World-Systems*, for which he also sought papal approval. The work was published in 1632. But he was accused of disobeying the decree of 1616. In 1633, he was found guilty of heresy and disobedience to the Church for treating Copernicus' claims as proven facts. He was imprisoned and forced to recant. Only 33 years before, in 1600, the Church had burned at the stake the philosopher Giordano Bruno for his heretical views. Despite his age and infirmities, Galileo published another work in 1638, the *Discourse Concerning Two New Sciences*, which contains his mechanics and the principle of inertia.

Philosophical Overview

Galileo made fundamental scientific advances in three areas. First, in astronomy, he built a powerful telescope and made many new significant observations, some of which provided evidence for the Copernican hypothesis.

Second, he opposed Aristotelian physics, replacing it with a quantifiable method. Aristotle's physics was based on the perceived qualities of objects and on verbal explanations. Under the influence of the atomism of the rediscovered ancient philosopher Lucretius, Galileo proposed that scientific investigations of nature should be based only on measurable qualities, such as weight, motion, number, size, and shape. Scientific results should be numerical and should consist in mathematically precise laws. Indeed, Galileo claimed that 'the Book of Nature is written in the mathematical characters.'

Galileo perceived that this view has some dramatic implications. It means that perceptual or secondary qualities, such as color, must be explicable in terms of the mathematical or primary properties of matter, such as motion, weight, size, and shape. It implies that all material objects differ only quantitatively. Consequently, Aristotle's four basic elements, earth, water, air, and fire, should be replaced with the single idea of matter, which has different degrees of the primary qualities. It also dispenses with the idea of a fifth element, ether, which composes the eternal celestial bodies. It implies that all matter is inert. Material things do not have inherent purposes or natural tendencies that explain their actions. This paved the way for Descartes' claim that all physical changes should be explained mechanically.

Third, Galileo developed the science of mechanics. Aristotle had claimed that heavier bodies fall faster than lighter ones because earthly bodies have a natural tendency to find their proper position in the scheme of things. According to a famous, but false, story, Galileo refuted Aristotle's theory publicly by dropping two bodies of unequal weight from the leaning tower of Pisa, which fell with equal speed. In actual fact, by employing mathematical analysis to repeated experiments on bodies rolling down inclines, Galileo showed that their motion was independent of their weight and he formulated the first version of the principle of inertia, a notion vital to the future of physics. The principle of inertia states that a body moving in a vacuum will continue its movement indefinitely, unless acted on by some external resisting force. In other words, force is required to bring about changes in velocity, and not just to maintain existing motion, as Aristotle had claimed. In 1638,

Galileo published the *Discourse Concerning Two New Sciences*, which contains an initial statement of the principle of inertia, later refined and extended by Descartes and Newton.

In summary, with these three advances, Galileo overturned the dominance of traditional Aristotelian physics, widened the divide between science and religion, and paved a new road forward for other scientists or natural philosophers.

SIDEREUS NUNCIUS (THE SIDEREAL MESSENGER)

First, in 1609, Galileo constructed a telescope through which he observed many new phenomena. He perceived that the night sky contained many more stars than are visible to the naked eye. He saw that the Milky Way was a huge cluster of stars, which suggested that the universe was much bigger than had previously been thought. He also observed that there were mountains on the moon, and he discovered four of the moons of Jupiter. His observations contradicted the idea that the planetary bodies, such as the stars, were just points of light. They no longer appeared to be the eternal celestial bodies of Aristotle's cosmology. The very idea of higher or celestial bodies was under threat. In 1610, Galileo published *The Sidereal Messenger*, in which he described these results, and which caused a stir in Europe. We have selected part of the introduction in order to give the reader a flavor and a sense of Galileo's publication.

ASTRONOMICAL MESSAGE

Containing and Explaining Observations Recently Made, With the Benefit of a New Spyglass, About the Face of the Moon, the Milky Way, and Nebulous Stars, about Innumerable Fixed Stars and also Four Planets hitherto never seen, and named MEDICEAN STARS

In this short treatise I propose great things for inspection and contemplation by every explorer of Nature. Great, I say, because of the excellence of the things themselves, because of their newness, unheard of through the ages, and also because of the instrument with the benefit of which they make themselves manifest to our sight.

Certainly it is a great thing to add to the countless multitude of fixed stars visible hitherto by natural means and expose to our eyes innumerable others never seen before, which exceed tenfold the number of old and known ones.

It is most beautiful and pleasing to the eye to look upon the lunar body, distant from us about sixty terrestrial diameters, from so near as if it were distant by only two of these measures, so that the diameter of the same Moon appears as if it were thirty times, the surface nine-hundred times, and the solid body about twenty-seven thousand times larger than when observed only with the naked eye. Anyone will then understand with the certainty of the senses that the Moon is by no means endowed with a smooth and polished surface, but is rough and uneven and, just as the face of the Earth itself, crowded everywhere with vast prominences, deep chasms, and convolutions.

Moreover, it seems of no small importance to have put an end to the debate about the Galaxy or Milky Way and to have made manifest its essence to the senses as well as the intellect; and it will be pleasing and most glorious to demonstrate clearly that the substance of those stars called nebulous up to now by all astronomers is very different from what has hitherto been thought.

But what greatly exceeds all admiration, and what especially impelled us to give notice to all astronomers and philosophers, is this, that we have discovered four wandering stars, known or observed by no one before us. These, like Venus and Mercury around the Sun, have their periods around a certain star notable among the number of known ones, and now precede, now follow, him, never digressing from him beyond certain limits. All these things were discovered and observed a few days ago by means of a glass contrived by me after I had been inspired by divine grace.

Perhaps more excellent things will be discovered in time, either by me or by others, with the help of a similar instrument, the form and construction of which, and the occasion of whose invention, I shall first mention briefly, and then I shall review the history of the observations made by me.

About 10 months ago a rumor came to our ears that a spyglass had been made by a certain Dutchman by means of which visible objects, although far removed from the eye of the observer, were distinctly perceived as though nearby. About this truly wonderful effect some accounts were spread abroad, to which some gave credence while others denied them. The rumor was confirmed to me a few days later by a letter from Paris from the noble Frenchman Jacques Badovere. This finally caused me to apply myself totally to investigating the principles and figuring out the means by which I might arrive at the invention of a similar instrument, which I achieved shortly afterward on the basis of the science of refraction. And first I prepared a lead tube in whose ends I fitted two glasses, both plane on one side while the other side of one was spherically convex and of the other concave. Then,

applying my eye to the concave glass, I saw objects satisfactorily large and close. Indeed, they appeared three times closer and nine times larger than when observed with natural vision only. Afterward I made another more perfect one for myself that showed objects more than sixty times larger. Finally, sparing no labor or expense, I progressed so far that I constructed for myself an instrument so excellent that things seen through it appear about a thousand times larger and more than thirty times closer than when observed with the natural faculty only. It would be entirely superfluous to enumerate how many and how great the advantages of this instrument are on land and at sea. But having dismissed earthly things, I applied myself to explorations of the heavens. And first I looked at the Moon from so close that it was scarcely two terrestrial diameters distant. Next, with incredible delight I frequently observed the stars, fixed as well as wandering, and as I saw their huge number I began to think of, and at last discovered, a method whereby I could measure the distances between them. In this matter, it behooves all those who wish to make such observations to be forewarned. For it is necessary first that they prepare a most accurate glass that shows objects brightly, distinctly, and not veiled by any obscurity, and second that it multiply them at least four hundred times and show them twenty times closer. For if it is not an instrument such as that, one will try in vain to see all the things observed in the heavens by us and enumerated below.

STUDY QUESTIONS: GALILEI, *THE SIDEREAL MESSENGER*

1. How many more stars could Galileo see with his telescope?
2. Why is the fact that Galileo could see that the moon is not endowed with a smooth and polished surface significant?
3. How many times closer did things appear through Galileo's final telescope?

DIALOGUE ON THE GREAT WORLD-SYSTEMS

In 1632, Galileo published the *Dialogue on the Two Great World-Systems—Ptolemaic and Copernican*, in which he argued that the earth revolves around the sun. He took an earlier version of the manuscript to the pope, who consented to its publication so long as Galileo treated the Copernican claim only as a hypothesis.

Galileo Galilei, from *Dialogue on the Great World-Systems*, revised translation by Giorgio de Santilla. Copyright 1953 by the University of Chicago. Reprinted by permission of the University of Chicago Press.

However, in the work, Galileo tries to make his own views patently clear while keeping to the letter of this papal condition. First, he addresses his preface to 'the discerning reader' and says, 'Complaints were to be heard that advisers who were totally unskilled in astronomical observations ought not clip the wings of reflecting intellects by means of rash prohibitions.' Second, in the dialogue, the two characters that defend the Copernican system are Salviatus and Sagredus, names of Galileo's friends. The third character, who rejects Copernicus, is called Simplicius, and often his remarks are simplistic and are treated as such. Galileo often uses irony in the dialogue.

After receiving complaints that in effect Galileo had treated the Copernican hypothesis as a fact, the inquisition prohibited further sales of the book and summoned Galileo. Galileo was 68 years old and ill. Under examination, he claimed to accept the Church's teaching and reject the Copernican hypothesis. He was found guilty of heresy and forced to repudiate publicly the Copernican theory. He was put under house imprisonment.

DAY 2

INTERLOCUTORS:
SALVIATUS, SAGREDUS, SIMPLICIUS

SALVIATUS: The digressions of yesterday, which led us out of the path of our principal discourse, were such and so many that I know not how I can recover the track in which I am to proceed without your assistance.

SAGREDUS: I do not wonder that you, who have your fancy charged and laden both with what has been, and is to be, spoken, should find yourself in some confusion. However, being only an auditor and having nothing to burden my memory except such things as I have heard, I may perhaps recover the first thread of our discourse. As far as my memory serves me, the sum of yesterday's conference was an examination of the principles of Ptolemy and Copernicus and which of their opinions is the more probable and rational; the former, which affirms the substance of the celestial bodies to be ingenerable, incorruptible, unalterable, impassible, and, in a word, exempt from all kind of change, save local motion, and therefore to be a *fifth essence* quite different from this of our elementary bodies, which are generable, corruptible, alterable, etc.; or else the latter, which, removing such differences among the parts of the world, holds the Earth to enjoy the same perfections as the other constitutive bodies of the universe and esteems it a movable and erratic globe, no less than the Moon, Jupiter, Venus, or any other planet. Lastly, we made many particular parallels between the Earth and the Moon; more with the Moon than with any

other planet, because we have greater and more sensibly detailed knowledge of it, as it is closer. Having, lastly, concluded this second opinion to be more probable than the first, I should think it best now to begin to examine whether the Earth is to be esteemed immovable, as has been believed till now by most men, or else movable, as some ancient philosophers and others for some time past have been of the opinion, and, if it be movable, to enquire what kind its motion may be.

SALV.: I see already what way I am to take, but, before we offer to proceed any further, I have to say something touching those last words you spoke—that the opinion which holds the Earth to be endowed with the same movements as other celestial bodies seems to be more true than the contrary. I affirmed no such thing, as I do not intend either to state a definite conclusion on any other of the controversial questions; but I only intended to produce on either part those reasons and answers, arguments and solutions, which have been hitherto thought upon by others, together with certain others which I have stumbled upon in my long searching thereinto, always remitting the decision to the judgment of my betters.

SAGR.: I was transported unawares by my own sense of the thing, and, believing that others ought to judge as I did, I assumed that conclusion universal, instead of particular. I confess I have erred, and all the more in that I do not know what Simplicius believes on this point.

SIMPLICIUS: I must confess that I have been ruminating all night of what passed yesterday, and, to say the truth, I have met with many acute, new, and plausible notions; yet I remain convinced by the authority of so many great writers and in particular. . . . I see you shaking your head, Sagredus, and grinning to yourself, as if I had uttered some great absurdity.

SAGR.: I not only grin but actually am ready to burst with holding myself from laughing outright, for you have put me in mind of a very pretty episode that I witnessed not many years since, together with some others of my worthy friends which I could name to you.

SALV.: It would be well that you told us what it was, so Simplicius may not still think that he is the point of your laughter.

SAGR.: Very well. One day at his home in Venice, I found a famous physician to whom some flocked for their studies, while others sometimes came thither out of curiosity to see certain bodies dissected by the hand of a no less learned than careful and experienced anatomist. It chanced upon that day, when I was there, that he was in search of the origin and stem of the nerves, about which there is a famous controversy between the Galenists and Peripatetics. The anatomist shewed how the great trunk of nerves, departing from the brain, their root, passed by the nape of the neck, extended themselves afterwards along the backbone, and branched out through all the body, while only a very small filament, as fine as a thread, went to the heart. Then he turned to a gentleman whom he knew to be a Peripatetic philosopher, and for whose sake he had uncovered and proved everything, and asked if he was satisfied and persuaded that the origin of the nerves was in the brain and not in the heart. The philosopher, after he had stood musing a while, answered: "You have made me see this business so plainly and sensibly that did not the text of Aristotle assert the contrary, which positively affirms the nerves to proceed from the heart, I should be constrained to confess your opinion to be true."

SIMP.: I would have you know, my Masters, that this controversy about the origin of the nerves is not yet so proved and decided, as some may perhaps persuade themselves.

SAGR.: Nor doubtless shall it ever be if it finds such contradictors; but what you say does not at all lessen the extravagance of the answer of that Peripatetic, who against such sensible experience did not produce other experiments or reasons of Aristotle but his bare authority and pure *ipse dixit*.

SIMP.: Aristotle would not have gained so great authority but for the force of his demonstrations and the profundity of his argument. It is requisite that we understand him, and not only understand him, but have so great a familiarity with his books, that we form a perfect idea of them in our minds, so that every saying of his may be always, as it were, present in our memory. He did not write for the vulgar, nor is he obliged to spin out his syllogisms in the trivial ordered method; on the contrary, using the perturbed order, he has sometimes placed the proof of one proposition among texts which seem to treat of quite another point. Therefore it is necessary to be master of all that vast system and to learn how to connect this passage with that and to combine this text with another far remote from it; he who has thus studied him will know how to gather from his books the demonstrations of every knowable deduction, because they contain all things.

SAGR.: But, good Simplicius, this reaching the desired conclusion by connecting several small extracts which you and other egregious philosophers easily find scattered throughout the texts of Aristotle I could do as well by the verses of Virgil or Ovid, composing patchworks of passages which explain all the affairs of men and secrets of Nature. But why do I talk of Virgil or any other poet? I have a little book much shorter than Aristotle or Ovid, in which are contained all the sciences, and with very little study one may gather out of it a most perfect system, and this is the alphabet. For there is no doubt but that he who knows how to couple and correctly dispose this and that vowel with the right consonants may gather thence the infallible answers to all doubts and deduce from them the principles of all sciences and arts. In the same manner the painter, from many simple colours laid individually upon his palette, proceeds, by mixing a little of this and a little of that with a little of a third, to represent lifelike men, plants, buildings, birds, fishes, or, in a word, counterfeiting whatever object is visible, though there be not on the palette, all the while, either eyes, feathers, fins, leaves, or stones. Even more necessary it is that none of the things to be imitated, or any part of them, be actually among colours, if you would be able therewith to represent all things; for should there be among them, say, feathers, these would serve to represent nothing save birds and plumed creatures.

SALV.: And there are certain gentlemen yet living and in health who were present when a professor in a famous Academy, hearing the description of the Telescope, said that the invention was taken from Aristotle, though he had not yet seen it. Having his works brought, he turned to a place where the philosopher gives the reason why, from the bottom of a very deep well, one may see the stars in heaven at noonday. Then addressing himself to the company: "See here," says he, "the well, which represents the tube, see here the gross vapours, from whence is taken the invention of the crystals, and see here lastly the sight fortified by the passage of the rays through a diaphanous but more dense and obscure medium."

SAGR.: This is a way to comprehend all things knowable, much like that whereby a piece of marble is one or even a thousand very beautiful statues; but the difficulty lies in being able to discover them. . . .

SIMP.: I believe, and in part I know, that in the world there are very extravagant minds whose vanities ought not to redound to the prejudice of Aristotle, of whom I think you speak sometimes with too little respect. Were it only for his antiquity and the great name that he has acquired in the opinions of so many famous men, they should render him honourable with all that profess themselves learned.

SALV.: You do not state the matter rightly, Simplicius. It is those pusillanimous followers of his who would give us cause to think less of him, should we consent to applaud their silly arguments. And you, please tell me, are you so simple as not to realize that, had Aristotle been present and heard the doctor who tried to make him author of the Telescope, he would have been much more displeased with him than with those who laughed at the doctor and his comments? Do you question whether Aristotle, had he but seen the new discoveries in heaven, would not have changed his opinions, amended his books, and embraced the more sensible doctrine, rejecting those silly gulls who go about so timidly to defend whatever he has said? Do those defenders consider that, if Aristotle were

such a one as they fancy him to themselves, he would be a man of an untractable wit, an obstinate mind, a barbarous soul, a stubborn will, who, accounting all other men as silly sheep, would have his oracles preferred before the senses, before experience, and before Nature herself? It is the sectators of Aristotle that have given him this authority and not he who has usurped or taken it upon himself. All because it is easier for a man to skulk under another's shield than to shew himself openly, they tremble and are afraid to stir one step from him; rather than admit some alterations in the heaven of Aristotle, they will impertinently deny those they behold in the heaven of Nature.

SIMP.: But in case we should give up Aristotle, who is to be our guide in philosophy? Name you some author.

SALV.: We need a guide in unknown and uncouth parts, but in clear thoroughfares, and in open plains, only the blind stand in need of a leader; and, for such, it is better that they stay at home. But he who has eyes in his head and in his mind has to use these for his guide. Yet mistake me not, thinking that I speak this because I am against hearing Aristotle; for, on the contrary, I commend the reading and diligent study of him and only blame the servilely giving one's self up a slave to him, so as blindly to subscribe to whatever he delivers, and receive it for an inviolable decree without search of any further reason. This is an abuse that carries with it the other extreme disorder that people will no longer take pains to understand the validity of his demonstrations. And what is more shameful in public disputes than, while someone is treating of demonstrable conclusions, to have someone else come up with a passage of Aristotle, quite often irrelevant, and with that stop the mouth of his opponent? But, if you will continue to study in this manner, I would have you lay aside the name of philosophers and call yourselves either historians or doctors of memory, for it is not fit that those who never philosophize should usurp the honourable title of philosophers. But it is best for us to return to shore and not launch out further into a boundless gulf, out of which we should not be able to get before night. Therefore, Simplicius, come with arguments and demonstrations of your own, or of Aristotle, but bring us no more texts and naked authorities, for our disputes are about the sensible world and not a paper one. Now in our discourses of yesterday we retrieved the Earth from darkness and exposed it to the open sky, showing that the attempt to number it among those which we call celestial bodies was not a position so compromised and vanquished that it had no life left in it. It follows next that we proceed to examine what probability there is for holding its entire globe fixed and wholly immovable; what likelihood there is for making it movable with some motion; and of what kind that may be. And since I am doubtful in this question, while Simplicius is resolute, as Aristotle is, for its immobility, he shall one by one produce the arguments in favour of their opinion, and I will allege the answers and reasons on the contrary part; next, Sagredus shall tell us his thoughts and to which side he finds himself inclined.

SAGR.: Content, provided always that I may reserve myself the liberty of alleging what straight natural reason shall sometimes dictate to me.

SALV.: Let our contemplation begin therefore with this view: that, whatever motion may be ascribed to the Earth as a whole, it is necessary that it be to us, as partakers of it, altogether imperceptible, so long as we have regard only to terrestrial things. On the other hand, it is equally necessary that the same motion should appear common to all other bodies and visible objects separated from the Earth and that therefore do not participate in it. So that the true method of finding it, and, once found, to know what it is, is to consider and observe if in bodies separated from the Earth one may discover any appearance of motion which equally suits all the rest of them. For a motion that is only seen, for example, in the Moon, and has nothing to do with Venus or Jupiter or any other stars, cannot in any way belong to the Earth or to any other save the Moon alone. Now there is a most general and grand motion above all others, and it is that by which the Sun, the Moon, the other planets, and the fixed stars, and, in a word the whole Universe, except only the Earth, appear to move from the east towards the west in the space of twenty-four hours; and this, at first sight, might as well belong to the Earth alone, as, on the other hand, to all the rest of the world, except the Earth; for the same phenomena will appear in the one case as in the other. Hence it is that Aristotle and Ptolemy, having hit upon this consideration when they go about to prove the Earth to be immovable, argue only against this diurnal motion; except that Aristotle hints something in obscure terms against another motion ascribed to it by an Ancient, of whom we shall speak in its place.

SAGR.: I very well perceive the necessity of your conclusion; but I meet with a doubt from which I do not know how to free myself. It is that, since Copernicus assigns another motion to the Earth beside the diurnal, which, according to the rule even now laid down, ought to be imperceptible to us but visible in all the rest of the world, I might necessarily infer either that he has manifestly erred in assigning the Earth a motion to which there does not appear a general correspondence in heaven or else that, if there be such a congruity therein, Ptolemy has failed in not confuting it, as he has done in the other.

SALV.: You have good cause for your doubts, and, when we come to treat of the other motion, you shall see how far Copernicus excelled Ptolemy in clearness and elevation of intellect in that he saw what the other did not; I mean the admirable correspondence whereby this motion reflected itself in all the other celestial bodies. But for the present we will suspend this particular and return to our first consideration.

Beginning, then, with more general things, I will propose those reasons which seem to favour the mobility of the Earth and then await the answers which Simplicius shall make. *First,* if we consider only the immense magnitude of the starry sphere compared to the smallness of the terrestrial globe, and weigh the velocity of the motions which must in a day and night make an entire revolution, I cannot persuade myself that there is any man who believes it more reasonable and credible that it is the celestial sphere that turns round, while the terrestrial globe stands still.

SAGR.: If in the totality of effects which may in Nature depend upon such like motions, there should follow in one hypothesis exactly all the same consequences as in the other. I would esteem at first inspection, that he who should hold it more rational to make the whole Universe move, in order to keep the Earth from moving, is less rea-sonable than he who being at the top of the dome of your Cathedral in Florence, in order to behold the city and the fields about it, should desire that the whole country might turn round, so that he might not be put to the trouble to turn his head. And surely the conveniences that could be drawn from this position would have to be many and great in order to equate in my mind, and to over-come, this absurdity in such manner as to make it more credible than the former. But perhaps Aristo-tle, Ptolemy, and Simplicius must find certain advantage therein, which they would do well to communicate to us also, if any such there be; or else they had better declare that there neither is nor can be any.

SALV.: I have not been able, much as I have thought upon it, to find any diversity in it, and indeed I think I have found that no such diversity can be; I even esteem it to no purpose to seek further after it. Therefore, observe: motion is motion and oper-ates as motion by how much relation it has to things which want motion; but in those things which all equally partake of it, it operates nothing and is as if it never were. Thus the merchandises with which a ship is laden move only as the ship leaves Venice and sails by Corfu, Crete, and Cyprus for Aleppo. Venice, Corfu, and Crete stand still, not moving with the ship. But the distance between Venice and Syria is as nothing to the chests, bales, and other parcels in respect to the ship itself, as nothing alters between them. But if a bale of the cargo were moved one inch from a chest, this alone would be a greater motion for that bale in respect to the chest, and to the ship, than the whole voyage of more than two thousand miles made by them together.

SIMP.: This doctrine is good, sound, and altogether Peripatetic.

SALV.: I hold it to be much more ancient, and sus-pect that Aristotle, in receiving it from some good school, did not fully understand it and that there-fore, having delivered it with some alteration, it has been an occasion of confusion, owing to those who would defend whatever he says. And when he wrote that, whatsoever moves, does move upon something immovable, I suppose that he equivo-cated and meant that, whatever moves, moves

with respect to something immovable; this propo-sition admits no doubt, and the other many.

SAGR.: Pray you, make no digression but proceed in the discourse you began.

SALV.: It being manifest therefore that the notion which is common to many movables is meaning-less and null in the relation of those movables between themselves, because among themselves they make no changes, and is operative only in the relation that those movables have to other things which want that motion; and, since we have divided the Universe in two parts, one of which is necessarily movable and the other immovable, then whatever may depend upon or be required from such a motion may as well be done by mak-ing the Earth alone move as all the rest of the world. For the operation of such a motion consists in nothing else, save in the relation which is between the celestial bodies as a whole and the Earth, and this relation only exchanges its terms. Now if, for obtaining the same effect *ad unguem,* it will be all one whether the Earth alone or the whole Universe moves with the same motion, who would believe that Nature (which by common consent does not work by many things what may be done by few) has chosen to make innumerable most vast bodies move with an inconceivable velocity, to perform that which might be done by the moderate motion of one alone about its own centre?

SIMP.: I do not well understand how this grand motion can be as nothing for the Sun, the Moon, the other planets and the innumerable multitude of fixed stars. Or why you should say that it is no purpose for the Sun to pass from one meridian to another, to rise above this horizon, to set beneath that other, to make day and night; and I will say the same as to the like variations made by the Moon, the other planets, and the fixed stars themselves.

SALV.: All these alterations instanced by you are nothing, except in relation to the Earth; and, to see that this is true, just imagine the Earth removed, and there will be no such thing in the world as the rising or the setting of the Sun or Moon, or horizons, days or nights, nor will such a motion cause any change between the Moon and Sun, or any other star whatever, whether fixed or erratic. But all these changes have relation to the Earth, and all import nothing else than that they should shew the Sun now to China, anon to Persia, then to Egypt, Greece, France, Spain, America, etc. And the same for the Moon and the rest of the celestial bodies. This same effect falls out exactly in the same manner if, without troubling so great a part of the Universe, the terrestrial globe be made to revolve in itself. But—and this augments the difficulty when you ascribe this great motion to heaven—you must of necessity make it *contrary* to the particular motion of all the spheres of the planets, each of which admittedly has its peculiar motion from the west towards the east. Then you have to say they are hurried to the contrary part, i.e., from east to west, by this most furious diurnal motion; whereas, on the contrary, by having the Earth move in itself, the contrariety of motions is taken away, and the sole motion from west to east is accommodated to all appearances and exactly satisfies every phenomenon.

SIMP.: As to the contrariety of motions it would import little, for Aristotle demonstrates that circular motions are not contrary to one another and that theirs cannot be truly called contrariety.

SALV.: Does Aristotle demonstrate this, or does he not rather barely affirm it, as serving for some certain design of his? If contraries be those things that destroy one another, as he himself affirms, I do not see how two bodies that encounter each other in a circular line should less prejudice each other than if they interfered in a straight line.

SAGR.: Hold a little, I pray you. Tell me, Simplicius, when two knights encounter each other, tilting in open field, or when two whole squadrons, or two fleets at sea, make up to grapple, and are broken and sunk, do you call these encounters contrary to each other?

SIMP.: Yes, we say they are contrary.

SAGR.: How, then, is there no contrariety in circular motions? These motions, being made upon the surface of the Earth or water, which are, as you know, spherical, come to be circular. Can you tell, Simplicius, what those circular motions can be that are not contrary to each other? They are, if I mistake not, those of two tangent circles, where one of them being turned makes the other move the contrary way; but, if one of them shall be

within the other, it is impossible that they should not jostle each other, their motion being made towards different points.

SALV.: But be they contrary or not contrary, these are but altercations of words; and I know that it would be far more proper and agreeable with Nature if we could save all with only one motion than to introduce two that are opposite (if you will not call them contrary). Yet I do not censure this introduction of opposites as impossible or pretend from the denial thereof to infer a necessary demonstration but only the greater probability of the other.

A *third* reason which makes the Ptolemaic hypothesis less probable is that it most unreasonably confounds the order that we assuredly see among those celestial bodies of which the circumgyration is not questionable but most certain. And that order is that, the greater a sphere, the longer is its revolution. Thus Saturn, describing a greater circle than all the other planets, completes it in thirty years; Jupiter finishes its, that is less, in twelve years; Mars in two; the Moon run through its, so much less than the rest, in only a month. Nor do we see less sensibly that that one of the Medicean Stars which is nearest to Jupiter makes its revolution in a very short time, that is, in forty-two hours, or thereabouts, the next to that in three days and a half, the third in seven days, and the most remote in sixteen. And this rate holds well enough, nor will it alter at all when we assign the rotation of twenty-four hours to the terrestrial globe. But, if you would have the Earth immovable, it is necessary that, when you have passed from the short period of the Moon to the others successively bigger, until you come to that of Saturn, which is of thirty years, it is necessary, I say, that you pass to another sphere incomparably greater than that and make this accomplish an entire revolution in twenty-four hours. And this yet is the least disorder that can follow. For if anyone should pass from the sphere of Saturn to the starry orb, and make it so much bigger than that of Saturn, as proportion would require in respect of its own very slow motion of many thousands of years, then it must certainly be a jump much more absurd to skip from this to another still bigger one, the *Primum Mobile,* and to make it revolve in twenty-four hours.

But if the motion of the Earth is granted, the order of the periods will be exactly observed, and from the very slow sphere of Saturn we come to the fixed stars which are wholly immovable and so avoid a *fourth* difficulty we would have if the starry sphere be supposed movable. That is the immense disparity between the motions of those stars themselves, of which some would come to move most swiftly in most vast circles, others most slowly in circles very small, according as the former or the latter should be found nearer or more remote from the Poles. This is accompanied with still more inconveniences, because we see that those of whose motion there is no question have been made to move all on a great circle; also, because it seems to be an act done with no good consideration to constitute bodies that are designed to move circularly at immense distances from the centre and afterwards to make them move in very small circles.

And not only the magnitudes of the circles and consequently the velocity of the motions of these stars shall be most different from the circles and motions of those others, but (which shall be the *fifth* inconvenience) the self-same star shall successively vary its circles and velocities. For those which two thousand years since were in the Equator, and consequently described very vast circles, being in our days many degrees distant, must of necessity become slower and be reduced to move in lesser circles. And it is not altogether impossible but that a time may come in which some of them which in aforetime had continually moved shall be reduced by uniting with the pole to a state of rest and then, after some time of cessation, shall return to their motion again; whereas the other stars whose motion none doubt all describe the great circle of their sphere and in that maintain themselves without any variation.

The absurdity is further increased (which is the *sixth* inconvenience) in that no thought can comprehend what ought to be the solidity of that immense sphere, whose depth so steadfastly holds fixed such a multitude of stars, which are with so much concord carried about without ever changing site among themselves with so great disparity of motions. Or else, supposing the heavens to be fluid, as we are with more reason to believe, so that every star wanders to and fro in it by ways of its own, what rules shall regulate their motions, and to .what purpose, so that, seen from the Earth, they appear as though they were made by one single sphere? It is my opinion that they might so much more easily and more conveniently do that, by being constituted immovable, than by being made errant, by as much as it is easier to. number the blocks in the pavement of a piazza than a rout of boys which run up and down upon them.

Lastly, which is the *seventh* instance, if we attribute the diurnal motion to the highest heaven, it must be constituted of such a force and efficacy as to carry along with it the innumerable multitude of fixed stars, bodies of cast magnitude far bigger than the Earth, and, moreover, all the spheres of the planets, notwithstanding that both the first and the last by their own nature move the contrary way. And, beside all this, it must be granted that also the element of fire and the greater part of the air are likewise forcibly hurried along with the rest and that only the little globe of the Earth contumaciously and pertinaciously stands unmoved against such an impulse. This in my thinking is very difficult; nor can I see how the Earth, a suspended body equilibrated upon its centre, exposed indifferently to either motion or rest, and environed with a liquid ambient, should not yield also like the rest and be carried about. But we find none of these obstacles in making the Earth move, a small body and insensible, compared to the Universe, and therefore unable to offer it any violence.

STUDY QUESTIONS: GALILEI, *DIALOGUE ON THE GREAT WORLD-SYSTEMS*

1. How does the Ptolemaic system characterize the substance of celestial bodies?
2. What is the point that Galileo is making with the example of the anatomists? (A Peripatetic philosopher is an Aristotelian.)

3. How did someone manage to claim that the invention of the telescope was taken from Aristotle? How is this like the relation between a piece of marble and a statue? What was the point of this interchange?
4. Simplicius asks, 'But in case we should give up Aristotle, who is to be our guide in philosophy?' How does Salviatus reply to this question? How does Sagredus reply?
5. What is the true method of finding the motion of the earth? What method is Salviatus rejecting?
6. What was the point of the story of the man on top of the dome of the cathedral who wanted the whole country to turn around in order to avoid having to turn his head?
7. What was the point of the story of the ship laden with merchandise? What is the point that Galileo is trying to make about the nature of motion?
8. From these stories, Salviatus draws the conclusion that it is a simpler hypothesis to postulate a moving earth. This hypothesis is simpler than what? How does Salviatus draw this conclusion from the points established earlier?
9. What is the third reason why the Ptolemaic hypothesis is less probable?

Philosophical Bridges: The Influence of Galileo

Galileo had a huge influence on the development of physics. First, he challenged Aristotle's physics fundamentally, and on many fronts. This was the beginning of the end for Scholasticism and the popular worldview it embraced. For example, Aristotelian physics postulated a fundamental division between the earth and the celestial heavens. Galileo's telescope broke through this barrier: it showed that, like the earth, the heavens are made of inert matter.

Second, the events surrounding Galileo's condemnation deepened the divide between religion and science. Although most intellectuals remained Christians, many were more willing to rethink the role of the Church and to challenge the old view of the universe and the authoritarian conception of knowledge. In short, Galileo's guilty verdict contributed to the end of the Church's supremacy in defining knowledge.

Third, Galileo's outspoken condemnation of Aristotelian physics, his insistence that science must be based on quantifiable results and experimentation, and his utter rejection of authority as evidence articulated a new vision of science and gave courage to a new generation of researchers.

Galileo was the greatest member of a generation of other scientists with similar ideas. For example, Gassendi measured the speed of sound and developed a primitive molecular theory of heat. In 1636, his friend Marin Mersenne completed other work on the physics of sound using vibrating strings. In 1611, Kepler studied the refraction of light by lenses, and, in 1621, Willebrad Snell formulated the mathematically precise laws of refraction, which enabled the construction of better lenses.

Descartes also stands out as a scientific leader influenced by Galileo. By employing his geometrical conception of matter, tried to unify the work of his contemporaries into one overall theory of mechanical physics, which covered areas as diverse as the formation and movement of the planets, heat, light, magnetism, anatomy, and animal behavior.

Fourth, Galileo left physics with a problem. Unaware of the importance of Kepler's work, he had assumed that the planets orbit around the sun in circles, and he had mistakenly thought that their circular orbits could be explained in terms of inertia. However, as Descartes saw, the principle of inertia applies only to uniform motion in a straight line and not to circular and elliptical motion. Thus, how could the elliptical orbits of the planets be explained? The definitive answer for the period was Newton's theory of gravity.

Isaac Newton (1642–1727)

Biographical History

Sir Isaac Newton was born near Grantham in England during the year that Galileo died. With the help of an uncle, he entered Trinity College, Cambridge, to study and, later, to teach mathematics and physics. His early work was concerned with the nature of light and optics, as well as with the theory of calculus, which he called fluxions. In 1666, the year that the bubonic plague hit England, Newton discovered the calculus and the composition of light. After 1679, Newton began to work in the field of astronomy, which led eventually to the publication of the groundbreaking *Principia* in 1687. From 1661 to 1691, he also experimented in alchemy. He also worked extensively in theology. Newton moved to London when he was made warden of the Mint in 1695, and its master in 1699. In 1703, he was appointed president of the Royal Society, and in 1705, he was knighted by Queen Anne. After Newton died at the age of 85, Voltaire marveled that a mathematician was buried with the honors of a king. Of his own work, Newton said, 'To myself I seem to have been only like a boy playing on the seashore . . . while the great ocean of truth lay all undiscovered before me.'

Philosophical Overview

In 1665–1666, Newton made his most famous mathematical finding, the calculus, also discovered by Leibniz. Newton's first work in physics was in optics. In 1666, he showed that sunlight is composed of light of the colors of the rainbow, each with a specific angle of refraction, which can be separated by a prism. As a result, he developed a corpuscular theory of light, whose velocity he calculated as 190,000 miles per second. His *Opticks* was published in 1704.

Also in 1666, Newton began to conceive of the gravity of the earth extending to the orbit of the moon. Voltaire portrays Newton as discovering gravity that year after seeing an apple fall from a tree. The story is probably false. Between 1679 and 1684, Newton worked out the mathematical details of his theory of gravity, using the results of Kepler and Brahe. He formulated the law according to which the force of gravitational attraction between two bodies varies inversely with the square of the distance between them and directly as the product of their masses. He showed how this law explains the elliptical orbits of the planets around the sun, as described by Kepler. This result led to one of the most important scientific works of all time, the *Principia*, published in 1687.

Of course, Newton's system had its critics. Leibniz, Berkeley, and, later, Kant criticized Newton's assumption that space and time are absolute, as well as his mysterious idea of action at a distance without any intervening causal mechanism, as postulated by the force of gravity. Nevertheless, with Newton, the promise of natural science to explain the workings of the universe with a few simple principles seemed to have been fulfilled. Eventually, Newton's mechanics usurped Descartes' physics, and it remained the dominant macrophysical paradigm until Albert Einstein's theories of special and general relativity in the early twentieth century.

PRINCIPIA

Newton's greatest work, the *Mathematical Principles of Natural Philosophy*, or the *Principia*, was published in 1687. He advances some definitions and scholium in which Newton explains the notions of absolute space, time, and motion. He then states the axioms of his physics, his three laws of motion. The first law states that every body continues in its state of rest, or uniform motion in a straight line, unless it is moved to change that state by external forces. The second law states that the change of motion is proportional to the external force and is made in the direction of the straight line in which that force is applied. The third law states that, for every action, there is an equal and opposite reaction.

Newton shows how these three laws, together with the principle of gravity, explain a huge range of natural phenomena, extending from the orbits of the planets to the relative density of the earth, and from the force of the tides to the flattening of the earth at the poles.

DEFINITIONS

1.

Quantity of matter is a measure of matter that arises from its density and volume jointly.

2.

Quantity of motion is a measure of motion that arises from the velocity and the quantity of matter jointly.

3.

Inherent force of matter is the power of resisting by which every body, so far as it is able, perseveres in its state either of resting or of moving uniformly straight forward.

4.

Impressed force is the action exerted on a body to change its state either of resting or of moving uniformly straight forward.

5.

Centripetal force is the force by which bodies are drawn from all sides, are impelled, or in any way tend, toward some point as to a center.

6.

The absolute quantity of centripetal force is the measure of this force that is greater or less in proportion to the efficacy of the cause propagating it from a center through the surrounding regions.

7.

The motive quantity of centripetal force is the measure of this force that is proportional to the motion which it generates in a given time.

8.

The accelerative quantity of centripetal force is the measure of this force that is proportional to the velocity which it generates in a given time.

SCHOLIUM

Thus far it has seemed best to explain the senses in which less familiar words are to be taken in this treatise. Although time, space, place, and motion are very familiar to everyone, it must be noted that these quantities are popularly conceived solely with reference to the objects of sense perception. And this is the source of certain preconceptions; to eliminate them it is useful to distinguish these quantities into absolute and relative, true and apparent, mathematical and common.

1. Absolute, true, and mathematical time, in and of itself and of its own nature, without reference to anything external, flows uniformly and by another name is called duration. Relative, apparent, and common time is any sensible and external measure (precise or imprecise) of duration by means of motion; such a measure—for example, an hour, a day, a month, a year—is commonly used instead of true time.

2. Absolute space, of its own nature without reference to anything external, always remains homogeneous and immovable. Relative space is any movable measure or dimension of this absolute space; such a measure or dimension is determined by our senses from the situation of the space with respect to bodies and is popularly used for immovable space, as in the case of space under the earth or in the air or in the heavens, where the dimension is determined from the situation of the space with respect to the earth. Absolute and relative space are the same in species and in magnitude, but they do not always remain the same numerically. For example, if the earth moves, the space of our air, which in a relative sense and with respect to the earth always remains the same, will now be one part of the absolute space into which the air passes, now another part of it, and thus will be changing continually in an absolute sense.

3. Place is the part of space that a body occupies, and it is, depending on the space, either absolute or relative. I say the part of space, not the position of the body or its outer surface. For the places of equal solids are always equal, while their surfaces are for the most part unequal because of the dissimilarity of shapes; and positions, properly speaking, do not have quantity and are not so much places as attributes of places. The motion of a whole is the same as the sum of the motions of the parts; that is, the change in position of a whole from its place is the same as the sum of the changes in position of its parts from their places, and thus the place of a whole is the same as the sum of the places of the parts and therefore is internal and in the whole body.

4. Absolute motion is the change of position of a body from one absolute place to another; relative motion is change of position from one relative place to another. Thus, in a ship under sail, the relative place of a body is that region of the ship in which the body happens to be or that part of the whole interior of the ship which the body fills and which accordingly moves along with the ship, and relative rest is the continuance of the body in that same region of the ship or same part of its interior. But true rest is the continuance of a body in the same part of that unmoving space in which the ship itself, along with its interior and all its contents, is moving. Therefore, if the earth is truly at rest, a body that is relatively at rest on a ship will move truly and absolutely with the velocity with which the ship is moving on the earth. But if the earth is also moving, the true and absolute motion of the body will arise partly from the true motion of the earth in unmoving space and partly from the relative motion of the ship on the earth. Further, if the body is also moving relatively on the ship, its true motion will arise partly from the true motion of the earth in unmoving space and partly from the relative motions both of the ship on the earth and of the body on the ship, and from these relative motions the relative motion of the body on the earth will arise. For example, if that part of the earth where the ship happens to be is truly moving eastward with a velocity of 10,010 units, and the ship is being borne westward by sails and wind with a velocity of 10 units, and a sailor is walking on the ship toward the east with a velocity of 1 unit, then the sailor will be moving truly and absolutely in unmoving space toward the east with a velocity of 10,001 units and relatively on the earth toward the west with a velocity of 9 units.

In astronomy, absolute time is distinguished from relative time by the equation of common time. For natural days, which are commonly considered equal for the purpose of measuring time, are actually unequal. Astronomers correct this inequality in order to measure celestial motions on the basis of a truer time. It is possible that there is no uniform motion by which time may have an exact measure. All motions can be accelerated and retarded, but the flow of absolute time cannot be changed. The duration or perseverance of the existence of things is the same, whether their motions are rapid or slow or null:

accordingly, duration is rightly distinguished from its sensible measures and is gathered from them by means of an astronomical equation. Moreover, the need for using this equation in determining when phenomena occur is proved by experience with a pendulum clock and also by eclipses of the satellites of Jupiter.

Just as the order of the parts of time is unchangeable, so, too, is the order of the parts of space. Let the parts of space move from their places, and they will move (so to speak) from themselves. For times and spaces are, as it were, the places of themselves and of all things. All things are placed in time with reference to order of succession and in space with reference to order of position. It is of the essence of spaces to be places, and for primary places to move is absurd. They are therefore absolute places, and it is only changes of position from these places that are absolute motions.

But since these parts of space cannot be seen and cannot be distinguished from one another by our senses, we use sensible measures in their stead. For we define all places on the basis of the positions and distances of things from some body that we regard as immovable, and then we reckon all motions with respects to these places, insofar as we conceive of bodies as being changed in position with respect to them. Thus, instead of absolute places and motions we use relative ones, which is not inappropriate in ordinary human affairs, although in philosophy abstraction from the senses is required. For it is possible that there is no body truly at rest to which places and motions may be referred.

Moreover, absolute and relative rest and motion are distinguished from each other by their properties, causes, and effects. It is a property of rest that bodies truly at rest are at rest in relation to one another. And therefore, since it is possible that some body in the regions of the fixed stars or far beyond is absolutely at rest, and yet it cannot be known from the position of bodies in relation to one another in our regions whether or not any of these maintains a given position with relation to that distant body, true rest cannot be defined on the basis of the position of bodies in relation to one another.—

It is a property of motion that parts which keep given positions in relation to wholes participate in the motions of such wholes. For all the parts of bodies revolving in orbit endeavor to recede from the axis of motion, and the impetus of bodies moving forward arises from the joint impetus of the individual parts. Therefore, when bodies containing others move, whatever is relatively at rest within them also moves. And thus true and absolute motion cannot be determined by means of change of position from the vicinity of bodies that are regarded as being at rest. For the exterior bodies ought to be regarded not only as being at rest but also as being truly at rest. Otherwise all contained bodies, besides being subject to change of position from the vicinity of the containing bodies, will participate in the true motions of the containing bodies and, if there is no such change of position, will not be truly at rest but only be regarded as being at rest. For containing bodies are to those inside them as the outer part of the whole to the inner part or as the shell to the kernel. And when the shell moves, the kernel also, without being changed in position from the vicinity of the shell, moves as a part of the whole.

A property akin to the preceding one is that when a place moves, whatever is placed in it moves along with it, and therefore a body moving away from a place that moves participates also in the motion of its place. Therefore, all motions away from places that move are only parts of whole and absolute motions, and every whole motion is compounded of the motion of a body away from its initial place, and the motion of this place away from its place, and so on, until an unmoving place is reached, as in the above-mentioned example of the sailor. Thus, whole and absolute motions can be determined only by means of unmoving places, and therefore in what has preceded I have referred such motions to unmoving places and relative motions to movable places. Moreover, the only places that are unmoving are those that all keep given positions in relation to one another from infinity to infinity and therefore always remain immovable and constitute the space that I call immovable.

The causes which distinguish true motions from relative motions are the forces impressed upon bodies to generate motion. True motion is neither generated nor changed except by forces impressed upon the moving body itself, but relative motion can be generated and changed without the impression of forces upon this body. For the impression of forces solely on other bodies with which a given body has a relation is enough, when the other bodies yield, to produce a change in that relation which constitutes the relative rest or motion of this body. Again, true motion is always changed by forces impressed upon a moving body, but relative motion is not necessarily changed by such forces. For if the same forces are impressed upon a moving body and also upon other bodies with which it has a relation, in such a way that the relative position is maintained, the relation that constitutes the relative motion will also be maintained. Therefore, every relative motion can be changed while the true motion is preserved, and can be preserved while the true one is changed, and thus true motion certainly does not consist in relations of this sort.

The effects distinguishing absolute motion from relative motion are the forces of receding from the axis of circular motion. For in purely relative circular motion these forces are null, while in true and absolute circular motion they are larger or smaller in proportion to the quantity of motion. If a bucket is hanging from a very long cord and is continually turned around until the cord becomes twisted tight, and if the bucket is thereupon filled with water and is at rest along with the water and then, by some sudden force, is made to turn around in the opposite direction and, as the cord unwinds, perseveres for a while in this motion; then the surface of the water will at first be level, just as it was before the vessel began to move. But after the vessel, by the force gradually impressed upon the water, has caused the water also to begin revolving perceptibly, the water will gradually recede from the middle and rise up the sides of the vessel, assuming a concave shape (as experience has shown me), and, with an ever faster motion, will rise further and further until, when it completes its revolutions in the same times as the vessel, it is relatively at rest in the vessel. The rise of the water reveals its endeavor to recede from the axis of motion, and from such an endeavor one can find out and measure the true and absolute circular motion of the water, which here is the direct opposite of its relative motion. In the beginning, when the relative motion of the water in the vessel was greatest, that motion was not giving rise to any endeavor to recede from the axis; the water did not seek the circumfer-

ence by rising up the sides of the vessel but remained level, and therefore its true circular motion had not yet begun. But afterward, when the relative motion of the water decreased, its rise up the sides of the vessel revealed its endeavor to recede from the axis, and this endeavor showed the true circular motion of the water to be continually increasing and finally becoming greatest when the water was relatively at rest in the vessel. Therefore, that endeavor does not depend on the change of position of the water with respect to surrounding bodies, and thus true circular motion cannot be determined by means of such changes of position. The truly circular motion of each revolving body is unique, corresponding to a unique endeavor as its proper and sufficient effect, while relative motions are innumerable in accordance with their varied relations to external bodies and, like relations, are completely lacking in true effects except insofar as they participate in that true and unique motion. Thus, even in the system of those who hold that our heavens revolve below the heavens of the fixed stars and carry the planets around with them, the individual parts of the heavens, and the planets that are relatively at rest in the heavens to which they belong, are truly in motion. For they change their positions relative to one another (which is not the case with things that are truly at rest), and as they are carried around together with the heavens, they participate in the motions of the heavens and, being parts of revolving wholes, endeavor to recede from the axes of those wholes.

Relative quantities, therefore, are not the actual quantities whose names they bear but are those sensible measures of them (whether true or erroneous) that are commonly used instead of the quantities being measured. But if the meanings of words are to be defined by usage, then it is these sensible measures which should properly be understood by the terms "time," "space," "place," and "motion," and the manner of expression will be out of the ordinary and purely mathematical if the quantities being measured are understood here. Accordingly those who there interpret these words as referring to the quantities being measured do violence to the Scriptures. And they no less corrupt mathematics and philosophy who confuse true quantities with their relations and common measures.

It is certainly very difficult to find out the true motions of individual bodies and actually to differentiate them from apparent motions, because the parts of that immovable space in which the bodies truly move make no impression on the senses. Nevertheless, the case is not utterly hopeless. For it is possible to draw evidence partly from apparent motions, which are the differences between the true motions, and partly from the forces that are the causes and effects of the true motions. For example, if two balls, at a given distance from each other with a cord connecting them, were revolving about a common center of gravity, the endeavor of the balls to recede from the axis of motion could be known from the tension of the cord, and thus the quantity of circular motion could be computed. Then, if any equal forces were simultaneously impressed upon the alternate faces of the balls to increase or decrease their circular motion, the increase or decrease of the motion could be known from the increased or decreased tension of the cord, and thus, finally, it could be discovered which faces of the balls the forces would have to be impressed upon for a maximum increase in the motion, that is, which were the posterior faces, or the ones that are in the rear in a circular motion. Further, once the faces that follow and the opposite faces that precede were known, the direction of the motion would be known. In this way both the quantity and the direction of this circular motion could be found in any immense vacuum, where nothing external and sensible existed with which the balls could be compared. Now if some distant bodies were set in that space and maintained given positions with respect to one another, as the fixed stars do in the regions of the heavens, it could not, of course, be known from the relative change of position of the balls among the bodies whether the motion was to be attributed to the bodies or to the balls. But if the cord was examined and its tension was discovered to be the very one which the motion of the balls required, it would be valid to conclude that the motion belonged to the balls and that the bodies were at rest, and then, finally, from the change of position of the balls among the bodies, to determine the direction of this motion. But in what follows, a fuller explanation will be given of how to determine true motions from their causes, effects, and apparent differences, and, conversely, of how to determine

from motions, whether true or apparent, their causes and effects. For this was the purpose for which I composed the following treatise.

AXIOMS, OR THE LAWS OF MOTION

Law 1   *Every body perseveres in its state of being at rest or of moving uniformly straight forward, except insofar as it is compelled to change its state by forces impressed.*

Projectiles persevere in their motions, except insofar as they are retarded by the resistance of the air and are impelled downward by the force of gravity. A spinning hoop, which has parts that by their cohesion continually draw one another back from rectilinear motions, does not cease to rotate, except insofar as it is retarded by the air. And larger bodies—planets and comets—preserve for a longer time both their progressive and their circular motions, which take place in spaces having less resistance.

Law 2   *A change in motion is proportional to the motive force impressed and takes place along the straight line in which that force is impressed.*

If some force generates any motion, twice the force will generate twice the motion, and three times the force will generate three times the motion, whether the force is impressed all at once or successively by degrees. And if the body was previously moving, the new motion (since motion is always in the same direction as the generative force) is added to the original motion if that motion was in the same direction or is subtracted from the original motion if it was in the opposite direction or, if it was in an oblique direction, is combined obliquely and compounded with it according to the directions of both motions.

Law 3   *To any action there is always an opposite and equal reaction; in other words, the actions of two bodies upon each other are always equal and always opposite in direction.*

Whatever presses or draws something else is pressed or drawn just as much by it. If anyone presses a stone with a finger, the finger is also pressed by the stone. If a horse draws a stone tied to a rope, the horse will (so to speak) also be drawn back equally toward the stone, for the rope, stretched out at both ends, will urge the horse toward the stone and the stone toward the horse by one and the same endeavor to go slack and will impede the forward motion of the one as much as it promotes the forward motion of the other. If some body impinging upon another body changes the motion of that body in any way by its own force, then, by the force of the other body (because of the equality of their mutual pressure), it also will in turn undergo the same change in its own motion in the opposite direction. By means of these actions, equal changes occur in the motions, not in the velocities—that is, of course, if the bodies are not impeded by anything else. For the changes in velocities that likewise occur in opposite directions are inversely proportional to the bodies because the motions are changed equally. This law is valid also for attractions, as will be proved in the next scholium.

BOOK 3

Rules for the Study of Natural Philosophy

Rule 1 *No more causes of natural things should be admitted than are both true and sufficient to explain their phenomena.*

As the philosophers say: Nature does nothing in vain, and more causes are in vain when fewer suffice. For nature is simple and does not indulge in the luxury of superfluous causes.

Rule 2 *Therefore, the causes assigned to natural effects of the same kind must be, so far as possible, the same.*

Examples are the cause of respiration in man and beast, or of the falling of stones in Europe and America, or of the light of a kitchen fire and the sun, or of the reflection of light on our earth and the planets.

Rule 3 *Those qualities of bodies that cannot be intended and remitted [i.e., qualities that cannot be increased and diminished] and that belong to all bodies on which experiments can be made should be taken as qualities of all bodies universally.*

For the qualities of bodies can be known only through experiments; and therefore qualities that square with experiments universally are to be regarded as universal qualities; and qualities that cannot be diminished cannot be taken away from bodies. Certainly idle fancies ought not to be fabricated recklessly against the evidence of experiments, nor should we depart from the analogy of nature, since nature is always simple and ever consonant with itself. The extension of bodies is known to us only through our senses, and yet there are bodies beyond the range of these senses; but because extension is found in all sensible bodies, it is ascribed to all bodies universally. We know by experience that some bodies are hard. Moreover, because the hardness of the whole arises from the hardness of its parts, we justly infer from this not only the hardness of the undivided particles of bodies that are accessible to our senses, but also of all other bodies. That all bodies are impenetrable we gather not by reason but by our senses. We find those bodies that we handle to be impenetrable, and hence we conclude that impenetrability is a property of all bodies universally. That all bodies are movable and persevere in motion or in rest by means of certain forces (which we call forces of inertia) we infer from finding these properties in the bodies that we have seen. The extension, hardness, impenetrability, mobility, and force of inertia of the whole arise from the extension, hardness, impenetrability, mobility, and force of inertia of each of the parts; and thus we conclude that every one of the least parts of all bodies is extended, hard, impenetrable, movable, and endowed with a force of inertia. And this is the foundation of all natural philosophy. Further, from phenomena we know that the divided, contiguous parts of bodies can be separated from one another, and from mathematics it is certain that the undivided parts can be distinguished into smaller parts by our reason.

But it is uncertain whether those parts which have been distinguished in this way and not yet divided can actually be divided and separated from one another by the forces of nature. But if it were established by even a single experiment that in the breaking of a hard and solid body, any undivided particle underwent division, we should conclude by the force of this third rule not only that divided parts are separable but also that undivided parts can be divided indefinitely.

Finally, if it is universally established by experiments and astronomical observations that all bodies on or near the earth gravitate [lit. are heavy] toward the earth, and do so in proportion to the quantity of matter in each body, and that the moon gravitates [is heavy] toward the earth in proportion to the quantity of its matter, and that our sea in turn gravitates [is heavy] toward the moon, and that all planets gravitate [are heavy] toward one another, and that there is a similar gravity [heaviness] of comets toward the sun, it will have to be concluded by this third rule that all bodies gravitate toward one another. Indeed, the argument from phenomena will be even stronger for universal gravity than for the impenetrability of bodies, for which, of course, we have not a single experiment, and not even an observation, in the case of the heavenly bodies. Yet I am by no means affirming that gravity is essential to bodies. By inherent force I mean only the force of inertia. This is immutable. Gravity is diminished as bodies recede from the earth.

Rule 4 *In experimental philosophy, propositions gathered from phenomena by induction should be considered either exactly or very nearly true notwithstanding any contrary hypotheses, until yet other phenomena make such propositions either more exact or liable to exceptions.*

This rule should be followed so that arguments based on induction may not be nullified by hypotheses.

STUDY QUESTIONS: NEWTON, *PRINCIPIA*

1. How does Newton define 'quantity of matter' and 'quantity of motion'?
2. How does Newton distinguish absolute and relative space?
3. What is the difference between absolute and relative motion?
4. How could one distinguish between the two in practice?
5. What was the point of the example of the bucket filled with water?
6. State and explain each of Newton's three laws of motion.
7. What are the four rules for the study of natural philosophy?
8. What purpose do these rules serve?

Philosophical Bridges: Newton's Influence

Newton's work forms the pinnacle of modern science. This is significant in two ways. First, it means that the most significant developments in physics after Newton are not Newtonian. Since Newton completed the work initiated by Kepler, Galileo, and Descartes, later breakthroughs, such as the theory of electromagnetism advanced by James Maxwell, led physics in a different direction. Second, Newton's achievement marks the beginning of the separation of philosophy and the natural sciences, especially physics. After Newton, philosophers were not physicists, despite some notable exceptions, such as Leibniz. The two disciplines separated partly because Newton's work attained a level of mathematical precision and experimental rigor that demanded specialization.

Newton's work exercised a tremendous influence on thought beyond physics. Although Berkeley, Leibniz, and Kant challenged some of the assumptions behind his physics, such as the postulation of absolute space, Newton's theories became a model for the natural sciences, which in turn became considered increasingly as the paradigm for all knowledge. Newton's theory explains a wide range of observable phenomena in terms of three laws of motion and the principle of gravity. Thinkers strove for the same comprehensive simplicity in their own theories in other fields of knowledge. For example, Hume sometimes portrayed his work as a continuation of Newtonian principles in the area of moral psychology, and the positivist Auguste Comte (1798–1857) argued that the methods of the natural sciences should be extended to the study of society through the formulation of appropriate causal laws.

Bibliography

Primary

Copernicus, Nicolaus, *On the Revolutions* (complete works), vol. 2, trans. Edward Rosen, John Hopkins, 1992

Galileo Galilei, *Sidereus Nuncius* (*The Sidereal Messenger*), trans. Albert Van Helden, University of Chicago Press, 1989

——, *Dialogue on the Great World Systems*, selection from Day 2, trans. G. de Santillana, University of Chicago Press, 1953

Johannes Kepler, *New Astronomy*, trans. W. H. Donahue, Cambridge University Press, 1992

Matthews, Michael, ed., *The Scientific Background to Modern Philosophy,* Hackett, 1989

Newton, Isaac, *Principia,* trans. I. B. Cohen and Anne Whitman, University of California Press, 1999

Secondary

Boas, Marie, *The Scientific Renaissance 1450–1630,* Harper & Row, 1962

Casper, Max, *Kepler,* Dover, 1993

Cohen, Bernard, *The Newtonian Revolution,* Cambridge University Press, 1980

Dyksterhuis, E. J., *The Mechanization of the World Picture,* Princeton University Press, 1986

Drake, Stillman, *Galileo at Work: His Scientific Biography,* University of Chicago Press, 1978

Thayer, H. S., *Newton's Philosophy of Nature* (selections), Hafner Publishing, 1953

Wartofsky, Marx, *Models Representations and the Scientific Understanding,* Reidel, 1979

SECTION II

◆ THE RATIONALISTS ◆

PROLOGUE

In seventeenth- and eighteenth-century Europe it seemed that there were two methods for acquiring scientific knowledge: mathematical reasoning and observation. Whereas Descartes stressed the importance of mathematics and mechanical explanation in science, Bacon emphasized science's experimental and observational aspects and its role in making useful predictions. This difference of emphasis led to the development of Rationalism and Empiricism.

Rationalism is roughly the view that reason, without the aid of sense perception, can give us knowledge of the world. Reason can discover self-evident axioms that govern the universe, and, in principle, all other knowledge can be deduced rationally from these axioms, the most important of which is the Principle of Sufficient Reason, which states that nothing happens without a reason. Rationalists, such as Descartes, Spinoza, and Leibniz, understand the Principle of Sufficient Reason to imply that there must be a complete explanation of everything that happens. For example, all physical laws must be derivable logically from a few self-evident fundamental principles. Furthermore, Rationalists tend to conceive of causation on the model of logical deduction. In other words, given the causes, the effect follows with logical necessity just as the conclusion of a valid argument follows logically from its premises. Given the totality of causes, the effect logically must be as it is.

Rationalism has three characteristics that result from the Principle of Sufficient Reason:

1. In its ideal form, knowledge is a deductive system of truths, analogous to a mathematical system. Mathematics provides the paradigm for knowledge because of its clarity and certainty. Furthermore, because everything must have a sufficient explanation, all truths are knowable a priori through reason.
2. Sense experience and observation are an inferior form of reasoning. Sense experience is unreliable as a source of knowledge; its ideas are confused, incomplete, and misleading, and they must be corrected by certain principles validated by reason. Spinoza calls sense perception 'conclusions without premises,' emphasizing that sense perception does not

reveal the causal and deductive connection between things, unlike knowledge gained through reasoning.

3. Because of their tendency to treat all truths as necessary, Rationalists have problems accounting for contingency in the world. Consequently, they either affirm determinism, as in the case of Spinoza, or have difficulties in trying to give an adequate explanation of contingency. Again, this is a consequence of their acceptance and use of the Principle of Sufficient Reason, which tends to assimilate causation to logical demonstration.

These common general features of Rationalism should not be taken as indicating uniformity of views. 'Rationalism' is a vague label imposed on the modern period after the fact. It is not a philosophical school. Moreover, although they share a common emphasis and general direction of thought, there are important differences among the three Rationalist philosophers, Descartes, Spinoza, and Leibniz.

RENÉ DESCARTES (1596–1650)

Biographical History

In 1616, after studying law at Poitiers in his native France, René Descartes began to travel, hoping to discover the knowledge contained 'in the great book of the world.' In Holland, he met Isaac Beckman, who stimulated Descartes' interests in mathematics and physics. Descartes then enlisted in the army. On November 10, 1619, stranded in a winter storm alone in a room, Descartes began to doubt all his beliefs. That night he had three dreams that he felt were divine indications of his philosophical mission to discover the unity of the sciences. During the 1620s, Descartes continued traveling in Germany, Holland, France, and Italy. In 1629, he decided to settle in Holland, where he experimented in optics and physiology, and visited universities to talk to mathematicians and doctors. By 1633, he had completed a work called *The World*, which explained 'all of physics,' and included topics such as heat, light, astronomy, and human physiology. Descartes withdrew the book when he heard of Galileo's condemnation by the Church. In 1637, he published the *Discourse on the Method for Conducting One's Reason Rightly*. Between 1638 and 1640, Descartes lived with his former servant, Hélène, who had borne him a daughter, Francine. The child died suddenly in 1640. In 1641, his main work, the *Meditations on First Philosophy*, was published with six sets of objections and his replies. Two years later, he began his celebrated correspondence with Princess Elizabeth of Bohemia. In 1644, he dedicated the *Principles of Philosophy* to Princess Elizabeth, and his last work, *The Passion of the Soul*, was inspired by his discussions with her. In 1649, he left for Sweden to act as tutor to Queen Christina. A few months later, he caught pneumonia and died.

Philosophical Overview

The main aims of Descartes' *Meditations* are, first, to build a secure foundation for knowledge and, in particular, for his physics and, second, to show that this physics is compatible with the two main claims of religion, namely, the existence of God and the soul.

The Method of Doubt

In the First Meditation, Descartes outlines his Method of Doubt. He realizes that many of his beliefs are unreliable and that knowledge must be based on certainty, which we can gain only by rejecting the uncertain. The ultimate aim of the method is to discover a secure foundation for knowledge and, more specifically, for the new physics. In other words, Descartes raises the question of doubt only to show how it should be answered. This answer will reveal how his own scientific approach is preferable to Scholasticism, as well as how science and religion can be reconciled.

Doubt does not require thinking that ones beliefs are false; it means suspending judgment as to their truth. In effect, Descartes' Method of Doubt amounts to withholding the judgment that anything in the external world corresponds to our ideas in the mind. It consists of three progressively radical arguments, the conclusion of each of which is to show that doubt is reasonable.

In the third stage of doubt, Descartes claims that he has no evidence to refute the claim that there is a supremely powerful and intelligent spirit, which does its utmost to deceive him. However, if there were a powerful deceiving demon, he (Descartes) would be mistaken even in thinking that his sense experiences correspond to external objects at all. The argument is as follows:

1. *I have no evidence that there is no powerful spirit deceiving me.*
2. *If there were such a demon, then all my beliefs would be mistaken.*
3. *If I have no evidence against the claim that a belief is mistaken, then that belief is open to reasonable doubt.*

---

4. *Therefore, all my beliefs are open to reasonable doubt.*

Regarding the first premise, consider the following two theories, A and B:

A. *The ideas that I now have are caused by material objects.*
B. *The ideas that I now have are caused by a deceiving demon.*

Premise 1 claims that there is no reason for thinking that theory A is more likely to be true than B. The two theories explain equally well the empirical data, namely, the sensory ideas that I am now having. Hence, there is no evidence that any one of the two theories is more likely to be true. This point forces us to distinguish between an idea perceived and the external cause of that idea. To see this consider two questions. First, can you imagine an experience exactly like the one that you are having now, except that it is not caused by external objects? We seem to be forced to answer 'Yes' because the external cause of the perception lies outside the perception itself. Second, do you have any evidence that your current experience is not in fact the duplicate? We seem forced to answer 'No' because we have admitted that the original and duplicate experiences are exactly alike. For Descartes, this skeptical argument presents a challenge, which requires that knowledge be placed on a secure rational foundation.

The Cogito

In the Second Meditation, Descartes claims that even a malicious demon could not deceive me into falsely believing that I do not exist. I cannot doubt that I exist without also supposing that I really do exist. Thus, I can be certain of my own existence merely from the fact that I am doubting. Since, doubt is only one kind of thought, the inference 'I doubt therefore I am' can be generalized to 'I think therefore I am' or 'Cogito ergo sum.'

Vindicating the Senses

After the Cogito, Descartes' *Meditations* follows two paths. Along the first, he tries to establish the existence and nature of the physical world. Along the second path, Descartes reveals the nature of the mind and, in the Sixth Meditation, its separation from the body.

At the end of the Second Meditation, Descartes can be certain that he exists and that his nature is to think. However, he has still not bridged the gap from this knowledge of his own mind to that of the external world. He cannot claim knowledge concerning the external world.

Descartes' strategy for bridging the knowledge gap between experience and the world consists of two steps. In the first step, Descartes tries to establish that if God exists, then he can treat his own faculties of judgment as reliable and be sure that clear and distinct ideas are true. In the second step, he offers two proofs of the existence of God. The combination of the two steps can be represented with the following argument.

1. *If God exists, then clear and distinct ideas are true.*
2. *God exists.*

---

3. *Therefore, clear and distinct ideas are true.*

In the above argument, the first premise is justified because God is a perfect being, and therefore, He is not a deceiver. However, He would be a deceiver if He allowed us to be mistaken with regard to our clear and distinct ideas. Thus, we can be sure that such ideas are true. The principle that clear and distinct ideas are true serves as a bridge between the realm of private ideas and the external world because it establishes what the external world is like solely on the basis of how ideas appear to the subject. If an idea is clear and distinct, then I can know that it is so while I am having the idea.

In this way, by the Sixth Meditation, Descartes has restored his knowledge of the world and answered the doubts of the First Meditation. From his search, he has learned three very important lessons. First, he has discovered that sense experience on its own is not a reliable way to gain knowledge; it has to be vindicated by reason. Second, the bridge principle that clear and distinct ideas are true furnishes us with a way of avoiding error: we should suspend our assent to ideas that are unclear or indistinct. This principle provides a foundation for his physics; the idea of the quantifiable properties of matter, such as shape and size, is clear and distinct. At the same time, it shows why the unclear and indistinct idea of Scholastic thought should be rejected. Third, he has shown how the new science can be reconciled with religion. The scientific study of matter must be grounded in clear methodological principles, which require us to show that God exists. Science requires the existence and knowledge of God.

The Real Distinction

The Sixth Meditation contains Descartes' reconstruction of knowledge: God exists and is no deceiver, and, therefore, we can be sure that our clear and distinct ideas are true. This principle has implications for the nature of matter. The only properties of matter are those that can be explained in terms of its essential attribute, extension. To prove that the essence of matter is extension, Descartes argues that a body can lose any of its properties, except extension, without ceasing to be a material body. The claim that matter is extension supports Descartes' mathematical view of science. Extension and motion are quantifiable, and are clear and distinct ideas. This means that Descartes' conception of matter is ultimately geometrical. Descartes argues that all physical phenomena can be explained by the motion of matter, and that all scientific explanation is purely mechanical and, ultimately, geometrical. Descartes' scientific work was very influential because he tries to apply the principles of mechanistic explanation to such a wide range of natural phenomena, such as planetary motion, light, the movement of the tides, and functions of the human body.

In the Second Meditation, Descartes argues that his essence is to think. He argues that he might lack every property except thought and consciousness, because the only thing that he knows for certain about his nature is that he thinks. Thus, his essence is to think. Descartes assumes that any property a substance possesses must be a mode or modification of its essential attribute. Given these points, Descartes tries to show that the mind and the body are distinct entities. This view is called 'mind/body dualism.'

MEDITATIONS ON THE FIRST PHILOSOPHY
In which the Existence of God
and the Distinction between Mind and Body are Demonstrated

In reading the *Meditations*, it is important to remember Descartes' overall goals and his strategy for achieving those aims. Descartes believed that his vision of a unified physical theory of the world based on geometry required a philosophical basis, because without it Scholasticism would continue to dominate European thought and thereby hamper progress.

His philosophical quest, as advanced in the *Meditations*, consists of two basic aims. First, Descartes provides a philosophical foundation for his physics; the foundation is both metaphysical and epistemological. Second, he attempts to prove that his physics is compatible with the basic doctrines of the Christian religion, despite appearances to the contrary.

To achieve his two general aims, Descartes has a simple argumentative strategy, which consists of two parts.

a. *In the first part, he tries to show that the only way to answer radical Skepticism is with a philosophy that provides a solid foundation at the same time for both his own physics and for the essentials of the Christian religion but not for Scholasticism. In effect, he argues that Scholasticism and materialistic atheism are both inadequate because neither can answer the radical Skepticism of the First Meditation. This line of argument is roughly as follows:*

1. *Radical Skepticism needs to be answered.*
2. *The only way to answer it is to demonstrate the principle that clear and distinct ideas are true.*
3. *This principle is true because God exists.*
4. *An epistemology based on this principle supports the geometrical conception of matter.*

This line of argument is pursued mainly in Meditations 1, 3, and 5.

b. *The second part consists in an argument designed to prove that the soul must be a substance distinct from matter. First, the distinction between mind and matter is implied by the very nature of doubt. Second, he argues that, given his modern geometric and anti-Scholastic view of matter, the essence of the mind and that of matter are necessarily different and that, therefore, the soul and the body are distinct. In other words, the new science with an inert conception of matter shows us that the soul is real. This line of argument is pursued in Meditations 2 and 6.*

To summarize, first, he first shows that there is a real skeptical problem. Second, he tries to solve that problem by proving that clear and distinct ideas are true by demonstrat-

R. Descartes, *Meditations*, complete, from *The Philosophical Works of Descartes, Volume 1*, translated by Elizabeth Haldane and G. Ross. Cambridge University Press, 1911.

ing the existence of God. In this way, he shows that his physics has a solid foundation and that this requires, and therefore is compatible with, the existence of God. Third, he argues that a proper scientific understanding of matter reveals that the soul and body are distinct. In short, physics and religion are secure, but Scholasticism is left without foundations.

MEDITATION I

Of the Things Which May Be Brought Within the Sphere of the Doubtful

It is now some years since I detected how many were the false beliefs that I had from my earliest youth admitted as true, and how doubtful was everything I had since constructed on this basis; and from that time I was convinced that I must once for all seriously undertake to rid myself of all the opinions which I had formerly accepted, and commence to build anew from the foundation, if I wanted to establish any firm and permanent structure in the sciences. But as this enterprise appeared to be a very great one, I waited until I had attained an age so mature that I could not hope that at any later date I should be better fitted to execute my design. This reason caused me to delay so long that I should feel that I was doing wrong were I to occupy in deliberation the time that yet remains to me for action. To-day, then, since very opportunely for the plan I have in view I have delivered my mind from every care [and am happily agitated by no passions] and since I have procured for myself an assured leisure in a peaceable retirement, I shall at last seriously and freely address myself to the general upheaval of all my former opinions.

Now for this object it is not necessary that I should show that all of these are false—I shall perhaps never arrive at this end. But inasmuch as reason already persuades me that I ought no less carefully to withhold my assent from matters which are not entirely certain and indubitable than from those which appear to me manifestly to be false, if I am able to find in each one some reason to doubt, this will suffice to justify my rejecting the whole. And for that end it will not be requisite that I should examine each in particular, which would be an endless undertaking; for owing to the fact that the destruction of the foundations of necessity brings with it the downfall of the rest of the edifice, I shall only in the first place attack those principles upon which all my former opinions rested.

All that up to the present time I have accepted as most true and certain I have learned either from the senses or through the senses; but it is sometimes proved to me that these senses are deceptive, and it is wiser not to trust entirely to any thing by which we have once been deceived.

But it may be that although the senses sometimes deceive us concerning things which are hardly perceptible, or very far away, there are yet many others to be met with as to which we cannot reasonably have any doubt, although we recognise them by their means. For example, there is the fact that I am here, seated by the fire, attired in a dressing gown, having this paper in my hands and other similar matters. And how could I deny that these hands and this body are mine, were it not perhaps that I compare myself to certain persons, devoid of sense, whose cerebella are so troubled and clouded by the violent vapours of black bile, that they constantly assure us that they think they are kings when they are really quite poor, or that they are clothed in purple when they are really without covering, or who imagine that they have an earthenware head or are nothing but pumpkins or are made of glass. But they are mad, and I should not be any the less insane were I to follow examples so extravagant.

At the same time I must remember that I am a man, and that consequently I am in the habit of sleeping, and in my dreams representing to myself the same things or sometimes even less probable things, than do those who are insane in their waking moments. How often has it happened to me that in the night I dreamt that I found myself in this particular place, that I was dressed and seated near the fire, whilst in reality I was lying undressed in bed! At this moment it does indeed seem to me that it is with eyes awake that I am looking at this paper; that this head which I move is not asleep, that it is deliberately and of set purpose that I extend my hand and perceive it; what happens in sleep does not appear so clear nor so distinct as does all this. But in thinking over this I remind myself that on many occasions I have in sleep been deceived by similar illusions, and in dwelling carefully on this reflection I see so manifestly that there are no certain indications by which we may clearly distinguish wakefulness from sleep that I am lost in astonishment. And my astonishment is such that it is almost capable of persuading me that I now dream.

Now let us assume that we are asleep and that all these particulars, e.g. that we open our eyes, shake our head, extend our hands, and so on, are but false delusions; and let us reflect that possibly neither our hands nor our whole body are such as they appear to us to be. At the same time we must at least confess that the things which are represented to us in sleep are like painted representations which can only have been formed as the counterparts of something real and true, and that in this way those general things at least, i.e. eyes, a head, hands, and a whole body, are not imaginary things, but things really existent. For, as a matter of fact, painters, even when they study with the greatest skill to represent sirens and satyrs by forms the most strange and extraordinary, cannot give them natures which are entirely new, but merely make a certain medley of the members of different animals; or if their imagination is extravagant enough to invent something so novel that nothing similar has ever before been seen, and that then their work represents a thing purely fictitious and absolutely false, it is certain all the same that the colours of which this is composed are necessarily real. And for the same reason, although these general things, to wit, [a body], eyes, a head, hands, and such like, may be imaginary, we are bound at the same time to confess that there are at least some other objects yet more simple and more universal, which are real and true; and of these just in the same way as with certain real colours, all these images of things which dwell in our thoughts, whether true and real or false and fantastic, are formed.

To such a class of things pertains corporeal nature in general, and its extension, the figure of extended things, their quantity or magnitude and number, as also the place in which they are, the time which measures their duration, and so on.

That is possibly why our reasoning is not unjust when we conclude from this that Physics, Astronomy, Medicine and all other sciences which have as their end the consideration of composite things, are very dubious and uncertain; but that Arithmetic, Geometry and other sciences of that kind which only treat of things that are very simple and very general, without taking great trouble to ascertain whether they are actually existent or not, contain some measure of certainty and an element of the indubitable. For whether I am awake or asleep, two and three together always form five, and the square can never have more than four sides, and it does not seem possible that truths so clear and apparent can be suspected of any falsity [or uncertainty].

Nevertheless I have long had fixed in my mind the belief that an all-powerful God existed by whom I have been created such as I am. But how do I know that He has not brought it to pass that there is no earth, no heaven, no extended body, no magnitude, no place, and that nevertheless [I possess the perceptions of all these things and that] they seem to me to exist just exactly as I now see them? And, besides, as I sometimes imagine that others deceive themselves in the things which they think they know best, how do I know that I am not deceived every time that I add two and three, or count the sides of a square, or judge of things yet simpler, if anything simpler can be imagined? But possibly God has not desired that I should be thus deceived, for He is said to be supremely good. If, however, it is contrary to His goodness to have made me such that I constantly deceive myself, it would also appear to be contrary to His goodness to permit me to be sometimes deceived, and nevertheless I cannot doubt that He does permit this.

There may indeed be those who would prefer to deny the existence of a God so powerful, rather than believe that all other things are uncertain. But let us not oppose them for the present, and grant that all that is here said of a God is a fable; nevertheless in whatever way they suppose that I have arrived at the state of being that I have reached—whether they attribute it to fate or to accident, or make out that it is by a continual succession of antecedents, or by some other method—since to err and deceive oneself is a defect, it is clear that the greater will be the probability of my being so imperfect as to deceive myself ever, as is the Author to whom they assign my origin the less powerful. To these reasons I have certainly nothing to reply, but at the end I feel constrained to confess that there is nothing in all that I formerly believed to be true, of which I cannot in some measure doubt, and that not merely through want of thought or through levity, but for reasons which are very powerful and maturely considered; so that henceforth I ought not the less carefully to refrain from giving credence to these opinions than to that which is manifestly false, if I desire to arrive at any certainty [in the sciences].

But it is not sufficient to have made these remarks, we must also be careful to keep them in mind. For these ancient and commonly held opinions still revert frequently to my mind, long and familiar custom having given them the right to occupy my mind against my inclination and rendered them almost masters of my belief; nor will I ever lose the habit of deferring to them or of placing my confidence in them, so long as I consider them as they really are, i.e. opinions in some measure doubtful, as I have just shown, and at the same time highly probable, so that there is much more reason to believe in than to deny them. That is why I consider that I shall not be acting amiss, if, taking of set purpose a contrary belief, I allow myself to be deceived, and for a certain time pretend that all these opinions are entirely false and imaginary, until at last, having thus balanced my former prejudices with my latter [so that they cannot divert my opinions more to one side than to the other], my judgment will no longer be dominated by bad usage or turned away from the right knowledge of the truth. For I am assured that there can be neither peril nor error in this course, and that I cannot at present yield too much to distrust, since I am not considering the question of action, but only of knowledge.

I shall then suppose, not that God who is supremely good and the fountain of truth, but some evil genius not less powerful than deceitful, has employed his whole energies in deceiving me; I shall consider that the heavens, the earth, colours, figures, sound, and all other external things are nought but the illusions and dreams of which this genius has availed himself in order to lay traps for my credulity; I shall consider myself as having no hands, no eyes, no flesh, no blood, nor any senses, yet falsely believing myself to possess all these things; I shall remain obstinately attached to this idea, and if by this means it is not in my power to arrive at the knowledge of any truth, I may at least do what is in my power [i.e. suspend my judgment], and with firm purpose avoid giving credence to any false thing, or being imposed upon by this arch deceiver, however powerful and

deceptive he may be. But this task is a laborious one, and insensibly a certain lassitude leads me into the course of my ordinary life. And just as a captive who in sleep enjoys an imaginary liberty, when he begins to suspect that his liberty is but a dream, fears to awaken, and conspires with these agreeable illusions that the deception may be prolonged, so insensibly of my own accord I fall back into my former opinions, and I dread awakening from this slumber, lest the laborious wakefulness which would follow the tranquillity of this repose should have to be spent not in daylight, but in the excessive darkness of the difficulties which have just been discussed.

MEDITATION II

Of the Nature of the Human Mind; and That It Is More Easily Known Than the Body

The Meditation of yesterday filled my mind with so many doubts that it is no longer in my power to forget them. And yet I do not see in what manner I can resolve them; and, just as if I had all of a sudden fallen into very deep water, I am so disconcerted that I can neither make certain of setting my feet on the bottom, nor can I swim and so support myself on the surface. I shall nevertheless make an effort and follow anew the same path as that on which I yesterday entered, i.e. I shall proceed by setting aside all that in which the least doubt could be supposed to exist, just as if I had discovered that it was absolutely false; and I shall ever follow in this road until I have met with something which is certain, or at least, if I can do nothing else, until I have learned for certain that there is nothing in the world that is certain. Archimedes, in order that he might draw the terrestrial globe out of its place, and transport it elsewhere, demanded only that one point should be fixed and immoveable; in the same way I shall have the right to conceive high hopes if I am happy enough to discover one thing only which is certain and indubitable.

I suppose, then, that all the things that I see are false; I persuade myself that nothing has ever existed of all that my fallacious memory represents to me. I consider that I possess no senses; I imagine that body, figure, extension, movement and place are but the fictions of my mind. What, then, can be esteemed as true? Perhaps nothing at all, unless that there is nothing in the world that is certain.

But how can I know there is not something different from those things that I have just considered, of which one cannot have the slightest doubt? Is there not some God, or some other being by whatever name we call it, who puts these reflections into my mind? That is not necessary, for is it not possible that I am capable of producing them myself? I myself, am I not at least something? But I have already denied that I had senses and body. Yet I hesitate, for what follows from that? Am I so dependent on body and senses that I cannot exist without these? But I was persuaded that there was nothing in all the world, that there was no heaven, no earth, that there were no minds, nor any bodies: was I not then likewise persuaded that I did not exist? Not at all; of a surety I myself did exist since I persuaded myself of something [or merely because I thought of something]. But there is some deceiver or other, very powerful and very cunning, who ever employs his ingenuity in deceiving me. Then without doubt I exist also if he deceives me, and let him deceive me as much as he will, he can never cause me to be nothing so long as I think that I am something. So that after having reflected well and carefully examined all things, we must come to the definite conclusion that this proposition: I am, I exist, is necessarily true each time that I pronounce it, or that I mentally conceive it.

But I do not yet know clearly enough what I am, I who am certain that I am; and hence I must be careful to see that I do not imprudently take some other object in place of myself, and thus that I do not go astray in respect of this knowledge that I hold to be the most certain and most evident of all that I have formerly learned. That is why I shall now consider anew what I believed myself to be before I embarked upon these last reflections; and of my former opinions I shall withdraw all that might even in a small degree be invalidated by the reasons which I have just brought forward, in order that there may be nothing at all left beyond what is absolutely certain and indubitable.

What then did I formerly believe myself to be? Undoubtedly I believed myself to be a man. But what is a man? Shall I say a reasonable animal? Certainly not; for then I should have to inquire what an animal is, and what is reasonable; and thus from a single question I should insensibly fall into an infinitude of others more difficult; and I should not wish to waste the little time and leisure remaining to me in trying to unravel subtleties like these. But I shall rather stop here to consider the thoughts which of themselves spring up in my mind, and which were not inspired by anything beyond my own nature alone when I applied myself to the consideration of my being. In the first place, then, I considered myself as having a face, hands, arms, and all that system of members composed of bones and flesh as seen in a corpse which I designated by the name of body. In addition to this I considered that I was nourished, that I walked, that I felt, and that I thought, and I referred all these actions to the soul: but I did not stop to consider what the soul was, or if I did stop, I imagined that it was something extremely rare and subtle like a wind, a flame, or an ether, which was spread throughout my grosser parts. As to body I had no manner of doubt about its nature, but thought I had a very clear knowledge of it; and if I had desired to explain it according to the notions that I had then formed of it, I should have described it thus: By the body I understand all that which can be defined by a certain figure: something which can be confined in a certain place, and which can fill a given space in such a way that every other body will be excluded from it; which can be perceived either by touch, or by sight, or by hearing, or by taste, or by smell: which can be moved in many ways not, in truth, by itself, but by something which is foreign to it, by which it is touched [and from which it receives impressions]: for to have the power of self-movement, as also of feeling or of thinking, I did not consider to appertain to the nature of body: on the contrary, I was rather astonished to find that faculties similar to them existed in some bodies.

But what am I, now that I suppose that there is a certain genius which is extremely powerful, and, if I may say so, malicious, who employs all his powers in deceiving me? Can I affirm that I possess the least of all those things which I have just said pertain to the nature of body? I pause to consider, I revolve all these things in my mind, and I find none of which I can say that it pertains to me. It would be tedious to stop to enumerate them. Let us pass to the attributes of soul and see if there is any one which is in me? What of nutrition or walking [the first mentioned]? But if it is so that I have no body it is also true that I can neither walk nor take nourishment. Another attribute is sensation. But one cannot feel without body, and besides I have thought I perceived many things during sleep that I recognised in my waking moments as not having been experienced at all. What of thinking? I find here that thought is an attribute that belongs to me; it alone cannot be separated from me. I am, I exist, that is certain. But how often? Just when I think; for it might possibly be the case if I ceased entirely to think, that I should likewise cease altogether to exist. I do not now admit anything which is not necessarily true: to speak accurately I am not more than a thing which thinks, that is to say a mind or a soul, or an understanding, or a reason, which are terms whose significance was formerly unknown to me. I am, however, a real thing and really exist; but what thing? I have answered: a thing which thinks.

And what more? I shall exercise my imagination [in order to see if I am not something more]. I am not a collection of members which we call the human body: I am not a subtle air distributed through these members, I am not a wind, a fire, a vapour, a breath, nor anything at all which I can imagine or conceive; because I have assumed that all these were nothing. Without changing that supposition I find that I only leave myself certain of the fact that I am somewhat. But perhaps it is true that these same things which I supposed were non-existent because they are unknown to me, are really not different from the self which I know. I am not sure about this, I shall not dispute about it now; I can only give judgment on things that are known to me. I know that I exist, and I inquire what I am, I whom I know to exist. But it is very certain that the knowledge of my existence taken in its precise significance does not depend on things whose existence is not yet known to me; consequently it does not depend on those which I can feign in imagination. And indeed the very term *feign* in imagination proves to me my error, for I really do this if I image myself a something, since to imagine is nothing else than to contemplate the figure or image of a corporeal thing. But I already know for certain that I am, and that it may be that all these images, and, speaking generally, all things that relate to the nature of body are nothing but dreams [and chimeras]. For this reason I see clearly that I have as little reason to say, 'I shall stimulate my imagination in order to know more distinctly what I am,' than if I were to say,

'I am now awake, and I perceive somewhat that is real and true: but because I do not yet perceive it distinctly enough, I shall go to sleep of express purpose, so that my dreams may represent the perception with greatest truth and evidence.' And, thus, I know for certain that nothing of all that I can understand by means of my imagination belongs to this knowledge which I have of myself, and that it is necessary to recall the mind from this mode of thought with the utmost diligence in order that it may be able to know its own nature with perfect distinctness.

But what then am I? A thing which thinks. What is a thing which thinks? It is a thing which doubts, understands, [conceives], affirms, denies, wills, refuses, which also imagines and feels.

Certainly it is no small matter if all these things pertain to my nature. But why should they not so pertain? Am I not that being who now doubts nearly everything, who nevertheless understands certain things, who affirms that one only is true, who denies all the others, who desires to know more, is averse from being deceived, who imagines many things, sometimes indeed despite his will, and who perceives many likewise, as by the intervention of the bodily organs? Is there nothing in all this which is as true as it is certain that I exist, even though I should always sleep and though he who has given me being employed all his ingenuity in deceiving me? Is there likewise any one of these attributes which can be distinguished from my thought, or which might be said to be separated from myself? For it is so evident of itself that it is I who doubts, who understands, and who desires, that there is no reason here to add anything to explain it. And I have certainly the power of imagining likewise; for although it may happen (as I formerly supposed) that none of the things which I imagine are true, nevertheless this power of imagining does not cease to be really in use, and it forms part of my thought. Finally, I am the same who feels, that is to say, who perceives certain things, as by the organs of sense, since in truth I see light, I hear noise, I feel heat. But it will be said that these phenomena are false and that I am dreaming. Let it be so; still it is at least quite certain that it seems to me that I see light, that I hear noise and that I feel heat. That cannot be false; properly speaking it is what is in me called feeling; and used in this precise sense that is no other thing than thinking.

From this time I begin to know what I am with a little more clearness and distinction than before; but nevertheless it still seems to me, and I cannot prevent myself from thinking, that corporeal things, whose images are framed by thought, which are tested by the senses, are much more distinctly known than that obscure part of me which does not come under the imagination. Although really it is very strange to say that I know and understand more distinctly these things whose existence seems to me dubious, which are unknown to me, and which do not belong to me, than others of the truth of which I am convinced, which are known to me and which pertain to my real nature, in a word, than myself. But I see clearly how the case stands: my mind loves to wander, and cannot yet suffer itself to be retained within the just limits of truth. Very good, let us once more give it the freest rein, so that, when afterwards we seize the proper occasion for pulling up, it may the more easily be regulated and controlled.

Let us begin by considering the commonest matters, those which we believe to be the most distinctly comprehended, to wit, the bodies which we touch and see; not indeed bodies in general, for these general ideas are usually a little more confused, but let us consider one body in particular. Let us take, for example, this piece of wax: it has been taken quite freshly from the hive, and it has not yet lost the sweetness of the honey which it contains; it still retains somewhat of the odour of the flowers from which it has been culled; its colour, its figure, its size are apparent; it is hard, cold, easily handled, and if you strike it with the finger, it will emit a sound. Finally all the things which are requisite to cause us distinctly to recognise a body, are met with in it. But notice that while I speak and approach the fire what remained of the taste is exhaled, the smell evaporates, the colour alters, the figure is destroyed, the size increases, it becomes liquid, it heats, scarcely can one handle it, and when one strikes it, no sound is emitted. Does the same wax remain after this change? We must confess that it remains; none would judge otherwise. What then did I know so distinctly in this piece of wax? It could certainly be nothing of all that the senses brought to my notice, since all these things which fall under taste, smell, sight, touch, and hearing, are found to be changed, and yet the same wax remains.

Perhaps it was what I now think, viz. that this wax was not that sweetness of honey, nor that agreeable scent of flowers, nor that particular whiteness, nor that figure, nor that sound, but simply a body which a little while before appeared to me as perceptible under these forms, and which is now perceptible under others. But what, precisely, is it that I imagine when I form such conceptions? Let us attentively consider this, and, abstracting from all that does not belong to the wax, let us see what remains. Certainly nothing remains excepting a certain extended thing which is flexible and movable. But what is the meaning of flexible and movable? Is it not that I imagine that this piece of wax being round is capable of becoming square and of passing from a square to a triangular figure? No, certainly it is not that, since I imagine it admits of an infinitude of similar changes, and I nevertheless do not know how to compass the infinitude by my imagination, and consequently this conception which I have of the wax is not brought about by the faculty of imagination. What now is this extension? Is it not also unknown? For it becomes greater when the wax is melted, greater when it is boiled, and greater still when the heat increases; and I should not conceive [clearly] according to truth what wax is, if I did not think that even this piece that we are considering is capable of receiving more variations in extension than I have ever imagined. We must then grant that I could not even understand through the imagination what this piece of wax is, and that it is my mind alone which perceives it. I say this piece of wax in particular, for as to wax in general it is yet clearer. But what is this piece of wax which cannot be understood excepting by the [understanding or] mind? It is certainly the same that I see, touch, imagine, and finally it is the same which I have always believed it to be from the beginning. But what must particularly be observed is that its perception is neither an act of vision, nor of touch, nor of imagination, and has never been such although it may have appeared formerly to be so, but only an intuition of the mind, which may be imperfect and confused as it was formerly, or clear and distinct as it is at present, according as my attention is more or less directed to the elements which are found in it, and of which it is composed.

Yet in the meantime I am greatly astonished when I consider [the great feebleness of mind] and its proneness to fall [insensibly] into error; for although without giving expression to my thoughts I consider all this in my own mind, words often impede me and I am almost deceived by the terms of ordinary language. For we say that we see the same wax, if it is present, and not that we simply judge that it is the same from its having the same colour and figure. From this I should conclude that I knew the wax by means of vision and not simply by the intuition of the mind; unless by chance I remember that, when looking from a window and saying I see men who pass in the street, I really do not see them, but infer that what I see is men, just as I say that I see wax. And yet what do I see from the window but hats and coats which may cover automatic machines? Yet I judge these to be men. And similarly solely by the faculty of judgment which rests in my mind, I comprehend that which I believed I saw with my eyes.

A man who makes it his aim to raise his knowledge above the common should be ashamed to derive the occasion for doubting from the forms of speech invented by the vulgar; I prefer to pass on and consider whether I had a more evident and perfect conception of what the wax was when I first perceived it, and when I believed I knew it by means of the external senses or at least by the common sense as it is called, that is to say by the imaginative faculty, or whether my present conception is clearer now that I have most carefully examined what it is, and in what way it can be known. It would certainly be absurd to doubt as to this. For what was there in this first perception which was distinct? What was there which might not as well have been perceived by any of the animals? But when I distinguish the wax from its external forms, and when, just as if I had taken from it its vestments, I consider it quite naked, it is certain that although some error may still be found in my judgment, I can nevertheless not perceive it thus without a human mind.

But finally what shall I say of this mind, that is, of myself, for up to this point I do not admit in myself anything but mind? What then, I who seem to perceive this piece of wax so distinctly, do I not know myself, not only with much more truth and certainty, but also with much more distinctness and clearness? For if I judge that the wax is or exists from the fact that I see it, it certainly follows much more clearly that I am or that I exist myself from the fact that I see

it. For it may be that what I see is not really wax, it may also be that I do not possess eyes with which to see anything; but it cannot be that when I see, or (for I no longer take account of the distinction) when I think I see, that I myself who think am nought. So if I judge that the wax exists from the fact that I touch it, the same thing will follow, to wit, that I am; and if I judge that my imagination, or some other cause, whatever it is, persuades me that the wax exists, I shall still conclude the same. And what I have here remarked of wax may be applied to all other things which are external to me [and which are met with outside of me]. And further, if the [notion or] perception of wax has seemed to me clearer and more distinct, not only after the sight or the touch, but also after many other causes have rendered it quite manifest to me, with how much more [evidence] and distinctness must it be said that I now know myself, since all the reasons which contribute to the knowledge of wax, or any other body whatever, are yet better proofs of the nature of my mind! And there are so many other things in the mind itself which may contribute to the elucidation of its nature, that those which depend on body such as these just mentioned, hardly merit being taken into account.

But finally here I am, having insensibly reverted to the point I desired, for, since it is now manifest to me that even bodies are not properly speaking known by the senses or by the faculty of imagination, but by the understanding only, and since they are not known from the fact that they are seen or touched, but only because they are understood, I see clearly that there is nothing which is easier for me to know than my mind. But because it is difficult to rid oneself so promptly of an opinion to which one was accustomed for so long, it will be well that I should halt a little at this point, so that by the length of my meditation I may more deeply imprint on my memory this new knowledge.

MEDITATION III

Of God: That He Exists

I shall now close my eyes, I shall stop my ears, I shall call away all my senses, I shall efface even from my thoughts all the images of corporeal things, or at least (for that is hardly possible) I shall esteem them as vain and false; and thus holding converse only with myself and considering my own nature, I shall try little by little to reach a better knowledge of and a more familiar acquaintanceship with myself. I am a thing that thinks, that is to say, that doubts, affirms, denies, that knows a few things, that is ignorant of many [that loves, that hates], that wills, that desires, that also imagines and perceives; for as I remarked before, although the things which I perceive and imagine are perhaps nothing at all apart from me and in themselves, I am nevertheless assured that these modes of thought that I call perceptions and imaginations, inasmuch only as they are modes of thought, certainly reside [and are met with] in me.

And in the little that I have just said, I think I have summed up all that I really know, or, at least all that hitherto I was aware that I knew. In order to try to extend my knowledge further, I shall now look around more carefully and see whether I cannot still discover in myself some other things which I have not hitherto perceived. I am certain that I am a thing which thinks; but do I not then likewise know what is requisite to render me certain of a truth? Certainly in this first knowledge there is nothing that assures me of its truth, excepting the clear and distinct perception of that which I state, which would not indeed suffice to assure me that what I say is true, if it could ever happen that a thing which I conceived so clearly and distinctly could be false; and accordingly it seems to me that already I can establish as a general rule that all things which I perceive very clearly and very distinctly are true.

At the same time I have before received and admitted many things to be very certain and manifest, which yet I afterwards recognised as being dubious. What then were these things? They were the earth, sky, stars and all other objects which I apprehended by means of the senses. But what did I clearly [and distinctly] perceive in them? Nothing more than that the ideas or thoughts of these things were presented to my mind. And not even now do I deny that these ideas are met with in me. But there was yet another thing which I affirmed, and which, owing to the habit which I had formed of believing it, I thought I perceived very clearly, although in truth I did not perceive it at all, to wit, that there were objects outside of me from which these ideas proceeded, and to which they were entirely similar. And it was in this that I erred, or, if perchance my judgment was correct, this was not due to any knowledge arising from my perception.

But when I took anything very simple and easy in the sphere of arithmetic or geometry into consideration, e.g. that two and three together made five, and other things of the sort, were not these present to my mind so clearly as to enable me to affirm that they were true? Certainly if I judged that since such matters could be doubted, this would not have been so for any other reason than that it came into my mind that perhaps a God might have endowed me with such a nature that I may have been deceived even concerning things which seemed to me most manifest. But every time that this preconceived opinion of the sovereign power of a God presents itself to my thought, I am constrained to confess that it is easy to Him, if He wishes it, to cause me to err, even in matters in which I believe myself to have the best evidence. And, on the other hand, always when I direct my attention to things which I believe myself to perceive very clearly, I am so persuaded of their truth that I let myself break out into words such as these: Let who will deceive me, He can never cause me to be nothing while I think that I am, or some day cause it to be true to say that I have never been, it being true now to say that I am, or that two and three make more or less than five, or any such thing in which I see a manifest contradiction. And, certainly, since I have no reason to believe that there is a God who is a deceiver, and as I have not yet satisfied myself that there is a God at all, the reason for doubt which depends on this opinion alone is very slight, and so to speak metaphysical. But in order to be able altogether to remove it, I must inquire whether there is a God as soon as the occasion presents itself; and if I find that there is a God, I must also inquire whether He may be a deceiver; for without a knowledge of these two truths I do not see that I can ever be certain of anything.

And in order that I may have an opportunity of inquiring into this in an orderly way [without interrupting the order of meditation which I have proposed to myself, and which is little by little to pass from the notions which I find first of all in my mind to those which I shall later on discover in it] it is requisite that I should here divide my thoughts into certain kinds, and that I should consider in which of these kinds there is, properly speaking, truth or error to be found. Of my thoughts some are, so to speak, images of the things, and to these alone is the title 'idea' properly applied; examples are my thought of a man or of a chimera, of heaven, of an angel, or [even] of God. But other thoughts possess other forms as well. For example in willing, fearing, approving, denying, though I always perceive something as the subject of the action of my mind, yet by this action I always add something else to the idea which I have of that thing; and of the thoughts of this kind some are called volitions or affections, and others judgments.

Now as to what concerns ideas, if we consider them only in themselves and do not relate them to anything else beyond themselves, they cannot properly speaking be false; for whether I imagine a goat or a chimera, it is not less true that I imagine the one than the other. We must not fear likewise that falsity can enter into will and into affections, for although I may desire evil things, or even things that never existed, it is not the less true that I desire them. Thus there remains no more than the judgments which we make, in which I must take the greatest care not to deceive myself. But the principal error and the commonest which we may meet with in them, consists in my judging that the ideas which are in me are similar or conformable to the things which are outside me; for without doubt if I considered the ideas only as certain modes of my thoughts, without trying to relate them to anything beyond, they could scarcely give me material for error.

But among these ideas, some appear to me to be innate, some adventitious, and others to be formed [or invented] by myself; for, as I have the power of understanding what is called a thing, or a truth, or a thought, it appears to me that I hold this power from no other source than my own nature. But if I now hear some sound, if I see the sun, or feel heat, I have hitherto judged that these sensations proceeded from certain things that exist outside of me; and finally it appears to me that sirens, hippogryphs, and the like, are formed out of my own mind. But again I may possibly persuade myself that all these ideas are of the nature of those which I term adventitious, or else that they are all innate, or all fictitious: for I have not yet clearly discovered their true origin.

And my principal task in this place is to consider, in respect to those ideas which appear to me to proceed from certain objects that are outside me, what are the reasons which cause me to think them similar to these objects. It seems indeed in the first place that I am taught this lesson by nature; and secondly, I

experience in myself that these ideas do not depend on my will nor therefore on myself—for they often present themselves to my mind in spite of my will. Just now, for instance, whether I will or whether I do not will, I feel heat, and thus I persuade myself that this feeling, or at least this idea of heat, is produced in me by something which is different from me, i.e. by the heat of the fire near which I sit. And nothing seems to me more obvious than to judge that this object imprints its likeness rather than anything else upon me.

Now I must discover whether these proofs are sufficiently strong and convincing. When I say that I am so instructed by nature, I merely mean a certain spontaneous inclination which impels me to believe in this connection, and not a natural light which makes me recognise that it is true. But these two things are very different; for I cannot doubt that which the natural light causes me to believe to be true, as, for example, it has shown me that I am from the fact that I doubt, or other facts of the same kind. And I possess no other faculty whereby to distinguish truth from falsehood, which can teach me that what this light shows me to be true is not really true, and no other faculty that is equally trustworthy. But as far as [apparently] natural impulses are concerned, I have frequently remarked, when I had to make active choice between virtue and vice, that they often enough led me to the part that was worse; and this is why I do not see any reason for following them in what regards truth and error.

And as to the other reason, which is that those ideas must proceed from objects outside me, since they do not depend on my will, I do not find it any the more convincing. For just as these impulses of which I have spoken are found in me, notwithstanding that they do not always concur with my will, so perhaps there is in me some faculty fitted to produce these ideas without the assistance of any external things, even though it is not yet known by me; just as, apparently, they have hitherto always been found in me during sleep without the aid of any external objects.

And finally, though they did proceed from objects different from myself, it is not a necessary consequence that they should resemble these. On the contrary, I have noticed that in many cases there was a great difference between the object and its idea. I find, for example, two completely diverse ideas of the sun in my mind; the one derives its origin from the senses, and should be placed in the category of adventitious ideas; according to this idea the sun seems to be extremely small; but the other is derived from astronomical reasonings, i.e. is elicited from certain notions that are innate in me, or else it is formed by me in some other manner; in accordance with it the sun appears to be several times greater than the earth. These two ideas cannot, indeed, both resemble the same sun, and reason makes me believe that the one which seems to have originated directly from the sun itself, is the one which is most dissimilar to it.

All this causes me to believe that until the present time it has not been by a judgment that was certain [or premeditated], but only by a sort of blind impulse that I believed that things existed outside of, and different from me, which, but the organs of my senses, or by some other method whatever it might be, conveyed these ideas or images to me [and imprinted on me their similitudes].

But there is yet another method of inquiring whether any of the objects of which I have ideas within me exist outside of me. If ideas are only taken as certain modes of thought, I recognise amongst them no difference or inequality, and all appear to proceed from me in the same manner; but when we consider them as images, one representing one thing and the other another, it is clear that they are very different one from the other. There is no doubt that those which represent to me substances are something more, and contain so to speak more objective reality within them [that is to say, by representation participate in a higher degree of being or perfection] that those that simply represent modes or accidents; and that idea again by which I understand a supreme God, eternal, infinite, [immutable], omniscient, omnipotent, and Creator of all things which are outside of Himself, has certainly more objective reality in itself than those ideas by which finite substances are represented.

Now it is manifest by the natural light that there must at least be as much reality in the efficient and total cause as in its effect. For, pray, whence can the effect derive its reality, if not from its cause? And in what way can this cause communicate this reality to it, unless it possessed it in itself? And from this it follows, not only that something cannot proceed from nothing, but likewise that what is more perfect—that

is to say, which has more reality within itself—cannot proceed from the less perfect. And this is not only evidently true of those effects which possess actual or formal reality, but also of the ideas in which we consider merely what is termed objective reality. To take an example, the stone which has not yet existed not only cannot now commence to be unless it has been produced by something which possesses within itself, either formally or eminently, all that enters into the composition of the stone. [i.e. it must possess the same things or other more excellent things than those which exist in the stone] and heat can only be produced in a subject in which it did not previously exist by a cause that is of an order [degree or kind] at least as perfect as heat, and so in all other cases. But further, the idea of heat, or of a stone, cannot exist in me unless it has been placed within me by some cause which possesses within it at least as much reality as that which I conceive to exist in the heat or the stone. For although this cause does not transmit anything of its actual or formal reality to my idea, we must not for that reason imagine that it is necessarily a less real cause; we must remember that [since every idea is a work of the mind] its nature is such that it demands of itself no other formal reality than that which it borrows from my thought, of which it is only a mode [i.e. a manner or way of thinking]. But in order that an idea should contain some one certain objective reality rather than another, it must without doubt derive it from some cause in which there is at least as much formal reality as this idea contains of objective reality. For if we imagine that something is found in an idea which is not found in the cause, it must then have been derived from nought; but however imperfect may be this mode of being by which a thing is objectively [or by representation] in the understanding by its idea, we cannot certainly say that this mode of being is nothing, nor, consequently, that the idea derives its origin from nothing.

Nor must I imagine that, since the reality that I consider in these ideas is only objective, it is not essential that this reality should be formally in the causes of my ideas, but that it is sufficient that it should be found objectively. For just as this mode of objective existence pertains to ideas by their proper nature, so does the mode of formal existence pertain to the causes of those ideas (this is at least true of the first and principal) by the nature peculiar to them.

And although it may be the case that one idea gives birth to another idea, that cannot continue to be so indefinitely; for in the end we must reach an idea whose cause shall be so to speak an archetype, in which the whole reality [or perfection] which is so to speak objectively [or by representation] in these ideas is contained formally [and really]. Thus the light of nature causes me to know clearly that the ideas in me are like [pictures or] images which can, in truth, easily fall short of the perfection of the objects from which they have been derived, but which can never contain anything greater or more perfect.

And the longer and the more carefully that I investigate these matters, the more clearly and distinctly do I recognise their truth. But what am I to conclude from it all in the end? It is this, that if the objective reality of any one of my ideas is of such a nature as clearly to make me recognise that it is not in me either formally or eminently, and that consequently I cannot myself be the cause of it, it follows of necessity that I am not alone in the world, but that there is another being which exists, or which is the cause of this idea. On the other hand, had no such an idea existed in me, I should have had no sufficient argument to convince me of the existence of any being beyond myself; for I have made very careful investigation everywhere and up to the present time have been able to find no other ground.

But of my ideas, beyond that which represents me to myself, as to which there can here be no difficulty, there is another which represents a God, and there are others representing corporeal and inanimate things, other angels, other animals, and others again which represent to me men similar to myself.

As regards the ideas which represent to me other men or animals, or angels, I can however easily conceive that they might be formed by an admixture of the other ideas which I have of myself, of corporeal things, and of God, even although there were apart from me neither men nor animals, nor angels, in all the world.

And in regard to the ideas of corporeal objects, I do not recognise in them anything so great or so excellent that they might not have possibly proceeded from myself; for if I consider them more closely, and examine them individually, as I yesterday examined the idea of wax, I find that there is very little in them which I perceive clearly and distinctly. Magnitude or extension in length, breadth, or depth, I do so perceive; also figure which results from a termination of this extension, the situation which bodies of different figure preserve in relation to one another, and movement or change of situation; to which we may also add substance, duration and number. As to other things such as light, colours, sounds, scents, tastes, heat, cold and the other tactile qualities, they are thought by me with so much obscurity and confusion that I do not even know if they are true or false, i.e. whether the ideas which I form of these qualities are actually the ideas of real objects or not [or whether they only represent chimeras which cannot exist in fact]. For although I have before remarked that it is only in judgments that falsity, properly speaking, or formal falsity, can be met with, a certain material falsity may nevertheless be found in ideas, i.e. when these ideas represent what is nothing as though it were something. For example, the ideas which I have of cold and heat are so far from clear and distinct that by their means I cannot tell whether cold is merely a privation of heat, or heat a privation of cold, or whether both are real qualities, or are not such. And inasmuch as [since ideas resemble images] there cannot be any ideas which do not appear to represent some things, if it is correct to say that cold is merely a privation of heat, the idea which represents it to me as something real and positive will not be improperly termed false, and the same holds good of other similar ideas.

To these it is certainly not necessary that I should attribute any author other than myself. For if they are false, i.e. if they represent things which do not exist, the light of nature shows me that they issue from nought, that is to say, that they are only in me in so far as something is lacking to the perfection of my nature. But if they are true, nevertheless because they exhibit so little reality to me that I cannot even clearly distinguish the thing represented from nonbeing, I do not see any reason why they should not be produced by myself.

As to the clear and distinct idea which I have of corporeal things, some of them seem as though I might have derived them from the idea which I possess of myself, as those which I have of substance, duration, number, and such like. For [even] when I think that a stone is a substance, or at least a thing capable of existing of itself, and that I am a substance also, although I conceive that I am a thing that thinks and not one that is extended, and that the stone on the other hand is an extended thing which does not think, and that thus there is a notable difference between the two conceptions—they seem, nevertheless, to agree in this, that both represent substances. In the same way, when I perceive that I now exist and further recollect that I have in former times existed, and when I remember that I have various thoughts of which I can recognise the number, I acquire ideas of duration and number which I can afterwards transfer to any object that I please. But as to all the other qualities of which the ideas of corporeal things are composed, to wit, extension, figure, situation and motion, it is true that they are not formally in me, since I am only a thing that thinks; but because they are merely certain modes of substance [and so to speak the vestments under which corporeal substance appears to us] and because I myself am also a substance, it would seem that they might be contained in me eminently.

Hence there remains only the idea of God, concerning which we must consider whether it is something which cannot have proceeded from me myself. By the name God I understand a substance that is infinite [eternal, immutable], independent, all-knowing, all-powerful, and by which I myself and everything else, if anything else does exist, have been created. Now all these characteristics are such that the more diligently I attend to them, the less do they appear capable of proceeding from me alone; hence, from what has been already said, we must conclude that God necessarily exists.

For although the idea of substance is within me owing to the fact that I am substance, nevertheless I should not have the idea of an infinite substance—since I am finite—if it had not proceeded from some substance which was veritably infinite.

Nor should I imagine that I do not perceive the infinite by a true idea, but only by the negation of the finite, just as I perceive repose and darkness by the negation of movement and of light; for, on the contrary, I see that there is manifestly more reality in infinite substance than in finite, and therefore that in some way I have in me the notion of the infinite earlier than the finite—to wit, the notion of God before that of myself. For how would it be possible that I should know that I doubt and desire, that is to say, that something is lacking to me, and that I am not quite perfect, unless I had within me some idea of a Being more perfect than myself, in comparison with which I should recognise the deficiencies of my nature?

And we cannot say that this idea of God is perhaps materially false and that consequently I can derive it from nought [i.e. that possibly it exists in me because I am imperfect], as I have just said is the case with ideas of heat, cold, and other such things; for, on the contrary, as this idea is very clear and distinct and contains within it more objective reality than any other, there can be none which is of itself more true, nor any in which there can be less suspicion of falsehood. The idea, I say, of this Being who is absolutely perfect and infinite, is entirely true; for although, perhaps, we can imagine that such a Being does not exist, we cannot nevertheless imagine that His idea represents nothing real to me, as I have said of the idea of cold. This idea is also very clear and distinct; since all that I conceive clearly and distinctly of the real and the true, and of what conveys some perfection, is in its entirety contained in this idea. And this does not cease to be true although I do not comprehend the infinite, or though in God there is an infinitude of things which I cannot comprehend, nor possibly even reach in any way by thought; for it is of the nature of the infinite that my nature, which is finite and limited, should not comprehend it; and it is sufficient that I should understand this, and that I should judge that all things which I clearly perceive and in which I know that there is some perfection, and possibly likewise an infinitude of properties of which I am ignorant, are in God formally or eminently, so that the idea which I have of Him may become the most true, most clear, and most distinct of all the ideas that are in my mind.

But possibly I am something more than I suppose myself to be, and perhaps all those perfections which I attribute to God are in some way potentially in me, although they do not yet disclose themselves, or issue in action. As a matter of fact I am already sensible that my knowledge increases [and perfects itself] little by little, and I see nothing which can prevent it from increasing more and more into infinitude; nor do I see, after it has thus been increased [or perfected], anything to prevent my being able to acquire by its means all the other perfections of the Divine nature; nor finally why the power I have of acquiring these perfections, if it really exists in me, shall not suffice to produce the ideas of them.

At the same time I recognise that this cannot be. For, in the first place, although it were true that every day my knowledge acquired new degrees of perfection, and that there were in my nature many things potentially which are not yet there actually, nevertheless these excellences do not pertain to [or make the smallest approach to] the idea which I have of God in whom there is nothing merely potential [but in whom all is present really and actually]; for it is an infallible token of imperfection in my knowledge that it increases little by little. And further, although my knowledge grows more and more, nevertheless I do not for that reason believe that it can ever be actually infinite, since it can never reach a point so high that it will be unable to attain to any greater increase. But I understand God to be actually infinite, so that He can add nothing to His supreme perfection. And finally I perceive that the objective being of an idea cannot be produced by a being that exists potentially only, which properly speaking is nothing, but only by a being which is formal or actual.

To speak the truth, I see nothing in all that I have just said which by the light of nature is not manifest to anyone who desires to think attentively on the subject; but when I slightly relax my attention, my mind, finding its vision somewhat obscured and so to speak blinded by the images of sensible objects, I do not easily recollect the reason why the idea that I possess of a being more perfect than I, must necessarily have been placed in me by a being which is really more perfect; and this is why I wish here to go on to inquire whether I, who have this idea, can exist if no such being exists.

And I ask, from whom do I then derive my existence? Perhaps from myself or from my parents, or from some other source less perfect than God; for we can imagine nothing more perfect than God, or even as perfect as He is.

But [were I independent of every other and] were I myself the author of my being, I should doubt nothing and I should desire nothing, and finally no perfection would be lacking to me; for I should have bestowed on myself every perfection of which I possessed any idea and should thus be God. And it must not be imagined that those things that are lacking to me are perhaps more difficult of attainment than those which I already possess; for, on the contrary, it is quite evident that it was a matter of much greater difficulty to bring to pass that I, that is to say, a thing

or a substance that thinks, should emerge out of nothing, than it would be to attain to the knowledge of many things of which I am ignorant, and which are only the accidents of this thinking substance. But it is clear that if I had of myself possessed this greater perfection of which I have just spoken [that is to say, if I had been the author of my own existence], I should not at least have denied myself the things which are the more easy to acquire [to wit, many branches of knowledge of which my nature is destitute]; nor should I have deprived myself of any of the things contained in the idea which I form of God, because there are none of them which seem to me specially difficult to acquire: and if there were any that were more difficult to acquire, they would certainly appear to me to be such (supposing I myself were the origin of the other things which I possess) since I should discover in them that my powers were limited.

But though I assume that perhaps I have always existed just as I am at present, neither can I escape the force of this reasoning, and imagine that the conclusion to be drawn from this is, that I need not seek for any author of my existence. For all the course of my life may be divided into an infinite number of parts, none of which is in any way dependent on the other; and thus from the fact that I was in existence a short time ago it does not follow that I must be in existence now, unless some cause at this instant, so to speak, produces me anew, that is to say, conserves me. It is as a matter of fact perfectly clear and evident to all those who consider with attention the nature of time, that, in order to be conserved in each moment in which it endures, a substance has need of the same power and action as would be necessary to produce and create it anew, supposing it did not yet exist, so that the light of nature show us clearly that the distinction between creation and conservation is solely a distinction of the reason.

All that I thus require here is that I should interrogate myself, if I wish to know whether I possess a power which is capable of bringing it to pass that I who now am shall still be in the future; for since I am nothing but a thinking thing, or at least since thus far it is only this portion of myself which is precisely in question at present, if such a power did reside in me, I should certainly be conscious of it. But I am conscious of nothing of the kind, and by this I know clearly that I depend on some being different from myself.

Possibly, however, this being on which I depend is not that which I call God, and I am created either by my parents or by some other cause less perfect than God. This cannot be, because, as I have just said, it is perfectly evident that there must be at least as much reality in the cause as in the effect; and thus since I am a thinking thing, and possess an idea of God within me, whatever in the end be the cause assigned to my existence, it must be allowed that it is likewise a thinking thing and that it possesses in itself the idea of all the perfections which I attribute to God. We may again inquire whether this cause derives its origin from itself or from some other thing. For if from itself, it follows by the reasons before brought forward, that this cause must itself be God; for since it possesses the virtue of self-existence, it must also without doubt have the power of actually possessing all the perfections of which it has the idea, that is, all those which I conceive as existing in God. But if it derives its existence from some other cause than itself, we shall again ask, for the same reason, whether this second cause exists by itself or through another, until from one step to another, we finally arrive at an ultimate cause, which will be God.

And it is perfectly manifest that in this there can be no regression into infinity, since what is in question is not so much the cause which formerly created me, as that which conserves me at the present time.

Nor can we suppose that several causes may have concurred in my production, and that from one I have received the idea of one of the perfections which I attribute to God, and from another the idea of some other, so that all these perfections indeed exist somewhere in the universe, but not as complete in one unity which is God. On the contrary, the unity, the simplicity or the inseparability of all things which are in God is one of the principal perfections which I conceive to be in Him. And certainly the idea of this unity of all Divine perfections cannot have been placed in me by any cause from which I have not likewise received the ideas of all the other perfections; for this cause could not make me able to comprehend them as joined together in an inseparable unity without having at the same time caused me in some measure to know what they are [and in some way to recognise each one of them].

Finally, so far as my parents [from whom it appears I have sprung] are concerned, although all that I have ever been able to believe of them were true, that does not make it follow that it is they who conserve me, nor are they even the authors of my being in any sense, in so far as I am a thinking being; since what they did was merely to implant certain dispositions in that matter in which the self—i.e. the mind, which alone I at present identify with myself—is by me deemed to exist. And thus there can be no difficulty in their regard, but we must of necessity conclude from the fact alone that I exist, or that the idea of a Being supremely perfect—that is of God—is in me, that the proof of God's existence is grounded on the highest evidence.

It only remains to me to examine into the manner in which I have acquired this idea from God; for I have not received it through the senses, and it is never presented to me unexpectedly, as is usual with the ideas of sensible things when these things present themselves, or seem to present themselves, to the external organs of my senses; nor is it likewise a fiction of my mind, for it is not in my power to take from or to add anything to it; and consequently the only alternative is that it is innate in me, just as the idea of myself is innate in me.

And one certainly ought not to find it strange that God, in creating me, placed this idea within me to be like the mark of the workman imprinted on his work; and it is likewise not essential that the mark shall be something different from the work itself. For from the sole fact that God created me it is most probable that in some way he has placed his image and similitude upon me, and that I perceive this similitude (in which the idea of God is contained) by means of the same faculty by which I perceive myself—that is to say, when I reflect on myself I not only know that I am something [imperfect], incomplete and dependent on another, which incessantly aspires after something which is better and greater than myself, but I also know that He on whom I depend possesses in Himself all the great things towards which I aspire [and the ideas of which I find within myself], and that not indefinitely or potentially alone, but really, actually and infinitely; and that thus He is God. And the whole strength of the argument which I have here made use of to prove the existence of God consists in this, that I recognise that it is not possible that my nature should be what it is, and indeed that I should have in myself the idea of a God, if God did not veritably exist—a God, I say, whose idea is in me, i.e. who possesses all those supreme perfections of which our mind may indeed have some idea but without understanding them all, who is liable to no errors or defect [and who has none of all those marks which denote imperfection]. From this it is manifest that He cannot be a deceiver, since the light of nature teaches us that fraud and deception necessarily proceed from some defect.

But before I examine this matter with more care, and pass on to the consideration of other truths which may be derived from it, it seems to me right to pause for a while in order to contemplate God Himself, to ponder at leisure His marvellous attributes, to consider, and admire, and adore, the beauty of this light so resplendent, at least as far as the strength of my mind, which is in some measure dazzled by the sight, will allow me to do so. For just as faith teaches us that the supreme felicity of the other life consists only in this contemplation of the Divine Majesty, so we continue to learn by experience that a similar meditation, though incomparably less perfect, causes us to enjoy the greatest satisfaction of which we are capable in this life.

MEDITATION IV

Of the True and the False

I have been well accustomed these past days to detach my mind from my senses, and I have accurately observed that there are very few things that one knows with certainty respecting corporeal objects, that there are many more which are known to us respecting the human mind, and yet more still regarding God Himself; so that I shall now without any difficulty abstract my thoughts from the consideration of [sensible or] imaginable objects, and carry them to those which, being withdrawn from all contact with matter, are purely intelligible. And certainly the idea which I possess of the human mind inasmuch as it is a thinking thing, and not extended in length, width and depth, nor participating in anything pertaining to body, is incomparably more distinct than is the idea of any corporeal thing. And when I consider that I doubt, that is to say, that I am an incomplete and dependent being, the idea of a being that is complete and independent, that is of God, presents itself to my mind with so much distinctness and clearness—and from the fact alone that

this idea is found in me, or that I who possess this idea exist, I conclude so certainly that God exists, and that my existence depends entirely on Him in every moment of my life—that I do not think that the human mind is capable of knowing anything with more evidence and certitude. And it seems to me that I now have before me a road which will lead us from the contemplation of the true God (in whom all the treasures of science and wisdom are contained) to the knowledge of the other objects of the universe.

For, first of all, I recognise it to be impossible that He should ever deceive me; for in all fraud and deception some imperfection is to be found, and although it may appear that the power of deception is a mark of subtilty or power, yet the desire to deceive without doubt testifies to malice or feebleness, and accordingly cannot be found in God.

In the next place I experienced in myself a certain capacity for judging which I have doubtless received from God, like all the other things that I possess; and as He could not desire to deceive me, it is clear that He has not given me a faculty that will lead me to err if I use it aright.

And no doubt respecting this matter could remain, if it were not that the consequence would seem to follow that I can thus never be deceived; for if I hold all that I possess from God, and if He has not placed in me the capacity for error, it seems as though I could never fall into error. And it is true that when I think only of God [and direct my mind wholly to Him], I discover [in myself] no cause of error, or falsity; yet directly afterwards, when recurring to myself, experience shows me that I am nevertheless subject to an infinitude of errors, as to which, when we come to investigate them more closely, I notice that not only is there a real and positive idea of God or of a Being of supreme perfection present to my mind, but also, so to speak, a certain negative idea of nothing, that is, of that which is infinitely removed from any kind of perfection; and that I am in a sense something intermediate between God and nought, i.e. placed in such a manner between the supreme Being and non-being, that there is in truth nothing in me that can lead to error in so far as a sovereign Being has formed me; but that, as I in some degree participate likewise in nought or in non-being, i.e. in so far as I am not myself the supreme Being, and as I find myself subject to an infinitude of imperfections, I ought not to be astonished if I should fall into error. Thus do I recognise that error, in so far as it is such, is not a real thing depending on God, but simply a defect; and therefore, in order to fall into it, that I have no need to possess a special faculty given me by God for this very purpose, but that I fall into error from the fact that the power given me by God for the purpose of distinguishing truth from error is not infinite.

Nevertheless this does not quite satisfy me; for error is not a pure negation [i.e. is not the simple defect or want of some perfection which ought not to be mine], but it is a lack of some knowledge which it seems that I ought to possess. And on considering the nature of God it does not appear to me possible that He should have given me a faculty which is not perfect of its kind, that is, which is wanting in some perfection due to it. For if it is true that the more skilful the artizan, the more perfect is the work of his hands, what can have been produced by this supreme Creator of all things that is not in all its parts perfect? And certainly there is no doubt that God could have created me so that I could never have been subject to error; it is also certain that He ever wills what is best; is it then better that I should be subject to err than that I should not?

In considering this more attentively, it occurs to me in the first place that I should not be astonished if my intelligence is not capable of comprehending why God acts as He does; and that there is thus no reason to doubt of His existence from the fact that I may perhaps find many other things besides this as to which I am able to understand neither for what reason nor how God has produced them. For, in the first place, knowing that my nature is extremely feeble and limited, and that the nature of God is on the contrary immense, incomprehensible, and infinite, I have no further difficulty in recognising that there is an infinitude of matters in His power, the causes of which transcend my knowledge; and this reason suffices to convince me that the species of cause termed final, finds no useful employment in physical [or natural] things; for it does not appear to me that I can without temerity seek to investigate the [inscrutable] ends of God.

It further occurs to me that we should not consider one single creature separately, when we inquire as to whether the works of God are perfect, but should regard all his creations together. For the same thing which might possibly seem very imperfect with some semblance of reason if regarded by itself, is found to be very perfect if regarded as part of the whole universe; and although, since I resolved to doubt all things, I as yet have only know certainly my own existence and that of God, nevertheless since I have recognised the infinite power of God, I cannot deny that He may have produced many other things, or at least that He has the power of producing them, so that I may obtain a place as a part of a great universe.

Whereupon, regarding myself more closely, and considering what are my errors (for they alone testify to there being any imperfection in me), I answer that they depend on a combination of two causes, to wit, on the faculty of knowledge that rests in me, and on the power of choice or of free will—that is to say, of the understanding and at the same time of the will. For by the understanding alone I [neither assert nor deny anything, but] apprehend the ideas of things as to which I can form a judgment. But no error is properly speaking found in it, provided the word error is taken in its proper signification; and though there is possibly an infinitude of things in the world of which I have no idea in my understanding, we cannot for all that say that it is deprived of these ideas [as we might say of something which is required by its nature], but simply it does not possess these; because in truth there is no reason to prove that God should have given me a greater faculty of knowledge than He has given me; and however skilful a workman I represent Him to be, I should not for all that consider that He was bound to have placed in each of His works all the perfections which He may have been able to place in some. I likewise cannot complain that God has not given me a free choice or a will which is sufficient, ample and perfect, since as a matter of fact I am conscious of a will so extended as to be subject to no limits. And what seems to me very remarkable in this regard is that of all the qualities which I possess there is no one so perfect and so comprehensive that I do not very clearly recognise that it might be yet greater and more perfect. For, to take an example, if I consider the faculty of comprehension which I possess, I find that it is of a very small extent and extremely limited, and at the same time I find the idea of another faculty much more ample and even infinite, and seeing that I can form the idea of it, I recognise from this very fact that it pertains to the nature of God. If in the same way I examine the memory, the imagination, or some other faculty, I do not find any which is not small and circumscribed, while in God it is immense [or infinite]. It is free-will alone or liberty of choice which I find to be so great in me that I can conceive no other idea to be more great; it is indeed the case that it is for the most part this will that causes me to know that in some manner I bear the image and similitude of God. For although the power of will is incomparably greater in God than in me, both by reason of the knowledge and the power which, conjoined with it, render it stronger and more efficacious, and by reason of its object, inasmuch as in God it extends to a great many things; it nevertheless does not seem to me greater if I consider it formally and precisely in itself: for the faculty of will consists alone in our having the power of choosing to do a thing or choosing not to do it (that is, to affirm or deny, to pursue or to shun it), or rather it consists alone in the fact that in order to affirm or deny, pursue or shun those things placed before us by the understanding, we act so that we are unconscious that any outside force constrains us in doing so. For in order that I should be free it is not necessary that I should be indifferent as to the choice of one or the other of two contraries; but contrariwise the more I lean to the one—whether I recognise clearly that the reasons of the good and true are to be found in it, or whether God so disposes my inward thought—the more freely do I choose and embrace it. And undoubtedly both divine grace and natural knowledge, far from diminishing my liberty, rather increase it and strengthen it. Hence this indifference which I feel, when I am not swayed to one side rather than to the other by lack of reason, is the lowest grade of liberty, and rather evinces a lack or negation in knowledge than a perfection of will: for if I always recognised clearly what was true and good, I should never have trouble in deliberating as to what judgment or choice I should make, and then I should be entirely free without ever being indifferent.

From all this I recognise that the power of will which I have received from God is not of itself the source of my errors—for it is very ample and very perfect of its kind—any more than is the power of understanding; for since I understand nothing but by the power which God has given me for understanding, there is no doubt that all that I understand, I understand as I ought, and it is not possible that I err in this. Whence then come my errors? They come from

the sole fact that since the will is much wider in its range and compass than the understanding, I do not restrain it within the same bounds, but extend it also to things which I do not understand: and as the will is of itself indifferent to these, it easily falls into error and sin, and chooses the evil for the good, or the false for the true.

For example, when I lately examined whether anything existed in the world, and found that from the very fact that I considered this question it followed very clearly that I myself existed, I could not prevent myself from believing that a thing I so clearly conceived was true: not that I found myself compelled to do so by some external cause, but simply because from great clearness in my mind there followed a great inclination of my will; and I believed this with so much the greater freedom or spontaneity as I possessed the less indifference towards it. Now, on the contrary, I not only know that I exist, inasmuch as I am a thinking thing, but a certain representation of corporeal nature is also presented to my mind; and it comes to pass that I doubt whether this thinking nature which is in me, or rather by which I am what I am, differs from this corporeal nature, or whether both are not simply the same thing; and I here suppose that I do not yet know any reason to persuade me to adopt the one belief rather than the other. From this it follows that I am entirely indifferent as to which of the two I affirm or deny, or even whether I abstain from forming any judgment in the matter.

And this indifference does not only extend to matters as to which the understanding has no knowledge, but also in general to all those which are not apprehended with perfect clearness at the moment when the will is deliberating upon them: for, however probable are the conjectures which render me disposed to form a judgment respecting anything, the simple knowledge that I have that those are conjectures alone and not certain and indubitable reasons, suffices to occasion me to judge the contrary. Of this I have had great experience of late when I set aside as false all that I had formerly held to be absolutely true, for the sole reason that I remarked that it might in some measure be doubted.

But if I abstain from giving my judgment on any thing when I do not perceive it with sufficient clearness and distinctness, it is plain that I act rightly and am not deceived. But if I determine to deny or affirm,

I no longer make use as I should of my free will, and if I affirm what is not true, it is evident that I deceive myself; even though I judge according to truth, this comes about only by chance, and I do not escape the blame of misusing my freedom; for the light of nature teaches us that the knowledge of the understanding should always precede the determination of the will. And it is in the misuse of the free will that the privation which constitutes the characteristic nature of error is met with. Privation, I say, is found in the act, in so far as it proceeds from me, but it is not found in the faculty which I have received from God, nor even in the act in so far as it depends on Him.

For I have certainly no cause to complain that God has not given me an intelligence which is more powerful, or a natural light which is stronger than that which I have received from Him, since it is proper to the finite understanding not to comprehend a multitude of things, and it is proper to a created understanding to be finite; on the contrary, I have every reason to render thanks to God who owes me nothing and who has given me all the perfections I possess, and I should be far from charging Him with injustice, and with having deprived me of, or wrongfully withheld from me, these perfections which He has not bestowed upon me.

I have further no reason to complain that He has given me a will more ample than my understanding, for since the will consists only of one single element, and is so to speak indivisible, it appears that its nature is such that nothing can be abstracted from it [without destroying it]; and certainly the more comprehensive it is found to be, the more reason I have to render gratitude to the giver.

And, finally, I must also not complain that God concurs with me in forming the acts of the will, that is the judgment in which I go astray, because these acts are entirely true and good, inasmuch as they depend on God; and in a certain sense more perfection accrues to my nature from the fact that I can form them, than if I could not do so. As to the privation in which alone the formal reason of error or sin consists, it has no need of any concurrence from God, since it is not a thing [or an existence], and since it is not related to God as to a cause, but should be termed merely a negation [according to the significance given to these words in the Schools]. For in fact it is not an imperfection in God that He has given me the liberty to give or withhold my assent from certain things as to which He has not placed a clear and distinct knowledge in my understanding; but it is without doubt an imperfection in me not to make a good use of my freedom, and to give my judgment readily on matters which I only understand obscurely. I nevertheless perceive that God could easily have created me so that I never should err, although I still remained free, and endowed with a limited knowledge, viz. by giving to my understanding a clear and distinct intelligence of all things as to which I should ever have to deliberate; or simply by His engraving deeply in my memory the resolution never to form a judgment on anything without having a clear and distinct understanding of it, so that I could never forget it. And it is easy for me to understand that, in so far as I consider myself alone, and as if there were only myself in the world, I should have been much more perfect than I am, if God had created me so that I could never err. Nevertheless I cannot deny that in some sense it is a greater perfection in the whole universe that certain parts should not be exempt from error as others are than that all parts should be exactly similar. And I have no right to complain if God, having placed me in the world, has not called upon me to play a part that excels all others in distinction and perfection.

And further I have reason to be glad on the ground that if He has not given me the power of never going astray by the first means pointed out above, which depends on a clear and evident knowledge of all the things regarding which I can deliberate, He has at least left within my power the other means, which is firmly to adhere to the resolution never to give judgment on matters whose truth is not clearly known to me; for although I notice a certain weakness in my nature in that I cannot continually concentrate my mind on one single thought, I can yet, by attentive and frequently repeated meditation, impress it so forcibly on my memory that I shall never fail to recollect it whenever I have need of it, and thus acquire the habit of never going astray.

And inasmuch as it is in this that the greatest and principal perfection of man consists, it seems to me that I have not gained little by this day's Meditation, since I have discovered the source of falsity and error. And certainly there can be no other source than that which I have explained; for as often as I so restrain my will within the limits of my knowledge that it forms no judgment except on matters which are clearly and distinctly represented to it by the understanding, I can never be deceived; for every clear and distinct conception is without doubt something, and hence cannot derive its origin from what is nought, but must of necessity have God as its author—God, I say, who being supremely perfect, cannot be the cause of any error; and consequently we must conclude that such a conception [or such a judgment] is true. Nor have I only learned to-day what I should avoid in order that I may not err, but also how I should act in order to arrive at a knowledge of the truth; for without doubt I shall arrive at this end if I devote my attention sufficiently to those things which I perfectly understand; and if I separate from these that which I only understand confusedly and with obscurity. To these I shall henceforth diligently give heed.

MEDITATION V

Of the Essence of Material Things, and Again, of God, That He Exists

Many other matters respecting the attributes of God and my own nature or mind remain for consideration; but I shall possibly on another occasion resume the investigation of these. Now (after first noting what must be done or avoided, in order to arrive at a knowledge of the truth) my principal task is to endeavour to emerge from the state of doubt into which I have these last days fallen, and to see whether nothing certain can be known regarding material things.

But before examining whether any such objects as I conceive exist outside of me, I must consider the ideas of them in so far as they are in my thought, and see which of them are distinct and which confused.

In the first place, I am able distinctly to imagine that quantity which philosophers commonly call continuous, or the extension in length, breadth, or depth, that is in this quantity, or rather in the object to which it is attributed. Further, I can number in it many different parts, and attribute to each of its parts many sorts of size, figure, situation and local movement, and, finally, I can assign to each of these movements all degrees of duration.

And not only do I know these things with distinctness when I consider them in general, but, likewise [however little I apply my attention to the matter], I discover an infinitude of particulars respecting numbers, figures, movements, and other such things, whose truth is so manifest, and so well accords with my nature, that when I begin to discover them, it seems to me that I learn nothing new, or recollect what I formerly knew—that is to say, that I for the first time perceive things which were already present to my mind, although I had not as yet applied my mind to them.

And what I here find to be most important is that I discover in myself an infinitude of ideas of certain things which cannot be esteemed as pure negations, although they may possibly have no existence outside of my thought, and which are not framed by me, although it is within my power either to think or not to think them, but which possess natures which are true and immutable. For example, when I imagine a triangle, although there may nowhere in the world be such a figure outside my thought, or ever have been, there is nevertheless in this figure a certain determinate nature, form, or essence, which is immutable and eternal, which I have not invented, and which in no wise depends on my mind, as appears from the fact that diverse properties of that triangle can be demonstrated, viz. that its three angles are equal to two right angles, that greatest side is subtended by the greatest angle, and the like, which now, whether I wish it or do not wish it, I recognise very clearly as pertaining to it, although I never thought of the matter at all when I imagined a triangle for the first time, and which therefore cannot be said to have been invented by me.

Nor does the objection hold good ·that possibly this idea of a triangle has reached my mind through the medium of my senses, since I have sometimes seen bodies triangular in shape; because I can form in my mind an infinitude of other figures regarding which we cannot have the least conception of their ever having been objects of sense, and I can nevertheless demonstrate various properties pertaining to their nature as well as to that of the triangle, and these must certainly all be true since I conceive them clearly. Hence they are something, and not pure negation; for it is perfectly clear that all that is true is something, and I have already fully demonstrated that all that I know clearly is true. And even although I had not demonstrated this, the nature of my mind is such that I could not prevent myself from holding them to be true so long as I conceive them clearly;

and I recollect that even when I was still strongly attached to the objects of sense, I counted as the most certain those truths which I conceived clearly as regards figures, numbers, and the other matters which pertain to arithmetic and geometry, and in general, to pure and abstract mathematics.

But now, if just because I can draw the idea of something from my thought, it follows that all which I know clearly and distinctly as pertaining to this object does really belong to it, may I not derive from this an argument demonstrating the existence of God? It is certain that I no less find the idea of God, that is to say, the idea of a supremely perfect Being, in me, than that of any figure or number whatever it is; and I do not know any less clearly and distinctly that an [actual and] eternal existence pertains to this nature than I know that all that which I am able to demonstrate of some figure or number truly pertains to the nature of this figure or number, and therefore, although all that I concluded in the preceding Meditations were found to be false, the existence of God would pass with me as at least as certain as I have ever held the truths of mathematics (which concern only numbers and figures) to be.

This indeed is not at first manifest, since it would seem to present some appearance of being a sophism. For being accustomed in all other things to make a distinction between existence and essence, I easily persuade myself that the existence can be separated from the essence of God, and that we can thus conceive God as not actually existing. But, nevertheless, when I think of it with more attention, I clearly see that existence can no more be separated from the essence of God than can its having its three angles equal to two right angles be separated from the essence of a [rectilinear] triangle, or the idea of a mountain from the idea of a valley; and so there is not any less repugnance to our conceiving a God (that is, a Being supremely perfect) to whom existence is lacking (that is to say, to whom a certain perfection is lacking), than to conceive of a mountain which has no valley.

But although I cannot really conceive of a God without existence any more than a mountain without a valley, still from the fact that I conceive of a mountain with a valley, it does not follow that there is such a mountain in the world; similarly although I conceive of God as possessing existence, it would seem that it does not follow that there is a God which

exists; for my thought does not impose any necessity upon things, and just as I may imagine a winged horse, although no horse with wings exists, so I could perhaps attribute existence to God, although no God existed.

But a sophism is concealed in this objection; for from the fact that I cannot conceive a mountain without a valley, it does not follow that there is any mountain or any valley in existence, but only that the mountain and the valley, whether they exist or do not exist, cannot in any way be separated one from the other. While from the fact that I cannot conceive God without existence, it follows that existence is inseparable from Him, and hence that He really exists; not that my thought can bring this to pass, or impose any necessity on things, but, on the contrary, because the necessity which lies in the thing itself, i.e. the necessity of the existence of God determines me to think in this way. For it is not within my power to think of God without existence (that is of a supremely perfect Being devoid of a supreme perfection) though it is in my power to imagine a horse either with wings or without wings.

And we must not here object that it is in truth necessary for me to assert that God exists after having presupposed that He possesses every sort of perfection, since existence is one of these, but that as a matter of fact my original supposition was not necessary, just as it is not necessary to consider that all quadrilateral figures can be inscribed in the circle; for supposing I thought this, I should be constrained to admit that the rhombus might be inscribed in the circle since it is a quadrilateral figure, which, however, is manifestly false. [We must not, I say, make any such allegations because] although it is not necessary that I should at any time entertain the notion of God, nevertheless whenever it happens that I think of a first and a sovereign Being, and, so to speak, derive the idea of Him from the storehouse of my mind, it is necessary that I should attribute to Him every sort of perfection, although I do not get so far as to enumerate them all, or to apply my mind to each one in particular. And this necessity suffices to make me conclude (after having recognised that existence is a perfection) that this first and sovereign Being really exists; just as though it is not necessary for me ever to imagine any triangle, yet, whenever I wish to consider a rectilinear figure composed only of three angles, it is absolutely essential that I should attribute to it all those properties which serve to bring about the conclusion that its three angles are not greater than two right angles, even although I may not then be considering this point in particular. But when I consider which figures are capable of being inscribed in the circle, it is in no wise necessary that I should think that all quadrilateral figures are of this number; on the contrary, I cannot even pretend that this is the case, so long as I do not desire to accept anything which I cannot conceive clearly and distinctly. And in consequence there is a great difference between the false suppositions such as this, and the true ideas born within me, the first and principal of which is that of God. For really I discern in many ways that this idea is not something factitious, and depending solely on my thought, but that it is the image of a true and immutable nature; first of all, because I cannot conceive anything but God himself to whose essence existence [necessarily] pertains; in the second place because it is not possible for me to conceive two or more Gods in this same position; and, granted that there is one such God who now exists, I see clearly that it is necessary that He should have existed from all eternity, and that He must exist eternally; and finally, because I know an infinitude of other properties in God, none of which I can either diminish or change.

For the rest, whatever proof or argument I avail myself of, we must always return to the point that it is only those things which we conceive clearly and distinctly that have the power of persuading me entirely. And although amongst the matters which I conceive of in this way, some indeed are manifestly obvious to all, while others only manifest themselves to those who consider them closely and examine them attentively; still, after they have once been discovered, the latter are not esteemed as any less certain than the former. For example, in the case of every right-angled triangle, although it does not so manifestly appear that the square of the base is equal to the squares of the two other sides as that this base is opposite to the greatest angle; still, when this has once been apprehended, we are just as certain of its truth as of the truth of the other. And as regards God, if my mind were not pre-occupied with prejudices, and if my thought did not find itself on all hands diverted by the continual pressure of sensible things, there would

be nothing which I could know more immediately and more easily than Him. For is there anything more manifest than that there is a God, that is to say, a Supreme Being, to whose essence alone existence pertains?

And although for a firm grasp of this truth I have need of a strenuous application of mind, at present I not only feel myself to be as assured of it as of all that I hold as most certain, but I also remark that the certainty of all other things depends on it so absolutely, that without this knowledge it is impossible ever to know anything perfectly.

For although I am of such a nature that as long as I understand anything very clearly and distinctly, I am naturally impelled to believe it to be true, yet because I am also of such a nature that I cannot have my mind constantly fixed on the same object in order to perceive it clearly, and as I often recollect having formed a past judgment without at the same time properly recollecting the reasons that led me to make it, it may happen meanwhile that other reasons present themselves to me, which would easily cause me to change my opinion, if I were ignorant of the facts of the existence of God, and thus I should have no true and certain knowledge, but only vague and vacillating opinions. Thus, for example, when I consider the nature of a [rectilinear] triangle, I who have some little knowledge of the principles of geometry recognise quite clearly that the three angles are equal to two right angles, and it is not possible for me not to believe this so long as I apply my mind to its demonstration; but so soon as I abstain from attending to the proof, although I still recollect having clearly comprehended it, it may easily occur that I come to doubt its truth, if I am ignorant of there being a God. For I can persuade myself of having been so constituted by nature that I can easily deceive myself even in those matters which I believe myself to apprehend with the greatest evidence and certainty, especially when I recollect that I have frequently judged matters to be true and certain which other reasons have afterwards impelled me to judge to be altogether false.

But after I have recognised that there is a God—because at the same time I have also recognised that all things depend upon Him, and that He is not a deceiver, and from that have inferred that what I perceive clearly and distinctly cannot fail to be true—although I no longer pay attention to the reasons for which I have judged this to be true, provided that I recollect having clearly and distinctly perceived it no contrary reason can be brought forward which could ever cause me to doubt of its truth; and thus I have a true and certain knowledge of it. And this same knowledge extends likewise to all other things which I recollect having formerly demonstrated, such as the truths of geometry and the like; for what can be alleged against them to cause me to place them in doubt? Will it be said that my nature is such as to cause me to be frequently deceived? But I already know that I cannot be deceived in the judgment whose grounds I know clearly. Will it be said that I formerly held many things to be true and certain which I have afterwards recognised to be false? But I had not had any clear and distinct knowledge of these things, and not as yet knowing the rule whereby I assure myself of the truth, I had been impelled to give my assent from reasons which I have since recognised to be less strong than I had at the time imagined them to be. What further objection can then be raised? That possibly I am dreaming (an objection I myself made a little while ago), or that all the thoughts which I now have are no more true than the phantasies of my dreams? But even though I slept the case would be the same, for all that is clearly present to my mind is absolutely true.

And so I very clearly recognise that the certainty and truth of all knowledge depends alone on the knowledge of the true God, in so much that, before I knew Him, I could not have a perfect knowledge of any other thing. And now that I know Him I have the means of acquiring a perfect knowledge of an infinitude of things, not only of those which relate to God Himself and other intellectual matters, but also of those which pertain to corporeal nature in so far as it is the object of pure mathematics [which have no concern with whether it exists or not].

MEDITATION VI

Of the Existence of Material Things, and Of the Real Distinction Between the Soul and Body of Man

Nothing further now remains but to inquire whether material things exist. And certainly I at least know that these may exist in so far as they are considered as the objects of pure mathematics, since in this aspect I perceive them clearly and distinctly. For there is no doubt that God possesses the power to produce everything that I am capable of perceiving with distinctness, and I have never deemed that anything was impossible for Him, unless I found a contradiction in attempting to conceive it clearly. Further, the faculty of imagination which I possess, and of which, experience tells me, I make use when I apply myself to the consideration of material things, is capable of persuading me of their existence; for when I attentively consider what imagination is, I find that it is nothing but a certain application of the faculty of knowledge to the body which is immediately present to it, and which therefore exists.

And to render this quite clear, I remark in the first place the difference that exists between the imagination and pure intellection [or conception]. For example, when I imagine a triangle, I do not conceive it only as a figure comprehended by three lines, but I also apprehend these three lines as present by the power and inward vision of my mind, and this is what I call imagining. But if I desire to think of a chiliagon, I certainly conceive truly that it is a figure composed of a thousand sides, just as easily as I conceive of a triangle that it is a figure of three sides only; but I cannot in any way imagine the thousand sides of a chiliagon [as I do the three sides of a triangle], nor do I, so to speak, regard them as present [with the eyes of my mind]. And although in accordance with the habit I have formed of always employing the aid of my imagination when I think of corporeal things, it may happen that in imagining a chiliagon I confusedly represent to myself some figure, yet it is very evident that this figure is not a chiliagon, since it in no way differs from that which I represent to myself when I think of a myriagon or any other many-sided figure; nor does it serve my purpose in discovering the properties which go to form the distinction between a chiliagon and other polygons. But if the question turns upon a pentagon, it is quite true that I can conceive its figure as well as that of a chiliagon without the help of my imagination; but I can also imagine it by applying the attention of my mind to each of its five sides, and at the same time to the space which they enclose. And thus I clearly recognise that I have need of a particular effort of mind in order to effect the act of imagination, such as I do not require in order to understand, and this particular effort of mind clearly manifests the difference which exists between imagination and pure intellection.

I remark besides that this power of imagination which is in one, inasmuch as it differs from the power of understanding, is in no wise a necessary element in my nature, or in [my essence, that is to say, in] the essence of my mind; for although I did not possess it I should doubtless ever remain the same as I now am, from which it appears that we might conclude that it depends on something which differs from me. And I easily conceive that if some body exists with which my mind is conjoined and united in such a way that it can apply itself to consider it when it pleases, it may be that by this means it can imagine corporeal objects; so that this mode of thinking differs from pure intellection only inasmuch as mind in its intellectual activity in some manner turns on itself, and considers some of the ideas which it possesses in itself; while in imagining it turns towards the body, and there beholds in it something conformable to the idea which it has either conceived of itself or perceived by the senses. I easily understand, I say, that the imagination could be thus constituted if it is true that body exists; and because I can discover no other convenient mode of explaining it, I conjecture with probability that body does exist; but this is only with probability, and although I examine all things with care, I nevertheless do not find that from this distinct idea of corporeal nature, which I have in my imagination, I can derive any argument from which there will necessarily be deduced the existence of body.

But I am in the habit of imagining many other things besides this corporeal nature which is the object of pure mathematics, to wit, the colours, sounds, scents, pain, and other such things, although less distinctly. And inasmuch as I perceive these things much better through the senses, by the medium of which, and by the memory, they seem to have reached my imagination, I believe that, in order to examine them more conveniently, it is right that I should at the same time investigate the nature of sense perception, and that I should see if from the ideas which I apprehend by this mode of thought, which I call feeling, I cannot derive some certain proof of the existence of corporeal objects.

And first of all I shall recall to my memory those matters which I hitherto held to be true, as having perceived them through the senses, and the foundations on which my belief has rested; in the next place I shall examine the reasons which have since obliged me to place them in doubt; in the last place I shall consider which of them I must now believe.

First of all, then, I perceived that I had a head, hands, feet, and all other members of which this body—which I considered as a part, or possibly even as the whole, of myself—is composed. Further I was sensible that this body was placed amidst many others, from which it was capable of being affected in many different ways, beneficial and hurtful, and I remarked that a certain feeling of pleasure accompanied those that were beneficial, and pain those which were harmful. And in addition to this pleasure and pain, I also experienced hunger, thirst, and other similar appetites, and also certain corporeal inclinations towards joy, sadness, anger, and other similar passions. And outside myself, in addition to extension, figure, and motions of bodies, I remarked in them hardness, heat, and all other tactile qualities, and further, light and colour, and scents and sounds, the variety of which gave me the means of distinguishing the sky, the earth, the sea, and generally all the other bodies, one from the other. And certainly, considering the ideas of all these qualities which presented themselves to my mind, and which alone I perceived properly or immediately, it was not without reason that I believed myself to perceive objects quite different from my thought, to wit, bodies from which those ideas proceeded; for I found by experience that these ideas presented themselves to me without my consent being requisite, so that I could not perceive any object, however desirous I might be, unless it were present to the organs of sense; and it was not in my power not to perceive it, when it was present. And because the ideas which I received through the senses were much more lively, more clear, and even, in their own way, more distinct than any of those which I could of myself frame in meditation, or than those I found impressed on my memory, it appeared as though they could not have proceeded from my mind, so that they must necessarily have been produced in me by some other things. And having no knowledge of those objects excepting the knowledge which the ideas themselves gave me, nothing was more likely to occur to my mind than that the objects were similar to the ideas which were caused. And because I likewise remembered that I had formerly made use of my senses rather than my reason, and recognised that the ideas which I formed of myself were not so distinct as those which I perceived through the senses, and that they were most frequently even composed of portions of these last, I persuaded myself easily that I had no idea in my mind which had not formerly come to me through the senses. Nor was it without some reason that I believed that this body (which by a certain special right I call my own) belonged to me more properly and more strictly than any other; for in fact I could never be separated from it as from other bodies; I experienced in it and on account of it all my appetites and affections, and finally I was touched by the feeling of pain and titillation of pleasure in its parts, and not in the parts of other bodies which were separated from it. But when I inquired, why, from some, I know not what, painful sensation, there follows sadness of mind, and from the pleasurable sensation there arises joy, or why this mysterious pinching of the stomach which I call hunger causes me to desire to eat, and dryness of throat causes a desire to drink, and so on, I could give no reason excepting that nature taught me so; for there is certainly no affinity (that I at least can understand) between the craving of the stomach and the desire to eat, any more than between the perception of whatever causes pain and the thought of sadness which arises from this perception. And in the same way it appeared to me that I had learned from nature all the other judgments which I formed regarding the objects of my senses, since I remarked that these judgments were formed in me before I had the leisure to weigh and consider any reasons which might oblige me to make them.

But afterwards many experiences little by little destroyed all the faith which I had rested in my senses; for I from time to time observed that those towers which from afar appeared to me to be round, more closely observed seemed square, and that colossal statues raised on the summit of these towers, appeared as quite tiny statues when viewed from the bottom; and so in an infinitude of other cases I found error in judgments founded on the external senses. And not only in those founded on the external senses, but even in those founded on the internal as well; for is there anything more intimate or more internal than pain? And yet I have learned from some persons whose arms or legs have been cut off, that they sometimes seemed to feel pain in the part which had been amputated, which made me think that I could not be quite certain that it was a certain member which pained me, even although I felt pain in it. And to those grounds of doubt I have lately added two others, which are very general; the first is that I never have believed myself to feel anything in waking moments which I cannot also sometimes believe myself to feel when I sleep, and as I do not think that these things which I seem to feel in sleep, proceed from objects outside of me, I do not see any reason why I should have this belief regarding objects which I seem to perceive while awake. The other was that being still ignorant, or rather supposing myself to be ignorant, of the author of my being, I saw nothing to prevent me from having been so constituted by nature that I might be deceived even in matters which seemed to me to be most certain. And as to the grounds on which I was formerly persuaded of the truth of sensible objects, I had not much trouble in replying to them. For since nature seemed to cause me to lean towards many things from which reason repelled me, I did not believe that I should trust much to the teachings of nature. And although the ideas which I receive by the senses do not depend on my will, I did not think that one should for that reason conclude that they proceeded from things different from myself, since possibly some faculty might be discovered in me—though hitherto unknown to me—which produced them.

But now that I begin to know myself better, and to discover more clearly the author of my being, I do not in truth think that I should rashly admit all the matters which the senses seem to teach us, but, on the other hand, I do not think that I should doubt them all universally.

And first of all, because I know that all things which I apprehend clearly and distinctly can be created by God as I apprehend them, it suffices that I am able to apprehend one thing apart from another clearly and distinctly in order to be certain that the one is different from the other, since they may be made to exist in separation at least by the omnipotence of God; and it does not signify by what power this separation is made in order to compel me to judge them to be different: and, therefore, just because I know certainly that I exist, and that meanwhile I do not remark that any other thing necessarily pertains to my nature or essence, excepting that I am a thinking thing, I rightly conclude that my essence consists solely in the fact that I am a thinking thing [or a substance whose whole essence or nature is to think]. And although possibly (or rather certainly, as I shall say in a moment) I possess a body with which I am very intimately conjoined, yet because, on the one side, I have a clear and distinct idea of myself inasmuch as I am only a thinking and unextended thing, and as, on the other, I possess a distinct idea of body, inasmuch as it is only an extended and unthinking thing, it is certain that this I [that is to say, my soul by which I am what I am], is entirely and absolutely distinct from my body, and can exist without it.

I further find in myself faculties employing modes of thinking peculiar to themselves, to wit, the faculties of imagination and feeling, without which I can easily conceive myself clearly and distinctly as a complete being; while, on the other hand, they cannot be so conceived apart from me, that is without an intelligent substance in which they reside, for [in the notion we have of these faculties, or, to use the language of the Schools] in their formal concept, some kind of intellection is comprised, from which I infer that they are distinct from me as its modes are from a thing. I observe also in me some other faculties such as that of change of position, the assumption of different figures and such like, which cannot be conceived, any more than can the preceding, apart from some substance to which they are attached, and consequently cannot exist without it; but it is very clear that these faculties, if it be true that they exist, must be attached to some corporeal or extended substance, and not to an intelligent substance, since in the clear and distinct conception of these there is some sort of extension found to be present, but no intellection at all. There is certainly further in me a certain passive faculty of perception, that is, of receiving and recognising the ideas of sensible things, but this would be useless to me [and I could in no way avail myself of it], if there were not either in me or in some other thing another active faculty capable of forming and producing these ideas. But this active faculty cannot exist in me [inasmuch as I am a thing that thinks] seeing that it does not presuppose thought, and also that those ideas are often produced in me without my contributing in any way to the same, and often even against my will; it is thus necessarily the case that the faculty resides in some substance different from me in which all the reality which is objectively in the ideas that are produced by this faculty is formally or eminently contained, as I remarked before. And this substance is either a body, that is, a corporeal nature in which there is contained formally [and

really] all that which is objectively [and by representation] in those ideas, or it is God Himself, or some other creature more noble than body in which that same is contained eminently. But, since God is no deceiver, it is very manifest that He does not communicate to me these ideas immediately and by Himself, nor yet by the intervention of some creature in which their reality is not formally, but only eminently, contained. For since He has given me no faculty to recognise that this is the case, but, on the other hand, a very great inclination to believe [that they are sent to me or] that they are conveyed to me by corporeal objects, I do not see how He could be defended from the accusation of deceit if these ideas were produced by causes other than corporeal objects. Hence we must allow that corporeal things exist. However, they are perhaps not exactly what we perceive by the senses, since this comprehension by the senses is in many instances very obscure and confused; but we must at least admit that all things which I conceive in them clearly and distinctly, that is to say, all things which, speaking generally, are comprehended in the object of pure mathematics, are truly to be recognised as external objects.

As to other things, however, which are either particular only, as, for example, that the sun is of such a figure, etc., or which are less clearly and distinctly conceived, such as light, sound, pain and the like, it is certain that although they are very dubious and uncertain, yet on the sole ground that God is not a deceiver, and that consequently He has not permitted any falsity to exist in my opinion which He has not likewise given me the faculty of correcting, I may assuredly hope to conclude that I have within me the means of arriving at the truth even here. And first of all there is no doubt that in all things which nature teaches me there is some truth contained; for by nature, considered in general, I now understand no other thing than either God Himself or else the order and disposition which God has established in created things; and by my nature in particular I understand no other thing than the complexus of all the things which God has given me.

But there is nothing which this nature teaches me more expressly [nor more sensibly] than that I have a body which is adversely affected when I feel pain, which has need of food or drink when I experience the feelings of hunger and thirst, and so on; nor can I doubt there being some truth in all this.

Nature also teaches me by these sensations of pain, hunger, thirst, etc., that I am not only lodged in my body as a pilot in a vessel, but that I am very closely united to it, and so to speak so intermingled with it that I seem to compose with it one whole. For if that were not the case, when my body is hurt, I, who am merely a thinking thing, should not feel pain, for I should perceive this wound by the understanding only, just as the sailor perceives by sight when something is damaged in his vessel; and when my body has need of drink or food, I should clearly understand the fact without being warned of it by confused feelings of hunger and thirst. For all these sensations of hunger, thirst, pain, etc. are in truth none other than certain confused modes of thought which are produced by the union and apparent intermingling of mind and body.

Moreover, nature teaches me that many other bodies exist around mine, of which some are to be avoided, and others sought after. And certainly from the fact that I am sensible of different sorts of colours, sounds, scents, tastes, heat, hardness, etc., I very easily conclude that there are in the bodies from which all these diverse sense-perceptions proceed certain variations which answer to them, although possibly these are not really at all similar to them. And also from the fact that amongst these different sense-perceptions some are very agreeable to me and other are disagreeable, it is quite certain that my body (or rather myself in my entirety, inasmuch as I am formed of body and soul) may receive different impressions agreeable and disagreeable from the other bodies which surround it.

But there are many other things which nature seems to have taught me, but which at the same time I have never really received from her, but which have been brought about in my mind by a certain habit which I have of forming inconsiderate judgments on things; and thus it may easily happen that these judgments contain some error. Take, for example, the opinion which I hold that all space in which there is nothing that affects [or makes an impression on] my senses is void; that in a body which is warm there is something entirely similar to the idea of heat which is in me; that in a white or green body there is the same whiteness or greenness that I perceive; that in a bitter or sweet body there is the same taste, and so on in other instances; that the stars, the towers, and all other distant bodies are of the same figure and size as they appear from far off to our eyes, etc. But in order that in this there should be nothing which I do not conceive distinctly, I should define exactly what I really understand when I say that I am taught somewhat by nature. For here I take nature in a more limited signification than when I term it the sum of all the things given me by God, since in this sum many things are comprehended which only pertain to mind (and to these I do not refer in speaking of nature) such as the notion which I have of the fact that what has once been done cannot ever be undone and an infinitude of such things which I know by the light of nature [without the help of the body]; and seeing that it comprehends many other matters besides which only pertain to body, and are no longer here contained under the name of nature, such as the quality of weight which it possesses and the like, with which I also do not deal; for in talking of nature I only treat of those things given by God to me as a being composed of mind and body. But the nature here described truly teaches me to flee from things which cause the sensation of pain, and seek after the things which communicate to me the sentiment of pleasure and so forth; but I do not see that beyond this it teaches me that from those diverse sense-perceptions we should ever form any conclusion regarding things outside of us, without having [carefully and maturely] mentally examined them beforehand. For it seems to me that it is mind alone, and not mind and body in conjunction, that is requisite to a knowledge of the truth in regard to such things. Thus, although a star makes no larger an impression on my eye than the flame of a little candle there is yet in me no real or positive propensity impelling me to believe that it is not greater than that flame; but I have judged it to be so from my earliest years, without any rational foundation. And although in approaching fire I feel heat, and in approaching it a little too near I even feel pain, there is at the same time no reason in this which could persuade me that there is in the fire something resembling this heat any more than there is in it something resembling the pain; all that I have any reason to believe from this is, that there is something in it, whatever it may be, which excites in me these sensations of heat or of pain. So also, although there are spaces in which I find nothing which excites my senses, I must not from that conclude that these spaces contain no body; for I see in this, as in other similar things, that I have been in the habit of perverting the order of nature, because these perceptions of sense having been placed within me by nature merely for the purpose of signifying to my mind what things are beneficial or hurtful to the composite whole of which it forms a part, and being up to that point sufficiently clear and distinct, I yet avail myself of them as though they were absolute rules by which I might immediately determine the essence of the bodies which are outside me, as to which, in fact, they can teach me nothing but what is most obscure and confused.

But I have already sufficiently considered how, notwithstanding the supreme goodness of God, falsity enters into the judgments I make. Only here a new difficulty is presented—one respecting those things the pursuit or avoidance of which is taught me by nature, and also respecting the internal sensations which I possess, and in which I seem to have sometimes detected error [and thus to be directly deceived by my own nature]. To take an example, the agreeable taste of some food in which poison has been intermingled may induce me to partake of the poison, and thus deceive me. It is true, at the same time, that in this case nature may be excused, for it only induces me to desire food in which I find a pleasant taste, and not to desire the poison which is unknown to it; and thus I can infer nothing from this fact, except that my nature is not omniscient, at which there is certainly no reason to be astonished, since man, being finite in nature, can only have knowledge the perfectness of which is limited.

But we not unfrequently deceive ourselves even in those things to which we are directly impelled by nature, as happens with those who when they are sick desire to drink or eat things hurtful to them. It will perhaps be said here that the cause of their deceptiveness is that their nature is corrupt, but that does not remove the difficulty, because a sick man is none the less truly God's creature than he who is in health; and it is therefore as repugnant to God's goodness for the one to have a deceitful nature as it is for the other. And as a clock composed of wheels and counterweights no less exactly observes the laws of nature when it is badly made, and does not show the time properly, than when it entirely satisfies the wishes of its maker, and as, if I consider the body of a man as being a sort of machine so built up and composed of nerves, muscles, veins, blood and skin, that though there were no mind in it at all, it would not cease to have the same motions as at present, exception being made of those movements which are due to the direction of the will, and in consequence depend upon the mind [as opposed to those which operate by the disposition of its organs], I easily recognise that it would be as natural to this body, supposing it to be, for example, dropsical, to suffer the parchedness of the throat which usually signifies to the mind the feeling of thirst, and to be disposed by this parched feeling to move the nerves and other parts in the way requisite for drinking, and thus to augment its malady and do harm to itself, as it is natural to it, when it has no indisposition, to be impelled to drink for its good by a similar cause. And although, considering the use to which the clock has been destined by its maker, I may say that it deflects from the order of its nature when it does not indicate the hours correctly; and as, in the same way, considering the machine of the human body as having been formed by God in order to have in itself all the movements usually manifested there, I have reason for thinking that it does not follow the order of nature when, if the throat is dry, drinking does harm to the conservation of health, nevertheless I recognise at the same time that this last mode of explaining nature is very different from the other. For this is but a purely verbal characterisation depending entirely on my thought, which compares a sick man and a badly constructed clock with the idea which I have a healthy man and a well made clock, and it is hence extrinsic to the things to which it is applied; but according to the other interpretation of the term nature I understand something which is truly found in things and which is therefore not without some truth.

But certainly although in regard to the dropsical body it is only so to speak to apply an extrinsic term when we say that its nature is corrupted, inasmuch as apart from the need to drink, the throat is parched; yet in regard to the composite whole, that is to say, to the mind or soul united to this body, it is not a purely verbal predicate, but a real error of nature, for it to have thirst when drinking would be hurtful to it. And thus it still remains to inquire how the goodness of God does not prevent the nature of man so regarded from being fallacious.

In order to begin this examination, then, I here say, in the first place, that there is a great difference between mind and body, inasmuch as body is by nature always divisible, and the mind is entirely indivisible. For, as a matter of fact, when I consider the mind, that is to say, myself inasmuch as I am only a thinking thing, I cannot distinguish in myself any parts, but apprehend myself to be clearly one and entire; and although the whole mind seems to be united to the whole body, yet if a foot, or an arm, or some other part, is separated from my body, I am aware that nothing has been taken away from my mind. And the faculties of willing, feeling, conceiving, etc. cannot be properly speaking said to be its parts, for it is one and the same mind which employs itself in willing and in feeling and understanding. But it is quite otherwise with corporeal or extended objects, for there is not one of these imaginable by me which my mind cannot easily divide into parts, and which consequently I do not recognise as being divisible; this would be sufficient to teach me that the mind or soul of man is entirely different from the body, if I had not already learned it from other sources.

I further notice that the mind does not receive the impressions from all parts of the body immediately, but only from the brain, or perhaps even from one of its smallest parts, to wit, from that in which the common sense is said to reside, which, whenever it is disposed in the same particular way, conveys the same thing to the mind, although meanwhile the other portions of the body may be differently disposed, as is testified by innumerable experiments which it is unnecessary here to recount.

I notice, also, that the nature of body is such that none of its parts can be moved by another part a little way off which cannot also be moved in the same way by each one of the parts which are between the two, although this more remote part does not act at all. As, for example, in the cord ABCD [which is in tension] if we pull the last part D, the first part A will not be moved in any way differently from what would be the case if one of the intervening parts B or C were pulled, and the last part D were to remain unmoved. And in the same way, when I feel pain in my foot, my knowledge of physics teaches me that this sensation is communicated by means of nerves dispersed through the foot, which, being extended like cords from there

to the brain, when they are contracted in the foot, at the same time contract the inmost portions of the brain which is their extremity and place of origin, and then excite a certain movement which nature has established in order to cause the mind to be affected by a sensation of pain represented as existing in the foot. But because these nerves must pass through the tibia, the thigh, the loins, the back and the neck, in order to reach from the leg to the brain, it may happen that although their extremities which are in the foot are not affected, but only certain ones of their intervening parts [which pass by the loins or the neck], this action will excite the same movement in the brain that might have been excited there by a hurt received in the foot, in consequence of which the mind will necessarily feel in the foot the same pain as if it had received a hurt. And the same holds good of all the other perceptions of our senses.

I notice finally that since each of the movements which are in the portion of the brain by which the mind is immediately affected brings about one particular sensation only, we cannot under the circumstances imagine anything more likely than that this movement, amongst all the sensations which it is capable of impressing on it, causes mind to be affected by that one which is best fitted and most generally useful for the conservation of the human body when it is in health. But experience makes us aware that all the feelings with which nature inspires us are such as I have just spoken of; and there is therefore nothing in them which does not give testimony to the power and goodness of the God [who has produced them]. Thus, for example, when the nerves which are in the feet are violently or more than usually moved, their movement, passing through the medulla of the spine to the inmost parts of the brain, gives a sign to the mind which makes it feel somewhat, to wit, pain, as though in the foot, by which the mind is excited to do its utmost to remove the cause of the evil as dangerous and hurtful to the foot. It is true that God could have constituted the nature of man in such a way that this same movement in the brain would have conveyed something quite different to the mind; for example, it might have produced consciousness of itself either in so far as it is in the brain, or as it is in the foot, or as it is in some other place between the foot and the brain, or it might finally have produced consciousness of anything else whatsoever; but none of all this would have contributed so well to the conservation of the body. Similarly, when we desire to drink, a certain dryness of the throat is produced which moves its nerves, and by their means the internal portions of the brain; and this movement causes in the mind the sensation of thirst, because in this case there is nothing more useful to us than to become aware that we have need to drink for the conservation of our health; and the same holds good in other instances.

From this it is quite clear that, notwithstanding the supreme goodness of God, the nature of man, inasmuch as it is composed of mind and body, cannot be otherwise than sometimes a source of deception. For if there is any cause which excites, not in the foot but in some part of the nerves which are extended between the foot and the brain, or even in the brain itself, the same movement which usually is produced when the foot is detrimentally affected, pain will be experienced as though it were in the foot, and the sense will thus naturally be deceived; for since the same movement in the brain is capable of causing but one sensation in the mind, and this sensation is much more frequently excited by a cause which hurts the foot than by another existing in some other quarter, it is reasonable that it should convey to the mind pain in the foot rather than in any other part of the body. And although the parchedness of the throat does not always proceed, as it usually does, from the fact that drinking is necessary for the health of the body, but sometimes comes from quite a different cause, as is the case with dropsical patients, it is yet much better that it should mislead on this occasion than if, on the other hand, it were always to deceive us when the body is in good health; and so on in similar cases.

And certainly this consideration is of great service to me, not only in enabling me to recognise all the errors to which my nature is subject, but also in enabling me to avoid them or to correct them more easily. For knowing that all my senses more frequently indicate to me truth than falsehood respecting the things which concern that which is beneficial to the body, and being able almost always to avail myself of many of them in order to examine one particular thing, and, besides that, being able to make use of my memory in order to connect the present with the past, and of my understanding which already has discovered all the causes of my errors, I ought no longer to fear that falsity may be found in matters every day presented to me by my sense. And I ought to set aside all the doubts of these past days as hyperbolical and ridiculous, particularly that very common uncertainty respecting sleep, which I could not distinguish from the waking state; for at present I find a very notable difference between the two, inasmuch as our memory can never connect our dreams one with the other, or with the whole course of our lives, as it unites events which happen to us while we are awake. And, as a matter of fact, if someone, while I was awake, quite suddenly appeared to me and disappeared as fast as do the images which I see in sleep, so that I could not know from whence the form came nor whither it went, it would not be without reason that I should deem it a spectre or a phantom formed by my brain [and similar to those which I form in sleep], rather than a real man. But when I perceive things as to which I know distinctly both the place from which they proceed, and that in which they are, and the time at which they appeared to me; and when, without any interruption, I can connect the perceptions which I have of them with the whole course of my life, I am perfectly assured that these perceptions occur while I am waking and not during sleep. And I ought in no wise to doubt the truth of such matters, if, after having called up all my senses, my memory, and my understanding, to examine them, nothing is brought to evidence by any one of them which is repugnant to what is set forth by the others. For because God is in no wise a deceiver, it follows that I am not deceived in this. But because the exigencies of action often oblige us to make up our minds before having leisure to examine matters carefully, we must confess that the life of man is very frequently subject to error in respect to individual objects, and we must in the end acknowledge the infirmity of our nature.

STUDY QUESTIONS: DESCARTES, *MEDITATIONS ON THE FIRST PHILOSOPHY*

1. What is Descartes' method of doubt? What is the point of this method?
2. What does Descartes mean by 'sound and correct judgments'?

3. Why does Descartes doubt the evidence from his senses?
4. Must Descartes refute each and every one of his opinions to overthrow them all? Why?
5. What reason does Descartes give that right now you cannot be sure you are not dreaming? What is it about your state of mind during a dream that makes this so?
6. Whether dreaming or awake, concepts such as *perceived extension* seem to apply. Can we, on the basis of this, know that extension is *real*? Why?
7. Why is geometry more certain than astronomy?
8. Could God deceive you about propositions such as 'a triangle has three sides' and '5 + 3 = 8'?
9. What is the point of Descartes' claim that an evil spirit might be deceiving him? Why is such a supposition reasonable?
10. Why is the question of *what* you are not the same as the assertion *that* you are?
11. How does Descartes conclude that he is a thinking thing, that is, a thing that thinks? What does the term 'thinking' mean?
12. What is the point of Descartes' wax example? What is it meant to show?
13. How does Descartes argue to the conclusion that what is very clearly and distinctly apprehended is true?
14. Why is the principle that clear and distinct ideas are true important for Descartes' philosophy?
15. Why must an efficient cause be at least as real as its effect?
16. Why does Descartes think the idea of an infinite substance has more objective reality than ideas concerning finite substances? How does he use this claim to prove the existence of God?
17. Which has the wider range—the will or the understanding? Why? What is the significance of this inequality?
18. Why must God be conceived as being perfect?
19. Why are existence and essence one and the same in God?
20. What are Descartes' arguments for the claim that the mind is a substance distinct from the body?

MEDITATIONS: OBJECTIONS AND REPLIES II, III, AND IV

Descartes' *Meditations* was first published in 1641. Once he had completed the manuscript, Descartes circulated it among his friends, and he asked Mersenne to collect and compile a set of objections, which were published, along with Descartes' replies, with the first edition of the book. Descartes' intention was to find the strongest objections possible and to leave the reader to judge whether his replies were adequate.

In all there are seven sets of objections, from which we have included selections from the most important three. The second set was collected and largely composed by Mersenne himself. The famous British philosopher and author of the *Leviathan*, Thomas Hobbes, wrote the third set of objections. The fourth set is by Antoine Arnauld (1612–1694), the leading Port Royal theologian and logician, who was friends with Pascal.

From *The Philosophical Works of Descartes, Volume II* translated by Elizabeth Haldane & G. Ross, Cambridge University Press, 1912.

The others were by Catholic theologian Johannes Caterus (the first set), the philosopher Pierre Gassendi (the fifth set), the Jesuit Pierre Bourdin (the seventh set), and Mersenne, who compiled the sixth set.

THE SECOND SET OF OBJECTIONS

Sir,

   Your endeavor to maintain the cause of the Author of all things against a new race of rebellious giants has sped so well, that henceforth men of worth may hope that in future there will be none who, after attentive study of your Meditations, will not confess that an eternal divine Being does exist, on whom all things depend. Hence we have decided to draw your attention to certain passages noted beneath and to request you to shed such light upon them that nothing will remain in your work which, if at all demonstrable, is not clearly proved. For, since you have for so many years so exercised your mind by continual meditation, that matters which to others seem doubtful and obscure are to you most evident, and you perhaps know them by a simple intuitive act of mind, without noticing the indistinctness that the same facts have for others, it will be well to bring before your notice those things which need to be more clearly and fully explained and demonstrated. This done, there will scarce remain anyone to deny that those arguments of yours, entered upon for the purpose of promoting the greater glory of God and vast benefit to all mankind, have the force of demonstrations.

   In the first place, pray remember that it was not as an actual fact and in reality, but merely by a mental fiction, that you so stoutly resisted the claim of all bodies to be more than phantasms, in order that you might draw the conclusion that you were merely a thinking being; for otherwise there is perhaps a risk you might believe that you could draw the conclusion that you were in truth nothing other than mind, or thought, or a thinking being. This we find worthy of mention only in connection with the first two Meditations, in which you show clearly that it is at least certain that you, who think, exist. But let us pause a little here. Up to this point you know that you are a being that thinks; but you do not know what this thinking thing is. What if that were a body which by its various motions and encounters produces that which we call thought? For, granted that you rejected the claim of every sort of body, you may have been deceived in this, because you did not rule out yourself, who are a body. For how will you prove

that a body cannot think, or that its bodily motions are not thought itself? Possibly even, the whole bodily system, which you imagine you have rejected, or some of its parts, say the parts composing the brain, can unite to produce those motions which we call thoughts. 'I am a thinking thing,' you say; but who knows but you are a corporeal motion, or a body in motion?

   Secondly, from the idea of a supreme being, which, you contend, cannot be by you produced, you are bold enough to infer the necessary existence of the supreme being from which alone can come that idea that your mind perceives. Yet we find in our own selves a sufficient basis on which alone to erect that said idea, even though that supreme being did not exist, or we were ignorant of its existence and did not even think of it though it did exist. Do I not see that I, in thinking, have some degree of perfection? And therefore I conclude that others besides me have a similar degree, and hence I have a basis on which to construct the thought of any number of degrees and so to add one degree of perfection to another to infinity, just as, given the existence of a single degree of light or heat, I can add and imagine fresh degrees up to infinity. Why, on similar reasoning, can I not add, to any degree of being that I perceive in myself any other degree I please, and out of the whole number capable of addition construct the idea of a perfect being? 'But' you say, 'an effect can have no degree of perfection or reality which has not previously existed in its cause.' In reply we urge (passing by the fact that experience shows us that flies and other animals, or even plants are produced by the sun, rain and the earth, in which life, a nobler thing than any merely corporeal grade of being, does not exist, and that hence an effect can derive from its cause some reality which yet is not found in the cause) that that idea is nothing but an entity of reason, which has no more nobility than your mind that thinks it. Besides this, how do you know that that idea would have come before your mind if you had not been nurtured among men of culture, but had passed all your life in some desert spot? Have you not derived it from reflections previously entertained, from books, from interchange of converse with your friends, etc., not from your own mind alone or from a supreme being who exists? You must therefore prove more clearly that that idea could not present itself to you unless a supreme being did exist; though when you show this we shall all confess ourselves vanquished. But it seems to be shown clearly that that idea springs from previous notions by the fact that the natives of Canada, the Hurons, and other savages, have no idea in their minds such as this, which is one that you can form from a previous survey of corporeal things, in such a way that your idea refers only to this corporeal world, which embraces all the perfections that you can imagine; hence you would have up to this point no grounds as yet for inferring more than an entirely perfect corporeal Entity, unless you were to add something else conducting us to the [knowledge of the] incorporeal or spiritual. Let us add that you can construct the idea of an angel (just as you can form the notion of supremely perfect being) without that idea being caused in you by a [really existing] angel; though the angel has more perfection than you have. But you do not possess the idea of God any more than that of an infinite number or of an infinite line; and though you did possess this, yet there could be no such number. Put along with this the contention that the idea of the unity and the simplicity of a sole perfection which embraces all other perfections, is merely the product of the reasoning mind, and is formed in the same way as other universal unities, which do not exist in fact but merely in the understanding, as is illustrated by the cases of generic, transcendental and other unities.

Thirdly, since you are not yet certain of the aforesaid existence of God, and yet according to your statement, cannot be certain of anything or know anything clearly and distinctly unless previously you know certainly and clearly that God exists, it follows that you cannot clearly and distinctly know that you are a thinking thing, since, according to you, that knowledge depends on the clear knowledge of the existence of God, the proof of which you have not yet reached at that point where you draw the conclusion that you have a clear knowledge of what you are.

Take this also, that while an Atheist knows clearly and distinctly that the three angles of a triangle are equal to two right, yet he is far from believing in the existence of God; in fact he denies it, because if God existed there would be a supreme existence, a highest good, i.e. an infinite Being. But the infinite in every type of perfection precludes the existence of anything else whatsoever it be, e.g. of every variety of entity and good, nay even every sort of non-entity and evil; whereas there are in existence many entities, many good things, as well as many non-entities and many evil things. We consider that you should give a

solution of this objection, lest the impious should still have some case left them.

Fourthly, you deny that God lies or deceives; whereas some schoolmen may be found who affirm this. . . . But if God could harden the heart of Pharaoh and blind his eyes, if He communicated to His Prophets a spirit of lying, whence do you conclude that we cannot be deceived by Him? May not God so deal with men as a physician treats his patients, or as a father his children, dissimulation being employed in both cases, and that wisely and with profit? For if God showed to us His truth undimmed, what eyes, what mental vision could endure it?

Yet it is true that it is not necessary for God to contrive deception in order for you to be deceived in the things which you think you clearly and distinctly perceive, if the cause of the illusion may reside in you yourself, provided only that you are unaware of the fact. What if your nature be such as to be continually, or at least very frequently, deceived? But what evidence is there that you are not deceived and cannot be deceived in those matters whereof you have clear and distinct knowledge? . . .

These, Sir, are the difficulties on which we request you to shed light, in order that it may be profitable for each and all to read your Meditations, containing as they do so much subtlety and, in our opinion, so much truth. This is why it would be well worth the doing if, hard upon your solution of the difficulties, you advanced as premises certain definitions, postulates and axioms, and thence drew conclusions, conducting the whole proof by the geometrical method, in the use of which you are so highly expert. Thus would you cause each reader to have everything in his mind, as it were at a single glance, and to be penetrated throughout with a sense of the Divine being.

REPLY TO THE SECOND SET OF OBJECTIONS

Gentlemen,

I had much pleasure in reading the criticisms you have passed on my little book dealing with First Philosophy; and I recognise the friendly disposition towards me that you display, united as it is with piety towards God and a zeal to promote His glory. I cannot be otherwise than glad not only that you should think my arguments worthy of your scrutiny, but also that you bring forward nothing in opposition to them to which I do not seem to be able quite easily to reply.

Firstly, you warn me *to remember that it was not actually but merely by a mental fiction that I rejected the claim of bodies to be more than phantasms, in order to draw the conclusion that I was merely a thinking being, so as to avoid thinking that it was a consequence of this that I was really nothing more than mind.* But in the Second Meditation I have already shown that I bore this in mind sufficiently; here are the words:—*But perhaps it is the case that these very things, which I thus suppose to be non-existent because they are unknown to me, do not in very truth differ from that self which I know. I cannot tell; this is not the subject I am now discussing, etc.* By these words I meant expressly to warn the reader that in that passage I did not as yet ask whether the mind was distinct from the body, but was merely investigating these properties of mind of which I am able to attain to sure and evident knowledge.

Who has ever had such an acquaintance with anything as to know that there was absolutely nothing in it of which he was not aware? But in proportion as we perceive more in anything, the better do we say we know it; thus we have more knowledge of those men with whom we have lived a long time, than of those whose face merely we have seen or whose name we have heard, even though they too are not said to be absolutely unknown. It is in this sense that I think I have demonstrated that the mind, considered apart from what is customarily attributed to the body, is better known than the body viewed as separate from the mind; and this alone was what I intended to maintain.

Further, since our previous ideas of what belongs to the mind have been wholly confused and mixed up with the ideas of sensible objects, and this was the first and chief reason why none of the propositions asserted of God and the soul could be understood with sufficient clearness, I thought I should perform something worth the doing if I showed how the properties or qualities of the soul are to be distinguished from those of the body.

Much time and many repetitions are required if we would, by forming the contrary habit of distinguishing intellectual from corporeal matters, for at least a few days, obliterate the life-long custom of confounding them. This appeared to me to be a very sound reason for treating of nothing further in the said (i.e. Second) Meditation.

But besides this you here ask *how I prove that a body cannot think.* Pardon me if I reply that I have not yet given ground for the raising of this question, for I first treat of it in the Sixth Meditation. Here are the words:—*In order that I may be sure that one thing is diverse from another, it is sufficient that I should be able to conceive the one apart from the other, etc.,* and shortly afterwards I say: *Although I have a body very closely conjoined with me, yet since, on the one hand, I have a clear and distinct idea of myself, in so far as I am a thinking thing and not extended; and, on the other hand, I have a distinct idea of the body in so far as it is an extended, not a thinking thing, it is certain that I* (that is the mind [or soul, by which I am what I am]) *am really distinct from my body and can exist without it.* It is easy from this to pass to the following:—*everything that can think is mind or is called mind, but, since mind and body are really distinct, no body is a mind; hence no body can think.*

But if any people deny that they have distinct ideas of mind and body, I can do nothing further than ask them to give sufficient attention to what is said in the Second Meditation. I beg them to note that the opinion they perchance hold, namely, that the parts of the brain join their forces with the soul to form thoughts, has not arisen from any positive ground, but only from the fact that they have never had experience of separation from the body, and have not seldom been hindered by it in their operations, and that similarly if anyone had from infancy continually worn irons on his legs, he would think that those irons were part of his own body and that he needed them in order to walk.

Secondly, when you say that *in ourselves there is a sufficient foundation on which to construct the idea of God,* your assertion in no way conflicts with my opinion. I myself at the end of the Third Meditation have expressly said that *this idea is innate in me,* or alternatively that it comes to me from no other source than myself. I admit that *we could form this very idea, though we did not know that a supreme being existed,* but not that we could do so *if it were in fact non-existent,* for on the contrary I have notified that *the whole force of my argument lies in the fact that the capacity for constructing such an idea could not exist in me, unless I were created by God.*

Neither does what you say about flies, plants, etc., tend to prove that there can be any degree of perfection in the effect which has not antecedently existed in the cause. For it is certain that either there is no perfection in animals that lack reason, which does not exist also in inanimate bodies; or that, if such do exist, it comes to them from elsewhere, and that sun, rain and earth are not their adequate causes.

There is also no more force in the objection you make in calling our idea of God an entity formed by thinking. For, firstly, it is not true that it is an *ens rationis* in the sense in which that means something non-existent, but only in the sense in which every mental operation is an *ens rationis*, meaning by this something that issues from thought; this entire world also could be called an entity formed by the divine thought, i.e. an entity created by a simple act of the divine mind. Secondly, I have already sufficiently insisted in various places that what I am concerned with is only the perfection of the idea or its objective reality which, not less than the objective artifice in the idea of a machine of highly ingenious device, requires a cause in which is actually contained everything that it, though only objectively, comprises.

I really do not see what can be added to make it clearer that that idea could not be present in my consciousness unless a supreme being existed.

That *there is nothing in the effect, that has not existed in a similar or in some higher form in the cause*, is a first principle than which none clearer can be entertained. The common truth *'from nothing, nothing comes'* is identical with it. For, if we allow that there is something in the effect which did not exist in the cause, we must grant also that this something has been created by nothing; again the only reason why nothing cannot be the cause of a thing, is that in such a cause there would not be the same thing as existed in the effect.

It is a first principle *that the whole of the reality or perfection that exists only objectively in ideas must exist in them formally or in a superior manner in their causes*. It is on this alone we wholly rely, when believing that things situated outside the mind have real existence; for what should have led us to suspect their existence except the fact that the ideas of them were borne in on the mind by means of the senses?

Now, from these arguments we derive it as a most evident conclusion that God exists. But for the sake of those whose natural light is so exceeding small that they do not see this first principle, viz. *that every perfection existing objectively in an idea must exist actually in something that causes that idea*, I have also demonstrated in a way more easily grasped an identical conclusion, from the fact that the mind possessing that

idea cannot be self-derived; and I cannot in consequence see what more is wanted to secure your admission that I have prevailed.

Moreover there is no force in your plea, that perchance the idea that conveys to me my knowledge of God has come *from notions previously entertained, from books, from conversations with friends, etc., not from my own mind alone*. For the argument takes the same course as it follows in my own case, if I raise the question whether those from whom I am said to have acquired the idea have derived it from themselves or from any one else; the conclusion will be always the same, that it is God from whom it first originated.

Thirdly, when I said that *we could know nothing with certainty unless we were first aware that God existed*, I announced in express terms that I referred only to the science apprehending such conclusions *as can recur in memory without attending further to the proofs which led me to make them*. Further, knowledge of first principles is not usually called science by dialecticians. But when we become aware that we are thinking beings, this is a primitive act of knowledge derived from no syllogistic reasoning. He who says, 'I think, hence I am, or exist,' does not deduce existence from thought by a syllogism, but, by a simple act of mental vision recognizes it as if it were a thing that is known *per se*. This is evident from the fact that if it were syllogistically deduced, the major premise, *that everything that thinks is, or exists*, would have to be known previously; but yet that has rather been learned from the experience of the individual—that unless he exists he cannot think. For our mind is so constituted by nature that general propositions are formed out of the knowledge of particulars.

Fourthly, *in denying that God lies, or is a deceiver*, I fancy that I am in agreement with all metaphysicians and theologians past and future. What you allege to the contrary refutes my position no more than, if I denied that anger existed in God, or that He was subject to other passions, you should bring forward in objection passages in Scripture where human attributes are ascribed to Him. Everyone knows the distinction between those modes of speaking of God that are suited to the vulgar understanding and do indeed contain some truth, a truth, however, relative to the human point of view,—modes of speaking which Holy Writ usually employs,—and those other expressions that give us the more bare and rigorous truth, though not that accommodated to the human mind. It is these latter that everyone should employ in philosophy, and it was my duty to use them specially in my Meditations, since not even there did I assume that there were as yet any men known to me, neither did I consider myself as consisting of mind and body, but as mind only. Hence, it is clear that I did not then speak of the lie that is expressed in words, but only of the internal formal ill-will which is contained in deception.

Nay, over and above this, there is the fact that sometimes we are really misled by the very natural instinct which God has given us, as in the case of the thirst of the dropsical patient. A man is moved to drink by a natural disposition that is given him by God in order to preserve his body; but one afflicted with dropsy is deceived by this natural disposition, for drink is hurtful to him. But how this is compatible with the benevolence and truthfulness of God, I have explained in the sixth Meditation.

In cases, however, that cannot be thus explained, viz. in the case of our clearest and most accurate judgments which, if false, could not be corrected by any that are clearer, or by any other natural faculty, I clearly affirm that we cannot be deceived. For, since God is the highest being He cannot be otherwise than the highest good and highest truth, and hence it is contradictory that anything should proceed from Him that positively tends towards falsity. But yet since there is nothing real in us that is not given by God (as was proved along with His existence) and we have, as well, a real faculty of recognizing truth, and distinguishing it from falsehood (as the mere existence in us of true and false ideas makes manifest), unless this faculty tended towards truth, at least when properly employed (i.e. when we give assent to none but clear and distinct perceptions, for no other correct use of this faculty can be imagined), God, who has given it to us, must justly be held to be a deceiver.

Thus you see that, after becoming aware of the existence of God, it is incumbent on us to imagine that he is a deceiver if we wish to cast doubt upon our clear and distinct perceptions; and since we cannot imagine that he is a deceiver, we must admit them all as true and certain.

It remains for me to thank you for your courtesy and candour in deigning to bring to my notice not only the difficulties that have occurred to you, but also those that can be brought forward by Atheists and peo-

ple of hostile intent. I see nothing in what you have brought forward of which I have not already in my Meditations given a solution and ruled out of court. (For those objections *about insects bred by the sun, about the natives of Canada, the people of Nineveh, the Turks,* etc., cannot occur to those who follow the way I have pointed out, and abstract for a time from everything due to the senses, in order to pay heed to the dictates of the pure and uncorrupted reason, and consequently I thought that I had adequately barred them out.)

Further, in the matter of the counsel you give me about *propounding my arguments in geometrical fashion, in order that the reader may perceive them as it were with a single glance*, it was worth while setting forth here the extent to which I have followed this method and that to which I intend in future to follow it.

ARGUMENTS DEMONSTRATING THE EXISTENCE OF GOD AND THE DISTINCTION BETWEEN SOUL AND BODY, DRAWN UP IN GEOMETRICAL FASHION

Definitions

I. *Thought* is a word that covers everything that exists in us in such a way that we are immediately conscious of it. Thus all the operations of will, intellect, imagination, and of the senses are thoughts. But I have added *immediately,* for the purpose of excluding that which is a consequence of our thought; for example, voluntary movement, which, though indeed depending on thought as on a causal principle, is yet itself not thought.

II. *Idea* is a word by which I understand the form of any thought, that form by the immediate awareness of which I am conscious of that said thought; in such a way that, when understanding what I say, I can express nothing in words, without that very fact making it certain that I possess the idea of that which these words signify. And thus it is not only images depicted in the imagination that I call ideas; nay, to such images I here decidedly refuse the title of ideas, in so far as they are pictures in the corporeal imagination, i.e. in some part of the brain. They are ideas only in so far as they constitute the form of the mind itself that is directed towards that part of the brain.

III. By the *objective reality of an idea* I mean that in respect of which the thing represented in the idea is an entity, in so far as that exists in the idea; and in the same way we can talk of objective perfection, objective device, etc. For whatever we perceive as being as it were in the objects of our ideas, exists in the ideas themselves objectively.

IV. To exist *formally* is the term applied where the same thing exists in the object of an idea in such a manner that the way in which it exists in the object is exactly like what we know of it when aware of it; it exists *eminently* when, though not indeed of identical quality, it is yet of such amount as to be able to fulfill the function of an exact counterpart.

V. Everything in which there resides immediately, as in a subject, or by means of which there exists anything that we perceive, i.e. any property, quality, or attribute, of which we have a real idea, is called a *Substance;* neither do we have any idea of substance itself, precisely taken, than that it is a thing in which this something that we perceive or which is present objectively in some of our ideas, exists formally or eminently. For by means of our natural light we know that a real attribute cannot be an attribute of nothing.

VI. That substance in which thought immediately resides I call *Mind.* I use the term 'mind' here rather than 'spirit,' as 'spirit' is equivocal and is frequently applied to what is corporeal.

VII. That substance, which is the immediate subject of extension in space and of the accidents that presuppose extension, e.g. figure, situation, movement in space etc., is called *Body.* But we must postpone till later on the inquiry as to whether it is one and the same substance or whether there are two diverse substances to which the names Mind and Body apply.

VIII. That substance which we understand to be supremely perfect and in which we conceive absolutely nothing involving defect or limitation of its perfection, is called *God.*

IX. When we say that any attribute is contained in the nature or concept of anything, that is precisely the same as saying that it is true of that thing or can be affirmed of it.

X. Two substances are said to be really distinct, when each of them can exist apart from the other.

Postulates

The *First* request I press upon my readers is a recognition of the weakness of the reasons on account of which they have hitherto trusted their senses, and the insecurity of all the judgments they have based upon

them. I beg them to revolve this in their minds so long and so frequently that at length they will acquire the habit of no longer reposing too much trust in them. For I deem that this is necessary in order to attain to a perception of the certainty of metaphysical truths [not dependent on the senses].

Secondly, I ask them to make an object of study of their own mind and all the attributes attaching to it, of which they find they cannot doubt, notwithstanding it be supposed that whatever they have at any time derived from their senses is false; and I beg them not to desist from attending to it, until they have acquired the habit of perceiving it distinctly and of believing that it can be more readily known than any corporeal thing.

Thirdly, I bid them carefully rehearse those propositions, intelligible *per se,* which they find they possess, e.g. *that the same thing cannot at the same time both be and not be; that nothing cannot be the efficient cause of anything,* and so forth; and thus employ in its purity, and in freedom from the interference of the senses, that clarity of understanding that nature has implanted in them, but which sensuous objects are wont to disturb and obscure. For by this means the truth of the following Axioms will easily become evident to them.

Fourthly, I postulate an examination of the ideas of those natures in which there is a complex of many coexistent attributes, such as e.g. the nature of the triangle or of the square, or of any other figure; and so too the nature of Mind, the nature of Body, and above all the nature of God, or of a supremely perfect entity. My readers must also notice that everything which we perceive to be contained in these natures can be truly predicated of the things themselves. For example, because the equality of its three angles to two right angles is contained in the idea of the Triangle, and divisibility is contained in the nature of Body or of extended thing (for we can conceive nothing that is extended as being so small as not to be capable of being divided in thought at least), we constantly assert that in every Triangle the angles are equal to two right angles, and that every Body is divisible.

Fifthly, I require my readers to dwell long and much in contemplation of the nature of the supremely perfect Being. Among other things they must reflect that while possible existence indeed attaches to the ideas of all other natures, in the case of the idea of God that existence is not possible but wholly necessary. For from this alone and without any train of reasoning they will learn that God exists, and it will be not less self evident to them than the fact that number two is even and number three odd, and similar truths. For there are certain truths evident to some people, without proof, that can be made intelligible to others only by a train of reasoning.

Sixthly, I ask people to go carefully over all the examples of clear and distinct perception, and likewise those that illustrate that which is obscure and confused, mentioned in my Meditations, and so accustom themselves to distinguish what is clearly known from what is obscure. For examples teach us better than rules how to do this; and I think that I have there either explained or at least to some extent touched upon all the instances of this subject.

Seventhly, and finally, I require them, in virtue of their consciousness that falsity has never been found in matters of clear perception, while, on the contrary, amidst what is only obscurely comprehended they have never come upon the truth, except accidentally, to consider it wholly irrational to regard as doubtful matters that are perceived clearly and distinctly by the understanding in its purity, on account of mere prejudices of the senses and hypotheses in which there is an element of the unknown. By doing so they will readily admit the truth and certainty of the following axioms. Yet I admit that several of them might have been much better explained and should have been brought forward as theorems if I had wished to be more exact.

Axioms or Common Principles

I. Nothing exists concerning which the question may not be raised—'what is the cause of its existence?' For this question may be asked even concerning God. Not that He requires any cause in order to exist, but because in the very immensity of His being lies the cause or reason why He needs no cause in order to exist.

II. The present time has no casual dependence on the time immediately preceding it. Hence, in order to secure the continued existence of a thing, no less a cause is required than that needed to produce it at the first.

III. A thing, and likewise an actually existing perfection belonging to anything, can never have *nothing*, or a non-existent thing, as the cause of its existence.

IV. Whatever reality or perfection exists in a thing, exists formally or else eminently in its first and adequate cause.

V. Whence it follows also that the objective reality of our ideas requires a cause in which the same reality is contained not indeed objectively, but formally or else eminently. We have to note that the admission of this axiom is highly necessary for the reason that we must account for our knowledge of all things, both of sensuous and of non-sensuous objects, and do so by means of it alone. For whence, e.g., comes our knowledge that there is a heaven? Because we behold it? But that vision does not reach the mind, except in so far as it is an idea, an idea, I say, inhering in the mind itself, and not an image depicted in the phantasy. But neither can we, in virtue of this idea, assert that there is a heaven, except because every idea needs to have some really existing cause of its objective reality; and this cause we judge to be the heaven itself, and so in other cases.

VI. There are diverse degrees of reality or (the quality of being an) entity. For substance has more reality than accident or mode; and infinite substance has more than finite substance. Hence there is more objective reality in the idea of substance than in that of accident; more in the idea of an infinite than in that of a finite substance.

VII. The will of a thinking being is borne, willingly indeed and freely (for that is of the essence of will), but none the less infallibly, towards the good that it clearly knows. Hence, if it knows certain perfections that it lacks, it will immediately give them to itself if they are in its power [for it will know that it is a greater good for it to posses them, than not to possess them].

VIII. That which can effect what is greater or more difficult, can also accomplish what is less.

IX. It is a greater thing to create or conserve substance than the attributes or properties of substance; it is not, moreover, a greater thing to create that than to conserve its existence, as I have already said.

X. Existence is contained in the idea or concept of everything, because we can conceive nothing except as existent, with this difference, that possible or contingent existence is contained in the concept of a limited thing, but necessary and perfect existence in the concept of a supremely perfect being.

PROPOSITION I

THE KNOWLEDGE OF THE EXISTENCE OF GOD PROCEEDS FROM THE MERE CONSIDERATION OF HIS NATURE

Demonstration

To say that something is contained in the nature or concept of anything is the same as to say that it is true of that thing (Def. IX). But necessary existence is contained in the concept of God (Ax. X). Hence it is true to affirm of God that necessary existence exists in Him, or that God Himself exists.

And this is the syllogism of which I made use above, in replying to the sixth objection. Its conclusion is self-evident to those who are free from prejudices, as was said in the fifth postulate, But, because it is not easy to arrive at such clearness of mind, we seek to establish it by other methods.

PROPOSITION II

A POSTERIORI DEMONSTRATION ON GOD'S EXISTENCE FROM THE MERE FACT THAT THE IDEA OF GOD EXISTS IN US

Demonstration

The objective reality of any of our ideas must have a cause, in which the very same reality is contained, not merely objectively but formally, or else eminently (Ax. V). But we do possess the idea of God (Deff. II and VIII), and the objective reality of this idea is contained in us neither formally nor eminently (Ax VI), nor can it be contained in anything other than God Himself (Def. VIII). Hence this idea of God, which exists in us, must have God as its cause, and hence God exists (Ax III).

PROPOSITION III

THE EXISTENCE OF GOD IS PROVED BY THE FACT THAT WE, WHO POSSESS THIS IDEA, OURSELVES EXIST

Demonstration

If I had the power of conserving my own existence, I should have had a proportionately great power of giv-

ing myself the perfections that I lack (Axx. VIII and IX); for they are only attributes of substance, whereas I am a substance. But I do not have the power of giving myself these perfections; otherwise I should already possess them (Ax. VII). Therefore I do not have the power of conserving myself.

Further, I cannot exist without being conserved, whilst I exist, either by myself, if I have that power, or by some other one who has that power (Axx. I and II); yet, though I do exist, I have not the power of conserving myself, as has just been proved. Consequently it is another being that conserves my existence.

Besides, He to whom my conservation is due contains within Himself formally or eminently everything that is in me (Ax. IV). But there exists in me the perception of many perfections that I do not possess, as well as of the idea of God (Deff. II and VIII). Therefore the perception of the same perfections exists in Him by whom I am conserved.

Finally this same Being cannot possess the perception of any perfections of which He is lacking, or which He does not possess within Himself either formally or eminently (Ax. VII). For, since He has the power of conserving me, as has been already said, He would have the power of bestowing these upon Himself, if He lacked them (Axx. VIII and IX). But He possesses the perception of all those that I lack, and which I conceive can exist in God alone, as has been lately proved. Therefore He possesses those formally or eminently within Himself, and hence is God.

COROLLARY

GOD HAS CREATED THE HEAVEN AND THE EARTH AND ALL THAT IN THEM IS. MOREOVER HE CAN BRING TO PASS WHATEVER WE CLEARLY CONCEIVE, EXACTLY AS WE CONCEIVE IT

Demonstration

This all follows clearly from the previous proposition. For in it we prove that God exists, from the fact that some one must exist in whom are formally or eminently all the perfections of which we have any idea. But we possess the idea of a power so great that by Him and Him alone, in whom this power is found, must heaven and earth be created, and a power such that likewise whatever else is apprehended by me as possible must be created by Him too. Hence concurrently with God's existence we have proved all this likewise about him.

PROPOSITION IV

THERE IS A REAL DISTINCTION BETWEEN MIND AND BODY

Demonstration

God can effect whatever we clearly perceive just as we perceive it (preceding Corollary). But we clearly perceive the mind, i.e. a thinking substance, apart from the body, i.e. apart from any extended substance (Post. II); and *vice versa* we can (as all admit) perceive body apart from mind. Hence, at least through the instrumentality of the Divine power, mind can exist apart from body, and body apart from mind.

But now, substances that can exist apart from each other, are really distinct (Def. X). But mind and body are substances (Deff. V, VI and VII), that can exist apart from each other (just proved). Hence there is a real distinction between mind and body.

Here it must be noted that I employed the Divine power as a means, not because any extraordinary power was needed to effect the separation of mind and body, but because, treating as I did of God alone in what precedes, there was nothing else for me to use. But our knowledge of the real distinctness of two things is unaffected by any question as to the power that disunites them.

THE THIRD SET OF OBJECTIONS WITH THE AUTHOR'S REPLY

First Objection

(In reference to Meditation I, *Concerning those matters that may be brought within the sphere of the doubtful.*)

It is sufficiently obvious from what is said in this Meditation, that we have no criterion for distinguishing dreaming from waking and from what the senses truly tell us; and that hence the images present to us when we are awake and using our senses are not accidents inhering in external objects, and fail to prove that such external objects do as a fact exist. And therefore, if we follow our senses without any train of reasoning, we shall be justified in doubting whether or not anything exists. Hence we acknowledge the truth of this Meditation. But, since Plato and other ancient

Philosophers have talked about this want of certitude in the matters of sense, and since the difficulty in distinguishing the waking state from dreams is a matter of common observations, I should have been glad if our author, so distinguished in the handling of modern speculations, had refrained from publishing those matters of ancient lore.

Reply

The reasons for doubt here admitted as true by this Philosopher were propounded by me only as possessing verisimilitude, and my reason for employing them was not that I might retail them as new, but partly that I might prepare my readers' minds for the study of intellectual matters and for distinguishing them from matters corporeal, a purpose for which such arguments seem wholly necessary; in part also because I intended to reply to these very arguments in the subsequent Meditations; and partly in order to show the strength of the truths I afterwards propound, by the fact that such metaphysical doubts cannot shake them. Hence, while I have sought no praise from their rehearsal, I believe that it was impossible for me to omit them, as impossible as it would be for a medical writer to omit the description of a disease when trying to teach the method of curing it.

Objection II

(In opposition to the Second Meditation, *Concerning the nature of the Human Mind.*)

I am a thing that thinks; *quite correct. From the fact that I think, or have an image, whether sleeping or waking, it is inferred that I am exercising thought; for I* think and I am exercising thought *mean the same thing. From the fact that I am exercising thought it follows that I am, since that which thinks is not nothing. But, where it is added, this is the mind, the spirit, the understanding, the reason, a doubt arises. For it does not seem to be good reasoning to say:* I am exercising thought, *hence I am* thought; *or I am using my intellect, hence I am intellect. For in the same way I might say,* I am walking; *hence I am the walking. It is hence an assumption on the part of M. Descartes that that which understands is the same as the exercise of understanding which is an act of that which understands, or, at least, that that which understands is the same as the understanding, which is a power possessed by that which thinks. Yet all Philosophers distinguish a subject* from its faculties and activities, i.e. from its properties and essences; for the entity itself is one thing, its essence another. Hence it is possible for a thing that thinks to be the subject of the mind, reason, or understanding, and hence to be something corporeal; and the opposite of this has been assumed, not proved. Yet this inference is the basis of the conclusion the M. Descartes seems to wish to establish.

In the same place he says, I know that I exist; the question is, who am I—the being that I know? It is certain that the knowledge of this being thus accurately determined does not depend on those things which I do not yet know to exist.

It is quite certain that the knowledge of this proposition, I exist, depends upon that other one, I think, as he has himself correctly shown us. But whence comes our knowledge of this proposition, I think? Certainly from that fact alone, that we can conceive no activity whatsoever apart from its subject, e.g. we cannot think of leaping apart from that which leaps, of knowing apart from a knower, or of thinking without a thinker.

And hence it seems to follow that that which thinks is something corporeal; for, as it appears, the subjects of all activities can be conceived only after a corporeal fashion, or as in material guise, as M. Descartes himself afterwards shows, when he illustrates by means of wax, this wax was understood to be always the same thing, i.e. the identical matter underlying the many successive changes, though its colour, consistency, figure and other activities were altered. Moreover it is not by another thought that I infer that I think; for though anyone may think that he has thought (to think so is precisely the same as remembering), yet we cannot think that we are thinking, nor similarly know that we know. For this would entail the repetition of the question an infinite number of times; whence do you know, that you know, that you know, that you know?

Hence, since the knowledge of this proposition, I exist, depends upon the knowledge of that other, I think, and the knowledge of it upon the fact that we cannot separate thought from a matter that thinks, the proper inference seems to be that that which thinks is material rather than immaterial.

Reply

Where I have said, this is the mind, the spirit, the intellect, or the reason, I understood by these names not merely faculties, but rather what is endowed with the

faculty of thinking; and this sense the two former terms commonly, the latter frequently bear. But I used them in this sense so expressly and in so many places that I cannot see what occasion there was for any doubt about their meaning.

Further, there is here no parity between walking and thinking; for walking is usually held to refer only to that action itself, while thinking applies now to the action, now to the faculty of thinking, and again to that in which the faculty exists.

Again I do not assert that that which understands and the activity of understanding are the same things, nor indeed do I mean that the thing that understands and the understanding are the same, if the term understanding be taken to refer to the faculty of understanding; they are identical only when the understanding means the thing itself that understands. I admit also quite gladly that, in order to designate that thing or substance, which I wished to strip of everything that did not belong to it, I employed the most highly abstract terms I could; just as on the contrary this Philosopher uses terms that are as concrete as possible, e.g. subject, matter, body, to signify that which thinks, fearing to let it be sundered from the body.

But I have no fear of anyone thinking that his method of coupling diverse things together is better adapted to the discovery of the truth than mine, that gives the greatest possible distinctness to every single thing. But, dropping the verbal controversy, let me look to the facts in dispute.

A thing that thinks, he says, may be something corporeal; and the opposite of this has been assumed; not proved. But really I did not assume the opposite, neither did I use it as a basis for my argument; I left it wholly undetermined until Meditation VI, in which its proof is given.

Next he quite correctly says, that we cannot conceive any activity apart from its subject, e.g. thought apart from that which thinks, since that which thinks is not nothing. But, wholly without any reason, and in opposition to the ordinary use of language and good Logic, he adds, hence it seems to follow that that which thinks is something corporeal; for the subjects of all activities are indeed understood as falling within the sphere of substance (or even, if you care, as wearing the guise of matter, viz. metaphysical matter), but not on that account are they to be defined as bodies.

On the other hand both logicians and as a rule all men are wont to say that substances are of two kinds, spiritual and corporeal. And all that I proved, when I took wax as an example, was that its colour, hardness, and figure did not belong to the formal nature of the wax itself [i.e. that we can comprehend everything that exists necessarily in the wax, without thinking of these]. I did not there treat either of the formal nature of the mind, or even of the formal nature of body.

Again it is irrelevant to say, as this Philosopher here does, that one thought cannot be the subject of another thought. Who, except my antagonist himself, ever imagined that it could? But now, for a brief explanation of the matter,—it is certain that no thought can exist apart from a thing that thinks; no activity, no accident can be without a substance in which to exist. Moreover, since we do not apprehend the substance itself immediately through itself, but by means only of the fact that it is the subject of certain activities, it is highly rational, and a requirement forced on us by custom, to give diverse names to those substances that we recognize to be the subjects of clearly diverse activities or accidents, and afterwards to inquire whether those diverse names refer to one and the same or to diverse things. But there are *certain* activities which we call *corporeal*, e.g. magnitude, figure, motion, and all those that cannot be thought of apart from extension in space; and the substance in which they exist is called *body*. It cannot be pretended that the substance that is the subject of figure is different from that which is the subject of spatial motion, etc., since all these activities agree in presupposing extension. Further, there are other activities, which we call *thinking* activities, e.g. understanding, willing, imagining, feeling, etc., which agree in falling under the description of thought, perception, or consciousness. The substance in which they reside we call a *thinking thing* or *the mind*, or any other name we care, provided only we do not confound it with corporeal substance, since thinking activities have no affinity with corporeal activities, and thought, which is the common nature in which the former agree, is totally different from extension, the common term for describing the latter.

But after we have formed two distinct concepts of those two substances, it is easy, from what has been said in the sixth Meditation, to determine whether they are one and the same or distinct.

Objection III

What then is there distinct from my thought? What can be said to be separate from me myself?

Perchance some one will answer the question thus— I, the very self that thinks, am held to be distinct from my own thought; and, though it is not really separate from me, my thought is held to be diverse from me, just in the way (as has been said before) that leaping is distinguished from the leaper. But if M. Descartes shows that he who understands and the understanding are identical we shall lapse back into the scholastic mode of speaking. The understanding understands, the vision sees, will wills, and by exact analogy, walking, or at least the faculty of walking will walk. Now all this is obscure, incorrect, and quite unworthy of M. Descartes' wonted clearness.

Reply

I do not deny that I, the thinker, am distinct from my own thought, in the way in which a thing is distinct from its mode. But when I ask, *what then is there distinct from my thought,* this is to be taken to refer to the various modes of thought there recounted, not to my substance; and when I add, *what can be said to be separate from me myself,* I mean only that these modes of thinking exist entirely in me. I cannot see on what pretext the imputation here of doubt and obscurity rests.

Objection IV

Hence it is left for me to concede that I do not even understand by the imagination what this wax is, but conceive it by the mind alone.

There is a great difference between imagining, i.e. having some idea, and conceiving with the mind, i.e. inferring, as the result of a train of reasoning, that something is, or exists. But M. Descartes has not explained to us the sense in which they differ. The ancient peripatetics also have taught clearly enough that substance is not perceived by the senses, but is known as a result of reasoning.

But what shall we now say, if reasoning chance to be nothing more than the uniting and stringing together of

names or designations by the word is? It will be a consequence of this that reason gives us no conclusion about the
nature of things, but only about the terms that designate
them, whether, indeed, or not there is a convention (arbitrarily made about their meanings) according to which we
join these names together. If this be so, as is possible, reasoning will depend on names, names on the imagination,
and imagination, perchance, as I think, on the motion of
the corporeal organs. Thus mind will be nothing but the
motions in certain parts of an organic body.

Reply

I have here explained the difference between imagination and a pure mental concept, as when in my
illustration I enumerated the features in wax that
were given by the imagination and those solely due to
a conception of the mind. But elsewhere also I have
explained how it is that one and the same thing, e.g. a
pentagon, is in one way an object of the understanding, in another way of the imagination [for example
how in order to imagine a pentagon a particular mental act is required which gives us this figure (i.e. its
five sides and the space they enclose) which we dispense with wholly in our conception]. Moreover, in
reasoning we unite not names but the things signified
by the names; and I marvel that the opposite can
occur to anyone. For who doubts whether a Frenchman and a German are able to reason in exactly the
same way about the same things, though they yet
conceive the words in an entirely diverse way? And
has not my opponent condemned himself in talking
of conversations arbitrarily made about the meanings
of words? For, if he admits that words signify anything, why will he not allow our reasonings to refer to
this something that is signified, rather than to the
words alone? But, really, it will be as correct to infer
that earth is heaven or anything else that is desired,
as to conclude that mind is motion [for there are no
other two things in the world between which there is
not as much agreement as there is between motion
and spirit, which are of two entirely different natures].

Objection V

In reference to the third Meditation—concerning
God—some of these (thoughts of man) are, so to
speak, images of things, and to these alone is the title

'idea' properly applied; examples are my thought of a
man, or of a Chimera, of Heavens, of an Angel, or
[even] of God.

When I think of a man, I recognize an idea, or
image, with figure and colour as its constituents; and
concerning this I can raise the question whether or not it
is the likeness of a man. So it is also when I think of the
heavens. When I think of the chimera, I recognize an
idea or image, being able at the same time to doubt
whether or not it is the likeness of an animal, which,
though it does not exist, may yet exist or has at some
other time existed.

But, when one thinks of an Angel, what is noticed in
the mind is now the image of a flame, now that of a fair
winged child, and this, I may be sure, has no likeness to
an Angel, and hence is not the idea of an Angel. But
believing that created beings exist that are the ministers of
God, invisible and immaterial, we give the name of Angel
to this object of belief, this supposed being, though the idea
used in imagining an Angel is, nevertheless, constructed
out of the ideas of visible things.

It is the same way with the most holy name of God; we
have no image, no idea corresponding to it. Hence we are
forbidden to worship God in the form of an image, lest we
should think we could conceive Him who is inconceivable.

Hence it appears that we have no idea of God. But
just as one born blind who has frequently been brought
close to a fire and has felt himself growing warm, recognizes that there is something which made him warm, and,
if he hears it called fire, concludes that fire exists, though he
has no acquaintance with its shape or colour, and has no
idea of fire nor image that he can discover in his mind; so a
man, recognizing that there must be some cause of his
images and ideas, and another previous cause of this cause
and so on continuously, is finally carried on to a conclusion, or to the supposition of some eternal cause, which,
never having begun to be, can have no cause prior to it;
and hence he necessarily concludes that something eternal
exists. But nevertheless he has no idea that he can assert to
be that of this eternal being, and he merely gives a name to
the object of his faith or reasoning and calls it God.

Since now it is from this portion, viz. that there is an
idea of God in our soul, M. Descartes proceeds to prove
the theorem that God (an all-powerful, all-wise Being, the
creator of the world) exists, he should have explained this
idea of God better, and he should have deduced from it not
only God's existence, but also the creation of the world.

Reply

Here the meaning assigned to the term idea is merely that of images depicted in the corporeal imagination; and, that being agreed on, it is easy for my critic to prove that there is no proper idea of Angel or of God. But I have, everywhere, from time to time, and principally in this place, shown that I take the term idea to stand for whatever the mind directly perceives; and so when I will or when I fear, since at the same time I perceive that I will and fear, that very volition and apprehension are ranked among my ideas. I employed this term because it was the term currently used by Philosophers for the forms of perception of the Divine mind, though we can discover no imagery in God; besides I had no other more suitable term. But I think I have sufficiently well explained what the idea of God is for those who care to follow my meaning; those who prefer to wrest my words from the sense I give them, I can never satisfy. The objection that here follows, relative to the creation of the world, is plainly irrelevant [for I proved that God exists, before asking whether there is a world created by him, and from the mere fact that God, i.e. a supremely perfect being exists, it follows that if there be a world it must have been created by him].

Objection VI

But other (thoughts) possess other forms as well. For example, in willing, fearing, affirming, denying, though I always perceive something as the subject of my thought, yet in my thought I embrace something more than the similitude of that thing; and, of the thoughts of this kind, some are called volitions or affections, and others judgments.

When a man wills or fears, he has indeed an image of the thing he fears or of the action he wills; but no explanation is given of what is further embraced in the thought of him who wills or fears. If indeed fearing be thinking, I fail to see how it can be anything other than the thought of the thing feared. In what respect does the fear produced by the onrush of a lion differ from the idea of the lion as it rushes on us, together with its effect (produced by such an idea in the heart), which impels the fearful man towards that animal motion we call flight? Now this motion of flight is not thought; whence we are left to infer that in

fearing there is no thinking since that which consists in the representation of the thing feared. The same account holds true of volition.

Further you do not have affirmation and negation without words and names; consequently brute creatures cannot affirm or deny, not even in thought, and hence are likewise unable to judge. Yet a man and a beast may have similar thoughts. For, when we assert that a man runs, our thought does not differ from that which a dog has when it sees its master running. Hence neither affirmation nor negation add anything to the bare thought, unless that increment be our thinking that the names of which the affirmation consists are the names of the same thing in [the mind of] him who affirms. But this does not mean that anything more is contained in our thought than the representation of the thing, but merely that that representation is there twice over.

Reply

It is self-evident that seeing a lion and fearing it at the same time is different from merely seeing it. So, too, it is one thing to see a man running, another thing to affirm to oneself that one sees it, an act that needs no language. I can see nothing here that needs an answer.

Objection VII

It remains for me to examine in what way I have received that idea from God. I have neither derived it from the senses; nor has it ever come to me contrary to my expectation, as the ideas of sensible things are wont to do, when these very things present themselves to the external organs of sense or seem to do so. Neither also has it been constructed as a fictitious idea by me, for I can take nothing from it and am quite unable to add to it. Hence the conclusion is left that it is innate in me, just as the idea of my own self is innate in me.

If there is no idea of God (now it has not been proved that it exists), as seems to be the case, the whole of this argument collapses. Further (if it is my body that is being considered) the idea of my own self proceeds [principally] from sight; but (if it is a question of the soul) there is no idea of the soul. We only infer by means of the reason that there is something internal in the human body, which imparts to it its animal motion, and by means of which it feels and moves; and this, whatever it be, we name the soul, without employing any idea.

Reply

If there is an idea of God (as it is manifest there is), the whole of this objection collapses. When it is said further that we have no idea of the soul but that we arrive at it by an inference of reason, that is the same as saying that there is not image of the soul depicted in the imagination, but that that which I have called its idea does, nevertheless, exist.

Objection VIII

But the other idea of the sun is derived from astronomical reasonings, i.e. is elicited from certain notions that are innate in me.

It seems that at one and the same time the idea of the sun must be single whether it is beheld by the eyes, or is given by our intelligence as many times larger than it appears. For this latter thought is not an idea of the sun, but an inference by argument that the idea of the sun would be many times larger if we viewed the sun from a much nearer distance.

But at different times the ideas of the sun may differ, e.g. when one looks at it with the naked eye and through a telescope. But astronomical reasonings do not increase or decrease the idea of the sun; rather they show that the sensible idea is misleading.

Reply

Here too what is said not to be an idea of the sun, but is, nevertheless, described, is exactly what I call an idea. [But as long as my critic refuses to come to terms with me about the meaning of words, none of his objections can be other than frivolous.]

Objection IX

For without doubt those ideas, which reveal substance to me, are something greater, and, so to speak, contain within them more objective reality than those which represent only modes or accidents. And again, that by means of which I apprehend a supreme God who is eternal, infinite, omniscient, all-powerful, and the creator of all else there is besides, assuredly possesses more objective reality than those ideas that reveal to us finite substances.

I have frequently remarked above that there is no idea either of God or of the soul; I now add that there is no idea of substance. For substance (the substance that is a material, subject to accidents and changes) is perceived and demonstrated by the reason alone, without yet being conceived by us, or furnishing us with any idea. If that is true, how can it be maintained that the ideas which reveal substance to me are anything greater or possess more objective reality than those revealing accidents to us? Further I pray M. Descartes to investigate the meaning of more reality. Does reality admit of more and less? Or, if he thinks that one thing can be more a thing than another, let him see how he is to explain it to our intelligence with the clearness called for in demonstration, and such as he himself has at other times employed.

Reply

I have frequently remarked that I give the name idea to that with which reason makes us acquainted just as I also do to anything else that is in any way perceived by us. I have likewise explained how reality admits of more and less: viz. in the way in which substance is greater than mode; and if there be real qualities or incomplete substances, they are things to a greater extent than modes are, but less than complete substances. Finally, if there be an infinite and independent substance, it is more a thing than a substance that is finite and dependent. Now all this is quite self-evident [and so needs no further explanation].

Objection X

Hence there remains alone the idea of God, concerning which we must consider whether it is not something that is capable of proceeding from me myself. By the name of God I understand a substance that is infinite [eternal, immutable], independent, all-knowing, all-powerful, and by which both I myself and everything else, if anything else does exist, have been created. Now all these characteristics are such that, the more diligently I attend to them, the less do they appear capable of proceeding from me alone; hence, from what has been already said, we must conclude that God necessarily exists.

When I consider the attributes of God, in order to gather thence the idea of God, and see whether there is anything contained in it that cannot proceed from ourselves, I find, unless I am mistaken, that what we assign

in thought to the name of God neither proceeds from ourselves nor needs to come from any other source than
external objects. For by the word God I mean a substance, *i.e. I understand that God exists (not by means of
an idea but by reasoning). This substance is* infinite
(*i.e. I can neither conceive nor imagine its boundaries or
extreme parts, without imagining further parts beyond
them); whence it follows that corresponding to the term*
infinite *there arises an idea not of the Divine infinity, but
of my own bounds or limitations. It is also* independent,
*i.e. I have no conception of a cause from which God orig-
inates; whence it is evident that I have no idea corresponding to the term* independent, *save the memory of my
own ideas with their commencement at divers times and
their consequent dependence.*

Wherefore to say that God is independent, *is merely
to day that God is to be reckoned among the number of
those things, of the origins of which we have no image.
Similarly to say that God is* infinite, *is identical with saying that He is among those objects of the limits of which
we have no conception. Thus any idea of God is ruled
out; for what sort of idea is that which has neither origin
nor termination?*

Take the term all-knowing. *Here I ask: what idea
does M. Descartes employ in apprehending the intellectual
activity of God?*

All-powerful. *So too, what is the idea by which we
apprehend power, which is relative to that which lies in the
future, i.e. does not exist? I certainly understand what
power is by means of an image, or memory of past events,
inferring it in this wise—Thus did He, hence thus was He
able to do; therefore as long as the same agent exists He
will be able to act so again, i.e. He has the power of acting. Now these are all ideas that can arise from external
objects.*

Creator of everything that exists. *Of creation
some image can be constructed by me out of the objects I
behold, e.g. the birth of a human being or its growth from
something small as a point to the size and figure it now
possesses. We have no other idea than this corresponding
to the term creator. But in order to prove creation it is not
enough to be able to imagine the creation of the world.
Hence although it had been demonstrated that an* infinite,
independent, all-powerful, *etc. being exists, nevertheless it does not follow that a creator exists. Unless anyone
thinks that it is correct to infer, from the fact that there is a
being which we believe to have created everything, that
hence the world was at some time created by him.*

*Further, when M. Descartes says that the idea of
God and that of the soul are innate in us, I should like to
know whether the minds of those who are in a profound
and dreamless sleep yet think. If not, they have at that
time no ideas. Whence no idea is innate, for what is
innate is always present.*

Reply

Nothing that we attribute to God can come from
external objects as a copy proceeds from its exemplar,
because in God there is nothing similar to what is
found in external things, i.e. in corporeal objects. But
whatever is unlike them in our thought [of God],
must come manifestly not from them, but from the
cause of that diversity existing in our thought [of
God].

Further I ask how my critic derives the intellectual comprehension of God from external things. But
I can easily explain the idea which I have of it, by
saying that by idea I mean whatever is the form of any
perception. For does anyone who understands something not perceive that he does so? and hence does he
not possess that form or idea of mental action? It is by
extending this indefinitely that we form the idea of
the intellectual activity of God; similarly also with
God's other attributes.

But, since we have employed the idea of God
existing in us for the purpose of proving His existence,
and such mighty power is comprised in this idea, that
we comprehend that it would be contradictory, if God
exists, for anything besides Him to exist, unless it were
created by Him; it clearly follows, from the fact that
His existence has been demonstrated, that it has been
also proved that the whole world, or whatever things
other than God exist, have been created by Him.

Finally when I say that an idea is innate in us [or
imprinted in our souls by nature], I do not mean that
it is always present to us. This would make no idea
innate. I mean merely that we possess the faculty of
summoning up this idea.

Objection XI

The whole force of the argument lies in this—that I
know I could not exist, and possess the nature I have,
that nature which puts me in possession of the idea of
God, unless God did really exist, the God, I repeat,
the idea of whom is found in me.

Since, then, it has not been proved that we possess an idea of God, and the Christian religion obliges us to believe that God is inconceivable, which amounts, in my opinion, to saying that we have no idea of Him, it follows that no proof of His existence has been effected, much less of His work of creation.

Reply

When it is said that we cannot conceive God, to conceive means to comprehend adequately. For the rest, I am tired of repeating how it is that we can have an idea of God. There is nothing in these objections that invalidates my demonstrations.

Objection XII

(Directed against the fourth Meditation, *Concerning the true and the false.*)

And thus I am quite sure that error, in so far as it is error, is nothing real, but merely defect. Hence in order to go astray, it is not necessary for me to have a faculty specially assigned to me by God for this purpose.

It is true that ignorance is merely a defect, and that we stand in need of no special positive faculty in order to be ignorant; but about error the case is not so clear. For it appears that stones and inanimate things are unable to err solely because they have no faculty of reasoning, or imagining. Hence it is a very direct inference that, in order to err, a faculty of reasoning, or at least of imagination is required; now both of these are positive faculties with which all beings that err, and only beings that err, have been endowed.

Further, M. Descartes says—I perceive that they (*viz. my mistakes*) depend upon the cooperation of two causes, viz. my faculty of cognition, and my faculty of choice, or the freedom of my will. *But this seems to be contradictory to what went before. And we must note here also that the freedom of the will has been assured without proof, and in opposition to the opinion of the Calvinists.*

Reply

Although in order to err the faculty of reasoning (or rather of judging, or affirming and denying) is required, because error is a lack of this power it does not hence follow that this defect is anything real, just as it does not follow that blindness is anything real, although stones are not said to be blind merely because they are incapable of vision. I marvel that in

these objections I have as yet found nothing that is properly argued out. Further I made no assumption concerning freedom which is not a matter of universal experience; our natural light makes this most evident and I cannot make out why it is said to be contradictory to previous statements.

But though there are many who, looking to the Divine foreordination, cannot conceive how that is compatible with liberty on our part, nevertheless no one, when he considered himself alone, fails to experience the fact that to will and to be free are the same thing [or rather that there is no difference between what is voluntary and what is free]. But this is no place for examining other people's opinions about this matter.

Objection XIII

For example, whilst I, during these days, sought to discuss whether anything at all existed, and noted that, from the very fact that I raised this question, it was an evident consequence that I myself existed, I could not indeed refrain from judging that what I understood so clearly was true; this was not owing to compulsion by some external force, but because the consequence of the great mental illumination was a strong inclination of the will, and I believed the above truth the more willingly and freely, the less indifferent I was towards it.

This term, great mental illumination, is metaphorical, and consequently is not adapted to the purposes of argument. Moreover everyone who is free from doubt claims to possess a similar illumination, and in his will there is the same inclination to believe that of which he does not doubt, as in that of one who truly knows. Hence while this illumination may be the cause that makes a man obstinately defend or hold some opinion, it is not the cause of his knowing it to be true.

Further, not only to know a thing to be true, but also to believe it or give assent to it, have nothing to do with the will. For, what is proved by valid argument or is recounted as credible, is believed by us whether we will or no. It is true that affirming and denying, maintaining or refuting propositions, are acts of will; but it does not follow on that account that internal assent depends upon the will.

Therefore the demonstrations of the truth that follows is not adequate—and it is in this misuse of our free-will, that this privation consists that constitutes the form of error.

Reply

It does not al all matter whether or not the term *great illumination* is proper to argument, so long as it is serviceable for explanation, as in fact it is. For no one can be unaware that by mental illumination is meant clearness of cognition, which perhaps is not possessed by everyone who thinks he possesses it. But this does not prevent it from being very different from a bigoted opinion, to the formation of which there goes no perceptual evidence.

Moreover when it is here said that when a thing is clearly perceived we give our assent whether we will or no, that is the same as saying that we desire what we clearly know to be good whether willing or unwilling; for the word *unwilling* finds no entrance in such circumstances, implying as it does that we will and do not will the same thing.

Objection XIV

(To the fifth Meditation, *On the essence of material things.*)

As, for example, when I imagine a triangle, though perhaps such a figure does no exist at all outside my thought, or never has existed, it has nevertheless a determinate nature, or essence, or immutable and eternal form, which is not a fiction of my construction, and does not depend on my mind, as is evident from the fact that various properties of that triangle may be demonstrated.

If the triangle exists nowhere at all, I do not understand how it can have any nature; for that which exists nowhere does not exist. Hence it has no existence or nature. The triangle in the mind comes from the triangle we have seen, or from one imaginatively constructed out of triangles we have beheld. Now when we have once called the thing (from which we think that the idea of triangle originates) by the name triangle, although the triangle itself perishes, yet the name remains. In the same way if, in our thought, we have once conceived that the angles of a triangle are together all equal to two right angles, and have given this other name to the triangle—possessed of three angles equal to two right angles—although there were no angle at all in existence, yet the name would remain; and the truth of this proposition will be of eternal duration—a triangle is possessed of three angles equal to two right angles. *But the nature of the triangle will not be of eternal duration, if it should chance that triangle perished.*

In like manner the proposition, man is animal, will be eternally true, because the names it employs are eternal, but if the human race were to perish there would no longer be a human nature.

Whence it is evident that essence in so far as it is distinguished from existence is nothing else than a union of names by means of the verb is. And thus essence without existence is a fiction of our mind. And it appears that as the image of a man in the mind is to the man so is essence to existence; or that the essence of Socrates bears to his existence the relation that this proposition, Socrates is a man, to this other, Socrates is or exists. Now the proposition, Socrates is a man, means when Socrates does not exist, merely the connection of its terms; and is, or to be, has underlying it the image of the unity of a thing designated by two names.

Reply

The distinction between essence and existence is known to all and all that is here said about eternal names in place of concepts or ideas of an eternal truth, has been already satisfactorily refuted.

Objection XV

(Directed against the sixth Meditation—*Concerning the existence of material things.*)

For since God has evidently given me no faculty by which to know this (*whether or not our ideas proceed from bodies*), but on the contrary has given me a strong propensity towards the belief that they do proceed from corporeal things, I fail to see how it could be made out that He is not a deceiver, if our ideas proceeded from some other source than corporeal things. Consequently corporeal objects must exist.

It is the common belief that no fault is committed by medical men who deceive sick people for their health's sake, nor by parents who mislead their children for their good; and that the evil in deception lies not in the falsity of what is said, but in the bad intent of those who practice it. M. Descartes must therefore look to this proposition, God can in no case deceive us, *taken universally, and see whether it is true; for if it is not true, thus universally taken, the conclusion,* hence corporeal things exist, *does not follow.*

Reply

For the security of my conclusion we do not need to assume that we can never be deceived (for I have gladly admitted that we are often deceived), but that we are not deceived when that error of ours would argue an intention to deceive on the part of God, an intention it is contradictory to impute to Him. Once more this is bad reasoning on my critic's part.

Final Objection

For now I perceive how great the difference is between the two (i.e. between waking and dreaming) from the fact that our dreams are never conjoined by our memory [with each other and] with the whole of the rest of our life's action [as happens with the things which occur in waking moments].

I ask whether it is really the case that one, who dreams he doubts whether he dreams or no, is unable to dream that his dream is connected with the idea of a long series of past events. If he can, those things which to the dreamer appear to be the actions of his past life may be regarded as true just as though he had been awake. Besides, since, as M. Descartes himself asserts, all certitude and truth in knowledge depend alone upon our knowing the true God, either it will be impossible for an Atheist to infer from the memory of his previous life that he wakes, or it will be possible for a man to know that he is awake, apart from knowledge of the true God.

Reply

One who dreams cannot effect a real connection between what he dreams and the ideas of past events, though he can dream that he does connect them. For who denies that in his sleep a man may be deceived? But yet when he has awakened he will easily detect his error.

But an Atheist is able to infer from the memory of his past life that he is awake; still he cannot know that this sign is sufficient to give him the certainty that he is not in error, unless he knows that it has been created by a God who does not deceive.

FOURTH SET OF OBJECTIONS

Letter to a Man of Note

Sir,

The favour you have done me I acknowledge, though I note that you expect a return for it. Kind though your action was, yet to let me share in the enjoyment of reading that most acute work only on condition I should disclose what I think of it, was to demand a requital, and surely a heavy one. Truly a hard condition, compliance with which the desire to acquaint myself with a fine piece of work has wrung from me, . . .

The first thing that here occurs to me to be worthy of remark is that our distinguished author should have taken as the foundation of the whole of his philosophy the doctrine laid down [before him] by St. Augustine, a man of most penetrating intellect and of such note, not only in the sphere of theology, but in that of philosophy as well. In 'De Libero arbitrio,' Book II, chap. 3., Alipius, when disputing with Euodius, setting about a proof of the existence of God, says: Firstly, to start with the things that are most evident, I ask you whether you yourself exist, or are you apprehensive lest in [answering] this question you are in error, when in any case, if you did not exist you could never be in error? *Similar to this are the words of our author:* But perhaps there exists an all-powerful being, extremely cunning, who deceives me, who intentionally at all times deceives me. There is then no doubt that I exist, if he deceives me. *But let us proceed, and, to pursue something more relevant to our purpose, let us discover now, from this principle, we can demonstrate the fact that our mind is [distinct and] separate from our body.*

I am able to doubt whether I have a body, nay, whether any body exists at all; yet I have no right to doubt whether I am, or exist, so long as I doubt or think.

Hence I, who doubt and think, am not a body; otherwise in entertaining doubt concerning body, I should doubt about myself.

Nay, even though I obstinately maintain that no body at all exists, the position taken up is unshaken: I am something, hence I am not a body.

This is really very acute, but someone could bring up the objection which our author urges against himself; the fact that I doubt about body or deny that body exists, does not bring it about that no body exists. Hence perhaps it happens that these very things which I suppose to be nothing, because they are unknown to me, yet do not in truth differ from that self which I do know. I know nothing about it, *he says,* I do not dispute this matter; [I can judge only about things that are known to me.] I know that I exist; I enquire who I, the known self, am; it is quite certain that the knowledge of this self thus precisely taken, does not depend on those things of the existence of which I am not yet acquainted.

The problem is: how it follows, from the fact that one is unaware that anything else [(except the fact of being a thinking thing)] belongs to one's essence, that nothing else really belongs to one's essence. *But, not to conceal my dullness, I have been unable to discover in the whole of Meditation II where he has shown this. Yet so far as I can conjecture, he attempts this proof in Meditation VI, because he believes that it is dependent on the possession of the clear knowledge of God to which in Meditation II he has not yet attained. Here is his proof:*

Because I know that all the things I clearly and distinctly understand can be created by God just as I conceive them to exist, it is sufficient for me to be able to comprehend one thing clearly and distinctly apart from another, in order to be sure that the one is diverse from the other, because at least God can isolate them; and it does not matter by what power that isolation is effected, in order that I may be obliged to think them different from one another. Hence because, on the one hand, I have a clear and distinct idea of myself in so far as I am a thinking being, and not extended, and on the other hand, a distinct idea of body, in so far as it is only an extended thing, not one that thinks, it is certain that I am in reality distinct from my body and can exist apart from it.

Here we must halt awhile; for on these few words the whole of the difficulty seems to hinge.

Firstly, in order to be true, the major premiss of that syllogism must be held to refer to the adequate notion of a thing [(i.e. the notion which comprises everything which may be known of the thing)], not to any notion, even a clear and distinct one.

But, if anyone cast doubt on the (minor) premiss here assumed, and contends that it is merely that your conception is inadequate when you conceive yourself [(i.e. your mind)] as being a thinking but not an extended thing, and similarly when you conceive yourself [(i.e. your body)] as being an extended and not a thinking thing, we must look to its proof in the previous part of the argument. For I do not reckon a matter like this to be so clear as to warrant us in assuming it as an indemonstrable first principle and in dispensing with proof.

Now as to the first part of the statement, namely, that you completely understand what body is, merely by thinking that it is extended, has figure, can move, etc., and by denying of it everything which belongs to the nature of mind, *this is of little value. For one who*

contends that the human mind is corporeal does not on that account believe that every body is a mind. Hence body would be so related to mind as genus is to species. But the genus can be conceived without the species, even although one deny of it whatsoever is proper and peculiar to the species; whence comes the common dictum of Logicians, 'the negation of the species does not negate the genus.' Thus, I can conceive figure without conceiving any of the attributes proper to the circle. Therefore, we must prove over and above this that the mind can be completely and adequately conceived apart from the body.

I can discover no passage in the whole work capable of effecting this proof, save the proposition laid down at the outset:—I can deny that there is any body or that any extended thing exists, but yet it is certain that I exist, so long as I make this denial, or think; hence I am a thing that thinks and not a body, and the body does not pertain to the knowledge of myself.

But the only result that I can see this to give, is that a certain knowledge of myself be obtained without a knowledge of the body. But it is not yet quite clear to me that this knowledge is complete and adequate, so as to make me sure that I am not in error in excluding the body from my essence. I shall explain by means of an example:—

Let us assume that a certain man is quite sure that the angle in a semicircle is a right angle and that hence the triangle made by this angle and the diameter is rightangled; but suppose he questions and has not yet firmly apprehended, nay, let us imagine that, misled by some fallacy, he denies that the square on its has is equal to the squares on the sides of the right-angled triangle. Now, according to our author's reasoning, he will see himself confirmed in his false belief. For, he will argue, while I clearly and distinctly perceive that this triangle is right-angled, I yet doubt whether the square on its base is equal to the square on its sides. Hence the equality of the square on the base to those on the sides does not belong to its essence.

Hence, that of which I doubt, or the removal of which leaves me with the idea still, cannot belong to its essence.

Besides, since I know that all things I clearly and distinctly understand can be created by God just as I conceive them to exist, it is sufficient for me, in order to be sure that one thing is distinct from another, to be able to comprehend the one clearly and distinctly apart from the other, because it can be isolated by God. *But I clearly and distinctly understand* that this triangle is right-angled, without comprehending that the square on its base is equal to the square on its sides. Hence God at least can create a right-angled triangle, the square on the base of which is not equal to the squares on its sides.

I do not see what reply can here be made, except that the man in question does not perceive clearly that the triangle is right-angled. But whence do I obtain any perception of the nature of my mind clearer than that which he has of the nature of the triangle? He is as sure that the triangle in a semicircle has one right angle (which is the notion of a right-angled triangle) as I am in believing that I exist because I think.

Hence, just as a man errs in not believing that the equality of the square on its base to the squares on its sides belongs to the nature of that triangle, which he clearly and distinctly knows to be right-angled, so why am I not perhaps in the wrong in thinking that nothing else belongs to my nature, which I clearly and distinctly know to be something that thinks, except the fact that I am this thinking being? Perhaps it also belongs to my essence to be something extended.

And certainly, some one will say it is no marvel if, in deducing my existence from the fact that I think, the idea that I form of the self, which is in this way an object of thought, represent me to my mind as merely a thinking being, since it has been derived from my thinking alone. And hence from this idea, no argument can be drawn to prove that nothing more belongs to my essence than what the idea contains.

In addition, it can be maintained that the argument proves too much and conducts us to the Platonic doctrine (refuted nevertheless by our author) that nothing corporeal belongs to the essence of man, who is hence entirely spirit, while his body is merely the vehicle of spirit; whence follows the definition of a man as a spirit that makes use of a body.

But if you reply that body is not absolutely excluded from my essence, but merely in so far precisely as I am a thinking being, the fear seems likely to arise that some one will entertain a suspicion that the knowledge of myself, in so far as I am a thinking being, is not the knowledge of anything fully and adequately conceived, but is known only inadequately and by a certain intellectual abstraction.

Hence, just as geometers conceive of a line as length without breadth, and of a surface as length and breadth together without depth, although there is no length apart from breadth, no breadth without depth, some one may

perhaps doubt whether everything that thinks is not likewise something extended; a thing in which, nevertheless, over and above the attributes common to other extended things, e.g. the possession of figure, motion, etc., is found this unique faculty of thinking. Whence it follows that while by an intellectual abstraction, it can be apprehended by means of this character alone and unaided as a thing that thinks, it is quite possible that in reality corporeal attributes are compatible with a thinking being; just as quantity can be mentally conceived by means of length alone, while it is possible that in reality breadth and depth go along with length in every quantity.

The difficulty is increased by the fact that this power of thinking seems to be attached to corporeal organs, since we can believe it to be asleep in infants, extinguished in the case of lunatics; and this is an objection strongly urged by those impious men whose aim is the soul's slaughter.

Thus far I have dealt with the distinctions between mind and body in real existence. But since M. Descartes has undertaken to prove the immortality of souls, it is right to ask whether that follows evidently from this separateness of existence. According to the principles of the vulgar philosophy that conclusion by no means can be drawn, for the common opinion is that the souls of animals are distinct from their bodies, but nevertheless perish with them.

I had carried my criticism to this point and was intending to show how, according to our author's principles, which I believed I had gathered from his method of philosophical enquiry, the immortality of the soul could be easily inferred from its distinctness from the body, when a new work, a little treatise bearing the fruit of our author's reflections, came into my hands; and this work not only throws much light on the whole, but in connection with this passage brings forward exactly what I was to adduce with a view to the solution of the above problem.

For in the matter of the souls of animals, in other passages he lets us know sufficiently well that they have no soul, but merely a body disposed in a certain manner and so compounded of various organs that all the actions we see them perform can be effected in it and by its means.

But I fear that this belief will not carry persuasion into men's minds, unless supported by the strongest evidence. For at the first blush, it seems incredible that there is any way by which, without any intervention of the soul, it can come to pass that the light reflected from the body of a wolf into the eyes of a sheep should excite into motion *the minute fibres of the optic nerves and by the penetration of this movement to the brain, discharge the animal spirits into the nerves in the manner requisite to make the sheep run off.*

REPLY TO THE FOURTH SET OF OBJECTIONS

I could not possibly desire any one to examine my writings who could show more insight and courtesy than the opponent whose criticisms you have forwarded. The gentleness with which he has treated me lets me see that he is well-disposed both to me and to the cause I maintain. Yet so accurately has he reconnoitred the positions he attacks, so thoroughly as he scrutinized them, that I am confident that nothing in the rest of the field has escaped his keen gaze. Further so acutely has he contested the points from which he has decided to withhold his approval, that I have no apprehension lest it be thought that complaisance has made him conceal anything. The result is, that instead of my being disturbesd by his objections, my feeling is rather one of gratification at not meeting with opposition in a greater number of places.

Reply to the First Part

The Nature of the Human Mind

I shall not take up time here by thanking my distinguished critic for bringing up to my aid the authority of St Augustine, and for expounding my arguments in a way which betokened a fear that others might not deem them strong enough.

I come first of all to the passage where my demonstration commences of how, *from the fact that I knew that nothing belongs to my essence* (i.e. to the essence of the mind alone) *beyond the fact that I am a thinking being, it follows that in actual truth nothing else does belong to it.* That was, to be sure, the place where I proved that God exists, that God, to wit, who can accomplish whatever I clearly and distinctly know to be possible.

For although much exists in me of which I am not yet conscious (for example in that passage I did, as a fact, assume that I was not yet aware that my mind had the power of moving the body, and that it was substantially united with it), yet since that which I do perceive is adequate to allow of my existing with it as my sole possession, I am certain that God could have created me without putting me in possession of those other attributes of which I am unaware. Hence it was that those other additional attributes were judged not to belong to the essence of the mind.

For in my opinion nothing without which a thing can still exist is comprised in its essence, and although mind belongs to the essence of man, to be united to a human body is in the proper sense no part of the essence of mind.

I must also explain what my meaning was in saying *that a real distinction cannot be inferred from the fact that one thing is conceived apart from another by means of the abstracting action of the mind when it conceives a thing inadequately, but only from the fact that each of them is comprehended apart form the other in a complete manner, or as a complete thing.*

By *a complete thing* I mean merely a substance endowed with those form or attributes which suffice to let me recognise that it is a substance.

For we do not have immediate cognition of substances, as has been elsewhere noted; rather from the mere fact that we perceive certain forms or attributes which must inhere in something in order to have existence, we name the thing in which they exist a *substance.*

For, as to be extended, divisible, possessed of figure, etc. are the forms or attributes by which I recognise that substance called *body;* so, to be a knowing, willing, doubting being, etc. are the·forms by which I recognize the substance called *mind;* and I know that thinking substance is a complete thing, no less than that which is extended.

But it can nowise be maintained that, in the words of M. Arnauld, *body is related to mind as genus is to species;* for although the genus can be apprehended apart from this or that specific difference, the species can by no means be thought apart from the genus.

For, to illustrate, we easily apprehend figure, without thinking at all of a circle (although that mental act is not distinct unless we refer to some specific figure, and it does not give up a complete thing, unless it embraces the nature of the body); but we are cognisant of no specific difference belonging to the circle, unless at the same time we think of figures.

But mind can be perceived clearly and distinctly, or sufficiently so to let it be considered to be a complete thing without any of those formed or attributes by which we recognize that body is a substance, as I think I have sufficiently shown in the Second Meditation; and the body is understood distinctly and as a complete thing apart from the attributes attaching to the mind.

Nevertheless, M. Arnauld here urges that *although a certain notion of myself can be obtained without a knowledge of the body, it yet does not thence result that this knowledge is complete and adequate, so as to make me sure that I am not in error in excluding the body from my essence.* He elucidates his meaning be taking as an illustration the triangle inscribed in a semicircle, which we can clearly and distinctly know to be right-angled, though we do not know, or even deny, that the square on its base is equal to the squares on its sides; and nevertheless we cannot thence infer that we can have a [right-angled] triangle, the square on the base of which is not equal to the squares on the sides.

Therefore, though I said that *it was sufficient to be able to apprehend one thing clearly and distinctly apart from another, etc.*, we cannot go on to complete the argument thus:—*but I clearly and distinctly apprehend this triangle, etc.* Firstly, because the ratio between the square on the base and those on the sides is not a complete thing. Secondly, because that ratio is clearly understood only in the case of the right-angled triangles. Thirdly, because the triangle itself cannot be distinctly apprehended if the ratio between the squares on the base and on the sides is denied.

But now I must explain how it is that, *from the mere fact that I apprehend one substance clearly and distinctly apart from another, I am sure that the one excludes the other.*

Really the notion of *substance* is just this—that which can exist by itself, without the aid of any other substance. No one who perceives two substances by means of two diverse concepts ever doubts that they are really distinct.

My opponent, however says, *I apprehend the triangle inscribed in the semicircle without knowing that the square on its base is equal to the square on the sides.* True, that triangle may indeed be apprehended although there is no thought of the ratio prevailing between the squares on the base and sides; but we can never think that this ratio must be denied. It is quite otherwise in the case of the mind where, not only do we understand that it exists apart from the body, but also

that all the attributes of the body may be denied of it; for reciprocal exclusion of one another belongs to the nature of substances.

There is no conflict between my theory and the point M. Arnauld next brings up, *that it is no marvel if, in deducing my existence from the fact that I think, the idea I thus form of myself represents me merely as a thinking being.* For, similarly when I examine the nature of body I find nothing at all in it that savour of thought; and there is no better proof of the distinctness of two things than if, when we study each separately, we find nothing in the one that does not differ from what we find in the other.

Further, I fail to see how this argument *proves too much.* For, in order to prove that one thing is really distinct from another, nothing less can be said, than that the divine power is able to separate one from the other. I thought I took sufficient care to prevent anyone thence inferring that *man was* merely *a spirit that makes use of a body;* for in this very Sixth Meditation in which I have dealt with the distinction between mind and body, I have at the same time proved that mind was substantially united with body; and I employed arguments, the efficacy of which in establishing this proof I cannot remember to have seen in any other case surpassed.

Finally, the fact that *the power of thinking is asleep in infants and in maniacs*—though not indeed *extinct,* yet troubled—should not make us believe that it is conjoined with the corporeal organs in such a way as to be incapable of existing apart from them. The fact that our thought is often in our experience impeded by them, does not allow us to infer that it is produced by them; for this there is not even the slightest proof.

I do not, however, deny that the close conjunction between soul and body of which our senses constantly give us experience, is the cause of our not perceiving their real distinction without attentive reflection. But, in my judgment, those who frequently revolve in their thought what was said in the Second Meditation, will easily persuade themselves that mind is distinguished from body not by a mere fiction or intellectual abstraction, but is known as a distinct thing because it is really distinct.

I make no reply to M. Arnauld's additions about the immortality of the soul, because they are not in conflict with my doctrine. As for the matter of the souls of brutes, this is not the place to treat the subject, and I could not, without taking in the whole of Physics, say more about them than in the explanations given in the fifth part of the discourse on Method. Yet, not to pass over the matter altogether, I should point out that the chief thing to note appears to me to be that motion is impossible alike in our own bodies and in those of the brutes, unless all the organs or instruments are present, by means of which it can be effected in a machine. Hence in our very selves the mind [(or the soul)] by no means moves the external limbs immediately, but merely directs the subtle fluid styled the animal spirits, that passes from the heart through the brain towards the muscles, and determines this fluid to perform definite motions, these animal spirits being in their own nature capable of being utilized with equal facility for many distinct actions. But the greater part of our motions do not depend on the mind at all. Such are the beating of the heart, the digestion of our food, nutrition, respiration when we are asleep, and even walking, singing and similar acts when we are awake, if performed without the mind attending to them. When a man in falling thrust out his hand to save his head he does that without his reason counseling him so to act, but merely because the sight of the impending fall penetrating to his brain, drives the animal spirits into the nerves in the manner necessary for this motion, and for producing it without the mind's desiring it, and as though it were the working of a machine. Now, when we experience this as a fact in ourselves, why should we marvel so greatly *if the light reflected from the body of a wolf into the eyes of a sheep* should be equally capable of exciting in it the motion of flight?

But if we wish by reasoning to determine whether any of the motions of brutes are similar to those which we accomplish with the aid of the mind, or whether they resemble those that depend alone upon the *influxus* of the animal spirits and the disposition of the organs, we must pay heed to the differences that prevail between the two classes: viz. those differences explained in the fifth part of the Discourse on Method, for I have been able to discover no others. Then it will be seen that all the actions of brutes resemble only those of ours that occur without the aid of the mind. Whence we are driven to conclude that

we can recognize no principle of motion in them beyond the disposition of their organs and the continual discharge of the animal spirits that are produced by the beat of the heart as it rarefies the blood. At the same time we shall perceive that we have had no cause for ascribing anything more to them, beyond that, not distinguishing these two principles of motion, when previously we have noted that the principle depending solely on the animal spirits and organs exists in ourselves and in the brutes alike, we have inadvisedly believed that the other principle, that consisting wholly of mind and thought, also existed in them.

SYNOPSIS OF THE SIX FOLLOWING MEDITATIONS

In the first Meditation I set forth the reasons for which we may, generally speaking, doubt about all things and especially about material things, at least so long as we have no other foundations for the sciences than those which we have hitherto possessed. But although the utility of a Doubt which is so general does not at first appear, it is at the same time very great, inasmuch as it delivers us from every kind of prejudice, and sets out for us a very simple way by which the mind may detach itself from the senses; and finally it makes it impossible for us ever to doubt those things which we have once discovered to be true.

In the second Meditation, mind, which making use of the liberty which pertains to it, takes for granted that all those things of whose existence it has the least doubt, are non-existent, recognizes that it is however absolutely impossible that it does not itself exist. This point is likewise of the greatest moment, inasmuch as by this means a distinction is easily drawn between the things which pertain to mind—that is to say to the intellectual nature—and those which pertain to body.

But because it may be that some expect from me in this place a statement of the reasons establishing the immortality of the soul, I feel that I should here make known to them that having aimed at writing nothing in all this Treatise of which I do not posses very exact demonstrations, I am obliged to follow a similar order to that made use of by the geometers, which is to begin by putting forward as premises all those things upon which the proposition that we seek depends, before coming to any conclusion regarding it. Now the first and principle matter which is requisite for thoroughly understanding the immortality of the soul is to form the clearest possible conception of it, and one which will be entirely distinct from all the conceptions which we may have of body; and in this Meditation this has been done. In addition to this it is requisite that we may be assured that all the things which we conceive clearly and distinctly are true in the very way in which we think them; and this could not be proven previously to the Fourth Meditation. Further we must have a distinct conception of corporeal nature, which is given partly in this Second, and partly in the Fifth and Sixth Meditations. And finally we should conclude from all this, that those things which we conceive clearly and distinctly as being diverse substances, as we regard mind and body to be, are really substance essentially distinct one from the other; and this is the conclusion of the Sixth Meditation. This is further confirmed in this same Meditation by the fact that we cannot conceive of body excepting in so far as it is divisible, while the mind cannot be conceived of excepting as indivisible. For we are not able to conceive of the half of a mind as we can do of the smallest of all bodies; so that we see that not only are their natures different but even in some respects contrary to one another. I have not however dealt further with this matter in this treatise, both because what I have said is sufficient to show clearly enough that the extinction of the mind does not follow from the corruption of the body, and also to give men the hope of another life after death, as also because the premises from which the immortality of the soul may be deduced depend on an elucidation of a complete system of Physics. This would mean to establish in the first place that all substances generally—that is to say all things which cannot exist without being created by God—are in their nature incorruptible, and that they can never cease to exist unless God, in denying to them his concurrence, reduce them to naught; and secondly that body, regarded generally, is a substance, which is the reason why is also cannot perish, but that the human body, inasmuch as it differs from other bodies, is composed only of a certain configuration of members and of other similar accidents, while the human mind is not similarly composed of any accidents, but is a pure substance. For although all the accidents of mind be changed, although, for instance, it think certain things, will others, perceive others, etc., despite all this it does not emerge from these changes another mind: the human body on the other hand becomes a different thing from the sole fact that the figure or form of any of its portions is found to be changed. From this it follows that the human body may indeed easily enough perish, but the

mind [or soul of man (I make no distinction between them)] is owing to its nature immortal.

In the third Meditation it seems to me that I have explained at sufficient length the principle argument of which I make use in order to prove the existence of God. But none the less, because I did not wish in that place to make use of any comparisons derived from corporeal things, so as to withdraw as much as I could the minds of readers from the senses, there may perhaps have remained many obscurities which, however, will, I hope, be entirely removed by the Replies which I have made to the Objections which have been set before me. Amongst others there is, for example, this one, 'How the idea in us of a being supremely perfect possesses so much objective reality [that is to say participates by representation in so many degrees of being and perfection] that it necessarily proceeds from a cause which is absolutely perfect. This is illustrated in these Replies by the comparison of a very perfect machine, the idea of which is found in the mind of some workman. For as the objective contrivance of this idea must have some cause, i.e. either the science of the workman or that of some other from whom he has received the idea, it is similarly impossible that the idea of God which is in us should not have God himself as its cause.

In the fourth Meditation it is shown that all these things which we very clearly and distinctly perceive are true, and at the same time it is explained in what the nature of error or falsity consists. This must of necessity be known both for the confirmation of the preceding truths and for the better comprehension of those that follow. (But it must meanwhile be remarked that I do not in any way there treat of sin—that is to say of the error which is committed in the pursuit of good and evil, but only of that which arises in the deciding between the true and the false. And I do not intend to speak of matters pertaining to the Faith or the conduct of life, but only of those which concern speculative truths, and which may be known by the sole aid of the light of nature.)

In the fifth Meditation corporeal nature generally is explained, and in addition to this the existence of God is demonstrated by a new proof in which there may possibly be certain difficulties also, but the solution of these will be seen in the Replies to the Objections. And further I show in what sense it is true to say that the certainty of geometrical demonstrations is itself dependent on the knowledge of God.

Finally, in the Sixth I distinguish the action of the understanding from that of the imagination; the marks by which this distinction is made are described. I here show that the mind of man is really distinct from the body, and at the same time that the two are so closely joined together that they form, so to speak, a single thing. All the errors which proceed from the senses are then surveyed, while the means of avoiding them are demonstrated, and finally all the reasons from which we may deduce the existence of material things are set forth. Not that I judge them to be very useful in establishing that which they prove, to wit, that there is in truth a world, that men possess bodies, and other such things which never have been doubted by anyone of sense; but because in considering these closely we come to see that they are neither so strong nor so evident as those arguments which lead us to the knowledge of our mind and of God; so that these last must be the most certain and most evident facts which can fall within the cognizance of the human mind. And this is the whole matter that I have tried to prove in these Meditations, for which reason I here omit to speak of many other questions with which I dealt incidentally in this discussion.

STUDY QUESTIONS: DESCARTES, MEDITATIONS: OBJECTIONS AND REPLIES II, III, AND IV

1. The second objector, Mersenne, asks of Descartes 'How do you know that you are not . . . a body which is in motion?' How does Descartes reply to this question?
2. How does Descartes reply to the thesis that God may deceive us, for example, when it is for our benefit? How does this thesis constitute a problem for Descartes?
3. The author of the second objections asks Descartes to present some of his arguments in a geometrical fashion. Please list the conclusions of these arguments. How does Descartes prove those conclusions?
4. In the third set of objections, Hobbes says, 'I might just as well say "I am walking, therefore I am a walk."' What is Hobbes' objection? How does Descartes reply to it?
5. How does Hobbes support his contention that we have no idea of God? How does Descartes reply to this claim?
6. What is Hobbes' objection to Descartes' claim that error is merely a defect? How does Descartes reply?
7. In the fourth set of objections, Arnauld doubts that the conception one has of oneself as a thinking and nonextended thing may be adequate. How does Descartes try to squash this doubt?
8. Arnauld tries to show that, from the facts that one can doubt the existence of material things and that one cannot doubt one exists, it does not follow that one is not material. He uses an example to illustrate this. What was the example? How does Descartes reply?
9. Arnauld points out that the people ordinarily think that the soul of brute animals is distinct from their bodies. For what argumentative purpose does Arnauld point this out? How does Descartes respond to this argument?

RULES FOR THE DIRECTION OF THE MIND

This was Descartes' first work. He started writing the book in 1620, but he abandoned the project in 1629. The aim of the book is to provide a method to guide the mind so that it can pass true and solid judgments on whatever it is investigating (Rule 1). Descartes' aim was to develop a method appropriate for all scientific investigation. He developed this method by reflecting on how certainty can be achieved in mathematics.

Later, writing in the Discourse about the earlier period of his life, Descartes claims that he had success applying his method: "By strictly observing the few rules I had chosen, I became very adept at unraveling all the questions" of geometry and arithmetic. The task he set himself was to develop from this method a general approach for all problem solving and investigation. Most investigators study haphazardly without method. Method means certain and easy-to-follow rules, which avoid error and, if used in the right order and way, will lead to as complete a knowledge as possible.

The work contains 21 rules for the direction of the mind, of which we have chosen 13. We have omitted all of Descartes' commentary on how to apply the rules, because the point of the selection is to give the student the briefest acquaintance with this aspect of Descartes' early thought.

RULE I.

The end of study should be to direct the mind towards the enunciation of sound and correct judgments on all matters that come before it.

RULE II.

Only those objects should engage our attention, to the sure and indubitable knowledge of which our mental powers seem to be adequate.

RULE III.

In the subjects we propose to investigate, our inquiries should be directed, not to what others have thought, nor to what we ourselves conjecture, but to what we can clearly and perspicuously behold and with certainty deduce; for knowledge is not won in any other way.

RULE IV.

There is need of a method for finding out the truth.

RULE V.

Method consists entirely in the order and disposition of the objects towards which our mental vision must be directed if we would find out any truth. We shall comply with it exactly if we reduce involved and obscure propositions step by step to those that are simpler, and then starting with the intuitive apprehension of all those that are absolutely simple, attempt to ascend to the knowledge of all others by precisely similar steps.

RULE VI.

In order to separate out what is quite simple from what is complex, and to arrange these matters methodically, we ought, in the case of every series in which we have deduced certain facts the one from the other, to notice which fact is simple, and to mark the interval, greater, less, or equal, which separates all the others from this.

RULE VII.

If we wish our science to be complete, those matters which promote the end we have in view must one and all be scrutinized by a movement of thought which is continuous and nowhere interrupted; they must also be included in an enumeration which is both adequate and methodical.

RULE VIII.

If in the matters to be examined we come to a step in the series of which our understanding is not sufficiently well able to have an intuitive cognition, we must stop short there. We must make no attempt to examine what follows; thus we shall spare ourselves superfluous labour.

RULE IX.

We ought to give the whole of our attention to the most insignificant and most easily mastered facts, and remain a long time in contemplation of them until we are accustomed to behold the truth clearly and distinctly.

RULE X.

In order that it may acquire sagacity the mind should be exercised in pursuing just those inquiries of which the solution has already been found by others; and it ought to traverse in a systematic way even the most trifling of men's inventions, though those ought to be preferred in which order is explained or implied.

RULE XI.

If, after we have recognized intuitively a number of simple truths, we wish to draw any inference from them, it is useful to run them over in a continuous and uninterrupted act of thought, to reflect upon their relations to one another, and to grasp together distinctly a number of these propositions so far as is possible at the same time. For this is a way of making our knowledge much more certain, and of greatly increasing the power of the mind.

RULE XII.

Finally we ought to employ all the aids of understanding, imagination, sense and memory, first for the purpose of having a distinct intuition of simple propositions; partly also in order to compare the propositions to be proved with those we know already, so that we may be able to recognize their truth; partly also in order to discover the truths, which should be compared with each other so that nothing may be left lacking on which human industry may exercise itself.

RULE XIII.

Once a 'question' is perfectly understood, we must free it of every conception superfluous to its meaning, state it in its simplest terms, and, having recourse to an enumeration, split it up into the various sections beyond which analysis cannot go in minuteness.

STUDY QUESTIONS: DESCARTES, *RULES FOR THE DIRECTION OF THE MIND*

1. What is the main aim of the rules?
2. What ought one to investigate? What does this rule out?
3. What is the essence of Descartes' method?
4. Why should we attend to what is more simple?
5. How can we train the mind in order to increase our intellectual capacity?
6. Why does Descartes recommend dividing a problem into its smallest possible parts?

Philosophical Bridges: The Cartesian Influence

Descartes set the agenda for much seventeenth- and eighteenth-century philosophy and science. As the leading pioneer in the fight to free philosophy and the fledgling sciences from the domination of medieval Scholasticism, he argued for the strategic importance of epistemology. This argument impressed later Empiricists, such as Locke, who also saw the definition of knowledge as vital to the progress of knowledge. At the same time, Descartes' project also included a metaphysical reconciliation of science and religion, and this aim influenced later Rationalists such as Spinoza and Leibniz. Let us consider these two points.

1. The Empiricist John Locke took to heart Descartes' insistence on the importance of epistemology. Furthermore, he adopted many features of Descartes' conception of perception and knowledge, including the claim that knowledge requires certainty and the thesis that one can perceive directly only one's own ideas. This latter proposition was one of the guiding principles of Locke's main work in epistemology, the *Essay*, as well as being the cornerstone of Berkeley's attack on the notion of material substance and of Hume's skeptical naturalism. In short, if Locke can be called the father of Empiricism, then Descartes is its grandfather.

2. At the same time, Descartes' metaphysics had a profound effect on the more Rationalistic philosophers of the seventeenth- and eighteenth-centuries. His aim of trying to reconcile a scientific worldview with a religious ontology survived even when his substance dualism was rejected. For instance, both Spinoza and Leibniz try to show that the principle of sufficient reason, as outlined by Descartes, explains the success of science but also necessitates the existence of God. They try to reconcile science and religion through metaphysics. Likewise, Descartes' definition of substance, as that which has independent existence, was a central premise in the arguments of Spinoza and Leibniz. In short, both pursue a Cartesian project and start with Cartesian premises, even though they arrive at metaphysical conclusions that oppose fundamentally Descartes' dualism.

By defining the agenda for much modern philosophy, Descartes has had a profound effect on contemporary thought. Indeed, one might characterize much late twentieth-century thinking as an attempt to escape its Cartesian legacy. Much recent philosophy is explicitly anti-Cartesian. This is especially evident in two related areas: epistemology and the philosophy of mind.

EPISTEMOLOGY

With his method of doubt, Descartes posed one of the great skeptical challenges in philosophy, namely, 'How can we have knowledge of the external world?' Some of the most important philosophy of the twentieth-century has been concerned with answering or dissolving this question by attacking its presuppositions. For example, in *Being and Time*, Martin Heidegger claims that Descartes' question presupposes a view of knowledge and perception that abstracts a person from the cares and concrete interactions that constitute our lives. In other words, we are not minds that live in a private mental world but rather beings who are thrown into and inhabit a social world that is populated by other people, and that also contains useful public objects. Wittgenstein also seeks to undermine Descartes' notion of essentially private mental objects. In his *Philosophical Investigations*, he argues that nothing could possibly count as making an error with regard to essentially private objects; the 'is'/'seems' distinction collapses. Because of this, an essentially private language is impossible.

Descartes' general strategy for answering his own skeptical question was to encounter a firm foundation for knowledge. Recent philosophers have criticized this foundationalist approach and also have rejected the goal of certainty. For example, in the *Quest for Certainty*, the American pragmatist John Dewey (1859–1952) argues that Cartesian certainty is a false goal because whether a belief is warranted depends on whether it is confirmed by the relevant communities of investigators. Such a warrant is not private; furthermore, it is a matter of degree, and is always open to revision.

PHILOSOPHY OF MIND

Until the 1950s, most philosophers accepted Descartes' introspective conception of the content of mental states. His thesis that we can only perceive our own ideas became a central claim of Empiricists, such as Locke, Berkeley, Hume, and, later, John Stuart Mill. Furthermore, some nineteenth-century idealists, such as Francis Bradley and Josiah Royce, also accepted this thesis, as did the early logical positivists, Bertrand Russell and even the common sense realist G. E. Moore. The acceptance of this claim also explains why much epistemology has been directed toward explaining how we can have knowledge of the external world, and also the philosophical fascination with idealism in the nineteenth century. After the 1960s, exponents of functionalist and causal theories of mind argued that the content of mental states cannot be defined purely introspectively but rather must be specified on the basis of the causal role of the mental state.

The most famous aspect of Descartes' philosophy of mind is his ontological mind/body dualism, which has been very influential, despite the fact that relatively few philosophers have espoused this view. Throughout the nineteenth-century, antimaterialist thinkers tended to argue for some version of idealism rather than Descartes' substance dualism. Nevertheless, Descartes' view has been influential in three ways. First, it accords with our Christian heritage, and partly for this reason, it has been a popular view, especially outside of academic philosophy. Second, within philosophy, substance mind/body dualism became a theory that philosophers had to dig deep to avoid. Since common sense seems to support dualism, philosophers who argue against it must try to offer an especially good explanation for rejecting it. In this way, Descartes' dualism had a powerful influence. Third, Descartes' dualism spurred vitalism in biology, the view that organisms are alive because of a nonphysical vital force, which became popular in nineteenth-century Britain.

SCIENCE AND MATHEMATICS

Descartes' geometrical and mechanical conception of physics reigned over Europe until it was eclipsed by Newton's more comprehensive system. Descartes' physics was so influential largely because it unified all the diverse scientific studies of the time, which had been perceived previously as disconnected investigations. The Cartesian ideal that the natural sciences should be a unity had an enduring influence even long after the specifics of Descartes' physics had been replaced. One might claim that Descartes was the first modern thinker to conceive of physics as a single body of knowledge. He was the first modern philosopher to suggest in some detail how areas as diverse as astronomy and physiology can be reduced to a few mechanical laws. Descartes' scientific vision was also so influential because it was mathematically based. He insisted that physics should be framed in terms of the clear and distinct ideas of mathematics. He also expounded the Euclidean ideal that mathematical theorems should be deducible from a few basic concepts and axioms, and embodied this ideal by formulating the principles of analytic geometry, which had an influence on Leibniz and nineteenth-century mathematicians such as Giuseppe Peano, George Boole and John Venn.

In summary, Descartes' work defined the direction of much philosophy at least up to the time of Kant. It influenced directly Hobbes, Locke, Malebranche, and Spinoza and, from there, many other thinkers. Descartes' theory of the passions had a direct impact on Spinoza's philosophy of the emotions.

BLAISE PASCAL (1632–1662)

Biographical History

Even as a child, Blaise Pascal was intensely interested in science. He listened to his father's conversations with Gassendi, Mersenne, and Descartes concerning physics and geometry. At the age of 15, the boy wrote a treatise on conic sections, and when he was 19 years old, Pascal invented a calculating machine, which used cogs and wheels. In 1648, he developed the mathematics of probability, also independently discovered by Pierre de Fermat.

In 1646, he began his famous work on the nature of vacuum. Two years earlier, Evangelista Torricelli had claimed to have produced a vacuum. This claim was rejected vehemently by both Cartesian and Aristotelian physicists, but after having worked on the problem for a year, Pascal confirmed Torricelli's hypothesis, thereby refuting the claim that nature abhors a vacuum. Pascal continued work on the vacuum and its implications for measuring barometric pressure and for hydraulics. In 1651, he wrote part of a treatise on the vacuum, of which only the preface remains.

Pascal continued working in mathematics and physics until 1654, when he underwent a personal crisis following the death of his father (1651) and his sister's retreat to a nunnery. This crisis culminated in a mystical conversion experience in November 1654. Thereafter, his passions turned to religion, fuelled by the reoccurrence of an illness that left him in severe pain for much of the time.

In 1654, Pascal became a member of the Port Royal community. Port Royal was a Catholic convent outside of Paris, which had been revived by the new young abbess, Jacqueline Arnauld. Due to her zeal, and with the help of her brother, Antoine, who wrote one of the objections to Descartes' *Meditations*, Port Royal became a religious and intellectual force in France. The movement ran high-quality schools, opened new convents, and won converts. Arnauld, who wrote a famous logic text, entered into high-profile conflict with the Jesuits. Port Royal embraced some of the doctrines of Jansenism, a form of mystical Puritanism, which the pope declared as heresy in 1653. The ensuing dispute divided France and absorbed the powerful intellect of Pascal. In 1656, in an attempt to defend Arnauld from censure, Pascal composed his *Provincial Letters*, supporting Jansenism, and attacking the Jesuits for moral and theological laxity. Partly because of their eloquence and passion, Pascal's letters had an immense influence on French public opinion, contributing to the decline of the Jesuits in France.

Philosophical Overview

In 1657, Pascal began to write his famous *Pensées*, a defense of religious belief, which was published posthumously in 1670. The work, which consists largely of aphorisms, was left unfinished. It was his original intention that the material of the *Pensées* would be part of a larger project, an *Apology for the Christian Religion*.

In the *Pensées*, Pascal describes the limits of science, claiming that science is based on reason, which in turn is based on the notoriously fallible senses. Reason cannot comprehend the relation between mind and body, the nature of morality and God, or the meaning of human life. Religion relies on feeling, rather than reason. Pascal writes, 'The heart has its reasons, which reason does not know.'

This does not mean that Pascal was against reason. Indeed, he wrote, 'Man is only a reed . . . , but he is a thinking reed. . . . Thus, all our dignity consists in thought.' His view is that reason has only a very limited role in religion.

PENSÉES

In the *Pensées*, Pascal challenges nonbelievers to his famous wager. Faith and religious belief cannot be proved. However, belief in God is a wise bet. Pascal weighs the costs and benefits of betting on the existence of God. On one hand, if God exists, the reward for faith is eternal salvation and the cost of unbelief is eternal damnation. On the other hand, if God does not exist, the believer has lost little and the nonbeliever has gained almost nothing. Pascal concludes, 'Wager, then, without hesitation that He exists.' He advises nonbelievers who find it difficult to believe to follow the customs of the Church, because belief will result!

Pascal conceived of his wager as a necessary alternative to the traditional metaphysical proofs of God's existence, such as Descartes' ontological argument. According to Pascal, God's existence cannot be proved. Furthermore, rational proofs do not bring conviction or faith, which comes through God's influence on the heart.

XIII. SUBMISSION AND USE OF REASON

167 Submission and use of reason; that is what makes true Christianity. (269)

173 If we submit everything to reason our religion will be left with nothing mysterious or supernatural.

If we offend the principles of reason our religion will be absurd and ridiculous. (273)

174 St Augustine. Reason would never submit unless it judged that there are occasions when it ought to submit.

It is right, then, that reason should submit when it judges that it ought to submit. (270)

175 One of the ways in which the damned will be confounded is that they will see themselves condemned by their own reason, by which they claimed to condemn the Christian religion. (563)

182 There is nothing so consistent with reason as this denial of reason. (272)

183 Two excesses: to exclude reason, to admit nothing but reason. (253)

185 Faith certainly tells us what the senses do not, but not the contrary of what they see; it is above, not against them. (265)

188 Reason's last step is the recognition that there are an infinite number of things which are beyond it. It is merely feeble if it does not go as far as to realize that.

If natural things are beyond it, what are we to say about supernatural things? (267)

190 *Preface.* The metaphysical proofs for the existence of God are so remote from human reasoning and so involved that they make little impact, and, even if they did help some people, it would only be for the moment during which they watched the demonstration, because an hour later they would be afraid they had made a mistake.

193 *Prejudice leading to error.* It is deplorable to see everybody debating about the means, never the end. Everyone thinks about how he will get on in his career, but when it comes to choosing a career or a country it is fate that decides for us.

SERIES II

[The Wager]

418 *Infinity—nothing.* Our soul is cast into the body where it finds number, time, dimensions; it reasons about these things and calls them natural, or necessary, and can believe nothing else.

Unity added to infinity does not increase it at all, any more than a foot added to an infinite measurement: the finite is annihilated in the presence of the infinite and becomes pure nothingness. So it is with our mind before God, with our justice before divine justice. There is not so great a disproportion between our justice and God's as between unity and infinity.

God's justice must be as vast as his mercy. Now his justice towards the damned is less vast and ought to be less startling to us than his mercy towards the elect.

We know that the infinite exists without knowing its nature, just as we know that it is untrue that numbers are finite. Thus it is true that there is an infinite number, but we do not know what it is. It is untrue that it is even, untrue that it is odd, for by adding a unit it does not change its nature. Yet it is a number, and every number is even or odd. (It is true that this applies to every finite number.)

Therefore we may well know that God exists without knowing what he is.

Is there no substantial truth, seeing that there are so many true things which are not truth itself?

Thus we know the existence and nature of the finite because we too are finite and extended in space.

We know the existence of the infinite without knowing its nature, because it too has extension but unlike us no limits.

But we do not know either the existence or the nature of God, because he has neither extension nor limits.

But by faith we know his existence, through glory we shall know his nature.

Now I have already proved that it is quite possible to know that something exists without knowing its nature.

Let us now speak according to our natural lights.

If there is a God, he is infinitely beyond our comprehension, since, being indivisible and without limits, he bears no relation to us. We are therefore incapable of knowing either what he is or whether he is. That being so, who would dare to attempt an answer to the question? Certainly not we, who bear no relation to him.

Who then will condemn Christians for being unable to give rational grounds for their belief, professing as they do a religion for which they cannot give rational grounds? They declare that it is a folly, *stultitiam*, in expounding it to the world, and then you complain that they do not prove it. If they did prove it they would not be keeping their word. It is by being without proof that they show they are not without sense. 'Yes, but although that excuses those who offer their religion as such, and absolves them from the criticism of producing it without rational grounds, it does not absolve those who accept it.' Let us then examine this point, and let us say: 'Either God is or he is not.' But to which view shall we be inclined? Reason cannot decide this question. Infinite chaos separates us. At the far end of this infinite distance a coin is being spun which will come down heads or tails. How will you wager? Reason cannot make you choose either, reason cannot prove either wrong.

Do not then condemn as wrong those who have made a choice, for you know nothing about it. 'No, but I will condemn them not for having made this particular choice, but any choice, for, although the one who calls heads and the other one are equally at fault, the fact is that they are both at fault: the right thing is not to wager at all.'

Yes, but you must wager. There is no choice, you are already committed. Which will you choose then? Let us see: since a choice must be made, let us see which offers you the least interest. You have two things to lose: the true and the good; and two things to stake: your reason and your will, your knowledge and your happiness; and your nature has two things to avoid: error and wretchedness. Since you must necessarily choose, your reason is no more affronted by choosing one rather than the other. That is one point cleared up. But your happiness? Let us weigh up the gain and the loss involved in calling heads that God exists. Let us assess the two cases: if you win you win everything, if you lose you lose nothing. Do not hesitate then; wager that he does exist. 'That is wonderful. Yes, I must wager, but perhaps I am wagering too much.' Let us see: since there is an equal chance of gain and loss, if you stood to win only two lives for one you could still wager, but supposing you stood to win three?

You would have to play (since you must necessarily play) and it would be unwise of you, once you are obliged to play, not to risk your life in order to win three lives at a game in which there is an equal chance of losing and winning. But there is an eternity of life and happiness. That being so, even though there were an infinite number of chances, of which only one were in your favour, you would still be right to wager one in order to win two; and you would be acting wrongly, being obliged to play, in refusing to stake one life against three in a game, where out of an infinite number of chances there is one in your favour, if there were an infinity of infinitely happy life to be won. But here there is an infinity of infinitely happy life to be won, one chance of winning against a finite number of chances of losing, and what you are staking is finite. That leaves no choice; wherever there is infinity, and where there are not infinite chances of losing against that of winning, there is no room for hesitation, you must give everything. And thus, since you are obliged to play, you must be renouncing reason if you hoard your life rather than risk it for an infinite gain, just as likely to occur as a loss amounting to nothing.

For it is no good saying that it is uncertain whether you will win, that it is certain that you are taking a risk, and that the infinite distance between the certainty of what you are risking and the uncertainty of what you may gain makes the finite good you are certainly risking equal to the infinite good that you are not certain to gain. This is not the case. Every gambler takes a certain risk for an uncertain gain, and yet he is taking a certain finite risk for an uncertain finite gain without sinning against reason. Here there is no infinite distance between the certain risk and the uncertain gain: that is not true. There is, indeed, an infinite distance between the certainty of winning and the certainty of losing, but the proportion between the uncertainty of winning and the certainty of what is being risked is in proportion to the chances of winning or losing. And hence if there are as many chances on one side as on the other you are playing for even odds. And in that case the certainty of what you are risking is equal to the uncertainty of what you may win; it is by no means infinitely distant from it. Thus our argument carries infinite weight, when the stakes are finite in a game where there are even chances of winning and losing and an infinite prize to be won.

This is conclusive and if men are capable of any truth this is it.

'I confess, I admit it, but is there really no way of seeing what the cards are?'—'Yes. Scripture and the rest, etc.'—'Yes, but my hands are tied and my lips are sealed; I am being forced to wager and I am not free; I am being held fast and I am so made that I cannot believe. What do you want me to do then?'—'That is true, but at least get it into your head that, if you are unable to believe, it is because of your passions, since reason impels you to believe and yet you cannot do so. Concentrate then not on convincing yourself by multiplying proofs of God's existence but by diminishing your passions. You want to find faith and you do not know the road. You want to be cured of unbelief and you

ask for the remedy: learn from those who were once bound like you and who now wager all they have. These are people who know the road you wish to follow, who have been cured of the affliction of which you wish to be cured: follow the way by which they began. They behaved just as if they did believe, taking holy water, having masses said, and so on. That will make you believe quite naturally, and will make you more docile.'—'But that is what I am afraid of.'—'But why? What have you to lose? But to show you that this is the way, the fact is that this diminishes the passions which are your great obstacles. . . .'

End of this address.

'Now what harm will come to you from choosing this course? You will be faithful, honest, humble, grateful, full of good works, a sincere, true friend. . . . It is true you will not enjoy noxious pleasures, glory and good living, but will you not have others?

'I tell you that you will gain even in this life, and that at every step you take along this road you will see that your gain is so certain and your risk so negligible that in the end you will realize that you have wagered on something certain and infinite for which you have paid nothing.'

'How these words fill me with rapture and delight!—'

'If my words please you and seem cogent, you must know that they come from a man who went down upon his knees before and after to pray this infinite and indivisible being, to whom he submits his own, that he might bring your being also to submit to him for your own good and for his glory: and that strength might thus be reconciled with lowliness.'   (233)

419   Custom is our nature. Anyone who grows accustomed to faith believes it, and can no longer help fearing hell, and believes nothing else.

Anyone accustomed to believe that the king is to be feared. . . .

Who then can doubt that our soul, being accustomed to see number, space, movement, believes in this and nothing else?   (419)

420   'Do you believe that it is impossible for God to be infinite and indivisible?'—'Yes.'—'Very

well, I will show you something infinite and indivisible: it is a point moving everywhere at an infinite speed.

'For it is one and the same everywhere and wholly present in every place. From this natural phenomenon which previously seemed impossible to you you should realize that there may be others which you do not yet know. Do not conclude from your apprenticeship that there is nothing left for you to learn, but that you still have an infinite amount to learn.' (231)

423 The heart has its reasons of which reason knows nothing: we know this in countless ways.
I say that it is natural for the heart to love the universal being or itself, according to its allegiance, and it hardens itself against either as it chooses. You have rejected one and kept the other. Is it reason that makes you love yourself? (277)

424 It is the heart which perceives God and not the reason. That is what faith is: God perceived by the heart, not by the reason. (278)

STUDY QUESTIONS: PASCAL, *PENSÉES*

1. Pascal says, 'There is nothing so consistent with reason as this denial of reason.' What does this mean? How would Pascal defend his claim?
2. What is reason's last step?
3. What is the main limitation of the metaphysical proofs of God's existence?
4. For what purpose does Pascal point out, 'Unity added to infinity does not increase it at all'?
5. What is Pascal's wager?
6. What is Pascal's advice to the person who is unable to believe?
7. What is it that we know in countless ways? What examples does Pascal himself provide of such knowledge?
8. How does Pascal define 'faith'?

Philosophical Bridges: Pascal's Influence

Apart from the influence of his mathematical and scientific works, Pascal's view of the importance of the feeling for our understanding of God influenced Jean-Jacques Rousseau (1712–1778), who conceived of natural religion as a spontaneous love of God and goodness, and who rejected the French Enlightenment emphasis on reason. In turn, Rousseau was a major inspiration for the nineteenth-century Romantic movement.

Pascal's engaged and biting style of writing influenced generations of French writers. Even the notorious critic of religion, Voltaire, called Pascal's *Letters* 'the best written book that has yet appeared in France.'

Baruch de Spinoza (1632–1677)

Biographical History

Baruch de Spinoza was born in the Jewish community of Amsterdam. His early education was almost entirely religious, but his later teachers included Manasseh ben Israel, a major figure in seventeenth-century Judaism who introduced Spinoza to non-Jewish learning. In 1656, Spinoza was excommunicated from the synagogue, and he began using the Latin version of his name, Benedict. His family disowned him, and he chose the trade of making and polishing lenses for spectacles, microscopes, and telescopes. From 1660 to 1663, Spinoza lived near Leiden, and he joined the study groups of the Collegiant sect, who were opposed to rigid orthodoxy. Spinoza worked on his major book, the *Ethics*, intermittently from 1662 to 1675. In the meantime, in 1663, he published the *Principles of the Philosophy of René Descartes*. In 1670, he moved to The Hague, where he spent the rest of his life. During his last years, Spinoza wrote a Hebrew grammar, a scientific treatise on the rainbow, and the *Tractatus Politicus*.

Philosophical Overview

Spinoza's aim in the *Ethics* is to present a new vision of ethics founded on metaphysics. He rejects Descartes' mind/body dualism, as well as a universe/God dualism. Instead, he argues that there is only one substance, Nature or God, and claims that the understanding of this oneness is the highest possible good.

Substance

The main point of Part I of the *Ethics* is that there can be only one substance, called 'God' or 'Nature.' God is not an entity distinct from the universe, and mind and matter are just two of the infinite attributes of the one substance. Substance exists in itself, independent of anything else, and 'is conceived through itself.' The only thing that qualifies as being conceived through itself is something that does not depend on any external causes, and that is Nature as a whole. Since everything must have a cause, substance must be its own cause, and, therefore, it must exist. However, only something infinite can be its own cause, and there can only be one infinite substance.

Spinoza tries to prove that God with infinite attributes necessarily exists, and that there can be only one such substance. To prove that there is only one substance, Spinoza argues that

A. *Substance must exist, or there exists at least one substance* (Ethics I.5 and I.7); *and*
B. *There can be only one substance* (Ethics I.14) *because substance must be infinite* (Ethics I.8 and I.11).

To prove that substance must exist, Spinoza demonstrates that it cannot be caused by anything but itself. This is true, he argues, because there cannot be two substances of the same kind (*Ethics* I.5), and that substances of different kinds cannot cause each other (*Ethics* I.6). To prove that only one substance can exist, Spinoza argues that substance has all infinite attributes (*Ethics* I.11), and there cannot be two substances with the same attribute (*Ethics* I.5). In conclusion, the only substance is Nature as a whole. The substance must be infinite and it necessarily exists, so it can be identified with God.

In effect, Spinoza shows how a Rationalistic view of explanation and the standard definition of 'substance' imply that there is only one substance. He defines substance as an independent existent, and his Rationalism interprets the word 'independent' so strictly that nothing but Nature as a whole counts as independent. Because he assimilates causation to logical implication, Spinoza assumes that the conception of any thing must include its explanation, which implies that no substance can be conceived in isolation. Descartes' philosophy is inconsistent because it involves the traditional definition of substance and the Rationalist view of causation, and yet it maintains that God is not the only substance. Descartes refers to minds and bodies as 'created substances,' which according to Spinoza is a contradiction in terms.

Finite Modes

Finite modes are what we normally call individual entities, such as particular persons and physical objects. According to Spinoza, these are not substances; they are merely modifications of the attributes of the one substance. This implies that finite modes are not real. They are not different parts of the one substance, because substance is indivisible, without any parts (*Ethics* I.13). Nature is really a single individual that exists necessarily and timelessly, and that is indivisible and infinite. The viewpoint of 'the common order of nature,' or our normal view of the world as consisting of many finite and transitory things, is just an illusion. Hence, Spinoza appears to mean that particular things are not really objects at all. They are properties of God, expressed in determinate ways. For example, this book is the attribute extension, modified in a specific way.

Causality and Science

According to Spinoza, God is the immanent cause of all things (*Ethics* I.18). The Divine Nature comprises the basic laws of physics through the nature of the attribute extension. However, he also claims that every finite mode must be conditioned by another finite mode ad infinitum (*Ethics* I.28). Combining these two statements, this means that any particular event is determined by an earlier state of the universe, given these general laws of Nature. In Spinoza's terminology, earlier finite modes and the Divine Nature jointly imply the existence of any finite mode. In this sense, God is the immanent cause of the world rather than being its transcendental creator.

In this way, Spinoza advocates the idea of a complete and unified physical science. Any physical change is a completely determined effect within a closed set of physical causes and laws, and this implies the possibility of a complete and scientific physical explanation of any physical event. This is a claim that Descartes' dualism must deny.

God has an infinite number of attributes. Spinoza defines an attribute as being that which the intellect perceives as the essence of substance. Because God is infinite, there are infinite ways of conceiving him. However, we are acquainted with only two attributes, thought and extension. Spinoza claims that each attribute must be conceived through itself (*Ethics* I.10). This means that, for instance, any physical event must be explained through the attribute of extension and its modes alone. The explanation should not involve a reference to the mental. Once again, this rebuts Descartes' dualism.

The Nature of the Mind

At *Ethics* II.7, Spinoza asserts that the order and connection of ideas are the same as the order and connection of extended things. Thought and extension are not two separate substances, but different attributes of the one substance. A spatially extended mode and the idea of that mode are one and the same, but are expressed through different attributes. There is only one chain of modes, but it can be viewed through the attributes. The same point applies to the relation between the human mind and body. The mind is the same mode as the body but apprehended through the attribute of thought rather than that of physical extension.

In this way, Spinoza rejects Descartes' substance dualism, replacing it with an attributive dualism, according to which thought and extension are two attributes of the one substance. Spinoza also rejects Descartes' claim that the mind and body interact. Since the mind and the body are the same mode, there can be no question of any interaction between them. In other words, according to Spinoza, we can view a human being through the attribute of extension as a material body, subject to and governed entirely by physical laws. Alternatively, we can conceive of a person through the attribute of thought as an idea, governed entirely by the laws of thought. These two ways of conceiving the same finite mode are self-contained, and, thus, there can be no interaction between the physical and the mental. The same point applies to the universe as a whole.

Ethics

Despite the fact that he appears to be a determinist, Spinoza does have a positive theory of human freedom, which is the basis of his ethical system. He contrasts freedom with constraint rather than with necessity. To act freely is not to act from an uncaused mental decision, but rather from the necessity of one's own nature. Human freedom resides in the power of reason to control the emotions, because reason is determined not by external causes but internally.

In the grip of passions, we appear to be under the power of external forces; but, as soon as we form a clear and distinct idea of a passion, it ceases to be one, and we are freed. In this way, a clear understanding that all things are necessary gives the mind power over the passions. This understanding, which liberates us from the bondage of negative emotions, instills in us an intellectual love of God.

THE ETHICS

Perhaps the most difficult part of *The Ethics* is Spinoza's argument that God with infinite attributes necessarily exists, and that there can be only one such substance. The argument has two basic parts:

1. *There is at least one substance, which exists necessarily (Ethics I.5 and I.7).*
2. *There can be only one infinite substance (Ethics I.8 and I.11).*

Proposition I.5: There cannot be two substances of the same nature or attribute.

Two substances with the same attributes cannot be distinguished by their attributes. Also, two such substances cannot be distinguished by their modifications, because substance must be conceived through itself.

Proposition I.7: It pertains to the nature of a substance to exist.

Substance cannot be caused by anything external to itself, so it must be its own cause. Therefore, existence belongs to its essence. A substance cannot be caused by something external to itself for two reasons. First, if it were, then knowledge of it would depend on knowledge of something else, which is impossible. Second, only a substance could be the external cause of another substance. But even this is impossible because there cannot be two substances with the same attribute (*Ethics* I.5); and substances with different attributes have nothing in common and, thus, could not causally affect each other.

Proposition I.8: Every substance is necessarily infinite.

It is impossible for a substance to be finite with respect to its attribute, because, if it were, it would have to be limited by something else with the same attribute, and there cannot be two substances with the same attribute (*Ethics* I.5).

Proposition I.11: God necessarily exists.

Spinoza defines God as a substance that has an infinite number of attributes. By *Ethics I.7*, substance must exist. Furthermore, there cannot be a cause of God's nonexistence. Such a cause could not come from God's own nature, for that would be an imperfection and God is all-perfect. But neither could such a cause come from anything outside God, for a substance of another nature could have nothing in common with God.

Proposition I.14: Except God, no substance can be conceived.

There can be no rational reason for another substance besides God, and everything that exists must be capable of explanation. Any substance besides God would have to be explicable in terms of one of God's infinite attributes, but in that case there would have to be two substances with the same attribute, which is impossible (*Ethics* I.5).

Part I
Concerning God

DEFINITIONS

I. By that which is *self-caused*, I mean that of which the essence involves existence, or that of which the nature is only conceivable as existent.

II. A thing is called *finite after its kind*, when it can be limited by another thing of the same nature; for instance, a body is called finite because we always conceive another greater body. So, also, a thought is limited by another thought, but a body is not limited by thought, nor a thought by body.

III. By *substance*, I mean that which is in itself, and is conceived through itself: in other words, that of which a conception can be formed independently of any other conception.

IV. By *attribute*, I mean that which the intellect perceives as constituting the essence of substance.

V. By *mode*, I mean the modifications of substance, or that which exists in, and is conceived through, something other than itself.

VI. By *God*, I mean a being absolutely infinite—that is, a substance consisting in infinite attributes, of which each expresses eternal and infinite essentiality.

Explanation.—I say absolutely infinite, not infinite after its kind: for, of a thing infinite only after its kind, infinite attributes may be denied; but that which is absolutely infinite, contains in its essence whatever expresses reality, and involves no negation.

VII. That thing is called free, which exists solely by the necessity of its own nature, and of which the action is determined by itself alone. On the other hand, that thing is necessary, or rather constrained, which is determined by something external to itself to a fixed and definite method of existence or action.

VIII. By *eternity*, I mean existence itself, in so far as it is conceived necessarily to follow solely from the definition of that which is eternal.

Explanation.—Existence of this kind is conceived as an eternal truth, like the essence of a thing, and, therefore, cannot be explained by means of continuance or time, though continuance may be conceived without a beginning or end.

AXIOMS

I. Everything which exists, exists either in itself or in something else.

II. That which cannot be conceived through anything else must be conceived through itself.

III. From a given definite cause an effect necessarily follows; and, on the other hand, if no definite cause be granted, it is impossible that an effect can follow.

IV. The knowledge of an effect depends on and involves the knowledge of a cause.

V. Things which have nothing in common cannot be understood, the one by means of the other; the conception of one does not involve the conception of the other.

VI. A true idea must correspond with its ideate or object.

VII. If a thing can be conceived as non-existing, its essence does not involve existence.

PROPOSITIONS

PROP. I. *Substance is by nature prior to its modifications.*

Proof.—This is clear from Deff. iii. and v.

PROP. II. *Two substances, whose attributes are different, have nothing in common.*

Proof.—Also evident from Def. iii. For each must exist in itself, and be conceived through itself; in other words, the conception of one does not imply the conception of the other.

PROP. III. *Things which have nothing in common cannot be one the cause of the other.*

Proof.—If they have nothing in common, it follows that one cannot be apprehended by means of the other (Ax. v.), and, therefore, one cannot be the cause of the other (Ax. iv.). Q.E.D.

PROP. IV. *Two or more distinct things are distinguished one from the other, either by the difference of the attributes of the substances, or by the difference of their modifications.*

Proof.—Everything which exists, exists either in itself or in something else (Ax. i.),—that is (by Deff. iii. and v.), nothing is granted in addition to the understanding, except substance and its modifications. Nothing is, therefore, given besides the understanding, by which several things may be distinguished one from the other, except the substances, or, in other words (see Ax. iv.), their attributes and modifications. Q.E.D.

PROP. V. *There cannot exist in the universe two or more substances having the same nature or attribute.*

Proof.—If several distinct substances be granted, they must be distinguished one from the other, either by the difference of their attributes, or by the difference of their modifications (Prop. iv.). If only by the difference of their attributes, it will be granted that there cannot be more than one with an identical attribute. If by the difference of their modifications— as substance is naturally prior to its modifications (Prop. i.),—it follows that setting the modifications aside, and considering substance in itself, that is truly, (Deff. iii. and vi.), there cannot be conceived one substance different from another,—that is (by Prop. iv.), there cannot be granted several substances, but one substance only. Q.E.D.

PROP. VI. *One substance cannot be produced by another substance.*

Proof.—It is impossible that there should be in the universe two substances with an identical attribute, *i.e.* which have anything common to them both (Prop. ii.), and, therefore (Prop. iii.), one cannot be the cause of another, neither can one be produced by the other. Q.E.D.

Corollary.—Hence it follows that a substance cannot be produced by anything external to itself. For in the universe nothing is granted, save substances and their modifications (as appears from Ax. i. and Deff. iii. and v.). Now (by the last Prop.) substance cannot be produced by another substance, therefore it cannot be produced by anything external to itself. Q.E.D. This is shown still more readily by the absurdity of the contradictory. For, if substance be produced by an external cause, the knowledge of it would depend on the knowledge of its cause (Ax. iv.), and (by Def. iii.) it would itself not be substance.

PROP. VII. *Existence belongs to the nature of substance.*

Proof.—Substance cannot be produced by anything external (Corollary, Prop. vi.), it must, therefore, be its own cause—that is, its essence necessarily involves existence, or existence belongs to its nature.

PROP. VIII. *Every substance is necessarily infinite.*

Proof.—There can only be one substance with an identical attribute, and existence follows from its nature (Prop. vii.); its nature, therefore, involves existence, either as finite or infinite. It does not exist as finite, for (by Def. ii.) it would then be limited by something else of the same kind, which would also necessarily exist (Prop. vii.); and there would be two substances with an identical attribute, which is absurd (Prop. v.). It therefore exists as infinite. Q.E.D.

Note I.—As finite existence involves a partial negation, and infinite existence is the absolute affirmation of the given nature, it follows (solely from Prop. vii.) that every substance is necessarily infinite.

Note II.—No doubt it will be difficult for those who think about things loosely, and have not been accustomed to know them by their primary causes, to comprehend the demonstration of Prop. vii: for such persons make no distinction between the modifications of substances and the substances themselves, and are ignorant of the manner in which things are produced; hence they attribute to substances the beginning which they observe in natural objects. Those who are ignorant of true causes, make complete confusion—think that trees might talk just as well as men—that men might be formed from stones as well as from seed; and imagine that any form might be changed into any other. So, also, those who confuse the two natures, divine and human, readily attribute human passions to the deity, especially so long as they do not know how passions originate in the mind. But, if people would consider the nature of substance, they would have no doubt about the truth of Prop. vii. In fact, this proposition would be a universal axiom, and accounted a truism. For, by substance, would be understood that which is in itself, and is conceived through itself—that is, something of which the conception requires not the conception of anything else; whereas modifications exist in something external to themselves, and a conception of them is formed by means of a conception of the thing in which they exist. Therefore, we may have true ideas of non-existent modifications; for, although they may have no *actual* existence apart from the conceiving intellect, yet their essence is so involved in something external to themselves that they may through it be conceived. Whereas the only truth substances can have, external to the intellect, must consist in their existence, because they are conceived through themselves. Therefore, for a person to say that he has a clear and distinct—that is, a true—idea of a substance, but that he is not sure whether such substance exists, would be the same as if he said that he had a true idea, but was not sure whether or no it was false (a little consideration will make this plain); or if anyone affirmed that substance is created, it would be the same as saying that a false idea was true—in short, the height of absurdity. It must, then, necessarily be admitted that the existence of substance as its essence is an eternal truth. And we can hence conclude by another process of reasoning—that there is but one such substance. I think that this may profitably be done at once; and, in order to proceed regularly with the demonstration, we must premise:—

1. The true definition of a thing neither involves nor expresses anything beyond the nature of the thing defined. From this it follows that—

2. No definition implies or expresses a certain number of individuals, inasmuch as it expresses nothing beyond the nature of the thing defined. For instance, the definition of a triangle expresses nothing beyond the actual nature of a triangle: it does not imply any fixed number of triangles.

3. There is necessarily for each individual existent thing a cause why it should exist.

4. This cause of existence must either be contained in the nature and definition of the thing defined, or must be postulated apart from such definition.

It therefore follows that, if a given number of individual things exist in nature, there must be some cause for the existence of exactly that number, neither more nor less. For example, if twenty men exist in the universe (for simplicity's sake, I will suppose them existing simultaneously, and to have had no predecessors), and we want to account for the existence of these twenty men, it will not be enough to show the cause of human existence in general; we must also show why there are exactly twenty men, neither more nor less: for a cause must be assigned for the existence of each individual. Now this cause cannot be contained in the actual nature of man, for the true definition of man does not involve any consideration of the number twenty. Consequently, the cause for the existence of these twenty men, and, consequently, of each of them, must necessarily be sought externally to each individual. Hence we may lay down the absolute rule, that everything which may consist of several individuals must have an external cause. And, as it has been shown already that existence appertains to the nature of substance, existence must necessarily be included in its definition; and from its definition alone existence must be deducible. But from its definition (as we have shown, Notes ii., iii.), we cannot infer the existence of several substances; therefore it follows that there is only one substance of the same nature. *Q.E.D.*

PROP. IX. *The more reality or being a thing has the greater the number of its attributes* (Def. iv.).

PROP. X. *Each particular attribute of the one substance must be conceived through itself.*

Proof.—An attribute is that which the intellect perceives of substance, as constituting its essence (Def. iv.), and, therefore, must be conceived through itself (Def. iii.). *Q.E.D.*

Note.—It is thus evident that, though two attributes are, in fact, conceived as distinct—that is, one without the help of the other—yet we cannot, therefore, conclude that they constitute two entities, or two different substances. For it is the nature of substance that each of its attributes is conceived through itself, inasmuch as all the attributes it has have always existed simultaneously in it, and none could be produced by any other; but each expresses the reality or being of substance. It is, then, far from an absurdity to ascribe several attributes to one substance: for nothing in nature is more clear than that each and every entity must be conceived under some attribute, and that its reality or being is in proportion to the number of its attributes expressing necessity or eternity and infinity. Consequently it is abundantly clear, that an absolutely infinite being must necessarily be defined as consisting in infinite attributes, each of which expresses a certain eternal and infinite essence.

If anyone now ask, by what sign shall he be able to distinguish different substances, let him read the following propositions, which show that there is but one substance in the universe, and that it is absolutely infinite, wherefore such a sign would be sought for in vain.

PROP. XI. *God, or substance, consisting of infinite attributes, of which each expresses eternal and infinite essentiality, necessarily exists.*

Proof.—If this be denied, conceive, if possible, that God does not exist: then his essence does not involve existence. But this (by Prop. vii.) is absurd. Therefore God necessarily exists.

Another proof.—Of everything whatsoever a cause or reason must be assigned, either for its existence, or for its non-existence—*e.g.* if a triangle exist, a reason or cause must be granted for its existence; if, on the contrary, it does not exist, a cause must also be granted, which prevents it from existing, or annuls its existence. This reason or cause must either be contained in the nature of the thing in question, or be external to it. For instance, the reason for the non-existence of a square circle is indicated in its nature, namely, because it would involve a contradiction. On the other hand, the existence of substance follows also solely from its nature, inasmuch as its nature involves existence. (See Prop. vii.)

But the reason for the existence of a triangle or a circle does not follow from the nature of those figures, but from the order of universal nature in extension. From the latter it must follow, either that a triangle necessarily exists, or that it is impossible that it should exist. So much is self-evident. It follows therefrom that a thing necessarily exists, if no cause or reason be granted which prevents its existence.

If, then, no cause or reason can be given, which prevents the existence of God, or which destroys his existence, we must certainly conclude that he necessarily does exist. If such a reason or cause should be given, it must either be drawn from the very nature of God, or be external to him—that is, drawn from another substance of another nature. For if it were of the same nature, God, by that very fact, would be admitted to exist. But substance of another nature could have nothing in common with God (by Prop. ii.), and therefore would be unable either to cause or to destroy his existence.

As, then, a reason or cause which would annul the divine existence cannot be drawn from anything external to the divine nature, such cause must perforce, if God does not exist, be drawn from God's own nature, which would involve a contradiction. To make such an affirmation about a being absolutely infinite and supremely perfect, is absurd; therefore, neither in the nature of God, nor externally to his nature, can a cause or reason be assigned which would annul his existence. Therefore, God necessarily exists. *Q.E.D.*

Another proof.—The potentiality of non-existence is a negation of power, and contrariwise the potentiality of existence is a power, as is obvious. If, then, that which necessarily exists is nothing but finite beings, such finite beings are more powerful than a being absolutely infinite, which is obviously absurd; therefore, either nothing exists, or else a being absolutely infinite necessarily exists also. Now we exist either in ourselves, or in something else which necessarily exists (see Axiom i. and Prop. vii.). Therefore a being absolutely infinite—in other words, God (Def. vi.)—necessarily exists. *Q.E.D.*

Note.—In this last proof, I have purposely shown God's existence *à posteriori,* so that the proof might be more easily followed, not because, from the same premises, God's existence does not follow *à priori.* For, as the potentiality of existence is a power, it follows that, in proportion as reality increases in the nature of a thing, so also will it increase its strength for existence. Therefore a being absolutely infinite, such as God, has from himself an absolutely infinite power of existence, and hence he does absolutely exist. Perhaps there will be many who will be unable to see the force of this proof, inasmuch as they are accustomed only to consider those things which flow from external causes. Of such things, they see that those which quickly come to pass—that is, quickly come into existence—quickly also disappear; whereas they regard as more difficult of accomplishment—that is, not so easily brought into existence—those things which they conceive as more complicated.

However, to do away with this misconception, I need not here show the measure of truth in the proverb, "What comes quickly, goes quickly," nor discuss whether, from the point of view of universal nature, all things are equally easy, or otherwise: I need only remark, that I am not here speaking of things, which come to pass through causes external to themselves, but only of substances which (by Prop. vi.) cannot be produced by any external cause. Things which are produced by external causes, whether they consist of many parts or few, owe whatsoever perfection or reality they possess solely to the efficacy of their external cause, and therefore their existence arises solely from the perfection of their external cause, not from their own. Contrariwise, whatsoever perfection is possessed by substance is due to no external cause; wherefore the existence of substance must arise solely from its own nature, which is nothing else but its essence. Thus, the perfection of a thing does not annul its existence, but, on the contrary, asserts it. Imperfection, on the other hand, does annul it; therefore we cannot be more certain of the existence of anything, than of the existence of a being absolutely infinite or perfect—that is, of God. For inasmuch as his essence excludes all imperfection, and involves absolute perfection, all cause for doubt concerning his existence is done away, and the utmost certainty on the question is given. This, I think, will be evident to every moderately attentive reader.

PROP. XII. *No attribute of substance can be conceived from which it would follow that substance can be divided.*

Proof.—The parts into which substance as thus conceived would be divided, either will retain the nature of substance, or they will not. If the former, then (by Prop. viii.) each part will necessarily be infinite, and (by Prop. vi.) self-caused, and (by Prop. v.) will perforce consist of a different attribute, so that, in that case, several substances could be formed out of one substance, which (by Prop. vi.) is absurd. Moreover, the parts (by Prop. ii.) would have nothing in common with their whole, and the whole (by Def. iv. and Prop. x.) could both exist and be conceived without its parts, which everyone will admit to be absurd. If we adopt the second alternative—namely, that the parts will not retain the nature of substance—then, if the whole substance were divided into equal parts, it would lose the nature of substance, and would cease to exist, which (by Prop. vii.) is absurd.

PROP. XIII. *Substance absolutely infinite is indivisible.*

Proof.—If it could be divided, the parts into which it was divided would either retain the nature of absolutely infinite substance, or they would not. If the former, we should have several substances of the same nature, which (by Prop. v.) is absurd. If the latter, then (by Prop. vii.) substance absolutely infinite could cease to exist, which (by Prop. xi.) is also absurd.

Corollary.—It follows, that no substance, and consequently no extended substance, in so far as it is substance, is divisible.

Note.—The indivisibility of substance may be more easily understood as follows. The nature of substance can only be conceived as infinite, and by a part of substance, nothing else can be understood than finite substance, which (by Prop. viii.) involves a manifest contradiction.

PROP. XIV. *Besides God no substance can be granted or conceived.*

Proof.—As God is a being absolutely infinite, of whom no attribute that expresses the essence of substance can be denied (by Def. vi.), and he necessarily exists (by Prop. xi.); if any substance besides God were granted, it would have to be explained by some attribute of God, and thus two substances with the same attribute would exist, which (by Prop. v.) is absurd; therefore, besides God no substance can be granted, or, consequently, be conceived. If it could be conceived, it would necessarily have to be conceived as existent; but this (by the first part of this proof) is absurd. Therefore, besides God no substance can be granted or conceived. Q.E.D.

Corollary I.—Clearly, therefore: 1. God is one, that is (by Def. vi.) only one substance can be granted in the universe, and that substance is absolutely infinite, as we have already indicated (in the note to Prop. x.).

Corollary II.—It follows: 2. That extension and thought are either attributes of God or (by Ax. i.) accidents (*affectiones*) of the attributes of God.

PROP. XV. *Whatsoever is, is in God, and without God nothing can be, or be conceived.*

Proof.—Besides God, no substance is granted or can be conceived (by Prop. xiv.), that is (by Def. iii.) nothing which is in itself and is conceived through itself. But modes (by Def. v.) can neither be, nor be conceived without substance; wherefore they can only be in the divine nature, and can only through it be conceived. But substances and modes form the sum total of existence (by Ax. i.), therefore, without God nothing can be, or be conceived. *Q.E.D.*

PROP. XVI. *From the necessity of the divine nature must follow an infinite number of things in infinite ways—that is, all things which can fall within the sphere of infinite intellect.*

Proof.—This proposition will be clear to everyone, who remembers that from the given definition of any thing the intellect infers several properties, which really necessarily follow therefrom (that is, from the actual essence of the thing defined); and it infers more properties in proportion as the definition of the thing expresses more reality, that is, in proportion as the essence of the thing defined involves more reality. Now, as the divine nature has absolutely infinite attributes (by Def. vi.), of which each expresses infinite essence after its kind, it follows that from the necessity of its nature an infinite number of things (that is, everything which can fall within the sphere of an infinite intellect) must necessarily follow. *Q.E.D.*

Corollary I.—Hence it follows, that God is the efficient cause of all that can fall within the sphere of an infinite intellect.

Corollary II.—It also follows that God is a cause in himself, and not through an accident of his nature.

Corollary III.—It follows, thirdly, that God is the absolutely first cause.

PROP. XVIII. *God is the indwelling and not the transient cause of all things.*

Proof.—All things which are, are in God, and must be conceived through God (by Prop. xv.), there-

fore (by Prop. xvi., Coroll. i.) God is the cause of those things which are in him. This is our first point. Further, besides God there can be no substance (by Prop. xiv.), that is nothing in itself external to God. This is our second point. God, therefore, is the indwelling and not the transient cause of all things. *Q.E.D.*

PROP. XXVIII.—*Every individual thing, or everything which is finite and has a conditioned existence, cannot exist or be conditioned to act, unless it be conditioned for existence and action by a cause other than itself, which also is finite, and has a conditioned existence; and likewise this cause cannot in its turn exist, or be conditioned to act, unless it be conditioned for existence and action by another cause, which also is finite, and has a conditioned existence, and so on to infinity.*

Proof.—Whatsoever is conditioned to exist and act, has been thus conditioned by God (by Prop. xxvi. and Prop. xxiv., Coroll.)

But that which is finite, and has a conditioned existence, cannot be produced by the absolute nature of any attribute of God; for whatsoever follows from the absolute nature of any attribute of God is infinite and eternal (by Prop. xxi.). It must, therefore, follow from some attribute of God, in so far as the said attribute is considered as in some way modified; for substance and modes make up the sum total of existence (by Ax. i. and Def. iii., v.), while modes are merely modifications of the attributes of God. But from God, or from any of his attributes, in so far as the latter is modified by a modification infinite and eternal, a conditioned thing cannot follow. Wherefore it must follow from, or be conditioned for, existence and action by God or one of his attributes, in so far as the latter are modified by some modification which is finite, and has a conditioned existence. This is our first point. Again, this cause or this modification (for the reason by which we established the first part of this proof) must in its turn be conditioned by another cause, which also is finite, and has a conditioned existence, and, again, this last by another (for the same reason); and so on (for the same reason) to infinity. *Q.E.D.*

Note.—As certain things must be produced immediately by God, namely those things which necessarily follow from his absolute nature, through the means of these primary attributes, which, nevertheless, can neither exist nor be conceived without God, it follows:— 1. That God is absolutely the proximate cause of those things immediately produced by him. I say absolutely, not after his kind, as is usually stated. For the effects of God cannot either exist or be conceived without a cause (Prop. xv. and Prop. xxiv., Coroll.). 2. That God cannot properly be styled the remote cause of individual things, except for the sake of distinguishing these from what he immediately produces, or rather from what follows from his absolute nature. For, by a remote cause, we understand a cause which is in no way conjoined to the effect. But all things which are, are in God, and so depend on God, that without him they can neither be nor be conceived.

Prop. XXIX. *Nothing in the universe is contingent, but all things are conditioned to exist and operate in a particular manner by the necessity of the divine nature.*

Proof.—Whatsoever is, is in God (Prop. xv.). But God cannot be called a thing contingent. For (by Prop. xi.) he exists necessarily, and not contingently. Further, the modes of the divine nature follow therefrom necessarily, and not contingently (Prop. xvi.); and they thus follow, whether we consider the divine nature absolutely, or whether we consider it as in any way conditioned to act (Prop. xxvii.). Further, God is not only the cause of these modes, in so far as they simply exist (by Prop. xxiv., Coroll.), but also in so far as they are considered as conditioned for operating in a particular manner (Prop. xxvi.). If they be not conditioned by God (Prop. xxvi.), it is impossible, and not contingent, that they should condition themselves; contrariwise, if they be conditioned by God, it is impossible, and not contingent, that they should render themselves unconditioned. Wherefore all things are conditioned by the necessity of the divine nature, not only to exist, but also to exist and operate in a particular manner, and there is nothing that is contingent. Q.E.D.

Note.—Before going any further, I wish here to explain, what we should understand by nature viewed as active (*natura naturans*), and nature viewed as passive (*natura naturata*). I say to explain, or rather call attention to it, for I think that, from what has been said, it is sufficiently clear, that by nature viewed as active we should understand that which is in itself, and is conceived through itself, or those attributes of substance, which express eternal and infinite essence, in other words (Prop. xiv., Coroll. i., and Prop. xvii., Coroll. ii.) God, in so far as he is considered as a free cause.

By nature viewed as passive I understand all that which follows from the necessity of the nature of God, or of any of the attributes of God, that is, all the modes of the attributes of God, in so far as they are considered as things which are in God, and which without God cannot exist or be conceived.

Prop. XXXII. *Will cannot be called a free cause, but only a necessary cause.*

Proof.—Will is only a particular mode of thinking, like intellect; therefore (by Prop. xxviii.) no volition can exist, nor be conditioned to act, unless it be conditioned by some cause other than itself, which cause is conditioned by a third cause, and so on to infinity. But if will be supposed infinite, it must also be conditioned to exist and act by God, not by virtue of his being substance absolutely infinite, but by virtue of his possessing an attribute which expresses the infinite and eternal essence of thought (by Prop. xxiii.). Thus, however it be conceived, whether as finite or infinite, it requires a cause by which it should be conditioned to exist and act. Thus (Def. vii.) it cannot be called a free cause, but only a necessary or constrained cause. Q.E.D.

Coroll. I.—Hence it follows, first, that God does not act according to freedom of the will.

Coroll. II.—It follows, secondly, that will and intellect stand in the same relation to the nature of God as do motion, and rest, and absolutely all natural phenomena, which must be conditioned by God (Prop. xxix.) to exist and act in a particular manner. For will, like the rest, stands in need of a cause, by which it is conditioned to exist and act in a particular manner. And although, when will or intellect be granted, an infinite number of results may follow, yet God cannot on that account be said to act from freedom of the will, any more than the infinite number of results from motion and rest would justify us in saying that motion and rest act by free will. Wherefore will no more appertains to God than does anything else in nature, but stands in the same relation to him as motion, rest, and the like, which we have shown to follow from the necessity of the divine nature, and to be conditioned by it to exist and act in a particular manner.

Prop. XXXIII. *Things could not have been brought into being by God in any manner or in any order different from that which has in fact obtained.*

Proof.—All things necessarily follow from the nature of God (Prop. xvi.), and by the nature of God are conditioned to exist and act in a particular way (Prop. xxix.). If things, therefore, could have been of a different nature, or have been conditioned to act in a different way, so that the order of nature would have been different, God's nature would also have been able to be different from what it now is; and therefore (by Prop. xi.) that different nature also would have perforce existed, and consequently there would have been able to be two or more Gods. This (by Prop. xiv., Coroll. i.) is absurd. Therefore things could not have been brought into being by God in any other manner, &c. *Q.E.D.*

Prop. XXXIV. *God's power is identical with his essence.*

Proof.—From the sole necessity of the essence of God it follows that God is the cause of himself (Prop. xi.) and of all things (Prop. xvi. and Coroll.). Wherefore the power of God, by which he and all things are and act, is identical with his essence. *Q.E.D.*

Part II

Of the Nature and Origin of the Mind

PREFACE

I now pass on to explaining the results, which must necessarily follow from the essence of God, or of the eternal and infinite being; not, indeed, all of them (for we proved in Part. i., Prop. xvi., that an infinite number must follow in an infinite number of ways), but only those which are able to lead us, as it were by the hand, to the knowledge of the human mind and its highest blessedness.

DEFINITIONS

I. By *body* I mean a mode which expresses in a certain determinate manner the essence of God, in so far as he is considered as an extended thing. (See Pt. i., Prop. xxv. Coroll.)

II. I consider as belonging to the essence of a thing that, which being given, the thing is necessarily given also, and, which being removed, the thing is necessarily removed also; in other words, that with-out which the thing, and which itself without the thing, can neither be nor be conceived.

III. By *idea,* I mean the mental conception which is formed by the mind as a thinking thing.

Explanation.—I say *conception* rather than perception, because the word perception seems to imply that the mind is passive in respect to the object; whereas conception seems to express an activity of the mind.

IV. By *an adequate idea,* I mean an idea which, in so far as it is considered in itself, without relation to the object, has all the properties or intrinsic marks of a true idea.

Explanation.—I say *intrinsic,* in order to exclude that mark which is extrinsic, namely, the agreement between the idea and its object (*ideatum*).

V. *Duration* is the indefinite continuance of existing.

Explanation.—I say *indefinite,* because it cannot be determined through the existence itself of the existing thing, or by its efficient cause, which necessarily gives the existence of the thing, but does not take it away.

VI. *Reality* and *perfection* I use as synonymous terms.

VII. By *particular things,* I mean things which are finite and have a conditioned existence; but if several individual things concur in one action, so as to be all simultaneously the effect of one cause, I consider them all, so far, as one particular thing.

AXIOMS

I. The essence of man does not involve necessary existence, that is, it may, in the order of nature, come to pass that this or that man does or does not exist.

II. Man thinks.

III. Modes of thinking, such as love, desire, or any other of the passions, do not take place, unless there be in the same individual an idea of the thing loved, desired, &c. But the idea can exist without the presence of any other mode of thinking.

IV. We perceive that a certain body is affected in many ways.

V. We feel and perceive no particular things, save bodies and modes of thought.

N.B. *The postulates are given after the conclusion of* Prop. xiii.

PROPOSITIONS

Prop. I. *Thought is an attribute of God, or God is a thinking thing.*

Proof.—Particular thoughts, or this or that thought, are modes which, in a certain conditioned manner, express the nature of God (Pt. i., Prop. xxv., Coroll.). God therefore possesses the attribute (Pt. i., Def. v.) of which the concept is involved in all particular thoughts, which latter are conceived thereby. Thought, therefore, is one of the infinite attributes of God, which express God's eternal and infinite essence (Pt. i., Def. vi.). In other words, God is a thinking thing. Q.E.D.

Prop. II. *Extension is an attribute of God, or God is an extended thing.*

Proof.—The proof of this proposition is similar to that of the last.

Prop. III. *In God there is necessarily the idea not only of his essence, but also of all things which necessarily follow from his essence.*

Proof.—God (by the first Prop. of this Part) can think an infinite number of things in infinite ways, or (what is the same thing, by Prop. xvi., Part i.) can form the idea of his essence, and of all things which necessarily follow therefrom. Now all that is in the power of God necessarily is. (Pt. i., Prop. xxxv.) Therefore, such an idea as we are considering necessarily is, and in God alone. Q.E.D. (Part i., Prop. xv.)

Prop. IV. *The idea of God, from which an infinite number of things follow in infinite ways, can only be one.*

Proof.—Infinite intellect comprehends nothing save the attributes of God and his modifications (Part i., Prop. xxx.). Now God is one (Part i., Prop. xiv., Coroll.). Therefore the idea of God, wherefrom an infinite number of things follow in infinite ways, can only be one. Q.E.D.

Prop. V. *The actual being of ideas owns God as its cause, only in so far as he is considered as a thinking thing, not in so far as he is unfolded in any other attribute; that is, the ideas both of the attributes of God and of particular things do not own as their efficient cause their objects (ideata) or the things perceived, but God himself in so far as he is a thinking thing.*

Proof.—This proposition is evident from Prop. iii. of this Part. We there drew the conclusion, that God can form the idea of his essence, and of all things which follow necessarily therefrom, solely because he is a thinking thing, and not because he is the object of his own idea. Wherefore the actual being of ideas owns for cause God, in so far as he is a thinking thing. It may be differently proved as follows: the actual being of ideas is (obviously) a mode of thought, that is (Part i., Prop. xxv., Coroll.) a mode which expresses in a certain manner the nature of God, in so far as he is a thinking thing, and therefore (Part i., Prop. x.) involves the conception of no other attribute of God, and consequently (by Part i., Ax. iv.) is not the effect of any attribute save thought. Therefore the actual being of ideas owns God as its cause, in so far as he is considered as a thinking thing, &c. Q.E.D.

Prop. VI. *The modes of any given attribute are caused by God, in so far as he is considered through the attribute of which they are modes, and not in so far as he is considered through any other attribute.*

Proof.—Each attribute is conceived through itself, without any other (Part i., Prop. x.); wherefore the modes of each attribute involve the conception of that attribute, but not of any other. Thus (Part i., Ax. iv.) they are caused by God, only in so far as he is considered through the attribute whose modes they are, and not in so far as he is considered through any other. Q.E.D.

Corollary.—Hence the actual being of things, which are not modes of thought, does not follow from the divine nature, because that nature has prior knowledge of the things. Things represented in ideas follow, and are derived from their particular attribute, in the same manner, and with the same necessity as ideas follow (according to what we have shown) from the attribute of thought.

Prop. VII. *The order and connection of ideas is the same as the order and connection of things.*

Proof.—This proposition is evident from Part i., Ax. iv. For the idea of everything that is caused depends on a knowledge of the cause, whereof it is an effect.

Corollary.—Hence God's power of thinking is equal to his realized power of action—that is, whatsoever follows from the infinite nature of God in the world of extension (*formaliter*), follows without exception in the same order and connection from the idea of God in the world of thought (*objective*).

Note.—Before going any further, I wish to recall to mind what has been pointed out above—namely, that whatsoever can be perceived by the infinite intellect as constituting the essence of substance, belongs altogether only to one substance: consequently, substance thinking and substance extended are one and the same substance, comprehended now through one attribute, now through the other. So, also, a mode of extension and the idea of that mode are one and the same thing, though expressed in two ways. This truth seems to have been dimly recognized by those Jews who maintained that God, God's intellect, and the things understood by God are identical. For instance, a circle existing in nature, and the idea of a circle existing, which is also in God, are one and the same thing displayed through different attributes. Thus, whether we conceive nature under the attribute of extension, or under the attribute of thought, or under any other attribute, we shall find the same order, or one and the same chain of causes—that is, the same things following in either case.

I said that God is the cause of an idea—for instance, of the idea of a circle,—in so far as he is a thinking thing; and of a circle, in so far as he is an extended thing, simply because the actual being of the idea of a circle can only be perceived as a proximate cause through another mode of thinking, and that again through another, and so on to infinity; so that, so long as we consider things as modes of thinking, we must explain the order of the whole of nature, or the whole chain of causes, through the attribute of thought only. And, in so far as we consider things as modes of extension, we must explain the order of the whole of nature through the attribute of extension only; and so on, in the case of other attributes. Wherefore of things as they are in themselves God is really the cause, inasmuch as he consists of infinite attributes. I cannot for the present explain my meaning more clearly.

PROP. IX. *The idea of an individual thing actually existing is caused by God, not in so far as he is infinite, but in so far as he is considered as affected by another idea of a thing actually existing, of which he is the cause, in so far as he is affected by a third idea, and so on to infinity.*

Proof.—The idea of an individual thing actually existing is an individual mode of thinking, and is distinct from other modes (by the Corollary and Note to Prop. viii. of this part); thus (by Prop. vi. of this part) it is caused by God, in so far only as he is a thinking thing. But not (by Prop. xxviii. of Part i.) in so far as

he is a thing thinking absolutely, only in so far as he is considered as affected by another mode of thinking; and he is the cause of this latter, as being affected by a third, and so on to infinity. Now, the order and connection of ideas is (by Prop. vii. of this book) the same as the order and connection of causes. Therefore of a given individual idea another individual idea, or God, in so far as he is considered as modified by that idea, is the cause; and of this second idea God is the cause, in so far as he is affected by another idea, and so on to infinity. *Q.E.D.*

Corollary.—Whatsoever takes place in the individual object of any idea, the knowledge thereof is in God, in so far only as he has the idea of the object.

Proof.—Whatsoever takes place in the object of any idea, its idea is in God (by Prop. iii. of this part), not in so far as he is infinite, but in so far as he is considered as affected by another idea of an individual thing (by the last Prop.); but (by Prop. vii. of this part) the order and connection of ideas is the same as the order and connection of things. The knowledge, therefore, of that which takes place in any individual object will be in God, in so far only as he has the idea of that object. *Q.E.D.*

PROP. X. *The being of substance does not appertain to the essence of man—in other words, substance does not constitute the actual being of man.*

Proof.—The being of substance involves necessary existence (Part i., Prop. vii.). If, therefore, the being of substance appertains to the essence of man, substance being granted, man would necessarily be granted also (II. Def. ii.), and, consequently, man would necessarily exist, which is absurd (II. Ax. i.). Therefore, &c. *Q.E.D.*

Note.—This proposition may also be proved from I. v., in which it is shown that there cannot be two substances of the same nature; for as there may be many men, the being of substance is not that which constitutes the actual being of man. Again, the proposition is evident from the other properties of substance—namely, that substance is in its nature infinite, immutable, indivisible, &c., as anyone may see for himself.

Corollary.—Hence it follows, that the essence of man is constituted by certain modifications of the attributes of God. For (by the last Prop.) the being of substance does not belong to the essence of man. That essence therefore (by i. 15) is something which is in God, and which without God can neither be nor be conceived, whether it be a modification (i. 25 Coroll.), or a mode which expresses God's nature in a certain conditioned manner.

Prop. XI. *The first element, which constitutes the actual being of the human mind, is the idea of some particular thing actually existing.*

Proof.—The essence of man (by the Coroll. of the last Prop.) is constituted by certain modes of the attributes of God, namely (by II. Ax. ii.), by the modes of thinking, of all which (by II. Ax. iii.) the idea is prior in nature, and, when the idea is given, the other modes (namely, those of which the idea is prior in nature) must be in the same individual (by the same Axiom). Therefore an idea is the first element constituting the human mind. But not the idea of a non-existent thing, for then (II. viii. Coroll.) the idea itself cannot be said to exist; it must therefore be the idea of something actually existing. But not of an infinite thing. For an infinite thing (I. xxi., xxii.), must always necessarily exist; this would (by II. Ax. i.) involve an absurdity. Therefore the first element, which constitutes the actual being of the human mind, is the idea of something actually existing. *Q.E.D.*

Corollary.—Hence it follows, that the human mind is part of the infinite intellect of God; thus when we say, that the human mind perceives this or that, we make the assertion, that God has this or that idea, not in so far as he is infinite, but in so far as he is displayed through the nature of the human mind, or in so far as he constitutes the essence of the human mind; and when we say that God has this or that idea, not only in so far as he constitutes the essence of the human mind, but also in so far as he, simultaneously with the human mind, has the further idea of another thing, we assert that the human mind perceives a thing in part or inadequately.

Note.—Here, I doubt not, readers will come to a stand, and will call to mind many things which will cause them to hesitate; I therefore beg them to accompany me slowly, step by step, and not to pronounce on my statements, till they have read to the end.

Prop. XII. *Whatsoever comes to pass in the object of the idea, which constitutes the human mind, must be perceived by the human mind, or there will necessarily be an idea in the human mind of the said occurrence. That is, if the object of the idea constituting the human mind be a*

body, *nothing can take place in that body without being perceived by the mind.*

Proof.—Whatsoever comes to pass in the object of any idea, the knowledge thereof is necessarily in God (II. ix. Coroll.), in so far as he is considered as affected by the idea of the said object, that is (II. xi.), in so far as he constitutes the mind of anything. Therefore, whatsoever takes place in the object constituting the idea of the human mind, the knowledge thereof is necessarily in God, in so far as he constitutes the nature of the human mind; that is (by II. xi. Coroll,) the knowledge of the said thing will necessarily be in the mind, in other words the mind perceives it.

Prop. XIII. *The object of the idea constituting the human mind is the body, in other words a certain mode of extension which actually exists, and nothing else.*

Proof.—If indeed the body were not the object of the human mind, the ideas of the modifications of the body would not be in God (II. ix. Coroll.) in virtue of his constituting our mind, but in virtue of his constituting the mind of something else; that is (II. xi. Coroll.) the ideas of the modifications of the body would not be in our mind: now (by II. Ax. iv.) we do possess the ideas of the modifications of the body. Therefore the object of the idea constituting the human mind is the body, and the body as it actually exists (II. xi.). Further, if there were any other object of the idea constituting the mind besides body, then, as nothing can exist from which some effect does not follow (I. xxxvi.) there would necessarily have to be in our mind an idea, which would be the effect of that other object (II. xi.); but (II. Ax. v.) there is no such idea. Wherefore the object of our mind is the body as it exists, and nothing else. *Q.E.D.*

Note.—We thus comprehend, not only that the human mind is united to the body, but also the nature of the union between mind and body. However, no one will be able to grasp this adequately or distinctly, unless he first has adequate knowledge of the nature of our body. The propositions we have advanced hitherto have been entirely general, applying not more to men than to other individual things, all of which, though in different degrees, are animated. For of everything there is necessarily an idea in God, of which God is the cause, in the same way as there is an idea of the human body; thus whatever we have asserted of the idea of the human body must necessarily also be asserted of the idea of everything else. Still, on the other hand, we cannot deny that ideas, like objects, differ one from the other, one being more excellent than another and containing more reality, just as the object of one idea is more excellent than the object of another idea, and contains more reality.

Wherefore, in order to determine, wherein the human mind differs from other things, and wherein it surpasses them, it is necessary for us to know the nature of its object, that is, of the human body. What this nature is, I am not able here to explain, nor is it necessary for the proof of what I advance, that I should do so. I will only say generally, that in proportion as any given body is more fitted than others for doing many actions or receiving many impressions at once, so also is the mind, of which it is the object, more fitted than others for forming many simultaneous perceptions; and the more the actions of one body depend on itself alone, and the fewer other bodies concur with it in action, the more fitted is the mind of which it is the object for distinct comprehension. We may thus recognize the superiority of one mind over others, and may further see the cause, why we have only a very confused knowledge of our body, and also many kindred questions, which I will, in the following propositions, deduce from what has been advanced. Wherefore I have thought it worth while to explain and prove more strictly my present statements. In order to do so, I must premise a few propositions concerning the nature of bodies.

LEMMA I. *Bodies are distinguished from one another in respect of motion and rest, quickness and slowness, and not in respect of substance.*

LEMMA II. *All bodies agree in certain respects.*

LEMMA III. *A body in motion or at rest must be determined to motion or rest by another body, which other body has been determined to motion or rest by a third body, and that third again by a fourth, and so on to infinity.*

Definition.—When any given bodies of the same or different magnitude are compelled by other bodies to remain in contact, or if they be moved at the same or different rates of speed, so that their mutual movements should preserve among themselves a certain fixed relation, we say that such bodies are in union, and that together they compose one body or individual, which is distinguished from other bodies by this fact of union.

LEMMA IV. *If from a body or individual, compounded of several bodies, certain bodies be separated, and if, at the same time, an equal number of other bodies of the same nature take their place, the individual will preserve its nature as before, without any change in its actuality (forma).*

LEMMA V. *If the parts composing an individual become greater or less, but in such proportion, that they all preserve the same mutual relations of motion and rest, the individual will still preserve its original nature, and its actuality will not be changed.*

LEMMA VI. *If certain bodies composing an individual be compelled to change the motion, which they have in one direction, for motion in another direction, but in such a manner, that they be able to continue their motions and their mutual communication in the same relations as before, the individual will retain its own nature without any change of its actuality.*

Proof.—This proposition is self-evident, for the individual is supposed to retain all that, which, in its definition, we spoke of as its actual being.

LEMMA VII. *Furthermore, the individual thus composed preserves its nature, whether it be, as a whole, in motion or at rest, whether it be moved in this or that direction; so long as each part retains its motion, and preserves its communication with other parts as before.*

Proof.—This proposition is evident from the definition of an individual prefixed to Lemma iv.

Note.—We thus see, how a composite individual may be affected in many different ways, and preserve its nature notwithstanding. Thus far we have conceived an individual as composed of bodies only distinguished one from the other in respect of motion and rest, speed and slowness; that is, of bodies of the most simple character. If, however, we now conceive another individual composed of several individuals of diverse natures, we shall find that the number of ways in which it can be affected, without losing its nature, will be greatly multiplied. Each of its parts would consist of several bodies, and therefore (by Lemma vi.) each part would admit, without change to its nature, of quicker or slower motion, and would consequently be able to transmit its motions more quickly or more slowly to the remaining parts. If we further conceive a third kind of individuals composed of individuals of this second kind, we shall find that they may be affected in a still greater number of ways without changing their actuality. We may easily proceed thus to infinity, and conceive the whole of nature as one individual, whose parts, that is, all bodies, vary in infinite ways, without any change in the individual as a whole. I should feel bound to explain and demonstrate this point at more length, if I were writing a special treatise on body. But I have already said that such is not my object, I have only touched on the question, because it enables me to prove easily that which I have in view.

POSTULATES

I. The human body is composed of a number of individual parts, of diverse nature, each one of which is in itself extremely complex.

II. Of the individual parts composing the human body some are fluid, some soft, some hard.

III. The individual parts composing the human body, and consequently the human body itself, are affected in a variety of ways by external bodies.

IV. The human body stands in need for its preservation of a number of other bodies, by which it is continually, so to speak, regenerated.

V. When the fluid part of the human body is determined by an external body to impinge often on another soft part, it changes the surface of the latter, and, as it were, leaves the impression thereupon of the external body which impels it.

VI. The human body can move external bodies, and arrange them in a variety of ways.

Prop. XIV. *The human mind is capable of perceiving a great number of things, and is so in proportion as its body is capable of receiving a great number of impressions.*

Proof.—The human body (by Post. iii. and vi.) is affected in very many ways by external bodies, and is capable in very many ways of affecting external bodies. But (II. xii.) the human mind must perceive all that takes place in the human body; the human mind is, therefore, capable of perceiving a great number of things, and is so in proportion, &c. *Q.E.D.*

Prop. XV. *The idea, which constitutes the actual being of the human mind, is not simple, but compounded of a great number of ideas.*

Proof.—The idea constituting the actual being of the human mind is the idea of the body (II. xiii.), which (Post. i.) is composed of a great number of complex individual parts. But there is necessarily in God the idea of each individual part whereof the body is composed (II. viii. Coroll.); therefore (II. vii.), the

idea of the human body is composed of these numerous ideas of its component parts. *Q.E.D.*

Prop. XVI. *The idea of every mode, in which the human body is affected by external bodies, must involve the nature of the human body, and also the nature of the external body.*

Proof.—All the modes, in which any given body is affected, follow from the nature of the body affected, and also from the nature of the affecting body (by Ax. i., after the Coroll. of Lemma iii.), wherefore their idea also necessarily (by I. Ax. iv.) involves the nature of both bodies; therefore, the idea of every mode, in which the human body is affected by external bodies, involves the nature of the human body and of the external body. *Q.E.D.*

Corollary I.—Hence it follows, first, that the human mind perceives the nature of a variety of bodies, together with the nature of its own.

Corollary II.—It follows, secondly, that the ideas, which we have of external bodies, indicate rather the constitution of our own body than the nature of external bodies. I have amply illustrated this in the Appendix to Part I.

Prop. XVII. *If the human body is affected in a manner which involves the nature of any external body, the human mind will regard the said external body as actually existing, or as present to itself, until the human body be affected in such a way, as to exclude the existence or the presence of the said external body.*

Proof.—This proposition is self-evident, for so long as the human body continues to be thus affected, so long will the human mind (II. xii.) regard this modification of the body—that is (by the last Prop.), it will have the idea of the mode as actually existing, and this idea involves the nature of the external body. In other words, it will have the idea which does not exclude, but postulates the existence or presence of the nature of the external body; therefore the mind (by II. xvi., Coroll. i.) will regard the external body as actually existing, until it is affected, &c. *Q.E.D.*

Corollary.—The mind is able to regard as present external bodies, by which the human body has once been affected, even though they be no longer in existence or present.

Note.—We thus see how it comes about, as is often the case, that we regard as present things which are not. It is possible that the same result may be brought about by other causes; but I think it suffices for me here to have indicated one possible explanation, just as well as if I had pointed out the true cause. Indeed, I do not think I am very far from the truth, for all my assumptions are based on postulates, which rest, almost without exception, on experience, that cannot be controverted by those who have shown, as we have, that the human body, as we feel it, exists (Coroll. after II. xiii.). Furthermore (II. vii. Coroll., II, xvi. Coroll. ii.), we clearly understand what is the difference between the idea, say, of Peter, which constitutes the essence of Peter's mind, and the idea of the said Peter, which is in another man, say, Paul. The former directly answers to the essence of Peter's own body, and only implies existence so long as Peter exists; the latter indicates rather the disposition of Paul's body than the nature of Peter, and, therefore, while this disposition of Paul's body lasts, Paul's mind will regard Peter as present to itself, even though he no longer exists. Further, to retain the usual phraseology, the modifications of the human body, of which the ideas represent external bodies as present to us, we will call the images of things, though they do not recall the figure of things. When the mind regards bodies in this fashion, we say that it imagines. I will here draw attention to the fact, in order to indicate where error lies, that the imaginations of the mind, looked at in themselves, do not contain error. The mind does not err in the mere act of imagining, but only in so far as it is regarded as being without the idea, which excludes the existence of such things as it imagines to be present to it. If the mind, while imagining non-existent things as present to it, is at the same time conscious that they do not really exist, this power of imagination must be set down to the efficacy of its nature, and not to a fault, especially if this faculty of imagination depend solely on its own nature—that is (I. Def. vii.), if this faculty of imagination be free.

PROP. XVIII. *If the human body has once been affected by two or more bodies at the same time, when the mind afterwards imagines any of them, it will straightway remember the others also.*

Proof.—The mind (II. xvii. Coroll.) imagines any given body, because the human body is affected and disposed by the impressions from an external body, in the same manner as it is affected when certain of its parts are acted on by the said external body; but (by our hypothesis) the body was then so disposed, that the mind imagined two bodies at once; therefore, it will also in the second case imagine two bodies at once, and the mind, when it imagines one, will straightway remember the other. *Q.E.D.*

Note.—We now clearly see what *Memory* is. It is simply a certain association of ideas involving the nature of things outside the human body, which association arises in the mind according to the order and association of the modifications (*affectiones*) of the human body. I say, first, it is an association of those ideas only, which involve the nature of things outside the human body: not of ideas which answer to the nature of the said things: ideas of the modifications of the human body are, strictly speaking (II. xvi.), those which involve the nature both of the human body and of external bodies. I say, secondly, that this association arises according to the order and association of the modifications of the human body, in order to distinguish it from that association of ideas, which arises from the order of the intellect, whereby the mind perceives things through their primary causes, and which is in all men the same. And hence we can further clearly understand, why the mind from the thought of one thing, should straightway arrive at the thought of another thing, which has no similarity with the first; for instance, from the thought of the word *pomum* (an apple), a Roman would straightway arrive at the thought of the fruit apple, which has no similitude with the articulate sound in question, nor anything in common with it, except that the body of the man has often been affected by these two things; that is, that the man has often heard the word *pomum*, while he was looking at the fruit; similarly every man will go on from one thought to another, according as his habit has ordered the images of things in his body. For a soldier, for instance, when he sees the tracks of a horse in sand, will at once pass from the thought of a horse to the thought of a horseman, and thence to the thought of war, &c.; while a countryman will proceed from the thought of a horse to the thought of a plough, a field, &c. Thus every man will follow this or that train of thought, according as he has been in the habit of conjoining and associating the mental images of things in this or that manner.

PROP. XIX. *The human mind has no knowledge of the body, and does not know it to exist, save through the ideas of the modifications whereby the body is affected.*

Proof.—The human mind is the very idea or knowledge of the human body (II. xiii.), which (II. ix.) is in God, in so far as he is regarded as affected by another idea of a particular thing actually existing: or, inasmuch as (Post. iv.) the human body stands in need of very many bodies whereby it is, as it were, continually regenerated; and the order and connection of ideas is the same as the order and connection of causes (II. vii.); this idea will therefore be in God, in so far as he is regarded as affected by the ideas of very many particular things. Thus God has the idea of the human body, or knows the human body, in so far as he is affected by very many other ideas, and not in so far as he constitutes the nature of the human mind; that is (by II. xi. Coroll.), the human mind does not know the human body. But the ideas of the modifications of body are in God, in so far as he constitutes the nature of the human mind, or the human mind perceives those modifications (II. xii.), and consequently (II. xvi.) the human body itself, and as actually existing; therefore the mind perceives thus far only the human body. *Q.E.D.*

Prop. XX. *The idea or knowledge of the human mind is also in God, following in God in the same manner, and being referred to God in the same manner, as the idea or knowledge of the human body.*

Proof.—Thought is an attribute of God (II. i.); therefore (II. iii.) there must necessarily be in God the idea both of thought itself and of all its modifications, consequently also of the human mind (II. xi.). Further, this idea or knowledge of the mind does not follow from God, in so far as he is infinite, but in so far as he is affected by another idea of an individual thing (II. ix.). But (II. vii.) the order and connection of ideas is the same as the order and connection of causes; therefore this idea or knowledge of the mind is in God and is referred to God, in the same manner as the idea or knowledge of the body. *Q.E.D.*

Prop. XXI. *This idea of the mind is united to the mind in the same way as the mind is united to the body.*

Proof.—That the mind is united to the body we have shown from the fact, that the body is the object of the mind (II. xii. and xiii.); and so for the same reason the idea of the mind must be united with its object, that is, with the mind in the same manner as the mind is united to the body. *Q.E.D.*

Note.—This proposition is comprehended much more clearly from what we said in the note to II. vii.

We there showed that the idea of body and body, that is, mind and body (II. xiii.), are one and the same individual conceived now under the attribute of thought, now under the attribute of extension; wherefore the idea of the mind and the mind itself are one and the same thing, which is conceived under one and the same attribute, namely, thought. The idea of the mind, I repeat, and the mind itself are in God by the same necessity and follow from him from the same power of thinking. Strictly speaking, the idea of the mind, that is, the idea of an idea, is nothing but the distinctive quality (*forma*) of the idea in so far as it is conceived as a mode of thought without reference to the object; if a man knows anything, he, by that very fact, knows that he knows it, and at the same time knows that he knows that he knows it, and so on to infinity. But I will treat of this hereafter.

Prop. XXII. *The human mind perceives not only the modifications of the body, but also the ideas of such modifications.*

Proof.—The ideas of the ideas of modifications follow in God in the same manner, and are referred to God in the same manner, as the ideas of the said modifications. This is proved in the same way as II. xx. But the ideas of the modifications of the body are in the human mind (II. xii.), that is, in God, in so far as he constitutes the essence of the human mind; therefore the ideas of these ideas will be in God, in so far as he has the knowledge or idea of the human mind, that is (II. xxi.), they will be in the human mind itself, which therefore perceives not only the modifications of the body, but also the ideas of such modifications. *Q.E.D.*

Prop. XXIII. *The mind does not know itself, except in so far as it perceives the ideas of the modifications of the body.*

Proof.—The idea or knowledge of the mind (II. xx.) follows in God in the same manner, and is referred to God ʿin the same manner, as the idea or knowledge of the body. But since (II. xix.) the human mind does not know the human body itself, that is (II. xi. Coroll.), since the knowledge of the human body is not referred to God, in so far as he constitutes the nature of the human mind; therefore, neither is the knowledge of the mind referred to God, in so far as he constitutes the essence of the human mind; therefore (by the same Coroll. II. xi.), the human mind thus far has no knowledge of itself. Further the ideas of the modifications, whereby the body is affected, involve the nature of the human body itself (II. xvi.), that is (II. xiii.), they agree with the nature of the mind; wherefore the knowledge of these ideas necessarily involves knowledge of the mind; but (by the last Prop.) the knowledge of these ideas is in the human mind itself; wherefore the human mind thus far only has knowledge of itself. *Q.E.D.*

PROP. XXIV.—*The human mind does not involve an adequate knowledge of the parts composing the human body.*

Proof.—The parts composing the human body do not belong to the essence of that body, except in so far as they communicate their motions to one another in a certain fixed relation (Def. after Lemma iii.), not in so far as they can be regarded as individuals without relation to the human body. The parts of the human body are highly complex individuals (Post. i.), whose parts (Lemma iv.) can be separated from the human body without in any way destroying the nature and distinctive quality of the latter, and they can communicate their motions (Ax. i., after Lemma iii.) to other bodies in another relation; therefore (II. iii.) the idea or knowledge of each part will be in God, inasmuch (II. ix.) as he is regarded as affected by another idea of a particular thing, which particular thing is prior in the order of nature to the aforesaid part (II. vii.). We may affirm the same thing of each part of each individual composing the human body; therefore, the knowledge of each part composing the human body is in God, in so far as he is affected by very many ideas of things, and not in so far as he has the idea of the human body only, in other words, the idea which constitutes the nature of the human mind (II. xiii.); therefore (II. xi. Coroll.), the human mind does not involve an adequate knowledge of the human body. *Q.E.D.*

PROP. XXV. *The idea of each modification of the human body does not involve an adequate knowledge of the external body.*

Proof.—We have shown that the idea of a modification of the human body involves the nature of an external body, in so far as that external body conditions the human body in a given manner. But, in so far as the external body is an individual, which has no reference to the human body, the knowledge or idea thereof is in God (II. ix.), in so far as God is regarded as affected by the idea of a further thing, which (II. vii.) is naturally prior to the said external body. Wherefore an adequate knowledge of the exter-

nal body is not in God, in so far as he has the idea of the modification of the human body; in other words, the idea of the modification of the human body does not involve an adequate knowledge of the external body. *Q.E.D.*

PROP. XXVI. *The human mind does not perceive any external body as actually existing, except through the ideas of the modifications of its own body.*

Proof.—If the human body is in no way affected by a given external body, then (II. vii.) neither is the idea of the human body, in other words, the human mind, affected in any way by the idea of the existence of the said external body, nor does it any manner perceive its existence. But, in so far as the human body is affected in any way by a given external body, thus far (II. xvi. and Coroll.) it perceives that external body. *Q.E.D.*

Corollary.—In so far as the human mind imagines an external body, it has not an adequate knowledge thereof.

Proof.—When the human mind regards external bodies through the ideas of the modifications of its own body, we say that it imagines (see II. xvii. note); now the mind can only imagine external bodies as actually existing. Therefore (by II. xxv.), in so far as the mind imagines external bodies, it has not an adequate knowledge of them. *Q.E.D.*

PROP. XXVII. *The idea of each modification of the human body does not involve an adequate knowledge of the human body itself.*

Proof.—Every idea of a modification of the human body involves the nature of the human body, in so far as the human body is regarded as affected in a given manner (II. xvi.). But, inasmuch as the human body is an individual which may be affected in many other ways, the idea of the said modification, &c. *Q.E.D.*

PROP. XXVIII. *The ideas of the modifications of the human body, in so far as they have reference only to the human mind, are not clear and distinct, but confused.*

Proof.—The ideas of the modifications of the human body involve the nature both of the human body and of external bodies (II. xvi.); they must involve the nature not only of the human body but also of its parts; for the modifications are modes (Post. iii.), whereby the parts of the human body, and, consequently, the human body as a whole are affected. But (by II. xxiv., xxv.) the adequate knowledge of external bodies, as also of the parts composing the human body, is not in God, in so far as he is regarded as affected by the human mind, but in so far as he is regarded as affected by other ideas. These ideas of modifications, in so far as they are referred to the human mind alone, are as consequences without premisses, in other words, confused ideas. *Q.E.D.*

Note.—The idea which constitutes the nature of the human mind is, in the same manner, proved not to be, when considered in itself alone, clear and distinct; as also is the case with the idea of the human mind, and the ideas of the ideas of the modifications of the human body, in so far as they are referred to the mind only, as everyone may easily see.

PROP. XXIX. *The idea of the idea of each modification of the human body does not involve an adequate knowledge of the human mind.*

Proof.—The idea of a modification of the human body (II. xxvii.) does not involve an adequate knowledge of the said body, in other words, does not adequately express its nature; that is (II. xiii.) it does not agree with the nature of the mind adequately; therefore (I. Ax. vi.) the idea of this idea does not adequately express the nature of the human mind, or does not involve an adequate knowledge thereof.

Corollary.—Hence it follows that the human mind, when it perceives things after the common order of nature, has not an adequate but only a confused and fragmentary knowledge of itself, of its own body, and of external bodies. For the mind does not know itself, except in so far as it perceives the ideas of the modifications of body (II. xxiii.). It only perceives its own body (II. xix.) through the ideas of the modifications, and only perceives external bodies through the same means; thus, in so far as it has such ideas of modification, it has not an adequate knowledge of itself (II. xxix.), nor of its own body (II. xxvii.), nor of external bodies (II. xxv.), but only a fragmentary and confused knowledge thereof (II. xxviii. and note.) *Q.E.D.*

Note.—I say expressly, that the mind has not an adequate but only a confused knowledge of itself, its own body, and of external bodies, whenever it perceives things after the common order of nature; that is, whenever it is determined from without, namely, by the fortuitous play of circumstance, to regard this or that; not at such times as it is determined from within, that is, by the fact of regarding several things at once, to understand their points of agreement, dif-

ference, and contrast. Whenever it is determined in anywise from within, it regards things clearly and distinctly, as I will show below.

PROP. XXXII. *All ideas, in so far as they are referred to God, are true.*

Proof.—All ideas which are in God agree in every respect with their objects (II. vii. Coroll.), therefore (I. Ax. vi.) they are all true. *Q.E.D.*

PROP. XXXIII. *There is nothing positive in ideas, which causes them to be called false.*

Proof.—If this be denied, conceive, if possible, a positive mode of thinking, which should constitute the distinctive quality of falsehood. Such a mode of thinking cannot be in God (II. xxxii.); external to God it cannot be or be conceived (I. xv.). Therefore there is nothing positive in ideas which causes them to be called false. *Q.E.D.*

PROP. XXXIV. *Every idea, which in us is absolute or adequate and perfect, is true.*

Proof.—When we say that an idea in us is adequate and perfect, we say, in other words (II. xi. Coroll.), that the idea is adequate and perfect in God, in so far as he constitutes the essence of our mind; consequently (II. xxxii.), we say that such an idea is true. *Q.E.D.*

PROP. XXXV. *Falsity consists in the privation of knowledge, which inadequate, fragmentary, or confused ideas involve.*

Proof.—There is nothing positive in ideas, which causes them to be called false (II. xxxiii); but falsity cannot consist in simple privation (for minds, not bodies, are said to err and to be mistaken), neither can it consist in absolute ignorance, for ignorance and error are not identical; wherefore it consists in the privation of knowledge, which inadequate, fragmentary, or confused ideas involve. *Q.E.D.*

Note.—In the note to II. xvii. I explained how error consists in the privation of knowledge, but in order to throw more light on the subject I will give an example. For instance, men are mistaken in thinking themselves free; their opinion is made up of consciousness of their own actions, and ignorance of the causes by which they are conditioned. Their idea of freedom, therefore, is simply their ignorance of any cause for their actions. As for their saying that human actions depend on the will, this is a mere phrase without any idea to correspond thereto. What the will is, and how it moves the body, they none of them know; those who boast of such knowledge, and feign dwellings and habitations for the soul, are wont to provoke either laughter or disgust. So, again, when we look at the sun, we imagine that it is distant from us about two hundred feet; this error does not lie solely in this fancy, but in the fact that, while we thus imagine, we do not know the sun's true distance or the cause of the fancy. For although we afterwards learn, that the sun is distant from us more than six hundred of the earth's diameters, we none the less shall fancy it to be near; for we do not imagine the sun as near us, because we are ignorant of its true distance, but because the modification of our body involves the essence of the sun, in so far as our said body is affected thereby.

PROP. XXXVI. *Inadequate and confused ideas follow by the same necessity, as adequate or clear and distinct ideas.*

Proof.—All ideas are in God (I. xv.), and in so far as they are referred to God are true (II. xxxii.) and (II. vii. Coroll.) adequate; therefore there are no ideas confused or inadequate, except in respect to a particular mind (cf. II. xxiv, and xxviii.); therefore all ideas, whether adequate or inadequate, follow by the same necessity (II. vi.). Q.E.D.

PROP. XL. *Whatsoever ideas in the mind follow from ideas which are therein adequate, are also themselves adequate.*

Proof.—This proposition is self-evident. For when we say that an idea in the human mind follows from ideas which are therein adequate, we say, in other words (II. xi. Coroll.), that an idea is in the divine intellect, whereof God is the cause, not in so far as he is infinite, nor in so far as he is affected by the ideas of very many particular things, but only in so far as he constitutes the essence of the human mind.

Note I.—I have thus set forth the cause of those notions, which are common to all men, and which form the basis of our ratiocination. But there are other causes of certain axioms or notions, which it would be to the purpose to set forth by this method of ours; for it would thus appear what notions are more useful than others, and what notions have scarcely any use at all. Furthermore, we should see what notions are common to all men, and what notions are only clear and distinct to those who are unshackled by prejudice, and

we should detect those which are ill-founded. Again we should discern whence the notions called *secondary* derived their origin, and consequently the axioms on which they are founded, and other points of interest connected with these questions. But I have decided to pass over the subject here, partly because I have set it aside for another treatise, partly because I am afraid of wearying the reader by too great prolixity. Nevertheless, in order not to omit anything necessary to be known, I will briefly set down the causes, whence are derived the terms styled *transcendental,* such as Being, Thing, Something. These terms arose from the fact, that the human body, being limited, is only capable of distinctly forming a certain number of images (what an image is I explained in II. xvii. note) within itself at the same time; if this number be exceeded, the images will begin to be confused; if this number of images, which the body is capable of forming distinctly within itself, be largely exceeded, all will become entirely confused one with another. This being so, it is evident (from II. Prop. xvii. Coroll. and xviii.) that the human mind can distinctly imagine as many things simultaneously, as its body can form images simultaneously. When the images become quite confused in the body, the mind also imagines all bodies confusedly without any distinction, and will comprehend them, as it were, under one attribute, namely, under the attribute of Being, Thing, &c. The same conclusion can be drawn from the fact that images are not always equally vivid, and from other analogous causes, which there is no need to explain here; for the purpose which we have in view it is sufficient for us to consider one only. All may be reduced to this, that these terms represent ideas in the highest degree confused. From similar causes arise those notions, which we call *general,* such as man, horse, dog, &c. They arise, to wit, from the fact that so many images, for instance, of men, are formed simultaneously in the human mind, that the powers of imagination break down, not indeed utterly, but to the extent of the mind losing count of small differences between individuals (*e.g.* colour, size, &c.) and their definite number, and only distinctly imagining that, in which all the individuals, in so far as the body is affected by them, agree; for that is the point, in which each of the said individuals chiefly affected the body; this the mind expresses by the name man, and this it predicates of an infinite number of particular individuals. For, as we have said, it is unable to imagine the definite number of individuals. We must, however, bear in mind, that these general notions are not formed by all men in the same way, but vary in each individual according as the point varies, whereby the body has been most often affected and which the mind most easily imagines or remembers. For instance, those who have most often regarded with admiration the stature of man, will by the name of man understand an animal of erect stature; those who have been accustomed to regard some other attribute, will form a different general image of man, for instance, that man is a laughing animal, a two-footed animal without feathers, a rational animal, and thus, in other cases, everyone will form general images of things according to the habit of his body.

It is thus not to be wondered at, that among philosophers, who seek to explain things in nature merely by the images formed of them, so many controversies should have arisen.

Note II.—From all that has been said above it is clear, that we, in many cases, perceive and form our general notions:—(1.) From particular things represented to our intellect fragmentarily, confusedly, and without order through our senses (II. xxix. Coroll.); I have settled to call such perceptions by the name of knowledge from the mere suggestions of experience. (2.) From symbols, *e.g.*, from the fact of having read or heard certain words we remember things and form certain ideas concerning them, similar to those through which we imagine things (II. xviii. note). I shall call both these ways of regarding things *knowledge of the first kind, opinion, or imagination.* (3.) From the fact that we have notions common to all men, and adequate ideas of the properties of things (II. xxxviii. Coroll., xxxix. and Coroll. and xl.); this I call *reason* and *knowledge of the second kind.* Besides these two kinds of knowledge, there is, as I will hereafter show, a third kind of knowledge, which we will call intuition. This kind of knowledge proceeds from an adequate idea of the absolute essence of certain attributes of God to the adequate knowledge of the essence of things. I will illustrate all three kinds of knowledge by a single example. Three numbers are given for finding a fourth, which shall be to the third as the second is to the first. Tradesmen without hesitation multiply the second by the third, and divide the product by the first; either because they have not forgotten the rule which they received from a master without any proof,

or because they have often made trial of it with simple numbers, or by virtue of the proof of the nineteenth proposition of the seventh book of Euclid, namely, in virtue of the general property of proportionals.

But with very simple numbers there is no need of this. For instance, one, two, three, being given, everyone can see that the fourth proportional is six; and this is much clearer, because we infer the fourth number from an intuitive grasping of the ratio, which the first bears to the second.

PROP. XLI. *Knowledge of the first kind is the only source of falsity, knowledge of the second and third kinds is necessarily true.*

Proof.—To knowledge of the first kind we have (in the foregoing note) assigned all those ideas, which are inadequate and confused; therefore this kind of knowledge is the only source of falsity (II. xxxv.). Furthermore, we assigned to the second and third kinds of knowledge those ideas which are adequate; therefore these kinds are necessarily true (II. xxxiv.). *Q.E.D.*

PROP. XLII. *Knowledge of the second and third kinds, not knowledge of the first kind, teaches us to distinguish the true from the false.*

Proof.—This proposition is self-evident. He, who knows how to distinguish between true and false, must have an adequate idea of true and false. That is (II. xl., note ii.), he must know the true and the false by the second or third kind of knowledge.

PROP. XLIII. *He, who has a true idea, simultaneously knows that he has a true idea, and cannot doubt of the truth of the thing perceived.*

Proof.—A true idea in us is an idea which is adequate in God, in so far as he is displayed through the nature of the human mind (II. xi. Coroll.). Let us suppose that there is in God, in so far as he is displayed through the human mind, an adequate idea, A. The idea of this idea must also necessarily be in God, and be referred to him in the same way as the idea A (by II. xx., whereof the proof is of universal application). But the idea A is supposed to be referred to God, in so far as he is displayed through the human mind; therefore, the idea of the idea A must be referred to God in the same manner; that is (by II. xi, Coroll.), the adequate idea of the idea A will be in the mind, which has the adequate idea A; therefore he, who has an adequate idea or knows a thing truly (II. xxxiv.), must at the same time have an adequate idea or true knowledge of his knowledge; that is, obviously, he must be assured. *Q.E.D.*

Note.—I explained in the note to II. xxi. what is meant by the idea of an idea; but we may remark that the foregoing proposition is in itself sufficiently plain. No one, who has a true idea, is ignorant that a true idea involves the highest certainty. For to have a true idea is only another expression for knowing a thing perfectly, or as well as possible. No one, indeed, can doubt of this, unless he thinks that an idea is something lifeless, like a picture on a panel, and not a mode of thinking—namely, the very act of understanding. And who, I ask, can know that he understands anything, unless he do first understand it? In other words, who can know that he is sure of a thing, unless he be first sure of that thing? Further, what can there be more clear, and more certain, than a true idea as a standard of truth? Even as light displays both itself and darkness, so is truth a standard both of itself and of falsity.

I think I have thus sufficiently answered these questions—namely, if a true idea is distinguished from a false idea, only in so far as it is said to agree with its object, a true idea has no more reality or perfection than a false idea (since the two are only distinguished by an extrinsic mark); consequently, neither will a man who has true ideas have any advantage over him who has only false ideas. Further, how comes it that men have false ideas? Lastly, how can anyone be sure, that he has ideas which agree with their objects? These questions, I repeat, I have, in my opinion, sufficiently answered. The difference between a true idea and a false idea is plain: from what was said in II. xxxv., the former is related to the latter as being is to not-being. The causes of falsity I have set forth very clearly in II. xix. and II. xxxv. with the note. From what is there stated, the difference between a man who has true ideas, and a man who has only false ideas, is made apparent. As for the last question—as to how a man can be sure that he has ideas that agree with their objects, I have just pointed out, with abundant clearness, that his knowledge arises from the simple fact, that he has an idea which corresponds with its object—in other words, that truth is its own standard. We may add that our mind, in so far as it perceives things truly, is part of the infinite intellect of God (II. xi. Coroll.); therefore, the clear and distinct ideas of the mind are as necessarily true as the ideas of God.

PROP. XLIV. *It is not in the nature of reason to regard things as contingent, but as necessary.*

Proof.—It is in the nature of reason to perceive things truly (II. xli.), namely (I. Ax. vi.), as they are in themselves—that is (I. xxix.), not as contingent, but as necessary. *Q.E.D.*

Corollary I.—Hence it follows, that it is only through our imagination that we consider things, whether in respect to the future or the past, as contingent.

Corollary II.—It is in the nature of reason to perceive things under a certain form of eternity (*sub quâdam œternitatis specie*).

PROP. XLVIII. *In the mind there is no absolute or free will; but the mind is determined to wish this or that by a cause, which has also been determined by another cause, and this last by another cause, and so on to infinity.*

Proof.—The mind is a fixed and definite mode of thought (II. xi.), therefore it cannot be the free cause of its actions (I. xvii. Coroll. ii.); in other words, it cannot have an absolute faculty of positive or negative volition; but (by I. xxviii.) it must be determined by a cause, which has also been determined by another cause, and this last by another, &c. *Q.E.D.*

Note.—In the same way it is proved, that there is in the mind no absolute faculty of understanding, desiring, loving, &c. Whence it follows, that these and similar faculties are either entirely fictitious, or are merely abstract or general terms, such as we are accustomed to put together from particular things. Thus the intellect and the will stand in the same relation to this or that idea, or this or that fore, this affirmation belongs to the essence of the idea of a triangle, and is nothing besides. What we have said of this volition (inasmuch as we have selected it at random) may be said of any other volition, namely, that it is nothing but an idea. *Q.E.D.*

Corollary.—Will and understanding are one and the same.

Proof.—Will and understanding are nothing beyond the individual volitions and ideas (II. xlviii. and note). But a particular volition and a particular idea are one and the same (by the foregoing Prop.); therefore, will and understanding are one and the same. *Q.E.D.*

. . . Volition, as "lapidity" to this or that stone, or as "man" to Peter and Paul. The cause which leads men to consider themselves free has been set forth in the Appendix to Part I. But, before I proceed further, I would here remark that, by the will to affirm and decide, I mean the faculty, not the desire. I mean, I repeat, the faculty, whereby the mind affirms or denies what is true or false, not the desire, wherewith the mind wishes for or turns away from any given thing. After we have proved, that these faculties of ours are general notions, which cannot be distinguished from the particular instances on which they are based, we must inquire whether volitions themselves are anything besides the ideas of things. We must inquire, I say, whether there is in the mind any affirmation or negation beyond that, which the idea, in so far as it is an idea, involves. On which subject see the following proposition, and II. Def. iii., lest the idea of pictures should suggest itself. For by ideas I do not mean images such as are formed at the back of the eye, or in the midst of the brain, but the conceptions of thought.

PROP. XLIX. *There is in the mind no volition or affirmation and negation, save that which an idea, inasmuch as it is an idea, involves.*

Proof.—There is in the mind no absolute faculty of positive or negative volition, but only particular volitions, namely, this or that affirmation, and this or that negation. Now let us conceive a particular volition, namely, the mode of thinking whereby the mind affirms, that the three interior angles of a triangle are equal to two right angles. This affirmation involves the conception or idea of a triangle, that is, without the idea of a triangle it cannot be conceived. It is the same thing to say, that the concept A must involve the concept B, as it is to say, that A cannot be conceived without B. Further, this affirmation cannot be made (II. Ax. iii.) without the idea of a triangle. Therefore, this affirmation can neither be nor be conceived, without the idea of a triangle. Again, this idea of a triangle must involve this same affirmation, namely, that its three interior angles are equal to two right angles. Wherefore, and *vice versâ*, this idea of a triangle can neither be nor be conceived without this affirmation, therefore, this affirmation belongs to the essence of the idea of a triangle, and is nothing besides. What we have said of this volition (inasmuch as we have selected it at random) may be said of any other volition, namely, that it is nothing but an idea. *Q.E.D.*

Corollary.—Will and understanding are one and the same.

Proof.—Will and understanding are nothing beyond the individual volitions and ideas (II. xlviii. and note). But a particular volition and a particular idea are one and the same (by the foregoing Prop.); therefore, will and understanding are one and the same. *Q.E.D.*

Part III
On the Origin and Nature of the Emotions

DEFINITIONS

I. By an *adequate* cause, I mean a cause through which its effect can be clearly and distinctly perceived. By an *inadequate* or partial cause, I mean a cause through which, by itself, its effect cannot be understood.

II. I say that we *act* when anything takes place, either within us or externally to us, whereof we are the adequate cause; that is (by the foregoing definition) when through our nature something takes place within us or externally to us, which can through our nature alone be clearly and distinctly understood. On the other hand, I say that we are passive as regards something when that something takes place within us, or follows from our nature externally, we being only the partial cause.

III. By *emotion* I mean the modifications of the body, whereby the active power of the said body is increased or diminished, aided or constrained, and also the ideas of such modifications.

N.B. If we can be the adequate cause of any of these modifications, I then call the emotion an activity, otherwise I call it a passion, or state wherein the mind is passive.

POSTULATES

I. The human body can be affected in many ways, whereby its power of activity is increased or diminished, and also in other ways which do not render its power of activity either greater or less.

N.B. This postulate or axiom rests on Postulate i. and Lemmas v. and vii., which see after II. xiii.

II. The human body can undergo many changes, and, nevertheless, retain the impressions or traces of objects (cf. II. Post. v.), and, consequently, the same images of things (see note II. xvii.).

PROP. I. *Our mind is in certain cases active, and in certain cases passive. In so far as it has adequate ideas it is necessarily active, and in so far as it has inadequate ideas, it is necessarily passive.*

Proof.—In every human mind there are some adequate ideas, and some ideas that are fragmentary and confused (II. xl. note). Those ideas which are adequate in the mind are adequate also in God, inasmuch as he constitutes the essence of the mind (II. xl. Coroll.), and those which are inadequate in the mind are likewise (by the same Coroll.) adequate in God, not inasmuch as he contains in himself the essence of the given mind alone, but as he, at the same time, contains the minds of other things. Again, from any given idea some effect must necessarily follow (I. 36); of this effect God is the adequate cause (III. Def. i.), not inasmuch as he is infinite, but inasmuch as he is conceived as affected by the given idea (II. ix.). But of that effect whereof God is the cause, inasmuch as he is affected by an idea which is adequate in a given mind, of that effect, I repeat, the mind in question is the adequate cause (II. xi. Coroll.). Therefore our mind, in so far as it has adequate ideas (III. Def. ii.), is in certain cases necessarily active; this was our first point. Again, whatsoever necessarily follows from the idea which is adequate in God, not by virtue of his possessing in himself the mind of one man only, but by virtue of his containing, together with the mind of that one man, the minds of other things also, of such an effect (II. xi. Coroll.) the mind of the given man is not an adequate, but only a partial cause; thus (III. Def. ii.) the mind, inasmuch as it has inadequate ideas, is in certain cases necessarily passive; this was our second point. Therefore our mind, &c. *Q.E.D.*

Corollary.—Hence it follows that the mind is more or less liable to be acted upon, in proportion as it possesses inadequate ideas, and, contrariwise, is more or less active in proportion as it possesses adequate ideas.

PROP. II. *Body cannot determine mind to think, neither can mind determine body to motion or rest or any state different from these, if such there be.*

Proof.—All modes of thinking have for their cause God, by virtue of his being a thinking thing, and not by virtue of his being displayed under any other attribute (II. vi.). That, therefore, which determines the mind to thought is a mode of thought, and not a mode of extension; that is (II. Def. i.), it is not body. This was our first point. Again, the motion and rest of a body must arise from another body, which has also been determined to a state of motion or rest by a third body, and absolutely everything which takes place in a body must spring from God, in so far as he is regarded as affected by some mode of extension, and not by some mode of thought (II. vi.); that is, it cannot spring from the mind, which is a mode of thought. This was our second point. Therefore body cannot determine mind, &c. *Q.E.D.*

Note.—This is made more clear by what was said in the note to II. vii., namely, that mind and body are one and the same thing, conceived first under the attribute of thought, secondly, under the attribute of extension. Thus it follows that the order or concatenation of things is identical, whether nature be conceived under the one attribute or the other; consequently the order of states of activity and passivity in our body is simultaneous in nature with the order of states of activity and passivity in the mind. The same conclusion is evident from the manner in which we proved II. xii.

PROP. III. *The activities of the mind arise solely from adequate ideas; the passive states of the mind depend solely on inadequate ideas.*

Proof.—The first element, which constitutes the essence of the mind, is nothing else but the idea of the actually existent body (II. xi. and xiii.), which (II. xv.) is compounded of many other ideas, whereof some are adequate and some inadequate (II. xxix. Coroll., II. xxxviii. Coroll.). Whatsoever therefore follows from the nature of mind, and has mind for its proximate cause, through which it must be understood, must necessarily follow either from an adequate or from an inadequate idea. But in so far as the mind (III. i.) has inadequate ideas, it is necessarily passive: wherefore the activities of the mind follow solely from adequate ideas, and accordingly the mind is only passive in so far as it has inadequate ideas. *Q.E.D.*

Note.—Thus we see, that passive states are not attributed to the mind, except in so far as it contains something involving negation, or in so far as it is regarded as a part of nature, which cannot be clearly and distinctly perceived through itself without other parts: I could thus show, that passive states are attributed to individual things in the same way that they are attributed to the mind, and that they cannot otherwise be perceived, but my purpose is solely to treat of the human mind.

PROP. IV. *Nothing can be destroyed, except by a cause external to itself.*

Proof.—This proposition is self-evident, for the definition of anything affirms the essence of that thing, but does not negative it; in other words, it postulates the essence of the thing, but does not take it away. So long therefore as we regard only the thing itself, without taking into account external causes, we shall not be able to find in it anything which could destroy it. Q.E.D.

PROP. V. *Things are naturally contrary, that is, cannot exist in the same object, in so far as one is capable of destroying the other.*

Proof.—If they could agree together or co-exist in the same object, there would then be in the said object something which could destroy it; but this, by the foregoing proposition, is absurd, therefore things, &c. Q.E.D.

PROP. VI. *Everything, in so far as it is in itself, endeavours to persist in its own being.*

Proof.—Individual things are modes whereby the attributes of God are expressed in a given determinate manner (I. xxv. Coroll.); that is (I. xxxiv.), they are things which express in a given determinate manner the power of God, whereby God is and acts; now no thing contains in itself anything whereby it can be destroyed, or which can take away its existence (III. iv.); but contrariwise it is opposed to all that could take away its existence (III. v.). Therefore, in so far as it can, and in so far as it is in itself, it endeavours to persist in its own being. Q.E.D.

PROP. VII. *The endeavour, wherewith everything endeavours to persist in its own being, is nothing else but the actual essence of the thing in question.*

Proof.—From the given essence of any thing certain consequences necessarily follow (I. xxxvi.), nor have things any power save such as necessarily follows from their nature as determined (I. xxix.); wherefore the power of any given thing, or the endeavour whereby, either alone or with other things, it acts, or endeavours to act, that is (III. vi.), the power or endeavour, wherewith it endeavours to persist in its own being, is nothing else but the given or actual essence of the thing in question. Q.E.D.

PROP. XXVIII. *We endeavour to bring about whatsoever we conceive to conduce to pleasure; but we endeavour to remove or destroy whatsoever we conceive to be truly repugnant thereto, or to conduce to pain.*

Proof.—We endeavour, as far as possible, to conceive that which we imagine to conduce to pleasure (III. xii.); in other words (II. xvii.) we shall endeavour to conceive it as far as possible as present or actually existing. But the endeavour of the mind, or the mind's power of thought, is equal to, and simultaneous with, the endeavour of the body, or the body's power of action. (This is clear from II. vii. Coroll. and II. xi. Coroll.). Therefore we make an absolute endeavour for its existence, in other words (which by III. ix. note come to the same thing) we desire and strive for it; this was our first point. Again, if we conceive that something, which we believed to be the cause of pain, that is (III. xiii. note), which we hate, is destroyed, we shall rejoice (III. xx.). We shall, therefore (by the first part of this proof), endeavour to destroy the same, or (III. xiii.) to remove it from us, so that we may not regard it as present; this was our second point. Wherefore whatsoever conduces to pleasure, &c. Q.E.D.

Part IV
Of Human Bondage

APPENDIX

What I have said in this Part concerning the right way of life has not been arranged, so as to admit of being seen at one view, but has been set forth piecemeal, according as I thought each Proposition could most readily be deduced from what preceded it. I propose, therefore, to rearrange my remarks and to bring them under leading heads.

I. All our endeavours or desires so follow from the necessity of our nature, that they can be understood either through it alone, as their proximate cause, or by virtue of our being a part of nature, which cannot be adequately conceived through itself without other individuals.

II. Desires, which follow from our nature in such a manner, that they can be understood through it alone, are those which are referred to the mind, in so far as the latter is conceived to consist of adequate ideas: the remaining desires are only referred to the mind, in so far as it conceives things inadequately, and their force and increase are generally defined not by the power of man, but by the power of things external to us: wherefore the former are rightly called actions, the latter passions, for the former always indicate our power, the latter, on the other hand, show our infirmity and fragmentary knowledge.

III. Our actions, that is, those desires which are defined by man's power or reason, are always good. The rest may be either good or bad.

IV. Thus in life it is before all things useful to perfect the understanding, or reason, as far as we can, and in this alone man's highest happiness or blessedness consists, indeed blessedness is nothing else but the contentment of spirit, which arises from the intuitive knowledge of God: now, to perfect the understanding is nothing else but to understand God, God's attributes, and the actions which follow from the necessity of his nature. Wherefore of a man, who is led by reason, the ultimate aim or highest desire, whereby he seeks to govern all his fellows, is that whereby he is brought to the adequate conception of himself and of all things within the scope of his intelligence.

V. Therefore, without intelligence there is not rational life: and things are only good, in so far as they aid man in his enjoyment of the intellectual life, which is defined by intelligence. Contrariwise, whatsoever things hinder man's perfecting of his reason, and capability to enjoy the rational life, are alone called evil.

VI. As all things whereof man is the efficient cause are necessarily good, no evil can befall man except through external causes; namely, by virtue of man being a part of universal nature, whose laws human nature is compelled to obey, and to conform to in almost infinite ways.

VII. It is impossible, that man should not be a part of nature, or that he should not follow her general order; but if he be thrown among individuals whose nature is in harmony with his own, his power of action will thereby be aided and fostered, whereas, if he be thrown among such as are but very little in harmony with his nature, he will hardly be able to accommodate himself to them without undergoing a great change himself.

VIII. Whatsoever in nature we deem to be evil, or to be capable of injuring our faculty for existing and enjoying the rational life, we may endeavour to remove in whatever way seems safest to us; on the other hand, whatsoever we deem to be good or useful for preserving our being, and enabling us to enjoy the rational life, we may appropriate to our use and employ as we think best. Everyone without exception may, by sovereign right of nature, do whatsoever he thinks will advance his own interest.

IX. Nothing can be in more harmony with the nature of any given thing than other individuals of the same species; therefore (cf. vii.) for man in the preservation of his being and the enjoyment of the rational life there is nothing more useful than his fellow-man who is led by reason. Further, as we know not anything among individual things which is more excellent than a man led by reason, no man can better display the power of his skill and disposition, than in so training men, that they come at last to live under the dominion of their own reason.

X. In so far as men are influenced by envy or any kind of hatred, one towards another, they are at variance, and are therefore to be feared in proportion, as they are more powerful than their fellows.

XI. Yet minds are not conquered by force, but by love and high-mindedness.

XII. It is before all things useful to men to associate their ways of life, to bind themselves together with such bonds as they think most fitted to gather them all into unity, and generally to do whatsoever serves to strengthen friendship.

XIII. But for this there is need of skill and watchfulness. For men are diverse (seeing that those who live under the guidance of reason are few), yet are they generally envious and more prone to revenge than to sympathy. No small force of character is therefore required to take everyone as he is, and to restrain one's self from imitating the emotions of others. But those who carp at mankind, and are more skilled in railing at vice than in instilling virtue, and who break rather than strengthen men's dispositions, are hurtful both to themselves and others. Thus many from too great impatience of spirit, or from misguided religious zeal, have preferred to live among brutes rather than among men; as boys or youths, who cannot peaceably endure the chidings of their parents, will enlist as soldiers and choose the hardships of war and the despotic discipline in preference to the comforts of home and the admonitions of their father: suffering any burden to be put upon them, so long as they may spite their parents.

XIV. Therefore, although men are generally governed in everything by their own lusts, yet their association in common brings many more advantages than drawbacks. Wherefore it is better to bear patiently the wrongs they may do us, and to strive to promote whatsoever serves to bring about harmony and friendship.

XV. Those things, which beget harmony, are such as are attributable to justice, equity, and honourable living. For men brook ill not only what is unjust or iniquitous, but also what is reckoned disgraceful, or that a man should slight the received customs of their society. For winning love those qualities are especially necessary which have regard to religion and piety (cf. IV. xxxvii. notes, i. ii. ; xlvi. note; and lxxiii. note).

XVI. Further, harmony is often the result of fear: but such harmony is insecure. Further, fear arises from infirmity of spirit, and moreover belongs not to the exercise of reason: the same is true of compassion, though this latter seems to bear a certain resemblance to piety.

XVII. Men are also gained over by liberality, especially such as have not the means to buy what is necessary to sustain life. However, to give aid to every poor man is far beyond the power and the advantage of any private person. For the riches of any private person are wholly inadequate to meet such a call. Again, an individual man's resources of character are too limited for him to be able to make all men his friends. Hence providing for the poor is a duty, which falls on the State as a whole, and has regard only to the general advantage.

XVIII. In accepting favours, and in returning gratitude our duty must be wholly different (cf. IV. lxx. note; lxxi. note).

XIX. Again, meretricious love, that is, the lust of generation arising from bodily beauty, and generally every sort of love, which owns anything save freedom of soul as its cause, readily passes into hate; unless indeed, what is worse, it is a species of madness; and then it promotes discord rather than harmony (cf. III. xxxi. Coroll.).

XX. As concerning marriage, it is certain that this is in harmony with reason, if the desire for physical union be not engendered solely by bodily beauty, but also by the desire to beget children and to train them up wisely; and moreover, if the love of both, to wit, of the man and of the woman, is not caused by bodily beauty only, but also by freedom of soul.

XXI. Furthermore, flattery begets harmony; but only by means of the vile offence of slavishness or treachery. None are more readily taken with flattery than the proud, who wish to be first, but are not.

XXII. There is in abasement a spurious appearance of piety and religion. Although abasement is the opposite to pride, yet is he that abases himself most akin to the proud (IV. lvii. note).

XXIII. Shame also brings about harmony, but only in such matters as cannot be hid. Further, as shame is a species of pain, it does not concern the exercise of reason.

XXIV. The remaining emotions of pain towards men are directly opposed to justice, equity, honour, piety, and religion; and, although indignation seems to bear a certain resemblance to equity, yet is life but lawless, where every man may pass judgment on another's deeds, and vindicate his own or other men's rights.

XXV. Correctness of conduct (*modestia*), that is, the desire of pleasing men which is determined by reason, is attributable to piety (as we said in IV. xxxvii. note i.). But, if it spring from emotion, it is ambition, or the desire whereby men, under the false cloak of piety, generally stir up discords and seditions. For he who desires to aid his fellows either in word or in deed, so that they may together enjoy the highest good, he, I say, will before all things strive to win them over with love: not to draw them into admiration, so that a system may be called after his name, nor to give any cause for envy. Further, in his conversation he will shrink from talking of men's faults, and will be careful to speak but sparingly of human infirmity: but he will dwell at length on human virtue or power, and the way whereby it may be perfected. Thus will men be stirred not by fear, nor by aversion, but only by the emotion of joy, to endeavour, so far as in them lies, to live in obedience to reason.

XXVI. Besides men, we know of no particular thing in nature in whose mind we may rejoice, and whom we can associate with ourselves in friendship or any sort of fellowship; therefore, whatsoever there be in nature besides man, a regard for our advantage does not call on us to preserve, but to preserve or destroy according to its various capabilities, and to adapt to our use as best we may.

XXVII. The advantage which we derive from things external to us, besides the experience and knowledge which we acquire from observing them, and from recombining their elements in different forms, is principally the preservation of the body; from this point of view, those things are most useful which can so feed and nourish the body, that all its parts may rightly fulfil their functions. For, in proportion as the body is capable of being affected in a greater variety of ways, and of affecting external bodies in a great number of ways, so much the more is the mind capable of thinking (IV. xxxviii. xxxix.). But there seem to be very few things of this kind in nature; wherefore for the due nourishment of the body we must use many foods of diverse nature. For the human body is composed of very many parts of different nature, which stand in continual need of varied nourishment, so that the whole body may be equally capable of doing everything that can follow from its own nature, and consequently that the mind also may be equally capable of forming many perceptions.

XXVIII. Now for providing these nourishments the strength of each individual would hardly suffice, if men did not lend one another mutual aid. But money has furnished us with a token for everything: hence it is with the notion of money, that the mind of the multitude is chiefly engrossed: nay, it can hardly conceive any kind of pleasure, which is not accompanied with the idea of money as cause.

XXIX. This result is the fault only of those, who seek money, not from poverty or to supply their necessary wants, but because they have learned the arts of gain, wherewith they bring themselves to great splendour. Certainly they nourish their bodies, according to custom, but scantily, believing that they lose as much of their wealth as they spend on the preservation of their body. But they who know the true use of money, and who fix the measure of wealth solely with regard to their actual needs, live content with little.

XXX. As, therefore, those things are good which assist the various parts of the body, and enable them to perform their functions; and as pleasure consists in an increase of, or aid to, man's power, in so far as he is composed of mind and body; it follows that all those things which bring pleasure are good. But seeing that things do not work with the object of giving us pleasure, and that their power of action is not tempered to suit our advantage, and, lastly, that pleasure is generally referred to one part of the body more than to the other parts; therefore most emotions of pleasure (unless reason and watchfulness be at hand), and consequently the desires arising therefrom, may become excessive. Moreover we may add that emotion leads us to pay most regard to what is agreeable in the present, nor can we estimate what is future with emotions equally vivid. (IV. xliv. note, and lx. note.)

XXXI. Superstition, on the other hand, seems to account as good all that brings pain, and as bad all that brings pleasure. However, as we said above (IV. xlv. note), none but the envious take delight in my infirmity and trouble. For the greater the pleasure whereby we are affected, the greater is the perfection whereto we pass, and consequently the more do we partake of the divine nature: no pleasure can ever be evil, which is regulated by a true regard for our advantage. But contrariwise he, who is led by fear and does good only to avoid evil, is not guided by reason.

XXXII. But human power is extremely limited, and is infinitely surpassed by the power of external causes; we have not, therefore, an absolute power of shaping to our use those things which are without us. Nevertheless, we shall bear with an equal mind all that happens to us in contravention to the claims of our own advantage, so long as we are conscious, that we have done our duty, and that the power which we possess is not sufficient to enable us to protect ourselves completely; remembering that we are a part of universal nature, and that we follow her order. If we have a clear and distinct understanding of this, that part of our nature which is defined by intelligence, in other words the better part of ourselves, will assuredly acquiesce in what befalls us, and in such acquiescence will endeavour to persist. For, in so far as we are intelligent beings, we cannot desire anything save that which is necessary, nor yield absolute acquiescence to anything, save to that which is true: wherefore, in so far as we have a right understanding of these things, the endeavour of the better part of ourselves is in harmony with the order of nature as a whole.

Part V

Of Human Freedom

AXIOMS

I. If two contrary actions be started in the same subject, a change must necessarily take place, either in both, or in one of the two, and continue until they cease to be contrary.

II. The power of an effect is defined by the power of its cause, in so far as its essence is explained or defined by the essence of its cause.

(This axiom is evident from III. vii.)

·Prop. I. *Even as thoughts and the ideas of things are arranged and associated in the mind, so are the modifications of body or the images of things precisely in the same way arranged and associated in the body.*

Proof.—The order and connection of ideas is the same (II. vii.) as the order and connection of things, and *vice versâ* the order and connection of things is the same (II. vi. Coroll. and vii.) as the order and connection of ideas. Wherefore, even as the order and connection of ideas in the mind takes place according to the order and association of modifications of the body (II. xviii.), so *vice versâ* (III. ii.) the order and connection of modifications of the body takes place in accordance with the manner, in which thoughts and the ideas of things are arranged and associated in the mind. *Q.E.D.*

Prop. II. *If we remove a disturbance of the spirit, or emotion, from the thought of an external cause, and unite it to other thoughts, then will the love or hatred towards that external cause, and also the vacillations of spirit which arise from these emotions, be destroyed.*

Proof.—That, which constitutes the reality of love or hatred, is pleasure or pain, accompanied by the idea of an external cause (Def. of the Emotions, vi. vii.); wherefore, when this cause is removed, the reality of love or hatred is removed with it; therefore these emotions and those which arise therefrom are destroyed. *Q.E.D.*

Prop. III. *An emotion, which is a passion, ceases to be a passion, as soon as we form a clear and distinct idea thereof.*

Proof.—An emotion, which is a passion, is a confused idea (by the general Def. of the Emotions). If, therefore, we form a clear and distinct idea of a given emotion, that idea will only be distinguished from the emotion, in so far as it is referred to the mind only, by reason (II. xxi. and note); therefore (III. iii.), the emotion will cease to be a passion. *Q.E.D.*

Corollary.—An emotion therefore becomes more under our control, and the mind is less passive in respect to it, in proportion as it is more known to us.

Prop. IV. *There is no modification of the body, whereof we cannot form some clear and distinct conception.*

Proof.—Properties which are common to all things can only be conceived adequately (II. xxxviii.); therefore (II. xii. and Lemma ii. after II. xiii.) there is no modification of the body, whereof we cannot form some clear and distinct conception. *Q.E.D.*

Corollary.—Hence it follows that there is no emotion, whereof we cannot form some clear and distinct conception. For an emotion is the idea of a modification of the body (by the general Def. of the Emotions), and must therefore (by the preceding Prop.) involve some clear and distinct conception.

Prop. VI. *The mind has greater power over the emotions and is less subject thereto, in so far as it understands all things as necessary.*

Proof.—The mind understands all things to be necessary (I. xxix.) and to be determined to existence and operation by an infinite chain of causes; therefore (by the foregoing Proposition), it thus far brings it about, that it is less subject to the emotions arising therefrom, and (III. xlviii.) feels less emotion towards the things themselves. *Q.E.D.*

Note.—The more this knowledge, that things are necessary, is applied to particular things, which we conceive more distinctly and vividly, the greater is the power of the mind over the emotions, as experience also testifies. For we see, that the pain arising from the loss of any good is mitigated, as soon as the man who has lost it perceives, that it could not by any means have been preserved. So also we see that no one pities an infant, because it cannot speak, walk, or reason, or lastly, because it passes so many years, as it were, in unconsciousness. Whereas, if most people were born full-grown and only one here and there as an infant, everyone would pity the infants; because infancy would not then be looked on as a state natural and necessary, but as a fault or delinquency in Nature; and we may note several other instances of the same sort.

PROP. VII. *Emotions which are aroused or spring from reason, if we take account of time, are stronger than those, which are attributable to particular objects that we regard as absent.*

Proof.—We do not regard a thing as absent, by reason of the emotion wherewith we conceive it, but by reason of the body being affected by another emotion excluding the existence of the said thing (II. xvii.). Wherefore, the emotion, which is referred to the thing which we regard as absent, is not of a nature to overcome the rest of a man's activities and power (IV. vi.), but is, on the contrary, of a nature to be in some sort controlled by the emotions, which exclude the existence of its external cause (IV. ix.). But an emotion which springs from reason is necessarily referred to the common properties of things (see the def. of reason in II. xl. note ii.), which we always regard as present (for there can be nothing to exclude their present existence), and which we always conceive in the same manner (II. xxxviii.). Wherefore an emotion of this kind always remains the same; and consequently (V. Ax. i.) emotions, which are contrary thereto and are not kept going by their external causes, will be obliged to adapt themselves to it more and more, until they are no longer contrary to it; to this extent the emotion which springs from reason is more powerful. *Q.E.D.*

PROP. X. *So long as we are not assailed by emotions contrary to our nature, we have the power of arranging and associating the modifications of our body according to the intellectual order.*

Proof.—The emotions, which are contrary to our nature, that is (IV. xxx.), which are bad, are bad in so far as they impede the mind from understanding (IV. xxvii.). So long, therefore, as we are not assailed by emotions contrary to our nature, the mind's power, whereby it endeavours to understand things (IV. xxvi.), is not impeded, and therefore it is able to form clear and distinct ideas and to deduce them one from another (II. xl. note ii. and xlvii. note); consequently we have in such cases the power of arranging and associating the modifications of the body according to the intellectual order. *Q.E.D.*

Note.—By this power of rightly arranging and associating the bodily modifications we can guard ourselves from being easily affected by evil emotions. For (V. vii.) a greater force is needed for controlling the emotions, when they are arranged and associated according to the intellectual order, than when they are uncertain and unsettled. The best we can do, therefore, so long as we do not possess a perfect knowledge of our emotions, is to frame a system of right conduct, or fixed practical precepts, to commit it to memory, and to apply it forthwith to the particular circumstances which now and again meet us in life, so that our imagination may become fully imbued therewith, and that it may be always ready to our hand. For instance, we have laid down among the rules of life (IV. xlvi. and note), that hatred should be overcome with love or high-mindedness, and not requited with hatred in return. Now, that this precept of reason may be always ready to our hand in time of need, we should often think over and reflect upon the wrongs generally committed by men, and in what manner and way they may be best warded off by high-mindedness: we shall thus associate the idea of wrong with the idea of this precept, which accordingly will always be ready for use when a wrong is done to us (II. xviii.) If we keep also in readiness the notion of our true advantage, and of the good which follows from mutual friendships, and common fellowships; further, if we remember that complete acquiescence is the result of the right way of life (IV. lii.), and that men, no less than everything else, act by the necessity of their nature: in such case I say the wrong, or the hatred, which commonly arises therefrom, will engross a very small part of our imagination and will be easily overcome; or, if the anger which springs from a grievous wrong be not overcome easily, it will nevertheless be overcome, though not without a spiritual conflict, far sooner than if we had not thus reflected on the subject beforehand. As is indeed evident from V. vi. vii. viii. We should, in the same way, reflect on courage as a means of overcoming fear; the ordinary dangers of life should frequently be brought to mind and imagined, together with the means whereby through readiness of resource and strength of mind we can avoid and overcome them. But we must note, that in arranging our thoughts and conceptions we should always bear in mind that which is good in every individual thing (IV. lxiii. Coroll. and III. lix.), in order that we may always be determined to action by an emotion of pleasure. For instance, if a man sees that he is too keen in the pursuit of honour, let him think over its right use, the end for which it should be pursued, and the means whereby he may attain it. Let him not think of its misuse, and its emptiness, and the fickleness of mankind, and the like, whereof no man thinks except through a morbidness of disposition; with thoughts like these do the most ambitious most torment themselves, when they despair of gaining the distinctions they hanker after, and in thus giving vent to their anger would fain appear wise. Wherefore it is certain that those, who cry out the loudest against the misuse of honour and the vanity of the world, are those who most greedily covet it. This is not peculiar to the ambitious, but is common to all who are ill-used by fortune, and who are infirm in spirit. For a poor man also, who is miserly, will talk incessantly of the misuse of wealth and of the vices of the rich; whereby he merely torments himself, and shows the world that he is intolerant, not only of his own poverty, but also of other people's riches. So, again, those who have been ill received by a woman they love think of nothing but the inconstancy, treachery, and other stock faults of the fair sex; all of which they consign to oblivion, directly they are again taken into favour by their sweetheart. Thus he who would govern his emotions and appetite solely by the love of freedom strives, as far as he can, to gain a knowledge of the virtues and their causes, and to fill his spirit with the joy which arises from the true knowledge of them: he will in no wise desire to dwell on men's faults, or to carp at his fellows, or to revel in a false show of freedom. Whosoever will diligently observe and practise these precepts (which indeed are not difficult) will verily, in a short space of time, be able, for the most part, to direct his actions according to the commandments of reason.

PROP. XIV. *The mind can bring it about, that all bodily modifications or images of things may be referred to the idea of God.*

Proof.—There is no modification of the body, whereof the mind may not form some clear and distinct conception (V. iv.); wherefore it can bring it about, that they should all be referred to the idea of God (I. xv.). *Q.E.D.*

PROP. XV. *He who clearly and distinctly understands himself and his emotions loves God, and so much the more in proportion as he more understands himself and his emotions.*

Proof.—He who clearly and distinctly understands himself and his emotions feels pleasure (III. liii.), and this pleasure is (by the last Prop.) accompa-

nied by the idea of God; therefore (Def. of the Emotions, vi.) such an one loves God, and (for the same reason) so much the more in proportion as he more understands himself and his emotions. *Q.E.D.*

PROP. XVI. *This love towards God must hold the chief place in the mind.*

Proof.—For this love is associated with all the modifications of the body (V. xiv.) and is fostered by them all (V. xv.); therefore (V. xi.), it must hold the chief place in the mind. *Q.E.D.*

PROP. XVII. *God is without passions, neither is he affected by any emotion of pleasure or pain.*

Proof.—All ideas, in so far as they are referred to God, are true (II. xxxii.), that is (II. Def. iv.) adequate; and therefore (by the general Def. of the Emotions) God is without passions. Again, God cannot pass either to a greater or to a lesser perfection (I. xx. Coroll. ii.); therefore (by Def. of the Emotions, ii. iii.) he is not affected by any emotion of pleasure or pain.

Corollary.—Strictly speaking, God does not love or hate anyone. For God (by the foregoing Prop.) is not affected by any emotion of pleasure or pain, consequently (Def. of the Emotions, vi. vii.) he does not love or hate anyone.

PROP. XVIII. *No one can hate God.*

Proof.—The idea of God which is in us is adequate and perfect (II. xlvi. xlvii.); wherefore, in so far as we contemplate God, we are active (III. iii.); consequently (III. lix.) there can be no pain accompanied by the idea of God, in other words (Def. of the Emotions, vii.), no one can hate God. *Q.E.D.*

Corollary.—Love towards God cannot be turned into hate.

Note.—It may be objected that, as we understand God as the cause of all things, we by that very fact regard God as the cause of pain. But I make answer, that, in so far as we understand the causes of pain, it to that extent (V. iii.) ceases to be a passion, that is, it ceases to be pain (III. lix.); therefore, in so far as we understand God to be the cause of pain, we to that extent feel pleasure.

PROP. XXIII. *The human mind cannot be absolutely destroyed with the body, but there remains of it something which is eternal.*

Proof.—There is necessarily in God a concept or idea, which expresses the essence of the human body (last Prop.), which, therefore, is necessarily something appertaining to the essence of the human mind

(II. xiii.). But we have not assigned to the human mind any duration, definable by time, except in so far as it expresses the actual existence of the body, which is explained through duration, and may be defined by time—that is (II. viii. Coroll.), we do not assign to it duration, except while the body endures. Yet, as there is something, notwithstanding, which is conceived by a certain eternal necessity through the very essence of God (last Prop.); this something, which appertains to the essence of the mind, will necessarily be eternal. Q.E.D.

Note.—This idea, which expresses the essence of the body under the form of eternity, is, as we have said, a certain mode of thinking, which belongs to the essence of the mind, and is necessarily eternal. Yet it is not possible that we should remember that we existed before our body, for our body can bear no trace of such existence, neither can eternity be defined in terms of time, or have any relation to time. But, notwithstanding, we feel and know that we are eternal. For the mind feels those things that it conceives by understanding, no less than those things that it remembers. For the eyes of the mind, whereby it sees and observes things, are none other than proofs. Thus, although we do not remember that we existed before the body, yet we feel that our mind, in so far as it involves the essence of the body, under the form of eternity, is eternal, and that thus its existence cannot be defined in terms of time, or explained through duration. Thus our mind can only be said to endure, and its existence can only be defined by a fixed time, in so far as it involves the actual existence of the body. Thus far only has it the power of determining the existence of things by time, and conceiving them under the category of duration.

PROP. XXIV. The more we understand particular things, the more do we understand God.

Proof.—This is evident from I. xxv. Coroll.

PROP. XXV. The highest endeavour of the mind, and the highest virtue is to understand things by the third kind of knowledge.

Proof.—The third kind of knowledge proceeds from an adequate idea of certain attributes of God to an adequate knowledge of the essence of things (see its definition II. xl. note ii.); and, in proportion as we understand things more in this way, we better understand God (by the last Prop.); therefore (IV. xxviii.) the highest virtue of the mind, that is (IV. Def. viii.)

the power, or nature, or (III. vii.) highest endeavour of the mind, is to understand things by the third kind of knowledge. Q.E.D.

PROP. XXVI. In proportion as the mind is more capable of understanding things by the third kind of knowledge, it desires more to understand things by that kind.

Proof.—This is evident. For, in so far as we conceive the mind to be capable of conceiving things by this kind of knowledge, we, to that extent, conceive it as determined thus to conceive things; and consequently (Def. of the Emotions, i.), the mind desires so to do, in proportion as it is more capable thereof. Q.E.D.

PROP. XXVII. From this third kind of knowledge arises the highest possible mental acquiescence.

Proof.—The highest virtue of the mind is to know God (IV. xxviii.), or to understand things by the third kind of knowledge (V. xxv.), and this virtue is greater in proportion as the mind knows things more by the said kind of knowledge (V. xxiv.): consequently, he who knows things by this kind of knowledge passes to the summit of human perfection, and is therefore (Def. of the Emotions, ii.) affected by the highest pleasure, such pleasure being accompanied by the idea of himself and his own virtue; thus (Def. of the Emotions, xxv.), from this kind of knowledge arises the highest possible acquiescence. Q.E.D.

PROP. XXVIII. The endeavour or desire to know things by the third kind of knowledge cannot arise from the first, but from the second kind of knowledge.

Proof.—This proposition is self-evident. For whatsoever we understand clearly and distinctly, we understand either through itself, or through that which is conceived through itself; that is, ideas which are clear and distinct in us, or which are referred to the third kind of knowledge (II. xl. note ii.) cannot follow from ideas that are fragmentary and confused, and are referred to knowledge of the first kind, but must follow from adequate ideas, or ideas of the second and third kind of knowledge; therefore (Def. of the Emotions, i.), the desire of knowing things by the third kind of knowledge cannot arise from the first, but from the second kind. Q.E.D.

PROP. XXIX. Whatsoever the mind understands under the form of eternity, it does not understand by virtue of conceiving the present actual existence of the body, but by virtue of conceiving the essence of the body under the form of eternity.

Proof.—In so far as the mind conceives the present existence of its body, it to that extent conceives duration which can be determined by time, and to that extent only has it the power of conceiving things in relation to time (V. xxi. II. xxvi.). But eternity cannot be explained in terms of duration (I. Def. viii. and explanation). Therefore to this extent the mind has not the power of conceiving things under the form of eternity, but it possesses such power, because it is of the nature of reason to conceive things under the form of eternity (II. xliv. Coroll. ii.), and also because it is of the nature of the mind to conceive the essence of the body under the form of eternity (V. xxiii.), for besides these two there is nothing which belongs to the essence of mind (II. xiii.). Therefore this power of conceiving things under the form of eternity only belongs to the mind in virtue of the mind's conceiving the essence of the body under the form of eternity. *Q.E.D.*

Note.—Things are conceived by us as actual in two ways; either as existing in relation to a given time and place, or as contained in God and following from the necessity of the divine nature. Whatsoever we conceive in this second way as true or real, we conceive under the form of eternity, and their ideas involve the eternal and infinite essence of God, as we showed in II. xlv. and note, which see.

Prop. XXX. *Our mind, in so far as it knows itself and the body under the form of eternity, has to that extent necessarily a knowledge of God, and knows that it is in God, and is conceived through God.*

Proof.—Eternity is the very essence of God, in so far as this involves necessary existence (I. Def. viii.). Therefore to conceive things under the form of eternity, is to conceive things in so far as they are conceived through the essence of God as real entities, or in so far as they involve existence through the essence of God; wherefore our mind, in so far as it conceives itself and the body under the form of eternity, has to that extent necessarily a knowledge of God, and knows, &c. *Q.E.D.*

Prop. XXXI. *The third kind of knowledge depends on the mind, as its formal cause, in so far as the mind itself is eternal.*

Proof.—The mind does not conceive anything under the form of eternity, except in so far as it conceives its own body under the form of eternity

(V. xxix.); that is, except in so far as it is eternal (V. xxi. xxiii.); therefore (by the last Prop.), in so far as it is eternal, it possesses the knowledge of God, which knowledge is necessarily adequate (II. xlvi.); hence the mind, in so far as it is eternal, is capable of knowing everything which can follow from this given knowledge of God (II. xl.), in other words, of knowing things by the third kind of knowledge (see Def. in II. xl. note ii.), whereof accordingly the mind (III. Def. i.), in so far as it is eternal, is the adequate or formal cause of such knowledge. *Q.E.D.*

Note.—In proportion, therefore, as a man is more potent in this kind of knowledge, he will be more completely conscious of himself and of God; in other words, he will be more perfect and blessed, as will appear more clearly in the sequel. But we must here observe that, although we are already certain that the mind is eternal, in so far as it conceives things under the form of eternity, yet, in order that what we wish to show may be more readily explained and better understood, we will consider the mind itself, as though it had just begun to exist and to understand things under the form of eternity, as indeed we have done hitherto; this we may do without any danger of error, so long as we are careful not to draw any conclusion, unless our premises are plain.

Prop. XXXII. *Whatsoever we understand by the third kind of knowledge, we take delight in, and our delight is accompanied by the idea of God as cause.*

Proof.—From this kind of knowledge arises the highest possible mental acquiescence, that is (Def. of the Emotions, xxv.), pleasure, and this acquiescence is accompanied by the idea of the mind itself (V. xxvii.), and consequently (V. xxx.) the idea also of God as cause. *Q.E.D.*

Corollary.—From the third kind of knowledge necessarily arises the intellectual love of God. From this kind of knowledge arises pleasure accompanied by the idea of God as cause, that is (Def. of the Emotions, vi.), the love of God; not in so far as we imagine him as present (V. xxix.), but in so far as we understand him to be eternal; this is what I call the intellectual love of God.

Prop. XXXIII. *The intellectual love of God, which arises from the third kind of knowledge, is eternal.*

Proof.—The third kind of knowledge is eternal (V. xxxi. I. Ax. iii.); therefore (by the same Axiom) the love which arises therefrom is also necessarily eternal. *Q.E.D.*

Note.—Although this love towards God has (by the foregoing Prop.) no beginning, it yet possesses all the perfections of love, just as though it had arisen as we feigned in the Coroll. of the last Prop. Nor is there here any difference, except that the mind possesses as eternal those same perfections which we feigned to accrue to it, and they are accompanied by the idea of God as eternal cause. If pleasure consists in the transition to a greater perfection, assuredly blessedness must consist in the mind being endowed with perfection itself.

PROP. XXXIV. *The mind is, only while the body endures, subject to those emotions which are attributable to passions.*

Proof.—Imagination is the idea wherewith the mind contemplates a thing as present (II. xvii. note); yet this idea indicates rather the present disposition of the human body than the nature of the external thing (II. xvi. Coroll. ii.). Therefore emotion (see general Def. of Emotions) is imagination, in so far as it indicates the present disposition of the body; therefore (V. xxi.) the mind is, only while the body endures, subject to emotions which are attributable to passions. *Q.E.D.*

Corollary.—Hence it follows that no love save intellectual love is eternal.

Note.—If we look to men's general opinion, we shall see that they are indeed conscious of the eternity of their mind, but that they confuse eternity with duration, and ascribe it to the imagination or the memory which they believe to remain after death.

PROP. XXXV. *God loves himself with an infinite intellectual love.*

Proof.—God is absolutely infinite (I. Def. vi.), that is (II. Def. vi.), the nature of God rejoices in infinite perfection; and such rejoicing is (II. iii.) accompanied by the idea of himself, that is (I. xi. and Def. i.), the idea of his own cause: now this is what we have (in V. xxxii. Coroll.) described as intellectual love.

PROP. XXXVI. *The intellectual love of the mind towards God is that very love of God whereby God loves himself, not in so far as he is infinite, but in so far as he can be explained through the essence of the human mind regarded under the form of eternity; in other words, the*

intellectual love of the mind towards God is part of the infinite love wherewith God loves himself.

Proof.—This love of the mind must be referred to the activities of the mind (V. xxxii. Coroll. and III. iii.); it is itself, indeed, an activity whereby the mind regards itself accompanied by the idea of God as cause (V. xxxii. and Coroll.); that is (I. xxv. Coroll. and II. xi. Coroll.), an activity whereby God, in so far as he can be explained through the human mind, regards himself accompanied by the idea of himself; therefore (by the last Prop.), this love of the mind is part of the infinite love wherewith God loves himself. *Q.E.D.*

Corollary.—Hence it follows that God, in so far as he loves himself, loves man, and, consequently, that the love of God towards men, and the intellectual love of the mind towards God are identical.

PROP. XXXVII. *There is nothing in nature, which is contrary to this intellectual love, or which can take it away.*

Proof.—This intellectual love follows necessarily from the nature of the mind, in so far as the latter is regarded through the nature of God as an eternal truth (V. xxxiii. and xxix.). If, therefore, there should be anything which would be contrary to this love, that thing would be contrary to that which is true; consequently, that, which should be able to take away this love, would cause that which is true to be false; an obvious absurdity. Therefore there is nothing in nature which, &c. *Q.E.D.*

PROP. XXXVIII. *In proportion as the mind understands more things by the second and third kind of knowledge, it is less subject to those emotions which are evil, and stands in less fear of death.*

Proof.—The mind's essence consists in knowledge (II. xi.); therefore, in proportion as the mind understands more things by the second and third kinds of knowledge, the greater will be the part of it that endures (V. xxix. and xxiii.), and, consequently (by the last Prop.), the greater will be the part that is not touched by the emotions, which are contrary to our nature, or in other words, evil (IV. xxx.). Thus, in proportion as the mind understands more things by the second and third kinds of knowledge, the greater will be the part of it, that remains unimpaired, and, consequently, less subject to emotions, &c. *Q.E.D.*

PROP. XXXIX. *He, who possesses a body capable of the greatest number of activities, possesses a mind whereof the greatest part is eternal.*

Proof.—He, who possesses a body capable of the greatest number of activities, is least agitated by those emotions which are evil (IV. xxxviii.)—that is (IV. xxx.), by those emotions which are contrary to our nature; therefore (V. x.), he possesses the power of arranging and associating the modifications of the body according to the intellectual order, and, consequently, of bringing it about, that all the modifications of the body should be referred to the idea of God; whence it will come to pass that (V. xv.) he will be affected with love towards God, which (V. xvi.) must occupy or constitute the chief part of the mind; therefore (V. xxxiii.), such a man will possess a mind whereof the chief part is eternal. *Q.E.D.*

PROP. XL. *In proportion as each thing possesses more of perfection, so is it more active, and less passive; and, vice versâ, in proportion as it is more active, so is it more perfect.*

Proof.—In proportion as each thing is more perfect, it possesses more of reality (II. Def. vi.), and, consequently (III. iii. and note), it is to that extent more active and less passive. This demonstration may be reversed, and thus prove that, in proportion as a thing is more active, so is it more perfect. *Q.E.D.*

Corollary.—Hence it follows that the part of the mind which endures, be it great or small, is more perfect than the rest. For the eternal part of the mind (V. xxiii. xxix.) is the understanding, through which alone we are said to act (III. iii.); the part which we have shown to perish is the imagination (V. xxi.), through which only we are said to be passive (III. iii. and general Def. of the Emotions); therefore, the former, be it great or small, is more perfect than the latter. *Q.E.D.*

PROP. XLI. *Even if we did not know that our mind is eternal, we should still consider as of primary importance piety and religion, and generally all things which, in Part IV., we showed to be attributable to courage and highmindedness.*

Proof.—The first and only foundation of virtue, or the rule of right living is (IV. xxii. Coroll. and xxiv.) seeking one's own true interest. Now, while we determined what reason prescribes as useful, we took no account of the mind's eternity, which has only become known to us in this Fifth Part. Although we were ignorant at that time that the mind is eternal, we nevertheless stated that the qualities attributable to courage and high-mindedness are of primary importance. Therefore, even if we were still ignorant of this doctrine, we should yet put the aforesaid precepts of reason in the first place. *Q.E.D.*

PROP. XLII. *Blessedness is not the reward of virtue, but virtue itself; neither do we rejoice therein, because we control our lusts, but, contrariwise, because we rejoice therein, we are able to control our lusts.*

Proof.—Blessedness consists in love towards God (V. xxxvi. and note), which love springs from the third kind of knowledge (V. xxxii. Coroll.); therefore this love (III. iii. lix.) must be referred to the mind, in so far as the latter is active; therefore (IV. Def. viii.) it is virtue itself. This was our first point. Again, in proportion as the mind rejoices more in this divine love or blessedness, so does it the more understand (V. xxxii.); that is (V. iii. Coroll.), so much the more power has it over the emotions, and (V. xxxviii.) so much the less is it subject to those emotions which are evil; therefore, in proportion as the mind rejoices in this divine love or blessedness, so has it the power of controlling lusts. And, since human power in controlling the emotions consists solely in the understanding, it follows that no one rejoices in blessedness, because he has controlled his lusts, but, contrariwise, his power of controlling his lusts arises from this blessedness itself. *Q.E.D.*

Note.—I have thus completed all I wished to set forth touching the mind's power over the emotions and the mind's freedom. Whence it appears, how potent is the wise man, and how much he surpasses the ignorant man, who is driven only by his lusts. For the ignorant man is not only distracted in various ways by external causes without ever gaining the true acquiescence of his spirit, but moreover lives, as it were unwitting of himself, and of God, and of things, and as soon as he ceases to suffer, ceases also to be.

Whereas the wise man, in so far as he is regarded as such, is scarcely at all disturbed in spirit, but, being conscious of himself, and of God, and of things, by a certain eternal necessity, never ceases to be, but always possesses true acquiescence of his spirit.

If the way which I have pointed out as leading to this result seems exceedingly hard, it may nevertheless be discovered. Needs must it be hard, since it is so seldom found. How would it be possible, if salvation were ready to our hand, and could without great labour be found, that it should be by almost all men neglected? But all things excellent are as difficult as they are rare.

STUDY QUESTIONS: SPINOZA, *THE ETHICS*

1. What is Spinoza's main aim in his *Ethics*?
2. What does Spinoza mean by 'God'? How does he define 'substance'?
3. What is Spinoza's argument for the claim that substance exists necessarily?
4. Why does God have infinite attributes?
5. Why is there only one substance? What is the argument?
6. What does Spinoza mean by 'finite modes'? How are they related to substance?
7. How are the basic laws of physics related to God?
8. How are thought and extension related?
9. Explain Spinoza's claim that the mind is the idea of the body.
10. What arguments would Spinoza give to refute Descartes' mind/body dualism?
11. Spinoza claims that all ideas, insofar as they are referred to God, are true (II.32). What does this mean? How does Spinoza try to support this? How does he account for falsity?
12. How does Spinoza define emotion?
13. Spinoza states that active states of mind arise solely from adequate ideas. How does Spinoza use this statement in relation to the overall aim of the *Ethics*?
14. The essence of a thing is its endeavor to persist in its own being (III.7). What does this mean? Why is this point important for Spinoza?
15. In the Appendix to Part IV, Spinoza claims that a certain kind of desire is always good. Which desires are those? How does this kind of desire relate to one's having an adequate conception of oneself?
16. How can an emotion cease to be a passion? What marks the difference between an emotion that is a passion and one that is not?
17. How can reason free a person from the passions? Why is such a freedom good?
18. How does the intellectual love of God arise? What is that love identical to?

Philosophical Bridges: Spinoza's Influence

Spinoza's main metaphysical conclusion is that there is only one substance. This rejection of a God/universe dualism makes Spinoza part of a long tradition of pantheism and deism that includes Friedrich Schelling, G. W. F. Hegel, and other nineteenth-century idealists who tend to regard God as the Absolute or the all-encompassing infinite totality. Hegel claimed that to be a philosopher, one must first be a Spinozist. Just as he repudiates a God/universe separation, Spinoza also rejects Descartes' mind/body distinction. Mind and body are two aspects of persons. This type of view has seemed attractive to many philosophers who are unwilling to accept either strict materialism or dualism. For example, the twentieth-century Oxford philosopher Peter Strawson argues in his book *Individuals* (1959) that 'person' is a basic or primitive concept and not a compound of mind and body. Mental and bodily predicates pick out two aspects of persons rather than two substances.

Perhaps the most consistently influential aspect of Spinoza's work is his ethical theory. This persistence is due to at least three factors:

1. First, Spinoza defines ethics in terms of personal development rather than moral requirements imposed by the needs of society. Ethics is a personal question of combating

negative and dehabilitating passions, such as hatred, fear, jealousy, and anger, within one-self and of cultivating an understanding that naturally breeds love. It is not merely a question of complying with social moral rules. This aspect of Spinoza's work has inspired recent writers such as Michel Foucault to distinguish ethics and morality.

2. Second, Spinoza's ethical theory is based on a metaphysical and spiritual vision of the universe, but it is not tied explicitly to a specific religious tradition. It has the majesty of a religious metaphysics but apparently without being doctrinaire. This has made it appealing to pantheists and deists. Spinoza sees the divine in nature rather than outside it; God is immanent rather than transcendental. In other words, nature has divine qualities, and our ethical lives should be a response to this facet of nature. This aspect of Spinoza's thinking appealed greatly to the Romantics of the nineteenth-century. The first romantic champion of Spinoza's *Ethics* was Friedrich Jacobi, around 1785, who made the work famous. From then on, it influenced many Romantic German thinkers such as Schelling (1775–1854) and especially the great German philosopher poet Johann Goethe (1749–1832), who said that he was 'converted' to the *Ethics* on first reading. From there, Spinoza's influence spread to Britain when the English poets Samuel Taylor Coleridge and William Wordsworth visited Germany in 1798 and passed the Romantic spirit in Spinoza onto Percy Bysshe Shelley and John Keats.

3. Recent ecological thinkers have drawn inspiration from a third aspect of Spinoza's ethics: the holism. For instance, 'deep ecology,' which was developed by Arne Naess in the 1970s, opposes so-called shallow approaches that characterize our environmental problems merely as the prevalence of pollution and the depletion of resources. Such views are superficial because they fail to identify our ecological predicament as constituted by an unhealthy way of life and unsustainable modes of thinking. Some deep ecologists argue that the conception of an individual as an entity separate from its environment is a mistaken metaphysical notion. The universe consists of parts within wholes, and the only genuine whole is the universe itself. Like Spinoza, some deep ecologists see the process of acquiring ecological awareness as a process of spiritual transformation through which one transcends the limited individualistic conception of the self.

In his own time, Spinoza's work had little immediate effect. It was considered atheistic. For instance, in 1732 Berkeley called him the 'great leader of our modern infidels,' and even Hume refers to the 'hideous hypothesis' of the famous atheist. The main exception was Leibniz, who was influenced strongly by Spinoza, whom he visited in October 1676.

Gottfried Leibniz (1646–1716)

Biographical History

Leibniz entered Leipzig University, in 1661, where he studied philosophy and law. During the rest of his life, he worked for various German nobles and European courts. A diplomat, mining engineer, and inventor, he also worked as a royal historian and librarian. As an academic, he was a world-famous philosopher, physicist, and mathematician, as well as a trained lawyer and a pioneer in logic.

In 1667, Leibniz was appointed to the court of the elector of Mainz, which involved him in various diplomatic missions, including one to Paris. During his four years in the

French capital, he studied with the mathematician Christian Huygens and developed a calculating machine that could multiply and divide. This intense activity culminated in his discovery of differential and integral calculus in 1676. However, it was not until 1684 that he published his findings, causing a controversy with Newton.

In 1676, Leibniz moved to Hanover to act as adviser and librarian to the duke of Brunswick, who set him the daunting task of researching a family history. This undertaking burdened Leibniz for the rest of his life, distracting him from his more fundamental projects. From 1687 to 1690, he traveled in Europe, investigating historical archives. In 1690, he returned to Hanover, where he spent most of the remainder of his life. He became close to the Duchess Sophie and her daughter, Sophie Charlotte (later queen of Prussia). His discussions with Sophie Charlotte resulted in his *Theodicy*.

By 1704, Leibniz had completed a commentary on Locke's *Essay Concerning Human Understanding*, but, in view of Locke's death, he declined to publish the critique. Leibniz proposed many practical ventures. Between 1679 and 1686, he designed windmills and pumps, and drafted extensive plans for draining the Harz silver mines. Later, he experimented with silk production. In 1700, he founded the Berlin Academy of Sciences. He also tried to encourage an alliance between the various Christian faiths and, later, between the Christian states.

Although Leibniz was a prolific writer, there is no single systematic exposition of his philosophy as a whole. His written works are only short summaries of part of his thought. He wrote much of his philosophy in letters and notes. His main metaphysical works are *Discourse on Metaphysics*, 1686; *New Essays Concerning Human Understanding*, 1704; *Theodicy*, 1710; and *Monadology*, 1710.

Philosophical Overview

Leibniz argues that the universe consists in an infinite number of mindlike, nonmaterial and independent monads, one of which is God. This conclusion is derived from his views of the proposition, truth, and substance. These views imply that space, time, and all relations are unreal. They also imply that infinitely divisible matter is also unreal.

Substance and Truth

Leibniz's philosophy begins with the claim that the concept of any individual substance must be entirely determinate and complete, and from which it is possible to infer all the properties of that individual. Without such a complete concept, we would be unable to distinguish a substance from all other possible individuals. In short, a substance must be individuated from all other possible individual substances by the sum total of its predicates. Leibniz distinguishes *the* concept of Caesar from *a* concept of Caesar. To have *the* concept of Caesar, one would need to have complete knowledge of every detail of his life, which only God can have.

From this conception of a substance, Leibniz derives his theory of truth. A proposition is true if and only if the predicate concept is contained in the subject concept. For example, in the 'the hairless man is bald,' the subject-concept ('the hairless man') contains the predicate-concept ('is bald'). Leibniz maintains that this applies to *all* true propositions, which appears to have the consequence that all true propositions are necessary.

Leibniz defends his analysis by arguing that although all propositions about the nature of an individual are necessarily true, those concerning its existence are contingent. For example, it is a contradiction to deny the essential truth that Adam was the first man. However, we can deny without contradiction that Adam ever existed. Propositions that assert actual existence are contingent because what exists depends on the free choice of God. In other words, there is an indefinite number of possible Adams, each one of which must be individuated by its own complete concept. However, only one of those possible Adams may exist, and which one does exist is a contingent truth, dependent on God's choice.

From this theory of truth, Leibniz derives the Principle of Sufficient Reason, which states that for every fact there must be a sufficient reason why things are so and not otherwise. To state the reason for the truth of any proposition requires giving an a priori proof of that proposition, which consists in showing that the subject contains the predicate. Contingent truths will have an analysis that is infinite.

Space and Time
Space Is Relational

In his letters to Samuel Clarke, Leibniz advocates a relational theory of space and time. This is opposed to the Newtonian absolute theory, according to which space is an unlimited whole that exists independently of objects. In contrast, Leibniz denies that space is like a container that exists logically prior to and independently of physical bodies; it is, rather, nothing except a system of spatial relations.

Leibniz argues that Newton's view contravenes the Principle of Sufficient Reason. It implies that all objects could have been differently situated in absolute space, while maintaining their positions relative to each other. Leibniz's theory implies that such a supposition is meaningless. Leibniz argues that Newton's theory contradicts the Principle of Sufficient Reason because God could have no possible reason for creating the physical universe in a different region of space or at a different period of time. Since everything must have a sufficient reason, it cannot make sense to say that the universe could have been created earlier or elsewhere. Therefore, the absolute theory is mistaken.

Likewise, Newton's theory violates the Principle of the Identity of Indiscernibles. Points of absolute space are clearly qualitatively similar in all respects (that is, they are indiscernible), and yet the absolute theory maintains that they are numerically distinct. Furthermore, Leibniz claims that the Newtonian idea of space and time as absolute and infinite entities contradicts the uniqueness of God. If God is the only infinite individual, space and time cannot be absolute and infinite.

Relations Are Ideal

Leibniz argues that all propositions can be reduced to the subject-predicate form. In a subject-predicate proposition, a property is affirmed or denied for the subject; for example, 'Adam was the first man.' However, relational propositions, such as 'X is to the left of Y,' are not of the subject-predicate form. According to Leibniz, all other types of proposition can be reduced to the subject-predicate form. This implies that all relations are merely ideal or mental constructions, which have their basis in the nonrelational properties of substances. In other words, what is affirmed by a relational proposition can be asserted with purely subject-predicate propositions.

These points have metaphysical importance. The ontological counterparts of subject-predicate propositions are substances and their properties. Because subject-predicate propositions are basic, the universe is describable completely by means of them. Thus, the universe ultimately consists only of substances and their properties, and all relations are ideal or unreal.

Therefore, Space Is Unreal

Leibniz argues that relations are not real; combined with the relational theory of space and time, this implies that space and time are unreal or ideal. This argument supports Leibniz's contention that reality consists of nonspatial substances. Space and time are appearances that have their real basis in the nature of substance.

Monads

Leibniz holds that there are infinitely many simple substances, which he calls 'monads.' These substances must be simple, because any thing with parts depends for its reality on those parts, and substances do not depend for their reality on anything else (Monadology, M, 2). The claim that substances are simple implies that material objects are not real, and that monads lack spatial extension. If all substances must be indivisible, then extended and divisible matter cannot be a substance.

Consequently, substances must be mindlike entities with mental states. This is because, insofar as reality appears to be extended, it must appear so to some mind. Therefore, reality consists solely of nonspatial monads and their mental states. This reality merely appears to consist of spatial physical objects. Reality is so perceived by the monads themselves. Spatial bodies are merely the appearances of and for mindlike monads.

Furthermore, Leibniz argues that these monads must have some strange properties. Like Spinoza, Leibniz denies the possibility of causal relations between substances. Substances cannot interact, because the proposition 'A acts on B' is relational and thus is ideal. Furthermore, each substance has its own complete concept, and this predetermines all its predicates at all times. It develops in accordance with its predetermined nature, which unfolds without any outside influence, except that of God (M, 11).

Nevertheless, each monad stands in relation to all other substances; the complete concept of substance A must contain its relations to all other things at all times. However, since all relations are ideal, they are reducible to the properties of each substance. In this sense, any individual substance expresses or mirrors the whole universe (M, 56).

Since there are in fact no causal relations between monads, this mirroring of monads cannot be explained causally. Each monad develops spontaneously and in isolation, in accordance with its predetermined nature. A change in any one monad is reflected in the changing state of any other monad because God determines the nature of each monad so that its state is coordinated in a preestablished harmony, without the need for interference (M, 51 and 78).

God and the Best

Leibniz tries to prove the existence of God. Given God's existence, Leibniz argues that this world must be the best of all possible worlds. All contingency in the world is due to God's free choice; God chooses which possible world to make actual. Nevertheless, we know a priori that God is perfect and that, being perfect, he chooses the best of all possible worlds. Thus, we know a priori that the actual world is the best of all possible worlds.

LETTERS TO ARNAULD

While he was in France from 1672 to 1676, Leibniz met the famous philosophers Arnauld and Malebranche. Antoine Arnauld (1612–1694) was the leading Port Royal theologian and logician, who was friends with Pascal and who wrote the Fourth Objections to Descartes' *Meditations*. Arnauld and Leibniz entered into a long correspondence, which has been published as a single volume. The first short extract is from Leibniz's letter dated 12 April 1686, and the second selection is from a letter dated 30 April 1687.

1 Moreover, some slight consideration of what I have said will show that it is evident *ex terminis*. For by the individual notion of Adam I undoubtedly mean a perfect representation of a particular Adam, with given individual conditions and distinguished thereby from an infinity of other possible persons very much like him, but yet different from him (just as every ellipse is different from the circle, however closely it approaches to it). God preferred him to all these others, because it pleased him to choose just this particular order of the universe; and all that follows from this decision of his is necessary only by a hypothetical necessity, and in no way derogates from the freedom of God nor from that of created minds. There is one possible Adam whose posterity is such and such, and an infinity of others whose posterity would be different; is it not the case that these possible Adams (if I may so speak of them) are different from one another, and that God has chosen only one of them, who is exactly our Adam?

2 It appears, too, that what constitutes the essence of an entity by aggregation is nothing but a manner of existence of the things of which it is composed; for example, what constitutes the essence of an army is simply a manner of existence of the men who compose it. This manner of existence, then, presupposes a substance, whose essence is not the manner of existence of a substance. Every machine, too, presupposes some substance in the pieces of which it is made; and there can be no plurality without true unities. To put it shortly, I maintain as axiomatic this identical proposition, whose differentiation can only be marked by the accentuation—namely, that that which is not truly *one* entity is not truly one *entity* either. It has always been held that unity and entity are reciprocal things. An entity is one thing, entities are quite another thing: but the plural presupposes the singular, and where there is no entity still less are there several entities. What could be more clearly stated? I therefore thought that I might be allowed to distinguish entities by aggregation from substances, since such entities have their unity in our mind only; which unity is based upon the relations or modes of genuine substances. If a machine is a substance, a circle of men holding one another's hands will be a substance too; so will an army, and so will every plurality of substances.

I do not mean that there is nothing substantial, or nothing but appearance, in the things which have no genuine unity; for I agree that they have always as much reality or substantiality as there is genuine unity in that of which they are composed.

You object, sir, that it may perhaps be of the essence of body not to have a true unity. But in that case it will be of the essence of body to be a phenomenon, deprived of all reality, like an ordered dream; for phenomena themselves, like a rainbow or a heap of stones, would be wholly imaginary, if they were not composed of entities with a genuine unity.

Leibniz, from *Leibniz: Philosophical Writings*, edited by G. H. R. Parkinson, translated by Mary Morris and G. H. R. Parkinson. First published by Everyman's Library in 1934. Reprinted by permission of Everyman's Library.

You say that you do not see what leads me to admit that there are such substantial terms, or rather corporeal substances, endowed with a genuine unity. It is because I do not conceive of any reality at all as without genuine unity. According to my view the notion of singular substance involves consequences which are incompatible with its being an entity by aggregation. I conceive of there being properties in substance which cannot be explained by extension, shape, and motion, besides the fact that there is no exact and fixed shape in bodies because of the actual subdivision of the continuum *ad infinitum*. Moreover, motion inasmuch as it is only a modification of extension and a change of neighbourhood, involves an imaginary element, so that it is not possible to determine to which of the subjects that change it belongs, unless we have recourse to the force in corporeal substance which is the cause of the motion. I admit that there is no need to mention these substances and qualities in order to explain particular phenomena, but neither is there any need to mention the concourse of God, the com-

position of the continuum, the plenum, and countless other things. We can explain mechanically, I fully admit, the particularities of nature; but this is after having discovered or presupposed the principles of mechanics themselves, which we cannot establish *a priori* except by metaphysical arguments; and even the difficulties *de compositione continui* will never be resolved so long as extension is regarded as constituting the substance of bodies, and we go on embarrassing ourselves by our own chimeras.

I think, too, that to allow genuine unity or substance to man almost alone is to be as limited in metaphysics as those people were in physics who confined the world within a ball. And as genuine substances are so many expressions of the whole universe taken in a certain sense, and so many reproductions of Divine works, it is in agreement with the greatness and beauty of these works of God, since these substances do not hinder one another from accomplishing as much in this universe as is possible and as much as superior reasons allow. . . .

STUDY QUESTIONS: LEIBNIZ, *LETTERS TO ARNAULD*

1. The notion of an individual has to be distinguished from what?
2. What is the main point that Leibniz wants to make concerning an aggregation?
3. 'That which is not truly *one* entity is not truly one *entity* either.' Please explain what Leibniz means by this. What support would he give in favor of it?
4. The claim that a singular substance must be simple has dramatic implications. What are those?

PRIMARY TRUTHS

Leibniz wrote this piece around 1686, the year that he composed the *Discourse on Metaphysics*. It is a remarkably compact explanation of many aspects of Leibniz's metaphysics and contains some elements that are not as explicit in the *Discourse* and the later *Monadology*. For example, it reveals his thinking concerning the infinite divisibility of the continuum and why something extended cannot be a substance. Additionally, Leibniz discusses briefly his theory of relations; he argues that there are no purely extrinsic denominations. In other words, relations must be based on the intrinsic properties of the substances involved. They can be reduced.

Leibniz, from *Leibniz: Philosophical Writings*, edited by G. H. R. Parkinson, translated by Mary Morris and G. H. R. Parkinson. First published by Everyman's Library in 1934. Reprinted by permission of Everyman's Library.

Primary truths are those which either state a term of itself or deny an opposite of its opposite. For example, 'A is A', or 'A is not not-A'; 'If it is true that A is B, it is false that A is not B, or that A is not-B'; again, 'Each thing is what it is', 'Each thing is like itself, or is equal to itself', 'Nothing is greater or less than itself'—and others of this sort which, though they may have their own grades of priority, can also be included under the one name of 'identities'.

All other truths are reduced to primary truths by the aid of definitions—i.e. by the analysis of notions; and this constitutes *a priori proof*, independent of experience. I will give an example. A proposition accepted as an axiom by mathematicians and all others alike is 'The whole is greater than its part', or 'A part is less than the whole'. But this is very easily demonstrated from the definition of 'less' or 'greater', together with the primitive axiom, that of identity. The 'less' is that which is equal to a part of another ('greater') thing. (This definition is very easily understood, and agrees with the practice of the human race when men compare things with one another, and find the excess by taking away something equal to the smaller from the larger.) So we get the following reasoning: a part is equal to a part of the whole (namely to itself: for everything, by the axiom of identity, is equal to itself). But that which is equal to a part of the whole is less than the whole (by the definition of 'less'); therefore a part is less than the whole.

The predicate or consequent, therefore, is always in the subject or antecedent, and this constitutes the nature of truth in general, or, the connexion between the terms of a proposition, as Aristotle also has observed. In identities this connexion and inclusion of the predicate in the subject is express, whereas in all other truths it is implicit and must be shown through the analysis of notions, in which *a priori* demonstration consists.

But this is true in the case of every affirmative truth, universal or particular, necessary or contingent, and in the case of both an intrinsic and an extrinsic denomination. And here there lies hidden a wonderful secret in which is contained the nature of contingency, or, the essential distinction between necessary and contingent truths; and by this also there is removed the difficulty about the fatal necessity of even those things which are free.

From these facts, which have not yet been sufficiently considered because of their excessive easiness, there follow many things of great importance. For from this there at once arises the accepted axiom, 'There is nothing without a reason', or, 'There is no effect without a cause'. For otherwise there would be a truth which could not be proved *a priori*, i.e. which is not analysed into identities; and this is contrary to the nature of truth, which is always, either expressly or implicitly, identical. It also follows that when in the data everything in one part is like everything in another part, then everything will be alike on both sides in the desiderata or consequences also. For no reason can be given for diversity, which must be sought from the data. A corollary, or rather an example of this, is the postulate of Archimedes at the beginning of his book on equilibrium; this states that when the arms of a balance and the weights placed on each side are equal, everything is in a state of equilibrium. Hence *there is a reason even for eternal things*. If it should be supposed that the world has existed from eternity, and that there have been only globules in it, a reason must be given why there should be globules rather than cubes.

From this it follows also that *there cannot be in nature two individual things which differ in number alone*. For it must be possible to give a reason why they are diverse, which must be sought from some difference in them. And so St. Thomas' recognition of the fact that separate intelligences never differ in number alone must be applied to other things as well; two perfectly similar eggs, or two perfectly similar leaves or blades of grass, will never be found. Perfect similarity, therefore, holds only in the case of incomplete and abstract notions, where things are not considered in all respects, but only with respect to a certain mode of consideration—as when we consider shapes only, and neglect the matter which has the shape. Consequently, in geometry two triangles are properly considered to be similar, although two material triangles which are perfectly alike are never found. We may also consider gold and other metals, salts, and many liquids as homogeneous bodies; but that can be admitted only as far as the senses are concerned, and even so is not exactly true.

It also follows that *there are no purely extrinsic denominations*, which have no foundation in the thing denominated. For the notion of the subject denominated must involve the notion of the predicate; consequently, as often as the denomination of the thing is changed, there must be some variation in the thing itself.

The complete or perfect notion of an individual substance involves all its predicates—past, present and future. For that a future predicate is future is true now, and so is contained in the notion of the thing. Therefore, in the perfect individual notion of Peter or Judas, considered under the aspect of possibility by abstracting the mind from the divine decree to create him, there are present and there are seen by God all the things that will happen to them, both necessary and free. From this it is manifest that God chooses, from an infinity of possible individuals, those which he thinks most consistent with the highest hidden ends of his wisdom. Nor is it exact to say that he decrees that Peter shall sin, or that Judas shall be damned; he decrees only that a Peter who will sin—certainly, indeed, though not necessarily but freely—and a Judas who will suffer damnation shall come into existence in preference to other possibles. In other words, God decrees that a possible notion shall become actual. And although the future salvation of Peter is also contained in his eternal possible notion, yet that is not without the concourse of grace; for in that same perfect notion of this possible Peter, the assistance of divine grace which is to be given to him is also contained under the aspect of possibility.

Every individual substance involves in its perfect notion the whole universe, and everything existing in it, past, present and future. For there is no thing on which some true denomination cannot be imposed from another, at all events a denomination of comparison and relation. But there is no purely extrinsic denomination. I show the same thing in many other interrelated ways.

Further, *all created individual substances are diverse expressions of the same universe, and of the same universal cause, namely God.* But these expressions vary in perfection, like different representations or projective drawings of the same town from different points of view.

Every created individual substance exercises physical action on, and is acted on by all others. For if a change is made in one, some corresponding change follows in

all the others, since the denomination is changed. This agrees with our experience of nature: for we see that in a vessel full of liquid (and the whole universe is such a vessel) a motion set up in the middle is propagated to the edges, although it becomes more and more imperceptible the farther it recedes from its point of origin.

Strictly, it can be said that *no created substance exercises on another a metaphysical action or influx.* For—to say nothing of the fact that it is impossible to explain how anything passes from one thing into the substance of another—it has already been shown that from the notion of any given thing all its future states already follow. What we call 'causes' are, in metaphysical rigour, merely concomitant requisites. This is illustrated by our experience of nature: for bodies recede from other bodies by the force of their own elasticity and not by any external force—even if another body is required for the elasticity, which arises from something intrinsic to the body itself, to be able to act.

Further, having posited the diversity of soul and body, we can explain their union from the above without the common hypothesis of an influx, which is unintelligible, and without the hypothesis of an occasional cause, which calls in a *Deus ex machina.* For God has from the beginning fashioned soul and body alike with such wisdom and such skill that, from the very first constitution or notion of each of these, all the things that happen in the one correspond perfectly of themselves to all the things that happen in the other, just as if they had passed from the one into the other. I call this the 'hypothesis of concomitance'. This is true of all substances in the whole universe, but it is not to be perceived in all of them, as it is in the soul and the body.

There is no vacuum. For the diverse parts of an empty space would be perfectly similar and congruent and could not be distinguished from one another, and so they would differ in number alone, which is absurd. In the same way in which it is proved that space is not a thing, it is also proved that time is not a thing.

There is no atom; on the contrary, there is no body so small that it is not actually subdivided. Whilst it is being acted on by all other bodies in the entire universe, and receives some effect from all of them (which must cause some variation in the body) it has also preserved all past impressions and contains in advance future impressions. If anyone says that the effect is contained in the motions impressed on the atom, which produce the effect in the whole without its being divided, it can be replied that not only must effects result in the atom from all the impressions of the universe, but it must also be possible in turn to infer from the atom the state of the whole universe, and from the effect the cause. But from the mere shape and motion of an atom we cannot infer back to the impressions by which the motion has reached it, since the same motion can be obtained from various impressions—to say nothing of the fact that no reason can be given why bodies of a certain degree of smallness are not divisible further.

From this it follows that *in every particle of the universe there is contained a world of infinite creatures*. However, the continuum is not divided into points, nor is it divided in all possible ways. Not into points, because points are not parts, but limits; not in all possible ways, because not all creatures are present in the same thing, but only a certain infinite progression of them—just as a man who supposes a straight line and any bisected part of it is establishing other divisions than a man who supposes a trisected part.

There is no actual determinate shape in things, for there is none which can satisfy infinite impressions. So neither a circle, nor an ellipse, nor any other line definable by us exists except in the intellect, nor any lines before they are drawn, or parts before they are cut off.

Extension and motion and bodies themselves, in so far as they consist of these alone, are not substances but true appearances, like rainbows and mock suns. For shapes do not exist objectively, and bodies, if they are considered as extension alone, are not one substance but several.

For the substance of bodies something without extension is required; otherwise there will be no principle of the reality of appearances, nor of true unity. Bodies are always held to be plural, and never one; therefore they are not really even plural. By means of a similar argument Cordemoy tried to prove that there are atoms; as these are excluded there remains something without extension, analogous to the soul, which was once called a form or species.

A corporeal substance can neither arise nor perish except by creation or annihilation. For since it once endures it will always endure, for there is no reason for a difference, and the dissolution of the parts of a body has nothing in common with the destruction of the body itself. Consequently, *things which have souls do not arise or perish, but are only transformed.*

STUDY QUESTIONS: LEIBNIZ, *PRIMARY TRUTHS*

1. How does Leibniz define a primary truth? How are other truths related to these?
2. What constitutes the nature of truth?
3. From these facts, 'there follow many things of great importance.' What follows from the nature of truth?
4. Why is the claim that there are no purely extrinsic denominations important for Leibniz?
5. No created substance exercises metaphysical action on another. What is the reasoning that supports this claim?
6. There is no atom. What is Leibniz's support for this claim?
7. Extension and motion and bodies are not substances but true appearances. What would Leibniz's argument be in favor of this claim?

NECESSARY AND CONTINGENT TRUTHS

(*c.* 1686)

Leibniz composed this piece around 1686. It supplements *Primary Truths*. Since Leibniz characterizes truth in terms of the subject containing the predicate, he needs to provide an explanation of the difference between necessary and contingent truths.

An affirmative truth is one whose predicate is in the subject; and so in every true affirmative proposition, necessary or contingent, universal or particular, the notion of the predicate is in some way contained in the notion of the subject, in such a way that if anyone were to understand perfectly each of the two notions just as God understands it, he would by that very fact perceive that the predicate is in the subject. From this it follows that all the knowledge of propositions which is in God, whether this is of the simple intelligence, concerning the essence of things, or of vision, concerning the existence of things, or mediate knowledge concerning conditioned existences, results immediately from the perfect understanding of each term which can be the subject or predicate of any proposition. That is, the *a priori* knowledge of complexes arises from the understanding of that which is not complex.

An *absolutely necessary* proposition is one which can be resolved into identical propositions, or, whose opposite implies a contradiction. I will cite a numerical example. I shall call every number which can be exactly divided by two, 'binary', and every one which can be divided by three or four 'ternary' or 'quaternary', and so on. Further, we may understand that every number is resolved into those which divide it exactly. I say, therefore, that the proposition 'A duodenary is a quarternary' is absolutely necessary, for it can be resolved into identical propositions in this way. A duodenary is a binary senary (by definition); a senary is a binary ternary (by definition). Therefore a duodenary is a binary binary ternary. Further, a binary binary is a quaternary (by definition); therefore a duodenary is a quaternary ternary. Therefore a duo-

denary is a quaternary; q.e.d. But even if other definitions were given, it could always be shown that the matter would come to this in the end. This type of necessity, therefore, I call metaphysical or geometrical. That which lacks such necessity I call contingent, but that which implies a contradiction, or whose opposite is necessary, is called *impossible*. The rest are called *possible*.

In the case of a contingent truth, even though the predicate is really in the subject, yet one never arrives at a demonstration or an identity, even though the resolution of each term is continued indefinitely. In such cases it is only God, who comprehends the infinite at once, who can see how the one is in the other, and can understand *a priori* the perfect reason for contingency; in creatures this is supplied *a posteriori,* by experience. So the relation of contingent to necessary truths is somewhat like the relation of surd ratios (namely, the ratios of incommensurable numbers) to the expressible ratios of commensurable numbers. For just as it can be shown that a lesser number is in a larger, by resolving each of the two into its largest common measure, so also propositions or truths of essence are demonstrated by carrying out a resolution of terms until one arrives at terms which, as is established by the definitions, are common to each term. But just as a larger number contains another which is incommensurable with it, though even if one continues to infinity with a resolution one will never arrive at a common measure, so in the case of a contingent truth you will never arrive at a demonstration, no matter how far you resolve the notions. The sole difference is that in the case of surd relations we can, none the less, establish demonstrations, by showing

Leibniz, from *Leibniz: Philosophical Writings,* edited by G. H. R. Parkinson, translated by Mary Morris and G. H. R. Parkinson. First published by Everyman's Library in 1934. Reprinted by permission of Everyman's Library.

that the error involved is less than any assignable error, but in the case of contingent truths not even this is conceded to a created mind. And so I think that I have disentangled a secret which had me perplexed for a long time; for I did not understand how a predicate could be in a subject, and yet the proposition would not be a necessary one. But the knowledge of geometry and the analysis of the infinite lit this light in me, so that I might understand that notions too can be resolved to infinity.

From this we learn that there are some propositions which pertain to the essences, and others to the existences of things. Propositions of essence are those which can be demonstrated by the resolution of terms; these are necessary, or virtually identical, and so their opposite is impossible, or virtually contradictory. The truth of these is eternal; not only will they hold whilst the world remains, but they would have held even if God had created the world in another way. Existential or contingent propositions differ entirely from these. Their truth is understood *a priori* by the infinite mind alone, and cannot be demonstrated by any resolution. These propositions are such as are true at a certain time; they express, not only what pertains to the possibility of things, but also what actually exists, or would exist contingently if certain things were granted—for example, that I am now alive, or that the sun is shining. For even if I say that the sun is shining at this hour in our hemisphere because its previous motion was such that, granted its continuation, this event would certainly follow, yet (to say nothing of the fact that its obligation to continue is not necessary) the fact that its motion was previously such is similarly a

contingent truth, for which again a reason must be sought. And this cannot be given in full except as a result of a perfect knowledge of all the parts of the universe—a task which surpasses all created powers. For there is no portion of matter which is not actually subdivided into others; so the parts of any body are actually infinite, and so neither the sun nor any other body can be known perfectly by a creature. Much less can we arrive at the end of our analysis if we seek the mover of each body which is moved, and again the mover of this; for we shall always arrive at smaller bodies without end. But God does not need this transition from one contingent to another contingent which is prior or more simple, a transition which can have no end. (Further, one contingent thing is not really the cause of another, even though it seems so to us.) Rather, in each individual substance, God perceives the truth of all its accidents from its very notion, without calling in anything extrinsic; for each one in its way involves all others, and the whole universe. So all propositions into which existence and time enter have as an ingredient the whole series of things, nor can 'now' or 'here' be understood except in relation to other things. Consequently, such propositions do not admit of demonstrations, i.e. of a terminable resolution by which their truth may appear. The same applies to all the accidents of individual created substances. Indeed, even if some one could know the whole series of the universe, even then he could not give a reason for it, unless he compared it with all other possibles. From this it is evident why no demonstration of a contingent proposition can be found, however far the resolution of notions is continued.

STUDY QUESTIONS: LEIBNIZ, NECESSARY AND CONTINGENT TRUTHS

1. What is an absolutely necessary proposition?
2. What is a contingent truth?
3. What is the difference between a necessary and a contingent truth?

DISCOURSE ON METAPHYSICS
(c. 1686)

This work was also written in 1686. For this reason, it does not contain the theory of monads, which is expounded in the later *Monadology*. Nevertheless, the *Discourse* does explain Leibniz's theory of truth and how that relates to his notion of a complete substance, which is required to individuate a substance. It also links these ideas to the Principle of Sufficient Reason, and thus to Leibniz's conception of God's choice.

8. To distinguish between the actions of God and the actions of creatures, an explanation is given of what constitutes the notion of an individual substance.

It is somewhat difficult to distinguish the actions of God from those of creatures. There are those who believe that God does everything; others imagine that he merely conserves the force which he has given to creatures. The sequel will show to what extent either of these can be said. Now, since actions and passions belong, strictly speaking, to individual substances (*actiones sunt suppositorum*), it will be necessary to explain what such a substance is. It is very true that when several predicates are attributed to one and the same subject, and this subject is not attributed to any other, one calls this subject an individual substance. But this is not enough, and such an explanation is only nominal. It is necessary, therefore, to consider what it is to be truly attributed to a certain subject. Now, it is agreed that every true predication has some basis in the nature of things, and when a proposition is not identical—that is, when the predicate is not contained expressly in the subject—it must be contained in it virtually. This is what philosophers call '*in-esse*', when they say that the predicate is 'in' the subject. The subject-term, therefore, must always include the predicate-term, in such a way that a man who understood the notion of the subject perfectly would also judge that the predicate belongs to it. That being so, we can say that it is the nature of an individual substance, or complete being, to have a notion so complete that it is sufficient to contain, and render deducible from itself, all the predicates of the subject to which this notion is

attributed. On the other hand, an accident is a being whose notion does not include all that can be attributed to the subject to which this notion is attributed. Take, for example, the quality of being a king, which belongs to Alexander the Great. This quality, when abstracted from its subject, is not sufficiently determinate for an individual and does not contain the other qualities of the same subject, nor everything that the notion of this prince contains. God, on the other hand, seeing the individual notion or *haecceitas* of Alexander, sees in it at the same time the foundation of and reason for all the predicates which can truly be stated of him—as, for example, that he is the conqueror of Darius and Porus—even to the extent of knowing *a priori*, and not by experience, whether he died a natural death or died by poison, which we can know only from history. Therefore, when one considers properly the connexion between things, one can say that there are in the soul of Alexander, from all time, traces of all that has happened to him, and marks of everything that will happen to him—and even traces of everything that happens in the universe—though no one but God can know all of them.

9. That every individual substance expresses the entire universe in its way, and that there are contained in its notion all the things that happen to it, together with all their circumstances and the entire series of external things.

From this, several notable paradoxes follow. One of these is that it is not true that two substances resemble each other entirely and are different in number alone (*solo numero*), and that what St. Thomas asserts in this connexion about angels or intelligences,

Leibniz, from *Leibniz: Philosophical Writings*, edited by G. H. R. Parkinson, translated by Mary Morris and G. H. R. Parkinson. First published by Everyman's Library in 1934. Reprinted by permission of Everyman's Library.

namely, that in these cases every individual is an *infima species* (*quod ibi omne individuum sit species infima*) is true of all substances, provided that one takes the specific difference in the way that geometers take it with respect to their figures. Another paradox is that a substance can begin only by creation, and perish only by annihilation; that one substance is not divided into two, nor is one made out of two, and that therefore the number of substances is neither increased nor diminished naturally, though substances are often transformed. Further, every substance is like an entire world and like a mirror of God, or of the whole universe, which each one expresses in its own way, very much as one and the same town is variously represented in accordance with different positions of the observer. Thus the universe is in a way multiplied as many times as there are substances, and in the same way the glory of God is redoubled by so many wholly different representations of his work. It can even be said that every substance bears in some way the stamp of the infinite wisdom and omnipotence of God, and imitates him as far as it is able. For it expresses, although confusedly, everything that happens in the universe, past, present and future, and this has some resemblance to infinite perception or knowledge. And as all other substances express that substance in their turn and agree with it, it can be said that it extends its power over all others, imitating the omnipotence of the Creator.

10. That the view that there are substantial forms has some solidity, but that these forms change nothing in phenomena, and must not be used to explain particular effects.

It seems that some knowledge of what we have just said was possessed by the ancients, and also by many able men, accustomed to profound meditation—some of them also praiseworthy for their holiness—who taught theology and philosophy several centuries ago. This knowledge made them introduce, and uphold, substantial forms, which are so decried today. But they are not so far from the truth, or so ridiculous, as the common run of our modern philosophers imagine. I agree that the consideration of these forms is of no value in the detail of physics, and must not be used in the explanation of particular phenomena. It is in this respect that our scholastics failed, and (following their example) the doctors of a past age. For they thought that they could explain the properties of bodies by mentioning forms and qualities, without going to the trouble of examining their method of operation—as if someone thought it sufficient to say that a timepiece has a time-indicative quality which comes from its form, without considering what all that consists in. That can indeed be sufficient for the man who buys the timepiece—provided that he abandon the care of it to another. But this shortcoming, and this misuse of forms, must not make us reject something the knowledge of which is so necessary in metaphysics that I maintain that without it first principles cannot be known properly, nor can the mind be raised high enough to know incorporeal natures and the wonders of God. However, we may make a comparison here. A geometer has no need to trouble his mind with the famous labyrinth of the composition of the continuum, and no moral philosopher, and still less a jurist or a politician, needs to trouble himself with the great difficulties which are found in reconciling free will with the providence of God. For the geometer can carry out all his demonstrations, and the politician can bring his deliberations to an end, without entering into these discussions—which are none the less necessary and important in philosophy and theology. In the same way, the physicist can explain his experiments by the use of simpler experiments that he has already made, or by demonstrations in geometry and mechanics, without the need of general considerations which belong to a different sphere. And if he uses the concourse of God, or some soul, archaeus or other thing of that nature, he is straying outside his proper limits, just as much as a man who, in the case of an important deliberation about what to do, tried to go into the great arguments about the nature of destiny and our freedom. Indeed, men make this mistake often enough without realising it, when they trouble their mind with thoughts about fate, and often are even turned away by this from some good resolution, or necessary concern.

11. That the meditations of the so-called Scholastic philosophers and theologians are not to be entirely despised.

I know that I am putting forward a great paradox in claiming to rehabilitate ancient philosophy to some extent, and to restore the rights of citizenship to substantial forms, which have practically been banished. But perhaps I shall not readily be condemned when it is known that I have thought carefully about modern philosophy, and that I have devoted much time to physical experiments and to geometrical demonstrations. I was for a long time persuaded of the emptiness of these entities, and was finally obliged to take them up again despite myself, and as it were by force. This was after I had myself conducted some researches which made me recognise that our modern philosophers do not do enough justice to St. Thomas and to other great men of that era, and that the views of the Scholastic philosophers and theologians have much more soundness than is imagined, provided that one uses them in a proper way and in their right place. I am even persuaded that if some precise and thoughtful mind were to take the trouble of clarifying and setting in order their thoughts, in the manner of analytic geometry, he would find in them a treasury of truths which are extremely important and wholly demonstrative.

12. That the notions which consist in extension include something imaginary, and cannot constitute the substance of a body.

But to take up again the thread of our discussion: I believe that anyone who will meditate on the nature of substance, as I have explained it above, will find that the entire nature of body does not consist in extension alone, that is to say in size, shape and motion. Rather, he will find that it is necessary to recognise in it something which has some relation to souls, and which is commonly called a substantial form, although this changes nothing in phenomena, any more than the soul of the lower animals does, if they have one. It can even be demonstrated that the notion of size, shape and motion is not as distinct as is imagined, and that it contains something that is imaginary and relative to our perceptions, just as is the case (though even more so) with colour, heat and other similar qualities, of which it may be doubted whether they are really found in the nature of things outside us. This is why qualities of these kinds cannot constitute any substance. And if there is no other principle of identity in bodies besides that which we have just mentioned, no body will ever last longer than a moment. However, the souls and substantial forms of other bodies are very different from intelligent souls. Only the latter know their actions, and not only do not perish naturally, but even retain perpetually the basis of the knowledge of what they are. It is this

which brings it about that they alone are capable of punishment and reward, and makes them citizens of the commonwealth of the universe, of which God is the monarch. It also follows that all other creatures must serve them, of which we shall speak at greater length presently.

13. Since the individual notion of each person includes, once and for all, everything that will ever happen to him, there are seen in this notion the a priori proofs of or reasons for the truth of each event, or why the one has occurred rather than the other. But these truths, though certain, are none the less contingent, being based on the free will of God and of creatures. It is true that their choice always has its reasons, but these incline without necessitating.

But before we go any further, it is necessary to try to answer a great difficulty which can be raised on the foundations that we have just laid. We have said that the notion of an individual substance contains, once and for all, everything that can ever happen to it, and that in considering this notion one can see in it everything that can truly be stated of it, as we can see in the nature of the circle all the properties that can be deduced from it. But it seems that this will destroy the difference between contingent and necessary truths, that human freedom will no longer hold, and that an absolute fatality will rule over all our actions as well as over all the rest of what happens in the world. To this I reply that one must distinguish between what is certain and what is necessary. Everyone agrees that future contingents are certain, since God foresees them, but it is not thereby admitted that they are necessary. But, it will be said, if some conclusion can be deduced infallibly from a definition or notion, it will be necessary. Now, we maintain that everything that is to happen to some person is already contained virtually in his nature or notion, as the properties of a circle are contained in its definition. So the difficulty still remains. To give a satisfactory answer to it, I assert that connexion or sequence is of two kinds. The one is absolutely necessary, whose contrary implies a contradiction; this kind of deduction holds in the case of eternal truths, such as those of geometry. The other is only necessary by hypothesis (*ex hypothesi*), and so to speak by accident; it is contingent in itself, since its contrary does not imply a contradiction.

This connexion is based, not on ideas pure and simple, and on the simple understanding of God, but on his free decrees and on the sequence of the universe. Let us give an example. Since Julius Caesar will become perpetual dictator and master of the republic, and will destroy the liberty of the Romans, this action is contained in his notion; for we are assuming that it is the nature of such a perfect notion of a subject to contain everything, so that the predicate is included in it, *ut possit inesse subjecto*. It could be said that it is not by virtue of this notion or idea that he must perform this action, since it belongs to him only because God knows everything. But it will be replied that his nature or form corresponds to this notion, and since God has imposed this personality on him, it is henceforth necessary for him to satisfy it. I could answer this by instancing future contingents; for they have no reality except in the understanding and will of God, and since God has given them this form in advance, they must correspond to it. However, I prefer to satisfy difficulties, rather than to excuse them by citing similar difficulties, and what I am about to say will throw light on both. This is where it is necessary to apply the distinction between connexions. I assert that that which happens in conformity with its antecedents is certain, but that it is not necessary, and that if someone were to do the opposite he would do nothing that is impossible in itself, although it is impossible by hypothesis (*ex hypothesi*) that that should happen. For if some human being could complete the whole demonstration by virtue of which he could prove the connexion between the subject who is Caesar, and the predicate which is his successful undertaking, he would indeed show that the future dictatorship of Caesar has its basis in his notion or nature, that one sees in it a reason why he decided to cross the Rubicon rather than halt there, why he won rather than lost the battle of Pharsalus, and that it was reasonable, and therefore certain, that that would happen. But he would not show that it is necessary in itself, or that the contrary implies a contradiction. (In much the same way it is reasonable, and certain, that God will always do the best, though the less perfect does not imply a contradiction.) For it will be found that this demonstration of this predicate of Caesar is not as absolute as those of arithmetic or geometry, but that it presupposes the

sequence of things that God has chosen freely, which is based on the primary free decree of God, namely, always to do that which is the most perfect, and on the decree which God has made (consequentially upon the first) with regard to human nature, which is that man will always do—but do freely—that which appears the best: Now, every truth which is based on decrees of these sorts is contingent, although it is certain. For these decrees do not alter the possibility of things and, as I have already said, although God's choice of the best is certain, that does not prevent the less perfect from being and remaining possible in itself, although it will not occur; for it is not its impossibility but its imperfection which makes God reject it. Now, nothing is necessary whose opposite is possible. One is therefore in a position to satisfy difficulties of these kinds, however great they may appear (and indeed they are no less urgent for all others who have ever discussed this matter) provided that one bears this in mind: that all contingent propositions have reasons for being thus rather than otherwise, or (what is the same thing) that they have *a priori* proofs of their truth which make them certain, and which show that the connexion between the subject and the predicate of these propositions has its basis in the nature of the one and of the other. But these proofs are not necessary demonstrations, for these reasons are based only on the principle of contingency or of the existence of things—that is, on that which is or appears the best among several things which are equally possible—whereas necessary truths are based on the principle of contradiction and on the possibility or impossibility of essences themselves, with no relation to the free will of God or of creatures.

14. God produces various substances according to the different views that he has of the universe, and through God's intervention the individual nature of each substance is such that what happens to one corresponds to what happens to all other, without any one actin immediately on any other.

Now that we have got to know in some way what the nature of substances consists in, it is necessary to try to explain the dependence they have on each other, and the way they act and are acted on. Now in the first place it is very clear that created substances depend on God, who conserves them and even produces them continually by a kind of emanation, as we produce our thoughts. For God, as it were, turns on all sides and in all ways the general system of phenomena which he finds it good to produce in order to manifest his glory, and regards all aspects of the world in all possible ways, since there is no relation which escapes his omniscience. The result of each view of the universe, as seen from a certain position, is a substance which expresses the universe in conformity with this view, if God finds it good to render his thought effective and to produce this substance. And as God's view is always a true one, our perceptions are true also; it is our judgements which come from us and deceive us. Now we have said above, and it follows from what we have just said, that each substance is like a world apart, independent of every other thing, except for God. Therefore all our phenomena, that is to say all the things that can ever happen to us, are only consequences of our being. These phenomena preserve a certain order, which conforms to our nature, or so to speak to the world which is in us, which means that we are able to make observations which are useful for regulating our conduct, which are justified by the success of future phenomena, and in this way we are often able to judge accurately about the future by means of the past. This would be enough for us to say that these phenomena are true, without our troubling ourselves as to whether they exist outside us, or whether others apperceive them too. However, it is very true that the perceptions or expressions of all substances correspond to one another, in such a way that each one, following with care certain reasons or laws which it has observed, agrees with another which does the same; it is just as when several men, who have agreed to meet together in some place on a certain prearranged day, can in fact do so if they wish. Now although all express the same phenomena, this is not to say that all their expressions are perfectly alike, but it is sufficient that they should be proportional; just as several spectators believe that they see the same thing, and do indeed understand one another, although each one sees and speaks in accordance with his point of view. Now it is God alone (from whom all individuals emanate continually and who sees the universe, not only as they see it, but also in quite a different way from all of them) who is the cause of this correspondence between their phenomena, and who brings it about that what is particular to one should be public to all; otherwise there would be no interconnexion. It could therefore be said in a way, and in a perfectly good sense (although remote from ordinary usage), that one particular substance never acts on another particular substance, nor is acted on by another, if one considers the fact that what happens to each is simply a consequence of its complete idea or notion alone, for this idea already contains all its predicates or events and expresses the entire universe. Really, nothing can happen to us apart from thoughts and perceptions, and all our future thoughts and perceptions are only consequences (although contingent consequences) of our preceding thoughts and perceptions, such that if I were able to consider distinctly everything that happens to or appears to me at the moment, I could see in it everything that will ever happen to or ever appear to me. This would not fail to occur, but would happen to me just the same, if everything outside me were destroyed, provided that there remained only God and myself. But as we attribute what we apperceive in a certain way to other things, as to causes acting on us, it is necessary to consider the basis of this judgement, and how much truth it has.

15. The action of one finite substance on another consists only in the increase of the degree of its expression, joined to the diminution of that of the other, in so far as God has formed them in advance in such a way that they agree with one another.

But without entering into a long discussion, it is sufficient for the moment, to reconcile metaphysical language with practice, to note that we attribute to ourselves (and rightly) the phenomena which we express more perfectly, and that we attribute to other substances what each one expresses best. Thus a substance which is of an infinite extent, in so far as it expresses everything, becomes limited by the more or less perfect manner of its expression. It is in this fashion that one can conceive the way in which substances hinder or limit one another, and consequently it can be said in this sense that they act on one another and are, so to speak, obliged to harmonise with one another. For it can happen that a change which increases the expression of one diminishes that of another. Now the virtue of a particular substance is to express well the glory of God, and it is through this that it is less limited. And when each thing exercises its virtue or power, that is to say when it acts, it changes for the better and extends itself in so far as it acts. When, therefore, a change occurs by which several substances are affected (and indeed every change concerns all substances) I believe that one can say that the one which, by this, immediately passes to a greater degree of perfection or a more perfect expression exercises its power and *acts,* and that which passes to a lesser degree of perfection displays its weakness and *is acted on.* I also maintain that every action of a substance which has perception involves some *pleasure* and every passion some *pain,* and vice versa. However, it can happen that a present advantage is destroyed by a greater evil which follows, from which arises the fact that one can sin in acting or exercising one's power and finding pleasure in it.

16. *God's extraordinary concourse is comprised in that which our essence expresses, for this expression extends to everything, but it surpasses the forces of our nature or our distinct expression, which is limited and follows certain subordinate maxims.*

It now only remains to explain how it is possible for God sometimes to have influence on men or on other substances by an extraordinary and miraculous concourse; for it seems that nothing can happen to them which is extraordinary or supernatural, in view of the fact that all the things that happen to them are only consequences of their nature. But it is necessary to recall what we said above about miracles in the universe: namely, that these are always in conformity with the universal law of general order, although they are above subordinate maxims. In so far as each person or substance is like a little world which expresses the great world, it can also be said that this extraordinary action of God on this substance does not cease to be miraculous, even though it is contained in the general order of the universe in so far as it is expressed by the essence or individual notion of the substance. This is why, if we include in our nature everything which it expresses, nothing is supernatural to it, for it extends to everything; for an effect always expresses its cause, and God is the true cause of substances. But as what our nature expresses more perfectly belongs to it in a special way (for, as I have just explained, it is that which constitutes its power, and

the fact that it is limited) there are many things that surpass the forces of our nature, and even those of all limited natures. Consequently, to speak more clearly, I assert that miracles and the acts of God's extraordinary concourse have this special feature: they cannot be foreseen by the reasoning of any created mind, however enlightened it may be, for the distinct comprehension of the general order surpasses all of them. On the other hand, all that one calls 'natural' depends on less general maxims, which creatures can understand. So that our words may be as unobjectionable as our meaning, it would be advantageous to link certain ways of speaking with certain thoughts. One could call our 'essence' or 'idea' that which contains all that we express, and as it expresses our union with God himself, it has no limits, and nothing surpasses it. But that which is limited in us could be called our 'nature' or our 'power', and in this respect what surpasses the natures of all created substances is supernatural.

17. *An example of a subordinate maxim or law of nature, where it is shown that God always regularly conserves the same force, but not the same quantity of motion— contrary to the Cartesians and several others.*

I have often mentioned subordinate maxims or laws of nature, and it seems advisable to give an example. Our modern philosophers commonly make use of the famous rule that God always conserves the same quantity of motion in the world. This is indeed very plausible, and in the past I regarded it as indubitable. Since then, however, I have recognised the nature of the error. Descartes, and many other able mathematicians, have believed that the quantity of motion—that is, the speed multiplied by the size of that which moves—agrees perfectly with the motive force, or, to speak geometrically, that forces are in a compound ratio of speeds and of bodies. Now, it is reasonable that the same force should always be conserved in the universe. Thus, when one pays attention to phenomena, one sees clearly that perpetual mechanical motion cannot occur; for if it were to do so, then the force of a machine (which is always diminished slightly by friction and must soon come to an end) would restore itself, and consequently would increase of itself, without any new impulse from outside. One notes also that the force of a body is diminished only to the extent that it gives some of it to some contiguous bodies, or to its own parts in so far as they have a separate motion. Thus it has been believed that what can be said of force could also be said of the quantity of motion. To show the difference between these, *I assume* that a body, falling from a certain height, acquires the force to rise again to that height if its direction takes it that way, at any rate if there are no obstacles. For example, a pendulum would rise again to the exact height from which it has descended, if the resistance of the air and some other slight obstacles did not diminish a little the force that it has acquired. *I assume* also that as much force is needed to raise a body A, of one pound, to the height CD of four fathoms, as to raise a body B of four pounds to a height of one fathom. All this is granted by our modern philosophers. It is therefore evident that the body A, having fallen from the height CD, has acquired exactly as much force as the body B, having fallen from the height EF. For the body (B), having arrived at F, and having (by the first supposition) the force to rise again as far as E, has in consequence the force to raise a body of four pounds (i.e. its own body) to the height EF of one fathom. Similarly the body (A), having arrived at D, and having the force to rise again as far as C, has the force to raise a body of one pound (i.e. its own body) to the height CD of four fathoms. Therefore (by the second supposition) the force of these two bodies is equal. Let us now see if the quantity of motion is also the same on both sides. Here, however, we shall be surprised to find a very great difference. It has been demonstrated by Galileo that the speed acquired by the fall CD is twice the speed acquired by the fall EF, although the

height is quadruple. Let us therefore multiply the body A, which is as 1, by its speed, which is as 2; the product or quantity of motion will be as 2. On the other hand let us multiply the body B, which is as 4, by its speed, which is as 1; the product or quantity of motion will be as 4. Therefore the quantity of motion of the body (A) at the point D is half the quantity of motion of the body (B) at the point F; and yet their forces are equal. There is, therefore, a great difference between quantity of motion and force; which is what was to be shown. By this one sees how force must be measured by the quantity of the effect which it can produce; for example, by the height to which a heavy body of a certain size and kind can be raised, which is very different from the speed which can be given to it. And to give it double the speed, more than double the force is needed. Nothing is simpler than this proof, and Descartes only fell into error here because he trusted his thoughts too much, when they were not yet sufficiently mature. But I am amazed that his followers have not noticed this error. I am afraid that they are gradually beginning to imitate some of the Aristotelians whom they mock, and, like them, are falling into the habit of consulting the books of their master rather than reason and nature.

23. To return to immaterial substances: it is explained how God acts on the understanding of minds, and whether we always have the idea of that of which we think.

I have found it relevant, in connexion with bodies, to lay some stress on these considerations about final causes, incorporeal natures and an intelligent cause, to make known their use in physics and in mathematics, both to rid mechanical philosophy of the irreligious nature which is ascribed to it, and to raise the minds of our philosophers from exclusively material considerations to nobler meditations. Now it will be timely to return from bodies to immaterial natures, and in particular to minds, and to say something about the method that God uses to enlighten them and to act on them. There is no room for doubt that certain laws of nature also exist here, about which I could speak more fully elsewhere. For the moment it will be sufficient to touch on the question of ideas, and whether we see everything in God, and how God is our light. Now it will be relevant to remark that the faulty employment of ideas is the occasion of many

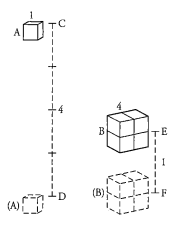

errors. For when one reasons about something, one imagines that one has an idea of that thing, and on this basis several philosophers, ancient and modern, have constructed a certain demonstration of the existence of God, a demonstration which is very imperfect. They say that I must have an idea of God or a perfect being, since I think of such a being and one cannot think without an idea. Now, the idea of this being includes all perfections, and existence is one of them; consequently this being exists. But this argument is insufficient, for we often think of impossible chimeras—for example, of the highest degree of speed, of the greatest number, of the meeting of the conchoid with its base or axis. It is therefore in this sense that it can be said that there are true and false ideas, as the thing in question is possible or not. One can only claim that one has an idea of a thing when one is sure of its possibility. Thus, the argument just mentioned proves at least that God exists necessarily, if he is possible. Indeed, this is an excellent privilege of the divine nature—that it needs only its possibility or essence in order to exist actually—and it is precisely this that one calls an *Ens a se*.

24. The nature of knowledge: clear or obscure, distinct or confused, adequate or inadequate, intuitive or suppositive. Of definitions: nominal, real, causal, essential.

In order to understand better the nature of ideas it is necessary to touch on the varieties of knowledge. When I can recognise one thing amongst others, without being able to say in what its differences or properties consist, my knowledge is *confused*. It is in this way that we sometimes know *clearly*, without being in any kind of doubt, if a poem or a picture is good or bad, because there is a *je ne sais quoi* which satisfies us or displeases us. But when I can explain the marks which I have, my knowledge is called *distinct*. Such is the knowledge possessed by an assayer, who distinguishes true from false gold by means of certain tests or marks which constitute the definition of gold. Distinct knowledge has degrees; for normally the notions which enter into the definition are themselves in need of definition and are known only confusedly. But when everything which enters into a definition or into distinct knowledge is itself known distinctly, right up to primitive notions, I call this knowledge *adequate*. When my mind understands distinctly and at the same time all the primitive ingredients of a notion, it has *intuitive* knowledge of it. This is very rare, the bulk of human knowledge being only confused or *suppositive*. There is also a distinction to be drawn between nominal and real definitions. I call a definition *nominal* when it is still possible to doubt whether the notion defined is possible. For example, if I say that an endless screw is a solid line whose parts are congruent, or can be superimposed on one another, someone who did not know from other sources what an endless screw is could doubt whether such a line is possible—though this is in fact a reciprocal property of the endless screw, for the other lines whose parts are congruent (and these are only the circumference of the circle and the straight line) are plane, that is to say can be described in a plane (*in plano*). This shows that every reciprocal property can serve as a nominal definition, but when the property enables us to know the possibility of the thing, it makes the definition real. Further, as long as one has only a nominal definition one cannot be certain of the consequences which one derives from it, for if it concealed some contradiction or impossibility, one could derive opposite conclusions from it. This is why truths do not depend on names and are not arbitrary, as some modern philosophers have believed. It must be added that there is a considerable difference between kinds of real definitions. When the possibility is proved only by experience, as in the definition of quick-silver—whose possibility one knows because one knows that there is indeed such a body, namely one which is a fluid, extremely heavy and yet very volatile—the definition is only real, and no more. But when the proof of possibility is *a priori*, the definition is both *real* and *causal*, as when it contains the possible generation of the thing. When the definition pushes the analysis to the end, right up to primitive notions, without presupposing anything which needs an *a priori* proof of its possibility, the definition is perfect or *essential*.

25. In what case our knowledge is joined with the contemplation of the idea.

Now it is evident that we have no idea of a notion when that notion is impossible. When the knowledge is only *suppositive*, then even when we have the idea we do not contemplate it. For such a notion is known only in the same way as notions which conceal an impossibility, and if it is possible, it is not by this manner of knowing that one learns of its possibility. For example, when I think of a thousand, or of a thousand-sided figure, I often do this without contemplating its idea (as when I say that a thousand is ten times a hundred) without giving myself the trouble of thinking what ten and a hundred are, because I *suppose* that I know this and I do not believe that I need to stop to conceive it at the moment. So it can very well happen, and indeed it very often does happen, that I deceive myself with regard to a notion which I suppose or believe myself to understand, although in reality it is impossible, or at any rate incompatible with the other notions with which I join it. And whether I deceive myself or not, this suppositive manner of conception remains the same. It is, therefore, only when our knowledge is *clear* in the case of confused notions, or *intuitive* in the case of distinct notions, that we see the entire idea.

26. *We have in us all ideas; and of Plato's reminiscence.*

In order to conceive properly what an idea is, we must forestall an equivocation. Several take the idea to be the form or difference of our thoughts, and in this way we have an idea in our mind only in so far as we think of it, and every time we think of it afresh, we have other ideas (though like the ones which have preceded them) of the same thing. Others, however, seem to take the idea to be an immediate object of thought or some permanent form which remains even when we do not contemplate it. And indeed our soul always has in it the quality of representing to itself any nature or form whatever, when the occasion for thinking of it presents itself. I believe that this quality of our soul, in so far as it expresses some nature, form or essence, is properly the idea of the thing, which is in us, and is always in us, whether we think of it or not. For our soul expresses God, the universe and all essences as well as all existences. This agrees with my principles; for nothing enters our mind naturally from outside, and our habit of thinking as if our soul received some messenger species and as if it had doors and windows is a bad one. We have in our mind all forms, and, indeed, we have them from all time; for the mind always expresses all its future thoughts and already thinks confusedly of all that it will ever think dis-

tinctly. We could never be informed of anything whose idea we do not already have in the mind—an idea which is like the matter from which this thought forms itself. Plato had an excellent appreciation of this when he put forward his theory of 'reminiscence', a theory which has much solidity provided that one takes it in the right way, that one rids it of the error of pre-existence, and does not imagine that the soul must at some previous time have known and thought distinctly what it learns and thinks now. He also confirmed his opinion by a fine experiment, introducing a little boy whom he leads imperceptibly to some very difficult geometrical truths regarding incommensurables, without teaching him anything, but simply asking relevant questions in an orderly way. This shows that our soul knows all this virtually, and only needs *attention* to know truths, and consequently that it has at least the ideas on which these truths depend. One can even say that it already possesses these truths, if one takes them as the relations of ideas.

27. *How our soul can be compared to blank tablets, and how our notions come from the senses.*

Aristotle preferred to compare our soul to tablets that are still blank, where there is space for writing, and he maintained that there is nothing in our understanding that does not come from the senses. This agrees more with popular notions, as is Aristotle's manner, whereas Plato is more profound. However, expressions of this kind, based on opinion or on practice, can pass into ordinary usage, much as we see that those who follow Copernicus do not cease saying that the sun rises and sets. I even find that one can often give them a good sense, according to which they have no falsity, as I have noted already that there is a way in which it can be said truly that particular substances act on each other. In the same sense it can be said that we receive knowledge from outside through the medium of our senses, because certain external things contain or express more particularly the reasons which determine our soul to certain thoughts. But when it is a matter of the precision of metaphysical truths, it is important to recognise the extent and the independence of our soul. This goes infinitely further than is commonly supposed, although in the ordinary usage of everyday life one attributes to it only that which one apperceives more clearly, and which belongs to us in a more particular way, for there is no point in going any further. However, it would be useful to choose terms which are proper to each sense, to avoid equivocation. Therefore those expressions which are in our soul, whether we conceive them or not, can be called *ideas*, but those which we conceive or form can be called *notions, conceptus*. But in whatever way one takes it, it is always false to say that all our notions come from the so-called external senses, for the notion that I have of myself and my thoughts, and consequently of being, substance, action, identity and many others, come from an internal experience.

28. God alone is the immediate object, existing outside us, of our perceptions, and he alone is our light.

Now, in strict metaphysical truth there is no external cause which acts on us except God alone, and it is God alone who communicates himself to us immediately by virtue of our continual dependence. From this it follows that there is no other external object which affects our soul and excites our perception immediately. Therefore we have in our soul the ideas of all things only by virtue of the continual action of God upon us, that is to say because every effect expresses its cause, and that thus the essence of our soul is a certain expression, imitation or image of the divine essence, thought and will, and of all the ideas that are contained therein. It can therefore be said that God alone is our immediate external object, and that we see all things by means of him. For example, when we see the sun and the stars, it is God who has given us and conserves for us the ideas of them, and who determines us by his ordinary concourse actually to think of them at the time when our senses are disposed in a certain way, following the laws that he has established. God is the sun and the light of souls, 'the Light which lighteth every man that cometh into the world' (*lumen illuminans omnem hominem venientem in hunc mundum*); and this view is not just held at the present day. After Holy Scripture and the Fathers of the Church, who have always been in favour of Plato rather than of Aristotle, I recall having previously remarked that from the time of the Scholastics several have believed that God is the light of the soul and, in their terminology,

the active intellect of the rational soul (*intellectus agens animae rationalis*). The Averroists have interpreted this in a bad sense, but others—among whom, I believe, are Guillaume de St. Amour and several mystical theologians—have taken it in a way which is worthy of God and capable of elevating the soul to the knowledge of its good.

29. However, we think immediately by means of our own ideas, and not by those of God.

However, I do not share the opinion of some able philosophers, who seem to maintain that our ideas themselves are in God, and not at all in us. In my view, this springs from the fact that they have not yet considered sufficiently what we have just explained here about substances, nor all the extent and independence of our soul, as a result of which it contains all that happens to it, and that it expresses God and, with him, all possible and actual beings, as an effect expresses its cause. It is therefore inconceivable that I should think by means of somebody else's ideas. The soul must also be affected actually in a certain way when it thinks of something, and there must be in it in advance not only the passive power of being able to be affected in this way, which is already entirely determined, but also an active power, by virtue of which it has always had in its nature marks of the future production of this thought and dispositions to produce it at its time. And all this already includes the idea contained in this thought.

30. How God inclines our soul without necessitating it; that we have no right to complain; that it must not be asked why Judas sins, since this free act is contained in his notion, but only why Judas the sinner is admitted to existence in preference to some other possible persons. Of imperfection or original limitation before sin, and of the degrees of grace.

The question of the action of God on the human will involves many very difficult considerations, which it would be tedious to pursue here. Roughly speaking, however, what can be said is as follows. God, in his ordinary concourse with our actions, does no more than follow the laws which he has established; that is to say, he conserves and continually produces our being in such a way that thoughts arise in us spontaneously or freely in the order implied by the notion of our individual substance, in which one could foresee them from all eternity. Further, God has decreed that the will shall always tend to the apparent good, expressing or limiting the will of God in certain particular respects, in regard to which this apparent good always has something of the genuine good in it. By virtue of this decree God determines our will to the choice of that which appears the best, without necessitating it in the least. For absolutely speaking it is in a state of indifference, in so far as this is opposed to necessity, and has the power of acting differently or even suspending its action entirely, both choices being and remaining possible. It therefore rests with the mind to take precautions against the surprises which come from appearances by means of a firm will to reflect, and only to act or judge in certain situations after thorough and mature deliberation. Nevertheless it is true, and even certain from all eternity, that a certain soul will not make use of this power in such and such a situation. But whose fault is that? Can the soul complain of anything but itself? For all such complaints made after the fact are unjust if they would have been unjust before the fact. Now could this soul, a little before sinning, fairly complain of God, as if he were determining it to sin? The determinations of God in these matters are things that cannot be foreseen; how, then, does it know that it is determined to sin, unless it is already actually sinning? It is only a matter of not willing, and God could not propose a condition which is easier or more just. Similarly, no judge seeks the reasons which have disposed a man to have an evil will; the judge only stops to consider how evil this will is. But perhaps it is certain, from all eternity, that I shall sin? Answer this yourself: perhaps it is not certain; and, without dreaming about that which you cannot know and which cannot bring you any kind of enlightenment, act according to your duty, which you do know. But someone else will say: how is it that this man will certainly commit this sin? The reply is easy: namely, that otherwise he would not be this man. For God sees from all time that there will be a certain Judas, whose notion or idea, which God has, contains this future free action. There therefore remains only this question: why such a Judas, the betrayer, who in God's idea is only possi-

ble, exists actually. But no reply may be expected to this question here on earth, apart from this general observation that must be made: that since God has found it good that he should exist, despite the sin which he foresaw, it is necessary that this evil is recompensed with interest in the universe at large, that God will draw out of it a greater good, and that it will be found that in sum this sequence of things, in which the existence of this sinner is contained, is the most perfect among all other possible kinds. But we cannot always explain the admirable economy of this choice whilst we are travellers in this world; it is enough for us to know it without understanding it. And it is here that it is time to recognise the 'depth of the riches' (altitudo divitiarum), the depth and the abyss of the divine wisdom, without seeking a detail which involves infinite considerations. However, it is clear that God is not the cause of evil. For not only did original sin seize hold of the soul after man's fall from innocence, but even before this there was an original limitation or imperfection, natural to all creatures, which makes them liable to sin, or capable of going wrong. So there is no more difficulty with regard to the supralapsarians than there is with regard to the others. And it is to this, in my view, that one must reduce the opinion of St. Augustine and others, that the root of evil is in nothingness, that is, in the privation or limitation of creatures, which God in his grace remedies by the degree of perfection which it pleases him to bestow. This grace of God, whether ordinary or extraordinary, has its degrees and its measures; in itself it is always efficacious in producing a certain proportionate effect; further, it is always sufficient, not only to guarantee us against sin, but even to produce salvation, assuming that man joins himself to it by that which comes from him. But it is not always sufficient to surmount the inclinations of man, for otherwise he would be without fault, and that is reserved for absolutely efficacious grace which is always victorious, whether by itself, or by the suitability of the circumstances.

32. The utility of these principles in matters of piety and religion.

For the rest, it seems that the thoughts that we have just expounded—and especially the great principle of the perfection of God's operations, and that of the notion of a substance which includes all that happens to it together with all their circumstances—are far from harming religion, but serve rather to strengthen it, to dispel great difficulties, to inflame souls with a divine love, and to elevate minds to the knowledge of incorporeal substances, much more than the hypotheses which have been seen hitherto. For it is seen clearly that all other substances depend on God, as thoughts emanate from our substance, that God is all in all, that he is united intimately with all creatures, though in proportion to their perfection, and that it is God alone who determines them from outside by his influence. Further, if to act is to determine immediately, it can be said in this sense, in the language of metaphysics, that God alone acts on me, and that God alone can do good or evil to me, other substances only contributing to the reason of these determinations, since God, having regard to them all, distributes his bounty and obliges them to harmonise with one another. Again, God alone brings about the liaison or communication between substances, and it is by him that the phenomena of any one tally with and agree with the phenomena of others, with the result that there is reality in our perceptions. In practice, however, one attributes action to particular reasons, in the sense which I have explained above, since it is not always necessary to mention the universal cause in particular cases. It is also seen that every substance has a perfect spontaneity (which becomes freedom in the case of intelligent substances), that everything which happens to it is a consequence of its idea or being, and that nothing determines it, apart from God alone. It is for this reason that a person of lofty mind and revered sanctity used to say that the soul ought often to think as if there were nothing but God and itself in the world. Now, nothing gives us a better understanding of immortality than this independence and extent of the soul, which gives it absolute protection from all external things; for it alone constitutes all its world and, together with God, is self-sufficient. It is as impossible that it should perish, except by annihilation, as it is impossible that the world, of which it is a living and perpetual expression, should destroy itself. It is therefore impossible that changes in that extended mass which is

called our body should do anything to the soul, or that the dissolution of this body should destroy what is indivisible.

33. *An explanation of the communication between soul and body, which has hitherto been regarded as inexplicable or miraculous, and of the origin of confused perceptions.*
We see also an unexpected elucidation of that great mystery, *the union of the soul and the body;* that is to say, how it happens that the passions and actions of the one are accompanied by the actions and passions, or the corresponding phenomena, of the other. For it is inconceivable that the one should have any influence on the other, and it is unreasonable simply to have recourse to the extraordinary operation of the universal cause in a matter which is ordinary and particular. But here is the real reason. We have said that everything that happens to the soul, and to each substance, is a consequence of its notion; therefore the very idea or essence of the soul implies that all that appears to it, all its perceptions, must arise in it spontaneously (*sponte*) from its own nature, and precisely in such a way that, of themselves, they correspond to what happens in the whole universe, but more particularly and more perfectly to what happens in the body which is assigned to it; for in some way and for a time the soul expresses the state of the universe, in accordance with the relation of other bodies to its own. This also explains how our body belongs to us, without being attached to our essence. And I believe that people who are capable of meditation will judge favourably of our principles for this very reason: that they can easily see the nature of the connexion between soul and body, which seems inexplicable in any other way. It is also seen that our sense-perceptions, even when they are clear, must necessarily contain some confused sensation. For as all bodies in the universe are in sympathy, our own receives the impression of all the others, and although our senses are related to everything, it is not possible for our soul to be able to attend to everything in particular. This is why our confused sensations are the result of an absolutely infinite variety of perceptions. This is very like the way in which the confused murmur which is heard by those who approach the seashore comes from the accumulation of the repercussions of innu-

merable waves. Now if, of several perceptions (which do not agree together, to make one) there is none which surpasses the others, and if they produce impressions which are almost equally strong, or equally capable of determining the attention of the soul, it can perceive them only confusedly.

34. Of the difference between minds and other substances, souls or substantial forms, and that the immortality which is demanded implies memory.

Assuming that the bodies which constitute an essential unity (*unum per se*), such as man, are substances and that they have substantial forms; assuming, too, that the beasts have souls, one has to admit that these souls and these substantial forms cannot entirely perish, any more than the atoms or ultimate particles of matter that are believed in by other philosophers. For no substance perishes, though it can become quite different. Further, they express the entire universe, though in a less perfect way than minds do. But the chief difference is that they know neither what they are nor what they do; consequently, being unable to reflect, they cannot discover necessary and universal truths. It is also for lack of reflexion on themselves that they have no moral quality; the result is that as they pass through a thousand transformations—much as we see a caterpillar change into a butterfly—it is morally or practically the same as if they were said to perish, and we can even say the same in terms of natural science, as when we say that bodies perish by their corruption. But the intelligent soul, knowing what it is and being able to say this 'I' which says so much, does not merely remain and subsist metaphysically (which it does more fully than the others), but also remains morally the same and constitutes the same personality. For it is the memory or knowledge of this 'I' which makes it capable of reward and punishment. Therefore the immortality which is demanded in morals and in religion does not consist solely in that perpetual subsistence, which belongs to all substances, for without the memory of what one has been it would be in no way desirable. Let us suppose that some individual were suddenly to become King of China, but on condition of forgetting what he has been, as if he had just been born anew. Is not this practically the same, or the same as far as the effects which can be apperceived, as if he were to be annihi-lated and a King of China were to be created in his place at the same moment? And this particular individual has no reason to desire this.

35. The excellence of minds; that God considers them in preference to other creatures; that minds express God rather than the world, and that other simple substances express the world rather than God.

But so that it can be judged by natural reasons that God will always conserve, not only our substance but also our personality, that is to say the memory and knowledge of what we are (though the distinct knowledge of this is sometimes suspended in sleep and in fainting fits) it is necessary to join morals to metaphysics. That is, it is necessary to consider God, not only as the principle and the cause of all substances and of all beings, but also as the chief of all persons or intelligent substances, and as the absolute monarch of the most perfect city or commonwealth, such as is that of the universe which is composed of all minds taken together, God himself being the most perfect of all minds, as he is the greatest of all beings. For it is certain that minds are the most perfect substances, and that they express the divinity best. And as the whole nature, end, virtue and function of substances is only to express God and the universe (as has been sufficiently explained), there is no room for doubt that the substances who express him with a knowledge of what they are doing, and are capable of knowing great truths that concern God and the universe, express him incomparably better than those natures which are merely animal or incapable of knowing truths, or are wholly without sensation and knowledge; and the difference between the substances which are intelligent and those which are not is as great as the difference between the mirror and the man who sees. And as God himself is the greatest and wisest of minds, it is easy to form the opinion that the beings with whom he can, so to speak, enter into conversation and even into social relations—communicating to them his opinions and his volitions in a particular way, such that they can know and love their benefactor—must concern him infinitely more than all other things, which can be considered only as the instruments of minds. In the same way, we see that all wise men have an infinitely higher regard for a human being than for any other thing, however precious it may be; and it seems that the greatest satisfaction which can be had by a soul which is in other respects content, is to see itself loved by others. In the case of God, however, there is this difference: that his glory and our worship can add nothing to his satisfaction, the knowledge that creatures have of him being only a consequence of his sovereign and perfect happiness, far from contributing to it or being its partial cause. However, that which is good and rational in finite minds is found eminently in him, and as we would praise a king who preferred to preserve the life of a man rather than that of the most precious and rare of his animals, we may not doubt that the most enlightened and most just of all monarchs shares the same opinion.

STUDY QUESTIONS: LEIBNIZ, *DISCOURSE ON METAPHYSICS*

1. What is the notion of an individual substance? For what reasons does Leibniz claim that it must be complete?
2. Why is substance indivisible?
3. How does Leibniz argue for the conclusion that every truth can be proved a priori?
4. How does he distinguish contingent and necessary propositions?
5. Why does Leibniz claim that one substance cannot causally influence another?
6. Why does Leibniz assert that each individual substance is like a little world or universe?

MONADOLOGY

Leibniz did not write one systematic exposition of his metaphysics. However, the *Monadology* perhaps comes closest to such a work. However, it does not explain explicitly Leibniz's arguments against the notion of material substance (but see M3, and 64–65). Nor does it contain his views on space and time, which are contained in the next selection, the "Letters to Clarke." In contrast, Leibniz's theory of truth is explained more fully in the previous selection, the *Discourse of Metaphysics*. Nevertheless, the *Monadology* does provide the main conclusions of his metaphysics, which is the theory of monads.

For these reasons, when reading this piece, it is important to bear in mind the other aspects of Leibniz's thought, which were explained in the philosophical overview. It is important to see that Leibniz's metaphysics as outlined in this work gains support from other aspects of his philosophy, such as his philosophy of language and of science.

1. The *monad*, of which we shall speak here, is nothing but a simple substance which enters into compounds; *simple*, that is to say, without parts.

2. And there must be simple substances, because there are compounds; for the compound is nothing but a collection or *aggregatum* of simples.

3. Now where there are no parts, there neither extension, nor shape, nor divisibility is possible. And these monads are the true atoms of nature and, in a word, the elements of things.

4. Moreover, there is no fear of dissolution, and there is no conceivable way in which a simple substance could perish in the course of nature.

5. For the same reason there is no way in which a simple substance could begin in the course of nature, since it cannot be formed by means of compounding.

Leibniz, from *Leibniz: Philosophical Writings*, edited by G. H. R. Parkinson, translated by Mary Morris and G. H. R. Parkinson. First published by Everyman's Library in 1934. Reprinted by permission of Everyman's Library.

6. Thus it may be said that monads can only begin and end all at once, that is to say they can only begin by creation and end by annihilation, whereas what is compound begins or ends by parts.

7. There is also no means of explaining how a monad can be altered or changed within itself by any other created thing, since it is impossible to displace anything in it or to conceive of the possibility of any internal motion being started, directed, increased, or diminished within it, as can occur in compounds, where change among the parts takes place. Monads have no windows, by which anything could come in or go out. Accidents cannot become detached, or wander about outside substances, as the 'sensible species' of the Scholastics used to do. Thus neither substance nor accident can enter a monad from without.

8. Monads, however, must have some qualities, otherwise they would not be beings at all. And if simple substances did not differ by their qualities, there would be no way of perceiving any change in things, since what is in the compound can only come from its simple ingredients; and if monads were without qualities, they would be indistinguishable from one another, since they do not differ in quantity either. And consequently, supposing space to be a plenum, each place would always only receive, when motion occurred, the equivalent of what it had before; and one state of things would be indistinguishable from another.

9. Indeed, every monad must be different from every other. For there are never in nature two beings which are precisely alike, and in which it is not possible to find some difference which is internal, or based on some intrinsic denomination.

10. I also take it as granted that every created thing, and consequently the created monad also, is subject to change, and indeed that this change is continual in each one.

11. It follows from what we have just said, that the natural changes of monads come from an *internal principle*, since an external cause would be unable to influence their inner being.

12. But besides the principle of change, there must be *differentiation within that which changes*, to constitute as it were the specification and variety of simple substances.

13. This differentiation must involve a plurality within the unity or the simple. For since every natural change takes place by degrees, something changes, and something remains; and consequently the simple must contain a large number of affections and relations, although it has no parts.

14. The passing state, which involves and represents a plurality within the unity or simple substance, is nothing other than what is called *perception*, which must be carefully distinguished from apperception or consciousness, as will appear presently. And herein lies the great mistake of the Cartesians, that they took no account of perceptions which are not apperceived. It is this also which made them believe that minds alone are monads, and that neither brutes nor other entelechies have souls. For the same reason also they fell into the common error of confusing death, properly so called, with a prolonged unconsciousness; and this made them favour the Scholastic conviction that souls are entirely separate from bodies, and even confirmed some ill-balanced minds in the opinion that souls are mortal.

15. The action of the internal principle which produces the change or passage from one perception to another may be called *appetition*; it is true that the appetite cannot always attain completely the whole of the perception towards which it tends, but it always attains something of it, and arrives at new perceptions.

16. We ourselves experience plurality within a simple substance, when we find that the least thought which we apperceive involves a variety in its object. So everyone who acknowledges that the soul is a simple substance must acknowledge this plurality within the monad; and M. Bayle should not have found any difficulty in this, as he does in his *Dictionary*, in the article 'Rorarius'.

17. We are moreover obliged to confess that *perception* and that which depends on it *cannot be explained mechanically*, that is to say by figures and motions. Suppose that there were a machine so constructed as to produce thought, feeling, and perception, we could imagine it increased in size while retaining the same proportions, so that one could enter as one might a mill. On going inside we should only see the parts impinging upon one another; we should not see anything which would explain a perception. The explanation of perception must therefore be sought in a simple substance, and not in a compound or in a machine. Moreover, there is nothing

else whatever to be found in the simple substance except just this, viz. perceptions and their changes. It is in this alone that all the *internal actions* of simple substances must consist.

18. We may give the name *entelechies* to all created simple substances or monads. For they have in themselves a certain perfection (ἔχουσι τὸ ἐνελέζ), there is a self-sufficiency (αὐτάρκεια) in them which makes them the sources of their internal actions—incorporeal automata, if I may so put it.

19. If we wish to give the name 'soul' to everything which has *perceptions* and *appetites* in the general sense I have just explained, all created simple substances or monads might be called souls; but as feeling is something more than a simple perception, I agree that the general name—monad or entelechy—should be enough for simple substances which have no more than that, and that those only should be called souls, whose perception is more distinct and is accompanied by memory.

20. For we experience within ourselves a state, in which we remember nothing and have no distinguishable perception; as when we fall into a swoon, or when we are overcome by a deep dreamless sleep. In this state the soul does not sensibly differ from a simple monad; but as this state is not permanent, and as the soul emerges from it, the soul is something more.

21. And it does not follow that when in that state the simple substance has no perception at all. Indeed, that is not possible for the above reasons; for it cannot perish, nor can it subsist without some affection in some way, and this affection is nothing but its perception.

29. But it is the knowledge of necessary and eternal truths which distinguishes us from mere animals, and gives us *reason* and the sciences, raising us to knowledge of ourselves and God. It is this in us which we call the rational soul or *mind.*

30. Further it is by the knowledge of necessary truths and by their abstractions that we are raised to *acts of reflection*, which make us think of what is called the *self*, and consider that this or that is within *us*. And it is thus that in thinking of ourselves, we think of being, of substance, of the simple and the compound, of the immaterial and of God himself, conceiving that what is limited in us, in him is limitless. And these acts of reflection provide the chief objects of our reasonings.

31. Our reasonings are based on two great principles: the *principle of contradiction*, by virtue of which we judge to be false that which involves a contradiction, and true that which is opposed or contradictory to the false;

32. and the *principle of sufficient reason*, by virtue of which we consider that no fact can be real or existing and no proposition can be true unless there is a sufficient reason, why it should be thus and not otherwise, even though in most cases these reasons cannot be known to us.

33. There are also two kinds of *truths*: truths of *reasoning* and truths of *fact*. Truths of reasoning are necessary and their opposite is impossible; those of fact are contingent and their opposite is possible. When a truth is necessary, the reason for it can be found by analysis, that is, by resolving it into simpler ideas and truths until the primary ones are reached.

34. It is in this way that in mathematics speculative *theorems* and practical *canons* are reduced by analysis to *definitions, axioms*, and *postulates*.

35. Finally there are simple ideas of which no definition can be given; there are also axioms and postulates, or in a word *primary principles*, which cannot be proved and have no need of proof. These are *identical propositions*, whose opposite contains an express contradiction.

36. But a *sufficient reason* also must be found in the case of *contingent truths* or *truths of fact*; that is to say, in the case of the series of things spread over the universe of created things; here resolution into particular reasons might go on into endless detail on account of the immense variety of things in nature and the division of bodies *ad infinitum*. There are an infinite number of shapes and motions, both present and past, which enter into the efficient cause of my present writing; and there are an infinite number of minute inclinations and dispositions of my soul, both present and past, which enter into its final cause.

37. And as all this differentiation involves only other prior or more differentiated contingent things, all of which need a similar analysis to explain them, we are no further advanced: and the sufficient or ultimate reason must be outside the succession or *series* of

this differentiation of contingent things, however infinite it may be.

38. This is why the ultimate reason of things must lie in a necessary substance, in which the differentiation of the changes only exists eminently as in their source; and this is what we call *God*.

39. Now since this substance is a sufficient reason of all this differentiation, which is itself likewise all connected, *there is only one God, and this God is enough.*

40. We may also judge that since this Supreme Substance, who is unique, universal, and necessary, has nothing outside himself independent of himself, and is a simple consequence of possible being, he must be incapable of being limited, and must contain just as much reality as is possible.

41. Whence it follows that God is absolutely perfect, since *perfection* is nothing but magnitude of positive reality, in the strict sense, setting aside the limits or bounds in things which are limited. And there, where there are no bounds, that is to say in God, perfection is absolutely infinite.

42. It follows also that created things owe their perfections to the influence of God, but that they owe their imperfections to their own nature, which is incapable of being without limits. For it is in this that they are distinguished from God.

43. It is true likewise, that in God is the source not only of existences but also of essences, in so far as they are real, that is of all the reality there is in possibility. This is because the Understanding of God is the region of eternal truths or of the ideas on which they depend, and because without him there would be nothing real in the possibilities—not only nothing existent, but also nothing possible.

44. For if there is a reality in essences or possibilities, or indeed in eternal truths, this reality must be founded on something existent and actual; and consequently on the existence of the Necessary Being in whom essence involves existence, or in whom it is enough to be possible in order to be actual.

45. Thus God alone (or the Necessary Being) has the privilege that he must exist if he is possible. And as nothing can prevent the possibility of that which has no limits, no negation, and consequently no contradiction, this alone is sufficient for us to know the existence of God *a priori*. We have proved it also by the reality of eternal truths. And we have now just proved it *a posteriori* also, since there exist contingent beings, which can only have their ultimate or sufficient reason in the Necessary Being, who has the reason for his existence in himself.

53. Now as there is an infinite number of possible universes in the ideas of God, and as only one can exist, there must be a sufficient reason for God's choice, determining him to one rather than to another.

54. And this reason can only be found in the *fitness,* or in the degrees of perfection, which these worlds contain, each possible world having the right to claim existence in proportion to the perfection which it involves.

55. And it is this which causes the existence of the best, which God knows through his wisdom, chooses through his goodness, and produces through his power.

56. Now this *connexion* or adaptation of all created things with each, and of each with all the rest, means that each simple substance has relations which express all the others, and that consequently it is a perpetual living mirror of the universe.

57. And just as the same town, when looked at from different sides, appears quite different and is, as it were, multiplied *in perspective,* so also it happens that because of the infinite number of simple substances, it is as if there were as many different universes, which are however but different perspectives of a single universe in accordance with the different points of view of each monad.

58. And this is the means of obtaining as much variety as possible, but with the greatest order possible; that is to say, it is the means of obtaining as much perfection as possible.

60. Moreover, there are evident from what I have just said the *a priori* reasons why things could not be otherwise than they are: namely, because God in regulating the whole had regard to each part, and particularly to each monad. The nature of the monad is representative, and consequently nothing can limit it to representing a part of things only, although it is true that its representation is confused as regards the detail of the whole universe and can only be distinct as regards a small part of things; that is to say as regards those which are either the nearest or the largest in relation to each of the monads; otherwise each monad would be a divinity. It is not in the object, but in the modification of the knowledge of the object, that monads are limited. In a confused way they all go towards the infinite, towards the whole; but they are limited and distinguished ·from one another by the degrees of their distinct perceptions.

61. And in this the compounds agree with the simples. For as the whole is a plenum, which means that the whole of matter is connected, and as in a plenum every movement has some effect on distant bodies in proportion to their distance, so that each body not only is affected by those which touch it, and is in some way sensitive to whatever happens to them, but also by means of them is sensitive to those which touch the first bodies by which it is itself directly touched; it follows that this communication stretches out indefinitely. Consequently every body is sensitive to everything which is happening in the universe, so much so that one who saw everything could read in each body what is happening everywhere, and even what has happened or what will happen, by observing in the present the things that are distant in time as well as in space; σύμπνοια πάντα, as Hippocrates said. But a soul can read in itself only what is distinctly represented there; it is unable to develop all at once all the things that are folded within it, for they stretch to infinity.

62. Thus although each created monad represents the whole universe, it represents more distinctly the body which is particularly affected by it, and whose entelechy it is: and as this body expresses the whole universe by the connexion of all matter in the plenum, the soul represents the whole universe also in representing the body which belongs to it in a particular way.

63. The body belonging to a monad, which is that body's entelechy or soul, constitutes together with the entelechy what may be called a *living thing*, and with the soul what is called an *animal*. Now this body of a living thing or animal is always organic; for since every monad is in its way a mirror of the universe, and since the universe is regulated in a perfect order, there must also be an order in that which represents it, that is to say in the perceptions of the soul,

and consequently in the body, according to which order the universe is represented therein.

64. Thus each organic body of a living thing is a kind of divine machine, or natural automaton, which infinitely surpasses all artificial automata. Because a machine which is made by the art of man is not a machine in each of its parts; for example, the tooth of a metal wheel has parts or fragments which as far as we are concerned are not artificial and which have about them nothing of the character of a machine, in relation to the use for which the wheel was intended. But the machines of nature, that is to say living bodies, are still machines in the least of their parts *ad infinitum*. This it is which makes the difference between nature and art, that is to say between Divine art and ours.

65. And the Author of nature was enabled to practise this divine and infinitely marvellous artifice, because each portion of matter is not only infinitely divisible, as the ancients recognised, but is also actually subdivided without limit, each part into further parts, of which each one has some motion of its own: otherwise it would be impossible for each portion of matter to express the whole universe.

66. Whence it is evident that there is a world of created beings—living things, animals, entelechies, and souls—in the least part of matter.

70. Thus we see that each living body has a dominant entelechy, which in the case of an animal is the soul, but the members of this living body are full of other living things, plants and animals, of which each has in turn its dominant entelechy or soul.

71. But we must not imagine, as some have done who have misunderstood my view, that each soul has a mass or portion of matter appropriate or attached to itself for ever, and that it consequently possesses other inferior living things, for ever destined to its service. For all bodies are in a perpetual flux like rivers, and parts are passing in and out of them continually.

72. Thus the soul only changes its body bit by bit and by degrees, so that it is never despoiled of all its organs all together; in animals there is often metamorphosis, but never metempsychosis, nor transmigration of souls: neither are there any entirely *separate souls*, nor *superhuman spirits* without bodies. God alone is entirely detached from body.

73. It is because of this also that there is never, strictly speaking, absolute generation nor perfect death, consisting in the separation of the soul. And what we call *generation* is a development and a growth, while what we call *death* is an envelopment and a diminution.

74. Philosophers have been much embarrassed over the origin of forms, entelechies or souls. But today when exact researches on plants, insects, and animals have revealed the fact that the organic bodies of nature are never produced from a chaos or from putrefaction, but always from seeds, wherein there was certainly some *preformation*, we conclude not only that the organic body was already present before conception, but also that there was a soul in this body; that, in a word, the animal itself was present, and that by means of conception it was merely prepared for a great transformation, so as to become an animal of another kind. We even see something of this kind apart from birth, as when worms become flies, and caterpillars become butterflies.

78. These principles provide me with a way of explaining naturally the union, or rather the conformity, of the soul and the organic body. The soul follows its own laws, and the body its own likewise, and they accord by virtue of the *harmony pre-established* among all substances, since they are all representations of one and the same universe.

79. Souls act according to the laws of final causes by appetitions, ends, and means. Bodies act according to the laws of efficient causes by motions. And the two kingdoms, of efficient and of final causes, are in harmony with one another.

80. Descartes recognised that souls cannot give force to bodies because there is always the same quantity of force in matter. He believed, however, that the soul could change the direction of bodies. But this is because in his day the law of nature was not known which affirms the conservation of the same total direction in matter. Had he noticed this, he would have stumbled upon my system of Pre-established Harmony.

81. Under this system, bodies act as though, *per impossible*, there were no souls: and souls act as if there were no bodies, and both act as if each influenced the other.

82. As for minds or rational souls, although I find that what I have just been saying is at bottom true of all living beings and animals (that is to say that the animal and the soul only begin with the world and do not come to an end any more than the world comes to an end), yet rational animals are peculiar in this, that their little spermatic animals, so long as they are that merely, have only ordinary or sensitive souls; but as soon as those which are, so to speak, elect arrive by an actual conception at human nature, then their sensitive souls are raised to the rank of reason and to the prerogative of minds.

83. Among other differences which exist between ordinary souls and minds, some of which I have already pointed out, there is also this, that souls in general are the living mirrors or images of the universe of created things, whereas minds are also images of the Divinity himself, or the Author of nature, capable of knowing the system of the universe, and of imitating something of it by architectonic patterns, each mind being as it were a little divinity in its own department.

84. This it is which renders minds capable of entering into a kind of society with God, and makes his relation to them not only that of an inventor to his machine (which is God's relation to the rest of created things) but also that of a prince to his subjects, and even of a father to his children.

STUDY QUESTIONS: LEIBNIZ, MONADOLOGY

1. What is a 'monad'? How many are there? How does Leibniz argue for their existence?
2. What is Leibniz's conception of substance?
3. Why does Leibniz claim that no two things can be exactly alike?
4. Why does Leibniz state that two monads are differentiated by their perceptions?
5. What distinguishes us from the animals, according to Leibniz?
6. How is the Principle of Sufficient Reason important for the definition of contingent truths?

7. According to what criteria does God choose which of the possible worlds to make actual?
8. Why does each created monad represent the whole universe?
9. What is the difference between a machine and a living body created by God?
10. What is preestablished harmony, and why is it necessary?

LETTERS TO CLARKE
Third and Fourth Letters

In the last year of his life, 1716, Leibniz expounded his theory of space and time in his letters to Clarke. In these letters, he advocates a relational theory of space and time, directly opposed to the Newtonian absolute theory put forward by Clarke. These letters have become a philosophical classic.

Leibniz argues for the relational theory by claiming that Newton's view contravenes the Principle of Sufficient Reason. He says that God could have no possible reason for creating the universe in a different region of space or at a different period of time. Since everything must have a sufficient reason, it cannot make sense to say that the universe could have been created earlier or elsewhere in space; these cannot be genuine alternatives, contrary to the claims of the absolute theory. Therefore, the theory is false.

Furthermore, Newton's theory is a violation of the Principle of the Identity of Indiscernibles. Points and empty regions of absolute space are clearly qualitatively similar in all respects (i.e., they are indiscernible), and yet the absolute theory maintains that they are numerically distinct.

Leibniz also challenges Newton's view on theological grounds. The Newtonian idea of space and time as absolute, infinite entities contradicts the uniqueness of God. If God is the only infinite individual, space and time cannot be absolute and infinite.

LEIBNIZ'S THIRD PAPER

1. According to the usual way of speaking, *mathematical principles* are those which consist in pure mathematics, for instance numbers, figures, arithmetic, geometry. But *metaphysical principles* concern more general notions, as for example cause and effect.

2. I am granted this important *principle, that nothing happens without a sufficient reason why it should be thus rather than otherwise.* But it is granted me in words and refused me in fact; which shows that the full force of it has not been properly understood; and in this connexion the author makes use of an example which exactly falls in with one of my demonstrations against real absolute space, the *idol* of some modern Englishman. I call it 'idol' not in a theological sense, but in the philosophical sense in which Chancellor Bacon used the word when he said, a long time ago, that there are *idola tribus, idola specus*.

3. These gentlemen maintain, then, that space is a real absolute being; but this leads them into great difficulties. For it appears that this being must be eternal and infinite. This is why there have been some who believed that it was God himself, or else his attribute, his immensity. But as it has parts, it is not a thing which can be appropriate to God.

4. As for me, I have more than once stated that I held *space* to be something purely relative, like *time*;

Leibniz, from *Leibniz: Philosophical Writings*, edited by G. H. R. Parkinson, translated by Mary Morris and G. H. R. Parkinson. First published by Everyman's Library in 1934. Reprinted by permission of Everyman's Library.

space being an order of co-existences as time is an order of successions. For space denotes in terms of possibility an order of things which exist at the same time, in so far as they exist together, and is not concerned with their particular ways of existing: and when we see several things together we perceive this order of things among themselves.

5. I have several proofs for refuting the conception of those who take *space* to be a substance, or at least an absolute being of some kind. But here I only wish to make use of the one which the present occasion requires. I say then that if space were an absolute being, there would happen something for which it would be impossible that there should be a sufficient reason, and this is contrary to our axiom. This is how I prove it. Space is something absolutely uniform, and without the things situated in it one point of space does not differ absolutely in any respect from another point of space. Now from this it follows that if we suppose that space is something in itself, other than the order of bodies among themselves, it is impossible that there should be a reason why God, preserving the same positions for bodies among themselves, should have arranged bodies in space thus and not otherwise, and why everything was not put the other way round (for instance) by changing east and west. But if space is nothing other than this order or relation, and is nothing whatever without bodies but the possibility of placing them in it, these two conditions, the one as things are, the other supposed the other way round, would not differ from one another: their difference exists only in our chimerical supposition of the reality of space in itself. But in truth the one would be just the same as the other, as they are absolutely indiscernible; and consequently there is no occasion to search after a reason for the preference of the one to the other.

6. The same is true of *time*. Suppose someone asks why God did not create everything a year sooner; and that the same person wants to infer from that that God did something for which there cannot possibly be a reason why he did it thus rather than otherwise, we should reply that his inference would be sound if time were something apart from temporal things, for it would be impossible that there should be reasons why things should have been applied to certain instants rather than to others, when their succession remained the same. But this itself proves that

instants apart from things are nothing, and that they only consist in the successive order of things; and if this remains the same, the one of the two states (for instance that in which the creation was imagined to have occurred a year earlier) would be nowise different and could not be distinguished from the other which now exists.

LEIBNIZ'S FOURTH PAPER

1. In things which are absolutely indifferent there is no choice and consequently no election or will, since choice must have some reason or principle.

2. A simple will without any motive (*a mere will*) is a fiction which is not only contrary to the perfection of God, but also chimerical and contradictory, incompatible with the definition of will and sufficiently refuted in my *Theodicy*.

3. It is indifferent whether three bodies which are equal and alike in every respect be placed in any order whatsoever, and consequently they never would be placed in order by Him who does nothing without wisdom. But also, being the Author of things, He will not produce any such; and consequently there are none in nature.

4. There are no two individuals indiscernible from one another. A clever gentleman, a friend of mine, when conversing with me in the presence of Her Electoral Highness in the garden at Herrenhausen, thought he would certainly find two leaves exactly alike. Her Electoral Highness challenged him to do so, and he spent a long time running about looking for them, but in vain. Two drops of water or milk looked at under the microscope will be found to be discernible. This is an argument against atoms, which, like the void, are opposed to the principles of a true metaphysic.

5. These great principles of a Sufficient Reason and of the Identity of Indiscernibles change the state of metaphysics, which by their means becomes real and demonstrative; whereas formerly it practically consisted of nothing but empty terms.

6. To suppose two things indiscernible is to suppose the same thing under two names. Thus the hypothesis that the universe should have originally had another position in time and place from that which it actually had, and yet all the parts of the universe should have had the same position with regard to one another as that which they have in fact received, is an impossible fiction.

7. The same reason which shows that space outside the world is imaginary proves that all empty space is something imaginary; for they differ only as the great from the small.

8. If space is a property or an attribute, it must be the property of some substance. Of what substance is the bounded empty space, which the supporters of this view suppose to exist between two bodies, the property or affection?

9. If infinite space is immensity, finite space will be the opposite of immensity, that is to say mensurability or bounded extension. Now extension must be the affection of something extended. But if this space is empty, it will be an attribute without a subject, an extension of no extended thing. This is why in mak-

ing space a property the author is accepting my position, according to which it is an order of things and not something absolute.

10. If space is an absolute reality, far from being a property or accident opposed to substance, it will have more subsistence than substances; God will be unable to destroy it, or even to change it in any respect. It will be not only immense in the whole, but also immutable and eternal in each of its parts. There will be an infinity of eternal things besides God.

11. To say that infinite space is without parts, is to say that it is not made up of finite spaces, and that infinite space might continue to exist though all finite spaces were reduced to nothing. It would be as if we were to say, on the Cartesian supposition of a corporeal extended universe without limits, that this universe might continue to exist though all the bodies which make it up were reduced to nothing.

STUDY QUESTIONS: LEIBNIZ, *LETTERS TO CLARKE*

1. How is his relational theory of space and time different from Newton's absolute theory?
2. What is the Principle of Sufficient Reason, and what role does it play in Leibniz's argument for the relational theory of space and time?
3. What is the Principle of the Identity of Indiscernibles? How does Leibniz argue for this principle? How does he employ the principle to argue against Newton?
4. How does the notion of absolute space contradict the idea of God?

Philosophical Bridges: Leibniz's Influence

Leibniz pioneered the field of formal logic. His work on formally deductive systems, in which he deduces propositions from axioms and definitions, was the most important advance in logic since Aristotle. In this way, Leibniz is a forerunner of the important breakthroughs in logic that occurred during the nineteenth century, such as the work of Georg Cantor, Boole, and Frege.

Leibniz's interest in logic was motivated by his wider project of creating an alphabet of human thought. Convinced that thought was calculation, Leibniz envisaged a calculating machine for propositions, which was a seventeenth-century version of the computer. The claim that thought is calculation, which formed the central axis of much of Leibniz's work, influenced greatly the British philosopher Bertrand Russell (1872–1970) and, largely through him, entered into twentieth-century philosophy of language. This is because, as Leibniz himself understood, the project of showing how thought is calculation requires uncovering the ideal structure of language through a process of analysis. In the process of elaborating this project, Leibniz created a slew of influential ideas in the philosophy of language. Among these are the following.

First, Leibniz's alphabet was the claim that all complex concepts can be analyzed or decomposed into a set of primitive ones that compose it. For example, the complex concept of a person is composed of the simpler concepts 'rational' and 'animal.' This view of philosophical analysis was predominant in much analytic philosophy until the mid-twentieth century. For instance, the British thinker G. E. Moore embraced a similar conception of analysis at the beginning of the twentieth century, and the logical positivist Rudolf Carnap adopted a similar view of concepts in his work *The Logical Construction of the World* (1928).

Second, Leibniz argued that all propositions are reducible to the subject-predicate form. He tried to show how relational statements could be so reduced. This view has been influential in two respects. Leibniz attempts to uncover the logical structure of language, a project that was important in much twentieth-century analytic philosophy of language. Additionally, he attempts to do so because he thinks that the structure of language mirrors that of the world; the fact that the subject-predicate proposition form is basic reflects the fact that the world consists only of substances and their monadic properties. In other words, we can investigate ontology by studying language. In both of these ways, Leibniz is a forerunner of some twentieth-century philosophy of language.

Third, Leibniz's notion of possible worlds has become an indispensable element of some analytic philosophy. Recent writers such as the contemporary American philosopher David Lewis have advocated that the notion and existence of possible worlds are necessary to explain the meaning of counterfactual sentences, such as 'If you had lit a match, then the gas would have exploded.' Other philosophers have worked on developing formal semantics that explains the meaning of sentences in terms of possible worlds.

Fourth, Leibniz defined analytic truths as ones in which the concept of the predicate is included as part of the concept of the subject. This definition was adopted by Kant and was regarded as the standard definition more or less until the 1940s.

Leibniz was a towering influence in many fields. For instance, in mathematics he discovered differential and integral calculus independently of Newton. In logic, he developed what were later called Euler circles or Venn diagrams to represent visually logical relations. He tried to represent logical inferences numerically, an extremely powerful tool used by Kurt Gödel in 1930 to prove the incompleteness of arithmetic. Leibniz's metaphysics was reformulated and systematized by Christian von Wolff, and in this form it became prominent in Germany prior to around 1790, after which time Kant's thinking tended to dominate the stage.

BIBLIOGRAPHY

GENERAL

Atherton, Margaret, *Women Philosophers of the Early Modern Period*, Hackett, 1994

Bennett, Jonathan, *Learning from Six Philosophers: Descartes, Spinoza, Leibniz, Locke, Berkeley, Hume*, Clarendon Press, 2001

Cottingham, John, *The Rationalists*, Oxford University Press, 1988

Emmanuel, Steven M., *The Blackwell Guide to the Modern Philosophers: From Descartes to Nietzsche*, Blackwell, 2001

Garber, Daniel, and Michael Ayers, eds., *The Cambridge History of Seventeenth-Century Philosophy*, Cambridge University Press, 1998

Loeb, Louis E., *From Descartes to Hume: Continental Metaphysics and the Development of Modern Philosophy*, Cornell University Press, 1981

Pereboom, Derek, ed., *The Rationalists: Critical Essays on Descartes, Spinoza, and Leibniz*, Rowman & Littlefield, 1999

Schacht, Richard, *Classical Modern Philosophers: Descartes to Kant*, Routledge, 1993

Thomson, Garrett, *Bacon to Kant: An Introduction to Modern Philosophy*, Waveland Press, 2001

———, *On Modern Philosophy*, Wadsworth, 2003

Yolton, John, *Perception and Reality: A History from Descartes to Kant*, Cornell University Press, 1996

DESCARTES
Primary

Descartes: Philosophical Writings, trans. John Cottingham, Robert Stroothoff, Dugald Murdoch, and Anthony Kenny, 3 vols., Cambridge University Press, 1988

Secondary

Chappell, Vere, ed., *Descartes's Meditations*, Rowman & Littlefield, 1997

Cottingham, John, *Descartes*, Blackwell, 1986

———, ed., *The Cambridge Companion to Descartes*, Cambridge University Press, 1992

Gaukroger, Stephen, *Descartes: An Intellectual Biography*, Clarendon Press, 1997

Kenny, Anthony, *Descartes*, Random House, 1968

Ree, Jonathan, *Descartes*, Allen Lane, 1974

Sorrell, Tom, *Descartes*, Oxford University Press, 1978

Thomson, Garrett, *On Descartes*, Wadsworth, 2000

Williams, Bernard, *Descartes the Project of Pure Enquiry*, Pelican, 1978

Wilson, Margaret, *Descartes*, Routledge & Kegan Paul, 1978

SPINOZA
Primary

The Collected Works of Spinoza, ed. E. Curley, Princeton University Press, 1985

Ethics, trans. R. H. M. Elwes, in *The Works of Benedict de Spinoza*, Dover, 1955

A Political Treatise, trans. R. Elwes, Dover, 1951

A Spinoza Reader, ed. E. Curley, Princeton University Press, 1994

Secondary

Allison, Henry, *Benedict de Spinoza: An Introduction*, Yale University Press, 1987

Bennett, Jonathan, *A Study of Spinoza's Ethics*, Hackett, 1985

Curley, E. M., *Spinoza's Metaphysics*, Cambridge University Press, 1969

———, *Behind the Geometrical Method: A Reading of Spinoza's Ethics*, Princeton University Press, 1988

Delahunty, R. J., *Spinoza, Arguments of the Philosophers*, Routledge, 1985

Hampshire, Stuart, *Spinoza*, Baltimore, 1962

Parkinson, H. R., *Spinoza's Theory of Knowledge*, Oxford University Press, 1954

Scruton, R., *Spinoza*, Oxford University Press, 1986

LEIBNIZ
Primary

The Leibniz-Arnauld Correspondence, trans. H. Mason, Manchester, 1967

The Leibniz-Clarke Correspondence, ed. H. Alexander, Manchester, 1956

Leibniz Philosophical Writings, ed. G. Parkinson, Rowman & Littlefield, 1973

Philosophical Papers and Letters, ed. L. Loemker, Reidel, 1969

New Essays on Human Understanding, ed. P. Remnant and J. Bennett, Cambridge University Press, 1982

Theodicy, trans. E. M. Huggard, Open Court, 1985

Secondary

Adams, Robert Merrihew, *Leibniz: Determinist, Theist, Idealist*, Oxford University Press, 1994

Broad, C. D., *Leibniz: An Introduction*, Cambridge University Press, 1975

Brown, Stuart, *Leibniz*, University of Minnesota University Press, 1984

Jolley, N., ed., *The Cambridge Companion to Leibniz*, Cambridge University Press, 1995

———, *Leibniz and Locke: A Study of the New Essays on Human Understanding*, Clarendon Press, 1984

Mates, Benson, *The Philosophy of Leibniz*, Oxford University Press, 1986

Parkinson, G. H. R., *Logic and Reality in Leibniz' Metaphysics*, Garland, 1985

Rescher, Nicholas, *Leibniz: An Introduction to His Philosophy*, Blackwell, 1979

Ross, George MacDonald, *Leibniz*, Oxford University Press, 1984

Thomson, Garrett, *On Leibniz*, Wadsworth, 2000

SECTION III

❖ THE EMPIRICISTS ❖

PROLOGUE

The development of science in seventeenth-century Europe depended on both mathematical reasoning and observation. Whereas the Rationalists stressed the importance of the former, the Empiricists emphasized the latter. Empiricism is the view that all knowledge and concepts originate from experience. Bacon, Hobbes, Locke, Berkeley, and Hume are called Empiricists because they share common concerns and assumptions, but not because they followed a specific school of thought. The central claims of Empiricism are as follows.

All Ideas Are Derived from Experience

All complex ideas are built from the simple ideas that we receive from experience. Consequently, there are no innate ideas or concepts. This view involves an atomistic conception of experience. All ideas are either complex or simple. Any complex idea is composed of simple ideas; and by definition, these simples cannot be broken down any further. If there were an idea that could not be derived from experience, then we would not be justified in using it to make judgments about experience. For example, Hume argues that, as traditionally conceived, the ideas of cause, substance, and self cannot be derived from experience, and he concludes that beliefs based on such ideas are not justifiable.

We Can Perceive Directly Only Our Own Ideas

We are immediately aware *only* of our own ideas, as a given in experience. Consequently, we are not immediately aware of external objects.

Reason Is Not a Source of Knowledge About the World

We can have no a priori knowledge of the world. Hume, in particular, makes this thesis explicit by distinguishing between relations of ideas and matters of fact. A priori reasoning is possible only concerning the relations between concepts, and such reasoning does not give us knowledge of matters of fact or of the world. In other words, we cannot have knowledge of the world through a priori reasoning alone. To have knowledge of facts, we must resort to experience. Hume's distinction undermines Rationalism.

All Meaningful Words Stand for Ideas

In the *Enquiry*, Hume says, 'When we entertain any suspicion that a philosophical term is employed without any meaning or idea, we need but inquire, from what impression is that supposed idea derived?' In other words, words stand for ideas, which are derived from sense experience.

The preceding four claims articulate the basic pillars of modern Empiricism. However, this does not mean that each Empiricist philosopher endorses all of them. These broad similarities do not indicate any uniformity in the views of the Empiricists. Sometimes, the similarities between an Empiricist and a Rationalist are just as important as the similarities between two Rationalists.

Francis Bacon (1561–1626)

Biographical History

At the age of 23, Bacon became a member of the English Parliament. However, it was not until after the death of Queen Elizabeth in 1603 that he was appointed Attorney General and, in 1618, Lord Chancellor of England. Three years later, he was found guilty of accepting bribes, and he lost all political power; he was banished from the court and was forced to sell his London mansion. The *Essays* appeared in 1597, and his first book, the *Advancement of Learning*, was published in 1605. In 1610, he wrote *New Atlantis*, concerning the cooperative nature of scientific research. *Novum Organum* was published in 1620. After his impeachment, Bacon wrote two works on natural history: *Historia Ventorum* (1622) and *Historia Vitae et Mortis* (1623). Bacon died in 1626, after catching a cold whilst experimenting on stuffing a dead chicken with snow.

Philosophical Overview

Bacon envisioned scientific knowledge as a new world or continent for which he would try to provide the map. According to Bacon's vision, knowledge should be used to control nature for the benefit and liberation of humanity. This was humanity's new mission, the worldly counterpart of spiritual salvation. Bacon saw himself as articulating the principles for the dawn of a new era, and sweeping aside the stagnant Scholastic view of knowledge that dominated Europe. However, Bacon's work does not argue for a systematic metaphysical theory to replace Scholasticism. Rather, it consists in voicing this vision and finding the means to bring it about.

As such, Bacon had three major philosophical ambitions. First, he tried to classify all kinds of knowledge. Second, he wanted to undermine the popular misconceptions of learning. Third, he presented a new method for the systematic advancement of scientific knowledge.

The Criticism of False Learning

Bacon's aim in the first part of the *Advancement of Learning* is to remove obstacles to the methodological progress of science, and for this purpose he criticizes three misleading schools of learning.

1. Dominant at the time was Aristotelian Scholasticism, which Bacon calls the 'disputatious' style of learning, which fruitlessly speculates about theology. Also, Bacon criticizes the Scholastics for overemphasis on deduction, which cannot yield new knowledge, and for too little emphasis on observation, which can. Most Scholastic philosophers try to preserve tradition rather than seek new knowledge.
2. He also criticizes the humanism of his time, which he calls the 'delicate' style of learning. He accuses it of indifference to the serious business of science, and for preoccupation with vacuous eloquence and polite morality.
3. The third problematic style of learning is that of the occultists. Despite their desire to master nature, the occultists uncritically accept myths and fables. In contrast, scientific knowledge should be based on rational procedure and observation that anyone could critically accept.

The New Method of Induction

Bacon claims that science should be based on his new method of eliminative induction, which he contrasts with simple enumerative induction. In enumerative induction, one derives an unrestricted general conclusion from an observed finite set of singular cases. From the fact that one has seen a few white swans, one concludes rashly that all swans are white. In contrast, the scientist should seek counterinstances in order to try to falsify a hypothesis, which can be eliminated. The scientific method should be eliminative and not enumerative.

Bacon's example of his method at work is the discovery of the nature of heat. First, draw up three lists: a list of hot things that are otherwise unalike; a list of cold things, which are otherwise like the hot things; and, finally, a list of things of varying degrees of heat. By carefully comparing these tables, one can reject some suggestions as to the nature of heat, and make a first affirmation as to its nature. Second, from a number of such affirmations of the lowest degree of generality, one can suggest laws that are slightly more general and so on. Third, any proposed law or hypothesis should be tested in new circumstances. One must try to falsify it, and, if one cannot, the hypothesis is to that extent confirmed. In particular, one should look for experiments that hasten the process of induction by allowing one to reject quickly false hypotheses. For example, Bacon mentioned 'prerogative instances,' which separate the characteristics found in both hot and cold bodies. By applying this method consistantly, one may conclude that heat is the rapid irregular motion of the small parts of bodies.

Bacon contrasts his method with that of the Scholastics. On one hand, his method begins from the observation of particulars and, by eliminative induction, builds systematically toward more general conclusions. On the other hand, the Scholastic method, which involves reasoning deductively from the general to the particular, is weak because it assumes general knowledge of nature that, in fact, must be acquired through elimination.

The Theory of Forms

According to Bacon, science is the investigation of 'the form of a simple nature.' For instance, the form of heat is both a necessary and sufficient condition of heat. The form of heat is always present in hot things, is always absent in cold things, and varies with the degree of heat. These forms are arrangements of matter. Bacon thinks we should explain observable properties in terms of the fine structure of matter. The form of gold is that configuration of matter that constitutes gold. This revolutionary idea was adopted and developed by Descartes, Hobbes, and Locke.

NOVUM ORGANUM

The first part of the reading, *The Great Instauration*, situates the *Novum Organum* in the context of Bacon's wider plans. Bacon envisaged a huge six-part program of work. The first two parts are philosophically the most important, and Bacon never achieved much beyond them. The first part of the plan is the classification of knowledge, which is found in the *Advancement of Learning*. The second part is in the *Novum Organum* itself, where Bacon sets out his new basis for scientific learning, which he calls 'the new method of induction.'

The first book of the *Novum Organum* contains Bacon's famous discussion of the idols of the mind. Scientific progress also requires that we overcome the erroneous tendencies of the mind, which are the four idols.

1. *The idols of the tribe are intellectual weaknesses generally inherent in human nature. With the aid of instruments and careful systematic observation, we can correct these defects because 'the senses suffice for knowledge.'*
2. *The idols of the cave are personal prejudices and biases.*
3. *The idols of the marketplace are those tendencies to error due to the bewitchment of the mind by language. 'Words are but the images of matter,' and we should not suppose that they reflect things truly.*
4. *The idols of the theater are the accepted, but mistaken, schools of philosophy, which we have discussed earlier.*

PROŒMIUM

Francis of Verulam

Reasoned thus with himself and judged it to be for the interest of the present and future generations that they should be made acquainted with his thoughts.

Being convinced that the human intellect makes its own difficulties, not using the true helps which are at man's disposal soberly and judiciously, whence follows manifold ignorance of things, and by reason of that ignorance mischiefs innumerable, he thought all trial should be made, whether that commerce between the mind of man and the nature of things, which is more precious than anything on earth, or at least than anything that is of the earth, might by any means be restored to its prefect and original condition, or if that may not be, yet reduced to a better condition than that in which it now is. Now that the errors which have hitherto prevailed, and which will prevail for ever should (if the mind be left to go its own way) either by the natural force of the understanding or by help of the aids and instruments of Logic, one by one correct themselves, was a thing

not to be hoped for, because the primary notions of things which the mind readily and passively imbibes, stores up, and accumulates (and it is from them that all the rest flow) are false, confused, and overhastily abstracted from the facts; nor are the secondary and subsequent notions less arbitrary and inconstant; whence it follows that the entire fabric of human reason, which we employ in the inquisition of nature, is badly put together and built up, and like some magnificent structure without any foundation. For while men are occupied in admiring and applauding the false powers of the mind, they pass by and throw away those true powers, which, if it be supplied with the proper aids and can itself be content to wait upon nature instead of vainly affecting to overrule her, are within its reach. There was but one course left, therefore—to try the whole thing anew upon a better plan, and to commence a total reconstruction of sciences, arts, and all human knowledge, raised upon the proper foundations. And this, though in the project and undertaking it may seem a thing infinite and beyond the powers of man, yet when it comes to be dealt with it will be found sound and sober, more so than what has been done hitherto. For of this there is some issue; whereas in what is now done in the matter of science there is only a whirling round about, and perpetual agitation, ending where it began.

Preface

That the state of knowledge is not prosperous nor greatly advancing; and that a way must be opened for the human understanding entirely different from any hitherto known, and other helps provided, in order that the mind may exercise over the nature of things the authority which properly belongs to it.

It seems to me that men do not rightly understand either their store or their strength, but overrate the one and underrate the other. Hence it follows that either from an extravagant estimate of the value of the arts which they possess they seek no further, or else from too mean an estimate of their own powers they spend their strength in small matters and never put it fairly to the trial in those which go to the main. These are as the pillars of fate set in the path of knowledge, for men have neither desire nor hope to encourage them to penetrate further. And since opinion of store is one of the chief causes of want, and satisfaction with the present induces neglect of provisions for the future, it becomes a thing not only useful but absolutely necessary, that the excess of honour and admiration with which our existing stock of inventions is regarded be in the very entrance and threshold of the work, and that frankly and without circumlocution, stripped off, and men be duly warned not to exaggerate or make too much of them. For let a man look carefully into all that variety of books with which the arts and sciences abound, he will find everywhere endless repetitions of the same thing, varying in the method of treatment but not new in substance, insomuch that the whole stock, numerous as it appears at first view, proves on examination to be but scanty. And for its value and utility it must be plainly avowed that that wisdom which we have derived principally from the Greeks is but like the boyhood of knowledge, and has the characteristic property of boys: it can talk, but it cannot generate, for it is fruitful of controversies but barren of works. So that the state of learning as it now is appears to be

represented to the life in the old fable of Scylla, who had the head and face of a virgin, but her womb was hung round with barking monsters, from which she could not be delivered. For in like manner the sciences to which we are accustomed have certain general positions which are specious and flattering, but as soon as they come to particulars, which are as the parts of generation, when they should produce fruit and works, then arise contentions and barking disputations, which are the end of the matter and all the issue they can yield. Observe also that if sciences of this kind had any life in them, that could never have come to pass which has been the case now for many ages—that they stand almost at a stay, without receiving any augmentations worthy of the human race; insomuch that many times not only what was asserted once is asserted still, but what was a question once is a question still, and instead of being resolved by discussion is only fixed and fed; and all the tradition and succession of schools is still a succession of masters and scholars, not of inventors and those who bring to further perfection the things invented. In the mechanical arts we do not find it so; they, on the contrary, as having in them some breath of life, are continually growing and becoming more perfect. As originally invented they are commonly rude, clumsy, and shapeless; afterwards they acquire new powers and more commodious arrangements and constructions; in so far that men shall sooner leave the study and pursuit of them and turn to something else, than they arrive at the ultimate perfection of which they are capable. Philosophy and the intellectual sciences, on the contrary, stand like status, worshipped and celebrated but not moved or advanced. Nay, they sometimes flourish most in the hands of the first author, and afterwards degenerate. For when men have once made over their judgements to others' keeping, and (like those senators whom they called *Pedarii*) have agreed to support some one person's opinion, from that time they make no enlargement of the sciences themselves, but fall to the servile office of embellishing certain individual authors and increasing their retinue. . . .

Lastly, I would address one general admonition to all, that they consider what are the true ends of knowledge, and that they seek it not either for pleasure of the mind, or for contention, or for superiority to others, or for profit, or fame, or power, or any of these inferior things, but for the benefit and use of life; and that they perfect and govern it in charity. For it was from lust of power that the angels fell, from lust of knowledge that man fell, but of charity there can be no excess, neither did angel or man ever come in danger by it.

The requests I have to make are these. Of myself I say nothing, but in behalf of the business which is in hand I entreat men to believe that it is not an opinion to be held but a work to be done; and to be well assured that I am labouring to lay the foundation, not of any sect or doctrine, but of human utility and power. Next, I ask them to deal fairly by their own interests, and laying aside all emulations and prejudices in favour of this or that opinion, to join in consultation for the common good, and being now freed and guarded by the securities and helps which I offer from the errors and impediments of the way, to come forward themselves and take part in that which remains to be done. Moreover, to be of good hope, nor to imagine that this Instauration of mine is a thing infinite and beyond the power of man, when it is in fact the true end and termination of infinite error; and seeing also that it is by no means forgetful of the conditions of mortality and humanity (for it does not suppose that the work can be altogether completed within one generation, but provides for its being taken up by another); and finally that it seeks for the sciences not arrogantly in the little cells of human wit but with reverence in the greater world. But it is the empty things that are vast; things solid are most contracted and lie in little room. And now I have only one favour more to ask (else injustice to me may perhaps imperil the business itself)—that men will consider well how far, upon that which I must needs assert (if I am to be consistent with myself) they are entitled to judge and decide upon these doctrines of mine; inasmuch as all that premature human reasoning which anticipates inquiry, and is abstracted from the facts rashly and sooner than is fit, is by me rejected (so far as the inquisition of nature is concerned) as a thing uncertain, confused, and ill built up; and I cannot be fairly asked to abide by the decision of a tribunal which is itself on its trial.

The Plan of the Work

The work is in six Parts:—

1. The Division of the Sciences.
2. The New Organon; or Directions concerning the Interpretation of Nature.
3. The Phenomena of the Universe; or a Natural and Experimental History for the foundation of Philosophy.
4. The Ladder of the Intellect.
5. The Forerunners; or Anticipations of the New Philosophy.
6. The New Philosophy; or Active Science.

The arguments of the several parts.

It being part of my design to set everything forth, as far as may be, plainly and perspicuously (for nakedness of the mind is still, as nakedness of the body once was, the companion of innocence and simplicity), let me first explain the order and plan of the work. I distribute it into six parts.

The first part exhibits a summary or general description of the knowledge which the human race at present possesses. For I thought it good to make some pause upon that which is received, that thereby the old may be more easily made perfect and the new more easily approached. And I hold the improvement of that which we have to be as much an object as the acquisition of more. Besides which it will make me the better listened to, for "He that is ignorant (says the proverb) receives not the words of knowledge, unless thou first tell him that which is in his own heart." We will therefore make a coasting voyage along the shores of the arts and sciences received, not without importing into them some useful things by the way.

Having thus coasted past the ancient arts, the next point is to equip the intellect for passing beyond. To the second part therefore belongs the doctrine concerning the better and more perfect use of human reason in the inquisition of things, and the true helps of the understanding, that thereby (as far as the condition of mortality and humanity allows) the intellect may be raised and exalted, and made capable of overcoming the difficulties and obscurities of nature. The art which I introduce with this view (which I call *Interpretation of Nature*) is a kind of logic, though the difference between it and the ordinary logic is great;

indeed immense. For the ordinary logic professes to contrive and prepare helps and guards for the understanding as mine does, and in this one point they agree. But mine differs from it in three points especially; viz. in the end aimed at; in the order of demonstration; and in the starting point of the inquiry.

For the end which this science of mine proposes is the invention not of arguments but of arts, not of things in accordance with principles but of principles themselves, not of probable reasons but of designations and directions for works. And as the intention is different, so accordingly is the effect, the effect of the one being to overcome an opponent in argument, of the other to command nature in action.

In accordance with this end is also the nature and order of the demonstrations. For in the ordinary logic almost all the work is spent about the syllogism. Of induction the logicians seem hardly to have taken any serious thought, but they pass it by with a slight notice, and hasten on to the formulæ of disputation. I on the contrary reject demonstration by syllogism, as acting too confusedly, and letting nature slip out of its hands. For although no one can doubt that things which agree in a middle term agree with one another (which is a proposition of mathematical certainty), yet it leaves an opening for deception, which is this. The syllogism consists of propositions; propositions of words; and words are the tokens and signs of notions. Now if the very notions of the mind (which are as the soul of words and the basis of the whole structure) be improperly and over-hastily abstracted from facts, vague, not sufficiently definite, faulty, in short, in many ways, the whole edifice tumbles. I therefore reject the syllogism; and that not only as regards principles (for to principles the logicians themselves do not apply it) but also as regards middle propositions, which, though obtainable no doubt by the syllogism, are, when so obtained, barren of works, remote from practice, and altogether unavailable for the active department of the sciences. Although therefore I leave to the syllogism and these famous and boasted modes of demonstration their jurisdiction over popular arts and such as are matter of opinion (in which department I leave all as it is), yet in dealing with the nature of things I use induction throughout, and that in the minor propositions as well as the major.

For I consider induction to be that form of demonstration which upholds the sense, and closes with nature, and comes to the very brink of operation, if it does not actually deal with it.

Hence it follows that the order of demonstration is likewise inverted. For hitherto the proceeding has been to fly at once from the sense and particulars up to the most general propositions, as certain fixed poles for the argument to turn upon, and from these to derive the rest by middle terms, a short way, no doubt, but precipitate, and one which will never lead to nature, though it offers an easy and ready way to disputation. Now my plan is to proceed regularly and gradually from one axiom to another, so that the most general are not reached till the last, but then when you do come to them, you find them to be not empty notions but well defined, and such as nature would really recognise as her first principles, and such as lie at the heart and marrow of things.

But the greatest change I introduce is in the form itself of induction and the judgment made thereby. For the induction of which logicians speak, which proceeds by simple enumeration, is a puerile thing; concludes at hazard; is always liable to be upset by a contradictory instance; takes into account only what is known and ordinary; and leads to no result.

Nor what the sciences stand in need of is a form of induction which shall analyse experience and take it to pieces, and by a due process of exclusion and rejection lead to an inevitable conclusion. And if that ordinary mode of judgment practised by the logicians was so laborious, and found exercise for such great wits, how much more labour must we be prepared to bestow upon this other, which is extracted not merely out of the depths of the mind but out of the very bowels of nature.

The sense fails in two ways. Sometimes it gives no information, sometimes it gives false information. For first, there are very many things which escape the sense, even when best disposed and no way obstructed, by reason either of the subtlety of the whole body, or the minuteness of the parts, or distance of place, or slowness or else swiftness of motion, or familiarity of the object, or other causes. And again when the sense does apprehend a thing, its apprehension is not much to be relied upon. For the testimony and information of the sense has reference always to man, not to the universe; and it is a great error to assert that the sense is the measure of things.

To meet these difficulties, I have sought on all sides diligently and faithfully to provide helps for the sense—substitutes to supply its failures, rectifications to correct its errors; and this I endeavour to accomplish not so much by instruments as by experiments. For the subtlety of experiments is far greater than that of the sense itself, even when assisted by exquisite instruments; such experiments, I mean, as are skilfully and artificially devised for the express purpose of determining the point in question. To the immediate and proper perception of the sense therefore I do not give much weight, but I contrive that the office of the sense shall be only to judge of the experiment, and that the experiment itself shall judge of the thing. And thus I conceive that I perform the office of a true priest of the sense (from which all knowledge in nature must be sought, unless men mean to go mad) and a not unskilful interpreter of its oracles; and that while others only profess to uphold and cultivate the sense, I do so in fact. Such then are the provisions I make for finding the genuine light of nature and kindling and bringing it to bear. And they would be sufficient of themselves, if the human intellect were even and like a fair sheet of paper with no writing on it. But since the minds of men are strangely possessed and beset, so that there is no true and even surface left to reflect the genuine rays of things, it is necessary to seek a remedy for this also.

Now the idols, or phantoms, by which the mind is occupied are either adventitious or innate. The adventitious come into the mind from without; namely, either from the doctrines and sects of philosophers or from perverse rules of demonstration. But the innate are inherent in the very nature of the intellect, which is far more prone to error than the sense is. For let men please themselves as they will in admiring and almost adoring the human mind, this is certain, that as an uneven mirror distorts the rays of objects according to its own figure and section, so the mind, when it receives impressions of objects through the sense, cannot be trusted to report them truly, but in forming its notions mixes up its own nature with the nature of things.

And as the first two kinds of idols are hard to eradicate, so idols of this last kind cannot be eradicated at all. All that can be done is to point them out, so that this insidious action of the mind may be marked and

reproved (else as fast as old errors are destroyed new ones will spring up out of the ill complexion of the mind itself, and so we shall have but a change of errors, and not a clearance), and to lay it down once for all as a fixed and established maxim, that the intellect is not qualified to judge except by means of induction, and induction in its legitimate form. This doctrine then of the expurgation of the intellect to qualify it for dealing with truth is comprised in three refutations: the refutation of the Philosophies; the refutation of the Demonstrations; and the refutation of the Natural Human Reason. The explanation of which things, and of the true relation between the nature of things and the nature of the mind, is as the strewing and decoration of the bridal chamber of the Mind and the Universe, the Divine Goodness assisting, out of which marriage let us hope (and be this the prayer of the bridal song) there may spring helps to man, and a line and race of inventions that may in some degree subdue and overcome the necessities and miseries of humanity. This is the second part of the work.

But I design not only to indicate and mark out the ways, but also to enter them. And therefore the third part of the work embraces the Phenomena of the Universe; that is to say, experience of every kind, and such a natural history as may serve for a foundation to build philosophy upon. For a good method of demonstration or form of interpreting nature may keep the mind from going astray or stumbling, but it is not any excellence of method that can supply it with the material of knowledge. Those however who aspire not to guess and divine, but to discover and know, who propose not to devise mimic and fabulous worlds of their own, but to examine and dissect the nature of this very world itself must go to facts themselves for everything. Nor can the place of this labour and search and worldwide perambulation be supplied by any genius or meditation or argumentation; no, not if all men's wits could meet in one. This therefore we must have, or the business must be for ever abandoned. But up to this day such has been the condition of men in this matter that it is no wonder if nature will not give herself into their hands.

Lastly, knowing how much the sight of man's mind is distracted by experience and history, and how hard it is at the first (especially for minds either tender or preoccupied) to become familiar with nature, I not unfrequently subjoin observations of my own, being as the first offers, inclinations, and as it were glances of history towards philosophy, both by way of an assurance to men that they will not be kept for ever tossing on the waves of experience, and also that when the time comes for the intellect to being its work, it may find everything the more ready. By such a natural history then as I have described, I conceive that a safe and convenient approach may be made to nature, and matter supplied of good quality and well prepared for the understanding to work upon.

The
FIRST PART OF THE INSTAURATION,
Which Comprises The
DIVISIONS OF THE SCIENCES
Is Wanting.
But some account of them will be found in the Second Book of the "Proficience and Advancement of Learning, Divine and Human."

Next comes
The
SECOND PART OF THE INSTAURATION,
Which Exhibits
THE ART ITSELF OF INTERPRETING NATURE,
And Of The Truer Exercise Of The Intellect;
Not however in the form of a regular Treatise, but only a Summary digested into Aphorisms.

The
Second Part of the Work,
which is called
THE NEW ORGANON;
or
TRUE DIRECTIONS
concerning
THE INTERPRETATION OF NATURE

Preface

Those who have taken upon them to lay down the law of nature as a thing already searched out and understood, whether they have spoken in simple assurance or professional affectation, have therein done philosophy and the sciences great injury. For as they have been successful in inducing belief, so they have been effective in quenching and stopping inquiry; and have done more harm by spoiling and putting an end to other men's efforts then good by their own. Those on the other hand who have taken a contrary course, and asserted that absolutely nothing can be known—whether it were from hatred of the ancient sophists, or from uncertainty and fluctuation of mind, or even from a kind of fulness of learning, that they fell upon this opinion—have certainly advanced reasons for it that are not to be despised; but yet they have neither started from true principles nor rested in the just conclusion, zeal and affectation having carried them much too far. The more ancient of the Greeks (whose writings are lost) took up with better judgement a position between these two extremes—between the presumption of pronouncing on everything, and the despair of comprehending anything; and though frequently and bitterly complaining of the difficulty of inquiry and the obscurity of things, and like impatient horses champing the bit, they did not the less follow up their object and engage with Nature; thinking (it seems) that this very question, viz. whether or no anything can be known, was to be settled not by arguing, but by trying. And yet they too, trusting entirely to the force of their understanding, applied no rule, but made everything turn upon hard thinking and perpetual working and exercise of the mind.

Now my method, though hard to practise, is easy to explain; and it is this. I propose to establish progressive stages of certainty. The evidence of the sense, helped and guarded by a certain process of correction, I retain. But the mental operation which follows the act of sense I for the most part reject; and instead of it I open and lay out a new and certain path for the mind to proceed in, starting directly from the simple sensuous perception. The necessity of this was felt no doubt by those who attributed so much importance to Logic; showing thereby that they were in search of helps for the understanding, and had no confidence in the native and spontaneous process of the mind. But this remedy comes too late to do any good, when the mind is already, through the daily intercourse and conversation of life, occupied with unsound doctrines and beset on all sides by vain imaginations. And therefore that art of Logic, coming (as I said) too late to the rescue, and no way able to set matters right again, has had the effect of fixing errors rather then disclosing truth. There remains but one course for the recovery of a sound and healthy condition; namely, that the entire work of the understanding be commenced afresh, and the mind itself be from the very outset not left to take its own course, but guided at every step; and the business be done as if by machinery.

APHORISMS

concerning

THE INTERPRETATION OF NATURE

and

THE KINGDOM OF MAN

Aphorism

I

Man, being the servant and interpreter of Nature, can do and understand so much and so much only as he has observed in fact or in thought of the course of nature; beyond this he neither knows anything nor can do anything.

II

Neither the naked hand nor the understanding left to itself can effect much. It is by instruments and helps that the work is done, which are as much wanted for the understanding as for the hand. And as the instruments of the hand either give motion or guide it, so the instruments of the mind supply either suggestions for the understanding or cautions.

III

Human knowledge and human power meet in one, for where the cause is not known the effect cannot be produced. Nature to be commanded must be obeyed, and that which in contemplation is as the cause is in operation as the rule.

IV

Towards the effecting of works, all that man can do is to put together or put asunder natural bodies. The rest is done by nature working within.

VII

The productions of the mind and hand seem very numerous in books and manufactures. But all this variety lies in an exquisite subtlety and derivations from a few things already known; not in the number of axioms.

VIII

Moreover the works already known are due to chance and experiment rather than to sciences, for the sciences we now possess are merely systems for the nice ordering and setting forth of things already invented; not methods of invention or directions for new works.

IX

The cause and root of nearly all evils in the sciences in this, that while we falsely admire and extol the powers of the human mind we neglect to seek for its true helps.

X

The subtlety of nature is greater many times over than the subtlety of the senses and understanding, so that all those specious mediations, speculations, and glosses in which men indulge are quite from the purpose, only there is no one by to observe it.

XI

As the sciences which we now have do not help us in finding out new works, so neither does the logic which we now have help us in finding out new sciences.

XII

The logic now in use serves rather to fix and give stability to the errors which have their foundation in commonly received notions than to help the search after truth. So it does more harm than good.

XIII

The syllogism is not applied to the first principles of sciences, and is applied in vain to intermediate axioms, being no match for the subtlety of nature. It commands assent therefore to the proposition, but does not take hold of the thing.

XIV

The syllogism consists of propositions, propositions consist of words, words are symbols of notions. Therefore if the notions themselves (which is the root of the matter) are confused and overhastily abstracted from the facts, there can be no firmness in the superstructure. Our only hope therefore lies in a true induction.

XIX

There are and can be only two ways of searching into and discovering truth. The one flies from the senses and particulars to the most general axioms, and from these principles, the truth of which it takes for settled and immovable, proceeds to judgement and to the discovery of middle axioms. And this way is now in fashion. The other derives axioms from the senses and particulars, rising by a gradual and unbroken ascent, so that it arrives at the most general axioms last of all. This is the true way, but as yet untried.

XX

The understanding left to itself takes the same course (namely, the former) which it takes in accordance with logical order. For the mind longs to spring up to positions of higher generality, that it may find rest there; and so after a little while wearies of experiment. But this evil is increased by logic because of the order and solemnity of its disputations.

XXI

The understanding left to itself, in a sober, patient, and grave mind, especially if it be not hindered by received doctrines, tries a little that other way, which is the right one, but with little progress, since the understanding, unless directed and assisted, is a thing unequal and quite unfit to contend with the obscurity of things.

XXII

Both ways set out from the senses and particulars, and rest in the highest generalities, but the difference between them is infinite. For the one just glances at experiment and particulars in passing, the other dwells duly and orderly among them. The one, again, begins at once by establishing certain abstract and useless generalities, the other rises by gradual steps to that which is prior and better known in the order of nature.

XXXVIII

The idols and false notions which are now in possession of the human understanding, and have taken deep root therein, not only so beset men's minds that

truth can hardly find entrance, but even after entrance obtained, they will again in the very instauration of the sciences meet and trouble us, unless men being forewarned of the danger fortify themselves as far as may be against their assaults.

XXXIX

There are four classes of Idols which beset men's minds. To these for distinction's sake I have assigned names, calling the first class *Idols of the Tribe;* the second, *Idols of the Cave;* the third, *Idols of the Market-place;* the fourth, *Idols of the Theatre*.

XL

The formation of ideas and axioms by true induction is no doubt the proper remedy to the applied for the keeping off and clearing away of idols. To point them our, however, is of great use, for the doctrine of Idols is to the Interpretation of Nature what the doctrine of the refutation of Sophisms is to common Logic.

XLI

The *Idols of the Tribe* have their foundation in human nature itself and in the tribe or race of men. For it is a false assertion that the sense of man is the measure of things. On the contrary, all perceptions as well of the sense as of the mind are according to the measure of the individual and not according to the measure of the universe. And the human understanding is like a false mirror, which, receiving rays irregularly, distorts and discolours the nature of things by mingling its own nature with it.

XLII

The *Idols of the Cave* are the idols of the individual man. For every one (besides the errors common to human nature in general) has a cave or den of his own, which refracts and discolours the light of nature, owing either to his own proper and peculiar nature, or to his education and conversation with others, or to the reading of books, and the authority of those whom he esteems and admires, or to the differences of impressions, accordingly as they take place in a mind preoccupied and predisposed or in a mind indifferent and settled, or the like. So that the spirit of man (according as it is meted out to different individuals) is in fact a thing variable and full of perturbation, and governed as it were by chance. Whence it was well observed by Heraclitus that men look for sciences in their own lesser worlds and not in the greater or common world.

XLIII

There are also Idols formed by the intercourse and association of men with each other, which I call *Idols of the Marketplace* on account of the commerce and consort of men there. For it is by discourse that men associate, and words are imposed according to the apprehension of the vulgar. And therefore the ill and unfit choice of words wonderfully obstructs the understanding. Nor do the definitions or explanations, wherewith in some things learned men are wont to guard and defend themselves, by any means set the matter right. But words plainly force and overrule the understanding, and throw all into confusion, and lead men away into numberless empty controversies and idle fancies.

XLIV

Lastly, there are Idols which have immigrated into men's minds from the various dogmas of philosophies and also from wrong laws of demonstration. These I call *Idols of the Theatre*, because in my judgement all the received systems are but so many stage-plays, representing worlds of their own creation after an unreal and scenic fashion. Nor is it only of the systems now in vogue or only of the ancient sects and philosophies that I speak, for many more plays of the same kind may yet be composed and in like artificial manner set forth, seeing that errors the most widely different have nevertheless causes for the most part alike. Neither again do I mean this only of entire systems, but also of many principles and axioms in science, which by tradition, credulity, and negligence have come to be received.

But of these several kinds of Idols I must speak more largely and exactly, that the understanding may be duly cautioned.

XLV

The human understanding is of its own nature prone to suppose the existence of more order and regularity in the world than it finds. And though there be many things in nature which are singular and unmatched, yet it devises for them parallels and conjugates and relatives which do not exist. Hence the fiction that all celestial bodies move in perfect circles, spirals and dragons being (except in name) utterly rejected.

XLVI

The human understanding when it has once adopted an opinion (either as being the received opinion or as being agreeable to itself) draws all things else to support and agree with it. And though there be a greater number and weight of instances to be found on the other side, yet these it either neglects and despises, or else by some distinction sets aside and rejects, in order that by this great and pernicious predetermination the authority of its former conclusions may remain inviolate. And therefore it was a good answer that was made by one who when they showed him hanging in a temple a picture of those who had paid their vows as having escaped shipwreck, and would have him say whether he did not now acknowledge the power of the gods. "Aye," asked he again, "but where are they painted that were drowned after their vows?" And such is the way of all superstition, whether in astrology, dreams, omens, divine judgements, or the like, wherein men, having a delight in such vanities, mark the events where they are fulfilled, but where they fail, though this happen much oftener, neglect and pass them by. But with far more subtlety does this mischief insinuate itself into philosophy and the sciences, in which the first conclusion colours and brings into conformity with itself all that come after, though far sounder and better. Besides, independently of that delight and vanity which I have described, it is the peculiar and perpetual error of the human intellect to be more moved and excited by affirmative than by negatives; whereas it ought properly to hold itself indifferently disposed towards both alike. Indeed in the establishment of any true axiom, the negative instance is the more forcible of the two.

XLVII

The human understanding is moved by those things most which strike and enter the mind simultaneously and suddenly, and so fill the imagination; and then it feigns and supposes all other things to be somehow, though it cannot see how, similar to those few things by which it is surrounded. But for that going to and fro to remote and heterogeneous instances, by which axioms are tried as in the fire, the intellect is altogether slow and unfit, unless it be forced thereto by severe laws and overruling authority.

XLVIII

The human understanding is unquiet; it cannot stop or rest, and still presses onward, but in vain. Therefore it is that we cannot conceive of any 'end or limit to the world, but always as of necessity it occurs to us that there is something beyond. . . .

But this inability interferes more mischievously in the discovery of causes, for although the most general principles in nature ought to be held merely positive, as they are discovered, and cannot with truth be referred to a cause, nevertheless the human understanding being unable to rest still seeks something prior in the order of nature. And then it is that in struggling towards that which is further off it falls back upon that which is more nigh at hand; namely, on final causes, which have relation clearly to the nature of man rather than to the nature of the universe, and from this source have strangely defiled philosophy.

L

But by far the greatest hindrance and aberration of the human understanding proceeds from the dulness, incompetency, and deceptions of the senses; in that things which strike the sense outweigh things which do not immediately strike it, though they be more important. Hence it is that speculation commonly ceases where sight ceases; insomuch that of things invisible there is little or no observation. Hence all the working of the spirits inclosed in tangible bodies lies hid and unobserved of men. So also all the more subtle changes of form in the parts of coarser substances (which they commonly call alteration, though it is in truth local motion through exceedingly small spaces) is in like manner unobserved. And yet unless theses two things just mentioned be searched out and brought to light, nothing great can be achieved in nature, as far as the production of works is concerned. So again the essential nature of our common air and of all bodies less dense then air (which are very many) is almost unknown. For the sense by itself is a thing infirm and erring; neither can instruments for enlarging or sharpening the senses do much; but all the truer kind of interpretation of nature is effected by instances and experiments fit and apposite; wherein the sense decides touching the experiment only, and the experiment touching the point in nature and the thing itself.

LII

Such then are the idols which I call *Idols of the Tribe,* and which take their rise either from the homogeneity of the substance of the human spirit, or from its preoccupation, or from its narrowness, or from its restless motion, or from an infusion of the affections, or from the incompetency of the senses, or from the mode of impression.

LIII

The *Idols of the Cave* take their rise in the peculiar constitution, mental or bodily, of each individual, and also in education, habit, and accident. Of this kind there is a great number and variety, but I will instance those the pointing out of which contains the most important caution, and which have most effect disturbing the clearness of the understanding.

LIV

Men become attached to certain particular sciences and speculations, either because they fancy themselves the authors and inventors thereof, or because they have bestowed the greatest pains upon them and become most habituated to them. But men of this kind, if they betake themselves to philosophy and contemplations of a general character, distort and colour them in obedience to their former fancies, a thing especially to be noticed in Aristotle, who made his natural philosophy a mere bond-servant to his logic, thereby rendering it contentious and well nigh useless. The race of chemists again out of a few experiments of the furnace have built up a fantastic philosophy, framed with reference to a few things, and Gilbert also, after he had employed himself most laboriously in the study and observation of the loadstone, proceeded at once to construct an entire system in accordance with his favourite subject.

LV

There is one principal and as it were radical distinction between different minds in respect of philosophy and the science, which is this: that some minds are stronger and apter to mark the differences of things, others to mark their resemblances. The steady and acute mind can fix its contemplations and dwell and fasten on the subtlest distinctions, the lofty and discursive mind recognises and puts together the finest and most general resemblances. Both kinds however easily err in excess, by catching the one at gradations the other at shadows.

LVIII

Let such then be our provision and contemplative prudence for keeping off and dislodging the *Idols of the Cave*, which grow for the most part either out of the predominance of a favourite subject, or out of an excessive tendency to compare or to distinguish, or out of partiality for particular ages, or out of the largeness or minuteness of the objects contemplated. And generally let every student of nature take this as a rule, that whatever his mind seizes and dwells upon with peculiar satisfaction is to be held in suspicion, and that so much the more care is to be taken in dealing with such questions to keep the understanding even and clear.

LIX

But the *Idols of the Market-place* are the most troublesome of all, idols which have crept into the understanding through the alliances of words and names. For men believe that their reason governs words, but it is also true that words react on the understanding, and this it is that has rendered philosophy and the sciences sophistical and inactive. Now words, being commonly framed and applied according to the capacity of the vulgar, follow those lines of division which are most obvious to the vulgar understanding. And whenever an understanding of greater acuteness or a more diligent observation would alter those lines to suit the true divisions of nature, words stand in the way and resist the change. Whence it comes to pass that the high and formal discussions of learned men end oftentimes in disputes about words and names, with which (according to the use and wisdom of the mathematicians) it would be more prudent to begin, and so by means of definitions reduce them to order. Yet even definitions cannot cure this evil in dealing with natural and material things; since and definitions themselves consist of words, and those words beget others, so that it is necessary to recur to individual instances, and those in due series and order, as I shall say presently when I come to the method and scheme for the formation of notions and axioms.

LX

The idols imposed by words on the understanding are of two kinds. They are either names of things which do not exist (for as there are things left unnamed through lack of observation, so likewise are there names which result from fantastic suppositions and to which nothing in reality corresponds), or they are names of things which exist, but yet confused and ill-defined and hastily and irregularly derived from realities. Of the former kind are Fortune, the Prime Mover, Planetary Orbits, Element of Fire, and like fictions which owe their origin to false and idle theories. And this class of idols is more easily expelled, because to get rid of them it is only necessary that all theories should be steadily rejected and dismissed as obsolete.

But the other class, which springs out of a faulty and unskilful abstraction, is intricate and deeply rooted. Let us take for example such a word as *humid,* and see how far the several things which the word is used to signify agree with each other; and we shall find the word *humid* to be nothing else than a mark loosely and confusedly applied to denote a variety of actions which will not bear to be reduced to any constant meaning. For it both signifies that which easily spreads itself round any other body; and that which in itself is indeterminate and cannot solidise; and that which readily yields in every direction; and that which easily divides and scatters itself; and that which easily unites and collects itself; and that which readily flows and is put in motion; and that which readily clings to another body and wets it; and that which is easily reduced to a liquid, or being solid easily melts. Accordingly when you come to apply the word, if you take it in one sense, flame is humid; if in another, air is not humid; if in another, fine dust is humid; if in another, glass is humid. So that it is easy to see that the notion is taken by abstraction only from water and common and ordinary liquids without any due verification.

LXI

But the *Idols of the Theatre* are not innate, nor do they steal into the understanding secretly, but are plainly impressed and received into the mind from the play-books of philosophical systems and the perverted rules of demonstration. To attempt refutations in this case would be merely inconsistent with what I have already said, for since we agree neither upon principles nor upon demonstrations there is no place for argument. And this is so far well, inasmuch as it leaves the honour of the ancients untouched. For they are no wise disparaged, the question between them and me being only as to the way. For as the saying is, the lame man who keeps the right road outstrips the runner who takes a wrong one. Nay, it is obvious that when a man runs the wrong way, the more active and swift he is the further he will go astray.

But the course I propose for the discovery of sciences is such as leaves but little to the acuteness and strength of wits, but places all wits and understandings nearly on a level. For as in the drawing of a straight line or a perfect circle much depends on the steadiness and practice of the hand, if it be done by aim of hand only, but if with the aid of rule or compass, little or nothing; so is it exactly with my plan. But though particular confutations would be of no avail, yet touching the sects and general divisions of such systems I must say something, something also touching the external signs which show that they are unsound, and finally something touching the causes of such great infelicity and of such lasting and general agreement in error, that so the access to truth may be made less difficult, and the human understanding may the more willingly submit to its purgation and dismiss its idols.

LXII

Idols of the Theatre, or of Systems, are many, and there can be and perhaps will be yet many more. For were it not that now for many ages men's minds have been busied with religion and theology, and were it not that civil governments, especially monarchies, have been averse to such novelties, even in matters speculative, so that men labour therein to the peril and harming of their fortunes, not only unrewarded but exposed also to contempt and envy, doubtless there would have arisen many other philosophical sects like to those which in great variety flourished once among the Greeks. For as on the phenomena of the heavens many hypotheses may be constructed, so likewise (and more also) many various dogmas may be set up and established on the phenomena of philosophy. And in the plays of this philosophical theatre you may observe the same thing which is found in the

theatre of the poets, that stories invented for the stage are more compact and elegant, and more as one would wish them to be than true stories out of history.

In general however there is taken for the material of philosophy either a great deal out of a few things, or a very little out of many things, so that on both sides philosophy is based on too narrow a foundation of experiment and natural history, and decides on the authority of too few cases. For the Rational School of philosophers snatches from experience a variety of common instances, neither duly ascertained nor diligently examined and weighed, and leaves all the rest to meditation and agitation of wit.

There is also another class of philosophers, who having bestowed much diligent and careful labour on a few experiments, have thence made bold to educe and construct systems, wresting all other facts in a strange fashion to conformity therewith.

And there is yet a third class, consisting of those who out of faith and veneration mix their philosophy with theology and traditions, among whom the vanity of some has gone so far aside as to seek the origin of sciences among spirits and genii. So that this parent stock of errors—this false philosophy—is of three kinds: the Sophistical, the Empirical, and the Superstitious.

LXVIII

So much concerning the several classes of Idols, and their equipage: all of which must be renounced and put away with a fixed and solemn determination, and the understanding thoroughly freed and cleansed; the entrance into the kingdom of man, founded on the sciences, being not much other than the entrance into the kingdom of heaven, whereinto none may enter except as a little child.

LXIX

But vicious demonstrations are as the strongholds and defences of Idols; and those we have in logic do little else than make the world the bond-slave of human thought, and human thought the bond-slave of words. Demonstrations truly are in effect the philosophies themselves and the sciences. For such as *they* are, well or ill established, such are the systems of philosophy and the contemplations which follow. Now in the whole of the process which leads from the sense and objects to axioms and conclusions, the demonstrations which we use are deceptive and incompetent. This process consists of four parts, and has as many faults. In the first place, the impressions of the sense itself are faulty, for the sense both fails us and deceives us. But its shortcomings are to be supplied, and its deceptions to be corrected. Secondly, notions are ill drawn from the impressions of the senses, and are indefinite and confused, whereas they should be definite and distinctly bounded. Thirdly, the induction is amiss which infers the principles of sciences by simple enumeration, and does not, as it ought, employ exclusions and solutions (or separations) of nature. Lastly, that method of discovery and proof according to which the most general principles are first established, and then intermediate axioms are tried and proved by them, is the parent of error and the curse of all science. Of these things, however, which now I do but touch upon, I will speak more largely, when, having performed these expiations and purgings of the mind, I come to set forth the true way for the interpretation of nature.

LXX

But the best demonstration by far is experience, if it go not beyond the actual experiment. For if it be transferred to other cases which are deemed similar, unless such transfer be made by a just and orderly process, it is a fallacious thing. But the manner of making experiments which men now use is blind and stupid. . . .

For it generally happens that men make their trials carelessly, and as it were in play, slightly varying experiments already known, and, if the thing does not answer, growing weary and abandoning the attempt. And even if they apply themselves to experiments more seriously and earnestly and laboriously, still they spend their labour in working out some one experiment, as Gilbert with the magnet, and the chemists with gold, a course of proceeding not less unskilful in the design than small in the attempt. For no one successfully investigates the nature of a thing in the thing itself; the inquiry must be enlarged, so as to become more general.

And even when they seek to educe some science or theory from their experiments, they nevertheless almost always turn aside with overhasty and unseasonable eagerness to practice, not only for the sake of

the uses and fruits of the practice, but from impatience to obtain in the shape of some new work an assurance for themselves that it is worth their while to go on, and also to show themselves off to the world, and so raise the credit of the business in which they are engaged.

XCV

Those who have handled sciences have been either men of experiment or men of dogmas. The men of experiment are like the ant; they only collect and use; the reasoners resemble spiders, who make cobwebs out of their own substance. But the bee takes a middle course; it gathers its material from the flowers of the garden and of the filed, but transforms and digests it by a power of its own. Not unlike this is the true business of philosophy, for it neither relies solely or chiefly on the powers of the mind, nor does it take the matter which it gathers from natural history and mechanical experiments and lay it up in the memory whole, as it finds it, but lays it up in the understanding altered and digested. Therefore from a closer and purer league between these two faculties, the experimental and the rational, (such as has never yet been made) much may be hoped.

XCVIII

Now for grounds of experience—since to experience we must come—we have as yet had either none or very weak ones; no search has been made to collect a store of particular observations sufficient either in number, or in kind, or in certainty, to inform the understanding, or in any way adequate. On the contrary, men of learning, but easy withal and idle, have taken for the construction or for the confirmation of their philosophy certain rumours and vague fames or airs of experience, and allowed to these the weight of lawful evidence. And just as if some kingdom or state were to direct its counsels and affairs, not by letters and reports from ambassadors and trustworthy messengers, but by the gossip of the streets; such exactly is the system of management introduced into philosophy with relation to experience. Nothing duly investigated, nothing verified, nothing counted, weighted, or measured is to be found in natural history, and what in observation is loose and vague is in information deceptive and treacherous. And if any one thinks that this is a strange thing to say, and something like an unjust complaint, seeing that Aristotle, himself so great a man and supported by the wealth of so great a king, has composed so accurate a history of animals, and that others with greater diligence, though less pretence, have made many additions, while others, again, have compiled copious histories and descriptions of metals, plants, and fossils, it seems that he does not rightly apprehend what it is that we are now about. For a natural history which is composed for its own sake is not like one that is collected to supply the understanding with information for the building up of philosophy. They differ in many ways but especially in this, that the former contains the variety of natural species only, and not experiments of the mechanical arts. For even as in the business of life a man's disposition and the secret workings of his mind and affections are better discovered when he is in trouble than at other times, so likewise the secrets of nature reveal themselves more readily under the vexations of art than when they go their own way. Good hopes may therefore be conceived of natural philosophy, when natural history, which is the basis and foundation of it, has been drawn up on a better plan, but not till then.

XCIX

Again, even in the great plenty of mechanical experiments there is yet a great scarcity of those which are of most use for the information of the understanding. For the mechanic, not troubling himself with the investigation of truth, confines his attention to those things which bear upon his particular work, and will not either raise his mind or stretch out his hand for anything else. But then only will there be good ground of hope for the further advance of knowledge, when there shall be received and gathered together into natural history a variety of experiments, which are of no use in themselves, but simply serve to discover causes and axioms, which I call "*Experimenta lucifera*," experiments of *light*, to distinguish them from those which I call "*fructifera*," experiments of *fruit*.

Now experiments of this kind have one admirable property and condition: they never miss or fail. For since they are applied, not for the purpose of

producing any particular effect, but only of discovering the natural cause of some effect, they answer the end equally well whichever way they turn out, for they settle the question.

CIII

But after this store of particulars has been set out duly and in order before our eyes, we are not to pass at once to the investigation and discovery of new particulars or works; or at any rate if we do so we must not stop there. For although I do not deny that when all the experiments of all the arts shall have been collected and digested, and brought within one man's knowledge and judgment, the mere transferring of the experiments of one art to others may lead, by means of that experience which I term *literate*, to the discovery of many new things of service to the life and state of man, yet it is no great matter that can be hoped from that, but from the new light of axioms, which having been educed from those particulars by a certain method and rule, shall in their turn point out the way again to new particulars, greater things may be looked for. For our road does not lie on a level, but ascends and descends, first ascending to axioms, then descending to works.

CIV

The understanding must not however be allowed to jump and fly from particulars to remote axioms and of almost the highest generality (such as the first principles, as they are called, of arts and things), and taking stand upon them as truths that cannot be shaken, proceed to prove and frame the middle axioms by reference to them, which has been the practice hitherto, the understanding being not only carried that way by a natural impulse but also by the use of syllogistic demonstration trained and inured to it. But then, and then only, may we hope well of the sciences, when in a just scale of ascent and by successive steps not interrupted or broken, we rise from particulars to lesser axioms, and then to middle axioms, one above the other, and last of all to the most general. For the lowest axioms differ but slightly from bare experience, while the highest and most general (which we now have) are notional and abstract and without solidity. But the middle are the true and solid and living axioms, on which depend the affairs and fortunes of men; and above them again, last of all, those which are indeed the most general, such I mean as are not abstract, but of which those intermediate axioms are really limitations.

The understanding must not therefore be supplied with wings, but rather hung with weights to keep it from leaping and flying. Now this has never yet been done; when it is done, we may entertain better hopes of the sciences.

CV

In establishing axioms another form of induction must be devised than has hitherto been employed, and it must be used for proving and discovering not first principles (as they are called) only, but also the lesser axioms, and the middle, and indeed all. For the induction which proceeds by simple enumeration is childish; its conclusions are precarious and exposed to peril from a contradictory instance; and it generally decides on too small a number of facts, and on those only which are at hand. But the induction which is to be available for the discovery and demonstration of sciences and arts must analyse nature by proper rejections and exclusions, and then, after a sufficient number of negatives, come to a conclusion on the affirmative instances, which has not yet been done or even attempted, save only by Plato, who does indeed employ this form of induction to a certain extent for the purpose of discussing definitions and ideas. But in order to furnish this induction or demonstration well and duly for its work, very many things are to be provided which no mortal has yet thought of; insomuch that greater labour will have to be spent in it than has hitherto been spent on the syllogism. And this induction must be used not only to discover axioms, but also in the formation of notions. And it is in this induction that our chief hope lies.

CVI

But in establishing axioms by this kind of induction, we must also examine and try whether the axiom so established be framed to the measure of those particulars only from which it is derived, or whether it be larger and wider. And if it be larger and wider, we must observe whether by indicating to us new particulars it confirm that wideness and largeness as by a collateral security, that we may not

either stick fast in things already known, or loosely grasp at shadows and abstract forms, not at things solid and realised in matter. And when this process shall have come into use, then at last shall we see the dawn of a solid hope.

CVII

And here also should be remembered what was said above concerning the extending of the range of natural philosophy to take in the particular sciences, and the referring or bringing back of the particular sciences to natural philosophy; that the branches of knowledge may not be severed and cut off from the stem. For without this the hope of progress will not be so good.

CVIII

So much then for the removing of despair and the raising of hope through the dismissal or rectification of the errors of past time. We must now see what else there is to ground hope upon. And this consideration occurs at once, that if many useful discoveries have been made by accident or upon occasion, when men were not seeking for them but were busy about other things, no one can doubt but that when they apply themselves to seek and make this their business, and that too by method and in order and not by desultory impulses, they will discover far more. For although it may happen once or twice that a man shall stumble on a thing by accident which, when taking great pains to search for it, he could not find, yet upon the whole it unquestionably falls out the other way. And therefore far better things, and more of them, and at shorter intervals, are to be expected from man's reason and industry and direction and fixed application than from accident and animal instinct and the like, in which inventions have hitherto had their origin.

CXXX

And now it is time for me to propound the art itself of interpreting nature, in which, although I conceive that I have given true and most useful precepts, yet I do not say either that it is absolutely necessary (as if nothing could be done without it) or that it is perfect. For I am of opinion that if men had ready at hand a just history of nature and experience, and laboured diligently thereon, and if they could bind themselves to two rules, the first, to lay aside received opinions and notions, and the second, to refrain the mind for a time from the highest generalisations, and those next to them, they would be able by the native and genuine force of the mind, without any other art, to fall into my form of interpretation. For interpretation is the true and natural work of the mind when freed from impediments. It is true however that by my precepts everything will be in more readiness, and must more sure.

Nor again do I mean to say that no improvement can be made upon these. On the contrary, I that regard the mind not only in its own faculties but in its connection with things, must needs hold that the art of discovery may advance as discoveries advance.

THE SECOND BOOK OF APHORISMS

concerning

THE INTERPRETATION OF NATURE

and

THE KINGDOM OF MAN

Aphorism

I

On a given body to generate and superinduce a new nature or new natures is the work and aim of Human Power. Of a given nature to discover the form, or true specific difference, or nature-engendering nature, or source of emanation (for these are the terms which come nearest to a description of the thing) is the work and aim of Human Knowledge. Subordinate to these primary works are two others that are secondary and of inferior mark: to the former, the transformation of concrete bodies, so far as this is possible; to the latter, the discovery, in every case of generation and motion, of the *latent process* carried on from the manifest efficient and the manifest material to the form which is engendered; and in like manner the discovery of the *latent configuration* of bodies at rest and not in motion.

II

In what an ill condition human knowledge is at the present time is apparent even from the commonly received maxims. It is a correct position that "true knowledge is knowledge by causes." And causes again are not improperly distributed into four kinds: the material, the formal, the efficient, and the final. But of these the final cause rather corrupts than advances

the sciences, except such as have to do with human action. The discovery of the formal is despaired of. The efficient and the material (as they are investigated and received, that is, as remote causes, without reference to the latent process leading to the form) are but slight and superficial, and contribute little, if anything, to true and active science. Nor have I forgotten that in a former passage I noted and corrected as an error of the human mind the opinion that Forms give existence. For though in nature nothing really exists beside individual bodies, performing pure individual acts according to a fixed law, yet in philosophy this very law and the investigation, discovery, and explanation of it is the foundation as well of knowledge as of operation. And it is this law, with its clauses, that I mean when I speak of *Forms*, a name which I the rather adopt because it has grown into use and become familiar.

III

If a man be acquainted with the cause of any nature (as whiteness or heat) in certain subjects only, his knowledge is imperfect, and if he be able to superinduce an effect on certain substances only (of those susceptible of such effect), his power is in like manner imperfect. Now if a man's knowledge be confined to the efficient and material causes (which are unstable causes, and merely vehicles, or causes which convey the form in certain cases) he may arrive at new discoveries in reference to substances in some degree similar to one another, and selected beforehand, but he does not touch the deeper boundaries of things. But whosoever is acquainted with Forms embraces the unity of nature in substances the most unlike, and is able therefore to detect and bring to light things never yet done, and such as neither the vicissitudes of nature, nor industry in experimenting, nor accident itself would ever have brought into act, and which would never have occurred to the thought of man. From the discovery of Forms therefore result truth in speculation and freedom in operation.

IV

Although the roads to human power and to human knowledge lie close together, and are nearly the same, nevertheless on account of the pernicious and inveterate habit of dwelling on abstractions, it is safer to begin and raise the sciences from those foundations which have relation to practice, and to let the active part itself be as the seal which prints and determines the contemplative counterpart. We must therefore consider, if a man wanted to generate and superinduce any nature upon a given body, what kind of rule or direction or guidance he would most wish for, and express the same in the simplest and least abstruse language. For instance, if a man wishes to superinduce upon silver the yellow colour of gold or an increase of weight (observing the laws of matter), or transparency on an opaque stone, or tenacity on glass, or vegetation on some substance that is not vegetable, we must consider, I say, what kind of rule or guidance he would most desire. And in the first place, he will undoubtedly wish to be directed to something which will not deceive him in the result, nor fail him in the trial. Secondly, he will wish for such a rule as shall not tie him down to certain means and particular modes of operation. For perhaps he may not have those means, nor be able conveniently to procure them. And if there be other means and other methods for producing the required nature (beside the one prescribed) these may perhaps be within his reach, and yet he shall be excluded by the narrowness of the rule, and get no good from them. Thirdly, he will desire something to be shown him, which is not as difficult as the thing proposed to be done, but comes nearer to practice.

For a true and perfect rule of operation then the direction will be *that it be certain, free, and disposing or leading to action.* And this is the same thing with the discovery of the true Form. For the Form of a nature is such that given the Form the nature infallibly follows. Therefore it is always present when the nature is present, and universally implies it, and is constantly inherent in it. Again, the Form is such that if it be taken away the nature infallibly vanishes. Therefore it is always absent when the nature is absent, and implies its absence, and inheres in nothing else. Lastly, the true Form is such that it deduces the given nature from some source of being which is inherent in more natures, and which is better known in the natural order of things then the Form itself. For a true and perfect axiom of knowledge then the direction and precept will be, *that another nature be discovered which is convertible with the given nature, and yet is a limitation of a more general nature, as of a true and real genus.* Now these two directions, the one active the other contem-

plative, are one and the same thing; and what in operation is most useful, that in knowledge is most true.

V

The rule or axiom for the transformation of bodies is of two kinds. The first regards a body as a troop or collection of simple natures. In gold, for example, the following properties meet. It is yellow in colour; heavy up to a certain weight; malleable or ductile to a certain degree of extension; it is not volatile, and loses none of its substance by the action of fire; it turns into a liquid with a certain degree of fluidity; it is separated and dissolved by particular means; and so on for the other natures which meet in gold. This kind of axiom, therefore, deduces the thing from the forms of simple natures. For he who knows the forms of yellow, weight, ductility, fixity, fluidity, solution, and so on, and the methods of superinducing them, and their gradations and modes, will make it his care to have them joined together in some body, whence may follow the transformation of that body into gold. And this kind of operation pertains to the first kind of action. For the principle of generating some one simple nature is the same as that of generating many, only that a man is more fettered and tied down in operation, if more are required, by reason of the difficulty of combining into one so many natures, which do not readily meet, except in the beaten and ordinary paths of nature. It must be said however that this mode of operation (which looks to simple natures though in a compound body) proceeds from what in nature is constant and eternal and universal, and opens broad roads to human power, such as (in the present state of things) human thought can scarcely comprehend or anticipate.

The second kind of axiom, which is concerned with the discovery of the *latent process,* proceeds not by simple natures, but by compound bodies, as they are found in nature in its ordinary course. As, for instance, when inquiry is made from what beginnings and by what method and by what process gold or any other metal or stone is generated, from its first menstrua and rudiments up to the perfect mineral; or in like manner by what process herbs are generated, from the first concretion of juices in the ground or from seeds up to the formed plant, with all the successive motions and diverse and continued efforts of nature. So also in the inquiry concerning the process of development in the generation of animals, from coition to birth; and in like manner of other bodies.

VI

But this Latent Process of which I speak is quite another thing than men, preoccupied as their minds now are, will easily conceive. For what I understand by it is not certain measures or signs or successive steps of process in bodies, which can be seen, but a process perfectly continuous, which for the most part escapes the sense.

For instance, in all generation and transformation of bodies, we must inquire what is lost and escapes; what remains, what is added; what is expanded, what contracted; what is united, what separated; what is continued, what cut off; what propels, what hinders; what predominates, what yields; and a variety of other particulars.

Again, not only in the generation or transformation of bodies are these points to be ascertained, but also in all other alterations and motions it should in like manner be inquired what goes before, what comes after; what is quicker, what more tardy; what produces, what governs motion; and like points—all which nevertheless in the present state of the sciences (the texture of which is as rude as possible and good for nothing) are unknown and unhandled. For seeing that every natural action depends on things infinitely small, or at least too small to strike the sense, no one can hope to govern or changes nature until he has duly comprehended and observed them.

VII

In like manner the investigation and discovery of the *latent configuration* in bodies is a new thing, no less than the discovery of the Latent Process and of the Form. For as yet we are but lingering in the outer courts of nature, nor are we preparing ourselves a way into her inner chambers. Yet no one can endow a given body with a new nature, or successfully and aptly transmute it into a new body, unless he has attained a competent knowledge of the body so to be altered or transformed. Otherwise he will run into methods which, if not useless, are at any rate difficult and perverse and unsuitable to the nature of the body on which he is operating. It is clear therefore that to this also a way must be opened and laid out.

And it is true that upon the anatomy of organized bodies (as of man and animals) some pains have been well bestowed and with good effect; and a subtle thing it seems to be, and a good scrutiny of nature. Yet this kind of anatomy is subject to sight and sense, and has place only in organized bodies. And besides it is a thing obvious and easy when compared with the true anatomy of the Latent Configuration in bodies which are thought to be of uniform structure, especially in things that have a specific character and their parts, as iron, stone, and again in parts of uniform structure in plants and animals, as the root, the leaf, the flower, flesh, blood, and bones. But even in this kind, human industry has not been altogether wanting; for this is the very thing aimed at in the separation of bodies of uniform structure by means of distillations and other modes of analysis: that the complex structure of the compound may be made apparent by bringing together its several homogeneous parts. And this is of use too, and conduces to the object we are seeking, although too often fallacious in its results, because many natures which are in fact newly brought out and superinduced by fire and heat and other modes of solution are taken to be the effect of separation merely, and to have subsisted in the compound before. And after all, this is but a small part of the work of discovering the true Configuration in the compound body; which Configuration is a thing far more subtle and exact, and such as the operation of fire rather confounds than brings out and makes distinct.

Therefore a separation and solution of bodies must be effected, not by fire indeed, but by reasoning and true induction, with experiments to aid, and by a comparison with other bodies, and a reduction to simple natures and their Forms, which meet and mix in the compound.

X

Having thus set up the mark of knowledge, we must go on to precepts, and that in the most direct and obvious order. Now my directions for the interpretation of nature embrace two generic divisions, the one how to educe and form axioms from experience, the other how to deduce and derive new experiments from axioms. The former again is divided into three ministrations, a ministration to the sense, a ministration to the memory, and a ministration to the mind or reason.

For first of all we must prepare a *Natural and Experimental History*, sufficient and good, and this is the foundation of all; for we are not to imagine or suppose, but to discover, what nature does or may be made to do.

But natural and experimental history is so various and diffuse that it confounds and distracts the understanding, unless it be ranged and presented to view in a suitable order. We must therefore form *Tables and Arrangements of Instances*, in such a method and order that the understanding may be able to deal with them.

And even when this is done, still the understanding, if left to itself and its own spontaneous movements, is incompetent and unfit to form axioms, unless it be directed and guarded. Therefore in the third place we must use *Induction*, true and legitimate induction, which is the very key of interpretation. But of this, which is the last, I must speak first, and then go back to the other ministrations.

XI

The investigation of Forms proceeds thus: a nature being given, we must first of all have a muster or presentation before the understanding of all known instances which agree in the same nature, though in substances the most unlike. And such collection must be made in the manner of a history, without premature speculation, or any great amount of subtlety. For example, let the investigation be into the Form of Heat.

XII

Secondly, we must make a presentation to the understanding of instances in which the given nature is wanting, because the Form, as stated above, ought no less to be absent when the given nature is absent, than present when it is present. But to note all these would be endless.

The negatives should therefore be subjoined to the affirmatives, and the absence of the given nature inquired of in those subjects only that are most akin to the others in which it is present and forthcoming. This I call the *Table of Deviation, or of Absence in Proximity*.

XIII

Thirdly, we must make a presentation to the understanding of instances in which the nature under inquiry is found in different degrees, more or less,

which must be done by making a comparison either of its increase and decrease in the same subject, or of its amount in different subjects, as compared one with another. For since the Form of a thing is the very thing itself, and the thing differs from the form no otherwise than as the apparent differs from the real, or the external from the internal, or the thing in reference to man from the thing in reference to the universe, it necessarily follows that no nature can be taken as the true form unless it always decrease when the nature in question decreases, and in like manner always increase when the nature in question increases. This Table therefore I call the *Table of Degrees* or the *Table of Comparison*.

XIV

How poor we are in history any one may see from the foregoing tables, where I not only insert sometimes mere traditions and reports (though never without a note of doubtful credit and authority) in place of history proved and instances certain, but am also frequently forced to use the words "Let trial be made," or "Let it be further inquired."

XV

The work and office of these three tables I call the Presentation of Instances to the Understanding. Which presentation having been made, Induction itself must be set at work; for the problem is, upon a review of the instances, all and each, to find such a nature as is always present or absent with the given nature, and always increases and decreases with it, and which is, as I have said, a particular case of a more general nature. Now if the mind attempt this affirmatively from the first, as when left to itself it is always wont to do, the result will be fancies and guesses and notions ill defined, and axioms that must be mended every day, unless like the schoolmen we have a mind to fight for what is false, though doubtless these will be better or worse according to the faculties and strength of the understanding which is at work. To God, truly, the Giver and Architect of Forms, and it may be to the angels and higher intelligences, it belongs to have an affirmative knowledge of forms immediately and from the first contemplation. But this assuredly is more than man can do, to whom it is granted only to proceed at first by negatives, and at last to end in affirmatives, after exclusion has been exhausted.

XVI

We must make therefore a complete solution and separation of nature, not indeed by fire, but by the mind, which is a kind of divine fire. The first work therefore of true induction (as far as regards the discovery of Forms) is the rejection or exclusion of the several natures which are not found in some instance where the given nature is present, or are found in some instance where the given nature is absent, or are found to increase in some instance when the given nature decreases, or to decrease when the given nature increases. Then indeed after the rejection and exclusion has been duly made, there will remain at the bottom, all light opinions vanishing into smoke, a Form affirmative, solid and true and well defined. This is quickly said, but the way to come at it is winding and intricate. I will endeavour however not to overlook any of the points which may help us towards it.

XVIII

I must now give an example of the Exclusion or Rejection of natures which by the Tables of Presentation are found not to belong to the Form of Heat, observing in the meantime that not only each table suffices for the rejection of any nature, but even any one of the particular instances contained in any of the tables. For it is manifest from what has been said that any one contradictory instance overthrows a conjecture as to the Form. But nevertheless, for clearness' sake and that the use of the tables may be more plainly shown, I sometimes double or multiply an exclusion.

XIX

In the process of Exclusion are laid the foundations of true Induction, which however is not completed till it arrives at an Affirmative. Nor is the Exclusive part itself at all complete, nor indeed can it possibly be so at first. For Exclusion is evidently the rejection of simple natures; and if we do not yet possess sound and true notions of simple natures, how can the process of Exclusion be made accurate? Now some of the above-mentioned notions (as that of the nature of the elements, of the nature of heavenly bodies, of rarity) are vague and ill-defined. I, therefore, well knowing and nowise forgetting how great a work I am about (viz., that of rendering the human understanding a match for things and nature), do not rest satisfied with the precepts I have laid down, but proceed further to devise and supply more powerful aids for the use of the understanding, which I shall now subjoin. And assuredly in the Interpretation of Nature the mind should by all means be so prepared and disposed that while it rests and finds footing in due stages and degrees of certainty, it may remember withal (especially at the beginning) that what it has before it depends in great measure upon what remains behind.

XX

And yet since truth will sooner come out from error than from confusion, I think it expedient that the understanding should have permission, after the three Tables of First Presentation (such as I have exhibited) have been made and weighed, to make an essay of the Interpretation of Nature in the affirmative way; on the strength both of the instances given in the tables, and of any others it may meet with elsewhere. Which kind of essay I call the *Indulgence of the Understanding,* or the *Commencement of Interpretation,* or the *First Vintage.*

XXI

The Tables of First Presentation and the Rejection or process of Exclusion being completed, and also the First Vintage being made thereupon, we are to proceed to the other helps of the understanding in the Interpretation of Nature and true and perfect Induction. In propounding which, I mean, when Tables are necessary, to proceed upon the Instances of Heat and Cold, but when a smaller number of examples will suffice, I shall proceed at large; so that the inquiry may be kept clear, and yet more room be left for the exposition of the system.

I propose to treat then, in the first place, of *Prerogative Instances;* secondly, of the *Supports of Induction;* thirdly, of the *Rectification of Induction;* fourthly, of *Varying the Investigation according to the nature of the Subject;* fifthly, of *Prerogative Natures* with respect to Investigation, or of what should be inquired first and what last; sixthly, of the *Limits of Investigation,* or a Synopsis of all Nature in the Universe; seventhly, of the *Application to Practice,* or of things in their relation to Man; eighthly, of *Preparations for Investigation*; and lastly, of the *Ascending and Descending Scale of Axioms*.

LII

So much then for the Dignities or Prerogatives of Instances. It must be remembered however that in this Organum of mine I am handling logic, not philosophy. But since my logic aims to teach and instruct the understanding, not that it may with the slender tendrils of the mind snatch at and lay hold of abstract notions (as the common logic does), but that it may in very truth dissect nature, and discover the virtues and actions of bodies, with their laws as determined in matter—so that this science flows not merely from the nature of the mind, but also from the nature of things—no wonder that it is everywhere sprinkled and illustrated with speculations and experiments in nature, as examples of the art I teach. . . .

But now I must proceed to the supports and rectifications of Induction, and then to concretes, and Latent Processes, and Latent Configurations, and the rest, as set forth in order in the twenty-first Aphorism, that at length (like an honest and faithful guardian) I may hand over to men their fortunes, now their understanding is emancipated and come as it were of age; whence there cannot but follow an improvement in man's estate and an enlargement of his power over nature. For man by the fall fell at the same time from his state of innocency and from his dominion over creation. Both of these losses however can even in this life be in some part repaired, the former by religion and faith, the latter by arts and sciences. For creation was not by the curse made altogether and for ever a rebel, but in virtue of that charter "In the sweat of thy fact shalt thou eat bread," it is now by various labours (not certainly by disputations or idle magical ceremonies, but by various labours) at length and in some measures subdued to the supplying of man with bread, that is, to the uses of human life.

STUDY QUESTIONS: BACON, NOVUM ORGANUM

1. How, according to Bacon, should knowledge be used?
2. What are the main obstacles to methodological progress in science, as Bacon sees it?
3. What are the four idols of the mind?
4. What is Bacon's new method of induction? How does it work? What is its aim?
5. What is Bacon's theory of forms? How is it related to Plato's theory, and how is it different?
6. Why, according to Bacon, have logicians until his time focused almost exclusively on the syllogism? Why have they not paid sufficient attention to the problem of induction?
7. Why does human understanding exaggerate the order in the world? What is the remedy to this problem? Why is this important?
8. What is the greatest hindrance to human understanding?
9. How are experimentalists like ants? How are Rationalists like spiders? How is a philosopher, in contrast to both, like a bee?

Philosophical Bridges: Bacon's Influence

Bacon's influence was immense, but it was largely specific to the period shortly after he wrote. He accomplished three goals. He gave a trenchant critique of Scholastic study, he called for others to join in the construction of the new sciences for the future of humanity, and he began the project of building those sciences by reclassifying knowledge and outlining some of the principles of the new scientific method. Bacon's call to action was answered. One might regard the philosophies of Descartes and Hobbes (who worked as

Bacon's secretary for a while) as attempts to complete the huge project that Bacon envis-aged and initiated: that of constructing a new unified vision of science and giving it a metaphysical foundation. Bacon saw the way forward for the philosophy of the time.

For these reasons, the work of Bacon was later acknowledged as a decisive turning point in philosophy. For example, Leibniz called him the regenerator of philosophy. One of the great works of the French Enlightenment was the *Encyclopedia*, edited by Denis Diderot and Jean d'Alembert, the complete first edition of which consisted of 35 volumes, which appeared between 1751 and 1780. This work was dedicated to Francis Bacon, who, as Diderot says, 'proposed the plan of a universal dictionary of sciences and arts at a time when, so to speak' neither existed.

Thomas Hobbes (1588–1679)

Biographical History

After graduating from Magdalen Hall, Oxford, in 1608, Thomas Hobbes found work with the Cavendish family, whom he served most of his life. During his long life, England underwent a civil war, which resulted in the country becoming a republic for 11 years, until the restoration of the monarch Charles II, who Hobbes had tutored in France during the future king's exile. Hobbes lived during the time of both scientific and political revolu-tion, and he participated in both as an outspoken thinker.

Hobbes' philosophical path started in May 1630, in Geneva, when he became enam-ored of Euclid's geometrical method of reasoning, which for him was the model of scien-tific knowledge. In 1637, he wrote the *Little Treatise*, in which he tries to explain sense experience in terms of a general theory of motion. Meanwhile, his interests turned toward politics.

In 1640, after Parliament was dissolved, Hobbes published *The Elements of Law*. When Parliament reassembled, the royalist Hobbes fled to Paris, where he started work on the *Elements of Philosophy*, a three-volume work consisting of *De Cive* (1642), concerning the politics of civil society; *De Homine* (1658), an explanation of human thought, sensa-tion, and desire in terms of bodily movement; and *De Corpore* (1655), outlining the prin-ciples of physical motion. During the civil war in England, he remained in France. After his return to London in 1651, Hobbes published his most famous work, the *Leviathan*, which argues that the preservation of peace requires an absolute sovereign.

Toward the end of his life, many people considered that the Plague and the Fire of London of 1666 were acts of God against an irreligious age, and Hobbes was accused of atheism. In his eighties, he wrote two autobiographies, one in Latin verse, as well as a verse translation of the *Iliad* and the *Odyssey*. In 1679, he died at the age of 91.

Philosophical Overview

Hobbes' main philosophical aim is to show how politics should be regarded as a science similar to mechanics. Politics is the most useful science, because it can prevent war; peace requires a proper understanding of politics. Hobbes' philosophy is divided into three parts: the first concerning the nature of matter; the second, human psychology; and the third, politics. The principles of politics are based on those of psychology, which in turn are derived from mechanics.

The Nature of Matter

According to Hobbes, the universe consists only of matter in motion, and causal influence can be transmitted from one body to another only through motion. For example, heat is transmitted by the movement of particles. All causation is mechanistic. Hobbes' materialistic claim that everything that exists is physical can be seen as a consequence of his mechanistic view of causation. Anything nonphysical would not be able to have causal relations with anything physical because it could not participate in any physical causal mechanism. In this way, Hobbes claims that materialism is the logical consequence of the new science, and he tries to refute Descartes' dualism.

This mechanistic theory of causation is a complete break with the Scholastic view according to which things move in nature because of their natural ends or purposes. Hobbes asserts that purposes are only applicable to animate beings that have a will. Even more radically, Hobbes argues that, even in the case of animate beings, such final causes or purposes are really mechanical causes.

For the period, Hobbes' materialism was a very bold and unpopular view. He tries to answer various objections to the theory. One objection is that materialism precludes the possibility of God. In the *Leviathan*, Hobbes tries to explain religion in terms that are compatible with his mechanistic philosophy. God is a material being. In support of this view, Hobbes claims that the idea of a nonmaterial substance is contradictory. A substance is a body and, as such, must occupy space and be subject to change. This definition of the word 'body,' however, permits the possibility of intangible and invisible material bodies, which Hobbes calls 'spirits.' Furthermore, Hobbes excludes the study of God from science and philosophy. Theology cannot yield scientific knowledge because the idea of God is the conception of something without external cause. Furthermore, there is no idea of the infinite and, because of this, reason can only inform us of what God cannot be. Another objection to materialism is that it cannot account for conscious psychological states.

Psychological Theory

Hobbes' psychological theory has two parts: sensation and motivation.

1. *To show that materialism can be made compatible with the fact that we have conscious sensations, Hobbes argues that his view of causation implies that sensation must be a physical motion. Since sensations are caused, they must be an instance of matter in motion in the brain. Hobbes' theory of perception is realist because he assumes that physical objects exist independently of our perception of them. He does not explain objects in terms of our perceptions or ideas, but rather he explains ideas in terms of the movement of material bodies. For example, memory occurs when our organs retain some of the movement occasioned by the external object. Concentration happens when other external objects cannot register on the sense organs because the movement in the nerves caused by the first object is so strong. Hobbes explains the capacity to imagine something new, such as a centaur, a horse's body with a man's head, as similar to two currents converging to produce a third flow that is a combination of the two.*

2. *Hobbes' theory of motivation forms the bridge from his physical mechanics to his political philosophy, and it consists of three steps. The first step takes us from physics to psychology. Hobbes' physics includes the idea of instantaneous movement, that is, motion through a point in space, that lasts an instant of time. He calls this 'endeavor.' Our movements toward and away from the objects of desire and aversion are caused by such endeavors in the body. The second step introduces the ideas of pleasure and pain, which are movements of the blood around the heart caused by*

endeavors toward or away from things known by experience to be pleasurable or painful. These motions generate desire and aversion. In the third step, Hobbes defines six basic passions in terms of different types of desire and aversion, and pleasure and pain. Appetite and aversion presuppose the absence of their objects, whereas, love and hate presuppose the presence of their object. On this basis, Hobbes tries to explain other features of human psychological life. For example, joy is the feeling of pleasure based on the expectation of an end, and on the awareness of the personal power to produce that end.

THE LEVIATHAN

The *Leviathan* has two parts: the first contains Hobbes' psychology, which is based on his views of matter, and the second explains his political theory. The first part, which was explained in the Philosophical Overview, culminates in Chapter 14, where Hobbes argues that every person acts for his or her personal good. This egoism implies that natural conflict or war is inevitable, given that goods are scarce and that no one person is able to dominate all other people. Thus, people are naturally in a state of war with one another. Our natural plight is 'solitary, poor, nasty, brutish and short,' and, to avoid it, people make a covenant and agree to be governed by a sovereign in a commonwealth.

According to Hobbes' political theory, we form a government through a covenant, which is a contract through which individuals transfer certain natural rights to a sovereign in exchange for a gain, which is peace and security. We transfer to a sovereign all our natural rights. Furthermore, reason dictates, and God commands, us to seek peace, and this requires us to keep to that covenant, so long as others do so. In short, the inevitability of war explains why we should enter into a covenant in the first place. The idea of the moral laws of nature explain why we should abide by that covenant, and the concept of natural rights explains the nature of the covenant.

The covenant results in a government that is absolute. Although the sovereign is obliged to obey the laws of nature and ought to do his or her best to protect his or her subjects, nevertheless the sovereign must be above the civil law. A sovereign cannot give up his or her right to self-governance because, otherwise, he or she would not be the sovereign. Therefore, the sovereign is not part of society's covenant. The covenant is an agreement between the people to transfer to a sovereign their natural rights to enforce morality. Hobbes' theory hinges on the idea that the only alternative to this absolute conception of governmental power is something even worse: the natural state of war.

THE INTRODUCTION

NATURE, the art whereby God hath made and governs the world, is by the *art* of man, as in many other things, so in this also imitated, that it can make an artificial animal. For seeing life is but a motion of limbs, the beginning whereof is in some principal part within; why may we not say, that all *automata* (engines that move themselves by springs and wheels as doth a watch) have an artificial life? For what is the *heart,* but *a spring;* and the *nerves,* but so many *strings;*

and the *joints*, but so many *wheels*, giving motion to the whole body, such as was intended by the artificer? *Art* goes yet further, imitating that rational and most excellent work of nature, *man*. For by art is created that great LEVIATHAN called a COMMONWEALTH, or STATE, in Latin CIVITAS, which is but an artificial man; though of greater stature and strength than the natural, for whose protection and defense it was intended; and in which the *sovereignty* is an artificial *soul*, as giving life and motion to the whole body; the *magistrates*, and other *officers* of judicature and execution, artificial *joints*; *reward* and *punishment*, by which fastened to the seat of the sovereignty every joint and member is moved to perform his duty, are the *nerves*, that do the same in the body natural; the *wealth* and riches of all the particular members, are the *strength*; *salus populi*, the *people's safety*, its *business*; *counsellors*, by whom all things needful for it to know are suggested unto it, are the *memory*; *equity*, and *laws*, an artificial *reason* and *will*; *concord*, *health*; *sedition*, *sickness*; *and civil war, death*. Lastly, the *pacts* and *covenants*, by which the parts of this body politic were at first made, set together, and united, resemble that *fiat*, or the *let us make man*, pronounced by God in the creation.

To describe the nature of this artificial man, I will consider

First, the *matter* thereof, and the *artificer*; both which is *man*.

Secondly, *how*, and by what *covenants* it is made; what are the *rights* and just *power* or *authority* of a *sovereign*; and what it is that *preserveth* or *dissolveth* it.

Thirdly, what is a *Christian commonwealth*.

Lastly, what is the *kingdom of darkness*.

PART I

OF MAN

Chapter I

Of sense

Concerning the thoughts of man, I will consider them first singly, and afterwards in train, or dependence upon one another. Singly, they are every one a *representation* or *appearance*, of some quality, or other accident of a body without us, which is commonly called an *object*. Which object worketh on the eyes, ears, and other parts of a man's body; and by diversity of working produceth diversity of appearances.

The original of them all, is that which we call SENSE, for there is no conception in a man's mind, which hath not at first, totally or by parts, been begotten upon the organs of sense. The rest are derived from that original.

To know the natural cause of sense, is not very necessary to the business now in hand; and I have elsewhere written of the same at large. Nevertheless, to fill each part of my present method, I will briefly deliver the same in this place.

The cause of sense, is the external body, or object, which presseth the organ proper to each sense, either immediately, as in the taste and touch; or mediately, as in seeing, hearing, and smelling; which pressure, by the mediation of the nerves, and other strings and membranes of the body, continued inwards to the brain and heart, causeth there a resistance, or counter-pressure, or endeavour of the heart to deliver itself, which endeavour, because *outward*, seemeth to be some matter without. And this *seeming*, or *fancy*, is that which men call *sense*; and consisteth, as to the eye, in a *light*, or *colour figured*; to the ear, in a *sound*; to the nostril, in an *odour*; to the tongue and palate, in a *savour*; and to the rest of the body, in *heat*, *cold*, *hardness*, *softness*, and such other qualities as we discern by *feeling*. All which qualities, called *sensible*, are in the object, that causeth them, but so many several motions of the matter, by which it presseth our organs diversely. Neither in us that are pressed, are they any thing else, but divers motions; for motion produceth nothing but motion. But their appearance to us is fancy, the same waking, that dreaming. And as pressing, rubbing, or striking the eye, makes us fancy a light; and pressing the ear, produceth a din; so do the bodies also we see, or hear, produce the same by their strong, though unobserved action. For if those colours and sounds were in the bodies, or objects that cause them, they could not be severed from them, as by glasses, and in echoes by reflection, we see they are; where we know the thing we see is in one place, the appearance in another. And though at some certain distance, the real and very object seem invested with the fancy it begets in us; yet still the object is one thing, the image or fancy is another. So that sense, in all cases, is nothing else but original fancy, caused, as I have said, by the pressure, that is, by the motion, of external things upon our eyes, ears, and other organs thereunto ordained.

Chapter II

Of imagination

When a body is once in motion, it moveth, unless something else hinder it, eternally; and whatsoever hindereth it cannot in an instant, but in time, and by degrees, quite extinguish it; and as we see in the water, though the wind cease, the waves give not over rolling for a long time after: so also it happeneth in that motion, which is made in the internal parts of a man, then, when he sees, dreams, &c. For after the object is removed, or the eye shut, we still retain an image of the thing seen, though more obscure than when we see it. And this is it, the Latins call *imagination*, from the image made in seeing; and apply the same, though improperly, to all the other senses. But the Greeks call it *fancy*; which signifies *appearance*, and is as proper to one sense, as to another. IMAGINATION therefore is nothing but *decaying sense*; and is found in men, and many other living creatures, as well sleeping, as waking.

The imagination that is raised in man, or any other creature indued with the faculty of imagining, by words, or other voluntary signs, is that we generally call *understanding*; and is common to man and beast. For a dog by custom will understand the call, or the rating of his master; and so will many other beasts. That understanding which is peculiar to man, is the understanding not only his will, but his conceptions and thoughts, by the sequel and contexture of the names of things into affirmations, negations, and other forms of speech; and of this kind of understanding I shall speak hereafter.

Chapter III

Of the consequence or train of imaginations

By *Consequence*, or TRAIN of thoughts, I understand that succession of one thought to another, which is called, to distinguish it from discourse in words, *mental discourse*.

When a man thinketh on any thing whatsoever, his next thought after, is not altogether so casual as it seems to be. Not every thought to every thought succeeds indifferently. But as we have no imagination, whereof we have not formerly had sense, in whole, or in parts; so we have no transition from one imagination to another, whereof we never had the like before in our senses. The reason whereof is this. All fancies are motions within us, relics of those made in the sense: and those motions that immediately succeeded one another in the sense, continue also together after sense.

This train of thoughts, or mental discourse, is of two sorts. The first is *unguided, without design*, and inconstant; wherein there is no passionate thought, to govern and direct those that follow, to itself, as the end and scope of some desire, or other passion: in which case the thoughts are said to wander, and seem impertinent one to another, as in a dream. Such are commonly the thoughts of men, that are not only without company, but also without care of anything; though even then their thoughts are as busy as at other times, but without harmony; as the sound which a lute out of tune would yield to any man; or in tune, to one that could not play. And yet in this wild ranging of the mind, a man may ofttimes perceive the way of it, and the dependence of one thought upon another. For in a discourse of our present civil war, what could seem more impertinent, than to ask, as one did, what was the value of a Roman penny? Yet the coherence to me was manifest enough. For the thought of the war, introduced the thought of the delivering up the king to his enemies; the thought of that, brought in the thought of the delivering up of Christ; and that again the thought of the thirty pence, which was the price of that treason; and thence easily followed that malicious question, and all this in a moment of time; for thought is quick.

The second is more constant; as being *regulated* by some desire, and design. For the impression made by such things as we desire, or fear, is strong, and permanent, or, if it cease for a time, of quick return: so strong it is sometimes, as to hinder and break our sleep. From desire, ariseth the thought of some means we have seen produce the like of that which we aim at; and from the thought of that, the thought of means to that mean; and so continually, till we come to some beginning within our own power.

Chapter V

Of reason and science

When a man *reasoneth*, he does nothing else but conceive a sum total, from *addition* of parcels; or conceive a remainder, from *subtraction* of one sum from another; which, if it be done by words, is conceiving of the consequence of the names of all the parts, to the name of the whole; or from the names of the whole and one part, to the name of the other part. And though in some things, as in numbers, besides adding and subtracting, men name other operations, as *multiplying* and *dividing*, yet they are the same; for multiplication, is but adding together of things equal; and division, but subtracting of one thing, as often as we can. These operations are not incident to numbers only, but to all manner of things that can be added together, and taken one out of another. For as arithmeticians teach to add and subtract in *numbers*; so the geometricians teach the same in *lines*, *figures*, solid and superficial, *angles*, *proportions*, *times*, degrees of *swiftness*, *force*, *power*, and the like; the logicians teach the same in *consequences of words*; adding together two *names* to make an *affirmation*, and two *affirmations* to make a *syllogism*; and *many syllogisms* to make a *demonstration*; and from the *sum*, or *conclusion* of a *syllogism*, they subtract one *proposition* to find the other. Writers of politics add together *pactions* to find men's *duties*; and lawyers, *laws* and *facts*, to find what is *right* and *wrong* in the actions of private men. In sum, in what matter soever there is place for *addition* and *subtraction*, there also is place for *reason*; and where these have no place, there *reason* has nothing at all to do.

Out of all which we may define, that is to say determine, what that is, which is meant by this word *reason*, when we reckon it amongst the faculties of the mind. For REASON, in this sense, is nothing but *reckoning*, that is adding and subtracting, of the consequences of general names agreed upon for the *marking* and *signifying* of our thoughts; I say *marking* them when we reckon by ourselves, and *signifying*, when we demonstrate or approve our reckonings to other men.

The use and end of reason, is not the finding of the sum and truth of one, or a few consequences, remote from the first definitions, and settled significations of names, but to begin at these, and proceed from one consequence to another. For there can be no certainty of the last conclusion, without a certainty of all those affirmations and negations, on which it was grounded and inferred. As when a master of a family, in taking an account, casteth up the sums of all the bills of expense into one sum, and not regarding how each bill is summed up, by those that give them in account; nor what it is he pays for; he advantages himself no more, than if he allowed the account in gross, trusting to every of the accountants' skill and honesty: so also in reasoning of all other things, he that takes up conclusions, on the trust of authors, and doth not fetch them from the first items in every reckoning, which are the significations of names settled by definitions, loses his labour; and does not know anything, but only believeth.

When a man reckons without the use of words, which may be done in particular things, as when upon the sight of any one thing, we conjecture what was likely to have preceded, or is likely to follow upon it; if that which he thought likely to follow, follows not, or that which he thought likely to have preceded it, hath not preceded it, this is called *error*; to which even the most prudent men are subject. But when we reason in words of general signification, and fall upon a general inference which is false, though it be commonly called *error*, it is indeed an *absurdity*, or senseless speech. For error is but a deception, in presuming that somewhat is passed, or to come; of which, though it were not past, or not to come, yet there was no impossibility discoverable. But when we make a general assertion, unless it be a true one, the possibility of it is inconceivable. And words whereby we conceive nothing but the sound, are those we call *absurd*, *insignificant*, and *nonsense*. And therefore if a man should talk to me of a *round quadrangle*; or, *accidents of bread in cheese*; or *immaterial substance*; or of a *free subject*; *a free will*; or any *free*, but free from being hindered by opposition, I should not say he were in an error, but that his words were without meaning, that is to say, absurd.

And whereas sense and memory are but knowledge of fact, which is a thing past and irrevocable. *Science* is the knowledge of consequences, and dependence of one fact upon another: by which, out of that we can presently do, we know how to do something else when we will, or the like another time; because when we see how anything comes about, upon what causes, and by what manner; when the like causes come into our power, we see how to make it produce the like effects.

To conclude, the light of human minds is perspicuous words, but by exact definitions first snuffed, and purged from ambiguity; *reason* is the *pace;* increase of *science,* the *way;* and the benefit of mankind, the *end.* And, on the contrary, metaphors, and senseless and ambiguous words, are like *ignes fatui;* and reasoning upon them is wandering amongst innumerable absurdities; and their end, contention and sedition, or contempt.

Chapter VI

Of the interior beginnings of voluntary motions; commonly called the passions; and the speeches by which they are expressed

There be in animals, two sorts of *motions* peculiar to them: one called *vital;* begun in generation, and continued without interruption through their whole life; such as are the *course* of the *blood,* the *pulse,* the *breathing,* the *concoction, nutrition, excretion,* &c., to which motions there needs no help of imagination: the other is *animal motion,* otherwise called *voluntary motion,* as to *go,* to *speak,* to *move* any of our limbs, in such manner as is first fancied in our minds. That sense is motion in the organs and interior parts of man's body, caused by the action of the things we see, hear, &c.; and that fancy is but the relics of the same motion, remaining after sense, has been already said in the first and second chapters. And because *going, speaking,* and the like voluntary motions, depend always upon a precedent thought of *whither, which way,* and *what;* it is evident, that the imagination is the first internal beginning of all voluntary motion. And although unstudied men do not conceive any motion at all to be there, where the thing moved is invisible; or the space it is moved in is, for the shortness of it, insensible; yet that doth not hinder, but that such motions are. For let a space be never so little, that which is moved over a greater space, whereof that little one is part, must first be moved over that. These small beginnings of motion, within the body of man, before they appear in walking, speaking, striking, and other visible actions, are commonly called ENDEAVOUR.

This endeavour, when it is toward something which causes it, is called APPETITE, or DESIRE; the lat-

ter, being the general name; and the other oftentimes restrained to signify the desire of food, namely *hunger* and *thirst.* And when the endeavour is fromward something, it is generally called AVERSION.

That which men desire, they are also said to LOVE: and to HATE those things for which they have aversion. So that desire and love are the same thing; save that by desire, we always signify the absence of the object; by love, most commonly the presence of the same. So also by aversion, we signify the absence; and by hate, the presence of the object.

These things which we neither desire, nor hate, we are said to *contemn;* CONTEMPT being nothing else but an immobility, or contumacy of the heart, in resisting the action of certain things; and proceeding from that the heart is already moved otherwise, by other more potent objects; or from want of experience of them.

But whatsoever is the object of any man's appetite or desire, that is it which he for his part calleth *good:* and the object of his hate and aversion, evil; and of his contempt, *vile* and *inconsiderable.* For these words of good, evil, and contemptible, are ever used with relation to the person that useth them: there being nothing simply and absolutely so; nor any common rule of good and evil, to be taken from the nature of the objects themselves; but from the person of the man, where there is no commonwealth; or, in a commonwealth, from the person that representeth it; or from an arbitrator or judge, whom men disagreeing shall by consent set up, and make his sentence the rule thereof.

Pleasure therefore, or *delight,* is the apparence, or sense of good; and *molestation,* or *displeasure,* the apparence, or sense of evil. And consequently all appetite, desire, and love, is accompanied with some delight more or less; and all hatred and aversion, with more or less displeasure and offence.

When in the mind of man, appetites, and aversions, hopes, and fears, concerning one and the same thing, arise alternately; and divers good and evil consequences of the doing, or omitting the thing propounded, come successively into our thoughts; so that sometimes we have an appetite to it; sometimes an aversion from it; sometimes hope to be able to do it; sometimes despair, or fear to attempt it; the whole sum of desires, aversions, hopes and fears continued till the thing be either done, or thought impossible, is that we call DELIBERATION.

Therefore of things past, there is no *deliberation*; because manifestly impossible to be changed: nor of things known to be impossible, or thought so; because men know, or think such deliberation vain. But of things impossible, which we think possible, we may deliberate; not knowing it is in vain. And it is called *deliberation*; because it is a putting an end to the *liberty* we had of doing, or omitting, according to our own appetite, or aversion.

This alternate succession of appetites, aversions, hopes and fears, is no less in other living creatures than in man: and therefore beasts also deliberate.

Every *deliberation* is then said to *end*, when that whereof they deliberate, is either done, or thought impossible; because till then we retain the liberty of doing, or omitting; according to our appetite, or aversion.

In *deliberation*, the last appetite, or aversion, immediately adhering to the action, or to the omission thereof, is that we call the WILL; the act, not the faculty, of *willing*. And beasts that have *deliberation*, must necessarily also have *will*. The definition of the *will*, given commonly by the Schools, that it is a *rational appetite*, is not good. For if it were, then could there be no voluntary act against reason. For a *voluntary act* is that, which proceedeth from the *will*, and no other. But if instead of a rational appetite, we shall say an appetite resulting: from a precedent deliberation, then the definition is the same that I have given here. *Will*, therefore, *is the last appetite in deliberating*. And though we say in common discourse, a man had a will once to do a thing, that nevertheless he forbore to do; yet that is properly but an inclination, which makes no action voluntary; because the action depends not of it, but of the last inclination, or appetite. For if the intervenient appetites, make any action voluntary; then by the same reason all intervenient aversions, should make the same action involuntary; and so one and the same action, should be both voluntary and involuntary.

Chapter IX

Of the several subjects of knowledge

There are of KNOWLEDGE two kinds; whereof one is *knowledge of fact*: the other *knowledge of the consequence of one affirmation to another*. The former is nothing else, but sense and memory, and is *absolute knowledge*; as when we see a fact doing, or remember it done: and this is the knowledge required in a witness. The latter is called *science*; and is *conditional*; as when we know, that, *if the figure shown be a circle, then any straight line through the center shall divide it into two equal parts*. And this is the knowledge required in a philosopher; that is to say, of him that pretends to reasoning.

The register of *knowledge of fact* is called *history*. Whereof there be two sorts: one called *natural history*; which is the history of such facts, or effects of nature, as have no dependence on man's *will*; such as are the histories of *metals, plants, animals, regions*, and the like. The other, is *civil history*; which is the history of the voluntary actions of men in commonwealths.

The registers of science, are such *books* as contain the *demonstrations* of consequences of one affirmation, to another; and are commonly called *books of philosophy*.

Chapter XIII

Of the natural condition of mankind as concerning their felicity, and misery

Nature hath made men so equal, in the faculties of the body, and mind; as that though there be found one man sometimes manifestly stronger in body, or of quicker mind than another; yet when all is reckoned together, the difference between man, and man, is not so considerable, as that one man can thereupon claim to himself any benefit, to which another may not pretend, as well as he. For as to the strength of body, the weakest has strength enough to kill the strongest, either by secret machination, or by confederacy with others, that are in the same danger with himself.

And as to the faculties of the mind, setting aside the arts grounded upon words, and especially that skill of proceeding upon general, and infallible rules, called science; which very few have, and but in few things; as being not a native faculty, born with us; nor attained, as prudence, while we look after somewhat else, I find yet a greater equality amongst men, than that of strength. For prudence, is but experience; which equal time, equally bestows on all men, in those things they equally apply themselves unto. That which may perhaps make such equality incredible, is but a vain conceit of one's own wisdom, which almost all men think they have in a greater degree, than the vulgar; that is, than all men but themselves, and a few others, whom by fame, or for concurring with themselves, they approve. For such is the nature of men, that howsoever they may acknowledge many others to be more witty, or more eloquent, or more learned; yet they will hardly believe there be many so wise as themselves; for they see their own wit at hand, and other men's at a distance. But this proveth rather that men are in that point equal, than unequal. For there is not ordinarily a greater sign of the equal distribution of any thing, than that every man is contented with his share.

From this equality of ability, ariseth equality of hope in the attaining of our ends. And therefore if any two men desire the same thing, which nevertheless they cannot both enjoy, they become enemies; and in the way to their end, which is principally their own conservation, and sometimes their delectation only, endeavour to destroy, or subdue one another. And from hence it comes to pass, that where an invader hath no more to fear, than another man's single power; if one plant, sow, build, or possess a convenient seat, others may probably be expected to come prepared with forces united, to dispossess, and deprive him, not only of the fruit of his labour, but also of his life, or liberty. And the invader again is in the like danger of another.

And from this diffidence of one another, there is no way for any man to secure himself, so reasonable, as anticipation; that is, by force, or wiles, to master the persons of all men he can, so long, till he see no other power great enough to endanger him; and this is no more than his own conservation requireth, and is generally allowed. Also because there be some, that taking pleasure in contemplating their own power in the acts of conquest, which they pursue farther than their security requires; if others, that otherwise would be glad to be at ease within modest bounds, should not by invasion increase their power, they would not be able, long time, by standing only on their defense, to subsist. And by consequence, such augmentation of dominion over men being necessary to a man's conservation, it ought to be allowed him.

Again, men have no pleasure, but on the contrary a great deal of grief, in keeping company, where there is no power able to over-awe them all. For every man looketh that his companion should value him, at the same rate he sets upon himself: and upon all signs of contempt, or undervaluing, naturally endeavours, as far as he dares, (which amongst them that have no common power to keep them in quiet, is far enough to make them destroy each other), to extort a greater value from his contemners, by damage; and from others, by the example.

So that in the nature of man, we find three principal causes of quarrel. First, competition; second, diffidence; thirdly, glory.

The first, maketh men invade for gain; the second, for safety; and the third, for reputation. The first use violence, to make themselves masters of other men's persons, wives, children, and cattle; the second, to defend them; the third, for trifles, as a word, a smile, a different opinion, and any other sign of undervalue, either direct in their persons, or by reflection in their kindred, their friends, their nation, their profession, or their name.

Hereby it is manifest, that during the time men live without a common power to keep them all in awe, they are in that condition which is called war; and such a war, as is of every man, against every man. For WAR, consisteth not in battle only, or the act of fighting; but in a tract of time, wherein the will to contend by battle is sufficiently known: and therefore the notion of *time*, is to be considered in the nature of war; as it is in the nature of weather. For as the nature of foul weather, lieth not in a shower or two of rain; but in an inclination thereto of many days together: so the nature of war, consisteth not in actual fighting; but in the known disposition thereto, during all the time there is no assurance to the contrary. All other time is PEACE.

Whatsoever therefore is consequent to a time of war, where every man is enemy to every man; the same is consequent to the time, wherein men live without other security, than what their own strength, and their own invention shall furnish them withal. In such condition, there is no place for industry; because the fruit thereof is uncertain: and consequently no culture of the earth; no navigation, nor use of the commodities that may be imported by sea; no commodious building; no instruments of moving, and removing, such things as require much force; no knowledge of the face of the earth; no account of time; no arts; no letters; no society; and which is worst of all, continual fear, and danger of violent death; and the life of man, solitary, poor, nasty, brutish, and short.

To this war of every man, against every man, this also is consequent; that nothing can be unjust. The notions of right and wrong, justice and injustice have there no place. Where there is no common power, there is no law: where no law, no injustice. Force, and fraud, are in war the two cardinal virtues. Justice, and injustice are none of the faculties neither of the body, nor mind. If they were, they might be in a man that were alone in the world, as well as his senses, and passions. They are qualities, that relate to men in society, not in solitude. It is consequent also to the same condition, that there be no propriety, no dominion, no *mine* and *thine* distinct; but only that to be every man's, that he can get; and for so long, as he can keep it. And thus much for the ill condition, which man by mere nature is actually placed in; though with a possibility to come out of it, consisting partly in the passions, partly in his reason.

The passions that incline men to peace, are fear of death; desire of such things as are necessary to commodious living; and a hope by their industry to obtain them. And reason suggesteth convenient articles of peace, upon which men may be drawn to agreement. These articles, are they, which otherwise are called the Laws of Nature: whereof I shall speak more particularly, in the two following chapters.

Chapter XIV

Of the first and second natural laws, and of contracts

The RIGHT OF NATURE, which writers commonly call *jus naturale*, is the liberty each man hath, to use his own power, as he will himself, for the preservation of his own nature; that is to say, of his own life; and consequently, of doing anything, which in his own judgment, and reason, he shall conceive to be the aptest means thereunto.

By LIBERTY, is understood, according to the proper signification of the word, the absence of external impediments: which impediments, may oft take away part of a man's power to do what he would; but cannot hinder him from using the power left him, according as his judgment, and reason shall dictate to him.

A LAW OF NATURE, *lex naturalis*, is a precept or general rule, found out by reason, by which a man is forbidden to do that, which is destructive of his life, or taketh away the means of preserving the same; and to omit that, by which he thinketh it may be best preserved. For though they that speak of this subject, use to confound *jus*, and *lex*, *right* and *law*: yet they ought to be distinguished; because RIGHT, consisteth in liberty to do, or to forbear; whereas LAW, determineth, and bindeth to one of them: so that law, and right, differ as much, as obligation, and liberty; which in one and the same matter are inconsistent.

And because the condition of man, as hath been declared in the precedent chapter, is a condition of war of every one against every one; in which case every one is governed by his own reason; and there is nothing he can make use of, that may not be a help unto him, in preserving his life against his enemies; it followeth, that in such a condition, every man has a right to every thing; even to one another's body. And therefore, as long as this natural right of every man to every thing endureth, there can be no security to any man, how strong or wise soever he be, of living out the time, which nature ordinarily alloweth men to live. And consequently it is a precept, or general rule of reason, *that every man, ought to endeavour peace, as far as he has hope of obtaining it; and when he cannot obtain it, that he may seek, and use, all helps, and advantages of war.* The first branch of which rule, containeth the first, and fundamental law of nature; which is, *to seek peace, and follow it.* The second, the sum of the right of nature; which is, *by all means we can, to defend ourselves.*

From this fundamental law of nature, by which men are commanded to endeavour peace, is derived this second law; *that a man be willing, when others are so too, as far forth, as for peace, and defence of himself he shall think it necessary, to lay down this right to all things; and be contented with so much liberty against other men, as he would allow other men against himself.* For as long as every man holdeth this right, of doing any thing he liketh; so long are all men in the condition of war. But if other men will not lay down their right, as well as he; then there is no reason for anyone, to divest himself of his: for that were to expose himself to prey, which no man is bound to, rather than to dispose himself to peace. This is that law of the Gospel; *whatsoever you require that others should do to you, that do ye to them.* And that law of all men, *quod tibi fieri non vis, alteri ne feceris.*

To *lay down* a man's *right* to any thing, is to *divest* himself of the *liberty*, of hindering another of the benefit of his own right to the same. For he that renounceth, or passeth away his right, giveth not to any other man a right which he had not before; because there is nothing to which every man had not right by nature: but only standeth out of his way, that he may enjoy his own original right, without hindrance from him; not without hindrance from another. So that the effect which redoundeth to one man, by another man's defect of right, is but so much diminution of impediments to the use of his own right original.

Whensoever a man transferreth his right, or renounceth it; it is either in consideration of some right reciprocally transferred to himself; or for some other good he hopeth for thereby. For it is a voluntary act: and of the voluntary acts of every man, the object is some *good to himself*. And therefore there be some rights, which no man can be understood by any words, or other signs, to have abandoned, or transferred. As first a man cannot lay down the right of resisting them, that assault him by force, to take away his life; because he cannot be understood to aim thereby, at any good to himself.

The mutual transferring of right, is that which men call CONTRACT.

There is difference between transferring of right to the thing; and transferring, or tradition, that is delivery of the thing itself. For the thing may be delivered together with the translation of the right; as in buying and selling with ready-money; or exchange of goods, or lands: and it may be delivered some time after.

Again, one of the contractors, may deliver the thing contracted for on his part, and leave the other to perform his part at some determinate time after, and in the mean time be trusted; and then the contract on his part, is called PACT, or COVENANT: or both parts may contract now, to perform hereafter: in which cases, he that is to perform in time to come, being trusted, his performance is called *keeping of promise*, or faith; and the failing of performance, if it be voluntary, *violation of faith*.

Chapter XV

Of other laws of nature

From that law of nature, by which we are obliged to transfer to another, such rights, as being retained, hinder the peace of mankind, there followeth a third; which is this, *that men perform their covenants made:* without which, covenants are in vain, and but empty words; and the right of all men to all things remaining, we are still in the condition of war.

And in this law of nature, consisteth the fountain and original of JUSTICE. For where no covenant hath preceded, there hath no right been transferred, and every man has right to every thing; and consequently, no action can be unjust. But when a covenant is made, then to break it is *unjust:* and the definition of INJUSTICE, is no other than *the not performance of covenant*. And whatsoever is not unjust, is *just*.

These dictates of reason, men used to call by the name of laws, but improperly: for they are but conclusions, or theorems concerning what conduceth to the conservation and defence of themselves; whereas law, properly, is the word of him, that by right hath command over others. But yet if we consider the same theorems, as delivered in the word of God, that by right commandeth all things; then are they properly called laws.

Chapter XVI

Of persons, authors, and things personated

A PERSON, is he, *whose words or actions are considered, either as his own, or as representing the words or actions of another man, or of any other thing, to whom they are attributed, whether truly or by fiction*.

When they are considered as his own, then is he called a *natural person:* and when they are considered as representing the words and actions of another, then is he a *feigned* or *artificial person*.

Of persons artificial, some have their words and actions *owned* by those whom they represent. And then the person is the *actor;* and he that owneth his words and actions, is the AUTHOR: in which case the actor acteth by authority. For that which in speaking of goods and possessions, is called an *owner*, and in Latin *dominus*, in Greek χύριος, speaking of actions, is called author. And as the right of possession, is called dominion; so the right of doing any action, is called AUTHORITY. So that by authority, is always understood a right of doing any act; and *done by authority*, done by commission, or licence from him whose right it is.

From hence it followeth, that when the actor maketh a covenant by authority, he bindeth thereby the author, no less than if he had made it himself; and no less subjecteth him to all the consequences of the same. And therefore all that hath been said formerly, (chap. xiv) of the nature of covenants between man and man in their natural capacity, is true also when they are made by their actors, representers, or procurators, that have authority from them, so far forth as is in their commission, but no further.

And therefore he that maketh a covenant with the actor, or representer, not knowing the authority he hath, doth it at his own peril. For no man is obliged by a covenant, whereof he is not author; nor consequently by a covenant made against, or beside the authority he gave.

When the actor doth anything against the law of nature by command of the author, if he be obliged by former covenant to obey him, not he, but the author breaketh the law of nature; for though the action be against the law of nature; yet it is not his: but contrarily, to refuse to do it, is against the law of nature, that forbiddeth breach of covenant.

And he that maketh a covenant with the author, by mediation of the actor, not knowing what authority he hath, but only takes his word; in case such authority be not made manifest unto him upon demand, is no longer obliged: for the covenant made with the author, is not valid, without his counterassurance. But if he that so covenanteth, knew beforehand he was to expect no other assurance, than the actor's word; then is the covenant valid; because the actor in this case maketh himself the author. And therefore, as when the authority is evident, the covenant obligeth the author, not the actor; so when the authority is feigned, it obligeth the actor only; there being no author but himself.

PART II

OF COMMONWEALTH

Chapter XVII

Of the causes, generation, and definition of a commonwealth

The final cause, end, or design of men, who naturally love liberty, and dominion over others, in the introduction of that restraint upon themselves, in which we see them live in commonwealths, is the foresight of their own preservation, and of a more contented life thereby; that is to say, of getting themselves out from that miserable condition of war, which is necessarily consequent, as hath been shown in chapter xiii, to the natural passions of men, when there is no visible power to keep them in awe, and tie them by fear of punishment to the performance of their covenants, and observation of those laws of nature set down in the fourteenth and fifteenth chapters.

For the laws of nature, as *justice, equity, modesty, mercy*, and, in sum, *doing to others, as we would be done to*, of themselves, without the terror of some power, to cause them to be observed, are contrary to our natural passions, that carry us to partiality, pride, revenge, and the like. And covenants, without the sword, are but words, and of no strength to secure a man at all. Therefore notwithstanding the laws of nature, which every one hath then kept, when he has the will to keep them, when he can do it safely, if there be no power erected, or not great enough for our security; every man will, and may lawfully rely on his own strength and art, for caution against all other men. And in all places, where men have lived by small families, to rob and spoil one another, has been a trade, and so far from being reputed against the law of nature, that the greater spoils they gained, the greater was their honour; and men observed no other laws therein, but the laws of honour; that is, to abstain from cruelty, leaving to men their lives, and instruments of husbandry. And as small families did then; so now do cities and kingdoms which are but greater families, for their own security, enlarge their dominions, upon all pretences of danger, and fear of invasion, or assistance that may be given to invaders, and endeavour as much as they can, to subdue, or weaken their neighbours, by open force, and secret arts, for want of other caution, justly; and are remembered for it in after ages with honour.

It is true, that certain living creatures, as bees, and ants, live sociably one with another, which are therefore by Aristotle numbered amongst political creatures; and yet have no other direction, than their particular judgments and appetites; nor speech, whereby one of them can signify to another, what he thinks expedient for the common benefit: and therefore some man may perhaps desire to know, why mankind cannot do the same. To which I answer, . . .

First, that men are continually in competition for honour and dignity, which these creatures are not; and consequently amongst men there ariseth on that ground, envy and hatred, and finally war; but amongst these not so.

Secondly, that amongst these creatures, the common good differeth not from the private; and being by nature inclined to their private, they procure thereby the common benefit. But man, whose joy consisteth in comparing himself with other men, can relish nothing but what is eminent.

Thirdly, that these creatures, having not, as man, the use of reason, do not see, nor think they see any fault, in the administration of their common business; whereas amongst men, there are very many, that think themselves wiser, and able to govern the public, better than the rest; and these strive to reform and innovate, one this way, another that way; and thereby bring it into distraction and civil war.

Fourthly, that these creatures, though they have some use of voice, in making known to one another their desires, and other affections; yet they want that art of words, by which some men can represent to others, that which is good, in the likeness of evil; and evil, in the likeness of good; and augment, or diminish the apparent greatness of good and evil; discontenting men, and troubling their peace at their pleasure.

Fifthly, irrational creatures cannot distinguish between *injury*, and *damage*; and therefore as long as they be at ease, they are not offended with their fellows: whereas man is then most troublesome, when he is most at ease; for then it is that he loves to show his wisdom, and control the actions of them that govern the commonwealth.

Lastly, the agreement of these creatures is natural; that of men, is by covenant only, which is artificial; and therefore it is no wonder if there be somewhat else required, besides covenant, to make their agreement constant and lasting; which is a common power, to keep them in awe, and to direct their actions to the common benefit.

The only way to erect such a common power, as may be able to defend them from the invasion of foreigners, and the injuries of one another, and thereby to secure them in such sort, as that by their own industry, and by the fruits of the earth, they may nourish themselves and live contentedly; is, to confer all their power and strength upon one man, or upon one assembly of men, that may reduce all their wills, by plurality of voices, unto one will: which is as much as to say, to appoint one man, or assembly of men, to bear their person; and every one to own, and acknowledge himself to be author of whatsoever he that so beareth their person, shall act, or cause to be acted, in those things which concern the common peace and safety; and therein to submit their wills, every one to his will, and their judgments, to his judgment. This is more than consent, or concord; it is a real unity of them all, in one and the same person, made by covenant of every man with every man, in such manner, as if every man should say to every man, *I authorise and give up my right of governing myself, to this man, or to this assembly of men, on this condition, that thou give up thy right to him, and authorise all his actions in like manner.* This done, the multitude so united in one person, is called a COMMONWEALTH, in Latin CIVITAS. This is the generation of that great LEVIATHAN, or rather, to speak more reverently, of that *mortal god,* to which we owe under the *immortal God,* our peace and defence. For by this authority, given him by every particular man in the commonwealth, he hath the use of so much power and strength conferred on him, that by terror thereof, he is enabled to perform the wills of them all, to peace at home, and mutual aid against their enemies abroad. And in him consisteth the essence of the commonwealth; which, to define it, is *one person, of whose acts a great multitude, by mutual covenants one with another, have made themselves every one the author, to the end he may use the strength and means of them all, as he shall think expedient, for their peace and common defence.*

And he that carrieth this person, is called SOVEREIGN, and said to have *sovereign power;* and every one besides, his SUBJECT.

The attaining to this sovereign power, is by two ways. One, by natural force; as when a man maketh his children, to submit themselves, and their children, to his government, as being able to destroy them if they refuse; or by war subdueth his enemies to his will, giving them their lives on that condition. The other, is when men agree amongst themselves, to submit to some man, or assembly of men, voluntarily, on confidence to be protected by him against all others. This latter, may be called a political commonwealth, or commonwealth by *institution;* and the former, a commonwealth by *acquisition.* And first, I shall speak of a commonwealth by institution.

Chapter XVIII

Of the rights of sovereigns by institution

A *commonwealth* is said to be *instituted,* when a *multitude* of men do agree, and *covenant, every one, with every one,* that to whatsoever *man,* or *assembly of men,* shall be given by the major part, the *right to present* the person of them all, that is to say, to be their *representative;* every one, as well he that *voted for it,* as he that *voted against it,* shall *authorize* all the actions and judgments, of that man, or assembly of men, in the same manner, as if they were his own, to the end, to live peaceably amongst themselves, and be protected against other men.

From this institution of a commonwealth are derived all the *rights,* and *faculties* of him, or them, on whom sovereign power is conferred by the consent of the people assembled.

First, because they covenant, it is to be understood, they are not obliged by former covenant to anything repugnant hereunto. And consequently they that have already instituted a commonwealth, being thereby bound by covenant, to own the actions, and judgments of one, cannot lawfully make a new covenant, amongst themselves, to be obedient to any other, in any thing whatsoever, without his permission.

Secondly, because the right of bearing the person of them all, is given to him they make sovereign, by covenant only of one to another, and not of him to any of them; there can happen no breach of covenant on the part of the sovereign; and consequently none of his subjects, by any pretence of forfeiture, can be freed from his subjection. That he which is made sovereign maketh no covenant with his subjects beforehand, is manifest; because either he must make it with the whole multitude, as one party to the covenant; or he must make a several covenant with every man. With the whole, as one party, it is impossible; because as yet they are not one person: and if he make so many several covenants as there be men, those covenants after he hath the sovereignty are void; because what act soever can be pretended by any one of them for breach thereof, is the act both of

himself, and of all the rest, because done in the person, and by the right of every one of them in particular. Besides, if any one, or more of them, pretend a breach of the covenant made by the sovereign at his institution; and others, or one other of his subjects, or himself alone, pretend there was no such breach, there is in this case, no judge to decide the controversy; it returns therefore to the sword again; and every man recovereth the right of protecting himself by his own strength, contrary to the design they had in the institution.

Thirdly, because the major part hath by consenting voices declared a sovereign; he that dissented must now consent with the rest; that is, be contented to avow all the actions he shall do, or else justly be destroyed by the rest. For if he voluntarily entered into the congregation of them that were assembled, he sufficiently declared thereby his will, and therefore tacitly covenanted, to stand to what the major part should ordain: and therefore if he refuse to stand thereto, or make protestation against any of their decrees, he does contrary to his covenant, and therefore unjustly. And whether he be of the congregation, or not; and whether his consent be asked, or not, he must either submit to their decrees, or be left in the condition of war he was in before; wherein, he might without injustice be destroyed by any man whatsoever.

Fourthly, because every subject is by this institution author of all the actions, and judgments of the sovereign instituted; it follows, that whatsoever he doth, it can be no injury to any of his subjects; nor ought he to be by any of them accused of injustice. For he that doth anything by authority from another, doth therein no injury to him by whose authority he acteth: but by this institution of a commonwealth, every particular man is author of all the sovereign doth: and consequently he that complaineth of injury from his sovereign, complaineth of that whereof he himself is author; and therefore ought not to accuse any man but himself; no nor himself of injury; because to do injury to one's self, is impossible. It is true that they that have sovereign power may commit iniquity, but not injustice, or injury in the proper signification.

Fifthly, and consequently to that which was said last, no man that hath sovereign power can justly be put to death, or otherwise in any manner by his subjects punished. For seeing every subject is author of the actions of his sovereign; he punisheth another for the actions committed by himself.

And because the end of this institution, is the peace and defence of them all; and whosoever has right to the end, has right to the means; it belongeth of right, to whatsoever man, or assembly that hath the sovereignty, to be judge both of the means of peace and defence, and also of the hindrances, and disturbances of the same; and to do whatsoever he shall think necessary to be done, both beforehand, for the preserving of peace and security, by prevention of discord at home, and hostility from abroad; and, when peace and security are lost, for the recovery of the same. And therefore,

Sixthly, it is annexed to the sovereignty, to be judge of what opinions and doctrines are averse, and what conducing to peace; and consequently, on what occasions, how far, and what men are to be trusted withal, in speaking to multitudes of people; and who shall examine the doctrines of all books before they be published. For the actions of men proceed from their opinions; and in the well-governing of opinions, consisteth the well-governing of men's actions, in order to their peace, and concord.

Seventhly, is annexed to the sovereignty, the whole power of prescribing the rules, whereby every man may know, what goods he may enjoy, and what actions he may do, without being molested by any of his fellow-subjects; and this is it men call *propriety*.

Eighthly, is annexed to the sovereignty, the right of judicature; that is to say, of hearing and deciding all controversies, which may arise concerning law, either civil, or natural; or concerning fact. For without the decision of controversies, there is no protection of one subject, against the injuries of another.

Ninthly, is annexed to the sovereignty, the right of making war and peace with other nations, and commonwealths; that is to say, of judging when it is for the public good, and how great forces are to be assembled, armed, and paid for that end; and to levy money upon the subjects, to defray the expenses thereof.

Tenthly, is annexed to the sovereignty, the choosing of all counsellors, ministers, magistrates, and officers, both in peace and war. For seeing the sovereign is charged with the end, which is the common peace and defense, he is understood to have power to use such means, as he shall think most fit for his discharge.

Eleventhly, to the sovereign is committed the power of rewarding with riches, or honour, and of punishing with corporal or pecuniary punishment, or with ignominy, every subject according to the law he hath formerly made; or if there be no law made, according as he shall judge most to conduce to the encouraging of men to serve the commonwealth, or deterring of them from doing disservice to the same.

There are the rights, which make the essence of sovereignty; and which are the marks, whereby a man may discern in what man, or assembly of men, the sovereign power is placed, and resideth. For these are incommunicable, and inseparable. The power to coin money; to dispose of the estate and persons of infant heirs; to have praeemption in markets; and all other statute prerogatives, may be transferred by the sovereign; and yet the power to protect his subjects be retained. But if he transfer the *militia*, he retains the judicature in vain, for want of execution of the laws: or if he grant away the power of raising money; the *militia* is in vain; or if he give away the government of doctrines, men will be frighted into rebellion with the fear of spirits. And so if we consider any one of the said rights, we shall presently see, that the holding of all the rest will produce no effect, in the conservation of peace and justice, the end for which all commonwealths are instituted. And this division is it, whereof it is said, a *kingdom divided in itself cannot stand*: for unless this division precede, division into opposite armies can never happen. If there had not first been an opinion received of the greatest part of England, that these powers were divided between the King, and the Lords, and the House of Commons, the people had never been divided and fallen into this civil war; first between those that disagreed in politics; and after between the dissenters about the liberty of religion; which have so instructed men in this point of sovereign right, and there be few now in England that do not see, that these rights are inseparable, and will be so generally acknowledged at the next return of peace; and so continue, till their miseries are forgotten; and no longer, except the vulgar be better taught than they have hitherto been.

And because they are essential and inseparable rights, it follows necessarily, that in whatsoever words any of them seem to be granted away, yet if the sovereign power itself be not in direct terms renounced, and the name of sovereign no more given by the grantees to him that grants them, the grant is void: for when he has granted all he can, if we grant back the sovereignty, all is restored, as inseparably annexed thereunto.

This great authority being indivisible, and inseparably annexed to the sovereignty, there is little ground for the opinion of them, that say of sovereign kings, though they be *singulis majores,* of greater power than every one of their subjects, yet they be *universis minores,* of less power than them all together. For if by *all together,* they mean not the collective body as one person, then *all together,* and *every one,* signify the same; and the speech is absurd. But if by *all together,* they understand them as one person, which person the sovereign bears, then the power of all together, is the same with the sovereign's power; and so again the speech is absurd: which absurdity they see well enough, when the sovereignty is in an assembly of the people; but in a monarch they see it not; and yet the power of sovereignty is the same in whomsoever it be placed.

And as the power, so also the honour of the sovereign, ought to be greater, than that of any, or all the subjects. For in the sovereignty is the fountain of honour.

Chapter XIX

Of the several kinds of commonwealth by institution, and of succession to the sovereign power

The difference of commonwealths, consisteth in the difference of the sovereign, or the person representative of all and every one of the multitude. And because the sovereignty is either in one man, or in an assembly of more than one; and into that assembly either every man hath right to enter, or not every one, but certain men distinguished from the rest; it is manifest, there can be but three kinds of commonwealth. For the representative must needs be one man, or more: and if more, then it is the assembly of all, or but of a part. When the representative is one man, then is the commonwealth a MONARCHY: when an assembly of all that will come together, then it is a DEMOCRACY, or popular commonwealth: when an assembly of a part only, then it is called an ARISTOCRACY. Other kind of commonwealth there can be none: for either one, or more, or all, must have the sovereign power, which I have shown to be indivisible, entire.

It is manifest, that men who are in absolute liberty, may, if they please, give authority to one man, to represent them every one; as well as give such authority to any assembly of men whatsoever; and consequently may subject themselves, if they think good, to a monarch, as absolutely, as to any other representative. Therefore, where there is already erected a sovereign power, there can be no other representative of the same people, but only to certain particular ends, by the sovereign limited. For that were to erect two sovereigns; and every man to have his person represented by two actors, that by opposing one another, must needs divide that power, which, if men will live in peace, is indivisible; and thereby reduce the multitude into the condition of war, contrary to the end for which all sovereignty is instituted. And therefore as it is absurd, to think that a sovereign assembly, inviting the people of their dominion, to send up their deputies, with power to make known their advice, or desires, should therefore hold such deputies, rather than themselves, for the absolute representatives of the people: so it is absurd also, to think the same in a monarchy.

The difference between these three kinds of commonwealth, consisteth not in the difference of power; but in the difference of convenience; or aptitude to produce the peace, and security of the people; for which end they were instituted. And to compare monarchy with the other two, we may observe; first, that whosoever beareth the person of the people, or is one of that assembly that bears it, beareth also his own natural person. And though he be careful in his politic person to procure the common interest; yet he is more, or no less careful to procure the private good of himself, his family, kindred and friends; and for the most part, if the public interest chance to cross the private, he prefers the private: for the passions of men, are commonly more potent than their reason. From whence it follows, that where the public and private interest are most closely united, there is the public most advanced. Now in monarchy, the private interest is the same with the public. The riches, power, and honour of a monarch arise only from the riches, strength and reputation of his subjects.

Secondly, that a monarch receiveth counsel of whom, when, and where he pleaseth; and consequently may hear the opinion of men versed in the matter about which he deliberates, of what rank or quality soever, and as long before the time of action, and with as much secrecy, as he will. But when a sovereign assembly has need of counsel, none are admitted but such as have a right thereto from the beginning

Thirdly, that the resolutions of a monarch, are subject to no other inconstancy, than that of human nature; but in assemblies, besides that of nature, there ariseth an inconstancy from the number. For the absence of a few, that would have the resolution once taken, continue firm, which may happen by security, negligence, or private impediments, or the diligent appearance of a few of the contrary opinion, undoes to-day, all that was concluded yesterday.

Fourthly, that a monarch cannot disagree with himself, out of envy, or interest; but an assembly may; and that to such a height, as may produce a civil war.

Fifthly, that in monarchy there is this inconvenience; that any subject, by the power of one man, for the enriching of a favourite or flatterer, may be deprived of all he possesseth; which I confess is a great and inevitable inconvenience.

Sixthly, that it is an inconvenience in monarchy, that the sovereignty may descend upon an infant, or one that cannot discern between good and evil: and consisteth in this, that the use of his power, must be in the hand of another man, or of some assembly of men, which are to govern by his right, and in his name; as curators, and protectors of his person, and authority.

Chapter XXI

Of the liberty of subjects

LIBERTY, or FREEDOM, signifieth, properly, the absence of opposition; by opposition, I mean external impediments of motion; and may be applied no less to irrational, and inanimate creatures, than to rational. For whatsoever is so tied, or environed, as it cannot move but within a certain space, which space is determined by the opposition of some external body, we say it hath not liberty to go further. And so of all living creatures, whilst they are imprisoned, or restrained, with walls, or chains; and of the water whilst it is kept in by banks, or vessels, that otherwise would spread itself into a larger space, we use to say, they are not at liberty, to move in such manner, as without those external impediments they would. But when the impediment of motion, is in the constitution of the thing itself, we use not to say; it wants the liberty; but the power to move; as when a stone lieth still, or a man is fastened to his bed by sickness.

And according to this proper, and generally received meaning of the word, a FREEMAN, *is he, that in those things, which by his strength and wit he is able to do, is not hindered to do what he has a will to*. But when the words *free*, and *liberty*, are applied to any thing but bodies, they are abused; for that which is not subject to motion is not subject to impediment: and therefore, when it is said, for example, the way is free, no liberty of the way is signified, but of those that walk in it without stop.

But as men, for the attaining of peace, and conservation of themselves thereby, have made an artificial man, which we call a commonwealth; so also have they made artificial chains, called *civil laws*, which they themselves, by mutual covenants, have fastened at one end, to the lips of that man, or assembly, to whom they have given the sovereign power; and at the other end to their own ears. These bonds, in their own nature but weak, may nevertheless be made to hold, by the danger, though not by the difficulty of breaking them.

In relation to these bonds only it is, that I am to speak now, of the *liberty* of *subjects*. For seeing there is no commonwealth in the world, wherein there be rules enough set down, for the regulating of all the actions, and words of men; as being a thing impossible: it followeth necessarily, that in all kinds of actions by the laws praetermitted, men have the liberty, of doing what their own reasons shall suggest, for the most profitable to themselves. For if we take liberty in the proper sense, for corporal liberty; that is to say, freedom from chains and prison; it were very absurd for men to clamour as they do, for the liberty they so manifestly enjoy. Again, if we take liberty, for an exemption from laws, it is no less absurd, for men to demand as they do, that liberty, by which all other men may be masters of their lives. And yet, as absurd as it is, this is it they demand; not knowing that the laws are of no power to protect them, without a sword in the hands of a man, or men, to cause those laws to be put in execution. The liberty of a subject, lieth therefore only in those things, which in regulating their actions, the sovereign hath praetermitted: such as is the liberty to buy, and sell, and otherwise contract with one another; to choose their own abode, their own diet, their own trade of life, and institute their children as they themselves think fit; and the like.

Nevertheless we are not to understand, that by such liberty, the sovereign power of life and death, is either abolished, or limited. For it has been already shown, that nothing the sovereign representative can do to a subject, on what pretence soever, can properly be called injustice, or injury; because every subject is author of every act the sovereign doth; so that he never wanteth right to anything, otherwise, than as he himself is the subject of God, and bound thereby to observe the laws of nature.

But it is an easy thing, for men to be deceived, by the specious name of liberty; and for want of judgment to distinguish, mistake that for their private inheritance, and birth-right, which is the right of the public only. And when the same error is confirmed by the authority of men in reputation for their writings on this subject, it is no wonder if it produce sedition, and change of government.

To come now to the particulars of the true liberty of a subject; that is to say, what are the things, which though commanded by the sovereign, he may nevertheless, without injustice, refuse to do; we are to consider, what rights we pass away, when we make a commonwealth; or, which is all one, what liberty we deny ourselves, by owning all the actions, without exception, of the man, or assembly, we make our sovereign. For in the act of our *submission*, consisteth both our *obligation*, and our *liberty*.

First therefore, seeing sovereignty by institution, is by covenant of every one to every one; and sovereignty by acquisition, by covenants of the vanquished to the victor, or child to the parent; it is manifest, that every subject has liberty in all those things, the right whereof cannot by covenant be transferred. I have shewn before in the 14th chapter, that covenants, not to defend a man's own body, are void. Therefore,

If the sovereign command a man, though justly condemned, to kill, wound, or maim himself; or not to resist those that assault him; or to abstain from the use of food, air, medicine, or any other thing, without which he cannot live; yet hath that man the liberty to disobey.

If a man be interrogated by the sovereign, or his authority, concerning a crime done by himself, he is not bound, without assurance of pardon, to confess it; because no man, as I have shown in the same chapter, can be obliged by covenant to accuse himself.

Again, the consent of a subject to sovereign power, is contained in these words, I *authorise, or take upon me, all his actions*; in which there is no restriction at all, of his own former natural liberty: for by allowing him to *kill me*, I am not bound to kill myself when he commands me.

As for other liberties, they depend on the silence of the law. In cases where the sovereign has prescribed no rule, there the subject hath the liberty to do, or forbear, according to his own discretion. And therefore such liberty is in some places more, and in some less; and in some times more, in other times less, according as they that have the sovereignty shall think most convenient.

The obligation of subjects to the sovereign, is understood to last as long, and no longer, than the power lasteth, by which he is able to protect them. For the right men have by nature to protect themselves, when none else can protect them, can by no covenant be relinquished. The sovereignty is the soul of the commonwealth; which once departed from the body, the members do no more receive their motion from it. The end of obedience is protection; which, wheresoever a man seeth it, either in his own, or in another's sword, nature applieth his obedience to it, and his endeavour to maintain it.

STUDY QUESTIONS: HOBBES, *THE LEVIATHAN*

1. How, according to Hobbes, is cause transmitted throughout the universe?
2. What is his mechanistic explanation of religion?
3. What are the two parts of Hobbes' psychological theory? How are they related?
4. Why do people make a covenant to be governed?
5. What is his theory of government? What obligation does the sovereign have over his or her subjects?
6. What does Hobbes mean by Nature?
7. How are all thoughts representations or appearances? What is mental discourse? How does it proceed? What does Hobbes mean by 'rationality,' and how does it work?

8. What is his view of the passions? How are they related to reason and action?
9. What are the various sorts of power?
10. What is a person? How does Hobbes define personhood?
11. What does he mean by 'commonwealth'? What is its aim? How are sovereign and subject related?
12. How does Hobbes define 'liberty'?

Philosophical Bridges: Hobbes' Influence

Hobbes' main philosophical aim was to make political theory scientific. He envisaged a unified body of knowledge that starts with the principles of mechanics and works up to include psychology and, finally, political theory. This vision has had an enormous impact. For example, in the 1850s the French positivist Auguste Comte argued that sociology should study society scientifically by formulating general laws that govern the functioning of societies. Like Hobbes before him, Comte thinks that the scientific study of society would be very beneficial. In the twentieth century, some of the logical positivists argued that the study of society should follow the same methodology as that of the natural sciences. Of course, these Hobbesian ideas are disputed by thinkers who claim that the study of society, unlike that of nature, must be interpretive (i.e., hermeneutical) rather than purely causal.

Hobbes was a materialist. He argued that everything that exists, including the conscious mind, is made up of matter. This was a brave position to take in public in seventeenth-century Europe, and Hobbes' defense of materialism opened the way for later defenders of the view such as the French Enlightenment thinker Julien la Mettrie (1709–51), who argued for a materialism in his work *Man, a Machine*. Hobbes also argued that all thought was computational; it is akin to adding, subtracting, and multiplying. This conception of reason influenced Leibniz, who took it very much to heart and, as a result, developed many of the concepts necessary for the creation of logical formal systems. The Latin translation of Hobbes' *Leviathan* had an impact on the thought of Spinoza, who saw in it the seeds of his own thesis that the order and connection of ideas are the same as the order and connection of spatially extended things. Hobbes' discussion of the emotions also influenced Spinoza.

Like Spinoza after him, Hobbes was known popularly as an atheist. This aspect of his reputation was historically important; it opened the way for others to challenge religious orthodoxy. After Hobbes' *Leviathan* (1651), deism became quite popular among educated people. As a religion, deism requires only belief in an impersonal God. A deist may conceive of God as nature or as the force that set the mechanical universe into motion, and typically would reject all other aspects of Christian teaching. In this way, Hobbes paved the way for Locke's reinterpretation of Christianity and Hume's atheism.

Hobbes' general approach to politics is based on the premise that a group of self-interested rational beings will have a reason to cooperate and establish a system of enforceable laws. This kind of approach has appeal because apparently it can explain moral concepts such as justice without having to postulate anything beyond individual rational self-interest. This line is inherent in recent attempts to explain apparently altruistic behavior and social arrangements in purely individualistic economic terms, such as game theory. For example, most recently, some of Hobbes' ideas are echoed in David Gauthier's *Morality by Agreement* (1986), which argues that moral constraints arise when people resolve to cooperate for mutual benefit. The most immediate influence of Hobbes' political work was Locke's *A Treatise Concerning Civil Government*, which in effect continues in the same tradition, despite the important differences between the two theories.

JOHN LOCKE (1632–1704)

Biographical History

Through family contacts, Locke had the good fortune to study at Westminster School and Christ Church, Oxford, where he met the chemist Sir Robert Boyle, who introduced him to the 'new science,' chemistry. Boyle's innovative emphasis on experiment contrasted sharply with Locke's formal studies in Scholastic philosophy. Although Locke trained to be a doctor, in 1666, he met Lord Ashley, an important politician, and became his secretary. When Ashley was appointed the Lord Chancellor of England in 1672, Locke became secretary to the Council of Trade and Plantations. In 1675, he moved to France for several years, where he met important philosophers, including Gassendi. During Locke's time abroad, Ashley, now long fallen from power, had been plotting against the succession of the Catholic James II to the throne and, when Ashley was arrested, Locke fled to Holland. He did not return to England until 1689, after James II had been replaced in a bloodless revolution by the Protestant king of Holland, William of Orange. During his five years of exile in Holland, Locke completed his *Essay Concerning Human Understanding* and *A Letter Concerning Toleration*, and worked on *Two Treatises on Civil Government*. In 1689, Locke was appointed the commissioner of appeals, but from then until his death in 1704, he spent most of his time in philosophical study, staying with his friends, the philosopher Lady Masham and her husband.

Philosophical Overview

After discussing 'the principles of morality and revealed religion' with some friends, in 1671, Locke decided to write the *Essay Concerning Human Understanding* to investigate the nature and limits of knowledge. Locke calls his philosophical approach 'the new way of ideas' (I.II.8). The center of his theory is that all ideas are derived from experience. He shows this, first, by arguing against innate ideas and, second, by showing how our ideas are derived from experience. His theory of knowledge aims to avoid the extremes of groundless speculation and universal Skepticism, to clarify the prospects of the new sciences, and to show how moral knowledge is possible. The essay is divided into four books:

1. *The first contains arguments against innate ideas.*
2. *The second shows how the complex ideas of substances, modes, and relations are formed. It contains discussions of primary and secondary qualities, the mind-body relation, and personal identity.*
3. *The third book contains Locke's theory of language and his distinction between real and nominal essence.*
4. *In the fourth book, Locke explains his theory of knowledge.*

Book II

Locke claims that all ideas come from sensation and reflection. Through sensation, the mind receives simple ideas of sensible qualities (such as that of yellow) from external objects. By reflecting on how the mind reacts to these ideas of sense, we acquire psychological ideas (such as that of thinking). Complex ideas are composed out of simple ones by various operations of the mind:

1. *The idea of substances and modes are formed when simple ideas are compounded.*
2. *When simple ideas are compared, they become the idea of relations.*
3. *General ideas are formed by the mental operation of abstraction.*

After Locke has argued for the distinction between primary and secondary qualities, he divides complex ideas into three categories: ideas of modes, ideas of substances, and ideas of relations. To maintain his Empiricist theory, Locke must argue that all complex ideas can be derived from simple ideas. He does this case by case.

Book III

This examines the relations between words and ideas. Locke repudiates the Scholastic view that the essences of natural kinds can be grasped by reasoning from definitions. According to Locke, words stand for ideas in the mind of the person who uses them, rather than for the properties of things. The use of words is for the communication of ideas, and the purpose of definition is to clarify these ideas rather than to refer to real essences or Platonic forms. General words do not name universal entities, such as Plato's Forms, because only particulars exist. Rather, general words name general ideas, and Locke tries to provide an Empiricist account of the formation of general ideas and the meaning of general words.

Locke rejects the Platonic view because it assumes falsely that there are essential natures common to all things of one kind. Locke rejects this assumption by distinguishing between real and nominal essence.

1. *The nominal essence of a substance type, such as gold, is an abstract idea of something having certain observable characteristics. We classify an object as a piece of gold because of its yellow shining color, its weight, and so on. We associate this complex idea, which is formed by abstraction, with the name 'gold'.*
2. *In contrast, the real essence of gold is its internal constitution, which is generally unknown. The observable characteristics of gold causally depend on the real essence of gold.*

However, because the real essence of things is unknown, it does not constitute the actual basis of our classifications, which depend on nominal essences. Since the nominal essence is an abstract idea of the mind, such classifications involve an arbitrary element and are to some extent arbitrary because they depend on the selections made by our attention. On the other hand, Locke admits that classifications have some basis in real similarities, and, thus, they are not entirely arbitrary. Nevertheless, words do not refer to the real essence of things. They can only signify ideas.

According to Locke, the failure to distinguish between real and nominal essence leads to a false view of knowledge. The Scholastic method of disputing definitions is a fruitless method of inquiry, because definitions only determine nominal essences. In contrast, the primary purpose of definition is really to clarify what idea a word stands for, in order to make communication clearer.

Book IV

Knowledge requires certainty and justification. Beliefs that are merely probable do not count as knowledge. In Chapter II of Book IV, Locke describes three different degrees of knowledge. Intuitive knowledge is an immediate perception of agreement between ideas, that leaves no room for doubt (e.g., 'Three is greater than two'). Demonstrative knowledge requires intervening steps, as in a mathematical or logical proof. Sensitive knowledge of particular external objects through the senses is less certain than demonstrative knowledge (IV.II.14).

Although Locke thinks that sensitive knowledge is possible, his definition of knowledge destroys the hope that science will enlarge our knowledge of nature. Scientific progress will be useful, but it can provide only probable belief and opinion rather than true knowledge, because 'our faculties are not fitted to penetrate into the internal fabric and real essences of bodies' (IV.XII.11). Locke sharply contrasts the gloomy prospects for scientific knowledge with those for morality. Moral knowledge can be demonstrated and, therefore, can be known with certainty. He says, 'Hence I think I may conclude that morality is the proper science and business of mankind in general' (IV.III.11).

AN ESSAY CONCERNING HUMAN UNDERSTANDING

It is important to understand the overarching aims that Locke had for his *Essay*. The impetus for the work arose from some inconclusive discussions that Locke had with friends about the nature of morality and religion in 1671. The historical context for Locke's work is that he was born into a Europe torn by religious wars between Protestants and Catholics. It was a time of scientific, political, and religious transformation. During this time of strife, Locke was a champion of toleration. He was against authoritarianism and the repression of individual free thought. Above all, Locke was concerned to demonstrate the importance of morality as a force for freedom in both politics and religion. He saw the need to avoid the extremes of dogmatic fanaticism on the one hand, and pessimistic Skepticism on the other. We need to assess carefully the capacities of science, religion, and morality to give us real knowledge. Such an assessment must be based on principles, which are argued for in the *Essay*, such as that there are no innate ideas (Book I), all ideas must be acquired from experience (Book II), words can refer only to ideas (Book III), and knowledge requires certainty (Book IV).

Given these general aims, some aspects of the argumentative structure of the *Essay* become clearer. By showing in detail how all ideas can be derived from experience in Book II, Locke repudiates appeals to authority and dogma. Given that all ideas are so derived, he shows in Book III that we cannot refer to the real essence of things but only to nominal essences. Words can refer only to ideas and not directly to objects. In Book IV, he claims that the term 'knowledge' requires the perceiving of a truth with certainty. Consequently, science may give us useful beliefs about the world that are probably true, but such beliefs do not count as knowledge of real essences. In contrast, we can have knowledge of moral claims because morality does not aim to give us knowledge of the real essence of natural objects. Like mathematics, it concerns a priori truths that can be grasped by reason with certainty.

BOOK I

OF INNATE NOTIONS

Chapter I

Introduction

1. Since it is the *understanding* that sets man above the rest of sensible beings, and gives him all the advantage and dominion which he has over them, it is certainly a subject, even for its nobleness, worth our labour to inquire into. The understanding, like the eye, whilst it makes us see and perceive all other things, takes no notice of itself; and it requires art and pains to set it at a distance and make it its own object. But whatever be the difficulties that lie in the way of

this inquiry, whatever it be that keeps us so much in the dark to ourselves, sure I am that all the light we can let in upon our own minds, all the acquaintance we can make with our own understandings, will not only be very pleasant, but bring us great advantage, in directing our thoughts in the search of other things.

2. This, therefore, being my *purpose*, to inquire into the original, certainty, and extent of human knowledge, together with the grounds and degrees of belief, opinion, and assent: I shall not at present meddle with the physical consideration of the mind; or trouble myself to examine wherein its essence consists; or by what motions of our spirits or alterations of our bodies we come to have any sensation by our organs, or any *ideas* in our understandings; and whether those *ideas* do in their formation, any or all of them, depend on matter or no. These are speculations which, however curious and entertaining, I shall decline, as lying out of my way in the design I am now upon. It shall suffice to my present purpose to consider the discerning faculties of a man, as they are employed about the objects which they have to do with. And I shall imagine I have not wholly misemployed myself in the thoughts I shall have on this occasion, if, in this historical, plain method, I can give any account of the ways whereby our understandings come to attain those notions of things we have, and can set down any measures of the certainty of our knowledge, or the grounds of those persuasions which are to be found amongst men, so various, different, and wholly contradictory; and yet asserted somewhere or other with such assurance and confidence that he that shall take a view of the opinions of mankind, observe their opposition, and at the same time consider the fondness and devotion wherewith they are embraced, the resolution and eagerness wherewith they are maintained, may perhaps have reason to suspect that either there is no such thing as truth at all, or that mankind hath no sufficient means to attain a certain knowledge of it.

3. It is therefore worth while to search out the *bounds* between opinion and knowledge, and examine by what measures, in things whereof we have no certain knowledge, we ought to regulate our assent and moderate our persuasions. In order whereunto I shall pursue this following method:

First, I shall inquire into the *original* of those *ideas,* notions, or whatever else you please to call them, which a man observes and is conscious to himself he has in his mind; and the ways whereby the understanding comes to be furnished with them.

Secondly, I shall endeavour to show what *knowledge* the understanding hath by those *ideas,* and the certainty, evidence, and extent of it.

Thirdly, I shall make some inquiry into the nature and grounds of *faith* or *opinion:* whereby I mean that assent which we give to any proposition as true, of whose truth yet we have no certain knowledge. And here we shall have occasion to examine the reasons and degrees of *assent.*

4. If by this inquiry into the nature of the understanding, I can discover the powers thereof: *how far* they reach; to what things they are in any degree proportionate; and where they fail us, I suppose it may be of use to prevail with the busy mind of man to be more cautious in meddling with things exceeding its comprehension; to stop when it is at the utmost extent of its tether; and to sit down in a quiet ignorance of those things which upon examination are found to be beyond the reach of our capacities. We should not then perhaps be so forward, out of an affectation of an universal knowledge, to raise questions and perplex ourselves and others with disputes about things to which our understandings are not suited, and of which we cannot frame in our minds any clear or distinct perceptions, or whereof (as it has perhaps too often happened) we have not any notions at all. If we can find out how far the understanding can extend its view, how far it has faculties to attain certainty, and in what cases it can only judge and guess, we may learn to content ourselves with what is attainable by us in this state.

6. *Knowing the extent of our capacities will hinder us from useless curiosity, skepticism, and idleness.* When we know our own *strength,* we shall know better what to undertake with hopes of success. And when we have well surveyed the *powers* of our own minds and made some estimate what we may expect from them, we shall not be inclined either to sit still, and not set our thoughts on work at all in despair of knowing anything nor, on the other side, question everything and disclaim all knowledge, because some things are not to be understood. . . .

Our business here is not to know all things, but those which concern our conduct. If we can find out those measures by which a rational creature, put in that state in which man is in this world, may and ought to govern his opinions and actions depending thereon, we need not be troubled that some other things escape our knowledge.

7. This was that which gave the first *rise* to this *Essay* concerning the *understanding*. For I thought that the first step towards satisfying several inquiries the mind of man was very apt to run into was to take a survey of our own understandings, examine our own powers, and see to what things they were adapted. Till that was done I suspected we began at the wrong end and in vain sought for satisfaction in a quiet and sure possession of truths that most concerned us, whilst we let loose our thoughts into the vast ocean of *Being,* as if all that boundless extent were the natural and undoubted possession of our understandings, wherein there was nothing exempt from its decisions or that escaped its comprehension. Thus men, extending their inquiries beyond their capacities, and letting their thoughts wander into those depths where they can find no sure footing, it is no wonder that they raise questions and multiply disputes, which, never coming to any clear resolution, are proper only to continue and increase their doubts and to confirm them at last in perfect scepticism. Whereas, were the capacities of our understandings well considered, the extent of our knowledge once discovered, and the horizon found which sets the bounds between the enlightened and dark parts of things, between what is and what is not comprehensible by us, men would perhaps with less scruple acquiesce in the avowed ignorance of the one, and employ their thoughts and discourse with more advantage and satisfaction in the other.

8. Thus much I thought necessary to say concerning the occasion of this inquiry into human understanding. But, before I proceed on to what I have thought on this subject, I must here in the entrance beg pardon of my reader for the frequent use of the word *idea,* which he will find in the following treatise. It being that term which, I think, serves best to stand for whatsoever is the object of the understanding when a man thinks, I have used it to express whatever is meant by *phantasm, notion, species,* or whatever it is which the mind can be employed about in thinking; and I could not avoid frequently using it.

I presume it will be easily granted me that there are such *ideas* in men's minds: everyone is conscious of them in himself, and men's words and actions will satisfy him that they are in others.

Our first inquiry then shall be how they come into the mind.

Chapter II

No Innate Principles in the Mind

1. It is an established opinion amongst some men that there are in the *understanding* certain *innate principles,* some primary notions, κοιναὶ ἔννοιαι, characters, as it were, stamped upon the mind of man, which the soul receives in its very first being and brings into the world with it. It would be sufficient to convince unprejudiced readers of the falseness of this supposition, if I should only show (as I hope I shall in the following parts of this discourse) how men, barely by the use of their natural faculties, may attain to all the knowledge they have, without the help of any innate impressions, and may arrive at certainty without any such original notions or principles. For I imagine anyone will easily grant that it would be impertinent to suppose the *ideas* of colours innate in a creature to whom God has given sight, and a power to receive them by the eyes, from external objects; and no less unreasonable would it be to attribute several truths to the impressions of nature and innate characters, when we may observe in ourselves faculties, fit to attain as easy and certain knowledge of them, as if they were originally imprinted on the mind.

But because a man is not permitted without censure to follow his own thoughts in the search of truth, when they lead him ever so little out of the common road, I shall set down the reasons that made me doubt of the truth of that opinion, as an excuse for my mistake, if I be in one; which I leave to be considered by those who, with me, dispose themselves to embrace truth, wherever they find it.

2. There is nothing more commonly taken for granted than that there are certain principles, both *speculative* and *practical* (for they speak of both), universally agreed upon by all mankind: which therefore, they argue, must needs be constant impressions which the souls of men receive in their first beings, and which they bring into the world with them, as necessarily and really as they do any of their inherent faculties.

3. This argument, drawn from *universal consent,* has this misfortune in it, that if it were true in matter

of fact that there were certain truths wherein all mankind agreed, it would not prove them innate, if there can be any other way shown how men may come to that universal agreement, in the things they do consent in, which I presume may be done.

4. But, which is worse, this argument of universal consent, which is made use of to prove innate principles, seems to me a demonstration that there are none such: because there are none to which all mankind give an universal assent. I shall begin with the speculative, and instance in those magnified principles of demonstration, *Whatsoever is, is* and *It is impossible for the same thing to be and not to be*, which of all others I think have the most allowed title to innate. These have so settled a reputation of maxims universally received that it will, no doubt, be thought strange if anyone should seem to question it. But yet I take liberty to say that these propositions are so far from having an universal assent, that there are a great part of mankind to whom they are not so much as known.

5. For, first, it is evident that all *children* and *idiots* have not the least apprehension or thought of them. And the want of that is enough to destroy that universal assent which must needs be the necessary concomitant of all innate truths: it seeming to me near a contradiction to say that there are truths imprinted on the soul which it perceives or understands not: imprinting, if it signify anything, being nothing else but the making certain truths to be perceived. For to imprint anything on the mind, without the mind's perceiving it, seems to me hardly intelligible. If therefore *children* and *idiots* have souls, have minds, with those impressions upon them, they must unavoidably perceive them, and necessarily know and assent to these truths; which since they do not, it is evident that there are no such impressions. For if they are not notions naturally imprinted, how can they be innate? And if they are notions imprinted, how can they be unknown? To say a notion is imprinted on the mind, and yet at the same time to say that the mind is ignorant of it, and never yet took notice of it, is to make this impression nothing. No proposition can be said to be in the mind, which it never yet knew, which it was never yet conscious of. For if any one may, then by the same reason all propositions that are true and the mind is capable ever of assenting to, may be said to be in the mind and to be imprinted: since, if

any one can be said to be in the mind which it never yet knew, it must be only because it is capable of knowing it; and so the mind is of all truths it ever shall know. Nay, thus truths may be imprinted on the mind which it never did nor ever shall know; for a man may live long, and die at last in ignorance of many truths which his mind was capable of knowing, and that with certainty. So that if the capacity of knowing be the natural impression contended for, all the truths a man ever comes to know will, by this account, be every one of them innate; and this great point will amount to no more, but only to a very improper way of speaking; which, whilst it pretends to assert the contrary, says nothing different from those who deny innate principles. For nobody, I think, ever denied that the mind was capable of knowing several truths. The capacity they say is innate, the knowledge acquired. But then to what end such contest for certain innate maxims? If truths can be imprinted on the understanding without being perceived, I can see no difference there can be between any truths the mind is capable of knowing, in respect of their original: they must all be innate, or all adventitious. In vain shall a man go about to distinguish them. He therefore that talks of innate notions in the understanding, cannot (if he intend thereby any distinct sort of truths) mean such truths to be in the understanding as it never perceived, and is yet wholly ignorant of. For if these words (*to be in the understanding*) have any propriety, they signify to be understood. So that to be in the understanding and not to be understood, to be in the mind and never to be perceived, is all one as to say: anything is and is not in the mind or understanding. If therefore these two propositions, *Whatsoever is, is* and *It is impossible for the same thing to be and not to be*, are by nature imprinted, children cannot be ignorant of them; infants, and all that have souls, must necessarily have them in their understandings, know the truth of them, and assent to it.

BOOK II

OF IDEAS

Chapter I

Of Ideas in General, and Their Original

1. Every man being conscious to himself that he thinks, and that which his mind is applied about whilst thinking being the *ideas* that are there, it is past doubt that men have in their minds several *ideas* such as are those expressed by the words *whiteness, hardness, sweetness, thinking, motion, man, elephant, army, drunkenness* and others: it is in the first place then to be inquired, how he comes by them? I know it is a received doctrine that men have native *ideas* and original characters stamped upon their minds in their very first being. This opinion I have at large examined already; and, I suppose, what I have said in the foregoing book will be much more easily admitted when I have shown whence the understanding may get all the *ideas* it has, and by what ways and degrees they may come into the mind; for which I shall appeal to everyone's own observation and experience.

2. Let us then suppose the mind to be, as we say, white paper void of all characters, without any *ideas*. How comes it to be furnished? Whence comes it by that vast store which the busy and boundless fancy of man has painted on it with an almost endless variety? Whence has it all the materials of reason and knowledge? To this I answer, in one word, from *experience*; in that all our knowledge is founded, and from that it ultimately derives itself. Our observation, employed either about *external sensible objects, or about the internal operations of our minds perceived and reflected on by ourselves, is that which supplies our understandings with all the materials of thinking*. These two are the fountains of knowledge, from whence all the *ideas* we have, or can naturally have, do spring.

3. First, *our senses*, conversant about particular sensible objects, do *convey into the mind* several distinct *perceptions* of things, according to those various ways wherein those objects do affect them. And thus we come by those *ideas* we have of *yellow, white, heat, cold, soft, hard, bitter, sweet*, and all those which we call sensible qualities; which when I say the senses convey into the mind, I mean, they from external objects convey into the mind what produces there those *perceptions*. This great source of most of the *ideas* we have, depending wholly upon our senses, and derived by them to the understanding, I call SENSATION.

4. Secondly, the other fountain from which experience furnisheth the understanding with *ideas* is the *perception of the operations of our own minds* within us, as it is employed about the *ideas* it has got; which operations, when the soul comes to reflect on and

consider, do furnish the understanding with another set of *ideas*, which could not be had from things without. And such are *perception, thinking, doubting, believing, reasoning, knowing, willing*, and all the different actings of our own minds; which we, being conscious of and observing in ourselves, do from these receive into our understandings as distinct *ideas* as we do from bodies affecting our senses. This source of *ideas* every man has wholly in himself; and though it be not sense, as having nothing to do with external objects, yet it is very like it, and might properly enough be called internal sense. But as I call the other *sensation*, so I call this REFLECTION, the *ideas* it affords being such only as the mind gets by reflecting on its own operations within itself. By REFLECTION then, in the following part of this discourse, I would be understood to mean that notice which the mind takes of its own operations, and the manner of them, by reason whereof there come to be *ideas* of these operations in the understanding. These two, I say, viz. external material things as the objects of SENSATION, and the operations of our own minds within as the objects of REFLECTION, are to me the only originals from whence all our *ideas* take their beginnings. The term *operations* here I use in a large sense, as comprehending not barely the actions of the mind about its *ideas*, but some sort of passions arising sometimes from them, such as is the satisfaction or uneasiness arising from any thought.

5. The understanding seems to me not to have the least glimmering of any *ideas* which it doth not receive from one of these two. *External objects furnish the mind with the* ideas *of sensible qualities*, which are all those different perceptions they produce in us; and the *mind furnishes the understanding with* ideas *of its own operations*.

These, when we have taken a full survey of them and their several modes, combinations, and relations, we shall find to contain all our whole stock of *ideas*, and that we have nothing in our minds which did not come in one of these two ways. Let anyone examine his own thoughts and thoroughly search into his understanding and then let him tell me whether all the original *ideas* he has there are any other than of the objects of his *senses*, or of the operations of his mind, considered as objects of his *reflection*. And how great a mass of knowledge soever he imagines to be lodged there, he will, upon taking a strict view, see that he has *not any* idea *in his mind but what one of these two have imprinted*, though perhaps, with infinite variety compounded and enlarged by the understanding, as we shall see hereafter.

6. He that attentively considers the state of a *child*, at his first coming into the world, will have little reason to think him stored with plenty of *ideas*, that are to be the matter of his future knowledge. It is by degrees he comes to be furnished with them. And though the *ideas* of obvious and familiar qualities imprint themselves before the memory begins to keep a register of time and order, yet it is often so late before some unusual qualities come in the way, that there are few men that cannot recollect the beginning of their acquaintance with them. And if it were worthwhile, no doubt a child might be so ordered as to have but a very few, even of the ordinary *ideas*, till he were grown up to a man. But all that are born into the world being surrounded with bodies that perpetually and diversely affect them, variety of *ideas*, whether care be taken about it or no, are imprinted on the minds of children. *Light* and *colours* are busy at hand everywhere when the eye is but open; *sounds* and some *tangible qualities* fail not to solicit their proper senses and force an entrance to the mind; but yet, I think it will be granted easily that, if a child were kept in a place where he never saw any other but black and white till he were a man, he would have no more *ideas* of scarlet or green than he that from his childhood never tasted an oyster or a pineapple has of those particular relishes.

7. Men then come to be furnished with fewer or more simple *ideas* from without, according as the *objects* they converse with afford greater or less variety; and from the operation of their minds within, according as they more or less *reflect* on them. For, though he that contemplates the operations of his mind cannot but have plain and clear *ideas* of them: yet, unless he turn his thoughts that way and consider them *attentively*, he will no more have clear and distinct *ideas* of all the *operations of his mind*, and all that may be observed therein, than he will have all the particular *ideas* of any landscape, or of the parts and motions of a clock, who will not turn his eyes to it and with attention heed all the parts of it. The picture or clock may be so placed that they may

come in his way every day, but yet he will have but a confused *idea* of all the parts they are made up of, till he *applies himself with attention* to consider them each in particular.

8. And hence we see the reason why it is pretty late before most children get *ideas* of the operations of their own minds; and some have not any very clear or perfect *ideas* of the greatest part of them all their lives. Because, though they pass there continually, yet, like floating visions, they make not deep impressions enough to leave in the mind clear, distinct, lasting *ideas*, till the understanding turns inwards upon itself, *reflects* on its own *operations*, and makes them the object of its own contemplation. Children, when they come first into it, are surrounded with a world of new things which, by a constant solicitation of their senses, draw the mind constantly to them, forward to take notice of new and apt to be delighted with the variety of changing objects. Thus the first years are usually employed and diverted in looking abroad. Men's business in them is to acquaint themselves with what is to be found without; and so growing up in a constant attention to outward sensations, seldom make any considerable reflection on what passes within them, till they come to be of riper years; and some scarce ever at all.

9. To ask *at what time a man has first any* ideas is to ask when he begins to perceive: having *ideas* and perception being the same thing. I know it is an opinion that the soul always thinks, and that it has the actual perception of *ideas* in itself constantly, as long as it exists; and that actual thinking is as inseparable from the soul as actual extension is from the body; which if true, to inquire after the beginning of a man's *ideas* is the same as to inquire after the beginning of his soul.

Chapter II

Of Simple Ideas

1. The better to understand the nature, manner, and extent of our knowledge, one thing is carefully to be observed concerning the *ideas* we have, and that is that *some* of them are *simple* and *some complex*.

Though the qualities that affect our senses are, in the things themselves, so united and blended that there is no separation, no distance between them, yet it is plain the *ideas* they produce in the mind enter by the senses simple and unmixed. For, though the sight and touch often take in from the same object, at the same time, different *ideas*, as a man sees at once motion and colour, the hand feels softness and warmth in the same piece of wax: yet the simple *ideas* thus united in the same subject are as perfectly distinct as those that come in by different senses. The coldness and hardness which a man feels in a piece of *ice* being as distinct *ideas* in the mind as the smell and whiteness of a lily, or as the taste of sugar, and smell of a rose; and there is nothing can be plainer to a man than the clear and distinct perception he has of those simple *ideas*; which, being each in itself uncompounded, contains in it nothing but *one uniform appearance* or conception in the mind, and is not distinguishable into different *ideas*.

2. These simple *ideas*, the materials of all our knowledge, are suggested and furnished to the mind only by those two ways above mentioned, viz. *sensation* and *reflection*. When the understanding is once stored with these simple *ideas*, it has the power to repeat, compare, and unite them, even to an almost infinite variety, and so can make at pleasure new complex *ideas*. But it is not in the power of the most exalted wit or enlarged understanding, by any quickness or variety of thought, to *invent or frame one new simple* idea in the mind, not taken in by the ways before mentioned; nor can any force of the understanding *destroy* those that are there, the dominion of man in this little world of his own understanding being much what the same as it is in the great world of visible things; wherein his power, however managed by art and skill, reaches no further than to compound and divide the materials that are made to his hand, but can do nothing towards the making the least particle of new matter, or destroying one atom of what is already in being. The same inability will everyone find in himself, who shall go about to fashion in his understanding any simple *idea*, not received in by his senses from external objects, or by reflection from the operations of his own mind about them. I would have anyone try to fancy any taste which had never affected his palate, or frame the *idea* of a scent he had never smelt; and when he can do this, I will also conclude that a blind man hath *ideas* of colours and a deaf man true distinct notions of sounds.

Chapter III

Of Ideas of One Sense

1. The better to conceive the *ideas* we receive from sensation, it may not be amiss for us to consider them in reference to the different ways whereby they make their approaches to our minds and make themselves perceivable by us.

First, then, There are some which come into our minds by *one sense* only.

Secondly, There are others that convey themselves into the mind *by more senses than one.*

Thirdly, Others that are had from *reflection* only.

Fourthly, There are some that make themselves way and are suggested to the mind *by all the ways of sensation and reflection.*

We shall consider them apart under these several heads.

First, There are *some* ideas *which have admittance only through one sense,* which is peculiarly adapted to receive them. Thus light and colours, as white, red, yellow, blue, with their several degrees or shades and mixtures, as green, scarlet, purple, sea-green, and the rest, come in only by the eyes. All kinds of noises, sounds, and tones, only by the ears. The several tastes and smells, by the nose and palate. And if these organs or the nerves which are the conduits to convey them from without to their audience in the brain, the mind's presence-room (as I may so call it), are any of them so disordered as not to perform their functions, they have no postern to be admitted by, no other way to bring themselves into view and be perceived by the understanding.

The most considerable of those belonging to the touch are heat and cold, and solidity; all the rest—consisting almost wholly in the sensible configuration, as smooth and rough; or else, more or less firm adhesion of the parts, as hard and soft, tough and brittle—are obvious enough.

Chapter V

Of Simple Ideas of Divers Senses

The *ideas* we get by more than one sense are of *space* or *extension, figure, rest,* and *motion.* For these make perceivable impressions, both on the eyes and touch; and we can receive and convey into our minds the *ideas* of the extension, figure, motion, and rest of bodies, both by seeing and feeling. But having occasion to speak more at large of these in another place, I here only enumerate them.

Chapter VI

Of Simple Ideas of Reflection

1. The mind, receiving the *ideas* mentioned in the foregoing chapters from without, when it turns its view inward upon itself and observes its own actions about those *ideas* it has, takes from thence other *ideas*, which are as capable to be the objects of its contemplation as any of those it received from foreign things.

2. The two great and principal actions of the mind, which are most frequently considered, and which are so frequent that everyone that pleases may take notice of them in himself, are these two:

Perception, or *Thinking;* and
Volition, or *Willing.*

The power of thinking is called the *understanding* and the power of volition is called the *will,* and these two powers or abilities in the mind are denominated *faculties.* Of some of the modes of these simple *ideas* of reflection, such as are *remembrance, discerning, reasoning, judging, knowledge, faith,* etc., I shall have occasion to speak hereafter.

Chapter VII

Of Simple Ideas of Both Sensation and Reflection

1. There be other simple *ideas* which convey themselves into the mind by all the ways of sensation and reflection, viz:

Pleasure or *Delight,* and its opposite.
Plain, or *Uneasiness.*
Power.
Existence.
Unity.

2. *Delight* or *uneasiness,* one or other of them, join themselves to almost all our *ideas* both of sensation and reflection: and there is scarce any affection of our senses from without, any retired thought of our mind within, which is not able to produce in us *pleasure* or *pain.* By *pleasure* and *pain* I would be understood to signify whatsoever delights or molests us, whether it arises from the thoughts of our minds, or anything operating on our bodies. For, whether we call it satisfaction, delight, pleasure, happiness, etc., on the one side, or uneasiness, trouble, pain, torment, anguish, misery, etc., on the other, they are still but different degrees of the same thing, and belong to the *ideas* of *pleasure* and *pain,* delight or uneasiness; which are the names I shall most commonly use for those two sorts of *ideas.*

7. *Existence* and *unity* are two other *ideas* that are suggested to the understanding by every object without, and every *idea* within. When *ideas* are in our minds, we consider them as being actually there, as well as we consider things to be actually without us; which is, that they exist or have *existence.* And whatever we can consider as one thing, whether a real being or *idea,* suggests to the understanding the *idea* of *unity.*

8. *Power* also is another of those simple *ideas* which we receive from *sensation and reflection.* For, observing in ourselves that we can at pleasure move several parts of our bodies which were at rest; the effects, also, that natural bodies are able to produce in one another occurring every moment to our senses, we both these ways get the *idea* of *power.*

9. Besides these there is another *idea,* which, though suggested by our senses, yet is more constantly offered us by what passes in our own minds, and that is the *idea* of *succession.* For if we look immediately into ourselves, and reflect on what is observable there, we shall find our *ideas* always, whilst we are awake or have any thought, passing in train, one going and another coming, without intermission.

10. These, if they are not all, are at least (as I think) the most considerable of those *simple ideas* which the mind has, and out of which is made all its other knowledge, all which it receives only by the two forementioned ways of *sensation* and *reflection.*

Nor let anyone think these too narrow bounds for the capacious mind of man to expatiate in, which takes its flight further than the stars and cannot be confined by the limits of the world, that extends its thought often even beyond the utmost expansion of matter, and makes excursions into that incomprehensible *inane*. I grant all this, but desire anyone to assign any *simple idea* which is not *received from* one of *those inlets* before mentioned, or any *complex idea* not *made out of those simple ones*. Nor will it be so strange to think these few simple *ideas* sufficient to employ the quickest thought or largest capacity, and to furnish the materials of all that various knowledge and more various fancies and opinions of all mankind, if we consider how many words may be made out of the various composition of twenty-four letters; or if, going one step further, we will but reflect on the variety of combinations that may be made with barely one of the above-mentioned *ideas, viz.* number, whose stock is inexhaustible and truly infinite; and what a large and immense field doth extension alone afford the mathematicians!

Chapter VIII

Some Further Considerations Concerning Our Simple Ideas

7. To discover the nature of our *ideas* the better, and to discourse of them intelligibly, it will be convenient to distinguish them as they are *ideas* or perceptions in our minds, and as they are modification of matter in the bodies that cause such perceptions in us: that so we *may not* think (as perhaps usually is done) that they are exactly the images and *resemblances* of something inherent in the subject: most of those of sensation being in the mind no more the likeness of something existing without us, than the names that stand for them are the likeness of our *ideas*, which yet upon hearing they are apt to excite in us.

8. Whatsoever the mind perceives in itself, or is the immediate object of perception, thought, or understanding, that I call *idea*; and the power to produce any *idea* in our mind, I call *quality* of the subject wherein that power is. Thus a snowball having the power to produce in us the *ideas* of *white, cold,* and *round,* the powers to produce those *ideas* in us as they are in the snowball I call *qualities;* and as they are sensations or perceptions in our understandings, I call them *ideas;* which *ideas,* if I speak of sometimes as in the things themselves, I would be understood to mean those qualities in the objects which produce them in us.

9. Qualities thus considered in bodies are:

First, such as are utterly inseparable from the body, in what state soever it be; such as in all the alterations and changes it suffers, all the force can be used upon it, it constantly keeps; and such as sense constantly finds in every particle of matter which has bulk enough to be perceived; and the mind finds inseparable from every particle of matter, though less than to make itself singly be perceived by our senses. V.g., take a grain of wheat, divide it into two parts, each part has still *solidity, extension, figure,* and *mobility;* divide it again, and it retains still the same qualities; and so divide it on, till the parts become insensible: they must retain still each of them all those qualities. For division (which is all that a mill or pestle or any other body does upon another in reducing it to insensible parts) can never take away either solidity, extension, figure, or mobility from any body, but only makes two or more distinct separate masses of matter, of that which was but one before; all which distinct masses, reckoned as so many distinct bodies, after division make a certain number. These I call *original* or *primary qualities* of body; which I think we may observe to produce simple *ideas* in us, viz. solidity, extension, figure, motion or rest, and number.

10. Secondly, such *qualities* which in truth are nothing in the objects themselves but powers to produce various sensations in us by their *primary qualities,* i.e. by the bulk, figure, texture, and motion of their insensible parts, as colours, sounds, tastes, etc. These I call *secondary qualities*. To these might be added a third sort, which are allowed to be barely powers, though they are as much real qualities in the subject as those which I, to comply with the common way of speaking, call *qualities,* but for distinction, *secondary qualities*. For the power in fire to produce a new colour, or consistency in wax or clay, by its primary qualities, is as much a quality in fire as the power it has to produce in me a new *idea* or sensation of warmth or burning, which I felt not before, by the same primary qualities, viz. the bulk, texture, and motion of its insensible parts.

11. The next thing to be considered is how *bodies* produce *ideas* in us; and that is manifestly by *impulse,* the only way which we can conceive bodies operate in.

12. If then external objects be not united to our minds when they produce *ideas* in it and yet we per-

ceive *these original qualities* in such of them as singly fall under our senses, it is evident that some motion must be thence continued by our nerves or animal spirits, by some parts of our bodies, to the brains or the seat of sensation, there to *produce in our minds the particular* ideas *we have of them*. And since the extension, figure, number, and motion of bodies of an observable bigness may be perceived at a distance *by the sight*, it is evident some singly imperceptible bodies must come from them to the eyes, and thereby convey to the brain some *motion*, which produces these *ideas* which we have of them in us.

13. After the same manner that the *ideas* of these original qualities are produced in us, we may conceive that the *ideas of secondary qualities* are also *produced*, viz. *by the operation of insensible particles on our senses*. For it being manifest that there are bodies and good store of bodies, each whereof are so small that we cannot by any of our senses discover either their bulk, figure, or motion, as is evident in the particles of the air and water and others extremely smaller than those, perhaps as much smaller than the particles of air or water as the particles of air or water are smaller than peas or hail-stones: let us suppose at present that the different motions and figures, bulk and number, of such particles, affecting the several organs of our senses, produce in us those different sensations which we have from the colours and smells of bodies: v.g. that a violet, by the impulse of such insensible particles of matter, of peculiar figures and bulks, and in different degrees and modifications of their motions, causes the *ideas* of the blue colour and sweet scent of that flower to be produced in our minds. It being no more impossible to conceive that God should annex such *ideas* to such motions, with which they have no similitude, than that he should annex the *idea* of pain to the motion of a piece of steel dividing our flesh, with which that *idea* hath no resemblance.

14. What I have said concerning *colours* and *smells* may be understood also of *tastes* and *sounds, and other the like sensible qualities;* which, whatever reality we by mistake attribute to them, are in truth nothing in the objects themselves but powers to produce various sensations in us, and depend *on those primary qualities*, viz. bulk, figure, texture, and motion of parts, as I have said.

15. From whence I think it easy to draw this observation: that the *ideas of primary qualities* of bodies *are resemblances* of them, and their patterns do really exist in the bodies themselves; but the *ideas produced* in us *by* these *secondary qualities have no resemblance* of them at all. There is nothing like our *ideas* existing in the bodies themselves. They are, in the bodies we denominate from them, only a power to produce those sensations in us; and what is sweet, blue, or warm in *idea* is but the certain bulk, figure, and motion of the insensible parts in the bodies themselves, which we call so.

16. *Flame* is denominated *hot* and *light; snow, white* and *cold;* and *manna, white* and *sweet*, from the *ideas* they produce in us. Which qualities are commonly thought to be the same in those bodies that those *ideas* are in us, the one the perfect resemblance of the other, as they are in a mirror, and it would by most men be judged very extravagant if one should say otherwise. And yet he that will consider that *the same fire* that at one distance *produces* in us the sensation of *warmth* does, at a nearer approach, produce in us the far different sensation of *pain*, ought to bethink himself what reason he has to say that his *idea* of *warmth*, which was produced in him by the fire, is actually *in the fire;* and his *idea of pain*, which the same fire produced in him the same way, is *not* in the fire. Why are whiteness and coldness in snow, and pain not, when it produces the one and the other *idea* in us; and can do neither, but by the bulk, figure, number, and motion of its solid parts?

17. The particular *bulk, number, figure, and motion of the parts of fire or snow are really in them*, whether anyone's senses perceive them or no; and therefore they may be called *real qualities*, because they really exist in those bodies. But *light, heat, whiteness*, or *coldness are no more really in them than sickness or pain is in* manna. Take away the sensation of them; let not the eyes see light or colours, nor the ears hear sounds; let the palate not taste, nor the nose smell; and all colours, tastes, odours, and sounds, as they are such particular *ideas*, vanish and cease, and are reduced to their causes, i.e. bulk, figure, and motion of parts.

18. A piece of *manna* of a sensible bulk is able to produce in us the *idea* of a round or square figure; and by being removed from one place to another, the

idea of motion. This *idea* of motion represents it as it really is in the *manna* moving; a circle or square are the same, whether in *idea* or existence, in the mind or in the *manna*; and this, both *motion and figure, are really in the manna,* whether we take notice of them or no: this everybody is ready to agree to. Besides, *manna,* by the bulk, figure, texture, and motion of its parts, has a power to produce the sensations of sickness, and sometimes of acute pains or gripings in us. That these *ideas* of *sickness and pain are not in the* manna, but effects of its operations on us, and are nowhere when we feel them not: this also everyone readily agrees to. And yet men are hardly to be brought to think that *sweetness and whiteness are not really in manna,* which are but the effects of the operations of *manna,* by the motion, size, and figure of its particles, on the eyes and palate, as the pain and sickness caused by *manna* are confessedly nothing but the effects of its operations on the stomach and guts, by the size, motion, and figure of its insensible parts (for by nothing else can a body operate, as has been proved). . . .

These *ideas* being all effects of the operations of *manna* on several parts of our bodies by the size, figure, number, and motion of its parts, why those produced by the eyes and palate should rather be thought to be really in the *manna* than those produced by the stomach and guts; or why the pain and sickness, *ideas* that are the effects of *manna,* should be thought to be nowhere, when they are not felt: and yet the sweetness and whiteness, effects of the same *manna* on other parts of the body by ways equally as unknown, should be thought to exist in the *manna,* when they are not seen nor tasted, would need some reason to explain.

19. Let us consider the red and white colours in *porphyry.* Hinder light but from striking on it, and its colours vanish: it no longer produces any such *ideas* in us; upon the return of light it produces these appearances on us again. Can anyone think any real alterations are made in the *porphyry* by the presence or absence of light; and that those *ideas* of whiteness and redness are really in *porphyry* in the light, when it is plain *it has no colour in the dark?* It has, indeed, such a configuration of particles, both night and day, as are apt, by the rays of light rebounding from some parts of that hard stone, to produce in us the *idea* of

redness, and from others the *idea* of whiteness; but whiteness or redness are not in it at any time, but such a texture that hath the power to produce such a sensation in us.

20. Pound an almond, and the clear white *colour* will be altered into a dirty one, and the sweet *taste* into an oily one. What real alteration can the beating of the pestle make in any body, but an alteration of the *texture* of it?

21. *Ideas* being thus distinguished and understood, we may be able to give an account how the same water, at the same time, may produce the *idea* of cold by one hand and of heat by the other, whereas it is impossible that the same water, if those *ideas* were really in it, should at the same time be both hot and cold. For if we imagine *warmth* as it is *in our hands* to be *nothing but a certain sort and degree of motion in the minute particles of our nerves, or animal spirits,* we may understand how it is possible that the same water may at the same time produce the sensation of heat in one hand and cold in the other; which yet figure never does, that never producing the *idea* of a square by one hand which has produced the *idea* of a globe by another. But if the sensation of heat and cold be nothing but the increase or diminution of the motion of the minute parts of our bodies, caused by the corpuscles of any other body, it is easy to be understood that, if that motion be greater in one hand than in the other, if a body be applied to the two hands, which has in its minute particles a greater motion than in those of one of the hands, and a less than in those of the other, it will increase the motion of the one hand and lessen it in the other, and so cause the different sensations of heat and cold that depend thereon.

22. I have in what just goes before been engaged in physical inquiries a little further than perhaps I intended. But, it being necessary to make the nature of sensation a little understood; and to make the *difference between the qualities in bodies, and the* ideas *produced by them in the mind,* to be distinctly conceived, without which it were impossible to discourse intelligibly of them: I hope I shall be pardoned this little excursion into natural philosophy, it being necessary in our present inquiry to distinguish the *primary* and *real qualities* of bodies, which are always in them (viz. solidity, extension, figure, number, and motion or rest; and are sometimes perceived by us, viz. when the bodies they are in are big enough singly to be discerned), from those *secondary* and *imputed qualities*, which are but the powers of several combinations of those primary ones, when they operate without being distinctly discerned; whereby we also may come to know what *ideas* are, and what are not, resemblances of something really existing in the bodies we denominate from them.

23. The *qualities*, then, that are in *bodies*, rightly considered, are of *three sorts:*

First, The *bulk, figure, number, situation,* and *motion or rest* of their solid parts. Those are in them, whether we perceive them or no; and when they are of that size that we can discover them, we have by these an *idea* of the thing as it is in itself, as is plain in artificial things. These I call *primary qualities*.

Secondly, The *power* that is in any body, by reason of *its* insensible *primary qualities*, to operate after a peculiar manner on any of our senses, and thereby *produce in us* the *different ideas* of several colours, sounds, smells, tastes, etc. These are usually called sensible qualities.

Thirdly, The *power* that is in any body, *by* reason of the particular constitution of *its primary qualities, to* make such a *change* in the *bulk, figure, texture, and motion of another body,* as to make it operate on our senses differently from what it did before. Thus the sun has a power to make wax white, and fire to make lead fluid. These *are* usually called powers.

The first of these, as has been said, I think may be properly called *real, original,* or *primary qualities,* because they are in the things themselves, whether they are perceived or no; and upon their different modifications it is that the secondary qualities depend.

The other two are only powers to act differently upon other things, which powers result from the different modifications of those primary qualities.

24. But though *these two latter sorts of qualities are powers barely,* and nothing but powers relating to several other bodies and resulting from the different modifications of the original qualities, yet they are generally otherwise thought of. For *the second sort,* viz. the powers to produce several *ideas* in us by our senses, *are looked upon as real qualities in the things* thus affecting us; but *the third sort are called and esteemed barely powers,* v.g. the *idea* of heat or light which we

receive by our eyes or touch from the sun are commonly thought *real qualities* existing in the sun and something more than mere powers in it. But when we consider the sun in reference to wax, which it melts or blanches, we look upon the whiteness and softness produced in the wax not as qualities in the sun but effects produced by *powers* in it: whereas, if rightly considered, these qualities of light and warmth, which are perceptions in me when I am warmed or enlightened by the sun, are no otherwise in the sun than the changes, made in the wax when it is blanched or melted, are in the sun. They are all of them equally powers in the sun, depending on its primary qualities; whereby it is able in the one case so to alter the bulk, figure, texture, or motion of some of the insensible parts of my eyes or hands as thereby to produce in me the *idea* of light or heat; and in the other, it is able so to alter the bulk, figure, texture, or motion of the insensible parts of the wax, as to make them fit to produce in me the distinct *ideas* of white and fluid.

25. The reason *why the one are ordinarily taken for real qualities and the other only for bare powers* seems to be because the *ideas* we have of distinct colours, sounds, etc., containing nothing at all in them of bulk, figure, or motion, we are not apt to think them the effects of these primary qualities which appear not to our senses to operate in their production, and with which they have not any apparent congruity or conceivable connexion. Hence it is that we are so forward to imagine that those *ideas* are the resemblances of something really existing in the objects themselves, since sensation discovers nothing of bulk, figure, or motion of parts in their production, nor can reason show how bodies by their bulk, figure, and motion should produce in the mind the *ideas* of blue or yellow, etc. But in the other case, in the operations of bodies changing the qualities one of another, we plainly discover that the quality produced hath commonly no resemblance with anything in the thing producing it; wherefore we look on it as a bare effect of power. For, though receiving the *idea* of heat or light from the sun, we are apt to think it is a perception and resemblance of such a quality in the sun: yet when we see wax or a fair face receive change of colour from the sun, we cannot imagine that to be the reception or resemblance of anything in the sun, because we find not those different colours in the sun itself. For, our senses being able to observe a likeness or unlikeness of sensible qualities in two different external objects, we forwardly enough conclude the production of any sensible quality in any subject to be an effect of bare power, and not the communication of any quality which was really in the efficient, when we find no such sensible quality in the thing that produced it. But our senses not being able to discover any unlikeness between the *idea* produced in us and the quality of the object producing it, we are apt to imagine that our *ideas* are resemblances of something in the objects, and not the effects of certain powers placed in the modification of their primary qualities, with which primary qualities the *ideas* produced in us have no resemblance.

Chapter IX

Of Perception

1. PERCEPTION, as it is the first faculty of the mind exercised about our *ideas,* so it is the first and simplest *idea* we have from reflection, and is by some called thinking in general. Though thinking, in the propriety of the *English* tongue, signifies that sort of operation in the mind about its *ideas,* wherein the mind is active, where it, with some degree of voluntary attention, considers anything. For in bare naked *perception,* the mind is, for the most part, only passive; and what it perceives, it cannot avoid perceiving.

2. *What perception is,* everyone will know better by reflecting on what he does himself, when he sees, hears, feels, etc., or thinks, than by any discourse of mine. Whoever reflects on what passes in his own mind cannot miss it. And if he does not reflect, all the words in the world cannot make him have any notion of it.

3. This is certain: that whatever alterations are made in the body, if they reach not the mind; whatever impressions are made on the outward parts, if they are not taken notice of within, there is no perception. Fire may burn our bodies with no other effect than it does a billet, unless the motion be continued to the brain, and there the sense of heat, or *idea* of pain, be produced in the mind; wherein consists *actual perception.*

4. How often may a man observe in himself that, whilst his mind is intently employed in the contemplation of some objects, and curiously surveying some *ideas* that are there, it takes no notice of impressions of sounding bodies made upon the organ of hearing, with the same alteration that used to be for the producing the idea of sound. A sufficient impulse there may be on the organ, but it not reaching the observation of the mind, there follows no perception; and though the motion that used to produce the *idea* of sound be made in the ear, yet no sound is heard. Want of sensation, in this case, is not through any defect in the organ, or that the man's ears are less affected than at other times when he does hear: but that which used to produce the *idea,* though conveyed in by the usual organ, not being taken notice of in the understanding, and so imprinting no *idea* on the mind, there follows no sensation. *So that wherever there is sense or perception, there some idea is actually produced, and present in the understanding.*

8. We are further to consider concerning perception that the *ideas we receive by sensation are often* in grown people *altered by the judgment,* without our taking notice of it. When we set before our eyes a round globe of any uniform colour, v.g. gold, alabaster, or jet, it is certain that the *idea* thereby imprinted in our mind is of a flat circle, variously shadowed, with several degrees of light and brightness coming to our eyes. But we having, by use, been accustomed to perceive what kind of appearance convex bodies are wont to make in us, what alterations are made in the reflections of light by the difference of the sensible figures of bodies: the judgment presently, by an habitual custom, alters the appearances into their causes. So that from that which truly is variety of shadow or colour, collecting the figure, it makes it pass for a mark of figure and frames to itself the perception of a convex figure and an uniform colour, when the *idea* we receive from thence is only a plane variously coloured, as is evident in painting. To which purpose I shall here insert a problem of that very ingenious and studious promoter of real knowledge, the learned and worthy Mr. *Molyneux,* which he was pleased to send me in a letter some months since; and it is this: *Suppose a man born blind, and now adult, and taught by his touch to distinguish between a cube and a sphere of the same metal, and* *nighly of the same bigness, so as to tell, when he felt one and the other, which is the cube, which the sphere. Suppose then the cube and sphere placed on a table, and the blind man to be made to see:* quaere, *whether by his sight, before he touched them, he could now distinguish and tell which is the globe, which the cube?* To which the acute and judicious proposer answers: *Not. For, though he has obtained the experience of how a globe, how a cube affects his touch, yet he has not yet obtained the experience that what affects his touch so or so must affect his sight so or so; or that a protuberant angle in the cube, that pressed his hand unequally, shall appear to his eye as it does in the cube.* I agree with this thinking gentleman, whom I am proud to call my friend, in his answer to this problem; and am of opinion that the blind man, at first sight, would not be able with certainty to say which was the globe, which the cube, whilst he only saw them, though he could unerringly name them by his touch, and certainly distinguish them by the difference of their figures felt. This I have set down and leave with my reader as an occasion for him to consider how much he may be beholding to experience, improvement, and acquired notions, where he thinks he has not the least use of or help from them; and the rather, because this observing *gentleman* further adds that, *having upon the occasion of my book proposed this to divers very ingenious men, he hardly ever met with one that at first gave the answer to it which he thinks true, till by hearing his reasons they were convinced.*

Of discerning, and other operations of the mind

4. The COMPARING them one with another, in respect of extent, degrees, time, place, or any other circumstances, is another operation of the mind about its *ideas,* and is that upon which depends all that large tribe of *ideas* comprehended under *relation;* which, of how vast an extent it is, I shall have occasion to consider hereafter.

6. The next operation we may observe in the mind about its *ideas* is COMPOSITION, whereby it puts together several of those simple ones it has received from sensation and reflection, and combines them into complex ones. Under this of composition may be reckoned also that of ENLARGING, wherein, though the composition does not so much appear as in more complex ones, yet it is nevertheless a putting several

ideas together, though of the same kind. Thus, by adding several units together, we make the *idea* of a dozen; and putting together the repeated *ideas* of several perches, we frame that of furlong.

9. The use of words then being to stand as outward marks of our internal *ideas,* and those *ideas* being taken from particular things, if every particular *idea* that we take in should have a distinct name, names must be endless. To prevent this, the mind makes the particular *ideas* received from particular objects to become general; which is done by considering them as they are in the mind such appearances, separate from all other existence and the circumstances of real existence, as time, place, or any other concomitant *ideas.* This is called ABSTRACTION, whereby *ideas* taken from particular beings become general representatives of all of the same kind; and their names, general names, applicable to whatever exists conformable to such abstract *ideas.* Such precise, naked appearances in the mind, without considering how, whence, or with what others they came there, the understanding lays up (with names commonly annexed to them) as the standards to rank real existences into sorts, as they agree with these patterns, and to *denominate* them accordingly. Thus the same colour being observed to-day in chalk or snow, which the mind yesterday received from milk, it considers that appearance alone, makes it a representative of all of that kind; and having given it the name *whiteness,* it by that sound signifies the same quality wheresoever to be imagined or met with; and thus universals, whether *ideas* or terms, are made.

Chapter XII

Of Complex Ideas

1. We have hitherto considered those *ideas* in the reception whereof the mind is only passive, which are those simple ones received from *sensation* and *reflection* before mentioned, whereof the mind cannot make one to itself, nor have any *idea* which does not wholly consist of them. But as the mind is wholly passive in the reception of all its simple *ideas,* so it exerts several acts of its own whereby out of its simple *ideas,* as the materials and foundations of the rest, the others are framed. The acts of the mind, wherein it exerts its power over its simple *ideas,* are chiefly these three:

(1) Combining several simple *ideas* into one compound one; and thus all complex *ideas* are made. (2) The second is bringing two *ideas*, whether simple or complex, together, and setting them by one another, so as to take a view of them at once, without uniting them into one; by which way it gets all its *ideas* of relations. (3) The third is separating them from all other *ideas* that accompany them in their real existence: this is called *abstraction;* and thus all its general *ideas* are made. This shows man's power, and its way of operation, to be much the same in the material and intellectual world. For the materials in both being such as he has no power over either to make or destroy, all that man can do is either to unite them together, or to set them by one another, or wholly separate them. I shall here begin with the first of these in the consideration of complex *ideas,* and come to the other two in their due places. As simple *ideas* are observed to exist in several combinations united together, so the mind has a power to consider several of them united together as one *idea,* and that not only as they are united in external objects, but as itself has joined them. *Ideas* thus made up of several simple ones put together, I call *complex,* such as are *beauty, gratitude, a man, an army, the universe;* which, though complicated of various simple *ideas,* or complex *ideas* made up of simple ones, yet are, when the mind pleases, considered each by itself as one entire thing, and signified by one name.

2. In this faculty of repeating and joining together its *ideas,* the mind has great power in varying and multiplying the objects of its thoughts, infinitely beyond what *sensation* or *reflection* furnished it with, but all this still confined to those simple *ideas* which it received from those two sources, and which are the ultimate materials of all its compositions. For simple *ideas* are all from things themselves, and of these *the mind can* have no more, nor other than what are suggested to it. It can have no other *ideas* of sensible qualities than what come from without by the senses; nor any *ideas* of other kind of operations of a thinking substance, than what it finds in itself. But when it has once got these simple *ideas* it is not confined barely to observation and what offers itself from without: it can, by its own power, put together those *ideas* it has and *make new complex ones,* which it never received so united.

3. *Complex ideas,* however compounded and decompounded, though their number be infinite and the variety endless wherewith fill and entertain the thoughts of men, yet I think they may be all reduced under these three heads:

1. *Modes.*
2. *Substances.*
3. *Relations.*

4. First, Modes I call such complex *ideas* which, however compounded, contain not in them the supposition of subsisting by themselves, but are considered as dependences on, or affections of substances; such are the *ideas* signified by the words *triangle, gratitude, murder,* etc. And if in this I use the word *mode* in somewhat a different sense from its ordinary signification, I beg pardon: it being unavoidable in discourses differing from the ordinary received notions either to make new words or to use old words in somewhat a new signification, the latter whereof in our present case is perhaps the more tolerable of the two.

5. Of these *modes,* there are two sorts which deserve distinct consideration: First, there are some which are only variations, or different combinations of the same simple *idea,* without the mixture of any other, as a dozen, or score; which are nothing but the *ideas* of so many distinct units added together; and these I call *simple modes* as being contained within the bounds of one simple *idea.* Secondly, there are others compounded of simple *ideas* of several kinds, put together to make one complex one: v.g. *beauty,* consisting of a certain composition of colour and figure, causing delight in the beholder; *theft,* which being the concealed change of the possession of anything, without the consent of the proprietor, contains, as is visible, a combination of several *ideas* of several kinds: and these I call *mixed modes.*

6. Secondly, the *ideas* of *substances* are such combinations of simple *ideas* as are taken to represent distinct particular things subsisting by themselves, in which the supposed or confused *idea* of substance, such as it is, is always the first and chief. Thus if to substance be joined the simple *idea* of a certain dull whitish colour, with certain degrees of weight, hardness, ductility, and fusibility, we have the *idea* of *lead;* and a combination of the *ideas* of a certain sort of figure, with the powers of motion, thought, and reasoning, joined to substance, make the ordinary *idea* of *a man*. Now of substances also, there are two sorts of *ideas*: one of single substances, as they exist separately, as of *a man* or *a sheep*; the other of several of those put together, as an *army* of men, or *flock* of sheep; which *collective* ideas *of* several *substances* thus put together are as much each of them one single *idea* as that of a man or an unit.

7. Thirdly, the last sort of complex *ideas* is that we call *relation*, which consists in the consideration and comparing one *idea* with another.

Of these several kinds we shall treat in their order.

8. If we will trace the progress of our minds, and with attention observe how it repeats, adds together, and unites its simple *ideas* received from sensation or reflection, it will lead us further than at first perhaps we should have imagined. And I believe we shall find, if we warily observe the originals of our notions, that even *the most abstruse ideas,* how remote soever they may seem from sense, or from any operation of our own minds, are yet only such as the understanding frames to itself, by repeating and joining together *ideas* that it had either from objects of sense, or from its own operations about them: so that those even large *and abstract* ideas *are derived from sensation or reflection,* being no other than what the mind, by the ordinary use of its own faculties, employed about *ideas* received from objects of sense or from the operations it observes in itself about them, may and does attain unto. This I shall endeavour to show in the *ideas* we have of *space*, *time*, and *infinity*, and some few other that seem the most remote from those originals.

Chapter XXI

Of Power

1. The mind—being every day informed by the senses of the alteration of those simple *ideas* it observes in things without; and taking notice how one comes to an end, and ceases to be, and another begins to exist which was not before; reflecting also on what passes within itself, and observing a constant change of its *ideas*, sometimes by the impression of outward objects on the senses, and sometimes by the determination of its own choice; and concluding

from what it has so constantly observed to have been, that the like changes will for the future be made in the same things, by like agents, and by the like ways—considers in one thing the possibility of having any of its simple *ideas* changed, and in another the possibility of making that change; and so comes by that *idea* which we call *power*. Thus we say fire has a *power* to melt gold, i.e. to destroy the consistency of its insensible parts, and consequently its hardness, and make it fluid; and gold has a *power* to be melted; that the sun has a *power* to blanch wax, and wax a *power* to be blanched by the sun, whereby the yellowness is destroyed, and whiteness made to exist in its room. In which, and the like cases, the *power* we consider is in reference to the change of perceivable *ideas*. For we cannot observe any alteration to be made in, or operation upon anything, but by the observable change of its sensible *ideas*, nor conceive any alteration to be made but by conceiving a change of some of its *ideas*.

2. *Power* thus considered is two-fold, viz. as able to make, or able to receive, any change; the one may be called *active,* and the other *passive power.* Whether matter be not wholly destitute of *active power*, as its author GOD is truly above all *passive power*, and whether the intermediate state of created spirits be not that alone which is capable of both *active* and *passive* power, may be worth consideration. I shall not now enter into that inquiry, my present business being not to search into the original of power but how we come by the *idea* of it. But since *active powers* make so great a part of our complex *ideas* of natural substances (as we shall see hereafter) and I mention them as such according to common apprehension, yet they being not, perhaps, so truly *active powers* as our hasty thoughts are apt to represent them, I judge it not amiss, by this intimation, to direct our minds to the consideration of GOD and spirits for the clearest *idea* of *active power.*

3. I confess *power includes in it some kind of relation* (a relation to action or change), as indeed which of our *ideas*, of what kind soever, when attentively considered, does not? For our *ideas* of extension, duration, and number, do they not all contain in them a secret relation of the parts? Figure and motion have something relative in them much more visibly; and sensible qualities, as colours and smells, etc., what are

they but the *powers* of different bodies in relation to our perception, etc.? And, if considered in the things themselves, do they not depend on the bulk, figure, texture, and motion of the parts? All which include some kind of relation in them. Our *idea* therefore of *power*, I think, may well have a place amongst other simple *ideas* and be considered as one of them, being one of those that make a principal ingredient in our complex *ideas* of substances, as we shall hereafter have occasion to observe.

4. We are abundantly furnished with the *idea* of *passive power* by almost all sorts of sensible things. In most of them we cannot avoid observing their sensible qualities, nay, their very substances, to be in a continual flux; and therefore with reason we look on them as liable still to the same change. Nor have we of *active power* (which is the more proper signification of the word *power*) fewer instances. Since whatever change is observed, the mind must collect a power somewhere able to make that change, as well as a possibility in the thing itself to receive it. But yet, if we will consider it attentively, bodies, by our senses, do not afford us so clear and distinct an *idea* of *active power*, as we have from reflection on the operations of our minds. For all *power* relating to action, and there being but two sorts of action whereof we have any *idea,* viz. thinking and motion, let us consider whence we have the clearest *ideas* of the *powers* which produce these actions. (1) Of thinking, body affords us no *idea* at all; it is only from reflection that we have that. (2) Neither have we from body any *idea* of the beginning of motion. A body at rest affords us no *idea* of any *active power* to move; and when it is set in motion itself, that motion is rather a passion than an action in it. For, when the ball obeys the stroke of a billiard stick, it is not any action of the ball, but bare passion; also when by impulse it sets another ball in motion that lay in its way, it only communicates the motion it had received from another, and loses in itself so much as the other received: which gives us but a very obscure *idea* of an *active power* of moving in body, whilst we observe it only to transfer, but not produce, any motion. For it is but a very obscure *idea* of *power* which reaches not the production of the action but the continuation of the passion. For so is motion in a body impelled by another, the continuation of the

alteration made in it from rest to motion being little more an action than the continuation of the alteration of its figure by the same blow is an action. The *idea* of the beginning of motion we have only from reflection on what passes in ourselves, where we find by experience that barely by willing it, barely by a thought of the mind, we can move the parts of our bodies which were before at rest. So that it seems to me we have from the observation of the operation of bodies by our senses but a very imperfect obscure *idea* of *active power*, since they afford us not any *idea* in themselves of the *power* to begin any action, either motion or thought. But if, from the impulse bodies are observed to make one upon another, anyone thinks he has a clear *idea* of *power*, it serves as well to my purpose, *sensation* being one of those ways whereby the mind comes by its *ideas;* only I thought it worthwhile to consider here by the way whether the mind doth not receive its *idea* of *active power* clearer from reflection on its own operations than it doth from any external sensation.

5. This, at least, I think evident: that we find in ourselves a *power* to begin or forbear, continue or end several actions of our minds and motions of our bodies, barely by a thought or preference of the mind ordering or, as it were commanding, the doing or not doing such or such a particular action. This *power* which the mind has thus to order the consideration of any *idea,* or the forbearing to consider it, or to prefer the motion of any part of the body to its rest, and *vice versa*, in any particular instance, is that which we call the *will*. The actual exercise of that power, by directing any particular action, or its forbearance, is that which we call *volition* or *willing*. The forbearance of that action, consequent to such order or command of the mind, is called *voluntary*. And whatsoever action is performed without such a thought of the mind is called *involuntary*. The power of perception is that which we call the *understanding*. Perception, which we make the act of the understanding, is of three sorts: (1) The perception of *ideas* in our minds. (2) The perception of the signification of signs. (3) The perception of the connexion or repugnancy, agreement or disagreement, that there is between any of our *ideas*. All these are attributed to the *understanding* or perceptive power, though it be the two latter only that use allows us to say we understand.

6. These powers of the mind, viz. of *perceiving* and of *preferring*, are usually called by another name; and the ordinary way of speaking is that the *understanding* and *will* are two *faculties* of the mind: a word proper enough, if it be used, as all words should be, so as not to breed any confusion in men's thoughts, by being supposed (as I suspect it has been) to stand for some real beings in the soul that performed those actions of understanding and volition. For when we say the *will* is the commanding and superior faculty of the soul; that it is or is not free; that it determines the inferior faculties; that it follows the dictates of the *understanding*, etc.; though these and the like expressions, by those that carefully attend to their own *ideas* and conduct their thoughts more by the evidence of things than the sound of words, may be understood in a clear and distinct sense: yet I suspect, I say, that this way of speaking of *faculties* has misled many into a confused notion of so many distinct agents in us, which had their several provinces and authorities and did command, obey, and perform several actions, as so many distinct beings; which has been no small occasion of wrangling, obscurity, and uncertainty in questions relating to them.

7. Everyone, I think, finds in himself a *power* to begin or forbear, continue or put an end to several actions in himself. From the consideration of the extent of this power of the mind over the actions of the man, which everyone finds in himself, arise the *ideas* of *liberty* and *necessity*.

8. All the actions that we have any *idea* of, reducing themselves, as has been said, to these two, viz. thinking and motion: so far as a man has a power to think or not to think, to move or not to move, according to the preference or direction of his own mind, so far is a man *free*. Wherever any performance or forbearance are not equally in a man's power, wherever doing or not doing will not equally follow upon the preference of his mind directing it, there he is not *free*, though perhaps the action may be voluntary. So that the *idea* of *liberty* is the *idea* of a power in any agent to do or forbear any particular action, according to the determination or thought of the mind, whereby either of them is preferred to the other; where either of them is not in the power of the agent to be produced by him according to his *volition*, there he is not at *liberty*: that agent is under *necessity*. So that *liberty* cannot be where there is no thought, no

volition, no will; but there may be thought, there may be will, there may be volition, where there is no *liberty*. A little consideration of an obvious instance or two may make this clear.

9. A tennis ball, whether in motion by the stroke of a racket, or lying still at rest, is not by anyone taken to be a *free agent*. If we inquire into the reason, we shall find it is because we conceive not a tennis ball to think, and consequently not to have any volition, or preference of motion to rest, or *vice versa*; and therefore has not *liberty,* is not a free agent; but all its both motion and rest come under our *idea* of *necessary*, and are so called. Likewise, a man falling into the water (a bridge breaking under him) has not herein liberty, is not a free agent. For though he has volition, though he prefers his not falling to falling, yet the forbearance of that motion not being in his power, the stop or cessation of that motion follows not upon his volition; and therefore therein he is not *free*. So a man striking himself or his friend by a convulsive motion of his arm, which it is not in his power by volition or the direction of his mind to stop or forbear, nobody thinks he has in this *liberty*; everyone pities him as acting by necessity and constraint.

10. Again, suppose a man be carried whilst fast asleep into a room where is a person he longs to see and speak with, and be there locked fast in, beyond his power to get out; he awakes and is glad to find himself in so desirable company, which he stays willingly in, i.e. prefers his stay to going away. I ask, is not this stay voluntary? I think nobody will doubt it; and yet being locked fast in, it is evident he is not at liberty not to stay, he has not freedom to be gone. So that *liberty is not an* idea *belonging to volition*, or preferring, but to the person having the power of doing or forbearing to do, according as the mind shall choose or direct. Our *idea* of liberty reaches as far as that power and no further. For wherever restraint comes to check that power, or compulsion takes away that indifferency of ability on either side to act or to forbear acting, there *liberty* and our notion of it, presently ceases.

11. We have instances enough and often more than enough in our own bodies. A man's heart beats and the blood circulates, which it is not in his power by any thought or volition to stop; and therefore in respect of these motions, where rest depends not on his choice nor would follow the determination of his mind if it should prefer it, he is not a *free agent*. Convulsive motions agitate his legs so that, though he *wills* it never so much, he cannot by any power of his mind stop their motion (as in that odd disease called *chorea Sancti Viti*), but he is perpetually dancing; he is not at liberty in this action but under as much necessity of moving as a stone that falls or a tennis ball struck with a racket. On the other side, a palsy or the stocks hinder his legs from obeying the determination of his mind if it would thereby transfer his body to another place. In all these there is want of *freedom*, though the sitting still even of a paralytic, whilst he prefers it to a removal, is truly voluntary. *Voluntary* then *is not opposed to necessary, but to involuntary*. For a man may prefer what he can do to what he cannot do; the state he is in, to its absence or change, though necessity has made it in itself unalterable.

12. As it is in the motions of the body, so it is in the thoughts of our minds: where anyone is such that we have power to take it up, or lay it by, according to the preference of the mind, there we are *at liberty*. A waking man, being under the necessity of having some *ideas* constantly in his mind, is not at *liberty* to think or not to think, no more than he is at *liberty* whether his body shall touch any other or no; but whether he will remove his contemplation from one *idea* to another is many times in his choice, and then he is, in respect of his *ideas*, as much at *liberty* as he is in respect of bodies he rests on; he can at pleasure remove himself from one to another. But yet some *ideas* to the mind, like some motions to the body, are such as in certain circumstances it cannot avoid, nor obtain their absence by the utmost effort it can use. A man on the rack is not at *liberty* to lay by the *idea* of pain, and divert himself with other contemplations; and sometimes a boisterous passion hurries our thoughts, as a hurricane does our bodies, without leaving us the liberty of thinking on other things, which we would rather choose. But as soon as the mind regains the power to stop or continue, begin or forbear any of these motions of the body without, or thoughts within, according as it thinks fit to prefer either to the other, we then consider the man as a *free agent* again.

13. Wherever thought is wholly wanting or the power to act or forbear according to the direction of thought, there *necessity* takes place. This, in an agent capable of volition when the beginning or continua-

tion of any action is contrary to that preference of his mind, is called *compulsion*; when the hindering or stopping any action is contrary to his volition, it is called *restraint*. Agents that have no thought, no volition at all, are in everything *necessary* agents.

14. If this be so (as I imagine it is), I leave it to be considered whether it may not help to put an end to that long agitated and, I think, unreasonable because unintelligible, question, viz. *whether man's will be free or no*. For if I mistake not, it follows from what I have said that the question itself is altogether improper; and it is as insignificant to ask whether man's *will* be free, as to ask whether his sleep be swift, or his virtue square: *liberty* being as little applicable to the *will*, as swiftness of motion is to sleep, or squareness to virtue. Everyone would laugh at the absurdity of such a question as either of these, because it is obvious that the modifications of motion belong not to sleep, nor the difference of figure to virtue; and when anyone well considers it, I think he will as plainly perceive that *liberty*, which is but a power, belongs only to agents and cannot be an attribute or modification of the *will*, which is also but a power.

15. Such is the difficulty of explaining and giving clear notions of internal actions by sounds that I must here warn my reader that *ordering, directing, choosing, preferring*, etc., which I have made use of, will not distinctly enough express *volition*, unless he will reflect on what he himself does when he *wills*. For example, *preferring*, which seems perhaps best to express the act of *volition*, does it not precisely. For though a man would prefer flying to walking, yet who can say he ever *wills* it? *Volition*, it is plain, is an act of the mind knowingly exerting that dominion it takes itself to have over any part of the man, by employing it in, or withholding it from, any particular action. And what is the *will* but the faculty to do this? And is that faculty anything more in effect than a power, the power of the mind to determine its thought to the producing, continuing, or stopping any action as far as it depends on us? For can it be denied that whatever agent has a power to think on its own actions, and to prefer their doing or omission either to other, has that faculty called *will*? *Will*, then, is nothing but such a power. *Liberty*, on the other side, is the power a man has to do or forbear doing any particular action according as its doing or forbearance has the actual preference in the mind; which is the same thing as to say according as he himself *wills* it.

16. It is plain then that the *will* is nothing but one power or ability, and *freedom* another power or ability, so that to ask whether the *will has freedom* is to ask whether one power has another power; one ability another ability: a question at first sight too grossly absurd to make a dispute, or need an answer. For who is it that sees not that *powers* belong only to *agents* and *are attributes only of substances, and not of powers* themselves? So that this way of putting the question (viz. whether the *will be free*) is in effect to ask whether the *will* be a substance, an agent, or at least to suppose it, since freedom can properly be attributed to nothing else. If freedom can with any propriety of speech be applied to power, it may be attributed to the power that is in a man to produce or forbear producing motion in parts of his body by choice or preference; which is that which denominates him free and is freedom itself. But if anyone should ask whether freedom were free, he would be suspected not to understand well what he said; and he would be thought to deserve *Midas's* ears, who, knowing that rich was a denomination from the possession of riches, should demand whether riches themselves were rich.

17. However, the *name faculty*, which men have given to this power called the *will*, and whereby they have been led into a way of talking of the *will* as acting, may, by an appropriation that disguises its true sense, serve a little to palliate the absurdity; yet the *will*, in truth, signifies nothing but a power or ability to prefer or choose; and when the *will*, under the name of a *faculty*, is considered, as it is, barely as an ability to do something, the absurdity in saying it is free or not free will easily discover itself. For if it be reasonable to suppose and talk of *faculties* as distinct beings that can act (as we do, when we say the *will* orders, and the *will* is free), it is fit that we should make a speaking *faculty*, and a walking *faculty*, and a dancing *faculty*, by which those actions are produced, which are but several modes of motion, as well as we make the *will* and *understanding* to be *faculties* by which the actions of choosing and perceiving are produced, which are but several modes of thinking. And we may as properly say that it is the singing *faculty* sings, and the dancing *faculty* dances, as that the *will* chooses, or that the understanding conceives; or, as is usual, that the *will* directs the understanding, or the understanding obeys or obeys not the *will*: it being altogether as proper and intelligible to say that

the power of speaking directs the power of singing, or the power of singing obeys or disobeys the power of speaking.

19. I grant that this or that actual thought may be the occasion of volition, or exercising the power a man has to choose, or the actual choice of the mind, the cause of actual thinking on this or that thing, as the actual singing of such a tune may be the occasion of dancing such a dance, and the actual dancing of such a dance the occasion of singing such a tune. But in all these it is not one *power* that operates on another, but it is the mind that operates and exerts these powers; it is the man that does the action, it is the agent that has power, or is able to do. For *powers* are relations, not agents; and *that which has the power or not the power to operate is that alone which is or is not free*, and not the power itself. For freedom, or not freedom, can belong to nothing but what has or has not a power to act.

21. To return, then, to the inquiry about liberty, I think *the question is not proper, whether the will be free, but whether a man be free*. Thus, I think,

(1) That so far as anyone can, by the direction or choice of his mind, preferring the existence of any action to the nonexistence of that action, and *vice versa*, make it to exist or not exist, so far he is *free*.

27. First then, it is carefully to be remembered that *freedom consists in the dependence of the existence or not-existence of any action upon our volition of it, and not in the dependence of any action or its contrary on our preference.* A man standing on a cliff is at liberty to leap twenty yards downwards into the sea, not because he has a power to do the contrary action, which is to leap twenty yards upwards, for that he cannot do; but he is therefore free because he has a power to leap or not to leap. But if a greater force than his either holds him fast or tumbles him down, he is no longer free in that case: because the doing or forbearance of that particular action is no longer in his power. He that is a close prisoner in a room twenty-foot-square, being at the north side of his chamber, is at liberty to walk twenty feet southward, because he can walk or not walk it; but is not, at the same time, at liberty to do the contrary, i.e. to walk twenty feet northward.

In this, then, consists freedom, viz. in our being able to act or not to act according as we shall choose or *will*.

Chapter XXII

Of Mixed Modes

1. Having treated of *simple modes* in the forego-ing chapters and given several instances of some of the most considerable of them, to show what they are and how we come by them, we are now in the next place to consider those we call *mixed modes;* such are the complex *ideas* we mark by the names *obligation, drunkenness,* a *lie,* etc.; which consisting of several combinations of simple *ideas* of different kinds, I have called *mixed modes,* to distinguish them from the more simple modes, which consist only of simple *ideas* of the same kind. These mixed modes, being also such combinations of simple *ideas* as are not looked upon to be characteristical marks of any real beings that have a steady existence, but scattered and independ-ent *ideas* put together by the mind, are thereby distin-guished from the complex *ideas* of substances.

2. That the mind, in respect of its simple *ideas,* is wholly passive and receives them all from the exis-tence and operations of things, such as sensation or reflection offers them, without being able to make any one *idea,* experience shows us. But if we attentively consider these *ideas* I call *mixed modes* we are now speaking of, we shall find their original quite different. *The mind* often *exercises an active power in making these* several *combinations;* for, it being once furnished with simple *ideas,* it can put them together in several compositions and so make variety of complex *ideas* without examining whether they exist so together in nature. And hence I think it is that these *ideas* are called *notions:* as if they had their original, and con-stant existence more in the thoughts of men than in the reality of things; and to form such *ideas,* it suf-ficed that the mind put the parts of them together, and that they were consistent in the understanding together, without considering whether they had any real being, though I do not deny but several of them might be taken from observation and the existence of several simple *ideas* so combined, as they are put together in the understanding. For the man who first framed the *idea* of *hypocrisy* might have either taken it at first from the observation of one who made show of good qualities which he had not, or else have framed that *idea* in his mind without having any such pattern to fashion it by. For it is evident that, in the beginning of languages and societies of men, several of those complex *ideas,* which were consequent to the consti-tutions established amongst them, must needs have been in the minds of men before they existed any-where else, and that many names that stood for such complex *ideas* were in use, and so those *ideas* framed, before the combinations they stood for ever existed.

3. Indeed, now that languages are made and abound with words standing for such combinations, *an usual way of getting these complex* ideas *is by the explication of those terms that stand for them.* For, con-sisting of a company of simple *ideas* combined, they may, by words for those simple *ideas,* be represented to the mind of one who understands those words, though that complex combination of simple *ideas* were never offered to his mind by the real existence of things. Thus a man may come to have the *idea* of *sacrilege* or *murder,* by enumerating to him the simple *ideas* which these words stand for, without ever seeing either of them committed.

Chapter XXIII

Of Our Complex Ideas of Substances

1. The mind being, as I have declared, furnished with a great number of the simple *ideas* conveyed in by the *senses,* as they are found in exterior things, or by *reflection* on its own operations, takes notice also that a certain number of these simple *ideas* go con-stantly together; which, being presumed to belong to one thing, and words being suited to common appre-hensions and made use of for quick dispatch, are called, so united in one subject, by one name; which, by inadvertency, we are apt afterward to talk of and consider as one simple *idea,* which indeed is a compli-cation of many *ideas* together: because, as I have said, not imagining how these simple *ideas* can subsist by themselves, we accustom ourselves to suppose some *substratum* wherein they do subsist, and from which they do result; which therefore we call *substance.*

2. So that if anyone will examine himself con-cerning his *notion of pure substance in general,* he will find he has no other *idea* of it at all, but only a suppo-sition of he knows not what support of such qualities which are capable of producing simple *ideas* in us; which qualities are commonly called *accidents.* If anyone should be asked what is the subject wherein

colour or weight inheres, he would have nothing to say but, the solid extended parts; and if he were demanded what is it that that solidity and extension adhere in, he would not be in a much better case than the *Indian* before-mentioned who, saying that the world was supported by a great elephant, was asked what the elephant rested on, to which his answer was, a great tortoise; but being again pressed to know what gave support to the broad-backed tortoise, replied, something, he knew not what. And thus here, as in all other cases where we use words without having clear and distinct *ideas*, we talk like children who, being questioned what such a thing is which they know not, readily give this satisfactory answer, that it is *something*; which in truth signifies no more, when so used, either by children or men, but that they know not what, and that the thing they pretend to know and talk of is what they have no distinct *idea* of at all, and so are perfectly ignorant of it and in the dark. The *idea* then we have, to which we give the general name substance, being nothing but the supposed, but unknown, support of those qualities we find existing, which we imagine cannot subsist *sine re substante*, without something to support them, we call that support *substantia*; which, according to the true import of the word, is, in plain *English, standing under* or *upholding*.

3. An obscure and relative *idea* of substance in general being thus made, we come to have the *ideas of particular sorts of substances* by collecting such combinations of simple *ideas* as are, by experience and observation of men's senses, taken notice of to exist together, and are therefore supposed to flow from the particular internal constitution or unknown essence of that substance. Thus we come to have the *ideas* of a man, horse, gold, water, etc.; of which substances, whether anyone has any other clear *idea*, further than of certain simple *ideas* co-existing together, I appeal to everyone's own experience. It is the ordinary qualities observable in iron, or a diamond, put together that make the true complex *idea* of those substances, which a smith or a jeweller commonly knows better than a philosopher; who, whatever substantial forms he may talk of, he no other *idea* of those substances than what is framed by a collection of those simple *ideas* which are to be found in them: only we must take notice that our complex *ideas* of substances, besides all these sim-

ple *ideas* they are made up of, have always the confused *idea* of *something* to which they belong, and in which they subsist; and therefore when we speak of any sort of substance, we say it is a *thing* having such or such qualities: as body is a *thing* that is extended, figured, and capable of motion; a spirit, a *thing* capable of thinking; and so hardness, friability, and power to draw iron, we say, are qualities to be found in a loadstone. These and the like fashions of sparking intimate that the substance is supposed always *something* besides the extension, figure, solidity, motion, thinking or other observable *ideas*, though we know not what it is.

4. Hence, when we talk or think of any particular sort of corporeal substances, as *horse, stone*, etc., though the *idea* we have of either of them be but the complication or collection of those several simple *ideas* of sensible qualities, which we use to find united in the thing called *horse* or *stone*: yet, because we cannot conceive how they should subsist alone, nor one in another, we suppose them existing in and supported by some common subject; *which support we denote by the name substance*, though it be certain we have no clear or distinct *idea* of that *thing* we suppose as support.

5. The same thing happens concerning the operations of the mind, viz. thinking, reasoning, fearing, etc., which we concluding not to subsist of themselves, nor apprehending how they can belong to body or be produced by it, we are apt to think these the actions of some other *substance*, which we call *spirit*; whereby yet it is evident that, having no other *idea* or notion of matter but *something* wherein those many sensible qualities which affect our senses do subsist, by supposing a substance wherein *thinking, knowing, doubting*, and a power of moving, etc., do subsist, *we have as clear a notion of the substance of spirit as we have of body*: the one being supposed to be (without knowing what it is) the *substratum* to those simple *ideas* we have from without; and the other supposed (with a like ignorance of what it is) to be the *substratum* to those operations which we experiment in ourselves within. It is plain then that the *idea* of corporeal *substance* in matter is as remote from our conceptions and apprehensions as that of spiritual *substance*, or *spirit*; and therefore, from our not having any notion of the *substance* of spirit, we can no more

conclude its non-existence than we can, for the same reason, deny the existence of body: it being as rational to affirm there is no body, because we have no clear and distinct idea of the *substance* of matter, as to say there is no spirit, because we have no clear and distinct *idea* of the *substance* of a spirit.

6. Whatever therefore be the secret and abstract nature of *substance* in general, all *the* ideas *we have of particular distinct sorts of substances* are nothing but several combinations of simple *ideas,* co-existing in such, though unknown, cause of their union as makes the whole subsist of itself. It is by such combinations of simple *ideas* and nothing else that we represent particular sorts of *substances* to ourselves; such are the *ideas* we have of their several species in our minds; and such only do we, by their specific names, signify to others, v.g. *man, horse, sun water, iron;* upon hearing which words, everyone who understands the language frames in his mind a combination of those several simple *ideas* which he has usually observed or fancied to exist together under that denomination, all which he supposes to rest in and be, as it were, adherent to that unknown common subject which inheres not in anything else. Though in the meantime it be manifest, and everyone upon inquiry into his own thoughts will find, that he has no other *idea* of any *substance,* v.g., let it be *gold, horse, iron, man, vitriol, bread,* but what he has barely of those sensible qualities which he supposes to inhere, with a supposition of such a *substratum* as gives, as it were, a support to those qualities or simple *ideas* which he has observed to exist united together. Thus, the *idea* of the *sun,* what is it but an aggregate of those several simple *ideas,* bright, hot, roundish, having a constant regular motion, at a certain distance from us, and perhaps some other: as he who thinks and discourses of the *sun* has been more or less accurate in observing those sensible qualities, *ideas,* or properties, which are in that thing which he calls the *sun.*

7. For he has the perfectest *idea* of any of the particular sorts of *substances,* who has gathered and put together most of those simple *ideas* which do exist in it; among which are to be reckoned its active powers and passive capacities, which, though not simple *ideas,* yet in this respect, for brevity's sake, may conveniently enough be reckoned amongst them. Thus, the power of drawing iron is one of the *ideas* of the complex one of that substance we call a *loadstone;* and a power to be so drawn is a part of the complex one we call *iron:* which powers pass for inherent qualities in those subjects. Because every *substance,* being as apt, by the powers we observe in it, to change some sensible qualities in other subjects as it is to produce in us those simple *ideas* which we receive immediately from it, does, by those new sensible qualities introduced into other subjects, discover to us those powers which do thereby mediately affect our senses, as regularly as its sensible qualities do it immediately: v.g. we immediately by our senses perceive in *fire* its heat and colour, which are, if rightly considered, nothing but powers in it to produce those *ideas* in us; we also by our senses perceive the colour and brittleness of *charcoal,* whereby we come by the knowledge of another power in fire, which it has to change the colour and consistency of wood. By the former, fire immediately, by the latter, it mediately discovers to us these several powers; which therefore we look upon to be a part of the qualities of fire, and so make them a part of the complex *idea* of it. For all those powers that we take cognizance of terminating only in the alteration of some sensible qualities in those subjects on which they operate, and so making them exhibit to us new sensible *ideas,* therefore it is that I have reckoned these powers amongst the simple *ideas* which make the complex ones of the sorts of *substances,* though these powers considered in themselves are truly complex *ideas.* And in this looser sense, I crave leave to be understood when I name any of these *potentialities amongst the simple ideas,* which we recollect in our minds when we think *of particular substances.* For the powers that are severally in them are necessary to be considered, if we will have true distinct notions of the several sorts of substances.

8. Nor are we to wonder that *powers make a great part of our complex* ideas *of substances,* since their secondary qualities are those which in most of them serve principally to distinguish substances one from another, and commonly make a considerable part of the complex *idea* of the several sorts of them. For, our senses failing us in the discovery of the bulk, texture, and figure of the minute parts of bodies, on which their real constitutions and differences depend, we are fain to make use of their secondary qualities as the characteristical notes and marks whereby to frame *ideas* of them in our minds and distinguish them one

from another: all which secondary qualities, as has been shown, are nothing but bare powers. For the colour and taste of *opium* are, as well as its soporific or anodyne virtues, mere powers, depending on its primary qualities, whereby it is fitted to produce different operations on different parts of our bodies.

9. *The* ideas *that make our complex ones of corporeal substances* are of these three sorts. *First,* the *ideas* of the primary qualities of things, which are discovered by our senses, and are in them even when we perceive them not; such are the bulk, figure, number, situation, and motion of the parts of bodies, which are really in them, whether we take notice of them or no. *Secondly,* the sensible secondary qualities, which, depending on these, are nothing but the powers those substances have to produce several *ideas* in us by our senses; which *ideas* are not in the things themselves otherwise than as anything is in its cause. *Thirdly,* the aptness we consider in any substance to give or receive such alterations of primary qualities, as that the substance so altered should produce in us different *ideas* from what it did before: these are called active and passive powers; all which powers, as far as we have any notice or notion of them, terminate only in sensible simple *ideas.* For whatever alteration a *loadstone* has the power to make in the minute particles of iron, we should have no notion of any power it had at all to operate on iron, did not its sensible motion discover it; and I doubt not but there are a thousand changes that bodies we daily handle have a power to cause in one another, which we never suspect, because they never appear in sensible effects.

10. *Powers* therefore justly *make a great part of our complex* ideas *of substances.* He that will examine his complex *idea* of gold will find several of its *ideas* that make it up to be only powers, as the power of being melted, but of not spending itself in the fire, of being dissolved in *aqua regia,* are *ideas* as necessary to make up our complex *idea* of gold as its colour and weight; which, if duly considered, are also nothing but different powers. For, to speak truly, yellowness is not actually in gold, but is a power in gold to produce that *idea* in us by our eyes, when placed in a due light; and the heat, which we cannot leave out of our *idea* of the sun, is no more really in the sun, than the white colour it introduces into wax. These are both equally powers in the sun, operating, by the motion and figure of its insensible parts, so on a man as to

make him have the *idea* of heat; and so on wax, as to make it capable to produce in a man the *idea* of white.

11. Had we senses acute enough to discern the minute particles of bodies and the real constitution on which their sensible qualities depend, I doubt not but they would produce quite different *ideas* in us; and that which is now the yellow colour of gold would then disappear, and instead of it we should see an admirable texture of parts, of a certain size and figure. This microscopes plainly discover to us; for what to our naked eyes produces a certain colour is, by thus augmenting the acuteness of our senses, discovered to be quite a different thing; and the thus altering, as it were, the proportion of the bulk of the minute parts of a coloured object to our usual sight produces different *ideas* from what it did before. Thus sand, or pounded glass, which is opaque and white to the naked eye, is pellucid in a microscope; and a hair seen this way loses its former colour and is in a great measure pellucid, with a mixture of some bright sparkling colours, such as appear from the refraction of diamonds and other pellucid bodies. Blood to the naked eye appears all red, but by a good microscope, wherein its lesser parts appear, shows only some few globules of red, swimming in a pellucid liquor; and how these red globules would appear, if glasses could be found that yet could magnify them a thousand or ten thousand times more, is uncertain.

14. But to return to the matter in hand, the *ideas* we have of substances and the ways we come by them: I say *our specific* ideas *of substances* are nothing else but *a collection of a certain number of simple* ideas, *considered as united in one thing.* These *ideas* of substances, though they are commonly called simple apprehensions, and the names of them simple terms, yet in effect are complex and compounded. Thus the *idea* which an *Englishman* signifies by the name *swan* is white colour, long neck, red beak, black legs, and whole feet, and all these of a certain size, with a power of swimming in the water, and making a certain kind of noise, and perhaps, to a man who has long observed this kind of birds, some other properties: which all terminate in sensible simple *ideas,* all united in one common subject.

15. Besides the complex *ideas* we have of material sensible substances, of which I have last spoken, by the simple *ideas* we have taken from those operations of our own minds which we experiment daily in our-selves, as thinking, understanding, willing, knowing and power of beginning motion, etc., coexisting in some substance, we are able to frame *the complex* idea *of an immaterial spirit*. And thus, by putting together the *ideas* of thinking, perceiving, liberty, and power of moving themselves and other things, we have as clear a perception and notion of immaterial substances as we have of material. For putting to-gether the *ideas* of thinking and willing, or the power of moving or qui-eting corporeal motion, joined to substance, of which we have no distinct *idea*, we have the *idea* of an immaterial spirit; and by putting together the *ideas* of coherent solid parts, and a power of being moved, joined with substance, of which likewise we have no positive *idea*, we have the *idea* of matter. The one is as clear and distinct an *idea* as the other: the *idea* of thinking, and moving a body, being as clear and dis-tinct *ideas* as the *ideas* of extension, solidity, and being moved. For our *idea* of substance is equally obscure, or none at all, in both: it is but a supposed I know not what, to support those *ideas* we call accidents. It is for want of reflection that we are apt to think that our senses show us nothing but material things. Every act of sensation, when duly considered, gives us an equal view of both parts of nature, the corporeal and spiri-tual. For whilst I know, by seeing or hearing, etc., that there is some corporeal being without me, the object of that sensation, I do more certainly know that there is some spiritual being within me that sees and hears. This, I must be convinced, cannot be the action of bare insensible matter; nor ever could be, without an immaterial thinking being.

Chapter XXVII

Of Identity And Diversity

1. Another occasion the mind often takes of comparing is the very being of things, when consider-ing anything as existing at any determined time and place, we compare it with itself existing at another time, and thereon form the *ideas* of *identity* and *divers-ity*. When we see anything to be in any place in any instant of time, we are sure (be it what it will) that it is that very thing, and not another which at that same time exists in another place, how like and undistinguishable soever it may be in all other re-

spects; and in this consists *identity*, when the *ideas* it is attributed to vary not at all from what they were that moment wherein we consider their former existence, and to which we compare the present. For we never finding nor conceiving it possible that two things of the same kind should exist in the same place at the same time, we rightly conclude that whatever exists any where at any time, excludes all of the same kind, and is there itself alone. When therefore we demand whether anything be the same or no, it refers always to something that existed such a time in such a place, which it was certain, at that instant, was the same with itself, and not other; from whence it follows that one thing cannot have tow beginnings of existence, nor two things one beginning: it being impossible for two things of the same kind to be or exist in the same instant in the very same place, or one and the same thing in different places. That, therefore, that had one beginning is the same thing; and that which had a different beginning in time and place from that is not the same, but diverse. That which has made the difficulty about this relation has been the little care and attention used in having precise notions of the things to which it is attributed.

2. We have the *ideas* but of three sorts of sub-stances: (1) God. (2) Finite intelligences. (3) *Bodies*. First, God is without beginning, eternal, unalterable, and everywhere, and therefore concerning his iden-tity there can be no doubt. Secondly, Finite spirits having had each its determinate time and place of beginning to exist, the relation to that time and place will always determine to each of them its identity, as long as it exists.

Thirdly, The same will hold of every particle of matter to which, no addition, or subtraction of matter being made, it is the same. For, though these three sorts of substances, as we term them, do not exclude one another out of the same place, yet we cannot conceive but that they must necessarily each of them exclude any of the same kind out of the same place; or else the notions and names of identity and diver-sity would be in vain, and there could be no such dis-tinction of substances, or anything else one from another. For example: could two bodies be in the same place at the same time, then those two parcels of matter must be one and the same, take them great or little; nay, all bodies must be one and the same. For by the same reason that two particles of matter may be in one place, all bodies may be in one place: which, when it can be supposed, takes away the distinction of identity and diversity of one and more, and renders it ridiculous. But it being a contradiction that two or more should be one, identity and diversity are relations and ways of comparing well-founded and of use to the understanding. All other things being but modes or relations ultimately terminated in substances, the identity and diversity of each particular existence of them too will be by the same way determined; only as to things whose existence is in succession, such as are the actions of finite beings, v.g. *motion* and *thought*, both which consist in a continued train of succession, concerning their diversity there can be no question: because each perishing the moment it begins, they cannot exist in different times or in different places, as permanent beings can at different times exist in distant places; and therefore no motion or thought, considered as at different times, can be the same, each part thereof having a different beginning of existence.

3. From what has been said, it is easy to discover what is so much inquired after, the *principium individuationis;* and that, it is plain, is existence itself, which determines a being of any sort to a particular time and place, incommunicable to two beings of the same kind. This, though it seems easier to conceive in simple substances or modes, yet, when reflected on, is not more difficult in compounded ones, if care be taken to what it is applied: v.g. let us suppose as atom, i.e. a continued body under one immutable superficies, existing in a determined time and place; it is evident, that, considered in any instant of its existence, it is in that instant the same with itself. For, being at that instant what it is, and nothing else, it is the same, and so must continue as long as its existence is continued; for so long it will be the same, and no other. In like manner, if two or more atoms be joined together into the same mass, every one of those atoms will be the same, by the foregoing rule; and whilst they exist united together, the mass consisting of the same atoms, must be the same mass, or the same body, let the parts be never so differently jumbled; but if one of these atoms be taken away, or one new one added, it is no longer that same mass or the same body. In the state of living creatures, their iden-

tity depends not on a mass of the same particles but on something else. For in them the variation of great parcels of matter alters not the identity: an oak growing from a plant to a great tree, and then lopped, is still the same oak; and a colt grown up to a horse, sometimes fat, sometimes lean, is all the while the same horse, though in both these cases there may be a manifest change of the parts, so that truly they are not either of them the same masses of matter, though they be truly one of them the same oak, and the other the same horse. The reason whereof is that, in these two cases of a mass of matter and a living body, *identity* is not applied to the same thing.

4. We must therefore consider wherein an oak differs from a mass of matter; and that seems to me to be in this: that the one is only the cohesion of particles of matter any how united; the other such a disposition of them as constitutes the part of an oak, and such an organization of those parts as is fit to receive and distribute nourishment, so as to continue and frame the wood, bark, and leaves, etc., of an oak, in which consists the vegetable life. That being then one plant which has such an organization of parts in one coherent body, partaking of one common life, it continues to be the same plant as long as it partakes of the same life, though that life be communicated to new particles of matter vitally united to the living plant, in a like continued organization, conformable to that sort of plants. For this organization, being at any one instant in any one collection of *matter,* is in that particular concrete distinguished from all other and is that individual life; which existing constantly from that moment both forwards and backwards, in the same continuity of insensibly succeeding parts united to the living body of the plant, it has that identity which makes the same plant and all the parts of its parts of the same plant during all the time that they exist united in that continued organization, which is fit to convey that common life to all the parts so united.

5. The case is not so much different in *brutes* but that anyone may hence see what makes an animal and continues it the same. Something we have like this in machines and may serve to illustrate it. For example, what is a watch? It is plain it is nothing but a fit organization or construction of parts to a certain end, which, when a sufficient force is added

to it, it is capable to attain. If we would suppose this machine one continued body, all whose organized parts were repaired, increased, or diminished by a constant addition or separation of insensible parts, with one common life, we should have something very much like the body of an animal, with this difference: that in an animal the fitness of the organization and the motion wherein life consists begin together, the motion coming from within; but in machines, the force, coming sensibly from without, is often away when the organ is in order and well-fitted to receive it.

6. This also shows wherein the identity of the same *man* consists: viz. in nothing but a participation of the same continued life, by constantly fleeting particles of matter, in succession vitally united to the same organized body. He that shall place the *identity* of man in anything else but, like that of other animals, in one fitly organized body, taken in any one instant and from thence continued under one organization of life in several successively fleeting particles of matter united to it, will find it hard to make an *embryo*, one of years, mad, and sober, the same man, by any supposition that will not make it possible for *Seth, Ismael, Socrates, Pilate, St. Austin,* and *Caesar Borgia* to be the same man. For if the *identity* of soul alone makes the same man, and there be nothing in the nature of matter why the same individual spirit may not be united to different bodies, it will be possible that those men living in instant ages, and of different tempers, may have been the same man: which way of speaking must be, from a very strange use of the word *man,* applied to an *idea* out of which body and shape are excluded. And that way of speaking would agree yet worse with the notions of those philosophers who allow of transmigration and are of opinion that the souls of men may, for their miscarriages, be detruded into the bodies of beasts, as fit habitations, with organs suited to the satisfaction of their brutal inclinations. But yet I think, nobody, could he be sure that the soul of *Heliogabalus* were in one of his hogs, would yet say that hog were a *man* or *Heliogabalus.*

7. It is not therefore unity of substance that comprehends all sorts of *identity* or will determine it in every case; but to conceive and judge of it aright, we must consider what *idea* the word it is applied to stands for: it being one thing to be the same *substance,* another the same *man,* and a third the

same *person,* if *person, man,* and *substance* are three names standing for three different *ideas;* for such as is the *idea* belonging to that name, such must be the *identity;* which, if it had been a little more carefully attended to, would possibly have prevented a great deal of that confusion which often occurs about this matter, with no small seeming difficulties, especially concerning *personal identity,* which therefore we shall in the next place a little consider.

9. This being premised, to find wherein *personal identity* consists, we must consider what *person* stands for; which, I think, is a thinking intelligent being that has reason and reflection and can consider itself as itself, the same thinking thing in different times and places; which it does only by that consciousness which is inseparable from thinking and, as it seems to me, essential to it: it being impossible for anyone to perceive without perceiving that he does perceive. When we see, hear, smell, taste, feel, meditate, or will anything, we know that we do so. Thus it is always as to our present sensations and perceptions, and by this everyone is to himself that which he calls *self*: it not being considered in this case whether the same *self* be continued in the same or divers substances. For since consciousness always accompanies thinking, and it is that that makes everyone to be what he calls *self,* and thereby distinguishes himself from all other thinking things: in this alone consists *personal identity,* i.e. the sameness of a rational being. And as far as this consciousness can be extended backwards to any past action or thought, so far reaches the identify of that *person:* it is the same *self* now it was then, and it is by the same *self* with this present one that now reflects on it, that that action was done.

10. But it is further inquired whether it be the same identical substance? This, few would think they had reason to doubt of, if these perceptions, with their consciousness, always remained present in the mind whereby the same thinking thing would be always consciously present and, as would be thought, evidently the same to itself. But that which seems to make the difficulty is this: that this consciousness being interrupted always by forgetfulness, there being no moment of our lives wherein we have the whole train of all our past actions before our eyes in one view, but even the best memories losing the sight of one part whilst they are viewing another; and we

sometimes, and that the greatest part of our lives, not reflecting on our past selves, being intent on our present thoughts, and in sound sleep having no thoughts at all, or at least none with that consciousness which remarks our waking thoughts; I say, in all these cases, our consciousness being interrupted, and we losing the sight of our past *selves*, doubts are raised whether we are the same thinking thing, i.e. the same substance, or no. Which, however reasonable or unreasonable, concerns not *personal identity* at all: the question being what makes the same *person*, and not whether it be the same identical substance, which always thinks in the same person; which, in this case, matters not at all: different substances, by the same consciousness (where they do partake in it) being united into one person, as well as different bodies by the same life are united into one animal, whose *identity* is preserved in that change of substance by the unity of one continued life. For, it being the same consciousness that makes a man be himself to himself, *personal identity* depends on that only, whether it be annexed only to one individual substance, or can be continued in a succession of several substances. For as far as any intelligent being can repeat the *idea* of any past action with the same consciousness it had of it at first, and with the same consciousness it has of any present action, so far it is the same *personal self*. For it is by the consciousness it has of its present thoughts and actions that it is *self* to *itself* now, and so will be the same *self* as far as the same consciousness can extend to actions past or to come, and would be by distance of time or change of substance no more two *persons* than a man be two men by wearing other clothes today than he did yesterday, with a long or short sleep between: the same consciousness uniting those distant actions into the same *person*, whatever substances contributed to their production.

13. But next, as to the first part of the question, whether, if the same thinking substance (supposing immaterial substances only to think) be changed, it can be the same person, I answer: That cannot be resolved but by those who know what kind of substances they are that do think, and whether the consciousness of past actions can be transferred from one thinking substance to another. I grant, were the same consciousness the same individual action, it could not; but, it being but a present representation of a past action, why it may not be possible that that may be represented to the mind to have been which really never was, will remain to be shown. And therefore how far the consciousness of past actions is annexed to any individual agent, so that another cannot possibly have it, will be hard for us to determine, till we know what kind of action it is that cannot be done without a reflex act of perception accompanying it, and how performed by thinking substances, who cannot think without being conscious of it. But that which we call the *same consciousness* not being the same individual act, why one intellectual substance may not have represented to it, as done by itself, what it never did, and was perhaps done by some other agent: why, I say, such a representation may not possibly be without reality of matter of fact, as well as several representations in dreams are, which yet whilst dreaming we take for true, will be difficult to conclude from the nature of things. And that it never is so will by us, till we have clearer views of the nature of thinking substances, be best resolved into the goodness of God, who, as far as the happiness or misery of any of his sensible creatures is concerned in it, will not, by a fatal error of theirs, transfer from one to another that consciousness which draws reward or punishment with it. How far this may be an argument against those who would place thinking in a system of fleeting animal spirits, I leave to be considered. But yet, to return to the question before us, it must be allowed that, if the same consciousness (which, as has been shown, is quite a different thing from the same numerical figure or motion in body) can be transferred from one thinking substance to another, it will be possible that two thinking substances may make but one person. For the same consciousness being preserved, whether in the same or different substances, the personal identity is preserved.

14. As to the second part of the question, whether, the same immaterial substance remaining, there may be two distinct persons, which question seems to me to be built on this: whether the same immaterial being, being conscious of the actions of its past duration, may be wholly stripped of all the consciousness of its past existence and lose it beyond the power of ever retrieving again and so, as it were beginning a new account from a new period, have a consciousness that cannot reach beyond this new state. All those who hold pre-existence are evidently of this mind, since they allow the soul to have no remaining consciousness of what it did in that pre-existent state, either wholly separate from body, or informing any other body; and if they should not, it is plain experience would be against them. So that, personal identity reaching no further than consciousness reaches, a pre-existent spirit, not having continued so many ages in a state of silence, must needs make different persons. Suppose a *Christian Platonist* or *Pythagorean* should, upon God's having ended all his works of creation the seventh day, think his soul hath existed ever since, and should imagine it has revolved in several human bodies, as I once met with one who was persuaded his had been the soul of *Socrates* (how reasonably I will not dispute; this I know, that in the post he filled, which was no inconsiderable one, he passed for a very rational man, and the press has shown that he wanted not parts or learning); would anyone say that he, being not conscious of any of *Socrates's* actions or thoughts, could be the same person with *Socrates?* Let anyone reflect upon himself and conclude that he has in himself an immaterial spirit, which is that which thinks in him and in the constant change of his body keeps him the same and is that which he calls himself; let him as suppose it to be the same soul that was in *Nestor* or *Thersites* at the siege of *Troy* (for souls being, as far as we know anything of them, in their nature indifferent to any parcel of matter, the supposition has no apparent absurdity in it), which it may have been, as well as it is now the soul of any other man; but he now having no consciousness of any of the actions either of *Nestor* or *Thersites,* does or can he conceive himself the same person with either of them? Can he be concerned in either of their actions, attribute them to himself, or think them his own, more than the actions of any other men that ever existed? So that, this consciousness not reaching to any of the actions of either of those men, he is no more one *self* with either of them than if the soul or immaterial spirit that now informs him had been created and began to exist, when it began to inform his present body, thought it were never so true that the same spirit that informed *Nestor's* or *Thersites's* body were numerically the same that now informs his. For this would no more make him the same person with *Nestor* than if some of the particles of matter that were once a part of *Nestor* were now a part of this man: the same immaterial

substance, without the same consciousness, no more making the same person by being united to any body than the same particle of matter, without consciousness, united to any body, makes the same person. But let him once find himself conscious of any of the actions of *Nestor,* he then finds himself the same person with *Nestor.*

15. And thus we may be able, without any difficulty, to conceive the same person at the resurrection, though in a body not exactly in make or parts the same which he had here, the same consciousness going along with the soul that inhabits it. But yet the soul alone, in the change of bodies, would scarce, to anyone but to him that makes the soul the *man,* be enough to make the same *man.* For should the soul of a prince, carrying with it the consciousness of the prince's past life, enter and inform the body of a cobbler as soon as deserted by his own soul, everyone sees he would be the same person with the prince, accountable only for the prince's actions; but who would say it was the same man? The body too goes to the making of the man and would, I guess, to everybody, determine the man in this case, wherein the soul, with all its princely thoughts about it, would not make another man: but he would be the same cobbler to everyone besides himself. I know that in the ordinary way of speaking, the same person and the same man stand for one and the same thing. And indeed, everyone will always have a liberty to speak as he pleases and to apply what articulate sounds to what *ideas* he thinks fit, and change them as often as he pleases. But yet when we will inquire what makes the same *spirit, man,* or *person,* we must fix the *ideas* of *spirit, man,* or *person* in our minds; and having resolved with ourselves what we mean by them, it will not be hard to determine in either of them or the like when it is the *same* and when not.

16. But though the same immaterial substance or soul does not alone, wherever it be, and in whatsoever state, make the same man: yet, it is plain, consciousness, as far as ever it can be extended, should it be to ages past, unites existences and actions very remote in time into the same person, as well as it does the existence and actions of the immediately preceding moment, so that whatever has the consciousness of present and past actions is the same person to whom they both belong. Had I the same consciousness that I saw the ark and *Noah's* flood as that I saw an overflowing of the *Thames* last winter, or as that I write now, I could no more doubt that I that write this now, that saw the *Thames* overflowed last winter, and that viewed the flood at the general deluge, was the same *self,* place that *self* in what substance you please, than I that write this am the same *myself* now whilst I write (whether I consist of all the same substance, material or immaterial, or no) that I was yesterday. For as to this point of being the same *self,* it matters not whether this present *self* be made up of the same or other substances, I being as much concerned and as justly accountable for any action that was done a thousand years since, appropriated to me now by this self-consciousness, as I am for what I did the last moment.

17. *Self* is that conscious thinking thing (whatever substance made up of, whether spiritual or material, simple or compounded, it matters not) which is sensible or conscious of pleasure and pain, capable of happiness or misery, and so is concerned for *itself,* as far as that consciousness extends. Thus everyone finds that, whilst comprehended under that consciousness, the little finger is as much a part of *itself* as what is most so. Upon separation of this little finger, should this consciousness go along with the little finger and leave the rest of the body, it is evident the little finger would be the *person,* the *same person;* and self then would have nothing to do with the rest of the body. As in this case it is the consciousness that goes along with the substance, when one part is separate from another, which makes the same *person* and constitutes this inseparable *self:* so it is in reference to substance remote in time. That with which the *consciousness* of this present thinking thing can join itself makes the same *person* and is one *self* with it, and with nothing else, and so attributes to *itself* and owns all the actions of that thing as its own, as far as that consciousness reaches, and no further; as everyone who reflects will perceive.

19. This may show us wherein *personal identity* consists: not in the identity of substance but, as I have said, in the identity of *consciousness,* wherein, if *Socrates* and the present mayor of *Queenborough* agree, they are the same person; if the same *Socrates* waking and sleeping do not partake of the same *consciousness, Socrates* waking and sleeping is not the same person. And to punish *Socrates* waking for what sleeping *Socrates* thought, and waking *Socrates* was

never conscious of, would be no more of right than to punish one twin for what his brother-twin did, whereof he knew nothing, because their outsides were so like that they could not be distinguished; for such twins have been seen.

20. But yet possibly it will still be objected, suppose I wholly lose the memory of some parts of my life beyond a possibility of retrieving them, so that perhaps I shall never be conscious of them again: yet am I not the same person that did those actions, had those thoughts that I once was conscious of, though I have now forgot them? To which I answer that we must here take notice what the word *I* is applied to, which, in this case, is the man only. And the same man being presumed to be the same person, *I* is easily here supposed to stand also for the same person. But if it be possible for the same man to have distinct incommunicable consciousness at different times, it is past doubt the same man would at different times make different persons; which, we see, is the sense of mankind in the solemnest declaration of their opinions, human laws not punishing the *mad man* for the *sober man's* actions, nor the *sober man* for what the *mad man* did, thereby making them two persons: which is somewhat explained by our way of speaking in *English* when we say such an one *is not himself,* or is *beside himself;* in which phrases it is insinuated, as if those who now, or at least first used them, thought that *self* was changed, the *self*-same persons was no longer in that man.

22. But is not a man drunk and sober the same person, why else is he punished for the act he commits when drunk, though he be never afterwards conscious of it? Just as much the same person as a man that walks and does other things in his sleep is the same persons and is answerable for any mischief he shall do in it. Human laws punish both, with a justice suitable to their way of knowledge; because, in these cases, they cannot distinguish certainly what is real, what counterfeit; and so that ignorance in drunkenness or sleep is not admitted as a plea. For, though punishment be annexed to personality, and personality to consciousness, and the drunkard perhaps be not conscious of what he did, yet human judicatures justly punish him, because the fact is proved against him, but want of consciousness cannot be proved for him. But in the Great Day, wherein the secrets of all hearts shall be laid open, it may be reasonable to think no one shall be made to answer for what he knows nothing of, but shall receive his doom, his conscience accusing or excusing him.

23. Nothing but consciousness can unite remote existences into the same person: the identity of substance will not do it; for whatever substance there is however framed, without consciousness there is no person; and a carcass may be a person, as well as any sort of substance be so, without consciousness.

Could we suppose two distinct incommunicable consciousnesses acting the same body, the one constantly by day, the other by night; and, on the other side, the same consciousness, acting by intervals, two distinct bodies: I ask, in the first case whether the *day-* and the *night-man* would not be two as distinct persons as *Socrates* and *Plato?* And whether, in the second case, there would not be one person in two distinct bodies, as much as one man is the same in two distinct clothings? Nor is it at all material to say that this same and this distinct *consciousness,* in the cases above mentioned, is owing to the same and distinct immaterial substances, bringing it with them to those bodies; which, whether true or no, alters not the case, since it is evident the *personal identity* would equally be determined by the consciousness, whether that consciousness were annexed to some individual immaterial substance or no. For, granting that the thinking substance in man must be necessarily supposed immaterial, it is evident that immaterial thinking thing may sometimes part with its past consciousness and be restored to it again, as appears in the forgetfulness men often have of their past actions; and the mind many times recovers the memory of a past consciousness, which it had lost for twenty years together. Make these intervals of memory and forgetfulness to take their turns regularly by day and night, and you have two persons with the same immaterial spirit, as much as in the former instance two persons with the same body. So that *self* is not determined by identity or diversity of substance, which it cannot be sure of, but only by identity of consciousness.

25. I agree the more probable opinion is that this consciousness is annexed to and the affection of one individual immaterial substance.

But let men, according to their divers hypotheses, resolve of that as they please. This every intelligent being, sensible of happiness or misery, must grant: that there is something that is *himself* that he is concerned for and would have happy; that this *self* has existed in a continued duration more than one instant, and therefore it is possible may exist, as it has done, months and years to come, without any certain bounds to be set to its duration; and may be the same *self* by the same consciousness, continued on for the future. And thus, by this consciousness, he finds himself to be the *same self* which did such or such an action some years since, by which he comes to be happy or miserable now. In all which account of *self,* the same numerical substance is not considered as making the same *self,* but the same continued consciousness, in which several substances may have been united and again separated from it, which, whilst they continued in a vital union with that wherein this consciousness then resided, made a part of that same *self.* Thus any part of our bodies, vitally united to that which is conscious in us, makes a part of our *selves;* but upon separation from the vital union, by which that consciousness is communicated, that which a moment since was part of our *selves* is now no more so than a part of another man's *self* is a part of me; and it is not impossible but in a little time may become a real part of another person. And so we have the same numerical substance become a part of two different persons, and the same person preserved under the change of various substances. Could we suppose any spirit wholly stripped of all its memory or consciousness of past actions, as we find our minds always are of a great part of ours, and sometimes of them all, the union or separation of such a spiritual substance would make no variation of personal identity, any more than that of any particle of matter does. Any substance vitally united to the present thinking being is a part of that very *same self* which now is; anything united to it by a consciousness of former actions makes also a part of the *same self* which is the same both then and now.

26. *Person,* as I take it, is the name for this *self.* Whatever a man finds what he calls *himself,* there, I think, another may say is the *same person.* It is a forensic term, appropriating actions and their merit, and so belongs only to intelligent agents, capable of a law, and happiness and misery. This personality extends *itself* beyond present existence to what is past, only by consciousness; whereby it becomes concerned and accountable, owns and imputes to *itself* past actions, just upon the same ground and for the same reason that it does the present. All which is founded in a concern for happiness, the unavoidable concomitant of consciousness: that which is conscious of pleasure and pain desiring that that self that is conscious should be happy. And therefore whatever past actions it cannot reconcile or appropriate to that present *self* by consciousness, it can be no more concerned in than if they had never been done; and to receive pleasure or pain, i.e., reward or punishment, on the account of any such action, is all one as to be made happy or miserable in its first being, without any demerit at all. For supposing a man punished now for what he had done in another life, whereof he could be made to have no consciousness at all, what difference is there between that punishment and being created miserable? And therefore conformable to this, the Apostle tells us, that at the Great Day, when everyone shall *receive according to his doings, the secrets of all hearts shall be laid open*. The sentence shall be justified by the consciousness all persons shall have that they *themselves*, in what bodies soever they appear, or what substances soever that consciousness adheres to, are the *same* that committed those actions and deserve that punishment for them.

BOOK III

Chapter II

Of the Signification of Words

1. Man, though he have great variety of thoughts, and such from which others as well as himself might receive profit and delight, yet they are all within his own breast, invisible and hidden from others, nor can of themselves be made to appear. The comfort and advantage of society not being to be had without communication of thoughts, it was necessary that man should find out some external sensible signs whereby those invisible *ideas*, which his thoughts are made up of, might be made known to others. For this purpose nothing was so fit, either for plenty or quickness, as these articulate sounds which with so much ease and variety he found himself able to make. Thus we may conceive how *words*, which were by nature so well adapted to that purpose, come to be made use of by men as *the signs of* their *ideas*: not by any natural connexion that there is between particular articulate sounds and certain *ideas*, for then there would be but

one language amongst all men; but by a voluntary imposition whereby such a word is made arbitrarily the mark of such an *idea*. The use, then, of words is to be sensible marks of *ideas*, and the *ideas* they stand for are their proper and immediate signification.

2. The use men have of these marks being either to record their own thoughts for the assistance of their own memory or, as it were, to bring out their *ideas* and lay them before the view of others: *words, in their primary or immediate signification, stand for nothing but the* ideas *in the mind of him that used them*, how imperfectly soever or carelessly those *ideas* are collected from the things which they are supposed to represent. When a man speaks to another, it is that the may be understood; and the end of speech is that those sounds, as marks, may make known his *ideas* to the hearer. That then which words are the marks of are the *ideas* of the speaker; nor can anyone apply them as marks, immediately, to anything else but the *ideas* that he himself hath, for this would be to make them signs of his own conceptions and yet apply them to other *ideas*, which would be to make them signs and not signs of his *ideas* at the same time, and so in effect to have no signification at all. Words being voluntary signs, they cannot be voluntary signs imposed by him on things he knows not. That would be to make them signs of nothing, sounds without signification. A man cannot make his words the signs either of qualities in things or of conceptions in the mind of another, whereof he has none in his own. Till he has some *ideas* of his own, he cannot suppose them to correspond with the conceptions of another man; nor can he use any signs for them: for thus they would be the signs of he knows not what, which is in truth to be the signs of nothing. But when he represents to himself other men's *ideas* by some of his own, if he consent to give them the same names that other men do, it is still to his own *ideas*: to *ideas* that he has, and not to *ideas* that he has not.

Chapter III

Of General Terms

1. All things that exist being particulars, it may perhaps be thought reasonable that words, which ought to be conformed to things, should be so too, I mean in their signification, but yet we find the quite contrary. The far *greatest part of words* that make all

languages *are general terms:* which has not been the effect of neglect or chance, but of reason and necessity.

2. *First, It is impossible that every particular thing should have a distinct peculiar name.* For, the signification and use of words depending on that connexion which the mind makes between its *ideas* and the sounds it uses as signs of them, it is necessary, in the application of names to things, that the mind should have distinct *ideas* of the things, and retain also the particular name that belongs to every one, with its peculiar appropriation to that *idea.* But it is beyond the power of human capacity to frame and retain distinct *ideas* of all the particular things we meet with: every bird and beast men saw, every tree and plant that affected the senses could not find a place in the most capacious understanding. If it be looked on as an instance of a prodigious memory that some generals have been able to call every soldier in their army by his proper name, we may easily find a reason why men have never attempted to give names to each sheep in their flock or crow that flies over their heads, much less to call every leaf of plants or grain of sand that came in their way by a peculiar name.

3. *Secondly,* If it were possible, *it would yet be useless,* because it would not serve to the chief end of language. Men would in vain heap up names of particular things, that would not serve them to communicate their thoughts. Men learn names and use them in talk with others only that they may be understood: which is then only done when, by use or consent, the sound I make by the organs of speech excites, in another man's mind who hears it, the *idea* I apply it to in mine when I speak it. This cannot be done by names applied to particular things, whereof I alone having the *ideas* in my mind, the names of them could not be significant or intelligible to another who was not acquainted with all those very particular things which had fallen under my notice.

4. *Thirdly,* But yet granting this also feasible (which I think is not), yet *a distinct name for every particular thing would not be of any great use for the improvement of knowledge,* which, though founded in particular things, enlarges itself by general views, to which things reduced into sorts, under general names, are properly subservient. These, with the names belonging to them, come within some compass and do not multiply every moment, beyond what either the mind can contain or use requires.

And therefore, in these, men have for the most part stopped, but yet not so as to hinder themselves from distinguishing particular things by appropriated names, where convenience demands it. And therefore in their own species, which they have most to do with and wherein they have often occasion to mention particular persons, they make use of proper names, and there distinct individuals have distinct denominations.

6. The next thing to be considered is *how general words come to be made.* For since all things that exist are only particulars, how come we by general terms, or where find we those general natures they are supposed to stand for? Words become general by being made the signs of general *ideas;* and *ideas* become general by separating from them the circumstances of time and place and any other *ideas* that may determine them to this or that particular existence. By this way of abstraction they are made capable of representing more individuals than one: each of which, having in it a conformity to that abstract *idea,* is (as we call it) of that sort.

9. That this is the *way whereby men first formed general* ideas, *and general names to them,* I think is so evident that there needs no other proof of it but the considering of a man's self, or others, and the ordinary proceedings of their minds in knowledge; and he that thinks general natures or notions are anything else but such abstract and partial *ideas* of more complex ones, taken at first from particular existences, will I fear be at a loss where to find them. For let anyone reflect and then tell me wherein does his *idea* of *man* differ from that of *Peter* and *Paul,* or his *idea* of *horse* from that of *Bucephalus,* but in the leaving out something that is peculiar to each individual, and retaining so much of those particular complex *ideas* of several particular existences as they are found to agree in. Of the complex *ideas* signified by the names *man* and *horse,* leaving out but those particulars wherein they differ, and retaining only those wherein they agree, and of those making a new distinct complex *idea,* and giving the name *animal* to it, one has a more general term that comprehends with man several other creatures. . . .

To conclude: this whole *mystery* of *genera* and *species,* which make such a noise in the schools and are with justice so little regarded out of them, is nothing else but abstract *ideas,* more or less comprehensive, with names annexed to them. In all which, this is constant and unvariable: that every more general term stands for such an *idea* as is but a part of any of those contained under it.

11. To return to general words: it is plain, by what has been said, that *general* and *universal* belong not to the real existence of things, but *are the inventions* and *creatures of the understanding*, made by it for its own use, *and concern only signs*, whether words or *ideas*. Words are general, as has been said, when used for signs of general *ideas*, and so are applicable indifferently to many particular things; and *ideas* are general when they are set up as the representatives of many particular things: but universality belongs not to things themselves, which are all of them particular in their existence, even those words and *ideas* which in their signification are general. When therefore we quit particulars, the generals that rest are only creatures of our own making: their general nature being nothing but the capacity they are put into, by the understanding, of signifying or representing many particulars. For the signification they have is nothing but a relation that, by the mind of man, is added to them.

15. But since the *essences* of things are thought by some (and not without reason) to be wholly unknown, it may not be amiss to consider the *several significations of the word essence*.

First, Essence may be taken for the being of anything whereby it is what it is. And thus the real internal, but generally (in Substances) unknown, constitution of things, whereon their discoverable qualities depend, may be called their *essence*. This is the proper original signification of the word, as is evident from the formation of it: *essentia*, in its primary notation, signifying properly *being*. And in this sense it is still used, when we speak of the *essence* of particular things, without giving them any name.

Secondly, The learning and disputes of the Schools having been much busied about *genus* and *species*, the word *essence* has almost lost its primary signification and, instead of the real constitution of things, has been almost wholly applied to the artificial constitution of *genus* and *species*. It is true, there is ordinarily supposed a real constitution of the sorts of things, and it is past doubt there must be some real constitution on which any collection of simple *ideas* co-existing must depend. But, it being evident that things are ranked under names into sorts or *species*, only as they agree to certain abstract *ideas* to which

we have annexed those names, the *essence* of each *genus* or sort comes to be nothing but that abstract *idea* which the general or *sortal* (if I may have leave so to call it from *sort*, as I do *general* from *genus*) name stands for. And this we shall find to be that which the word *essence* imports in its most familiar use. These two sorts of *essences*, I suppose, may not unfitly be termed the one the *real*, the other the *nominal essence*.

16. *Between the nominal essence and the name* there is so *near a connexion* that the name of any sort of things cannot be attributed to any particular being but what has this *essence*, whereby it answers that abstract *idea* whereof that name is the sign.

17. Concerning the real essences of corporeal substances (to mention those only) there are, if I mistake not, two opinions. The one is of those who, using the word *essence* for they know not what, suppose a certain number of those essences, according to which all natural things are made and wherein they do exactly every one of them partake, and so become of this or that *species*. The other and more rational opinion is of those who look on all natural things to have a real, but unknown, constitution of their insensible parts, from which flow those sensible qualities which serve us to distinguish them one from another, according as we have occasion to rank them into sorts, under common denominations. The former of the opinions, which supposes these· *essences* as a certain number of forms or moulds wherein all natural things that exist are cast and do equally partake, has, I imagine, very much perplexed the knowledge of natural things. The frequent productions of monsters in all the species of animals, and of changelings, and other strange issues of human birth carry with them difficulties not possible to consist with this *hypothesis*, since it is as impossible that two things partaking exactly of the same real *essence* should have different properties, as that two figures partaking in the same real *essence* of a circle should have different properties. But were there no other reason against it, yet the *supposition of essences that cannot be known* and the making them, nevertheless, to be that which distinguishes the species of things *is* so *wholly useless* and unserviceable to any part of our knowledge that that alone were sufficient to make us lay it by and content ourselves with such *essences* of the sorts or species of things as come within the reach of our knowledge: which, when seriously considered, will be found, as I have said, to be

nothing else but those abstract complex *ideas* to which we have annexed distinct general names.

18. *Essences* being thus distinguished into *nominal and real,* we may further observe that, *in the species of simple* ideas *and modes, they are always the same,* but *in substances always quite different.* Thus, a figure including a space between three lines is the real as well as nominal *essence* of a triangle, it being not only the abstract *idea* to which the general name is annexed, but the very *essentia* or being of the thing itself, that foundation from which all its properties flow, and to which they are all inseparably annexed. But it is far otherwise concerning that parcel of matter which makes the ring on my finger, wherein these two *essences* are apparently different. For it is the real constitution of its insensible parts, on which depend all those properties of colour, weight, fusibility, fixedness, etc., which makes it to be *gold* or gives it a right to that name which is therefore its nominal *essence,* since nothing can be called *gold* but what has a conformity of qualities to that abstract complex *idea* to which that name is annexed. But this distinction of *essences* belonging particularly to substances, we shall, when we come to consider their names, have an occasion to treat of more fully. . . .

Chapter V

Of the Names of Mixed Modes and Relations

2. The first particularity I shall observe in them is that the abstract *ideas* or, if you please, the essences of the several species *of mixed modes are made by the understanding,* wherein they differ from those of simple *ideas;* in which sort the mind has no power to make any one, but only receives such as are presented to it by the real existence of things operating upon it.

3. In the next place, these *essences of the species of mixed modes are* not only *made by the mind,* but made *very arbitrarily,* made without patterns, or reference to any real existence. Wherein they differ from those of substances, which carry with them the supposition of some real being, from which they are taken, and to which they are conformable.

Chapter VI

Of the Names of Substances

2. The measure and boundary of each sort or *species,* whereby it is constituted that particular sort and distinguished from others, is that we call its *essence,* which *is* nothing but that *abstract* idea *to which the name is annexed;* so that everything contained in that *idea* is essential to that sort. This, though it be all the *essence* of natural substances that we know or by which we distinguish them into sorts, yet I call it by a peculiar name, the *nominal essence,* to distinguish it from that real constitution of substances upon which depends this *nominal essence* and all the properties of that sort; which, therefore, as has been said, may be called the *real essence:* v.g. the *nominal essence* of *gold* is that complex *idea* the word *gold* stands for, let it be for instance a body yellow, of a certain weight, malleable, fusible, and fixed. But the *real essence* is the constitution of the insensible parts of that body on which those qualities and all the other properties of *gold* depend. How far these two are different, though they are both called *essence,* is obvious at first sight to discover.

26. Since then it is evident that we sort and name substances by their *nominal* and not by their real *essences,* the next thing to be considered is how and by whom these *essences* come to be made. As to the latter, it is evident they *are made by the mind,* and not by nature: for were they nature's workmanship, they could not be so various and different in several men as experience tells us they are. For if we will examine it, we shall not find the nominal essence of any one *species* of substances in all men the same: no, not of that which of all others we are the most intimately acquainted with. It could not possibly be that the abstract *idea* to which the name *man* is given should be different in several men, if it were of nature's making, and that to one it should be *animal rationale,* and to another *animal implume bipes latis unguibus.*

28. But though these *nominal essences of substances* are made by the mind, they are *not yet made so arbitrarily as those of mixed modes.* To the making of any nominal essence it is necessary, *first,* that the *ideas* whereof it consists have such an union as to make but one *idea,* how compounded soever. *Secondly,* that the particular *ideas* so united be exactly the same, neither more nor less. For if two abstract complex *ideas* differ either in number or sorts of their component parts, they make two different, and not one and the same essence. In the first of these, the mind, in making its complex *ideas* of substances, only follows nature and puts none together which are not supposed to have an union in nature. Nobody joins the voice of a sheep with the shape of a horse, nor the colour of lead with the weight and fixedness of gold, to be the complex *ideas* of any real substances, unless he has a mind to fill his head with *chimeras* and his discourse with unintelligible words. Men, observing certain qualities always joined and existing together, therein copied nature, and of *ideas* so united made their complex ones of substances. For though men may make what complex *ideas* they please and give what names to them they will, yet if they will be understood when they speak of things really existing, they must in some degree conform their *ideas* to the things they would speak of; or else men's language will be like that of *Babel,* and every man's words, being intelligible only to himself, would no longer serve to conversation and the ordinary affairs of life, if the ideas they stand for be not some way answering the common appearances and agreement of substances as they really exist.

Chapter IX

Of the Imperfection of Words

5. Words having naturally no signification, the *idea* which each stands for must be learned and retained by those who would exchange thoughts and hold intelligible discourse with other in any language. But this is hardest to be done where,

First, The *ideas* they stand for are very complex, and made up of a great number of *ideas* put together.

Secondly, Where the *ideas* they stand for have no certain connexion in nature, and so no settled standard anywhere in nature existing, to rectify and adjust them by.

Thirdly, Where the signification of the word is referred to a standard, which standard is not easy to be known.

Fourthly, Where the signification of the word and the real essence of the thing are not exactly the same.

These are difficulties that attend the signification of several words that are intelligible. Those which are not intelligible at all, such as names standing for any simple *ideas* which another has not organs or faculties to attain, as the names of colours to a blind man or sounds to a deaf man, need not here be mentioned.

In all these cases, we shall find an imperfection in words, which I shall more at large explain in their particular application to our several sorts of *ideas;* for, if we examine them, we shall find that the *names of mixed modes are most liable to doubtfulness and imperfection, for the two first of these reasons, and the names of substances chiefly for the two latter.*

Chapter X

Of the Abuse of Words

4. *Men* having been *accustomed* from their cradles *to learn words* which are easily got and retained *before they knew* or had framed *the complex ideas* to which they were annexed, or which were to be found in the things *they* were thought to *stand* for, they *usually continue to do so* all their lives; and without taking the pains necessary to settle in their minds determined *ideas,* they use their words for such unsteady and confused notions as they have, contenting themselves with the same words other people use, as if their very sound necessarily carried with it constantly the same meaning. This, though men make a shift with in the ordinary occurrences of life, where they find it necessary to be understood, and therefore they make signs till they are so: yet this insignificancy in their words, when they come to reason concerning either their tenets or interest, manifestly fills their discourse with abundance of empty unintelligible noise and jargon, especially in moral matters, where the words for the most part standing for arbitrary and numerous collections of *ideas* not regularly and permanently united in nature, their bare sounds are often only thought on, or at least very obscure and uncertain notions annexed to them. Men take the words they find in use amongst their neighbours, and that they may not seem ignorant what they stand for, use them confidently without much troubling their heads about a certain fixed meaning, whereby, besides the ease of it, they obtain this advantage: that as in such discourses they seldom are in the right, so they are as seldom to be convinced that they are in the wrong, it being all one to go about to draw those men out of their mistakes, who have no settled notions, as to dispossess a vagrant of his habitation who has no settled abode. This I guess to be so, and everyone may observe in himself and others whether it be or no.

BOOK IV

OF KNOWLEDGE AND OPINION

Chapter I

Of Knowledge in General

1. Since *the mind*, in all its thoughts and reasonings, hath no other immediate object but its own *ideas*, which it alone does or can contemplate, it is evident that our knowledge is only conversant about them.

2. *Knowledge* then seems to me to be nothing but *the perception of the connexion and agreement, or disagreement and repugnancy, of any of our ideas*. In this alone it consists. Where this perception is, there is knowledge; and where it is not, there, though we may fancy, guess, or believe, yet we always come short of knowledge. For when we know that *white is not black*, what do we else but perceive that these two *ideas* do not agree? When we possess ourselves with the utmost security of the demonstration that *the three angles of a triangle are equal to two right ones*, what do we more but perceive that equality to two right ones does necessarily agree to and is inseparable from the three angles of a triangle?

3. But to understand a little more distinctly wherein this agreement or disagreement consists, I think we may reduce it all to these four sorts:

1. *Identity*, or *diversity*.
2. *Relation*.
3. *Co-existence*, or *necessary connexion*.
4. *Real existence*.

4. *First*, As to the first sort of agreement or disagreement, viz. *identity* or *diversity*. It is the first act of the mind, when it has any sentiments or *ideas* at all, to perceive its *ideas*, and so far as it perceives them, to know each what it is, and thereby also to perceive their difference and that one is not another. This is so absolutely necessary that without it there could be no knowledge, no reasoning, no imagination, no distinct thoughts at all. By this the mind clearly and infallibly perceives each *idea* to agree with itself and to be what it is, and all distinct *idea* to disagree, i.e. the one not to be the other; and this is does without pains, labour, or deduction, but at first view, by its natural power of perception and distinction. And though men of art have reduced this into those general rules, *What is, is*,

and *It is impossible for the same thing to be and not to be*, for ready application in all cases wherein there may be occasion to reflect on it: yet it is certain that the first exercise of this faculty is about particular *ideas*. A man infallibly knows, as soon as ever he has them in his mind, that the *ideas* he calls *white* and *round* are the very *ideas* they are, and that they are not other *ideas* which he calls *red* or *square*. Nor can any maxim or proposition in the world make him know it clearer or surer than he did before, and without any such general rule. This then is the first agreement or disagreement which the mind perceives in its *ideas*, which it always perceives at first sight; and if there ever happen any doubt about it, it will always be found to be about the names and not the *ideas* themselves, whose identity and diversity will always be perceived as soon and as clearly as the *ideas* themselves are; nor can it possibly be otherwise.

5. *Secondly*, The next sort of agreement or disagreement the mind perceives in any of its *ideas* may, I think, be called *relative*, and is nothing but *the perception of the relation between any two ideas*, of what kind soever, whether substances, modes or any other. For, since all distinct *ideas* must eternally be known not to be the same, and so be universally and constantly denied one of another, there could be no room for any positive knowledge at all if we could not perceive any relation between our *ideas* and find out the agreement or disagreement they have one with another, in several ways the mind takes of comparing them.

6. *Thirdly*, The third sort of agreement or disagreement to be found in our *ideas*, which the perception of the mind is employed about, is *co-existence* or *non-co-existence* in the same subject; and this belongs particularly to substances. Thus when we pronounce, concerning *gold*, that it is fixed, our knowledge of this truth amounts to no more but this: that fixedness, or a power to remain in the fire unconsumed, is an *idea* that always accompanies and is joined with that particular sort of yellowness, weight, fusibility, malleableness, and solubility in *aqua regia*, which make our complex *idea* signified by the word *gold*.

7. *Fourthly*, The fourth and last sort is that of *actual real existence* agreeing to any *idea*. Within these four sorts of agreement or disagreement is, I suppose, contained all the knowledge we have or are capable of; for all the inquiries that we can make concerning any

of our *ideas*, all that we know or can affirm concerning any of them is that it is or is not the same with some other; that it does or does not always co-exist with some other *idea* in the same subject; that it has this or that relation to some other *idea;* or that it has a real existence without the mind. Thus, *Blue is not yellow* is of identity. *Two triangles upon equal bases between two parallels are equal* is of relation. *Iron is susceptible of magnetical impressions* is of co-existence. GOD *is* is of real existence. Though identity and co-existence are truly nothing but relations, yet they are so peculiar ways of agreement or disagreement of our *ideas* that they deserve well to be considered as distinct heads and not under relation in general, since they are so different grounds of affirmation and negation; as will easily appear to anyone who will but reflect on what is said in several places of this Essay. I should now proceed to examine the several degree of our knowledge, but that it is necessary first to consider the different acceptations of the word *knowledge*.

Chapter II

Of the Degrees of Our Knowledge

1. All our knowledge consisting, as I have said, in the view the mind has of its own *ideas*, which is the utmost light and greatest certainty we, with our faculties and in our way of knowledge, are capable of, it may not be amiss to consider a little the degree of its evidence. The different clearness of our knowledge seems to me to lie in the different way of perception the mind has of the agreement or disagreement of any of its *ideas*. For if we will reflect on our own ways of thinking, we shall find that sometimes the mind perceives the agreement or disagreement of two *ideas* immediately by themselves, without the intervention of any other; and this I think we may call *intuitive knowledge*. For in this the mind is at no pains of proving or examining but perceives the truth as the eye doth light, only by being directed toward it. Thus the mind perceives that *white* is not *black,* that a *circle* is not a *triangle,* that *three* are more than *two* and equal to *one* and *two.* Such kind of truths the mid perceives at the first sight of the *ideas* together, by bare *intuition,* without the intervention of any other *idea;* and this kind of knowledge is the clearest and most certain that human frailty is capable of. This part of knowl-

edge is irresistible and, like bright sunshine, forces itself immediately to be perceived, as soon as ever the mind turns its view that way; and leaves no room for hesitation, doubt, or examination, but the mind is presently filled with the clear light of it. It is on this *intuition* that depends all the certainty and evidence of all our knowledge, which certainty everyone finds to be so great that he cannot imagine, and therefore not require, a greater; for a man cannot conceive himself capable of a greater certainty than to know that any *idea* in his mind is such as he perceives it to be, and that two *ideas* wherein he perceives a difference are different and not precisely the same. He that demands a greater certainty than this demands he knows not what, and shows only that he has a mid to be a sceptic without being able to be so. Certainty depends so wholly on this intuition that in the next degree of *knowledge,* which I call *demonstrative,* this intuition is necessary in all the connexions of the intermediate *ideas,* without which we cannot attain knowledge and certainty.

2. The next degree of knowledge is where the mind perceives the agreement or disagreement of any *ideas,* but not immediately. Though, wherever the mind perceives the agreement or disagreement of any of its *ideas,* there be certain knowledge: yet it does not always happen that the mind sees that agreement or disagreement which there is between them, even where it is discoverable; and in that case, remains in ignorance, and at most gets no further than a probable conjecture. The reason why the mind cannot always perceive presently the agreement or disagreement of two *ideas* is because those *ideas,* concerning whose agreement or disagreement the inquiry is made, cannot by the mind be so put together as to show it. In this case then, when the mind cannot so bring its *ideas* together as by their immediate comparison and as it were juxtaposition or application one to another, to perceive their agreement or disagreement, it is fain, by the intervention of other *ideas* (one or more, as it happens) to discover the agreement or disagreement which it searches; and this is that which we call *reasoning.* Thus the mind, being willing to know the agreement or disagreement in bigness between the three angles of a triangle and two right once, cannot by an immediate view and comparing them do it, because the three angles of a triangle

cannot be brought at once and be compared with any one or two angles; and so of this the mind has no immediate, no intuitive knowledge. In this case the mind is fain to find out some other angles to which the three angles of a triangle have an equality, and finding those equal to two right ones, comes to know their equality to two right ones.

3. Those intervening *ideas* which serve to show the agreement of any two others are called *proofs*; and where the agreement or disagreement is by this means plainly and clearly perceived, it is called *demonstration*; it being *shown* to the understanding, and the mind made see that it is so. A quickness in the mind to find out these intermediate *ideas* (that shall discover the agreement or disagreement of any other) and to apply them right is, I suppose, that which is called *sagacity*.

4. *This knowledge by intervening proofs*, though it be certain, yet the evidence of it is *not* altogether *so clear* and bright, nor the assent so ready, *as in intuitive* knowledge. For, though in *demonstration* the mind does at last perceive the agreement or disagreement of the *ideas* it considers, yet it is not without pain and attention: there must be more than one transient view to find it. A steady application and pursuit is required to this discovery, and there must be a progression by steps and degrees, before the mind can in this way arrive at certainty and come to perceive the agreement or repugnancy between two *ideas* that need proofs and the use of reason to show it.

14. These two, viz. intuition and demonstration, are the degrees of our knowledge; whatever comes short of one of these, with what assurance soever embraced, is but faith or opinion, but not knowledge, at least in all general truths. There is, indeed, another *perception* of the mind, employed about *the particular existence of finite beings* without us, which, going beyond bare probability and yet not reaching perfectly to either of the foregoing degrees of certainty, passes under the name of knowledge. There can be nothing more certain than that the *idea* we receive from an external object is in our minds: this is intuitive knowledge. But whether there be anything more than barely that *idea* in our minds, whether we can thence certainly infer the existence of anything without us which corresponds to that *idea* is that whereof some men think there may be a question made: because men may have such *ideas* in their

minds, when no such thing exists, no such object affects their senses. But yet here I think we are provided with an evidence that puts us past doubting: for I ask anyone whether he be not invincibly conscious to himself of a different perception, when he looks on the sun by day and thinks on it by night, when he actually tastes wormwood or smells a rose or only thinks on that savour or odour? We as plainly find the difference there is between any *idea* revived in our minds by our own memory and actually coming into our minds by our senses, as we do between any two distinct *ideas*. If anyone say a dream may do the same thing, and all these *ideas* may be produced in us without any external objects, he may please to dream that I make him this answer: (1) That it is no great matter whether I remove his scruple or no: where all is but dream, reasoning and arguments are of no use, truth and knowledge nothing. (2) That I believe he will allow a very manifest difference between dreaming of being in the fire and being actually in it. But yet if he be resolved to appear so sceptical as to maintain that what I call being actually in the fire is nothing but a dream, and that we cannot thereby certainly know that any such thing as fire actually exists without us, I answer: that we certainly finding that pleasure or pain follows upon the application of certain objects to us whose existence we perceive or dream that we perceive by our senses, this certainty is as great as our happiness or misery, beyond which we have no concernment to know or to be. So that, I think, we may add to the two former sorts of *knowledge* this also of the existence of particular external objects, by that perception and consciousness we have of the actual entrance of *ideas* from them, and allow these *three degrees of knowledge*, viz. *intensive, demonstrative, and sensitive*, in each of which there are different degrees and ways of evidence and certainty.

Chapter III

Of the Extent of Human Knowledge

1. Knowledge, as has been said, lying in the perception of the agreement or disagreement of any of our *ideas*, it follows from hence that:

First, We can have *knowledge* no further than we have *ideas*.

2. *Secondly,* That we can have no *knowledge* further than we can have perception of that agreement or disagreement; which perception being: (1) either by *intuition*, or the immediate comparing any two *ideas*; or (2) by *reason*, examining the agreement or disagreement of two *ideas* by the intervention of some others; or (3) by *sensation*, perceiving the existence of particular things.

6. From all which it is evident that *the extent of our knowledge* comes not only short of the reality of things, but even of the extent of our own *ideas*. Though our knowledge be limited to our *ideas* and cannot exceed them either in extent or perfection; we have the *ideas* of *matter* and *thinking*, but possibly shall never be able to know whether any mere material being thinks or no: it being impossible for us, by the contemplation of our own *ideas*, without revelation, to discover whether Omni-potency has not given to some systems of matter, fitly disposed, a power to perceive and think, or else joined and fixed to matter, so disposed, a thinking immaterial substance: it being, in respect of our notions, not much more remote from our comprehension to conceive that GOD can, if he pleases, superadd to matter a faculty of thinking, than that he should superadd to it another substance with a faculty of thinking, since we know not wherein thinking consists, nor to what sort of substances the Almighty has been pleased to give that power, which cannot be in any created being but merely by the good pleasure and bounty of the Creator. For I see no contradiction in it that the first eternal thinking Being should, if he pleased, give to certain systems of created senseless matter, put together as he thinks fit, some degrees of sense, perception, and thought: though, as I think I have proved, *lib. IV, ch. x*, it is no less than a contradiction to suppose matter (which is evidently in its own nature void of sense and thought) should be that eternal first thinking being. . . .

I say not this that I would any way lessen the belief of the soul's immateriality; I am not here speaking of probability but knowledge, and I think not only that it becomes the modesty of philosophy not to pronounce magisterially where we want that evidence that can produce knowledge, but also that it is of use to us to discern how far our knowledge does reach; for the state we are at present in not being that of vision, we must, in many things, content ourselves with faith and probability; and in the present question about the immateriality of the soul,

if our faculties cannot arrive at demonstrative certainty, we need not think it strange. All the great ends of morality and religion are well enough secured without philosophical proofs of the soul's immateriality, since it is evident that he who made us at first begin to subsist here, sensible intelligent beings, and for several years continued us in such a state, can and will restore us to the like state of sensibility in another world and make us capable there to receive the retribution he has designed to men, according to their doings in this life.

16. But *as to the powers of substances* to change the sensible qualities of other bodies, which make a great part of our inquires about them and is no inconsiderable branch of our knowledge: I doubt, as to these, whether *our knowledge reaches much* further than our experience, or whether we can come to the discovery of most of these powers and be certain that they are in any subject by the connexion with any of those *ideas* which to us make its essence. Because the active and passive powers of bodies and their ways of operating consisting in a texture and motion of parts which we cannot by any means come to discover, it is but in very few cases we can be able to perceive their dependence on or repugnance to any of those *ideas* which make our complex one of that sort of things. I have here instanced in the corpuscularian hypothesis, as that which is thought to go furthest in an intelligible explication of the qualities of bodies; and I fear the weakness of human understanding is scarce able to substitute another which will afford us a fuller and clearer discovery of the necessary connexion and *co-existence* of the powers which are to be observed united in several sorts of them.

18. As to the third sort of our knowledge, viz. the *agreement or disagreement of any of our ideas in any other relation*; this, as it is the largest field of our knowledge, so it is hard to determine how far it may extend.

Chapter IV

Of the Reality of Knowledge

3. It is evident the mind knows not things immediately, but only by the intervention of the *ideas* it has of them. *Our knowledge*, therefore, is *real* only so far as there is a conformity between our *ideas* and the reality of things. But what shall be here the criterion?

How shall the mind, when it perceives nothing but its own *ideas*, known that they agree with things themselves? This, thought it seems not to want difficulty, yet I think, there be two sorts of *ideas* that we may be assured agree with things.

4. *First,* The first are simple *ideas* which, since the mind, as has been shown, can by no means make to itself, must necessarily be the product of things operating on the mind in a natural way and producing therein those perceptions which by the wisdom and will of our Maker they are ordained and adapted to. From whence it follows that *simple* ideas *are not fictions* of our fancies, but the natural and regular productions of things without us, really operating upon us, and so carry with them all the conformity which is intended or which our state requires; for they represent to us things under those appearances which they are fitted to produce in us: whereby we are enabled to distinguish the sorts of particular substances, to discern the states they are in, and so to take them for our necessities and apply them to our uses. Thus the *idea* of whiteness or bitterness, as it is in the mind, exactly answering that power which is in any body to produce it there, has all the real conformity it can or ought to have with things without us. And this conformity between our simple *ideas* and the existence of things is sufficient for real knowledge.

5. *Secondly,* All our *complex* ideas, *except those of substances,* being *archetypes* of the mind's own making, not intended to be the copies of anything nor referred to the existence of anything as to their originals, *cannot want any conformity necessary to real knowledge.* For that which is not designed to represent anything but itself can never be capable of a wrong representation nor mislead us from the true apprehension of anything by its dislikeness to it; and such, excepting those of substances, are all our complex *ideas.* Which, as I have shown in another place, are combinations of *ideas* which the mind, by its free choice, puts together, without considering any connexion they have in nature. And hence it is that in all these sorts the *ideas* themselves are considered as the *archetypes,* and things no otherwise regarded but as they are conformable to them. So that we cannot but be infallibly certain that all the knowledge we attain concerning these *ideas* is real and reaches things themselves. Because in all our thoughts, reasonings, and discourses of this kind, we intend things

no further than as they are conformable to our *ideas.* So that in these we cannot miss of a certain undoubted reality.

7. And hence it follows that *moral knowledge* is as *capable of real certainty* as mathematics. For certainty being but the perception of the agreement or disagreement of our *ideas,* and demonstration nothing but the perception of such agreement by the intervention of other *ideas* or mediums, our *moral ideas,* as well as mathematical, being *archetypes* themselves and so adequate and complete *ideas,* all the agreement or disagreement which we shall find in them will produce real knowledge, as well as in mathematical figures.

12. I say then that, to have *ideas* of *substances* which, by being conformable to things, may afford us *real* knowledge, it is not enough, as in modes, to put together such *ideas* as have no inconsistency, though they did never before so exist: v.g., the *ideas* of *sacrilege* or *perjury,* etc., were as real and true *ideas* before, as after, the existence of any such fact. But *our ideas of substances,* being supposed copies and referred to *archetypes* without us, must still be taken from something that does or has existed: they must not consist of *ideas* put together at the pleasure of our thoughts, without any real pattern they were taken from, though we can perceive no inconsistency in such a combination. The reason whereof is because, we knowing not what real constitution it is of substances whereon our simple *ideas* depend, and which really is the cause of the strict union of some of them one with another and the exclusion of others, there are very few of them that we can be sure are or are not inconsistent in nature, any further than experience and sensible observation reaches. Herein, therefore, is founded the *reality* of our knowledge concerning *substances:* that all our complex *ideas* of them must be such, and such only, as are made up of such simple ones as have been discovered to co-exist in nature. And our *ideas,* being thus true though not perhaps very exact copies, are yet the subjects of *real* (as far as we have any) *knowledge* of them. Which (as has been already shown) will not be found to reach every far; but so far as it does, it will still be *real knowledge.* Whatever *ideas* we have, the agreement we find they have with others will still be knowledge. If those *ideas* be abstract, it will be general knowledge. But to make it *real* concerning substances, the *ideas* must be taken from the real existence of things. Whatever simple *ideas* have been found to co-exist in any substance, these we may with confidence join together again and so make abstract *ideas* of substances. For whatever have once had an union in nature may be united again.

Chapter IX

Of Our Knowledge of Existence

1. Hitherto we have only considered the essence of things; let us proceed now to inquire concerning our knowledge of the *existence* of things, and how we come by it. I say, then, that we have the knowledge of *our own existence* by intuition, of the *existence of* GOD by demonstration, and of other things by sensation.

3. As for *our own existence,* we perceive it so plainly and so certainly that it neither needs nor is capable of any proof. For nothing can be more evidence to us than our own existence. *I think, I reason, I feel pleasure and pain:* can any of these be more evident to me than my own existence? If I doubt of all other things, that very doubt makes me perceive my own *existence,* and will not suffer me to doubt of that. For if I know *I feel pain,* it is evident I have as certain perception of my own existence as of the existence of the pain I feel; or, if I know *I doubt,* I have as certain perception of the existence of the thing doubting, as of that thought which I call *doubt.* Experience then convinces us that *we have an intuitive knowledge of our own existence* and an internal infallible perception that we are. In every act of sensation, reasoning, or thinking, we are conscious to ourselves of our own being and, in this matter, come not short of the highest degree of *certainty.*

Chapter X

Of Our Knowledge of the Existence of a God

2. I think it is beyond question that *man has a clear perception of his own being:* he knows certainly that he exists and that he is something. He that can doubt whether he be anything or no, I speak not to, no more than I would argue with pure nothing, or endeavour to convince nonentity that it were something. If anyone pretends to be so sceptical as to deny his own existence (for really to doubt of it is manifestly impossible), let him for me enjoy his beloved happiness of being nothing, until hunger or

some other pain convince him of the contrary. This, then, I think I may take for a truth, which everyone's certain knowledge assures him of, beyond the liberty of doubting, viz. that he is something that actually exists.

3. In the next place, man knows, by an intuitive certainty, that bare *nothing can no more produce any real being than it can be equal to two right angles.* If a man knows not that nonentity, or the absence of all being, cannot be equal to two right angles, it is impossible he should know any demonstration in *Euclid.* If, therefore, we know there is some real being, and that nonentity cannot produce any real being, it is an evident demonstration that from eternity there has been something, since what was not from eternity had a beginning, and what had a beginning must be produced by something else.

4. Next, it is evident that what had its being and beginning from another must also have all that which is in and belongs to its being from another too. All the powers it has must be owing to and received from the same source. This eternal source, then, of all being must also be the source and original of all power: and so *this eternal being must be also the most powerful.*

5. Again, a man finds in himself *perception* and *knowledge.* We have then got one step further, and we are certain now that there is not only some being, but some knowing, intelligent being in the world.

There was a time, then, when there was no knowing being, and when knowledge began to be; or else there has been also *a knowing being from eternity.* If it be said there was a time when no being had any knowledge, when that eternal being was void of all understanding, I reply that then it was impossible there should ever have been any knowledge: it being as impossible that things wholly void of knowledge, and operating blindly and without any perception, should produce a knowing being, as it is impossible that a triangle should make itself three angles bigger than two right ones. For it is as repugnant to the *idea* of senseless matter that it should put into itself sense, perception, and knowledge, as it is repugnant to the *idea* of a triangle that it should put into itself greater angles than two right ones.

6. Thus, from the consideration of ourselves and what we infallibly find in our own constitutions, our reason leads us to the knowledge of this certain and evident truth: that *there is an eternal, most powerful, and most knowing being,* which whether anyone will please to call *God,* it matters not. The thing is evident, and, from this *idea* duly considered, will easily be deduced all those other attributes which we ought to ascribe to this eternal being.

8. There is no truth more evident than that *something* must be *from eternity.* I never yet heard of anyone so unreasonable, or that could suppose so manifest a contradiction, as a time wherein there was perfectly nothing: this being of all absurdities the greatest, to imagine that pure nothing, the perfect negation and absence of all beings, should ever produce any real existence.

It being then unavoidable for all rational creatures to conclude that something has existed from eternity, let us next see what kind of thing that must be.

9. There are but two sorts of beings in the world that man knows or conceives.

First, Such as are purely material, without sense, perception, or thought, as the clippings of our beards, and parings of our nails.

Secondly, Sensible, thinking, perceiving beings, such as we find ourselves to be. Which, if you please, we will hereafter call *cogitative and incogitative* beings; which to our present purpose, if for nothing else, are perhaps better terms than material and immaterial.

10. If, then, there must be something eternal, let us see what sort of being it must be. And to that, it is very obvious to reason that it must necessarily be a *cogitative* being. For it is as impossible to conceive that ever bare incogitative matter should produce a thinking intelligent being, as that nothing should of itself produce matter.

11. If, therefore, it be evident that *something* necessarily must *exist from eternity,* it is also as evident that *that something must* necessarily *be a cogitative being:* for it is as impossible that incogitative matter should produce a cogitative being as that nothing, or the negation of all being, should produce a positive being or matter.

12. Though this discovery of the *necessary existence of an eternal mind* does sufficiently lead us into the knowledge of God, since it will hence follow that all other knowing beings that have a beginning must depend on him, and have no other ways of knowledge or extent of power than what he gives them; and

therefore, if he made those, he made also the less excellent pieces of this universe, all inanimate beings: whereby his *omniscience, power,* and *providence* will be established, and all his other attributes necessarily follow; yet, to clear up this a little further, we will see what doubts can be raised against it.

Chapter XI

Of Our Knowledge of the Existence of Other Things

1. The knowledge of our own being we have by institution. The existence of a God, reason clearly makes known to us, as has been shown.

The *knowledge of the existence* of any other thing we can have only by *sensation:* for, there being no necessary connexion of *real existence* with any *idea* a man hath in his memory, nor of any other existence but that of God with the existence of any particular man, no particular man can know the *existence* of any other being but only when, by actual operating upon him, it makes itself perceived by him. For the having the *idea* of anything in our mind no more proves the existence of that thing, than the picture of a man evidences his being in the world, or the visions of a dream make thereby a true history.

3. *The notice we have by our senses of the existing of things without us,* though it be not altogether so certain as our intuitive knowledge or the deductions of our reason employed about the clear abstract *ideas* of our own minds, yet it is an assurance that *deserves the name of knowledge.* If we persuade ourselves that our faculties act and inform us right concerning the existence of those objects that affect them, it cannot pass for an ill-grounded confidence: for I think nobody can, in earnest, be so sceptical as to be uncertain of the existence of those things which he sees and feels. At least, he that can doubt so far (whatever he may have with his own thoughts) will never have any controversy with me, since he can never be sure I say anything contrary to his opinion. As to myself, I think God has given me assurance enough of the existence of things without me, since, by their different application, I can produce in myself both pleasure and pain, which is one great concernment of my present state. This is certain: the confidence that our faculties do not herein deceive us is the greatest assurance we are capable of concerning the existence

of material beings. For we cannot act anything but by our faculties, nor talk of knowledge itself but by the help of those faculties which are fitted to apprehend even what knowledge is. But besides the assurance we have from our senses themselves, that they do not err in the information they give us of the existence of things without us when they are affected by them, we are further confirmed in this assurance by other concurrent reasons.

4. First, it is plain those perceptions are produced in us by exterior causes affecting our senses, because *those that want the organs of any sense never can have the* ideas *belonging to that sense* produced in their minds.

5. *Secondly,* Because *sometimes I find that I cannot avoid the having those* ideas *produced in my mind.*

6. *Thirdly,* Add to this, that *many of those* ideas *are produced in us with pain, which afterwards we remember without the least offence.* Thus, the pain of heat or cold, when the *idea* of it is revived in our minds, gives us no disturbance, which when felt was very troublesome, and is again when actually repeated: which is occasioned by the disorder the external object causes in our bodies when applied to it:

7. *Fourthly,* Our *senses* in many cases bear *witness* to the truth of each other's report concerning the existence of sensible things without us.

8. But yet, if after all this anyone will be so sceptical as to distrust his senses and to affirm that all we see and here, feel and taste, think and do during our whole being is but the series and deluding appearances of a long dream, whereof there is no reality, and therefore will question the existence of all things or our knowledge of anything: I must desire him to consider that, if all be a dream, then he doth but dream that he makes the question, and so it is not much matter that a waking man should answer him.

9. In fine then, when our senses do actually convey into our understanding any *idea,* we cannot but be satisfied that there doth something at that time really exist without us which doth affect our senses, and by them give notice of itself to our apprehensive faculties, and actually produce that *idea* which we then perceive; and we cannot so far distrust their testimony as to doubt that such collections of simple *ideas,* as we have observed by our senses to be united together, do really exist together. But *this knowledge extends as far as the present testimony of our senses,* employed about particular objects that do then affect them, *and no further.*

10. Whereby yet we may observe how foolish and vain a thing it is for a man of a narrow knowledge who, having reason given him to judge of the different evidence and probability of things and to be swayed accordingly, how *vain,* I say, it is *to expect demonstration* and certainty *in things not capable of it,* and refuse assent to very rational propositions and act contrary to very plain and clear truths because they cannot be made out so evident as to surmount every the least (I will not say reason, but) pretence of doubting. He that, in the ordinary affairs of life, would admit of nothing but direct plain demonstration would be sure of nothing in this world but of perishing quickly. The wholesomeness of his meat or drink would not give him reason to venture on it, and I would fain know what it is he could do upon such grounds as were capable of no doubt, no objection.

Chapter XII

Of the Improvement of Our Knowledge

7. *We must,* therefore, if we will proceed as reason advises, *adapt our methods of inquiry to the nature of the* ideas *we examine* and the truth we search after. General and certain truths are only founded in the habitudes and relations of abstract *ideas.* A sagacious and methodical application of our thoughts, for the finding our these relations, is the only way to discover all that can be put with truth and certainty concerning them into general propositions.

9. In our search after the knowledge of *substances,* our want of *ideas* that are suitable to such a way of proceeding obliges us to a quite different method. We advance not here as in the other (whether our abstract *ideas* are real as well as nominal essences), by contemplating our *ideas* and considering their relations and correspondences: that helps us very little, for the reasons that in another place we have at large set down. By which I think it is evident that substances afford matter of very little general knowledge; and the bare contemplation of their abstract *ideas* will carry us but a very little way in the search of truth and certainty. What, then, are we to do for the improvement of our *knowledge in substantial*

beings? Here we are to take a quite contrary course, the want of *ideas* of their real *essence* sends us from our own thoughts to the things themselves as they exist. *Experience here must teach me* what reason cannot; and it is by trying alone that I can certainly know what other qualities coexist with those of my complex *idea,* v.g. whether that *yellow, heavy, fusible* body I call *gold* be *malleable* or no; which experience (which way ever it prove, in that particular body I examine) makes me not certain that it is so in all or any other *yellow, heavy, fusible* bodies but that which I have tried. Because it is no consequence one way or the other from my complex *idea:* the necessity or inconsistency of *malleability* hath no visible connexion with the combination of that *colour, weight,* and *fusibility* in any body. What I have said here of the nominal essence of *gold,* supposed to consist of a body of such a determinate *colour, weight,* and *fusibility,* will hold true if *malleableness, fixedness,* and *solubility* in *aqua regia* be added to it. Our reasonings from these *ideas* will carry us but a little way in the certain discovery of the other properties in those masses of matter wherein all these are to be found. Because the other properties of such bodies depending not on these, but on that unknown real essence on which these also depend, we cannot by them discover the rest: we can go no further than the simple *ideas* of our nominal essence will carry us, which is very little beyond themselves and so afford us but very sparingly any certain, universal, and useful truths. . . .

Here again for assurance I must apply myself to *experience:* as far as that reaches I may have certain knowledge, but no further.

11. From whence it is obvious to conclude that, since our faculties are not fitted to penetrate into the internal fabric and real essences of bodies, but yet plainly discover to us the being of a GOD and the knowledge of ourselves, enough to lead us into a full and clear discovery of our duty and great concernment, it will become us, as rational creatures, to employ those faculties we have about what they are most adapted to, and follow the direction of nature where it seems to point us out the way. For it is rational to conclude that our proper employment lies in those inquiries, and in that sort of knowledge which is most suited to our natural capacities and carries in it our greatest interest, i.e. the condition of our eternal estate. Hence I think I may conclude that *morality* is *the proper science and business of mankind in general* (who are both concerned and fitted to search out their *summum bonum*) as several arts, conversant about several parts of nature, are the lot and private talent of particular men, for the common use of human life and their own particular subsistence in this world.

STUDY QUESTIONS: LOCKE, *AN ESSAY CONCERNING HUMAN UNDERSTANDING*

1. What are Locke's main aims in his *Essay?*
2. What does Locke mean by 'idea'?
3. Why does Locke think that the concept of an innate idea is absurd?
4. What are the objects of sensation? What is the difference between reflection and sensation?
5. What does Locke mean by 'simple ideas'? Why can the mind neither create nor destroy them? Why do we have names for only a few of them?
6. What are the operations of the mind about its ideas? How are complex ideas made by the mind from simple ones?
7. Why does Locke assert that we can only perceive directly our own ideas?
8. How does Locke distinguish primary from secondary qualities?
9. What is the distinction between ideas and qualities?
10. How do bodies produce ideas in us? How do secondary qualities produce ideas? Why are ideas of primary qualities resemblances, whereas the ideas of secondary qualities are not?
11. What is the third type of quality in bodies, and how is it related to primary and secondary qualities?

12. How does Locke explain the notion of cause?
13. How does Locke explain the notion of substance? Would Locke agree that the notion of a pure substratum can be acquired from experience?
14. What is the principle of individuation?
15. How does Locke argue against the view that the soul constitutes a person's identity?
16. What does he mean by 'same consciousness'? Why, according to Locke, does consciousness and not substance constitute personal identity?
17. What is Locke's main aim in Book II of the *Essay*?
18. When Locke claims that words can stand only for ideas, what does he mean to exclude?
19. How does Locke try to explain communication?
20. How does Locke distinguish real from nominal essence? What is the significance and aim of the distinction?
21. How does Locke classify knowledge?
22. What is a requirement of knowledge?
23. What are the main conclusions of the *Essay*?

A TREATISE CONCERNING THE TRUE ORIGINAL EXTENT AND END OF CIVIL GOVERNMENT
Second Treatise

Locke wrote his political theory in response to the English civil war of 1642 and the revolution of 1689, in which James II was deposed and replaced by William and Mary. The theory consists of three main elements:

1. *His critique of the claim that kings have a divine right to rule*
2. *The theory of consent that gives governments their legitimacy*
3. *The theory of property: how people acquire the right to own private property*

In the First Treatise, Locke tries to refute the claims of Sir Robert Filmer, who argued that, the right of kings to rule over their subjects was divine. In the Second Treatise, Locke argues that the basis of political power is a social contract, which establishes a civil society governed by laws and not the authority of God.

Prior to the formation of any civil society, people obeyed the moral law only insofar as they happened to be rational. In this state of nature, any person may punish any other for acting immorally according to his or her judgment. The state of nature is, therefore, unstable and insecure. In order for people to live together in a more secure environment, common agreement about the enforcement of morality is needed, and, for this, people need openly stated and commonly known expectations of each other. This requires laws enforced by a political power. Furthermore, such laws are required for the sake of our prosperity, because property rights can be upheld with security and peace only with public and enforceable laws. Locke claims that these are the reasons why we form civil society.

Individuals form such a society by agreeing to a social contract according to which they give up their right to enforce morality to a government, in exchange for security for themselves and their property. This analysis of the origin of society shows the purpose of government. It is for the mutual preservation of life, liberty, and property. It also shows the limitations of government: government should not control and rule. It should serve. In conrast to Hobbes, it follows that the individual should give up his or her rights to the minimum degree necessary for the mutual protection of the members of society.

Locke also tries to explain how individual property rights can be justified. How can the idea of humanity as a whole receiving God's gift be compatible with private property? The essence of Locke's answer is labor. Labor belongs to the person who works, and by applying labor to raw materials and other unowned things, a person can make those things his or her private property. The person acquires private property rights over land, minerals, and energy through his or her work.

Our private property rights have important political implications. For example, Locke claims that a monarch cannot legitimately levy taxes on his or her own authority. The monarch requires the consent of the people or of their legislative. However, according to Locke, property rights are not absolute. They are limited by other moral obligations, such as the duty not to waste and to promote the common good.

Economic development necessitates the existence of contracts and property laws to regulate commerce, and such laws require the existence of a government. As the wealth of society increases, leaders are more likely to act in their own self-interest, and so we need to balance the power of government.

CHAPTER 1

Of Civil Government

3. *Political power,* then, I take to be a *right* of making laws and penalties of death, and consequently all less penalties for the regulating and preserving of property, and of employing the force of the community, in the execution of such laws, and in the defence of the commonwealth from foreign injury, and all this only for the public good.

CHAPTER 2

Of the State of Nature

4. To understand political power, right, and derive it from its original, we must consider what state all men are naturally in, and that is, a *state of perfect freedom* to order their actions, and dispose of their possessions and persons, as they think fit, within the bounds of the law of nature; without asking leave, or depending upon the will of any other man.

A *state* also of *equality,* wherein all the power and jurisdiction is reciprocal, no one having more than another; there being nothing more evident, than that creatures of the same species and rank, promiscuously born to all the same advantages of nature, and the use of the same faculties, should also be equal one amongst another without subordination or subjection; unless the lord and master of them all should, by any manifest declaration of his will, set one above another, and confer on him, by an evident and clear appointment, an undoubted right to dominion and sovereignty.

6. But though this be *a state of liberty,* yet *it is not a state of licence:* though man in that state have an uncontrolable liberty to dispose of his person or possessions, yet he has not liberty to destroy himself, or so much as any creature in his possession, but where some nobler use than its bare preservation calls for it. The *state of nature* has a law of nature to govern it, which obliges every one: And reason, which is that law, teaches all mankind, who will but consult it, that

being all *equal and independent*, no one ought to harm another in his life, health, liberty, or possessions. For men being all the workmanship of one omnipotent and infinitely wise Maker; all the servants of one sovereign master, sent into the world by his order, and about his business; they are his property, whose workmanship they are, made to last during his, not another's pleasure. And being furnished with like faculties, sharing all in one community of nature, there cannot be supposed any such subordination among us, that may authorize us to destroy another, as if we were made for one another's uses, as the inferior ranks of creatures are for ours. Every one, as he is *bound to preserve himself*, and not to quit his station wilfully, so by the like reason, when his own preservation comes not in competition, ought he, as much as he can, *to preserve the rest of mankind,* and may not, unless it be to do justice to an offender, take away or impair the life, or what tends to the preservation of life, the liberty, health, limb, or goods of another.

7. And that all men may be restrained from invading others rights, and from doing hurt to one another, and the law of nature be observed, which willeth the peace and *preservation of all mankind,* the *execution* of the law of nature is, in that state, put into every man's hands, whereby every one has a right to punish the transgressors of that law to such a degree as may hinder its violation. For the *law of nature* would, as all other laws that concern men in this world, be in vain, if there were no body that in the state of nature had a *power to execute* that law, and thereby preserve the innocent and restrain offenders. And if any one in the state of nature may punish another for any evil he has done, every one may do so. For in that *state of perfect equality*, where naturally there is no superiority of jurisdiction of one over another, what any may do in prosecution of that law, every one must needs have a right to do.

8. And thus, in the state of nature, *one man comes by a power over another;* but yet no absolute or arbitrary power, to use a criminal, when he has got him in his hands, according to the passionate heats, or boundless extravagancy of his own will; but only to retribute to him, so far as calm reason and conscience dictate, what is proportionate to his *transgression,* which is so much as may serve for *reparation* and *restraint.* For these two are the only reasons, why one

man may lawfully do harm to another, which is that we call *punishment.*

In transgressing the law of nature, the offender declares himself to live by another rule than that of reason and common equity, which is that measure God has set to the actions of men, for their mutual security; and so he becomes dangerous to mankind, the tie, which is to secure them from injury and violence, being slighted and broken by him. Which being a trespass against the whole species, and the peace and safety of it, provided for by the law of nature; every man upon this score, by the right he hath to preserve mankind in general, may restrain, or, where it is necessary, destroy things noxious to them, and so may bring such evil on any one, who hath transgressed that law, as may make him repent the doing of it, and thereby deter him, and by his example others, from doing the like mischief. And in this case, and upon this ground, *every man hath a right to punish the offender, and be executioner of the law of nature.*

11. From these *two distinct rights,* the one of punishing the *crime for restraint,* and preventing the like offence, which right of punishing is in every body; the other of taking reparation, which belongs only to the injured party; comes it to pass that the magistrate, who by being magistrate, hath the common right of punishing put into his hands, can often, where the public good demands not the execution of the law, *remit* the punishment of criminal offences by his own authority, but yet cannot *remit* the satisfaction due to any private man, for the damage he has received. That, he who has suffered the damage has a right to demand in his own name, and he alone can remit: The damnified person has this power of appropriating to himself the goods or service of the offender, *by right of self-preservation,* as every man has a power to punish the crime, to prevent its being committed again, *by the right he has of preserving all mankind;* and doing all reasonable things he can in order to that end:

14. It is often asked as a mighty objection, *where are,* or ever were, there any *men in such a state of nature?* To which it may suffice as an answer at present: That since all princes and rulers of independent governments, all through the world, are in a state of nature, it is plain the world never was, nor ever will

be, without numbers of men in that state. I have named all governors of independent communities, whether they are, or are not, in league with others. For it is not every compact that puts an end to the state of nature between men, but only this one of agreeing together mutually to enter into one community, and make one body politic; other promises and compacts men may make one with another, and yet still be in the state of nature.

CHAPTER 3

Of the State of War

16. The *state of war* is a state of *enmity* and *destruction*: And therefore declaring by word or action, not a passionate and hasty, but a sedate settled design upon another man's life, *puts him in a state of war* with him against whom he has declared such an intention, and so has exposed his life to the other's power to be taken away by him, or any one that joins with him in his defence, and espouses his quarrel: it being reasonable and just I should have a right to destroy that which threatens me with destruction. For *by the fundamental law of nature, man being to be preserved* as much as possible, when all cannot be preserved, the safety of the innocent is to be preferred: And one may destroy a man who makes war upon him, or has discovered an enmity to his being, for the same reason that he may kill a *wolf* or a *lion;* because such men are not under the ties of the common law of reason, have no other rule, but that of force and violence, and so may be treated as beasts of prey, those dangerous and noxious creatures, that will be sure to destroy him whenever he falls into their power.

17. And hence it is, that he who attempts to get another man into his absolute power, does thereby *put himself into a state of war* with him; it being to be understood as a declaration of a design upon his life. For I have reason to conclude, that he who would get me into his power without my consent, would use me as he pleased when he got me there, and destroy me too when he had a fancy to it; for no body can desire to *have me in his absolute power* unless it be to compel me by force to that which is against the right of my freedom, i.e. make me a slave. To be free from such force is the only security of my preservation; and reason bids me look on him, as an enemy to my preservation, who would take away that freedom

which is the fence to it; so that he who makes an *attempt to enslave* me, thereby puts himself into a state of war with me. He that, in the state of nature, *would take away the freedom* that belongs to any one in that state, must necessarily to supposed to have a design to take away every thing else, that *freedom* being the foundation of all the rest: As he that, in the state of society, would take away the freedom belonging to those of that society or commonwealth, must be supposed to design to take away from them every thing else, and so be looked on as *in a state of war.*

19. And here we have the plain *difference between the state of nature and the state of war;* which however some men have confounded, are as far distant, as a state of peace, good will, mutual assistance and preservation, and a state of enmity, malice, violence and mutual destruction, are one from another. Men living together according to reason, without a common superior on earth, with authority to judge between them, is *properly the state of nature.* But force, or a declared design of force, upon the person of another, where there is no common superior on earth to appeal to for relief, *is the state of war:* And it is the want of such an appeal gives a man the right of war even against an aggressor, though he be in society and a fellow subject. Thus a *thief,* whom I cannot harm, but by appeal to the law, for having stolen all that I am worth, I may kill, when he sets on me to rob me but of my horse or coat; because the law, which was made for my preservation, where it cannot interpose to secure my life from present force, which, if lost, is capable of no reparation, permits me my own defence, and the right of war, a liberty to kill the aggressor, because the aggressor allows not time to appeal to our common judge, nor the decision of the law, for remedy in a case where the mischief may be irreparable. *Want of a common judge with authority, puts all men in a state of nature: Force without right, upon a man's person, makes a state of war,* both where there is, and is not, a common judge.

21. To avoid this state of war (wherein there is no appeal but to heaven, and wherein every the least difference is apt to end, where there is no authority to decide between the contenders) is one great reason of men's putting themselves into society, and quitting the state of nature. For where there is an authority, a power on earth, from which relief can be had by ap-

peal, there the continuance of the state of war is excluded, and the controversy is decided by that power.

CHAPTER 5

Of Property

27. Though the earth, and all inferior creatures, be common to all men, yet every man has a property in his own person: this no body has any right to but himself. The labour of his body, and the work of his hands, we may say, are properly his. Whatsoever then he removes out of the state that nature hath provided, and left it in, he hath mixed his labour with, and joined to it something that is his own, and thereby makes it his property. It being by him removed from the common state nature hath placed it in, it hath by this labour something annexed to it, that excludes the common right of other men. For this labour being the unquestionable property of the labourer, no man but he can have a right to what that is once joined to, at least where there is enough, and as good, left in common for others.

34. God gave the world to men in common; but since he gave it them for their benefit, and the greatest conveniences of life they were capable to draw from it, it cannot be supposed he meant it should always remain common and uncultivated. He gave it to the use of the industrious and rational, (and *labour* was to be *his title* to it) not to the fancy or covetousness of the quarrelsome and contentious. He that had as good left for his improvement, as was already taken up, needed not complain, ought not to meddle with what was already improved by another's labour: If he did, it is plain he desired the benefit of another's pains, which he had no right to, and not the ground which God had given him in common with others to labour on, and whereof there was as good left, as that already possessed, and more than he knew what to do with, or his industry could reach to.

36. The *measure of property* nature has well set by the extent of men's *labour, and the conveniences of life:* No man's labour could subdue or appropriate all; nor could his enjoyment consume more than a small part; so that it was impossible for any man, this way, to entrench upon the right of another, or acquire to himself a property to the prejudice of his neighbor, who would still have room for as good and as large a possession—after the other had taken out his—as before it was appropriated. This measure did confine every man's possession to a very moderate proportion, and such as he might appropriate to himself without injury to anybody, in the first ages of the world, when men were more in danger to be lost by wandering from their company in the then vast wilderness of the earth than to be straitened for want of room to plant in. And the same measure may be allowed still without prejudice to anybody, as full as the world seems. . . .

51. And thus, I think, it is very easy to conceive, without any difficulty *how labour could at first begin a title of property* in the common things of nature, and how the spending it upon our uses bounded it. So that there could then be no reason of quarrelling about title, nor any doubt about the largeness of possession it gave. Right and conveniency went together; for as a man had a right to all he could employ his labour upon, so he had no temptation to labour for more than he could make use of. This left no room for controversy about the title, nor for encroachment on the right of others; what portion a man carved to himself, was easily seen; and it was useless, as well as dishonest, to carve himself too much, or take more than he needed.

CHAPTER 7

Of Political or Civil Society

87. Man being born, as has been proved, with a title to perfect freedom, and an uncontrolled enjoyment of all the rights and privileges of the law of nature, equally with any other man, or number of men in the world, hath by nature a power, not only to preserve his property, that is, his life, liberty, and estate, against the injuries and attempts of other men; but to judge of and punish the breaches of that law in others, as he is persuaded the offence deserves, even with death itself, in crimes where the heinousness of the fact, in his opinion, requires it. But because no *political* society can be, nor subsist, without having in itself the power to preserve the property, and, in order thereunto, punish the offences of all those of that society; there and there only is *political society,* where every one of the members hath

quitted his natural power, resigned it up into the hands of the community in all cases that excludes him not from appealing for protection to the law established by it. And thus all private judgment of every particular member being excluded, the community comes to be umpire by settled standing rules, indifferent, and the same to all parties; and by men having authority from the community, for the execution of those rules, decides all the differences that may happen between any members of that society concerning any matter of right; and punishes those offences which any member hath committed against the society, with such penalties as the law has established, whereby it is easy to discern, who are, and who are not, in *political society* together. Those who are united into one body, and have a common established law and judicature to appeal to, with authority to decide controversies between them, and punish offenders, *are in civil society* one with another: but those who have no such common appeal, I mean on earth, are still in the state of nature, each being, where there is no other, judge for himself, and executioner: which is, as I have before shewed, the perfect *state of nature*.

88. And thus the commonwealth comes by a power to set down what punishment shall belong to the several transgressions which they think worthy of it, committed amongst the members of that society, (which is the *power of making laws*) as well as it has the power to punish any injury done unto any of its members, by any one that is not of it, (which is the power of war and peace,) and all this for the preservation of the property of all the members of that society, as far as is possible. But though every man who has entered into civil society, and is become a member of any commonwealth, has thereby quitted his power to punish offences against the law of nature, in prosecution of his own private judgment; yet with the judgment of offences, which he has given up to the legislative in all cases, where he can appeal to the magistrate, he has given a right to the commonwealth to employ his force, for the execution of the judgments of the commonwealth whenever he shall be called to it; which indeed are his own judgments, they being made by himself, or his representative. And herein we have the original of the legislative and executive power of civil society, which is to judge by standing laws, how far offences are to be punished, when committed within the commonwealth; and also to determine, by occasional judgments founded on the present circumstances of the fact, how far injuries from without are to be vindicated; and in both these to employ all the force of all the members, when there shall be need.

89. Whenever therefore any number of men are so united into one society, as to quit every one his executive power of the law of nature, and to resign it to the public, there and there only is a political, or civil society. And this is done, wherever any number of men, in the state of nature, enter into society to make one people, one body politic, under one supreme government; or else when any one joins himself to, and incorporates with any government already made. For hereby he authorizes the society, or, which is all one, the legislative thereof, to make laws for him, as the public good of the society shall require; to the execution whereof, his own assistance (as to his own degrees) is due. And this puts men out of a state of nature into that of a commonwealth, by setting up a judge on earth, with authority to determine all the controversies, and redress the injuries that may happen to any member of the commonwealth: which judge is the legislative, or magistrate appointed by it. And wherever there are any number of men, however associated, that have no such decisive power to appeal to, there they are still in the state of nature.

90. Hence it is evident, that absolute monarchy, which by some men is counted the only government in the world, is indeed inconsistent with civil society, and so can be no form of civil government at all; for the end of civil society being to avoid and remedy these inconveniencies of the state of nature, which necessarily follow from every man's being judge in his own case, by setting up a known authority, to which every one of that society may appeal upon any injury received, or controversy that may arise, and which every one of the society ought to obey; wherever any persons are, who have not such an authority to appeal to for the decision of any difference between them, there those persons are still *in the state of nature*. And so is every *absolute prince*, in respect of those who are under his dominion.

91. For he being supposed to have all, both legislative and executive power in himself alone, there is no judge to be found, no appeal lies open to any one,

who may fairly, and indifferently, and with authority decide, and from whose decision relief and redress may be expected of any injury or inconveniency that may be suffered from the prince, or by his order: so that such a man, however intitled, *czar*, or *grand seignior,* or how you please, is as much *in the state of nature*, with all under his dominion, as he is with the rest of mankind. For wherever any two men are, who have no standing rule, and common judge to appeal to on earth, for the determination of controversies of right betwixt them, there they are still *in the state of nature*, and under all the inconveniencies of it, with only this woful difference to the subject, or rather slave of an absolute prince; that whereas in the ordinary state of nature he has a liberty to judge of his right, and according to the best of his power, to maintain it; now, whenever his property is invaded by the will and order of his monarch, he has not only no appeal, as those in society ought to have, but, as if he were degraded from the common state of rational creatures, is denied a liberty to judge of, or to defend his right; and so is exposed to all the misery and inconveniencies that a man can fear from one, who being in the unrestrained state of nature, is yet corrupted with flattery, and armed with power.

CHAPTER 8

Of the Beginning of Political Societies

95. Men being, as has been said, by nature, all free, equal, and independent, no one can be put out of this estate, and subjected to the political power of another, without his own consent. The only way, whereby any one divests himself of his natural liberty, and puts on the *bonds of civil society,* is by agreeing with other men to join and unite into a community, for their comfortable, safe, and peaceable living one amongst another, in a secure enjoyment of their properties, and a greater security against any, that are not of it. This any number of men may do, because it injures not the freedom of the rest; they are left as they were in the liberty of the state of nature. When any number of men have so *consented to make one community or government,* they are thereby presently incorporated, and make *one body politic,* wherein the *majority* have a right to act and conclude the rest.

96. For when any number of men have, by the consent of every individual, made a *community,* they have thereby made that *community* one body, with a power to act as one body, which is only by the will and determination of the majority. For that which acts any community, being only the *consent* of the individuals of it, and it being necessary to that which is one body to move one way; it is necessary the body should move that way whither the greater force carries it, which is the *consent of the majority:* or else it is impossible it should act or continue one body, one community, which the consent of every individual that united into it, agreed that it should; and so every one is bound by that consent to be concluded by the majority. And therefore we see, that in assemblies, impowered to act by positive laws, where no number is set by that positive law which impowers them, the *act of the majority* passes for the act of the whole, and of course determines, as having, by the law of nature and reason, the power of the whole.

97. And thus every man, by consenting with others to make one body politic under one government, puts himself under an obligation, to every one of that society, to submit to the determination of the majority, and to be concluded by it; or else this *original compact,* whereby he with others incorporate into one society, would signify nothing, and be no compact, if he be left free, and under no other ties than he was in before in the state of nature. For what appearance would there be of any compact? What new engagement if he were no farther tied by any decrees of the society, than he himself thought fit, and did actually consent to? This would be still as great a liberty, as he himself had before his compact, or any one else in the state of nature hath, who may submit himself, and consent to any acts of it if he thinks fit.

98. For if *the counsel of the majority* shall not, in reason, be received as *the act of the whole,* and concluded every individual; nothing but the consent of every individual can make any thing to be the act of the whole: But such a consent is next to impossible ever to be had, if we consider the infirmities of health, and avocations of business, which in a number, though much less than that of a commonwealth, will necessarily keep many away from the public assembly. To which if we add the variety of opinions, and contrariety of interests, which unavoidably happen in all collections of men, the coming into society upon such terms, would be only like Cato's coming into the theatre, only to go out again. Such a constitution as this would make the mighty *leviathan* of a shorter duration, than the feeblest creatures, and not let it outlast the day it was born in: which cannot be supposed, till we can think, that rational creatures should desire and constitute societies only to be dissolved. For where the majority cannot conclude the rest, there they cannot act as one body, and consequently will be immediately dissolved again.

99. Whosoever therefore out of a state of nature unite into a community, must be understood to give up all the power, necessary to the ends for which they unite into society, to the majority of the community, unless they expressly agreed in any number greater than the majority. And this is done by barely agreeing to *unite into one political society*, which is *all the compact* that is, or needs be, between the individuals, that enter into, or make up a commonwealth. And thus that, which begins and actually *constitutes any political society*, is nothing, but the consent of any number of freemen capable of a majority, to unite and incorporate into such a society. And this is that, and that only, which did, or could give beginning to any lawful government in the world.

CHAPTER 9

Of the Ends of Political Society and Government

123. If man in the state of nature be so free, as has been said; if he be absolute lord of his own person and possession, equal to the greatest, and subject to no body, why will he part with his freedom? why will he give up this empire, and subject himself to the dominion and control of any other power? To which it is obvious to answer, that though in the state of nature he hath such a right, yet the enjoyment of it is very uncertain, and constantly exposed to the invasion of others. For all being kings as much as he, every man his equal, and the greater part no strict observers of equity and justice, the enjoyment of the property he has in this state is very unsafe, very unsecure. This makes him willing to quit this condition, which, however free, is full of fears and continual dangers: and it is not without reason, that he seeks out, and is willing to join in society with others, who are already united, or have a mind to unite, for the mutual preservation of their lives, liberties, and estates, which I call by the general name, property.

124. The great and *chief end*, therefore, of men's uniting into commonwealths, and putting themselves under government, *is the preservation of their property*. To which in the state of nature there are many things wanting.

First, There wants an established, settled, known law, received and allowed by common consent to be the standard of right and wrong, and the common measure to decide all controversies between them. For though the law of nature be plain and intelligible to all rational creatures; yet men being biassed by their interest, as well as ignorant for want of studying it, are not apt to allow of it as a law binding to them in the application of it to their particular cases.

125. Secondly, In the state of nature there wants *a known and indifferent judge*, with authority to determine all differences according to the established law. For every one in that state being both judge and executioner of the law of nature, men being partial to themselves, passion and revenge is very apt to carry them too far, and with too much heat, in their own cases; as well as negligence, and unconcernedness, to make them too remiss in other men's.

126. Thirdly, In the state of nature, there often wants power to back and support the sentence when right, and to give it due execution. They who by any injustice offended, will seldom fail, where they are able, by force to make good their injustice; such resistance many times makes the punishment dangerous, and frequently destructive, to those who attempt it.

127. Thus mankind, notwithstanding all the privileges of the state of nature, being but in an ill condition, while they remain in it, are quickly driven into society. Hence it comes to pass that we seldom find any number of men live any time together in this state. The inconveniencies that they are therein exposed to, by the irregular and uncertain exercise of the power every man has of punishing the transgressions of others, make them take sanctuary under the established laws of government, and therein seek *the preservation of their property*. It is this makes them so willingly give up every one his single power of punishing, to be exercised by such alone, as shall be appointed to it amongst them; and by such rules as the community, or those authorized by them to that purpose, shall agree on. And in this we have the original *right and rise of both the legislative and executive power*, as well as of the governments and societies themselves.

STUDY QUESTIONS: *LOCKE, A TREATISE CONCERNING CIVIL GOVERNMENT*

1. How does Locke define the *state of perfect freedom?* How is it related to the state of nature? How are these related to Locke's notion of civil government?
2. What is Locke's view of private property? How is it related to labor?
3. What does he mean by civil society? Why is absolute monarchy, in Locke's view, inconsistent with civil society?
4. What is the chief end of forming a government and entering a commonwealth?

Philosophical Bridges: Locke's Influence

In the *Essay Concerning Human Understanding,* Locke formulates the basic Empiricist principle that all concepts are derived from the simple ideas of sense and reflection. This same principle forms the starting premise of the philosophies of Berkeley and Hume, as well as other seventeenth- and eighteenth-century Empiricists. This is why Locke is sometimes referred to as the father of Empiricism: he originated a tradition that includes Mill in the nineteenth century and the logical positivists in the twentieth century, as well as Berkeley and Hume.

Locke's *Essay* had an important influence on the development of psychology in Britain. Until the later part of the nineteenth century, much psychology was broadly Empiricist and associationist. According to this view, the mind consists in a collection of ideas that can be associated into wider wholes. Much of this approach has its roots in Locke, who can be regarded as a founder of empirical psychology.

The French edition of Locke's *Essay* was published in 1700, and it was lauded as a great psychological work. For example, Voltaire, who visited England from 1726 to 1729, claimed that Locke laid open the anatomy of the soul. Locke's work became an inspiration to the French Enlightenment in more general terms, too. For example, Étienne Condillac (1715–1780) adapted Locke's Empiricist ideas in order to argue against the metaphysical systems of Spinoza and Leibniz. Perhaps, the popularity of Locke's work was in part due to its tone: Locke argues for revolutionary ideas in quietly reasonable terms in the areas of epistemology and philosophy of religion, as well as politics.

Book II of Locke's *Essay* attempts to provide an overall and systematic explanation of human concepts and knowledge based on sense experience and reflection. It has had a powerful influence because of its extensive scope. Locke deals with many important concepts within his explanatory scheme, and often the details of his treatment have been influential. For example, his discussions on space, time, infinity, substance, and cause have all had a significant impact on later thinkers. We shall focus briefly on three of the most famous of such examples.

First, Locke's distinction between primary and secondary qualities is often regarded as defining a central philosophical issue because it concerns the division between appearance and reality. Locke's idea is that the primary qualities, such as size and shape, are the real and nonrelative properties of an object, whereas its secondary qualities are relative to our perceptual capacities. In his book on Descartes, the British philosopher Bernard Williams argues that this kind of view is necessitated by an absolute conception of reality and the claim that science seeks knowledge of reality so conceived. In short, reality consists only of matter and its measurable primary qualities. Other thinkers, opposed to such a move, argue that secondary qualities are a part of reality as much as the primary ones and reject the absolute conception of reality.

Second, Locke distinguished real and nominal essence, and a similar distinction has been canvassed in contemporary philosophy. The real essence of, for example, gold consists of certain arrangements of the primary qualities of the minute particles of that substance type. The real essence of each substance provides a scientific basis for explaining why all instances of gold share common observable properties. The contemporary philosophers Hilary Putnam (in 'Meaning and Reference') and Saul Kripke (*Naming and Necessity*) have argued that natural kind terms such as 'gold' refer to the real essence of gold, even when this real essence was not known.

Third, Locke's discussion of personal identity has been influential for both its content and style. By employing puzzle examples, such as the hypothetical cases of the cobbler and the prince in Book II (Ch. 27.15), Locke set the tone of much of the debate in this area. For example, two contemporary writers in this field, Robert Nozick (*Philosophical Explanations*) and Derek Parfit (*Reasons and Persons*), use a host of puzzle cases to dispute both materialist and psychological theories of personal identity.

Book III of the *Essay* is one of the first works to provide explicitly a communicative theory of linguistic meaning. Locke's conception of language as a means of communication initiated a tradition that includes the recent work of H. P. Grice, who tries to explain sentence meaning in terms of the communicative intentions of speakers ('Meaning,' *Philosophical Review*, 1957)

Locke's political philosophy has had an immense influence on political thought and practice. Locke's political ideas moved to France when Voltaire returned home in 1729 and when Baron Montesquieu (1689–1755) visited England that same year. Rousseau's political theory, which helped ignite the French Revolution, owed much to Locke, as did the Declaration of the Rights of Man issued in 1789 by the new French Assembly, before the revolution took a violent turn in 1792. Locke's political philosophy inspired directly the U.S. Declaration of Independence, as well as the Bill of Rights, as did his arguments for the separation of church and state, and for religious toleration and liberty.

GEORGE BERKELEY (1685–1753)

Biographical History

At the age of 15 George Berkeley entered Trinity College, Dublin. In 1707, he published a work on mathematics and was made a fellow at Trinity. He also took holy orders in the Anglican Church. His *Essay Towards a New Theory of Vision* appeared in 1709, and, at the age of 25, the following year, he published A *Treatise Concerning the Principles of Human Knowledge*. Three years later, the *Three Dialogues Between Hylas and Philonous* was published.

In 1713, he moved to London, where he became friends with the city's intellectuals, including Alexander Pope and Jonathan Swift. In 1721, he published *An Essay Towards Preventing the Ruin of Great Britain*. He began to plan and solicit support for a college in Bermuda. In 1728, he sailed for America with his new wife, Anne, and purchased 100 acres of land near Newport, Rhode Island. During this peiod, Berkeley wrote *Alciphron*, a philosophical defense of Christianity. By 1732, the anticipated funds from England had not arrived, and Berkeley, disappointed, returned to London. In 1734, he was appointed bishop of Cloyne and returned to Ireland to live in his diocese for 18 years. In 1744, he published *Siris*, which promoted the medical use of tar water, made by boiling in water the tar from pine trees. Berkeley had seven children, three of whom died in infancy, and his eldest son survived only to age 14.

Philosophical Overview

Berkeley regards Locke's philosophy as skeptical and atheistic, two faults that he over-comes, dramatically, by denying the existence of material substance. Minds and their ideas are all that exist. Our ideas of sense perception are not caused by material objects that lie behind a veil of perception, but directly by God. What we call objects are simply our ideas of sense, which exist only in the mind.

The Argument from Illusion

The first step in Berkeley's attack on the existence of matter is the claim that we perceive only our own ideas. To argue for this conclusion, he appeals to the so-called argument from illusion to show that sensible qualities, or the qualities we perceive, are nothing but ideas. The argument is as follows:

1. *The real properties of an external object cannot change without the occurrence of a change in the object itself.*
2. *The colors I perceive can change without the occurrence of a change in the object itself.*

3. *Therefore, the colors I perceive are not the real properties of an external object.*

The first premise establishes a criterion or that the real properties of an external object must satisfy: if those properties change, there must be a corresponding change in the object itself. The second premise informs us that the colors we perceive fail that test or criterion. For instance, perceived color can change if we wear colored glasses or if the surrounding lighting is altered. Since the colors I perceive are not the real properties of an external object, they are only ideas.

Berkeley applies this argument to all the sensible qualities that we perceive. The sounds we hear, the tastes and smells we perceive, and the sensations of touch are all subject to illusion. This implies that all sensible qualities that we perceive are only ideas—or, in other words, that we only perceive our own ideas.

Berkeley uses this conclusion to present a dilemma. Prior to philosophical reflection, most of us would assent to the following two claims:

1. *We perceive objects, such as tables and trees, which exist in the external world; and*
2. *They possess sensible qualities such as shape, size, and color.*

The argument from illusion implies that these two assertions are inconsistent. If we insist that tables and trees are part of the external world, the argument shows that we never perceive them (because we perceive only our own ideas). If, on the other hand, we claim that we do perceive tables and trees, the argument from illusion shows that they are not part of the external world, because they must be merely ideas. In brief, either tables and chairs are only ideas or they are not perceived. Of these two alternatives, Berkeley argues for the first. It is contrary to common sense to assert that tables, and all other sensible objects, are never perceived, and he unhesitatingly draws the conclusion that they are merely ideas.

Primary and Secondary Qualities

To resist this argument one might appeal to Locke's distinction between primary and sec-ondary qualities, by distinguishing between, for example, sounds as they are perceived, and sound as it is in itself, which is a vibration in the air. In reply, Berkeley contends that the argument from illusion also applies to primary qualities. Shape, size, speed of motion, and solidity all vary according to the conditions of perception without requiring a change in the object and, therefore, are simply ideas in the mind.

Second, Berkeley attacks Locke's claim that primary qualities resemble our ideas of sense, by arguing that 'an idea can be like nothing but another idea.' In order to compare two things it is necessary to perceive them both. It does not make sense to talk of resemblance when there is no possibility of comparison. But, because we can perceive only our own ideas, it is impossible to compare an idea with a primary quality of an object, which cannot be perceived. In summary, Berkeley argues that the following three claims are inconsistent:

a. *Primary qualities resemble their ideas.*
b. *We can only perceive our own ideas.*
c. *The claim that two things resemble each other requires that they can be compared.*

Given that claims B and C are true, then claim A (the resemblance thesis) must be false.

Sensible Objects and Matter

Trees, rivers, and mountains are all sensible objects that, by definition, we perceive. However, the argument from illusion shows that we can only ever perceive our own ideas, which cannot exist unperceived. Therefore, sensible objects are only collections of ideas and cannot exist unperceived.

From this, Berkeley argues that either (a) the idea of material substance is a contradiction, or else (b) it is meaningless.

a. *On one hand, suppose that one claims, as Locke does, that material objects have sensible qualities or something resembling them. In this case, Berkeley argues that the concept of material substance involves a contradiction. It is contradictory to suppose that an idea could exist in anything but a mind; something inert, such as matter, cannot have sensible qualities, which are only ideas. Furthermore, the only thing that can resemble an idea is another idea. Therefore, matter cannot have anything resembling ideas.*
b. *On the other hand, suppose that one claims that material objects do not have sensible qualities. In this case, Berkeley argues that material substance is utterly unknowable. We can perceive only sensible qualities, which are ideas; and, therefore, if material objects do not have sensible qualities, then they must be unperceivable. In this case, since all knowledge is derived from perception, matter cannot be known. Given this, the idea of matter must be meaningless: something unperceivable and unknowable cannot be significantly talked about.*

Unperceived Objects and the Existence of God

If sensible objects are only ideas, and if the essence of an idea is to be perceived, then surely objects cease to exist when I do not perceive them. Is this true? Berkeley claims that an object unperceived by me can be said to exist because it is perceived by God.

Berkeley argues that this God hypothesis is better than Locke's theory that ideas of sense are caused by material objects. First, the idea of matter is a contradiction. Second, according to Locke, God creates matter, and matter causes ideas in us. Berkeley claims that his own explanation is simpler than Locke's: God directly creates ideas in our minds, without the need for matter as an intermediary. Third, matter cannot cause ideas because it is inert. By arguing that God directly causes our sensible ideas, Berkeley tries to destroy the atheism that he thinks is inherent in Locke's materialism.

The Spirit or Mind

According to Berkeley, the only substances are spirits or minds. A spirit is a simple undivided active being. Insofar as a mind perceives ideas, it has understanding; insofar as it produces ideas, it is a will. Berkeley claims that we can have no idea of spirit, because all ideas are passive and inert, and spirits or minds are essentially active. Nevertheless, we still know what the word 'spirit' means, because each of us is a spirit and is directly aware of his or her own being. We do have the notion of a spirit. Berkeley says, 'My own mind and own ideas, I have immediate knowledge of.'

A TREATISE CONCERNING THE PRINCIPLES OF HUMAN KNOWLEDGE

As you work through the details of Berkeley's argument for the conclusions that we can only perceive our own ideas and that material substance does not exist, it is important to bear in mind a few points. First, Berkeley felt assured of his conclusions because he was convinced that he had a series of sound arguments to support them. One aim in studying his text would be to understand the arguments sufficiently that you are willing to be persuaded by them. Second, it is tempting to dismiss Berkeley's conclusions without examining the arguments. This is what the famous English writer Dr. Samuel Johnson did when he kicked a stone and said, 'I hereby refute Berkeley.' Once you have understood Berkeley's arguments well enough that you are willing to be convinced by them, you may wish to turn a sharper critical light on those arguments. Try to find the problems with Berkeley's arguments. Third, Berkeley may have anticipated your objections. It is worth checking to see if he has and asking whether his reply is adequate. Finally, it is important to remember Berkeley's overall aims. He is reacting primarily against the philosophies of Hobbes and Locke, which he regards as materialistic and atheistic. In other words, he conceives of the universe as a spiritual place inhabited only by God and nonmaterial souls.

THE PREFACE

What I here make public has, a long and scrupulous inquiry, seemed to me evidently true and not unuseful to be known; particularly to those who are tainted with Scepticism, or want a demonstration of the existence and immateriality of God, or the natural immortality of the Soul. Whether it be so or no I am content the reader should impartially examine; since I do not think myself any farther concerned for the success of what I have written than as it is agreeable to truth. But, to the end this may not suffer, I make it my request that the reader suspend his judgment till he has once at least read the whole through, with that degree of attention and thought which the subject-matter shall seem to deserve. For, as there are some passages that, taken by themselves, are very liable (nor could it be remedied) to gross misinterpretation, and to be charged with most absurd consequences, which, nevertheless, upon an entire perusal will appear not to follow from them; so likewise, though the whole should be read over, yet, if this be done transiently, it is very probable my sense may be mistaken: but to a thinking reader, I flatter myself it will be throughout clear and obvious.

As for the characters of novelty and singularity which some of the following notions may seem to bear, it is, I hope, needless to make any apology on that account. He must surely be either very weak, or very little acquainted with the sciences, who shall reject a truth that is capable of demonstration, for no other reason but because it is newly known, and contrary to the prejudices of mankind.

Thus much I thought fit to premise, in order to prevent, if possible, the hasty censures of a sort of men who are too apt to condemn an opinion before they rightly comprehend it.

INTRODUCTION

1. Philosophy being nothing else but the study of Wisdom and Truth, it may with reason be expected that those who have spent most time and pains in it should enjoy a greater clam and serenity of mind, a greater clearness and evidence of knowledge, and be less disturbed with doubts and difficulties than other men. Yet, so it is, we see the illiterate bulk of mankind, that walk the highroad of plain common sense, and are governed by the dictates of nature, for the most part easy and undisturbed. To them nothing that is familiar appears unaccountable or difficult to comprehend. They complain not of any want of evidence in their senses, and are out of all danger of becoming Sceptics. But no sooner do we depart from sense and instinct to follow the light of a superior principle—to reason, mediate, and reflect on the nature of things, but a thousand scruples spring up in our minds, concerning those things which before we seemed fully to comprehend. Prejudices and errors of sense do from all parts discover themselves to our view; and, endeavouring to correct these by reason, we are insensibly drawn into uncouth paradoxes, difficulties, and inconsistencies, which multiply and grow upon us as we advance in speculation; till at length, having wandered through many intricate mazes, we find ourselves just where we were, or, which is worse, sit down in a forlorn Scepticism.

2. The cause of this is thought to be the obscurity of things, or the natural weakness and imperfection of our understandings. It is said the faculties we have are few, and those designed by nature for the support and pleasure of life, and not to penetrate into the inward essence and constitution of things: besides, the mind of man being finite, when it treats of things which partake of Infinity, it is not to be

wondered at if it run into absurdities and contradictions, out of which it is impossible it should ever extricate itself; it being of the nature of Infinite not to be comprehended by that which is finite.

3. But, perhaps, we may be too partial to ourselves in placing the fault originally in our faculties, and not rather in the wrong use we make of them. It is a hard thing to suppose that right deductions from true principles should ever end in consequences which cannot be maintained or made consistent. We should believe that God has dealt more bountifully with the sons of men than to give them a strong desire for that knowledge which he had placed quite out of their reach. This were not agreeable to the wonted indulgent methods of Providence, which, whatever appetites it may have implanted in the creatures, doth usually furnish them with such means as, if rightly made use of, will not fail to satisfy them. Upon the whole, I am inclined to think that the far greater part, if not all, of those difficulties which have hitherto amused philosophers, and blocked up the way to knowledge, are entirely owing to ourselves. We have first raised a dust, and then complain we cannot see.

4. My purpose therefore is, to try if I can discover what those Principles are which have introduced all that doubtfulness and uncertainty, those absurdities and contradictions, into the several sects of philosophy; insomuch that the wisest men have thought our ignorance incurable, conceiving it to arise from the natural dulness and limitation of our faculties. And surely it is a work well deserving our pains to make a strict inquiry concerning the First Principles of Human Knowledge; to sift and examine them on all sides: especially since there may be some grounds to suspect that those lets and difficulties, which stay and embarrass the mind in its search after truth, do not spring from any darkness and intricacy in the objects, or natural defect in the understanding, so much as from false Principles which have been insisted on, and might have been avoided.

5. How difficult and discouraging soever this attempt may seem, when I consider what a number of very great and extraordinary men have gone before me in the like designs, yet I am not without some hopes; upon the consideration that the largest views are not always the clearest, and that he who is short-

sighted will be obliged to draw the object nearer, and may, perhaps, by a close and narrow survey, discern that which had escaped far better eyes.

6. In order to prepare the mind of the reader for the easier conceiving what follows, it is proper to premise somewhat, by way of Introduction, concerning the nature and abuse of Language. But the unravelling this matter leads me in some measure to anticipate my design, by taking notice of what seems to have had a chief part in rendering speculation intricate and perplexed, and to have occasioned innumerable errors and difficulties in almost all parts of knowledge. And that is the opinion that the mind hath a power of framing *abstract* ideas or notions of things. He who is not a perfect stranger to the writings and disputes of philosophers must needs acknowledge that no small part of them are spent about abstract ideas. These are in a more especial manner thought to be the object of those sciences which go by the name of logic and metaphysics, and of all that which passes under the notion of the most abstracted and sublime learning; in all which one shall scarce find any question handled in such a manner as does not suppose their existence in the mind, and that it is well acquainted with them.

7. It is agreed on all hands that the *qualities* or *modes* of things do never really exist each of them apart by itself, and separated from all others, but are mixed, as it were, and blended together, several in the same object. But, we are told, the mind, being able to consider each quality singly, or abstracted from those other qualities with which it is united, does by that means frame to itself *abstract ideas*. For example, there is conceived by sight an object extended, coloured, and moved: this mixed or compound idea the mind resolving into its simple, constituent parts, and viewing each by itself, exclusive of the rest, does frame the abstract ideas of extension, colour, and motion. Not that it is possible for colour or motion to exist without extension; but only that the mind can frame to itself by abstraction the idea of color exclusive of extension, and of motion exclusive of both colour and extension.

8. Again, the mind having observed that in the particular extensions perceived by sense there is something common and alike in all, and some other things peculiar, as this or that figure or magnitude, which distinguish them one from another, it considers apart, or singles out by itself, that which is common; making thereof a most abstract idea of extension; which is neither line, surface, nor solid, nor has any figure or magnitude, but is an idea entirely prescinded from all these. So likewise the mind, by leaving out of the particular colours perceived by sense that which distinguishes them one from another, and retaining that only which is common to all, makes an idea of colour in abstract; which is neither red, nor blue, nor white, nor any other determinate colour. And, in like manner, by considering motion abstractedly, not only from the body moved, but likewise from the figure it describes, and all particular directions and velocities, the abstract idea of motion is framed; which equally corresponds to all particular motions whatsoever that may be perceived by sense.

9. And as the mind frames to itself abstract ideas of *qualities* or *modes*, so does it, by the same precision, or mental separation, attain abstract ideas of the more compounded *beings* which include several co-existent qualities. For example, the mind having observed that Peter, James, and John resemble each other in certain common agreements of shape and other qualities, leaves out of the complex or compound idea it has of Peter, James, and any other particular man, that which is peculiar to each, retaining only what is common to all, and so makes an abstract idea, wherein all the particulars equally partake; abstracting entirely from and cutting off all those circumstances and differences which might determine it to any particular existence. And after this manner it is said we come by the abstract idea of *man*, or, if you please, humanity, or human nature; wherein it is true there is included colour, because there is no man but has some colour, but then it can be neither white, nor black, nor any particular colour, because there is no one particular colour wherein all men partake. So likewise there is included stature, but then it is neither tall stature, nor low stature, nor yet middle stature, but something abstracted from all these. And so of the rest. Moreover, there being a great variety of other creatures that partake in some parts, but not all, of the complex idea of man, the mind, leaving out those parts which are peculiar to men, and retaining those only which are common to all the

living creatures, frames the idea of *animal*; which abstracts not only from all particular men, but also all birds, beasts, fishes, and insects. The constituent parts of the abstract idea of animal are body, life, sense, and spontaneous motion. By *body* is meant body without any particular shape or figure, there being no one shape or figure common to all animals; without covering, either of hair, or feathers, or scales, &c., nor yet naked: hair, feathers, scales, and nakedness being the distinguishing properties of particular animals, and for that reason left out of the abstract idea. Upon the same account, the spontaneous motion must be neither walking, nor flying, nor creeping; it is nevertheless a motion, but what that motion is it is not easy to conceive.

10. Whether others have this wonderful faculty of abstracting their ideas, they best can tell. For myself, [I dare be confident I have it not]. I find indeed I have a faculty of imagining, or representing to myself, the ideas of those particular things I have perceived, and of variously compounding and dividing them. I can imagine a man with two heads; or the upper parts of a man joined to the body of a horse. I can consider the hand, the eye, the nose, each by itself abstracted or separated from the rest of the body. But then whatever hand or eye I imagine, it must have some particular shape and colour. Likewise the idea of man that I frame to myself must be either of a white, or a black, or a tawny, a straight, or a crooked, a tall, or a low, or a middle-sized man. I cannot by any effort of thought conceive the abstract idea above described. And it is equally impossible for me to form the abstract idea of motion distinct from the body moving, and which is neither swift nor slow, curvilinear nor rectilinear; and the like may be said of all other abstract general ideas whatsoever. To be plain, I own myself able to abstract in one sense, as when I consider some particular parts or qualities separated from others, with which, though they are united in some object, yet it is possible they may really exist without them. But I deny that I can abstract from one another, or conceive separately, those qualities which it is impossible should exist so separated; or that I can frame a general notion, by abstracting from particulars in the manner aforesaid—which last are the two proper acceptations of *abstraction*. And there is ground to think most men

will acknowledge themselves to be in my case. The generality of men which are simple and illiterate never pretend to abstract notions. It is said they are difficult and not to be attained without pains and study. We may therefore reasonably conclude that, if such there be, they are confined only to the learned.

11. I proceed to examine what can be alleged in defence of the doctrine of abstraction, and try if I can discover what it is that inclines the men of speculation to embrace an opinion so remote from common sense as that seems to be. There has been a late [excellent and] deservedly esteemed philosopher[1] who, no doubt, has given it very much countenance, by seeming to think the having abstract general ideas is what puts the widest difference in point of understanding betwixt man and beast. 'The having of general ideas,' saith he, 'is that which puts a perfect distinction betwixt man and brutes, and is an excellency which the faculties of brutes do by no means attain unto. For it is evident we observe no foot-steps in them of making use of general signs for universal ideas; from which we have reason to imagine that they have not the faculty of abstracting, or making general ideas, since they have no use of words, or any other general signs.' And a little after:—'Therefore, I think, we may suppose, that it is in this that the species of brutes are discriminated from man: and it is that proper difference wherein they are wholly separated, and which at last widens to so wide a distance. For if they have any ideas at all, and are not bare machines (as some would have them), we cannot deny them to have some reason. It seems as evident to me that they do, some of them, in certain instances, reason, as that they have sense; but it is only in particular ideas, just as they receive them from their senses. They are the best of them tied up within those narrow bounds, and have not (as I think) the faculty to enlarge them by any kind of abstraction.'—*Essay on Human Understanding*, B. II. ch. 11. § 10 and 11. I readily agree with this learned author, that the faculties of brutes can by no means attain to abstraction. But then if this be made the distinguishing property of that sort of animals, I fear a great many of those that pass for men must be reckoned into their number. The reason that is here assigned, why we have no grounds to think brutes have abstract general ideas, is, that we observe in them no use of words, or any

other general signs; which is built on this supposition, to wit, that the making use of words implies having general ideas. From which it follows that men who use language are able to abstract or generalize their ideas. That this is the sense and arguing of the author will further appear by his answering the question he in another place puts: 'Since all things that exist are only particulars, how come we by general terms?' His answer is: 'Words become general by being made the signs of general ideas.'—*Essay on Human Understanding*, B. III. ch. 3. § 6. But it seems that a word becomes general by being made the sign, not of an abstract general idea, but of several particular ideas, any one of which it indifferently suggests to the mind. For example, when it is said 'the change of motion is proportional to the impressed force,' or that 'whatever has extension is divisible,' these propositions are to be understood of motion and extension in general; and nevertheless it will not follow that they suggest to my thoughts an *idea* of motion without a body moved, or any determinate direction and velocity; or that I must conceive an *abstract general idea* of extension, which is neither line, surface, nor solid, neither great nor small, black, white, nor red, nor of any other determinate colour. It is only implied that whatever particular motion I consider, whether it be swift or slow, perpendicular, horizontal, or oblique, or in whatever object, the axiom concerning it holds equally true. As does the other of every particular extension; it matters not whether line, surface, or solid, whether of this or that magnitude or figure.

12. By observing how ideas become general, we may the better judge how words are made so. And here it is to be noted that I do not deny absolutely there are *general ideas*, but only that there are any *abstract general ideas*. For, in the passages we have quoted wherein there is mention of general ideas, it is always supposed that they are formed by abstraction, after the manner set forth in section 8 and 9. Now, if we will annex a meaning to our words, and speak only of what we can conceive, I believe we shall acknowledge that an idea, which considered in itself is particular, becomes general, by being made to represent or stand for all other particular ideas of the same sort. To make this plain by an example. Suppose a geometrician is demonstrating the method of cutting a line in two equal parts. He draws, for instance, a black line of an inch in length: this, which in itself is a particular line, is nevertheless *with regard to its signification* general; since, as it is there used, it represents all particular lines whatsoever; so that what is demonstrated of it is demonstrated of all lines, or, in other words, of a line in general. And, as *that particular line* becomes general by being made a sign, so the *name* line, which taken absolutely is particular, by being a sign, is made general. And as the former owes its generality, not to its being the sign of an abstract or general line, but of all particular right lines that may possibly exist, so the latter must be thought to derive its generality from the same cause, namely, the various particular lines which it indifferently denotes.

13. To give the reader a yet clearer view of the nature of abstract ideas, and the uses they are thought necessary to, I shall add one more passage out of the *Essay on Human Understanding*, which is as follows:— 'Abstract ideas are not so obvious or easy to children, or the yet unexercised mind, as particular ones. If they seem so to grown men, it is only because by constant and familiar use they are made so. For, when we nicely reflect upon them, we shall find that general ideas are fictions and contrivances of the mind, that carry difficulty with them, and do not so easily offer themselves as we are apt to imagine. For example, does it not require some pains and skill to form the general idea of a triangle (which is yet none of the most abstract, comprehensive, and difficult); for it must be neither oblique nor rectangle, neither equilateral, equicrural, nor scalenon; but all and none of these at once? In effect, it is something imperfect, that cannot exist; an idea wherein some parts of several different and inconsistent ideas are put together. It is true the mind, in this imperfect state, has need of such ideas, and makes all the haste to them it can, for the conveniency of communication and enlargement of knowledge; to both which it is naturally very much inclined. But yet one has reason to suspect such ideas are marks of our imperfection. At least this is enough to shew that the most abstract and general ideas are not those that the mind is first and most easily acquainted with, nor such as its earliest knowledge is conversant about.'—B. iv. ch. 7. § 9. If any man has the faculty of framing in his mind such an idea of a triangle as is here described, it is in vain to pretend to dispute him out of it, nor would I go about it. All I desire is that the reader would fully and certainly inform himself whether he has such an idea or no. And this, methinks, can be no hard task for any one to perform. What more easy than for any one to look a little into his own thoughts, and there try whether he has, or can attain to have, an idea that shall correspond with the description that is here given of the general idea of a triangle—which is neither oblique nor rectangle, equilateral, equicrural nor scalenon, but all and none of these at once?

14. Much is here said of the difficulty that abstract ideas carry with them, and the pains and skill requisite to the forming them. And it is on all hands agreed that there is need of great toil and labour of the mind, to emancipate our thoughts from particular objects, and raise them to those sublime speculations that are conversant about abstract ideas. From all which the natural consequence should seem to be, that so difficult a thing as the forming abstract ideas was not necessary for *communication*, which is so easy and familiar to all sorts of men. But, we are told, if they seem obvious and easy to grown men, it is only because by constant and familiar use they are made so. Now, I would fain know at what time it is men are employed in surmounting that difficulty, and furnishing themselves with those necessary helps for discourse. It cannot be when they are grown up; for then it seems they are not conscious of any such painstaking. It remains therefore to be the business of their childhood. And surely the great and multiplied labour of framing abstract notions will be found a hard task for that tender age. Is it not a hard thing to imagine that a couple of children cannot prate together of their sugar-plums and rattles and the rest of their little trinkets, till they have first tacked together numberless inconsistencies, and so framed in their minds abstract general ideas, and annexed them to every common name they make use of?

15. Nor do I think them a whit more needful for the *enlargement of knowledge* than for communication. It is, I know, a point much insisted on, that all knowledge and demonstration are about universal notions, to which I fully agree. But then it does not appear to me that those notions are formed by abstraction in the manner premised—*universality*, so far as I can comprehend, not consisting in the absolute, positive nature or conception of anything, but in the relation it bears to the particulars signified or represented by it; by virtue whereof it is that things, names, or notions, being in their own nature *particular*, are *rendered universal*. Thus, when I demonstrate any proposition concerning triangles, it is supposed that I have in view the universal idea of a triangle: which ought not to be understood as if I could frame an *idea* of a triangle which was neither equilateral, nor scalenon, nor equicrural; but only that the particular triangle I consider, whether of this or that sort it matters not, doth equally stand for and represent all rectilinear triangles whatsoever, and is in that sense universal. All which seems very plain and not to include any difficulty in it.

16. But here it will be demanded, how we can know any proposition to be true of all particular triangles, except we have first seen it demonstrated of the abstract idea of a triangle which equally agrees to all? For, because a property may be demonstrated to agree to some one particular triangle, it will not thence follow that it equally belongs to any other triangle which in all respects is not the same with it. For example, having demonstrated that the three angles of an isosceles rectangular triangle are equal to two right ones, I cannot therefore conclude this affection agrees to all other triangles which have neither a right angle nor two equal sides. It seems therefore, that, to be certain this proposition is universally true, we must either make a particular demonstration for every particular triangle, which is impossible; or once for all demonstrate it of the abstract idea of a triangle, in which all the particulars do indifferently partake, and by which they are all equally represented. To which I answer, that, though the idea I have in view whilst I make the demonstration be, for instance, that of an isosceles rectangular triangle whose sides are of a determinate length, I may nevertheless be certain it extends to all other rectilinear triangles, of what sort or bigness soever. And that because neither the right angle, nor the equality, nor determinate length of the sides are at all concerned in the demonstration. It is true the diagram I have in view includes all these particulars; but then there is not the least mention made of *them* in the proof of the proposition. It is not said the three angles are equal to two right ones, because one of them is a right angle, or because the sides comprehending it

are of the same length. Which sufficiently shews that the right angle might have been oblique, and the sides unequal, and for all that the demonstration have held good. And for this reason it is that I conclude that to be true of any obliquangular or scalenon which I have demonstrated of a particular right-angled equicrural triangle, and not because I demonstrated the proposition of the abstract idea of a triangle. [And here it must be acknowledged that a man may *consider* a figure merely as triangular; without attending to the particular qualities of the angles, or relations of the sides. *So far he may abstract.* But this will never prove that he can frame an abstract, general, inconsistent *idea* of a triangle. In like manner we may consider Peter so far forth as man, or so far forth as animal, without framing the forementioned abstract idea, either of man or of animal; inasmuch as all that is perceived is not considered.]

17. It were an endless as well as an useless thing to trace the Schoolmen, those great masters of abstraction, through all the manifold inextricable labyrinths of error and dispute which their doctrine of abstract natures and notions seems to have led them into. What bickerings and controversies, and what a learned dust have been raised about those matters, and what mighty advantage has been from thence derived to mankind, are things at this day too clearly known to need being insisted on. And it had been well if the ill effects of that doctrine were confined to those only who make the most avowed profession of it. When men consider the great pains, industry, and parts that have for so many ages been laid out on the cultivation and advancement of the sciences, and that notwithstanding all this the far greater part of them remain full of darkness and uncertainty, and disputes that are like never to have an end; and even those that are thought to be supported by the most clear and congent demonstrations contain in them paradoxes which are perfectly irreconcilable to the understandings of men; and that, taking all together, a very small portion of them does supply any real benefit to mankind, otherwise than by being an innocent diversion and amusement—I say, the consideration of all this is apt to throw them into a despondency and perfect contempt of all study. But this may perhaps cease upon a view of the false Principles that have obtained in the world; amongst all which there is

none, methinks, hath a more wide influence over the thoughts of speculative men than this of *abstract general ideas*.

18. I come now to consider to *source* of this prevailing notion, and that seems to me to be *language*. And surely nothing of less extent than reason itself could have been the source of an opinion so universally received. The truth of this appears as from other reasons so also from the plain confession of the ablest patrons of abstract ideas, who acknowledge that they are made in order to naming; from which it is clear consequence that if there had been no such thing as speech or universal signs, there never had been any thought of abstraction. See B. iii. ch. 6. §39, and elsewhere of the *Essay on Human Understanding.*

Let us examine the manner wherein Words have contributed to the origin of that mistake.—First then, it is thought that every name has, or ought to have, one only precise and settled signification; which inclines men to think there are certain abstract determinate ideas that constitute the true and only immediate signification of each general name; and that it is by the mediation of these abstract ideas that a general name comes to signify any particular thing. Whereas, in truth, there is no such thing as one precise and definite signification annexed to any general name, they all signifying indifferently a great number of particular ideas. All which does evidently follow from what has been already said, and will clearly appear to any one by a little reflexion. To this it will be objected that every name that has a definition is thereby restrained to one certain signification. For example, a triangle is defined to be 'a plain surface comprehended by three right lines'; by which that name is limited to denote one certain idea and no other. To which I answer, that in the definition it is not said whether the surface be great or small, blank or white, nor whether the sides are long or short, equal or unequal, nor with what angles they are inclined to each other; in all which there may be great variety, and consequently there is no one settled idea which limits the signification of the word triangle. It is one thing for to keep a name constantly to the same *definition*, and another to make it stand everywhere for the same *idea*: the one is necessary, the other useless and impracticable.

19. But, to give a farther account how words came to produce the doctrine of abstract ideas, it must be observed that it is a received opinion that language has no other end but the communicating ideas, and that every significant name stands for an idea. This being so, and it being withal certain that names which yet are not thought altogether insignificant do not always mark out particular conceivable ideas, it is straightway concluded that they stand for abstract notions. That there are many names in use amongst speculative men which do not always suggest to others determinate, particular ideas, or in truth anything at all, is what nobody will deny. And a little attention will discover that it is not necessary (even in the strictest reasonings) that significant names which stand for ideas should, every time they are used, excite in the understanding the ideas they are made to stand for: in reading and discoursing, names being for the most part used as letters are in Algebra, in which, though a particular quantity be marked by each letter, yet to proceed right it is not requisite that in every step each letter suggest to your thoughts that particular quantity it was appointed to stand for.

20. Besides, the communicating of ideas marked by words is not the chief and only end of language, as is commonly supposed. There are other ends, as the raising of some passion, the exciting to or deterring from an action, the putting the mind in some particular disposition; to which the former is in many cases barely subservient, and sometimes entirely omitted, when these can be obtained without it, as I think doth not unfrequently happen in the familiar use of language. I entreat the reader to reflect with himself, and see if it doth not often happen, either in hearing, or reading a discourse, that the passions of fear, love, hatred, admiration, and disdain, and the like, arise immediately in his mind upon the perception of certain words, without any ideas coming between. At first, indeed, the words might have occasioned ideas that were fitting to produce those emotions; but, if I mistake not, it will be found that, when language is once grown familiar, the hearing of the sounds or sight of the characters is oft immediately attended with those passions which at first were wont to be produced by the intervention of ideas that are now quite omitted. May we not, for example, be affected with the promise of a *good thing*, though we

have not an idea of what it is? Or is not the being threatened with danger sufficient to excite a dread, though we think not of any particular evil likely to befall us, nor yet frame to ourselves an idea of danger in abstract? If any one shall join ever so little reflection of his own to what has been said, I believe that it will evidently appear to him that general names are often used in the propriety of language without the speakers designing them for marks of ideas in his own, which he would have them raise in the mind of the hearer. Even proper names themselves do not seem always spoken with a design to bring into our view the ideas of those individuals that are supposed to be marked by them. For example, when a schoolman tells me 'Aristotle hath said it,' all I conceive he means by it is to dispose me to embrace his opinion with the deference and submission which custom has annexed to that name. And this effect may be so instantly produced in the minds of those who are accustomed to resign their judgment to authority of the philosopher, as it is impossible any idea either of his person, writings, or reputations should go before. [So close and immediate a connexion may custom establish betwixt the very world Aristotle and the motions of assent and reverence in the minds of some men.] Innumerable examples of this kind may be given, but why should I insist on those things which every one's experience will, I doubt not, plentifully suggest unto him?

21. We have, I think, shewn the impossibility of Abstract Ideas. We have considered what has been said for them by their ablest patron; and endeavoured to shew they are of no use for those ends to which they are thought necessary. And lastly, we have traced them to the source from whence they flow, which appears evidently to be Language.

It cannot be denied that words are of excellent use, in that by their means all that stock of knowledge which has been purchased by the joint labours of inquisitive men in all ages and nations may be drawn into the view and made the possession of one single person. But [at the same time it must be owned that] most parts of knowledge have been [so] strangely perplexed and darkened by the abuse of words, and general ways of speech wherein they are delivered, [that it may almost be made a question whether language has contributed more to the hindrance or advancement of the sciences]. Since therefore words are so apt to impose on the understanding, [I am resolved in my inquiries to make as little use of them as possibly I can:] whatever ideas I consider, I shall endeavour to take them bare and naked into my view; keeping out of my thoughts, so far as I am able, those names which long and constant use hath so strictly united with them. From which I may expect to derive the following advantages:—

22. *First,* I shall be sure to get clear of all controversies purely verbal, the springing up of which weeds in almost all the sciences has been a main hindrance to the growth of true and sound knowledge. *Secondly,* this seems to be a sure way to extricate myself out of that fine and subtle net of abstract ideas, which has so miserably perplexed and entangled the minds of men; and that with this peculiar circumstance, that by how much the finer and more curious was the wit of any man, by so much the deeper was he likely to be ensnared and faster held therein. *Thirdly,* so long as I confine my thoughts to my own ideas, divested of words, I do not see how I can easily be mistaken. The objects I consider, I clearly and adequately know. I cannot be deceived in thinking I have an idea which I have not. It is not possible for me to imagine that any of my own ideas are alike or unlike that are not truly so. To discern the agreements or disagreements there are between my ideas, to see what ideas are included in my compound idea and what not, there is nothing more requisite than an attentive perception of what passes in my own understanding.

23. But the attainment of all these advantages does presuppose an entire deliverance from the deception of words; which I dare hardly promise myself, so difficult a thing it is to dissolve an union so early begun, and confirmed by so long a habit as that betwixt words and ideas. Which difficulty seems to have been very much increased by the doctrine of *abstraction.* For, so long as men thought *abstract* ideas were annexed to their words, it does not seem strange that they should use words for ideas; it being found an impracticable thing to lay aside the word, and retain the *abstract* idea in the mind; which in itself was perfectly inconceivable. This seems to me the principle cause why those who have so emphatically recommended to others the laying aside all use of words in their meditations, and contemplating their bare

ideas, have yet failed to perform it themselves. Of late many have been very sensible of the absurd opinions and significant disputes which grow out of the abuse of words. And, in order to remedy these evils, they advise well, that we attend to the ideas signified, and draw off our attention from the words which signify them. But, how good soever this advice may be they have given others, it is plain they could not have a due regard to it themselves, so long as they thought the only immediate use of words was to signify ideas, and that the immediate signification of every general name was a determinate abstract idea.

24. But these being known to be mistakes, a man may with greater ease prevent his being imposed on by words. He that knows he has no other than *particular* ideas, will not puzzle himself in vain to find out and conceive the *abstract* idea annexed to any name. And he that knows names do not always stand for ideas will spare himself the labour of looking for ideas where there are none to be had. It were, therefore, to be wished that every one would use his utmost endeavours to obtain a clear view of the ideas he would consider; separating from them all that dress and incumbrance of words which so much contribute to blind the judgment and divide the attention. In vain do we extend our view into the heavens and pry into the entrails of the earth, in vain do we consult the writings of learned men and trace the dark footsteps of antiquity. We need only draw the curtain of words, to behold the fairest tree of knowledge, whose fruit is excellent, and within the reach of our hand.

25. Unless we take care to clear the First Principles of Knowledge from the embarras and delusion of Words, we may make infinite reasonings upon them to no purpose; we may draw consequences from consequences, and be never the wiser. The farther we go, we shall only lose ourselves the more irrecoverably, and be the deeper entangled to difficulties and mistakes. Whoever therefore designs to read the following sheets, I entreat him that he would make my words the occasion of his own thinking, and endeavour to attain the same train of thoughts in reading that I had in writing them. By this means it will be easy for him to discover the truth or falsity of what I say. He will be out of all danger of being deceived by my words. And I do not see how he can be led into an error by considering his own naked, undisguised ideas.

OF THE PRINCIPLES
OF HUMAN KNOWLEDGE

Part First

1. It is evident to any one who takes a survey of the *objects of human knowledge*, that they are either *ideas* actually imprinted on the senses; or else such as are perceived by attending to the passions and operations of the mind; or lastly, *ideas* formed by help of memory and imagination—either compounding, dividing, or barely representing those originally perceived in the aforesaid ways. By sight I have the ideas of light and colours, with their several degrees and variations. By touch I perceive hard and soft, heat and cold, motion and resistance; and of all these more and less either as to quantity or degree. Smelling furnishes me with odours; the palate with tastes; and hearing conveys sounds to the mind in all their variety of tone and composition.

And as several of these are observed to accompany each other, they come to be marked by one name, and so to be reputed as one *thing*. Thus, for example, a certain colour, taste, smell, figure and consistence having been observed to go together, are accounted one distinct thing, signified by the name apple; other collections of ideas constitute a stone, a tree, a book, and the like sensible things; which as they are pleasing or disagreeable excite the passions of love, hatred, joy, grief, and so forth.

2. But, besides all that endless variety of ideas or objects of knowledge, there is likewise Something which knows or perceives them; and exercises divers operations, as willing, imagining, remembering, about them.

3. That neither our thoughts, nor passions, nor ideas formed by the imagination, exist without the mind is what everybody will allow. And to me it seems no less evident that the various sensations or ideas imprinted on the Sense, however blended or combined together (that is, whatever objects they compose), cannot exist otherwise than in a mind perceiving them. I think an intuitive knowledge may be obtained of this, by any one that shall attend to what is meant by the term *exist* when applied to sensible things. The table I write on I say exists; that is, I see and feel it: and if I were out of my study I should say it existed; meaning thereby that if I was in my study I might perceive it, or that some other spirit actually does perceive it. There was an odour, that is, it was smelt; there was a sound, that is, it was heard; a colour or figure, and it was perceived by sight or touch. This is all that I can understand by these and the like expressions. For as to what is said of the *absolute* existence of unthinking things, without any relation to their being perceived, that is to me perfectly unintelligible. Their *esse* is *percipi*; nor is it possible they should have any existence out of the minds or thinking things which perceive them.

4. It is indeed an opinion strangely prevailing amongst men, that houses, mountains, rivers, and in a word all sensible objects, have an existence, natural or real, distinct from their being perceived by the understanding. But, with how great an assurance and acquiescence soever this Principle may be entertained in the world, yet whoever shall find in his heart to call it in question may, if I mistake not, perceive it to involve a manifest contradiction. For, what are the forementioned objects but the things we perceive by sense? and what do we perceive besides our own ideas or sensations? and is it not plainly repugnant that any one of these, or any combination of them, should exist unperceived?

5. If we thoroughly examine this tenet it will, perhaps, be found at bottom to depend on the doctrine of *abstract ideas*. For can there be a nicer strain of abstraction than to distinguish the existence of sensible objects from their being perceived, so as to conceive them existing unperceived? Light and colours, heat and cold, extension and figures—in a word the things we see and feel—what are they but so many sensations, notions, ideas, or impressions of the sense? and is it possible to separate; even in thought, any of these from perception? For my part, I might as easily divide a thing from itself. I may, indeed, divide in my thoughts, or conceive apart from each other, those things which perhaps I never perceived by sense so divided. Thus, I imagine the trunk of a human body without the limbs, or conceive the smell of a rose without thinking on the rose itself. So far, I will not deny, I can abstract; if that may properly be called *abstraction* which extends only to the conceiving separately such objects as it is possible may really exist or be actually perceived asunder. But my conceiving or imagining power does not extend beyond

the possibility of real existence or perception. Hence, as it is impossible for me to see or feel anything without an actual sensation of that thing, so is it impossible for me to conceive in my thoughts any sensible thing or object distinct from the sensation or perception of it. [In truth, the object and the sensation are the same thing, and cannot therefore be abstracted from each other.]

6. Some truths there are so near and obvious to the mind that a man need only open his eyes to see them. Such I take this important one to be, viz. that all the choir of heaven and furniture of the earth, in a word all those bodies which compose the mighty frame of the world, have not any subsistence without a mind; that their *being* is to be perceived or known; that consequently so long as they are not actually perceived by me, or do not exist in my mind, or that of any other created spirit, they must either have no existence at all, or else subsist in the mind of some Eternal Spirit: it being perfectly unintelligible, and involving all the absurdity of abstraction, to attribute to any single part of them an existence independent of a spirit. [To be convinced of which, the reader need only reflect, and try to separate in his own thoughts the *being* of a sensible thing from its *being perceived*.]

7. From what has been said it is evident there is not any other Substance than *Spirit*, or that which perceives. But, for the fuller proof of this point, let it be considered the sensible qualities are colour, figure, motion, smell, taste, and such like, that is, the ideas perceived by sense. Now, for an idea to exist in an unperceiving thing is a manifest contradiction; for to have an idea is all one as to perceive: that therefore wherein colour, figure, and the like qualities exist must perceive them. Hence it is clear there can be no unthinking substance or *substratum* of those ideas.

8. But, say you, though the ideas themselves do not exist without the mind, yet there may be things like them, whereof they are copies or resemblances; which things exist without the mind, in an unthinking substance. I answer, an idea can be like nothing but an idea; a colour or figure can be like nothing but another colour or figure. If we look but never so little into our thoughts, we shall find it impossible for us to conceive a likeness except only between our ideas. Again, I ask whether those supposed *originals*, or external things, of which our ideas are the pictures or

representations, be themselves perceivable or no? If they are, then *they* are ideas, and we have gained our point: but if you say they are not, I appeal to any one whether it be sense to assert a colour is like something which is invisible; hard or soft, like something which is intangible; and so of the rest.

9. Some there are who make a distinction betwixt *primary* and *secondary* qualities. By the former they mean extension, figure, motion, rest, solidity or impenetrability, and number; by the latter they denote all other sensible qualities, as colours, sounds, tastes, and so forth. The ideas we have of these last they acknowledge not to be the resemblances of anything existing without the mind, or unperceived; but they will have our ideas of the *primary qualities* to be patterns or images of things which exist without the mind, in an unthinking substance which they call Matter. By Matter, therefore, we are to understand an inert, senseless substance in which extension, figure, and motion do actually subsist. But it is evident, from what we have already shewn, that extension, figure and motion are only ideas existing in the mind, and that an idea can be like nothing but another idea; and that consequently neither they nor their archetypes can exist in an unperceiving substance. Hence, it is plain that the very notion of what is called *Matter* or *corporeal substance*, involves a contradiction in it. [Insomuch that I should not think it necessary to spend more time in exposing its absurdity. But, because the tenet of the existence of Matter seems to have taken so deep a root in the minds of philosophers, and draws after it so many ill consequences, I choose rather to be thought prolix and tedious than omit anything that might conduce to the full discovery and extirpation of that prejudice.]

10. They who assert that figure, motion, and the rest of the primary or original qualities do exist without the mind, in unthinking substances, do at the same time acknowledge that colours, sounds, heat, cold, and suchlike secondary qualities, do not; which they tell us are sensations, existing in the mind alone, that depend on and are occasioned by the different size, texture, and motion of the minute particles of matter. This they take for an undoubted truth, which they can demonstrate beyond all exception. Now, if it be certain that those *original* qualities are inseparably united with the other sensible qualities, and not,

even in thought, capable of being abstracted from them, it plainly follows that *they* exist only in the mind. But I desire any one to reflect, and try whether he can, by any abstraction of thought, conceive the extension and motion of a body without all other sensible qualities. For my own part, I see evidently that it is not in my power to frame an idea of a body extended and moving, but I must withal give it some colour or other sensible quality, which is acknowledged to exist only in the mind. In short, extension, figure, and motion, abstracted from all other qualities, are inconceivable. Where therefore the other sensible qualities are, there must these be also, to wit, in the mind and nowhere else.

11. Again, *great* and *small*, *swift* and *slow*, are allowed to exist nowhere without the mind; being entirely relative, and changing as the frame or position of the organs of sense varies. The extension therefore which exists without the mind is neither great nor small, the motion neither swift nor slow; that is, they are nothing at all. But, say you, they are extension in general, and motion in general. Thus we see how much the tenet of extended moveable substances existing without the mind depends on that strange doctrine of *abstract ideas*. And here I cannot but remark how nearly the vague and indeterminate description of Matter, or corporeal substance, which the modern philosophers are run into by their own principles, resembles that antiquated and so much ridiculed notion of *materia prima*, to be met with in Aristotle and his followers. Without extension solidity cannot be conceived: since therefore it has been shewn that extension exists not in an unthinking substance, the same must also be true of solidity.

12. That *number* is entirely the creature of the mind, even though the other qualities be allowed to exist without, will be evident to whoever considers that the same thing bears a different denomination of number as the mind views it with different respects. Thus, the same extension is one, or three, or thirty-six, according as the mind considers it with reference to a yard, a foot, or an inch. Number is so visibly relative, and dependent on men's understanding, that it is strange to think how any one should give it an absolute existence without the mind. We say one book, one page, one line, &c.; all these are equally units, though some contain several of the others. And in each instance, it is plain, the unit relates to

some particular combination of ideas *arbitrarily* put together by the mind.

13. Unity I know some will have to be a simple or uncompounded idea, accompanying all other ideas into the mind. That I have any such idea answering the word *unity* I do not find; and if I had, methinks I could not miss finding it; on the contrary, it should be the most familiar to my understanding, since it is said to accompany all other ideas, and to be perceived by all the ways of sensation and reflexion. To say no more, it is an *abstract idea*.

14. I shall farther add, that, after the same manner as modern philosophers prove certain sensible qualities to have no existence in Matter, or without the mind, the same thing may be likewise proved of all other sensible qualities whatsoever. Thus, for instance, it is said that heat and cold are affections only for the mind, and not at all patterns of real beings, existing in the corporeal substances which excite them; for that the same body which appears cold to one hand seems warm to another. Now, why may we not as well argue that figure and extension are not patterns or resemblances of qualities existing in Matter; because to the same eye at different stations, or eyes of a different texture at the same station, they appear various, and cannot therefore be the images of anything settled and determinate without the mind? Again, it is proved that sweetness is not really in the sapid thing; because the thing remaining unaltered the sweetness is changed into bitter, as in case of a fever or otherwise vitiated palate. Is it not as reasonable to say that motion is not without the mind; since if the succession of ideas in the mind become swifter, the motion, it is acknowledged, shall appear slower, without any alteration in any external object?

15. In short, let any one consider those arguments which are thought manifestly to prove that colours and tastes exist only in the mind, and he shall find they may with equal force be brought to prove the same thing of extension, figure, and motion. Though it must be confessed this method of arguing does not so much prove that there is no extension or colour in an outward object, as that we do not know by sense which is the true extension or colour of the object. But the arguments foregoing plainly shew it to be impossible that any colour or extension at all, or other sensible quality whatsoever, should exist in an unthinking subject without the mind, or in truth that there should be any such thing as an outward object.

16. But let us examine a little the received opinion. It is said extension is a *mode* or *accident* of Matter, and that Matter is the *substratum* that supports it. Now I desire that you would explain to me what is meant by Matter's *supporting* extension. Say you, I have no idea of Matter; and therefore cannot explain it. I answer, though you have no positive, yet, if you have any meaning at all, you must at least have a relative idea of Matter; though you know not what it is, yet you must be supposed to know what relation it bears to accidents, and what is meant by its supporting them. It is evident *support* cannot here be taken in its usual or literal sense, as when we say that pillars support a building. In what sense therefore must it be taken? [For my part, I am not able to discover any sense at all that can be applicable to it.]

17. If we inquire into what the most accurate philosophers declare themselves to mean by *material substance,* we shall find them acknowledge they have no other meaning annexed to those sounds but the idea of Being in general, together with the relative notion of its supporting accidents. The general idea of Being appeareth to me the most abstract and incomprehensible of all other; and as for its supporting accidents, this, as we have just now observed, cannot be understood in the common sense of those words: it must therefore be taken in some other sense, but what that is they do not explain. So that when I consider the two parts or branches which make the signification of the words *material substance,* I am convinced there is no distinct meaning annexed to them. But why should we trouble ourselves any farther, in discussing this material *substratum* or support of figure and motion and other sensible qualities? Does it not suppose they have an existence without the mind? And is not this a direct repugnancy, and altogether inconceivable?

18. But, though it were possible that solid figured, moveable substances may exist without the mind, corresponding to the ideas we have of bodies, yet how is it possible for us to know this? Either we must know it by Sense or by Reason. As for our senses, by them we have the knowledge only of our sensations, ideas, or those things that are immediately perceived by sense, call them what you will: but they do not inform us that things exist without the mind, or unperceived, like to those which are perceived. This the materialists themselves acknowledge.—It remains therefore that if we have any knowledge at all of external things, it must be by reason inferring their existence from what is immediately perceived by sense. But [I do not see] what reason can induce us to believe the existence of bodies without the mind, from what we perceive, since the very patrons of Matter themselves do not pretend there is any necessary connexion betwixt them and our ideas? I say it is granted on all hands (and what happens in dreams, frensies, and the like, puts it beyond dispute) that it is possible we might be affected with all the ideas we have now, though no bodies existed without resembling them. Hence it is evident the supposition of external bodies is not necessary for the producing our ideas; since it is granted they are produced sometimes, and might possibly be produced always, in the same order we see them in at present, without their concurrence.

19. But, though we might possibly have all our sensations without them, yet perhaps it may be thought easier to conceive and explain the manner of their production, by supposing external bodies in their likeness rather than otherwise; and so it might be at least probable there are such things as bodies that excite their ideas in our minds. But neither can this be said. For, though we give the materialists their external bodies, they by their own confession are never the nearer knowing how our ideas are produced; since they own themselves unable to comprehend in what manner body can act upon spirit, or how it is possible it should imprint any idea in the mind. Hence it is evident the production of ideas or sensations in our minds, can be no reason why we should suppose Matter or corporeal substances; since that is acknowledged to remain equally inexplicable with or without this supposition. If therefore it were possible for bodies to exist without the mind, yet to hold they do so must needs be a very precarious opinion; since it is to suppose, without any reason at all, that God has created innumerable beings that are entirely useless, and serve to no manner of purpose.

20. In short, if there were external bodies, it is impossible we should ever come to know it; and if there were not, we might have the very same reasons to think there were that we have now. Suppose— what no one can deny possible—an intelligence, without the help of external bodies, to be affected with the same train of sensations or ideas that you are, imprinted in the same order and with like vividness in his mind. I ask whether that intelligence hath not all the reason to believe the existence of Corporeal Substances, represented by his ideas, and exciting them in his mind, that you can possibly have for believing the same thing? Of this there can be no question. Which one consideration were enough to make any reasonable person suspect the strength of whatever arguments he may think himself to have, for the existence of bodies without the mind.

21. Were it necessary to add any farther proof against the existence of Matter, after what has been said, I could instance several of those errors and difficulties (not to mention impieties) which have sprung from that tenet. It has occasioned numberless controversies and disputes in philosophy, and not a few of far greater moment in religion. But I shall not enter into the detail of them in this place, as well because I think arguments *a posteriori* are unnecessary for confirming what has been, if I mistake not, sufficiently demonstrated *a priori*, as because I shall hereafter find occasion to speak somewhat of them.

22. I am afraid I have given cause to think I am needlessly prolix in handling this subject. For, to what purpose is it to dilate on that which may be demonstrated with the utmost evidence in a line or two, to any one that is capable of the least reflexion? It is but looking into your own thoughts, and so trying whether you can conceive it possible for a sound, or figure, or motion, or colour to exist without the mind or unperceived. This easy trial may perhaps make you see that what you contend for is a downright contradiction. Insomuch that I am content to put the whole upon this issue:—If you can but conceive it possible for one extended moveable substance, or in general for any one idea, or anything like an idea, to exist otherwise than in a mind perceiving it, I shall readily give up the cause. And, as for all that compages of external bodies you contend for, I shall grant you its existence, though you cannot either give me any reason why you believe it exists, or assign any use to it when it is supposed to exist, I say, the bare possibility of your opinions being true shall pass for an argument that it is so.

23. But, say you, surely there is nothing easier than for me to imagine trees, for instance, in a park,

or books existing in a closet, and nobody by to perceive them. I answer, you may so, there is no difficulty in it. But what is all this, I beseech you, more than framing in your mind certain ideas which you call *books* and *trees*, and at the same time omitting to frame the idea of any one that may perceive them? But do not you yourself perceive or think of them all the while? This therefore is nothing to the purpose: it only shews you have the power of imagining; or forming ideas in your mind; but it does not shew that you can conceive it possible the objects of your thought may exist without the mind. To make out this, it is necessary that you conceive them existing unconceived or unthought of; which is a manifest repugnancy. When we do our utmost to conceive the existence of external bodies, we are all the while only contemplating our own ideas. But the mind, taking no notice of itself, is deluded to think it can and does conceive bodies existing unthought of, or without the mind, though at the same time they are apprehended by, or exist in, itself. A little attention will discover to any one the truth and evidence of what is here said, and make it unnecessary to insist on any other proofs against the existence of *material substance*.

24. [Could men but forbear to amuse themselves with words, we should, I believe, soon come to an agreement in this point.] It is very obvious, upon the least inquiry into our own thoughts, to know whether it be possible for us to understand what is meant by the *absolute existence of sensible objects in themselves*, or *without the mind*. To me it is evident those words mark out either a direct contradiction, or else nothing at all. And to convince others of this, I know no readier or fairer way than to entreat they would calmly attend to their own thoughts; and if by this attention the emptiness or repugnancy of those expressions does appear, surely nothing more is requisite for their conviction. It is on this therefore that I insist, to wit, that the *absolute existence of unthinking things* are words without a meaning, or which include a contradiction. This is what I repeat and inculcate, and earnestly recommend to the attentive thoughts of the reader.

25. All our ideas, sensations, notions, or the things which we perceive, by whatsoever names they may be distinguished, are visibly inactive: there is nothing of power or agency included in them. So that one idea or object of thought cannot produce or make any alteration in another. To be satisfied of the truth

of this, there is nothing else requisite but a bare observation of our ideas. For, since they and every part of them exist only in the mind, it follows that there is nothing in them but what is perceived: but whoever shall attend to his ideas, whether of sense or reflexion, will not perceive in them any power or activity; there is, therefore, no such thing contained in them. A little attention will discover to us that the very being of an idea implies passiveness and inertness in it; insomuch that it is impossible for an idea to do anything, or, strictly speaking, to be the cause of anything: neither can it be the resemblance or pattern of any active being, as is evident from sect. 8. Whence it plainly follows that extension, figure, and motion cannot be the cause of our sensations. To say, therefore, that these are the effects of powers resulting from the configuration, number, motion, and size of corpuscles, must certainly be false.

26. We perceive a continual succession of ideas; some are anew excited, others are changed or totally disappear. There is therefore, *some* cause of these ideas, whereon they depend, and which produces and changes them. That this cause cannot be any quality or idea or combination of *ideas,* is clear from the preceding section. It must therefore be a *substance;* but it has been shewn that there is no corporeal or material substance: it remains therefore that the cause of ideas is an incorporeal active substance or Spirit.

27. A Spirit is one simple, undivided, active being—as it perceives ideas it is called the *understanding,* and as it produces or otherwise operates about them it is called the *will.* Hence there can be no *idea* formed of a soul or spirit; for all ideas whatever, being passive and inert (vid. sect. 25), they cannot represent unto us, by way of image or likeness, that which acts. A little attention will make it plain to any one, that to have an idea which shall be *like* that active Principle of motion and change of ideas is absolutely impossible. Such is the nature of Spirit, or that which acts, that it cannot be of itself perceived, but only by the effects which it produceth. If any man shall doubt of the truth of what is here delivered, let him but reflect and try if he can frame the idea of any power or active being; and whether he has ideas of two principal powers, marked by the names *will* and *understanding,* distinct from each other, as well as from a third idea of Substance or Being in general, with a relative notion of its supporting or being the

subject of the aforesaid powers—which is signified by the name *soul* or *spirit.* This is what some hold; but, so far as I can see, the words *will,* [*understanding, mind,*] *soul, spirit,* do not stand for different ideas, or, in truth, for any idea at all, but for something which is very different from ideas, and which, being an agent, cannot be like unto, or represented by, any idea whatsoever. [Though it must be owned at the same time that we have some *notion* of soul, spirit, and the operations of the mind, such as willing, loving, hating—inasmuch as we know or understand the meaning of these words.]

28. I find I can excite ideas in my mind at pleasure, and vary and shift the scene as oft as I think fit. It is no more than *willing,* and straightway this or that idea arises in my fancy; and by the same power it is obliterated and makes way for another. This making and unmaking of ideas doth very properly denominate the mind active. Thus much is certain and grounded on experience: but when we talk of unthinking agents, or of exciting ideas exclusive of volition, we only amuse ourselves with words.

29. But, whatever power I may have over my own thoughts, I find the ideas actually perceived by Sense have not a like dependence of *my* will. When in broad daylight I open my eyes, it is not in my power to choose whether I shall see or no, or to determine what particular objects shall present themselves to my view: and so likewise as to the hearing and other senses; the ideas imprinted on them are not creatures of *my* will. There is therefore some other Will or Spirit that produces them.

30. The ideas of Sense are more strong, lively, and distinct than those of the Imagination; they have likewise a steadiness, order, and coherence, and are not excited at random, as those which are the effects of human wills often are, but in a regular train or series—the admirable connexion whereof sufficiently testifies the wisdom and benevolence of its Author. Now the set rules, or established methods, wherein the Mind we depend on excites in us the ideas of Sense, are called *the laws of nature;* and these we learn by experience, which teaches us that such and such ideas are attended with such and such other ideas, in the ordinary course of things.

31. This gives us a sort of foresight, which enables us to regulate our actions for the benefit of life. And without this we should be eternally at a loss: we

could not know how to act anything that might procure us the least pleasure, or remove the least pain of sense. That food nourishes, sleep refreshes, and fire warms us; that to sow in the seed-time is the way to reap in the harvest; and in general that to obtain such or such ends, such or such means are conducive—all this we know, not by discovering any *necessary connexion* between our ideas, but only by the observation of the *settled laws* of nature; without which we should be all in uncertainty and confusion, and a grown man no more know how to manage himself in the affairs of life than an infant just born.

32. And yet this consistent uniform working, which so evidently displays the Goodness and Wisdom of that Governing Spirit whose Will constitutes the laws of nature, is so far from leading our thoughts to Him, that it rather sends them wandering after second causes. For, when we perceive certain ideas of Sense constantly followed by other ideas, and we know this is not of our own doing, we forthwith attribute power and agency to the ideas themselves, and make one the cause of another, than which nothing can be more absurd and unintelligible. Thus, for example, having observed that when we perceive by sight a certain round luminous figure, we at the same time perceive by touch the idea or sensation called heat, we do from thence conclude the sun to be the *cause* of heat. And in like manner perceiving the motion and collision of bodies to be attended with sound, we are inclined to think the latter the *effect* of the former.

33. The ideas imprinted on the Senses by the Author of nature are called *real things*: and those excited in the imagination, being less regular, vivid, and constant, are more properly termed *ideas* or *images of* things, which they copy and represent. But then our *sensations*, be they never so vivid and distinct, are nevertheless ideas: that is, they exist in the mind, or are perceived by it, as truly as the ideas of its own framing. The ideas of Sense are allowed to have more reality in them, that is, to be more strong, orderly, and coherent than the creatures of the mind; but this is no argument that they exist without the mind. They are also less dependent on the spirit or thinking substance which perceives them, in that they are excited by the will of another and more powerful Spirit: yet still they are *ideas*: and certainly no idea, whether faint or strong, can exist otherwise than in a mind perceiving it.

34. Before we proceed any farther it is necessary we spend some time in answering Objections which may probably be made against the Principles we have hitherto laid down. In doing of which, if I seem too prolix to those of quick apprehensions, I desire I may be excused, since all men do not equally apprehend things of this nature; and I am willing to be understood by every one.

First, then, it will be objected that by the foregoing principles all that is real and substantial in nature is banished out of the world, and instead thereof a chimerical scheme of *ideas* takes place. All things that exist exist only in the mind; that is, they are purely notional. What therefore becomes of the sun, moon, and stars? What must we think of houses, rivers, mountains, trees, stones; nay, even of our own bodies? Are all these but so many chimeras and illusions on the fancy?—To all which, and whatever else of the same sort may be objected, I answer, that by the Principles premised we are not deprived of any one thing in nature. Whatever we see, feel, hear, or any wise conceive or understand, remains as secure as ever, and is as real as ever. There is a *rerum natura*, and the distinction between realities and chimeras retains its full force. This is evident from sect. 29, 30, and 33, where we have shewn what is meant by *real things*, in opposition to *chimeras* or *ideas of our own framing*; but then they both equally exist in the mind, and in that sense are alike *ideas*.

35. I do not argue against the existence of any one thing that we can apprehend, either by sense or reflection. That the things I see with my eyes and touch with my hands do exist, really exist, I make not the least question. The only thing whose existence we deny is that which *philosophers* call Matter or corporeal substance. And in doing of this there is no damage done to the rest of mankind, who, I dare say, will never miss it. The Atheist indeed will want the colour of an empty name to support his impiety; and the Philosophers may possibly find they have lost a great handle for trifling and disputation. [But that is all the harm that I can see done.]

36. If any man thinks this detracts from the existence or reality of things, he is very far from understanding what hath been premised in the plainest terms I could think of. Take here an abstract of what has been said:—There are spiritual substances, minds, or human souls, which will or excite ideas in them-

selves at pleasure; but these are faint, weak, and unsteady in respect of others they perceive by sense: which, being impressed upon them according to certain rules or laws of nature, speak themselves the effects of a Mind more powerful and wise than human spirits. These latter are said to have *more reality* in them than the former;—by which is meant that they are more affecting, orderly, and distinct, and that they are not fictions of the mind perceiving them. And in this sense the sun that I see by day is the real sun, and that which I imagine by night is the idea of the former. In the sense here given of *reality*, it is evident that every vegetable, star, mineral, and in general each part of the mundane system, is as much a *real being* by our principles as by any other. Whether others mean anything by the term *reality* different from what I do, I entreat them to look into their own thoughts and see.

37. It will be urged that thus much at least is true, to wit, that we take away all *corporeal substances*. To this my answer is, that if the word *substance* be taken in the vulgar sense, for a *combination* of sensible qualities, such as extension, solidity, weight, and the like—this we cannot be accused of taking away: but if it be taken in a philosophic sense, for the support of accidents or qualities without the mind—then indeed I acknowledge that we take it away, if one may be said to take away that which never had any existence, not even in the imagination.

38. But after all, say you, it sounds very harsh to say we eat and drink ideas, and are clothed with ideas. I acknowledge it does so—the word *idea* not being used in common discourse to signify the several combinations of sensible qualities which are called *things;* and it is certain that any expression which varies from the familiar use of language will seem harsh and ridiculous. But this doth not concern the truth of the proposition, which in other words is no more than to say, we are fed and clothed with those things which we perceive immediately by our senses. The hardness or softness, the colour, taste, warmth, figure, and suchlike qualities, which combined together constitute the several sorts of victuals and apparel, have been shewn to exist only in the mind that perceives them: and this is all that is meant by calling them *ideas;* which word, if it was as ordinarily used as *thing,* would sound no harsher nor more ridiculous than it. I am not for disputing about the propriety, but the truth of the expression. If therefore you agree with me

that we eat and drink and are clad with the immediate objects of sense, which cannot exist unperceived or without the mind, I shall readily grant it is more proper or conformable to custom that they should be called *things* rather than *ideas.*

39. If it be demanded why I make use of the word *idea,* and do not rather in compliance with custom call them *things;* I answer, I do it for two reasons:—First, because the term *thing,* in contradistinction to *idea,* is generally supposed to denote somewhat existing without the mind: Secondly, because *thing* hath a more comprehensive signification than *idea,* including spirits, or thinking things, as well as ideas. Since therefore the objects of sense exist only in the mind, and are withal thoughtless and inactive, I chose to mark them by the word *idea;* which implies those properties.

40. But, say what we can, some one perhaps may be apt to reply, he will still believe his senses, and never suffer any arguments, how plausible soever, to prevail over the certainty of them. Be it so; assert the evidence of sense as high as you please, we are willing to do the same. That what I see, hear, and feel doth exist, that is to say, is perceived by me, I no more doubt than I do of my own being. But I do not see how the testimony of sense can be alleged as a proof for the existence of anything which is *not* perceived by sense. We are not for having any man turn sceptic and disbelieve his senses; on the contrary, we give them all the stress and assurance imaginable; nor are there any principles more opposite to Scepticism than those we have laid down, as shall be hereafter clearly shewn.

41. *Secondly,* it will be objected that there is a great difference betwixt real fire for instance, and the idea of fire, betwixt dreaming or imagining oneself burnt, and actually being so. [If you suspect it to be only the idea of fire which you see, do but put your hand into it and you will be convinced with a witness.] This and the like may be urged in opposition to our tenets.—To all which the answer is evident from what hath been already said; and I shall only add in this place, that if real fire be very different from the idea of fire, so also is the real pain that it occasions very different from the idea of the same pain, and yet nobody will pretend that real pain either is, or can possibly be, in an unperceiving thing, or without the mind, any more than its idea.

42. *Thirdly*, it will be objected that we see things actually without or at a distance from us, and which consequently do not exist in the mind; it being absurd that those things which are seen at the distance of several miles should be as near to us as our own thoughts.—In answer to this, I desire it may be considered that in a dream we do oft perceive things as existing at a great distance off, and yet for all that, those things are acknowledged to have their existence only in the mind.

43. But, for the fuller clearing of this point, it may be worth while to consider how it is that we perceive distance, and things placed at a distance, by sight. For, that we should in truth *see* external space, and bodies actually existing in it, some nearer, others farther off, seems to carry with it some opposition to what hath been said of their existing nowhere without the mind. The consideration of this difficulty it was that gave birth to my *Essay towards a New Theory of Vision*, which was published not long since. Wherein it is shewn that distance or outness is neither immediately of itself perceived by sight, nor yet apprehended or judged of by lines and angles, or anything that hath a necessary connexion with it; but that it is only suggested to our thoughts by certain visible ideas, and sensations attending vision, which in their own nature have no manner of similitude or relation either with distance or things placed at a distance; but, by a connexion taught us by experience, they come to signify and suggest them to us, after the same manner that words of any language suggest the ideas they are made to stand for. Insomuch that a man born blind, and afterwards made to see, would not, at first sight, think the things he saw to be without his mind, or at any distance from him. See sect. 41 of the forementioned treatise.

44. The ideas of sight and touch make two species entirely distinct and heterogeneous. The former are marks and prognostics of the latter. That the proper objects of sight neither exist without the mind, nor are the images of external things, was shewn even in that treatise. Though throughout the same the contrary be supposed true of *tangible objects*;—not that to suppose that vulgar error was necessary for establishing the notion therein laid down, but because it was beside my purpose to examine and refute it, in a discourse concerning *Vision*. So that in strict truth the ideas of sight, when we apprehend by them distance, and things placed at a distance, do not suggest or mark out to us things actually existing at a distance, but only admonish us what ideas of touch will be imprinted in our minds at such and such distances of time, and in consequence of such or such actions. It is, I say, evident, from what has been said in the foregoing parts of this Treatise, and in sect. 147 and elsewhere of the Essay concerning Vision, that visible ideas are the Language whereby the Governing Spirit on whom we depend informs us what tangible ideas he is about to imprint upon us, in case we excite this or that motion in our own bodies. But for a fuller information in this point I refer to the Essay itself.

45. *Fourthly*, it will be objected that from the foregoing principles it follows things are every moment annihilated and created anew. The objects of sense exist only when they are perceived: the trees therefore are in the garden, or the chairs in the parlour, no longer than while there is somebody by to perceive them. Upon shutting my eyes all the furniture in the room is reduced to nothing, and barely upon opening them it is again created.—In answer to all which, I refer the reader to what has been said in sect. 3, 4, &c.; and desire he will consider whether he means anything by the actual existence of an idea distinct from its being perceived. For my part, after the nicest inquiry I could make, I am not able to discover that anything else is meant by those words; and I once more entreat the reader to sound his own thoughts, and not suffer himself to be imposed on by words. If he can conceive it possible either for his ideas or their archetypes to exist without being perceived, then I give up the cause. But if he cannot, he will acknowledge it is unreasonable for him to stand up in defence of he knows not what, and pretend to charge on me as an absurdity, the not assenting to those propositions which at bottom have no meaning in them.

46. It will not be amiss to observe how far the received principles of philosophy are themselves chargeable with those pretended absurdities. It is thought strangely absurd that upon closing my eyelids all the visible objects around me should be reduced to nothing; and yet is not this what philosophers commonly acknowledge, when they agree on all hands that light and colours, which alone are the proper and immediate objects of sight, are mere sensations that exist no longer than they are perceived? Again, it may to some perhaps seem very incredible that things should be every moment creating; yet this very notion is commonly taught in the schools. For the Schoolmen, though they acknowledge the existence of Matter, and that the whole mundane fabric is framed out of it, are nevertheless of opinion that it cannot subsist without the divine conservation; which by them is expounded to be a continual creation.

47. Farther, a little thought will discover to us that, though we allow the existence of Matter or corporeal substance, yet it will unavoidably follow, from the principles which are now generally admitted, that the particular bodies, of what kind soever, do none of them exist whilst they are not perceived. For, it is evident, from sect. 11 and the following sections, that the Matter philosophers contend for is an incomprehensible Somewhat, which hath none of those particular qualities whereby the bodies falling under our senses are distinguished one from another. But, to make this more plain, it must be remarked that the infinite divisibility of Matter is now universally allowed, at least by the most approved and considerable philosophers, who on the received principles demonstrate it beyond all exception. Hence, it follows there is an infinite number of parts in each particle of Matter which are not perceived by sense. The reason therefore that any particular body seems to be of a finite magnitude, or exhibits only a finite number of parts to sense, is, not because it contains no more, since in itself it contains an infinite number of parts, but because the sense is not acute enough to discern them. In proportion therefore as the sense is rendered more acute, it perceives a greater number of parts in the object, that is, the object appears greater; and its figure varies, those parts in its extremities which were before unperceivable appearing now to bound it in very different lines and angles from those perceived by an obtuser sense. And at length, after various changes of size and shape, when the sense becomes infinitely acute, the body shall seem infinite. During all which there is no alternation in the body, but only in the sense. Each body therefore, considered in itself, is infinitely extended, and consequently void of all shape and figure. From which it follows that, though we should grant the existence of Matter to be never so certain, yet it is withal as certain, the materialists themselves are by their own principles forced to acknowledge, that neither the particular bodies perceived by sense, nor anything like them, exists without the mind. Matter, I say, and each particle thereof, is according to them infinite and shapeless; and it is the mind that frames all that variety of bodies which compose the visible world, any one whereof does not exist longer than it is perceived.

48. But, after all, if we consider it, the objection proposed in sect. 45 will not be found reasonably charged on the Principles we have premised, so as in truth to make any objection at all against our notions. For, though we hold indeed the objects of sense to be nothing else but ideas which cannot exist unperceived, yet we may not hence conclude they have no existence except only while they are perceived by *us*; since there may be some other spirit that perceives them though we do not. Wherever bodies are said to have no existence without the mind, I would not be understood to mean this or that particular mind, but all minds whatsoever. It does not therefore follow from the foregoing Principles that bodies are annihilated and created every moment, or exist not at all during the intervals between *our* perception of them.

49. *Fifthly*, it may perhaps be objected that if extension and figure exist only in the mind, it follows that the mind is extended and figured; since extension is a mode or attribute which (to speak with the Schools) is predicated of the subject in which it exists.—I answer, those qualities are in the mind only as they are perceived by it;—that is, not by way of *mode* or *attribute*, but only by way of *idea*. And it no more follows the soul or mind is extended, because extension exists in it alone, that it does that it is red or blue, because those colours are on all hands acknowledged to exist in it, and nowhere else. As to what philosophers say of subject and mode, that seems very groundless and unintelligible. For instance, in this proposition 'a die is hard, extended, and square,' they will have it that the word *die* denotes a subject or substance, distinct from the hardness, extension, and figure which are predicated of it, and in which they exist. This I cannot comprehend: to me a die seems to be nothing distinct from those things which are termed its modes or accidents. And, to say a die is hard, extended, and square is not to attribute those qualities to a subject distinct from and supporting them, but only an explication of the meaning of the word *die*.

50. *Sixthly,* you will say there have been a great many things explained by matter and motion; take away these and you destroy the whole corpuscular philosophy, and undermine those mechanical principles which have been applied with so much success to account for the phenomena. In short, whatever advances have been made, either by accident or modern philosophers, in the study of nature do all proceed on the supposition that corporeal substance or Matter doth really exist.—To this I answer that there is not any one phenomenon explained on that supposition which may not as well be explained without it, as might easily be made appear by an induction of particulars. To explain the phenomena, is all one as to shew why, upon such and such occasions, we are affected with such and such ideas. But how Matter should operate on a Spirit, or produce any idea in it, is what no philosopher will pretend to explain; it is therefore evident there can be no use of Matter in natural philosophy. Besides, they who attempt to account for things do it, not by corporeal substance, but by figure, motion, and other qualities; which are in truth no more than mere ideas, and therefore cannot be the cause of anything, as hath been already shewn. See sect. 25.

51. *Seventhly,* it will upon this be demanded whether it does not seem absurd to take away natural causes, and ascribe everything to the immediate operation of spirits? We must no longer say upon these principles that fire heats, or water cools, but that a spirit heats, and so forth. Would not a man be deservedly laughed at, who should talk after this manner?—I answer, he would so: in such things we ought to think with the learned, and speak with the vulgar. They who to demonstration are convinced of the truth of the Copernican system do nevertheless say 'the sun rises,' 'the sun sets,' or 'comes to the meridian'; and if they affected a contrary style in common talk it would without doubt appear very ridiculous. A little reflection on what is here said will make it manifest that the common use of language would receive no manner of alteration or disturbance from the admission of our tenets.

52. In the ordinary affairs of life, any phrases may be retained, so long as they excite in us proper sentiments, or dispositions to act in such a manner as is necessary for our well-being, how false soever they may be if taken in a strict and speculative sense. Nay, this is unavoidable, since, propriety being regulated by custom, language is suited to the received opinions, which are not always the truest. Hence it is impossible—even in the most rigid, philosophic reasonings—so far to alter the bent and genius of the tongue we speak as never to give a handle for cavillers to pretend difficulties and inconsistencies. But, a fair and ingenuous reader will collect the sense from the scope and tenor and connexion of a discourse, making allowances for those inaccurate modes of speech which use has made inevitable.

53. As to the opinion that there are no corporeal causes, this has been heretofore maintained by some of the Schoolmen, as it is of late by others among the modern philosophers; who though they allow Matter to exist, yet will have God alone to be the immediate efficient cause of all things. These men saw that amongst all the objects of sense there was none which had any power or activity included in it; and that by consequence this was likewise true of whatever bodies they supposed to exist without the mind, like unto the immediate objects of sense. But then, that they should suppose an innumerable multitude of created beings, which they acknowledge are not capable of producing any one effect in nature, and which therefore are made to no manner of purpose, since God might have done everything as well without them—this I say, though we should allow it possible, must yet be a very unaccountable and extravagant supposition.

54. In the *eighth* place, the universal concurrent assent of mankind may be thought by some an invincible argument in behalf of Matter, or the existence of external things. Must we suppose the whole world to be mistaken? And if so, what cause can be assigned of so widespread and predominant an error?—I answer, first, that, upon a narrow inquiry, it will not perhaps be found so many as is imagined do really believe the existence of Matter or things without the mind. Strictly speaking, to believe that which involves a contradiction, or has no meaning in it, is impossible; and whether the foregoing expressions are not of that sort, I refer it to the impartial examination of the reader. In one sense, indeed, men may be said to believe that Matter exists; that is, they act as if the immediate cause of their sensations, which affects them every moment, and is so nearly present to them, were some senseless unthinking being. But, that they should clearly apprehend any meaning marked by those words, and form thereof a settled speculative opinion, is what I am not able to conceive. This is not the only instance wherein men impose upon themselves, by imagining they believe those propositions which they have often heard, though at bottom they have no meaning in them.

55. But secondly, though we should grant a notion to be never so universally and stedfastly adhered to, yet this is but a weak argument of its truth to whoever considers what a vast number of prejudices and false opinions are everywhere embraced with the utmost tenaciousness, by the unreflecting (which are the far greater) part of mankind. There was a time when the antipodes and motion of the earth were looked upon as monstrous absurdities even by men of learning: and if it be considered what a small proportion they bear to the rest of mankind, we shall find that at this day those notions have gained but a very inconsiderable footing in the world.

56. But it is demanded that we assign a cause of this prejudice, and account for its obtaining in the world. To this I answer, that men knowing they perceived several ideas, whereof they themselves were not the authors, as not being excited from within, nor depending on the operation of their wills, this made them maintain *those* ideas or objects of perception, had an existence independent of and without the mind, without ever dreaming that a contradiction was involved in those words. But, philosophers having plainly seen that the immediate objects of perception do not exist without the mind, they in some degree corrected the mistake of the vulgar; but at the same time run into another, which seems no less absurd, to wit, that there are certain objects really existing without the mind, or having a subsistence distinct from being perceived, of which our ideas are only images or resemblances, imprinted by those objects on the mind. And this notion of the philosophers owes its origin to the same cause with the former, namely, their being conscious that *they* were not the authors of their own sensations; which they evidently knew were imprinted from without, and which therefore must have *some* cause, distinct from the minds on which they are imprinted.

57. But why they should suppose the ideas of sense to be excited in us by things in their likeness, and not rather have recourse to *Spirit*, which alone

can act, may be accounted for. First, because they were not aware of the repugnancy there is, as well in supposing things like unto our ideas existing without, as in attributing to them power or activity. Secondly, because the Supreme Spirit which excites those ideas in our minds, is not marked out and limited to our view by any particular finite collection of sensible ideas, as human agents are by their size, complexion, limbs, and motions. And thirdly, because His operations are regular and uniform. Whenever the course of nature is interrupted by a miracle, men are ready to own the presence of a Superior Agent. But, when we see things go on in the ordinary course, they do not excite in us any reflexion; their order and concatenation, though it be an argument of the greatest wisdom, power, and goodness in their Creator, is yet so constant and familiar to us, that we do not think them the immediate effects of a *Free Spirit*; especially since inconsistency and mutability in acting, though it be an imperfection, is looked on as a mark of *freedom*.

58. *Tenthly*, it will be objected that the notions we advance are inconsistent with several sound truths in philosophy and mathematics. For example, the motion of the earth is now universally admitted by astronomers as a truth grounded on the clearest and most convincing reasons. But, on the foregoing Principles, there can be no such thing. For, motion being only an idea, it follows that if it be not perceived it exists not: but the motion of the earth is not perceived by sense.—I answer, That tenet, if rightly understood, will be found to agree with the Principles we have premised: for, the question whether the earth moves or no amounts in reality to no more than this, to wit, whether we have reason to conclude, from what has been observed by astronomers, that if we were placed in such and such circumstances, and such or such a position and distance both from the earth and sun, we should perceive the former to move among the choir of the planets, and appearing in all respects like one of them: and this, by the established rules of nature, which we have no reason to mistrust, is reasonably collected from the phenomena.

59. We may, from the experience we have had of the train and succession of ideas in our minds, often make, I will not say uncertain conjectures, but sure and well-grounded predictions concerning the ideas we shall be affected with pursuant to a great train of actions; and be enabled to pass a right judgment of what would have appeared to us, in case we were placed in circumstances very different from those we are in at present. Herein consists the knowledge of nature, which may preserve its use and certainty very consistently with what hath been said. It will be easy to apply this to whatever objections of the like sort may be drawn from the magnitude of the stars, or any other discoveries in astronomy or nature.

60. In the *eleventh* place, it will be demanded to what purpose serves that curious organization of plants, and the animal mechanism in the parts of animals. Might not vegetables grow, and shoot forth leaves and blossoms, and animals perform all their motions, as well without as with all that variety of internal parts so elegantly contrived and put together;—which, being ideas, have nothing powerful or operative in them, nor have any *necessary* connexion with the effects ascribed to them? If it be a Spirit that immediately produces every effect by a *fiat*, or act of his will, we must think all that is fine and artificial in the works, whether of man or nature, to be made in vain. By this doctrine, though an artist hath made the spring and wheels, and every movement of a watch, and adjusted them in such a manner as he knew would produce the motions he designed; yet he must think all this done to no purpose, and that it is an Intelligence which directs the index, and points to the hour of the day. If so, why may not the Intelligence do it, without *his* being at the pains of making the movements and putting them together? Why does not an empty case serve as well as another? And how comes it to pass, that whenever there is any fault in the going of a watch, there is some corresponding disorder to be found in the movements, which being mended by a skilful hand all is right again? The like may be said of all the Clockwork of Nature, great part whereof is so wonderfully fine and subtle as scarce to be discerned by the best microscope. In short, it will be asked, how, upon our Principles, any tolerable account can be given, or any final cause assigned of an innumerable multitude of bodies and machines, framed with the most exquisite art, which in the common philosophy have very opposite uses assigned them, and serve to explain abundance of phenomena?

61. To all which I answer, first, that though there were some difficulties relating to the administration of Providence, and the uses by it assigned to the several parts of nature, which I could not solve by

the foregoing Principles, yet this objection could be of small weight against the truth and certainty of those things which may be proved *a priori*, with the utmost confidence and rigour of demonstration. Secondly, but neither are the received principles free from the like difficulties; for, it may still be demanded to what end God should take those roundabout methods of effecting things by instruments and machines, which no one can deny might have been effected by the mere command of His will, without all that *apparatus*. Nay, if we narrowly consider it, we shall find the objection may be retorted with greater force on those who hold the existence of those machines without the mind; for it has been made evident that solidity, bulk, figure, motion, and the like have no *activity* or *efficacy* in them, so as to be capable of producing any one effect in nature. See sect. 25. Whoever therefore supposes them to exist (allowing the supposition possible) when they are not perceived does it manifestly to no purpose; since the only use that is assigned to them, as they exist unperceived, is that they produce those perceivable effects which in truth cannot be ascribed to anything but Spirit.

62. But, to come nigher the difficulty, it must be observed that though the fabrication of all those parts and organs be not absolutely necessary to the producing any effect, yet it is necessary to the producing of things in a constant regular way, according to the laws of nature. There are certain general laws that run through the whole chain of natural effects: these are learned by the observation and study of nature, and are by men applied, as well to the framing artificial things for the use and ornament of life as to the explaining the various phenomena. Which explication consists only in shewing the conformity any particular phenomenon hath to the general laws of nature, or, which is the same thing, in discovering the *uniformity* there is in the production of natural effects; as will be evident to whoever shall attend to the several instances wherein philosophers pretend to account for appearances. That there is a great and conspicuous *use* in these regular constant methods of working observed by the Supreme Agent hath been shewn in sect. 31. And it is no less visible that a particular size, figure, motion, and disposition of parts are necessary, though not absolutely to the producing any effect, yet to the producing it according to the standing mechanical laws of nature. Thus, for instance, it

cannot be denied that God, or the Intelligence that sustains and rules the ordinary course of things, might if He were minded to produce a miracle, cause all the motions on the dial-plate of a watch, though nobody had ever made the movements and put them in it. But yet, if He will act agreeably to the rules of mechanism, by Him for wise ends established and maintained in the creation, it is necessary that those actions of the watchmaker, whereby *he* makes the movements and rightly adjusts them, precede the production of the aforesaid motions; as also that any disorder in them be attended with the perception of some corresponding disorder in the movements, which being once corrected all is right again.

63. It may indeed on some occasions be necessary that the Author of nature display His overruling power in producing some appearance out of the ordinary series of things. Such exceptions from the general rules of nature are proper to surprise and awe men into an acknowledgment of the Divine Being; but then they are to be used but seldom, otherwise there is a plain reason why they should fail of that effect. Besides, God seems to choose the convincing our reason of His attributes by the works of nature, which discover so much harmony and contrivance in their make, and are such plain indications of wisdom and beneficence in their Author, rather than to astonish us into a belief of His Being by anomalous and surprising events.

64. To set this matter in a yet clearer light, I shall observe that what has been objected in sect. 60 amounts in reality to no more than this:—*ideas* are not anyhow and at random produced, there being a certain order and connexion between them, like to that of cause and effect: there are also several combinations of them, made in a very regular and artificial manner, which seem like so many instruments in the hand of nature that, being hid as it were behind the scenes, have a secret operation in producing those appearances which are seen on the theatre of the world, being themselves discernible only to the curious eye of the philosopher. But, since one idea cannot be the cause of another, to what purpose is that connexion? And since those instruments, being barely *inefficacious* perceptions in the mind, are not subservient to the production of natural effects, it is demanded why they are made; or, in other words, what reason can be assigned why God should make

us, upon a close inspection into His works, behold so great variety of ideas, so artfully laid together, and so much according to rule; it not being credible that He would be at the expense (if one may so speak) of all that art and regularity to no purpose?

65. To all which my answer is, first, that the connexion of ideas does not imply the relation of *cause* and *effect,* but only of a mark or *sign* with the *thing signified.* The fire which I see is not the cause of the pain I suffer upon my approaching it, but the mark that forewarns me of it. In like manner the noise that I hear is not the effect of this or that motion or collision of the ambient bodies, but the sign thereof. Secondly, the reason why ideas are formed into machines, that is, artificial and regular combinations, is the same with that for combining letters into words. That a few original ideas may be made to signify a great number of effects and actions, it is necessary they be variously combined together. And to the end their use be permanent and universal, these combinations must be made by *rule,* and with *wise contrivance.* By this means abundance of information is conveyed unto us, concerning what we are to expect from such and such actions, and what methods are proper to be taken for the exciting such and such ideas. Which in effect is all that I conceive to be distinctly meant when it is said that, by discerning the figure, texture, and mechanism of the inward parts of bodies, whether natural or artificial, we may attain to know the several uses and properties depending thereon, or the nature of the thing.

66. Hence, it is evident that those things which, under the notion of a cause co-operating or concurring to the production of effects, are altogether inexplicable and run us into great absurdities, may be very naturally explained, and have a proper and obvious use assigned to them, when they are considered only as marks or signs for *our* information. And it is the searching after and endeavouring to understand this Language (if I may so call it) of the Author of Nature, that ought to be the employment of the natural philosopher; and not the pretending to explain things by *corporeal* causes, which doctrine seems to have too much estranged the minds of men from that Active Principle, that supreme and wise Spirit 'in whom we live, move, and have our being.'

67. In the *twelfth* place, it may perhaps be objected that—though it be clear from what has been said that there can be no such thing as an inert, senseless, extended, solid, figured, moveable Substance, existing without the mind, such as philosophers describe Matter; yet, if any man shall leave out of his idea of Matter the positive ideas of extension, figure, solidity and motion, and say that he means only by that word an inert, senseless substance, that exists without the mind, or unperceived, which is the *occasion* of our ideas, or at the presence whereof God is pleased to excite ideas in us—it doth not appear but that Matter taken in this sense may possibly exist.—In answer to which I say, first, that it seems no less absurd to suppose a substance without accidents, than it is to suppose accidents without a substance. But secondly, though we should grant this unknown substance may possibly exist, yet where can it be supposed to be? That it exists not in the mind is agreed; and that it exists not in place is no less certain, since all place or extension exists only in the mind, as hath been already proved. It remains therefore that it exists nowhere at all.

68. Let us examine a little the description that is here given us of Matter. It neither acts, nor perceives, nor is perceived: for this is all that is meant by saying it is an inert, senseless, unknown substance; which is a definition entirely made up of negatives, excepting only the relative notion of its standing under or supporting. But then it must be observed that it supports nothing at all, and how nearly this comes to the description of a *nonentity* I desire may be considered. But, say you, it is the *unknown occasion,* at the presence of which ideas are excited in us by the will of God. Now, I would fain know how anything can be present to us, which is neither perceivable by sense nor reflexion, nor capable of producing any idea in our minds, nor is at all extended, nor hath any form, nor exists in any place. The words 'to be present,' when thus applied, must needs be taken in some abstract and strange meaning, and which I am not able to comprehend.

69. Again, let us examine what is meant by *occasion.* So far as I can gather from the common use of language, that word signifies either the agent which produces any effect, or else something that is observed to accompany or go before it, in the ordinary course of things. But, when it is applied to Matter, as above described, it can be taken in neither of those senses; for Matter is said to be passive and inert, and so cannot be an agent or efficient cause. It is also unperceivable, as being devoid of all sensible qualities, and so cannot be the occasion of our perceptions in the latter sense; as when the burning my finger is said to be the occasion of the pain that attends it. What therefore can be meant by calling *matter* an *occasion?* This term is either used in no sense at all, or else in some very distant from its received signification.

70. You will perhaps say that Matter, though it be not perceived by us, is nevertheless perceived by God, to whom it is the occasion of exciting ideas in our minds. For, say you, since we observe our sensations to be imprinted in an orderly and constant manner, it is but reasonable to suppose there are certain constant and regular occasions of their being produced. That is to say, that there are certain permanent and distinct parcels of Matter, corresponding to our ideas, which, though they do not excite them in our minds, or anywise immediately affect us, as being altogether passive, and unperceivable to us, they are nevertheless to God, by whom they *are* perceived, as it were so many occasions to remind Him when and what ideas to imprint on our minds: that so things may go on in a constant uniform manner.

71. In answer to this, I observe that, as the notion of Matter is here stated, the question is no longer concerning the existence of a thing distinct from *Spirit* and *idea,* from perceiving and being perceived; but whether there are not certain Ideas (of I know not what sort) in the mind of God, which are so many marks or notes that direct Him how to produce sensations in our minds in a constant and regular method: much after the same manner as a musician is directed by the notes of music to produce that harmonious train and composition of sound which is called a tune; though they who hear the music do not perceive the notes, and may be entirely ignorant of them. But this notion of Matter (which after all is the only intelligible one that I can pick from what is said of unknown occasions) seems too extravagant to deserve a confutation. Besides, it is in effect no objection against what we have advanced, viz. that there is no senseless unperceived substance.

72. If we follow the light of reason, we shall, from the constant uniform method of our sensations, collect the goodness and wisdom of the Spirit who excites them in our minds; but this is all that I can see reasonably concluded from thence. To me, I say, it is evident that the being of a Spirit—infinitely wise, good, and powerful—is abundantly sufficient to explain all the appearances of nature. But, as for *inert, senseless Matter*, nothing that I perceive has any the least connexion with it, or leads to the thoughts of it. And I would fain see any one explain any the meanest phenomenon in nature by it, or shew any manner of reason, though in the lowest rank of probability, that he can have for its existence; or even make any tolerable sense or meaning of that supposition. For, as to its being an occasion, we have, I think, evidently shewn that with regard to us it is no occasion. It remains therefore that it must be, if at all, the occasion to God of exciting ideas in us; and what this amounts to we have just now seen.

97. Beside the external existence of the objects of perception, another great source of errors and difficulties with regard to ideal knowledge is the doctrine of *abstract ideas*, such as it hath been set forth in the Introduction. The plainest things in the world, those we are most intimately acquainted with and perfectly know, when they are considered in an abstract way, appear strangely difficult and incomprehensible. Time, place, and motion, taken in particular or concrete, are what everybody knows; but, having passed through the hands of a metaphysician, they become too abstract and fine to be apprehended by men of ordinary sense. Bid your servant meet you at such a *time*, in such a *place*, and he shall never stay to deliberate on the meaning of those words. In conceiving that particular time and place, or the motion by which he is to get thither, he finds not the least difficulty. But if *time* be taken exclusive of all those particular actions and ideas that diversify the day, merely for the continuation of existence or duration in abstract, then it will perhaps gravel even a philosopher to comprehend it.

98. For my own part, whenever I attempt to frame a simple idea of *time*, abstracted from the succession of ideas in my mind, which flows uniformly, and is participated by all beings, I am lost and embrangled in inextricable difficulties. I have no notion of it at all: only I hear others say it is infinitely divisible, and speak of it in such a manner as leads me to harbour odd thoughts of my existence: since that doc-

trine lays one under an absolute necessity of thinking, either that he passes away innumerable ages without a thought, or else that he is annihilated every moment of his life: both which seem equally absurd. Time therefore being nothing, abstracted from the succession of ideas in our minds, it follows that the duration of any finite spirit must be estimated by the number of ideas or actions succeeding each other in that same spirit of mind. Hence, it is a plain consequence that the soul always thinks. And in truth whoever shall go about to divide in his thoughts or abstract the *existence* of a spirit from its *cogitation*, will, I believe, find it no easy task.

99. So likewise when we attempt to abstract *extension* and *motion* from all other qualities, and consider them by themselves, we presently lose sight of them, and run into great extravagances. [Hence spring those odd paradoxes, that the fire is not hot, nor the wall white; or that heat and colour are in the objects nothing but figure and motion.] All which depend on a twofold abstraction: first, it is supposed that extension, for example, may be abstracted from all other sensible qualities; and, secondly, that the entity of extension may be abstracted from its being perceived. But, whoever shall reflect, and take care to understand what he says, will, if I mistake not, acknowledge that all sensible qualities are alike *sensations*, and alike *real*; that where the extension is, there is the colour too, to wit, in his mind, and that their archetypes can exist only in some other *mind*: and that the objects of sense are nothing but those sensations, combined, blended, or (if one may so speak) concreted together; none of all which can be supposed to exist unperceived. [And that consequently the wall is as truly white as it is extended, and in the same sense.]

100. What it is for a man to be happy, or an object good, every one may think he knows. But to frame an abstract idea of happiness, prescinded from all particular pleasure, or of goodness from everything that is good, this is what few can pretend to. So likewise a man may be just and virtuous without having precise ideas of justice and virtue. The opinion that those and the like words stand for general notions, abstracted from all particular persons and actions, seems to have rendered morality difficult, and the study thereof of less use to mankind. [And in effect

one may make a great progress in school-ethics without ever being the wiser or better man for it, or knowing how to behave himself in the affairs of life more to the advantage of himself or his neighbours than he did before.] And in effect the doctrine of *abstraction* has not a little contributed towards spoiling the most useful parts of knowledge.

101. The two great provinces of speculative science conversant about ideas received from sense and their relations, are Natural Philosophy and Mathematics. With regard to each of these I shall make some observations.

And first I shall say somewhat of Natural Philosophy. On this subject it is that the sceptics triumph. All that stock of arguments they produce to depreciate our faculties and make mankind appear ignorant and low, are drawn principally from this head, namely, that we are under an invincible blindness as to the *true* and *real* nature of things. This they exaggerate, and love to enlarge on. We are miserably bantered, say they, by our senses, and amused only with the outside and shew of things. The real essence, the internal qualities and constitution of even the meanest object, is hid from our view: something there is in every drop of water, every grain of sand, which it is beyond the power of human understanding to fathom or comprehend. But, it is evident from what has been shewn that all this complaint is groundless, and that we are influenced by false principles to that degree as to mistrust our senses, and think we know nothing of those things which we perfectly comprehend.

102. One great inducement to our pronouncing ourselves ignorant of the nature of things is, the current opinion that every thing includes *within itself* the cause of its properties: or that there is in each object an inward essence, which is the source whence its discernible qualities flow, and whereon they depend. Some have pretended to account for appearances by occult qualities; but of late they are mostly resolved into mechanical causes, to wit, the figure, motion, weight, and suchlike qualities, of insensible particles: whereas, in truth, there is no other agent or efficient cause than *spirit* it being evident that motion, as well as all other *ideas*, is perfectly inert. See sect. 25. Hence, to endeavour to explain the production of colours or sounds, by figure, motion, magnitude, and the like, must needs be labour in vain. And accordingly we see the attempts of that kind are not at all

satisfactory. Which may be said in general of those instances wherein one idea or quality is assigned for the cause of another. I need not say how many hypotheses and speculations are left out, and how much the study of nature is abridged by this doctrine.

103. The great mechanical principle now in vogue is *attraction*. That a stone falls to the earth, or the sea swells towards the moon, may to some appear sufficiently explained thereby. But how are we enlightened by being told this is done by attraction? Is it that that word signifies the manner of the tendency, and that it is by the mutual drawing of bodies instead of their being impelled or protruded towards each other? But nothing is determined of the manner or action, and it may as truly (for aught we know) be termed *impulse,* or *protrusion,* as *attraction.* Again, the parts of steel we see cohere firmly together, and this also is accounted for by attraction; but, in this, as in the other instances, I do not perceive that anything is signified besides the effect itself; for as to the manner of the action whereby it is produced, or the cause which produces it, these are not so much as aimed at.

104. Indeed, if we take a view of the several phenomena, and compare them together, we may observe some likeness and conformity between them. For example, in the falling of a stone to the ground, in the rising of the sea towards the moon, in cohesion and crystallization, there is something alike; namely, an union or mutual approach of bodies. So that any one of these or the like phenomena may not seem strange or surprising to a man who has nicely observed and compared the effects of nature. For that only is thought so which is uncommon, or a thing by itself, and out of the ordinary course of our observation. That bodies should tend towards the centre of the earth is not thought strange, because it is what we perceive every moment of our lives. But that they should have a like gravitation towards the centre of the moon may seem odd and unaccountable to most men, because it is discerned only in the tides. But a philosopher, whose thoughts take in a larger compass of nature, having observed a certain similitude of appearances, as well in the heavens as the earth, that argue innumerable bodies to have a mutual tendency towards each other, which he denotes by the general name *attraction*, whatever can be reduced to that, he thinks justly accounted for. Thus he explains the tides by the attraction of the terraqueous globe towards the moon; which to him doth not appear odd or anomalous, but only a particular example of a general rule or law of nature.

105. If therefore we consider the difference there is betwixt natural philosophers and other men, with regard to their knowledge of the phenomena, we shall find it consists, not in an exacter knowledge of the efficient cause that produces them—for that can be no other than the *will of a spirit*—but only in a greater largeness of comprehension, whereby analogies, harmonies, and agreements are discovered in the works of nature, and the particular effects explained, that is, reduced to general rules, see sect. 62: which rules, grounded on the analogy and uniformness observed in the production of natural effects, are most agreeable and sought after by the mind; for that they extend our prospect beyond what is present and near to us, and enable us to make very probable conjectures touching things that may have happened at very great distances of time and place, as well as to predict things to come: which sort of endeavour towards Omniscience is much affected by the mind.

106. But we should proceed warily in such things: for we are apt to lay too great a stress on analogies, and, to the prejudice of truth, humour that eagerness of the mind, whereby it is carried to extend its knowledge into general theorems. For example, gravitation or mutual attraction, because it appears in many instances, some are straightway for pronouncing *universal*; and that to attract and be attracted by every other body is an essential quality inherent in all bodies whatsoever. Whereas it is evident the fixed stars have no such tendency towards each other; and, so far is that gravitation from being *essential* to bodies that in some instances a quite contrary principle seems to shew itself; as in the perpendicular growth of plants, and the elasticity of the air. There is nothing necessary or essential in the case; but it depends entirely on the will of the Governing Spirit, who causes certain bodies to cleave together or tend towards each other according to various laws, whilst He keeps others at a fixed distance; and to some He gives a quite contrary tendency to fly asunder, just as He sees convenient.

107. After what has been premised, I think we may lay down the following conclusions. First, it is plain philosophers amuse themselves in vain, when they enquire for any natural efficient cause, distinct from a *mind* or *spirit*. Secondly, considering the whole creation is the workmanship of a *wise and good Agent*, it should seem to become philosophers to employ their thoughts (contrary to what some hold) about the final causes of things. [For, besides that this would prove a very pleasing entertainment to the mind, it might be of great advantage, in that it not only discovers to us the attributes of the Creator, but may also direct us in several instances to the proper uses and applications of things.] And I must confess I see no reason why pointing out the various ends to which natural things are adapted, and for which they were originally with unspeakable wisdom contrived, should not be thought one good way of accounting for them, and altogether worthy a philosopher. Thirdly, from what has been premised, no reason can be drawn why the history of nature should not still be studied, and observations and experiments made; which, that they are of use to mankind, and enable us to draw any general conclusions, is not the result of any immutable habitudes or relations between things themselves, but only of God's goodness and kindness to men in the administration of the world. See sects. 30 and 31. Fourthly, by a diligent observation of the phenomena within our view, we may discover the general laws of nature, and from them deduce other phenomena. I do not say *demonstrate*; for all deductions of that kind depend on a supposition that the Author of Nature always operates uniformly, and in a constant observance of those rules *we* take for principles, which we cannot evidently know.

108. [It appears from sect. 66, &c. that the steady consistent methods of nature may not unfitly be styled the Language of its Author, whereby He discovers His attributes to our view and directs us how to act for the convenience and felicity of life.] Those men who frame general rules from the phenomena, and afterwards derive the phenomena from those rules, seem to consider signs rather than causes. A man may well understand natural signs without knowing their analogy, or being able to say by what rule a thing is so or so. And, as it is very possible to write improperly, through too strict an observance of general grammar-rules; so, in arguing from general laws of nature, it is not impossible we may extend the analogy too far, and by that means run into mistakes.

109. [To carry on the resemblance.] As in reading other books a wise man will choose to fix his thoughts on the sense and apply it to use, rather than lay them out in grammatical remarks on the language; so, in perusing the volume of nature, methinks it is beneath the dignity of the mind to affect an exactness in reducing each particular phenomenon to general rules, or shewing how it follows from them. We should propose to ourselves nobler views, such as to recreate and exalt the mind with a prospect of the beauty, order, extent, and variety of natural things: hence, by proper inferences, to enlarge our notions of the grandeur, wisdom, and beneficence of the Creator: and lastly, to make the several parts of the creation, so far as in us lies, subservient to the ends they were designed for—God's glory, and the sustentation and comfort of ourselves and fellow-creatures.

110. [The best key for the aforesaid analogy, or natural Science, will be easily acknowledged to be a certain celebrated Treatise of *Mechanics*.] In the entrance of which justly admired treatise, Time, Space, and Motion are distinguished into *absolute* and *relative*, *true* and *apparent*, *mathematical* and *vulgar*: which distinction, as it is at large explained by the author, does suppose those quantities to have an existence without the mind: and that they are ordinarily conceived with relation to sensible things, to which nevertheless in their own nature they bear no relation at all.

111. As for *Time*, as it is there taken in an absolute, or abstracted sense, for the duration or perseverance of the existence of things, I have nothing more to add concerning it after what has been already said on that subject. Sects. 97 and 98. For the rest, this celebrated author holds there is an *absolute Space*, which, being unperceivable to sense, remains in itself similar and immoveable; and relative space to be the measure thereof, which, being moveable and defined by its situation in respect of sensible bodies, is vulgarly taken for immoveable space. *Place* he defines to be that part of space which is occupied by any body: and according as the space is absolute or relative so also is the place. *Absolute Motion* is said to be the translation of a body from absolute place to absolute place, as relative motion is from one relative place to another. And because the parts of absolute space do not fall under our senses, instead of them we are obliged to use their sensible measures; and so define both place and motion with respect to bodies which we regard as immoveable. But it is said, in philosophical matters we must abstract from our senses; since it may be that none of those bodies which seem to be quiescent are truly so; and the same thing which is moved relatively may be really at rest. As likewise one and the same body may be in relative rest and motion, or even moved with contrary relative motions at the same time, according as its place is variously defined. All which ambiguity is to be found in the apparent motions; but not at all in the true or absolute, which should therefore be alone regarded in philosophy. And the true we are told are distinguished from apparent or relative motions by the following properties. First, in true or absolute motion, all parts which preserve the same position with respect of the whole, partake of the motions of the whole. Secondly, the place being moved, that which is placed therein is also moved: so that a body moving in a place which is in motion doth participate the motion of its place. Thirdly, true motion is never generated or changed otherwise than by force impressed on the body itself. Fourthly, true motion is always changed by force impressed on the body moved. Fifthly, in circular motion, barely relative, there is no centrifugal force, which nevertheless, in that which is true or absolute, is proportional to the quantity of motion.

112. But, notwithstanding what hath been said, I must confess it does not appear to me that there can be any motion other than *relative*: so that to conceive motion there must be conceived at least two bodies; whereof the distance or position in regard to each other is varied. Hence, if there was one only body in being it could not possibly be moved. This seems evident, in that the idea I have of motion doth necessarily include relation.—[Whether others can conceive it otherwise, a little attention may satisfy them.]

113. But, though in every motion it be necessary to conceive more bodies than one, yet it may be that one only is moved, namely, that on which the force causing the change in the distance or situation of the bodies is impressed. For, however some may define relative motion, so as to term that body *moved* which changes its distance from some other body whether the force [or action] causing that change were impressed on it or no, yet, as relative motion is that which is perceived by sense, and regarded in the ordinary affairs of life, it follows that every man of common sense knows what it is as well as the best philosopher. Now, I ask any one whether, in his sense

of motion as he walks along the streets, the stones he passes over may be said to *move,* because they change distance with his feet? To me it appears that though motion includes a relation of one thing to another, yet it is not necessary that each term of the relation be denominated from it. As a man may think of somewhat which does not think, so a body may be moved to or from another body which is not therefore itself in motion, [I mean relative motion, for other I am not able to conceive.]

114. As the place happens to be variously defined, the motion which is related to it varies. A man in a ship may be said to be quiescent with relation to the sides of the vessel, and yet move with relation to the land. Or he may move eastward in respect of the one, and westward in respect of the other. In the common affairs of life, men never go beyond the Earth to define the place of any body; and what is quiescent in respect of *that* is accounted *absolutely* to be so. But philosophers, who have a greater extent of thought, and juster notions of the system of things, discover even the Earth itself to be moved. In order therefore to fix their notions, they seem to conceive the Corporeal World as finite, and the utmost unmoved walls or shell thereof to be the place whereby they estimate true motions. If we sound our own conceptions, I believe we may find all the absolute motion we can frame an idea of to be at bottom no other than relative motion thus defined. For, as has been already observed, absolute motion, exclusive of *all* external relation, is incomprehensible: and to this kind of relative motion all the above-mentioned properties, causes, and effects ascribed to absolute motion will, if I mistake not, be found to agree. As to what is said of the centrifugal force, that it does not at all belong to circular relative motion, I do not see how this follows from the experiment which is brought to prove it. See Newton's *Philosophiae Naturalis Principia Mathematica, in Schol. Def. VIII.* For the water in the vessel, at that time wheren it is said to have the greatest relative circular motion, hath, I think, no motion at all: as is plain from the foregoing section.

115. For, to denominate a body *moved,* it is requisite, first, that it change its distance or situation with regard to some other body: and secondly, that the force occasioning that change be applied to it. If either of these be wanting, I do not think that, agree-

ably to the sense of mankind, or the propriety of language, a body can be said to be in motion. I grant indeed that it is pos sible for us to think a body, which we see change its distance from some other, to be moved, though it have no force applied to it (in which sense there may be apparent motion); but then it is because the force causing the change of distance is imagined by us to be [applied or] impressed on that body thought to move. Which indeed shews we are capable of mistaking a thing to be in motion which is not, and that is all. [But it does not prove that, in the common acceptation of motion, a body is moved merely because it changes distance from another; since as soon as we are undeceived, and find that the moving force was not communicated to it, we no longer hold it to be moved. So, on the other hand, when one only body (the parts whereof preserve a given position between themselves) is imagined to exist, some there are who think that it can be moved all manner of ways, though without any change of distance or situation to any other bodies; which we should not deny, if they meant only that it might have an impressed force, which, upon the bare creation of other bodies, would produce a motion of some certain quantity and determination. But that an actual motion (distinct from the impressed force, or power, productive of change of place in case there were bodies present whereby to define it) can exist in such a single body, I must confess I am not able to comprehend.]

116. From what has been said, it follows that the philosophic consideration of motion doth not imply the being of an *absolute Space,* distinct from that which is perceived by sense, and related to bodies: which that it cannot exist without the mind is clear upon the same principles that demonstrate the like of all other objects of sense. And perhaps, if we inquire narrowly, we shall find we cannot even frame an idea of *pure Space exclusive of all body.* This I must confess seems impossible, as being a most abstract idea. When I excite a motion in some part of my body, if it be free or without resistance, I say there is *Space.* But if I find a resistance, then I say there is *Body:* and in proportion as the resistance to motion is lesser or greater, I say the space is more or less *pure.* So that when I speak of pure or empty space, it is not to be supposed that the word *space* stands for an idea distinct from, or conceivable without, body and motion. Though

indeed we are apt to think every noun substantive stands for a distinct idea that may be separated from all others; which hath occasioned infinite mistakes. When, therefore, supposing all the world to be annihilated besides my own body, I say there still remains *pure Space*; thereby nothing else is meant but only that I conceive it possible for the limbs of my body to be moved on all sides without the least resistance: but if that too were annihilated then there could be no motion, and consequently no Space. Some, perhaps, may think the sense of seeing doth furnish them with the idea of pure space; but it is plain from what we have elsewhere shewn, that the ideas of space and distance are not obtained by that sense. See the *Essay concerning Vision*.

117. What is here laid down seems to put an end to all those disputes and difficulties that have sprung up amongst the learned concerning the nature of *pure Space*. But the chief advantage arising from it is that we are freed from that dangerous dilemma, to which several who have employed their thoughts on that subject imagine themselves reduced, viz. of thinking either that Real Space is God, or else that there is something beside God which is eternal, uncreated, infinite, indivisible, immutable. Both which may justly be thought pernicious and absurd notions. It is certain that not a few divines, as well as philosophers of great note, have, from the difficulty they found in conceiving either limits or annihilation of space, concluded it must be *divine*. And some of late have set themselves particularly to shew that the incommunicable attributes of God agree to it. Which doctrine, how unworthy soever it may seem of the Divine Nature, yet I must confess I do not see how we can get clear of it, so long as we adhere to the received opinions.

118. Hitherto of Natural Philosophy. We come now to make some inquiry concerning that other great branch of speculative knowledge, to wit, Mathematics. These, how celebrated soever they may be for their clearness and certainty of demonstration, which is hardly anywhere else to be found, cannot nevertheless be supposed altogether free from mistakes, if in their principles there lurks some secret error which is common to the professors of those sciences with the rest of mankind. Mathematicians, though they deduce their theorems from a great height of evidence, yet their first principles are limited by the consideration of Quantity. And they do not ascend into any inquiry concerning those transcendental maxims which influence all the particular sciences; each part whereof, Mathematics not excepted, doth consequently participate of the errors involved in them. That the principles laid down by mathematicians are true, and their way of deduction from those principles clear and incontestible, we do not deny. But we hold there may be certain erroneous maxims of greater extent than the object of Mathematics, and for that reason not expressly mentioned, though tacitly supposed, throughout the whole progress of that science; and that the ill effects of those secret unexamined errors are diffused through all the branches thereof. To be plain, we suspect the mathematicians are no less deeply concerned than other men in the errors arising from the doctrine of abstract general ideas, and the existence of objects without the mind.

119. Arithmetic hath been thought to have for its object abstract ideas of *number*. Of which to understand the properties and mutual habitudes, is supposed no mean part of speculative knowledge. The opinion of the pure and intellectual nature of numbers in abstract has made them in esteem with those philosophers who seem to have affected an uncommon fineness and elevation of thought. It hath set a price on the most trifling numerical speculations, which in practice are of no use, but serve only for amusement; and hath heretofore so far infected the minds of some, that they have dreamed of mighty *mysteries* involved in numbers, and attempted the explication of natural things by them. But, if we narrowly inquire into our own thoughts, and consider what has been premised, we may perhaps entertain a low opinion of those high flights and abstractions, and look on all inquiries about numbers only as so many *difficiles nugae*, so far as they are not subservient to practice, and promote the benefit of life.

120. Unity in abstract we have before considered in sect. 13; from which, and what has been said in the Introduction, it plainly follows there is not any such idea. But, number being defined a *collection of units*, we may conclude that, if there be no such thing as unity, or unit in abstract, there are no *ideas* of number in abstract, denoted by the numeral names and figures. The theories therefore in Arithmetic, if they are abstracted from the names and figures, as likewise from all use and practice, as well as from the particu-

lar things numbered, can be supposed to have nothing at all for their object. Hence we may see how entirely the science of numbers is subordinate to practice, and how jejune and trifling it becomes when considered as a matter of mere speculation.

121. However, since there may be some who, deluded by the specious show of discovering abstracted verities, waste their time in arithmetical theorems and problems which have not any use, it will not be amiss if we more fully consider and expose the vanity of that pretence. And this will plainly appear by taking a view of Arithmetic in its infancy, and observing what it was that originally put men on the study of that science, and to what scope they directed it. It is natural to think that at first, men, for ease of memory and help of computation, made use of counters, or in writing of single strokes, points, or the like, each whereof was made to signify an unit, *i.e.* some one thing of whatever kind they had occasion to reckon. Afterwards they found out the more compendious ways of making one character stand in place of several strokes or points. And, lastly, the notation of the Arabians or Indians came into use; wherein, by the repetition of a few characters or figures, and varying the signification of each figure according to the place it obtains, all numbers may be most aptly expressed. Which seems to have been done in imitation of language, so that an exact analogy is observed betwixt the notation by figures and names, the nine simple figures answering the nine first numeral names and places in the former, corresponding to denominations in the latter. And agreeably to those conditions of the simple and local value of figures, were contrived methods of finding, from the given figures or marks of the parts, what figures and how placed are proper to denote the whole, or *vice versa*. And having found the sought figures, the same rule or analogy being observed throughout, it is easy to read them into words; and so the number becomes perfectly known. For then the number of any particular things is said to be known, when we know the name or figures (with their due arrangement) that according to the standing analogy belong to them. For, these signs being known, we can by the operations of arithmetic know the signs of any part of the particular sums signified by them; and thus computing in signs, (because of the connexion established betwixt them and the distinct multitudes of things, whereof one is taken for an unit), we may be able rightly to sum up, divide, and proportion the things themselves that we intend to number.

122. In Arithmetic, therefore, we regard not the *things* but the *signs;* which nevertheless are not regarded for their own sake, but because they direct us how to act with relation to things, and dispose rightly of them. Now, agreeably to what we have before observed of Words in general (sect. 19, Introd.), it happens here likewise, that abstract ideas are thought to be signified by numeral names or characters, while they do not suggest ideas of particular things to our minds. I shall not at present enter into a more particular dissertation on this subject; but only observe that it is evident from what has been said, those things which pass for abstract truths and theorems concerning numbers, are in reality conversant about no object distinct from particular numerable things; except only names and characters, which originally came to be considered on no other account but their being *signs*, or capable to represent aptly whatever particular things men had need to compute. Whence it follows that to study them for their own sake would be just as wise, and to as good purpose, as if a man, neglecting the true use or original intention and subserviency of language, should spend his time in impertinent criticisms upon words, or reasonings and controversies purely verbal.

123. From numbers we proceed to speak of *extension*, which, considered as relative, is the object of Geometry. The *infinite* divisibility of *finite* extension, though it is not expressly laid down either as an axiom or theorem in the elements of that science, yet is throughout the same everywhere supposed, and thought to have so inseparable and essential a connexion with the principles and demonstrations in Geometry that mathematicians never admit it into doubt, or make the least question of it. And as this notion is the source from whence do spring all those amusing geometrical paradoxes which have such a direct repugnancy to the plain common sense of mankind, and are admitted with so much reluctance into a mind not yet debauched by learning; so is it the principal occasion of all that nice and extreme subtilty, which renders the study of Mathematics so very difficult and tedious. Hence, if we can make it appear that no *finite* extension contains innumerable parts, or is infinitely divisible, it follows that we shall at

once clear the science of Geometry from a great number of difficulties and contradictions which have ever been esteemed a reproach to human reason, and withal make the attainment thereof a business of much less time and pains than it hitherto hath been.

124. Every particular finite extension which may possibly be the object of our thought is an *idea* existing only in the mind; and consequently each part thereof must be perceived. If, therefore, I cannot *perceive* innumerable parts in any finite extension that I consider, it is certain they are not contained in it. But it is evident that I cannot distinguish innumerable parts in any particular line, surface, or solid, which I either perceive by sense, or figure to myself in my mind. Wherefore I conclude they are not contained in it. Nothing can be plainer to me than that the extensions I have in view are no other than my own ideas; and it is no less plain that I cannot resolve any one of my ideas into an infinite number of other ideas; that is, that they are not infinitely divisible. If by *finite extension* be meant something distinct from a finite idea, I declare I do not know what that is, and so cannot affirm or deny anything of it. But if the terms *extension, parts,* and the like, are taken in any sense conceivable—that is, for *ideas,*—then to say a finite quantity or extension consists of parts infinite in number is so manifest and glaring a contradiction, that every one at first sight acknowledges it to be so. And it is impossible it should ever gain the assent of any reasonable creature who is not brought to it by gentle and slow degrees, as a converted Gentile to the belief of transubstantiation. Ancient and rooted prejudices do often pass into principles. And those propositions which once obtain the force and credit of a *principle*, are not only themselves, but likewise whatever is deducible from them, thought privileged from all examination. And there is no absurdity so gross, which, by this means, the mind of man may not be prepared to swallow.

125. He whose understanding is prepossessed with the doctrine of abstract general ideas may be persuaded that (whatever be thought of the ideas of sense) *extension in abstract* is infinitely divisible. And one who thinks the objects of sense exist without the mind will perhaps, in virtue thereof, be brought to admit that a line but an inch long may contain innumerable parts really existing, though too small to be discerned. These errors are grafted as well in the minds of geometricians as of other men, and have a like influence on their reasonings; and it were no difficult thing to shew how the arguments from Geometry made use of to support the infinite divisibility of extension are bottomed on them. [But this, if it be thought necessary, we may hereafter find a proper place to treat of in a particular manner.] At present we shall only observe in general whence it is the mathematicians are all so fond and tenacious of that doctrine.

126. It has been observed in another place that the theorems and demonstrations in Geometry are conversant about universal ideas (sect. 15, Introd.): where it is explained in what sense this ought to be understood, to wit, the particular lines and figures included in the diagram are supposed to stand for innumerable others of different sizes; or, in other words, the geometer considers them abstracting from their magnitude: which doth not imply that he forms an abstract idea, but only that he cares not what the particular magnitude is, whether great or small, but looks on that as a thing indifferent to the demonstration. Hence it follows that a line in the scheme but an inch long must be spoken of as though it contained ten thousand parts, since it is regarded not in itself, but as it is universal; and it is universal only in its signification, whereby it *represents* innumerable lines greater than itself, in which may be distinguished ten thousand parts or more, though there may not be above an inch in *it*. After this manner, the properties of the lines signified are (by a very usual figure) transferred to the sign; and thence, through mistake, thought to appertain to it considered in its own nature.

127. Because there is no number of parts so great but it is possible there may be a line containing more, the inch-line is said to contain parts more than any assignable number; which is true, not of the inch taken absolutely, but only for the things signified by it. But men, not retaining that distinction in their thoughts, slide into a belief that the small particular line described on paper contains in itself parts innumerable. There is no such thing as the ten thousandth part of an inch; but there is of a mile or diameter of the earth, which may be signified by that inch. When therefore I delineate a triangle on paper, and take one side, not above an inch for example in length, to be the radius, this I consider as divided into 10,000 or 100,000 parts, or more. For, though the ten thousandth part of that line considered in itself, is nothing at all, and consequently may be neglected without any error or inconveniency, yet these described lines, being only marks standing for greater quantities, whereof it may be the ten thousandth part is very considerable, it follows that, to prevent notable errors in practice, the radius must be taken of 10,000 parts, or more.

128. From what has been said the reason is plain why, to the end any theorem may become universal in its use, it is necessary we speak of the lines described on paper as though they contained parts which really they do not. In doing of which, if we examine the matter thoroughly, we shall perhaps discover that we cannot conceive an inch itself as consisting of, or being divisible into, a thousand parts, but only some other line which is far greater than an inch, and represented by it; and that when we say a line is *infinitely divisible*, we must mean *a line which is infinitely great*. What we have here observed seems to be the chief cause, why to suppose the *infinite* divisibility of *finite extension* has been thought necessary in geometry.

129. The several absurdities and contradictions which flowed from this false principle might, one would think, have been esteemed so many demonstrations against it. But, by I know not what logic, it is held that proofs *a posteriori* are not to be admitted against propositions relating to Infinity. As though it were not impossible even for an Infinite Mind to reconcile contradictions; or as if anything absurd and repugnant could have a necessary connexion with truth, or flow from it. But whoever considers the weakness of this pretence, will think it was contrived on purpose to humour the laziness of the mind, which had rather acquiesce in an indolent scepticism than be at the pains to go through with a severe examination of those principles it has ever embraced for true.

130. Of late the speculations about Infinites have run so high, and grown to such strange notions, as have occasioned no small scruples and disputes among the geometers of the present age. Some there are of great note who, not content with holding that finite lines may be divided into an infinite number of parts, do yet farther maintain, that each of those Infinitesimals is itself subdivisible into an infinity of other parts, or Infinitesimals of a second order, and so on *ad infinitum*. These, I say, assert there are Infinitesimals of Infinitesimals of Infinitesimals, without ever coming to an end. So that according to them an inch does not barely contain an infinite number of parts, but an infinity of an infinity of an infinity *ad infinitum* of parts. Others there be who hold all orders of Infinitesimals below the first to be nothing at all; thinking it with good reason absurd to imagine there is any positive quantity or part of extension which, though multiplied infinitely, can ever equal the smallest given extension. And yet on the other hand it seems no less absurd to think the square, cube, or other power of a positive real root, should itself be nothing at all; which they who hold Infinitesimals of the first order, denying all of the subsequent orders, are obliged to maintain.

131. Have we not therefore reason to conclude they are *both* in the wrong, and that there is in effect no such thing as parts infinitely small, or an infinite number of parts contained in any finite quantity? But you will say that if this doctrine obtains it will follow the very foundations of Geometry are destroyed, and those great men who have raised that science to so astonishing a height, have been all the while building a castle in the air. To this it may be replied, that whatever is useful in geometry, and promotes the benefit of human life, does still remain firm and unshaken on our Principles; that science considered as practical will rather receive advantage than any prejudice from what has been said. But to set this in a due light, [and shew how lines and figures may be measured, and their properties investigated, without supposing finite extension to be infinitely divisible,] may be the proper business of another place. For the rest, though it should follow that some of the more intricate and subtle parts of Speculative Mathematics may be pared off without any prejudice to truth, yet I do not see what damage will be thence derived to mankind. On the contrary, I think it were highly to be wished that men of great abilities and obstinate application would draw off their thoughts from those amusements, and employ them in the study of such things as lie nearer the concerns of life, or have a more direct influence on the manners.

132. If it be said that several theorems, undoubtedly true, are discovered by methods in which Infinitesimals are made use of, which could never have been if their existence included a contradiction in it:—I answer that upon a thorough examination it will not be found that in any instance it is necessary to make use of or conceive *infinitesimal* parts of *finite* lines, or even quantities less than the *minimum sensible*: nay, it will be evident this is never done, it being impossible. [And whatever mathematicians may think of Fluxions, or the Differential Calculus, and the like, a little reflexion will shew them that, in working by those methods, they do not conceive or imagine lines or surfaces less than what are perceivable to sense. They may indeed call those little and almost insensible quantities Infinitesimals, or Infinitesimals of Infinitesimals, if they please. But at bottom this is all, they being in truth finite; nor does the solution of problems require the supposing any other. But this will be more clearly made out hereafter.]

133. By what we have hitherto said, it is plain that very numerous and important errors have taken their rise from those false Principles which were impugned in the foregoing parts of this Treatise; and the opposites of those erroneous tenets at the same time appear to be most fruitful Principles, from whence do flow innumerable consequences, highly advantageous to true philosophy as well as to religion. Particularly *Matter*, or *the absolute existence of corporeal objects*, hath been shewn to be that wherein the most avowed and pernicious enemies of all knowledge, whether human or divine, have ever placed their chief strength and confidence. And surely if by distinguishing the real existence of unthinking things from their being perceived, and allowing them a subsistence of their own, out of the minds of spirits, no one thing is explained in nature, but on the contrary a great many inexplicable difficulties arise; if the supposition of Matter is barely precarious, as not being grounded on so much as one single reason; if its consequences cannot endure the light of examination and free inquiry, but screen themselves under the dark and general pretence of *infinites being incomprehensible*; if withal the removal of *this* Matter be not attended with the least evil consequence; if it be not even missed in the world, but everything as well, nay much easier conceived without it; if, lastly, both Sceptics and Atheists are for ever silenced upon supposing only spirits and ideas, and this scheme of things is perfectly agreeable both to Reason and Religion: methinks we may expect it should be admitted and firmly embraced, though it were proposed only as an *hypothesis*, and the existence of Matter had been allowed possible: which yet I think we have evidently demonstrated that it is not.

134. True it is that, in consequence of the foregoing Principles, several disputes and speculations which are esteemed no mean parts of learning are rejected as useless [and in effect conversant about nothing at all]. But how great a prejudice soever against our notions this may give to those who have already been deeply engaged, and made large advances in studies of that nature, yet by others we hope it will not be thought any just ground of dislike to the principles and tenets herein laid down, that they abridge the labour of study, and make human sciences more clear, compendious, and attainable than they were before.

135. Having despatched what we intended to say concerning the knowledge of *ideas*, the method we proposed leads us in the next place to treat of *spirits*; with regard to which, perhaps, human knowledge is not so deficient as is vulgarly imagined. The great reason that is assigned for our being thought ignorant of the nature of Spirits is our not having an *idea* of it. But, surely it ought not to be looked on as a defect in a human understanding that it does not perceive the idea of Spirit, if it is manifestly impossible there should be any such idea. And this if I mistake not has been demonstrated in section 27. To which I shall here add that a Spirit has been shewn to be the only substance or support wherein unthinking beings or ideas can exist: but that this *substance* which supports or perceives ideas should itself be an idea, or like an idea, is evidently absurd.

136. It will perhaps be said that we want a *sense* (as some have imagined) proper to know substances withal; which, if we had, we might know our own soul as we do a triangle. To this I answer, that in case we had a new sense bestowed upon us, we could only receive thereby some new *sensations* or *ideas of sense*. But I believe nobody will say that what he means by the terms *soul* and *substance* is only some particular sort of idea or sensation. We may therefore infer that, all things duly considered, it is not more reasonable to think our faculties defective, in that they do not furnish us with an *idea* of Spirit, or active thinking substance, than it would be if we should blame them for not being able to comprehend a *round square*.

137. From the opinion that Spirits are to be known after the manner of an idea or sensation have risen many absurd and heterodox tenets, and much scepticism about the nature of the soul. It is even probable that this opinion may have produced a doubt in some whether they had any soul at all distinct from their body; since upon inquiry they could not find they had an idea of it. That an *idea,* which is inactive, and the existence whereof consists in being perceived, should be the image or likeness of an agent subsisting by itself, seems to need no other refutation than barely attending to what is meant by those words. But perhaps you will say that though an idea cannot resemble a Spirit in its thinking, acting, or subsisting by itself, yet it may in some other respects; and it is not necessary that an idea or image be in all respects like the original.

138. I answer, If it does not in those mentioned, it is impossible it should represent it in any other thing. Do but leave out the power of willing, thinking, and perceiving ideas, and there remains nothing else wherein the idea can be like a spirit. For, by the word *spirit* we mean only that which thinks, wills, and perceives; this, and this alone, constitutes the signification of that term. If therefore it is impossible that any degree of those powers should be represented in an idea [or notion], it is evident there can be no idea [or notion] of a Spirit.

139. But it will be objected that, if there is no *idea* signified by the terms, *soul, spirit,* and *substance,* they are wholly insignificant, or have no meaning in them. I answer, those words do mean or signify a real thing; which is neither an idea nor like an idea, but that which perceives ideas, and wills, and reasons about them. What I am *myself,* that which I denote by the term *I,* is the same with what is meant by *soul,* or *spiritual substance.* [But if I should say that *I* was nothing, or that *I* was an *idea* or *notion,* nothing could be more evidently absurd than either of these propositions.] If it be said that this is only quarrelling at a word, and that, since the immediate significations of other names are by common consent called *ideas,* no reason can be assigned why that which is signified by the name *spirit* or *soul* may not partake in the same appellation. I answer, all the unthinking objects of the mind agree in that they are entirely passive, and their existence consists only in being perceived: whereas a *soul* or *spirit* is an active being, whose existence consists, not in being perceived, but in perceiving ideas and thinking. It is therefore necessary, in order to prevent equivocation and confounding natures perfectly disagreeing and unlike, that we distinguish between *spirit* and *idea.* See sect. 27.

140. In a large sense indeed, we may be said to have an idea [or rather a notion] of *spirit.* That is, we understand the meaning of the word, otherwise we could not affirm or deny anything of it. Moreover, as we conceive the ideas that are in the minds of other spirits by means of our own, which we suppose to be resemblances of them, so we know other spirits by means of our own soul: which in that sense is the image or idea of them; it having a like respect to other spirits that blueness or heat by me perceived has to those ideas perceived by another.

141. [The natural immortality of the soul is a necessary consequence of the foregoing doctrine. But before we attempt to prove this, it is fit that we explain the meaning of that tenet.] It must not be supposed that they who assert the natural immortality of the soul are of opinion that it is absolutely incapable of annihilation even by the infinite power of the Creator who first gave it being, but only that it is not liable to be broken or dissolved by the ordinary laws of nature or motion. They indeed who hold the soul of man to be only a thin vital flame, or system of animal spirits, make it perishing and corruptible as the body; since there is nothing more easily dissipated than such a being, which it is naturally impossible should survive the ruin of the tabernacle wherein it is inclosed. And this notion hath been greedily embraced and cherished by the worst part of mankind, as the most effectual antidote against all impressions of virtue and religion. But it hath been made evident that bodies, of what frame or texture soever, are barely passive ideas in the mind, which is more distant and heterogeneous from them than light is from darkness. We have shewn that the soul is indivisible, incorporeal, unextended; and it is consequently incorruptible. Nothing can be plainer than that the motions, changes, decays, and dissolutions which we hourly see befal natural bodies (and which is what we mean by the *course of nature*) cannot possibly affect an active, simple, uncompounded substance: such a being therefore is indissoluble by the force of nature; that is to say, *the soul of man is naturally immortal.*

142. After what has been said, it is, I suppose, plain that our souls are not to be known in the same manner as senseless, inactive objects, or by way of *idea. Spirits* and *ideas* are things so wholly different, that when we say 'they exist,' 'they are known,' or the like, these words must not be thought to signify anything common to both natures. There is nothing alike or common in them; and to expect that by any

multiplication or enlargement of our faculties, we may be enabled to know a spirit as we do a triangle, seems as absurd as if we should hope to *see a sound*. This is inculcated because I imagine it may be of moment towards clearing several important questions, and preventing some very dangerous errors concerning the nature of the soul.

[We may not, I think, strictly be said to have an *idea* of an active being, or of an action; although we may be said to have a *notion* of them. I have some knowledge or notion of *my mind,* and its acts about ideas; inasmuch as I know or understand what is meant by these words. What I know, that I have some notion of. I will not say that the terms *idea* and *notion* may not be used convertibly, if the world will have it so. But yet it conduceth to clearness and propriety, that we distinguish things very different by different names. It is also to be remarked that, all *relations* including an act of the mind, we cannot so properly be said to have an idea, but rather a notion, of the relations and habitudes between things. But if, in the modern way, the word *idea* is extended to *spirits*, and *relations*, and *acts*, this is, after all, an affair of verbal concern.]

143. It will not be amiss to add, that the doctrine of *abstract ideas* has had no small share in rendering those sciences intricate and obscure which are particularly conversant about spiritual things. Men have imagined they could frame abstract notions·of the *powers* and *acts* of the mind, and consider them prescinded as well from the mind or spirit itself, as from their respective objects and effects. Hence a great number of dark and ambiguous terms, presumed to stand for abstract notions, have been introduced into metaphysics and morality; and from these have grown infinite distractions and disputes amongst the learned.

144. But, nothing seems more to have contributed towards engaging men in controversies and mistakes with regard to the nature and operations of the mind, than the being used to speak of those things in terms borrowed from sensible ideas. For example, the will is termed the *motion* of the soul: this infuses a belief that the mind of man is as a ball in motion, impelled and determined by the objects of sense, as necessarily as that is by the stroke of a racket. Hence arise endless scruples and errors of dangerous consequence in morality. All which, I doubt not, may be cleared, and truth appear plain, uniform, and consistent, could but philosophers be prevailed on to

[depart from some received prejudices and modes of speech, and] retire into themselves, and attentively consider their own meaning. [But the difficulties arising on this head demands a more particular disquisition than suits with the design of this treatise.]

145. From what hath been said, it is plain that we cannot know the existence of *other spirits* otherwise than by their operations, or the ideas by them, excited in us. I perceive several motions, changes, and combinations of ideas, that inform me there are certain particular agents, like myself, which accompany them, and concur in their production. Hence, the knowledge I have of other spirits is not immediate, as is the knowledge of my ideas; but depending on the intervention of ideas, by me referred to agents or spirits distinct from myself, as effects or concomitant signs.

146. But, though there be some things which convince us human agents are concerned in producing them, yet it is evident to every one that those things which are called the Works of Nature, that is, the far greater part of the ideas or sensations perceived by us, are *not* produced by, or dependent on, the wills of *men*. There is therefore some other Spirit that causes them; since it is repugnant that they should subsist by themselves. See sect. 29. But, if we attentively consider the constant regularity, order, and concatenation of natural things, the surprising magnificence, beauty and perfection of the larger, and the exquisite contrivance of the smaller parts of the creation, together with the exact harmony and correspondence of the whole, but above all the never-enough-admired laws of pain and pleasure, and the instincts or natural inclinations, appetites, and passions of animals;—I say if we consider all these things, and at the same time attend to the meaning and import of the attributes One, Eternal, Infinitely Wise, Good, and Perfect, we shall clearly perceive that they belong to the aforesaid Spirit, 'who works all in all' and 'by whom all things consist.'

· **147.** Hence, it is evident that God is known as certainly and immediately as any other mind or spirit whatsoever, distinct from ourselves. We may even assert that the existence of God is far more evidently perceived than the existence of men; because the effects of Nature are infinitely more numerous and considerable than those ascribed to human agents. There is not any one mark that denotes a man, or effect produced by him, which does not more strongly evince the being of that Spirit who is the Author of Nature. For it is evident that, in affecting other persons, the will of man hath no other object than barely the motion of the limbs of his body; but that such a motion should be attended by, or excite any idea in the mind of another, depends wholly on the will of the Creator. He alone it is who, 'upholding all things by the word of His power,' maintains that intercourse between spirits whereby they are able to perceive the existence of each other. And yet this pure and clear Light which enlightens everyone is itself invisible [to the greatest part of mankind].

148. It seems to be a general pretence of the unthinking herd that they cannot *see* God. Could we but see Him, say they, as we see a man, we should believe that He is, and believing obey His commands. But alas, we need only open our eyes to see the Sovereign Lord of all things, with a *more* full and clear view than we do any one of our fellow-creatures. Not that I imagine we see God (as some will have it) by a direct and immediate view; or see corporeal things, not by themselves, but by seeing that which represents them in the essence of God; which doctrine is, I must confess, to me incomprehensible. But I shall explain my meaning. A human spirit or person is not perceived by sense, as not being an idea. When therefore we see the colour, size, figure, and motions of a man, we perceive only certain sensations or ideas excited in our own minds; and these being exhibited to our view in sundry distinct collections, serve to mark out unto us the existence of finite and created spirits like ourselves. Hence it is plain we do not see a man, if by *man* is meant, that which lives, moves, perceives, and thinks as we do: but only such a certain collection of ideas, as directs us to think there is a distinct principle of thought and motion, like to ourselves, accompanying and represented by it. And after the same manner we see God: all the difference is that, whereas some one finite and narrow assemblage of ideas denotes a particular human mind, whithersoever we direct our view we do at all times and in all places perceive manifest tokens of the Divinity; everything we see, hear, feel, or anywise perceive by sense, being a sign or affect of the power of God; as is our perception of those very motions which are produced by men.

149. It is therefore plain that nothing can be more evident to any one that is capable of the least reflexion than the existence of God, or a Spirit who is intimately present to our minds, producing in them all that variety of ideas or sensations which continually affect us, on whom we have an absolute and entire dependence, in short 'in whom we live, and move, and have our being.' That the discovery of this great truth, which lies so near and obvious to the mind, should be attained to by the reason of so very few, is a sad instance of the stupidity and inattention of men, who, though they are surrounded with such clear manifestations of the Deity, are yet so little affected by them that they seem, as it were, blinded with excess of light.

150. But you will say—Hath Nature no share in the production of natural things, and must they be all ascribed to the immediate and sole operation of God? I answer, If by *Nature* is meant only the *visible series* of effects or sensations imprinted on our minds according to certain fixed and general laws, then it is plain that Nature, taken in this sense, cannot produce anything at all. But if by *Nature* is meant some being distinct from God, as well as from the laws of nature and things perceived by sense, I must confess that word is to me an empty sound, without any intelligible meaning annexed to it. Nature, in this acceptation, is a vain chimera, introduced by those heathens who had not just notions of the omnipresence and infinite perfection of God. But it is more unaccountable that it should be received among Christians, professing belief in the Holy Scriptures, which constantly ascribe those effects to the immediate hand of God that heathen philosophers are wont to impute to Nature. 'The Lord, He causeth the vapours to ascend; He maketh lightnings with rain; He bringeth forth the wind out of His treasures.' Jerem. x. 13. 'He turneth the shadow of death into the morning, and maketh the day dark with night.' Amos. v. 8. 'He visiteth the earth, and maketh it soft with showers: He blesseth the springing thereof, and crowneth the year with His goodness; so that the pastures are clothed with flocks, and the valleys are covered over with corn.' See Psal. lxv. But, notwithstanding that this is the constant language of Scripture, yet we have I know not what aversion from believing that God concerns Himself so nearly in our affairs. Fain would we suppose Him at a great distance off, and substitute some blind, unthinking deputy in His stead; though (if we may believe Saint Paul) 'He be not far from every one of us.'

151. It will, I doubt not, be objected that the slow, gradual, and roundabout methods observed in

the production of natural things do not seem to have for their cause the *immediate* hand of an Almighty Agent: besides, monsters, untimely births, fruits blasted in the blossom, rains falling in desert places, miseries incident to human life, and the like, are so many arguments that the whole frame of nature is not immediately actuated and superintended by a Spirit of infinite wisdom and goodness. But the answer to this objection is in a good measure plain from sect. 62; it being visible that the aforesaid methods of nature are absolutely necessary in order to working by the most simple and general rules, and after a steady and consistent manner; which argues both the wisdom and goodness of God. [For, it doth hence follow that the finger of God is not so conspicuous to the resolved and careless sinner; which gives him an opportunity to harden in his impiety and grow ripe for vengeance. (Vid. sect. 57.)] Such is the artificial contrivance of this mighty machine of Nature that, whilst its motions and various phenomena strike on our senses, the Hand which actuates the whole is itself unperceivable to men of flesh and blood. 'Verily' (saith the prophet) 'thou art a God that hidest thyself.' Isaiah xlv. 15. But, though the Lord conceal Himself from the eyes of the sensual and lazy, who will not be at the least expense of thought, yet to an unbiassed and attentive mind, nothing can be more plainly legible than the intimate presence of an All-wise Spirit, who fashions, regulates, and sustains the whole system of Being. It is clear, from what we have elsewhere observed, that the operating according to general and stated laws is so necessary for our guidance in the affairs of life, and letting us into the secret of nature, that without it all reach and compass of thought, all human sagacity and design, could serve to no manner of purpose. It were even impossible there should be any such faculties or powers in the mind. See sect. 31. Which one consideration abundantly outbalances whatever particular inconveniences may thence arise.

152. We should further consider, that the very blemishes and defects of nature are not without their use, in that they make an agreeable sort of variety, and augment the beauty of the rest of the creation, as shades in a picture serve to set off the brighter and more enlightened parts. We would likewise do well to examine, whether our taxing the waste of seeds and embryos, and accidental destruction of plants and animals before they come to full maturity, as an

imprudence in the Author of nature, be not the effect of prejudice contracted by our familiarity with impotent and saving mortals. In *man* indeed a thrifty management of those things which he cannot procure without much pains and industry may be esteemed wisdom. But we must not imagine that the inexplicably fine machine of an animal or vegetable costs the great Creator any more pains or trouble in its production than a pebble does; nothing being more evident than that an Omnipotent Spirit can indifferently produce everything by a mere *fiat* or act of his will. Hence it is plain that the splendid profusion of natural things should not be interpreted weakness or prodigality in the Agent who produces them, but rather be looked on as an argument of the riches of His power.

153. As for the mixture of pain or uneasiness which is in the world, pursuant to the general laws of Nature, and the actions of finite, imperfect Spirits, this, in the state we are in at present, is indispensably necessary to our well-being. But our prospects are too narrow. We take, for instance, the idea of some one particular pain into our thoughts, and account it *evil*. Whereas, if we enlarge our view, so as to comprehend the various ends, connexions, and dependencies of things, on what occasions and in what proportions we are affected with pain and pleasure, the nature of human freedom, and the design with which we are put into the world; we shall be forced to acknowledge that those particular things which, considered in themselves, appear to be evil, have the nature of good, when considered as linked with the whole system of beings.

154. From what hath been said, it will be manifest to any considering person, that it is merely for want of attention and comprehensiveness of mind that there are any favourers of Atheism or the Manichean Heresy to be found. Little and unreflecting souls may indeed burlesque the works of Providence; the beauty and order whereof they have not capacity, or will not be at the pains, to comprehend. But those who are masters of any justness and extent of thought, and are withal used to reflect, can never sufficiently admire the divine traces of Wisdom and Goodness that shine throughout the economy of Nature. But what truth is there which glares so strongly on the mind that, by an aversion of thought, a wilful shutting of the eyes, we may not escape seeing it? Is it therefore to be wondered at, if the generality of men, who are ever intent on business or pleasure, and little used to fix or open the eye of their mind, should not have all that conviction and evidence of the Being of God which might be expected in reasonable creatures?

155. We should rather wonder that men can be found so stupid as to neglect, than that neglecting they should be unconvinced of such an evident and momentous truth. And yet it is to be feared that too many of parts and leisure, who live in Christian countries, are, merely through a supine and dreadful negligence, sunk into a sort of Atheism. [They cannot say there is not a God, but neither are they convinced that there is. For what else can it be but some lurking infidelity, some secret misgivings of mind with regard to the existence and attributes of God, which permits sinners to grow and harden in impiety?] Since it is downright impossible that a soul pierced and enlightened with a thorough sense of the omnipresence, holiness, and justice of that Almighty Spirit, should persist in a remorseless violation of His laws. We ought, therefore, earnestly to meditate and dwell on those important points; that so we may attain conviction without all scruple 'that the eyes of the Lord are in every place, beholding the evil and the good; that He is with us and keepeth us in all places whither we go, and giveth us bread to eat and raiment to put on;' that He is present and conscious to our innermost thoughts; and, that we have a most absolute and immediate dependence on Him. A clear view of which great truths cannot choose but fill our hearts with an awful circumspection and holy fear, which is the strongest incentive to Virtue, and the best guard against Vice.

156. For, after all, what deserves the first place in our studies is, the consideration of GOD and our DUTY; which to promote, as it was the main drift and design of my labours, so shall I esteem them altogether useless and ineffectual if, by what I have said, I cannot inspire my readers with a pious sense of the Presence of God; and, having shewn the falseness or vanity of those barren speculations which make the chief employment of learned men, the better dispose them to reverence and embrace the salutary truths of the Gospel; which to know and to practise is the highest perfection of human nature.

NOTES

[1]The reference is to Locke.

STUDY QUESTIONS: BERKELEY, A TREATISE CONCERNING THE PRINCIPLES OF HUMAN KNOWLEDGE

1. What are Berkeley's main qualms with Locke's philosophy, and how does he try to overcome them?
2. What is Berkeley's critique of the notion of abstract ideas? How does this critique pertain to Berkeley's main aims?
3. What is the contradiction in supposing that houses and mountains exist independently of being perceived?
4. For an idea to exist in an unperceiving thing is a contradiction, says Berkeley. What reason does he have for making that claim? Why is it important?
5. How does Berkeley respond to the distinction between primary and secondary qualities?
6. What are Berkeley's objections to the claim that matter is a substratum that supports extension?
7. If there were external bodies, then it would be impossible to know it, says Berkeley. How does he justify that claim?
8. In section 24, Berkeley says, 'Those words mark out either a direct contradiction, or else nothing at all.' What are the words in question? How does he support both parts of his claim?
9. How does Berkeley define 'matter'?
10. How does Berkeley define 'spirit'? Why is a mind or spirit distinct from an idea?

11. In what way is the idea of matter *contradictory?* In what way is it *meaningless?*
12. How does Berkeley distinguish between real things and imaginary things?
13. How does Berkeley respond to the objection that his theory means that we eat ideas and are clothed with ideas?
14. Must we suppose that the whole world is mistaken? How does Berkeley respond to this question?
15. How does Berkeley argue for the existence of God? What function does the notion of God play in his overall theory?
16. According to Berkeley, what is the problem with employing the concept of matter to explain natural phenomena (72)?
17. What is Berkeley's objection to the notion of gravitational attraction?
18. What are Berkeley's objections to the notions of absolute space and time?
19. How does Berkeley argue that his theory overcomes the paradoxes concerned with the infinite divisibility of finite extension?
20. How do Berkeley's views on abstract ideas relate to his criticisms of the concept of infinitesimals?

Philosophical Bridges: Berkeley's Influence

When it was first published, Berkeley's work was generally dismissed. As mentioned earlier, Dr. Johnson exemplifies the dismissive attitude when he kicked a stone and commented to James Boswell that he thereby refuted Berkeley. One of the thinkers who Berkeley first had an impact on, apart from Hume, was Arthur Schopenhauer (1788–1860), who agreed with Berkeley's thesis that we can perceive only our own ideas. Schopenhauer uses this claim as a premise in his argument that the noumenal reality behind sense appearances must consist in the one transcendent Will. Schopenhauer opens his work *The World as Will and Idea* as follows: 'The world is my idea.'

Berkeley's ideas began to have a wider impact during the second half of the nineteenth century; this was due to two factors. First, in 1871, a new edition of Berkeley's works was published in Britain by A. C. Fraser, which attracted more attention to his writings. That same year, John Stuart Mill published a paper on Berkeley, attributing to him an important philosophical breakthrough. Mill found Berkeley's explanation of the perception of visual depth compelling. Likewise, he was convinced by Berkeley's explanation of why objects appear to be outside the perceiver when they are really only ideas in the mind. Indeed, Mill's claim that objects are the permanent possibility of sensation can be regarded as a way to elaborate Berkeley's views but without appealing to God. Through Mill, Berkeley became recognized as an important thinker within the Empiricist tradition. Second, when Hegelian idealism became increasingly popular in many British and American universities, some philosophers, such as James Ferrier (1854), drew on the arguments of Berkeley to support this idealism as against materialism. For example, in the United States, around 1882, Royce agreed with Mill that Berkeley had proved that we can perceive only our own ideas, and used this epistemological point to advance a neo-Hegelian idealism.

More recently, the British philosopher Howard Robinson has attempted to defend many elements of Berkeley's immaterialism with arguments from analytic philosophy. See, for example, *Matter and Sense: A Critique of Contemporary Materialism* (1982).

DAVID HUME (1711–1776)

Biographical History

As a student at Edinburgh University, David Hume had 'an insurmountable aversion to everything but the pursuits of philosophy and general learning.' In 1734, he went to France for three years, where he completed the *Treatise on Human Nature*, published in 1739–1740. In 1745, he was denied the chair of philosophy at Edinburgh because of his unorthodox religious views. He became secretary to Lieutenant-General St. Clair, joining him on missions to Ireland, Vienna, and Turin. In 1748, he published *An Enquiry Concerning Human Understanding* and, in 1751, the *Enquiry Concerning the Principles of Morals*. Despite these publications, in 1752, he was rejected for a professorship at Glasgow University. Between 1754 and 1762, Hume wrote the popular six-volume *History of England*. In 1750, he became keeper of the law library in Edinburgh. In 1763, he returned to France for three years. Amongst his many friends in France were the Enlightenment thinkers Diderot, d'Alembert, and Rousseau and, in Scotland, the economist Adam Smith. Hume served as undersecretary of state for Scotland from 1767 to 1769. He spent the last years of his life in Edinburgh, working on the *Dialogues Concerning Natural Religion*.

Philosophical Overview

There are two general aspects to Hume's philosophy.

1. First, he is an epistemological Skeptic. Hume accepts the Empiricist principles inherent in Locke and Berkeley, and follows them to their logical conclusion: Skepticism, especially with regard to the notions of cause, objects, and self.
2. Second, he provides a study of human nature by showing how certain beliefs arise naturally through the nonrational or feeling side of our nature. Hume replaces rational justification with a naturalistic explanation. In this way, he aims to defeat rationalism with naturalism.

Typically, he gives a naturalistic and nonrationalistic account of the origins of certain beliefs after he has argued philosophically that these beliefs cannot be justified by appeal either to reason or to sense experience.

Ideas and Impressions

Hume divides perceptions into two kinds: impressions and ideas. All sensations, passions, and emotions are impressions; but to think of something is to form an idea of it. Ideas are faint copies of vivid impressions. All complex perceptions are made up of simple ones, and all simple ideas are derived from simple impressions. Therefore, all perceptions result from, or are, simple impressions.

This result is the basis for Hume's Skepticism. In the *Enquiry*, he says, 'When we entertain any suspicion that a philosophical term is employed without any meaning, we need to inquire from what impression is that supposed idea derived?' All meaningful words must stand for ideas.

In section III of the *Enquiry*, Hume claims that ideas and impressions do not occur haphazardly. They are bound together and united by association, which he compares to the force of gravity. Association works through three types of relations between our perceptions: resemblance, contiguity in time and place, and cause and effect. Because of these three relations, the mind passes naturally from one idea to another. Association connects our ideas and explains how all our beliefs and ideas are formed.

Judgments of Facts and Ideas

In section IV of the *Enquiry*, Hume divides all judgments into two exclusive and exhaustive groups: relations of ideas and matters of fact. The first includes 'every affirmation which is either intuitively or demonstratively certain,' such as 'A father is a male.' Such truths are discoverable by reason alone because they inform us exclusively about the logical relations between our ideas, and not at all concerning what actually exists. To deny such a truth is a contradiction. In contrast, judgments of matters of fact are not demonstratively certain because their denial is not a contradiction and their truth depends on what exists in the universe. This distinction became known as 'Hume's fork.' It denies the Rationalist assumption that reasoning is sufficient for knowledge of the world because reasoning alone cannot yield knowledge of matters of fact. This point is an important tool in the development of his philosophy.

The Causal Relation

Hume attacks the Rationalist conception of causation by applying this fork in three ways.

1. *To the scope of the causal relation:* Hume argues that the claim 'All events have a cause' cannot be justified. It cannot be justified empirically by observation because no one can observe all events. Neither can it be justified by reason, because it is not an analytic truth. 'All events have a cause' should not be confused with 'All effects have a cause.' The latter is a priori because it is analytic. The former is not. The ideas of an event and a cause are distinct, and, thus, we can conceive of an event that has no cause. Consequently, the idea of an uncaused event is not a logical contradiction, and Hume concludes that the Rationalist Principle of Sufficient Reason cannot be justified.

2. *To the nature of the causal relation:* Rationalists assume that causation requires the idea of a necessary connection between events. Hume thinks that the idea of such a necessary connection is without justification because we have no idea of such a connection. Empirically, there is no sense impression of such a necessary connection. We only ever perceive events following one after the other; we do not perceive any connection between them. Therefore, the idea cannot be justified by appeal to sense impressions. The idea cannot be justified by reason either. Any two events are logically separate. If one event, A, causes another event B, the two events are logically distinct, and there is no logical necessity that B should follow A. For example, it is not logically necessary that a stone thrown into the air should fall to the ground.

3. *To induction:* We acquire beliefs about the unobserved future, apparently, by reasoning inductively using the causal relation. We see that in the past, A has always been followed by B, and conclude that the next A will also be followed by B. Hume argues skeptically that inductive reasoning can never be justified. First, it cannot be justified deductively. Just because the sun has risen every day up to now does not imply logically that it will rise tomorrow. Second, inductive reasoning cannot be justified empirically. It presupposes that nature will continue in the same way in the future. A causal inference from past observations to the future implies that the course of nature will continue uniformly, as it has done in the past. However, this uniformity assumption itself cannot be justified empirically by induction. We cannot assert that, because nature has been consistently uniform in the past, it will continue to be uniform in the future. This would merely beg the question. Furthermore, the assumption that nature is uniform is not an analytic truth, and so it cannot be justified deductively.

Hume's general aim is to replace Rationalist justifications with naturalistic explanations. In this vein, Hume explains the idea of cause in terms of feelings of expectation that arise from custom and habit. In section V of the *Enquiry*, he says; 'All inferences from experience are effects of custom, not reasoning.' Because we are accustomed to certain conjunctions, we come to expect events to follow in a certain order. This expectation is spontaneous and natural, but it cannot be justified. Furthermore, the idea of causal necessity is derived from the feeling of inevitability that arises naturally when the mind is placed in certain conditions. The mind spreads or projects this feeling of necessity onto the events in the external world. In reality, what we call cause is simply an observed constant conjunction between events.

Material Bodies and Identity

In the *Treatise*, Hume tries to explain the origin of our belief in the continued and distinct existence of external objects or bodies.

According to Hume, we are aware only of our own perceptions. Thus, Hume seeks to explain the natural and common belief that our impressions themselves have a distinct and continued existence. He argues that these beliefs are not due to the senses or to reason, but rather to the imagination. First, the senses cannot be the source of our belief that objects continue to exist when unperceived. Nor can they be the origin of our belief in the distinct existence of bodies: the senses present us with impressions only, and not with the idea that these impressions are distinct from ourselves. Second, Hume argues that the popular belief in external objects cannot be justified by appeal to reason either. Inferences about such objects from our impressions require that there be an observed constant conjunction between our impressions and the objects, and such a conjunction could never be observed, because we can only perceive impressions.

The common belief in continuing and distinct existence has its origin in the imagination. The ordinary person attributes distinct and continuous existence to certain impressions, which are subsequently referred to as objects, when they exhibit constancy and coherence, which are features of series of impressions. A series of impressions has constancy when the impressions present themselves in the same order, which does not change when interrupted. For example, when I look at a scene of mountains, and then turn away, they have not changed when I look back again. In this way, an invariable and uninterrupted series of momentary impressions is taken to be an identical object because of the natural dispositions of the imagination. We suppose that the series of impressions continues in the same way, but unobserved, during the gaps when we were looking away.

Personal Identity

In Book 1, Section V, Part IV of the *Treatise*, Hume extends his Skepticism to the idea of a mental substance in which perceptions inhere. First, he points out that there is no impression from which such an idea can be derived. If the idea of a continuing self is derived directly from sense experience, there must be an impression of such a self. Hume notes that we are only directly aware of particular impressions, and that there is no impression of a self. All that we can find in introspection is a bundle of different perceptions in perpetual flux. Second, Hume argues that we cannot acquire knowledge of mental substance, nor indeed of any substance, from a priori reasoning. A priori reasoning can only inform us of the relations between our ideas; it cannot inform us of matters of fact.

Hume concludes that the idea of a mental substance cannot be justified by appealing either to the senses or to reason. Instead, we should explain the psychological origins of the ideas of the self and personal identity in terms of the workings of the imagination. Hume tries to explain how we regard a series of perceptions as constituting a single mind. The imagination regards a series of momentary and distinct impressions as a unitary, continuous self because of the resemblance between different perceptions, as well as because of causation. For example, when a series of perceptions seems to form a single causal chain, the imagination glides along the series, ignoring the differences between the perceptions, until it eventually regards the series as a single self extended through time. However, there really are no necessary connections between these distinct perceptions. The idea of personal identity is a natural and inevitable fiction of the imagination.

AN ENQUIRY CONCERNING HUMAN UNDERSTANDING

The *Enquiry* was published in 1748. Hume wrote in part to explain in a more accessible way some of the ideas that he expressed in the first part of the *Treatise on Human Nature,* which was published in 1739. In studying the *Enquiry,* it is important to see how the conclusions that he reaches later in the work depend on the principles that he tries to establish at the outset, which include the propositions that all ideas must be derived from impressions and that all judgments must concern either relations of ideas or matters of fact. His skeptical conclusions about causation and induction can be derived in part from those initial premises, and his views on liberty and necessity follow from those conclusions.

SECTION I

Of the Different Species of Philosophy

1 Moral philosophy, or the science of human nature, may be treated after two different manners; each of which has its peculiar merit, and may contribute to the entertainment, instruction, and reformation of mankind. The one considers man chiefly as born for action; and as influenced in his measures by taste and sentiment; pursuing one object, and avoiding another, according to the value which these objects seem to possess, and according to the light in which they present themselves. As virtue, of all objects, is allowed to be the most valuable, this species of philosophers paint her in the most amiable colours; borrowing all helps from poetry and eloquence, and treating their subject in an easy and obvious manner, and such as is best fitted to please the imagination, and engage the affections. They select the most striking observations and instances from common life; place opposite characters in a proper contrast; and alluring us into the paths of virtue by the views of glory and happiness, direct our steps in these paths by the soundest precepts and most illustrious examples. They make us *feel* the difference between vice and virtue; they excite and regulate our sentiments; and so they can but bend our hearts to the love of probity and true honour, they think, that they have fully attained the end of all their labours.

2 The other species of philosophers consider man in the light of a reasonable rather than an active being, and endeavour to form his understanding more than cultivate his manners. They regard human nature as a subject of speculation; and with a narrow scrutiny examine it, in order to find those principles, which regulate our understanding, excite our sentiments, and make us approve or blame any particular object, action, or behaviour. They think it a reproach to all literature, that philosophy should not yet have fixed, beyond controversy, the foundation of morals, reasoning, and criticism; and should for ever talk of truth and falsehood, vice and virtue,

beauty and deformity, without being able to determine the source of these distinctions. While they attempt this arduous task, they are deterred by no difficulties; but proceeding from particular instances to general principles, they still push on their enquiries to principles more general, and rest not satisfied till they arrive at those original principles, by which, in every science, all human curiosity must be bounded. Though their speculations seem abstract, and even unintelligible to common readers, they aim at the approbation of the learned and the wise; and think themselves sufficiently compensated for the labour of their whole lives, if they can discover some hidden truths, which may contribute to the instruction of posterity.

3   It is certain that the easy and obvious philosophy will always, with the generality of mankind, have the preference above the accurate and abstruse; and by many will be recommended, not only as more agreeable, but more useful than the other. It enters more into common life; moulds the heart and affections; and, by touching those principles which actuate men, reforms their conduct, and brings them nearer to that model of perfection which it describes. On the contrary, the abstruse philosophy, being founded on a turn of mind, which cannot enter into business and action, vanishes when the philosopher leaves the shade, and comes into open day; nor can its principles easily retain any influence over our conduct and behaviour. The feelings of our heart, the agitation of our passions, the vehemence of our affections, dissipate all its conclusions, and reduce the profound philosopher to a mere plebeian.

4   Man is a reasonable being; and as such, receives from science his proper food and nourishment: But so narrow are the bounds of human understanding, that little satisfaction can be hoped for in this particular, either from the extent or security of his acquisitions. Man is a sociable, no less than a reasonable being: But neither can he always enjoy company agreeable and amusing, or preserve the proper relish for them. Man is also an active being; and from that disposition, as well as from the various necessities of human life, must submit to business and occu-

pation: But the mind requires some relaxation, and cannot always support its bent to care and industry. It seems, then, that nature has pointed out a mixed kind of life as most suitable to human race, and secretly admonished them to allow none of these biasses to *draw* too much, so as to incapacitate them for other occupations and entertainments. Indulge your passion for science, says she, but let your science be human, and such as may have a direct reference to action and society. Abstruse thought and profound researches I prohibit, and will severely punish, by the pensive melancholy which they introduce, by the endless uncertainty in which they involve you, and by the cold reception which your pretended discoveries shall meet with, when communicated. Be a philosopher; but, amidst all your philosophy, be still a man.

8 Besides this advantage of rejecting, after deliberate enquiry, the most uncertain and disagreeable part of learning, there are many positive advantages, which result from an accurate scrutiny into the powers and faculties of human nature. It is remarkable concerning the operations of the mind, that, though most intimately present to us, yet, whenever they become the object of reflexion, they seem involved in obscurity; nor can the eye readily find those lines and boundaries, which discriminate and distinguish them. The objects are too fine to remain long in the same aspect or situation; and must be apprehended in an instant, by a superior penetration, derived from nature, and improved by habit and reflexion. It becomes, therefore, no inconsiderable part of science barely to know the different operations of the mind, to separate them from each other, to class them under their proper heads, and to correct all that seeming disorder, in which they lie involved, when made the object of reflexion and enquiry. This task of ordering and distinguishing, which has no merit, when performed with regard to external bodies, the objects of our senses, rises in its value, when directed towards the operations of the mind, in proportion to the difficulty and labour, which we meet with in performing it. And if we can go no farther than this mental geography, or delineation of the distinct parts

and powers of the mind, it is at least a satisfaction to go so far; and the more obvious this science may appear (and it is by no means obvious) the more contemptible still must the ignorance of it be esteemed, in all pretenders to learning and philosophy.

Nor can there remain any suspicion, that this science is uncertain and chimerical; unless we should entertain such a scepticism as is entirely subversive of all speculation, and even action. It cannot be doubted, that the mind is endowed with several powers and faculties, that these powers are distinct from each other, that what is really distinct to the immediate perception may be distinguished by reflexion; and consequently, that there is a truth and falsehood in all propositions on this subject, and a truth and falsehood, which lie not beyond the compass of human understanding. There are many obvious distinctions of this kind, such as those between the will and understanding, the imagination and passions, which fall within the comprehension of every human creature; and the finer and more philosophical distinctions are no less real and certain, though more difficult to be comprehended. Some instances, especially late ones, of success in these enquiries, may give us a juster notion of the certainty and solidity of this branch of learning. And shall we esteem it worthy the labour of a philosopher to give us a true system of the planets, and adjust the position and order of those remote bodies; while we affect to overlook those, who, with so much success, delineate the parts of the mind, in which we are so intimately concerned?

10 What though these reasonings concerning human nature seem abstract, and of difficult comprehension? This affords no presumption of their falsehood. On the contrary, it seems impossible, that what has hitherto escaped so many wise and profound philosophers can be very obvious and easy. And whatever pains these researches may cost us, we may think ourselves sufficiently rewarded, not only in point of profit but of pleasure, if, by that means, we can make any addition to our stock of knowledge, in subjects of such unspeakable importance.

But as, after all, the abstractedness of these speculations is no recommendation, but rather a disadvantage to them, and as this difficulty may perhaps be surmounted by care and art, and the avoiding of all unnecessary detail, we have, in the following enquiry, attempted to throw some light upon subjects, from which uncertainty has hitherto deterred the wise, and obscurity the ignorant. Happy, if we can unite the boundaries of the different species of philosophy, by reconciling profound enquiry with clearness, and truth with novelty! And still more happy, if, reasoning in this easy manner, we can undermine the foundations of an abstruse philosophy, which seems to have hitherto served only as a shelter to superstition, and a cover to absurdity and error!

SECTION II

Of the Origin of Ideas

11 Every one will readily allow, that there is a considerable difference between the perceptions of the mind, when a man feels the pain of excessive heat, or the pleasure of moderate warmth, and when he afterwards recalls to his memory this sensation, or anticipates it by his imagination. These faculties may mimic or copy the perceptions of the senses; but they never can entirely reach the force and vivacity of the original sentiment. The utmost we say of them, even when they operate with greatest vigour, is, that they represent their object in so lively a manner, that we could *almost* say we feel or see it: But, except the mind be disordered by disease or madness, they never can arrive at such a pitch of vivacity, as to render these perceptions altogether undistinguishable. All the colours of poetry, however splendid, can never paint natural objects in such a manner as to make the description be taken for a real landskip. The most lively thought is still inferior to the dullest sensation.

We may observe a like distinction to run through all the other perceptions of the mind. A man in a fit of anger, is actuated in a very different manner from one who only thinks of that emotion. If you tell me, that any person is in love, I easily understand your meaning, and form a just conception of his situation; but never can mistake that conception for the real disorders and agitations of the passion. When we reflect on our past sentiments and affections, our thought is a faithful mirror, and copies its objects truly; but the colours which it employs are faint and dull, in comparison of those in which our original perceptions were clothed. It requires no nice discernment or metaphysical head to mark the distinction between them.

12   Here therefore we may divide all the perceptions of the mind into two classes or species, which are distinguished by their different degrees of force and vivacity. The less forcible and lively are commonly denominated *Thoughts* or *Ideas*. The other species want a name in our language, and in most others; I suppose, because it was not requisite for any, but philosophical purposes, to rank them under a general term or appellation. Let us, therefore, use a little freedom, and call them *Impressions;* employing that word in a sense somewhat different from the usual. By the term *impression,* then, I mean all our more lively perceptions, when we hear, or see, or feel, or love, or hate, or desire, or will. And impressions are distinguished from ideas, which are the less lively perceptions, of which we are conscious, when we reflect on any of those sensations or movements above mentioned.

13   Nothing, at first view, may seem more unbounded than the thought of man, which not only escapes all human power and authority, but is not even restrained within the limits of nature and reality. To form monsters, and join incongruous shapes and appearances, costs the imagination no more trouble than to conceive the most natural and familiar objects. And while the body is confined to one planet, along which it creeps with pain and difficulty; the thought can in an instant transport us into the most distant regions of the universe; or even beyond the universe, into the unbounded chaos, where nature is supposed to lie in total confusion. What never was seen, or heard of, may yet be conceived; nor is any thing beyond the power of thought, except what implies an absolute contradiction.

But though our thought seems to possess this unbounded liberty, we shall find, upon a nearer examination, that it is really confined within very narrow limits, and that all this creative power of the mind amounts to no more than the faculty of compounding, transposing, augmenting, or diminishing the materials afforded us by the senses and experience. When we think of a golden mountain, we only join two consistent ideas, *gold,* and *mountain,* with which we were formerly acquainted. A virtuous horse we can conceive; because, from our own feeling, we can conceive virtue; and this we may unite to the figure and shape of a horse, which is an animal familiar to us. In short, all the materials of thinking are derived either from our outward or inward sentiment: the mixture and composition of these belongs alone to the mind and will. Or, to express myself in philosophical language, all our ideas or more feeble perceptions are copies of our impressions or more lively ones.

14   To prove this, the two following arguments will, I hope, be sufficient. First, when we analyze our thoughts or ideas, however compounded or sublime, we always find that they resolve themselves into such simple ideas as were copied from a precedent feeling or sentiment. Even those ideas, which, at first view, seem the most wide of this origin, are found, upon a nearer scrutiny, to be derived from it. The idea of God, as meaning an infinitely intelligent, wise, and good Being, arises from reflecting on the operations of our own mind, and augmenting, without limit, those qualities of goodness and wisdom. We may prosecute this enquiry to what length we please; where we shall always find, that every idea which we examine is copied from a similar impression. Those who would assert that this position is not universally true nor without exception, have only one, and that an easy method of refuting it; by producing that idea, which, in their opinion, is not derived from this source. It will then be incumbent on us, if we would maintain our doctrine, to produce the impression, or lively perception, which corresponds to it.

15   Secondly. If it happen, from a defect of the organ, that a man is not susceptible of any species of sensation, we always find that he is as little susceptible of the correspondent ideas. A blind man can form no notion of colours; a deaf man of sounds. Restore either of them that sense in which he is deficient; by opening this new inlet for his sensations, you also open an inlet for the ideas; and he finds no difficulty in conceiving these objects. The case is the same, if the object, proper for exciting any sensation, has never been applied to the organ. A Laplander or Negro has no notion of the relish of wine. And though there are few or no instances of a like deficiency in the mind, where a person has never felt or is wholly incapable of a sentiment or passion that belongs to his species; yet we find the same observation to take place in a less degree. A man of mild manners can form no idea of inveterate revenge or cruelty; nor can a selfish heart easily conceive the heights of friendship and generosity. It is readily allowed, that other beings may possess many senses of which we can have no conception; because the ideas of them have never been introduced to us in the only manner by which an idea can have access to the mind, to wit, by the actual feeling and sensation.

16   There is, however, one contradictory phenomenon, which may prove that it is not absolutely impossible for ideas to arise, independent of their correspondent impressions. I believe it will readily be allowed, that the several distinct ideas of colour, which enter by the eye, or those of sound, which are conveyed by the ear, are really different from each other; though, at the same time, resembling. Now if this be true of different colours, it must be no less so of the different shades of the same colour; and each shade produces a distinct idea, independent of the rest. For if this should be denied, it is possible, by the continual gradation of shades, to run a colour insensibly into what is most remote from it; and if you will not allow any of the means to be different, you cannot, without absurdity, deny the extremes to be the same. Suppose, therefore, a person to have enjoyed his sight for thirty years, and to have become perfectly acquainted with colours of all kinds except one particular shade of blue, for instance, which it never has been his fortune to meet with. Let all the different shades of that colour, except that single one, be placed before him, descending gradually from the deepest to the lightest; it is plain that he will perceive a blank, where that shade is wanting, and will be sensible that there is a greater distance in that place between the contiguous colours than in any other. Now I ask, whether it be possible for him, from his own imagination, to supply this deficiency, and raise up to himself the idea of that particular shade, though it had never been conveyed to him by his senses? I believe there are few but will be of opinion that he can: and this may serve as a proof that the simple ideas are not always, in every instance, derived from the correspondent impressions; though this instance is so singular, that it is scarcely worth our observing, and does not merit that for it alone we should alter our general maxim.

17   Here, therefore, is a proposition, which not only seems, in itself, simple and intelligible; but, if a proper use were made of it, might render every dispute equally intelligible, and banish all that jargon, which has so long taken possession of metaphysical reasonings, and drawn disgrace upon them. All ideas, especially abstract ones, are naturally faint and obscure: the mind has but a slender hold of them: they are apt to be confounded with other resembling ideas; and when we have often employed any term, though without a distinct meaning, we are apt to imagine it has a determinate idea annexed to it. On the contrary, all impressions, that is, all sensations, either outward or inward, are strong and vivid: the limits between them are more exactly determined: nor is it easy to fall into any error or mistake with regard to them. When we entertain, therefore, any suspicion that a philosophical term is employed without any meaning or idea (as is but too frequent), we need but enquire, *from what impression is that supposed idea derived?* And if it be impossible to assign any, this will serve to confirm our suspicion. By bringing ideas into so clear a light we may reasonably hope to

remove all dispute, which may arise, concerning their nature and reality.

SECTION III

Of the Association of Ideas

18 It is evident that there is a principle of connexion between the different thoughts or ideas of the mind, and that, in their appearance to the memory or imagination, they introduce each other with a certain degree of method and regularity. In our more serious thinking or discourse this is so observable, that any particular thought, which breaks in upon the regular tract or chain of ideas, is immediately remarked and rejected. And even in our wildest and most wandering reveries, nay in our very dreams, we shall find, if we reflect, that the imagination ran not altogether at adventures, but that there was still a connexion upheld among the different ideas, which succeeded each other. Were the loosest and freest conversation to be transcribed, there would immediately be observed something which connected it in all its transitions. Or where this is wanting, the person who broke the thread of discourse might still inform you, that there had secretly revolved in his mind a succession of thought, which had gradually led him from the subject of conversation. Among different languages, even where we cannot suspect the least connexion or communication, it is found, that the words, expressive of ideas, the most compounded, do yet nearly correspond to each other: a certain proof that the simple ideas, comprehended in the compound ones, were bound together by some universal principle, which had an equal influence on all mankind.

19 Thought it be too obvious to escape observation, that different ideas are connected together; I do not find that any philosopher has attempted to enumerate or class all the principles of association; a subject, however, that seems worthy of curiosity. To me, there appear to be only three principles of connexion among ideas, namely, *Resemblance, Contiguity* in time or place, and *Cause* or *Effect*.

That these principles serve to connect ideas will not, I believe, be much doubted. A picture naturally leads our thoughts to the original: the mention of one apartment in a building naturally introduces an enquiry or discourse concerning the other: and if we think of a wound, we can scarcely forbear reflecting on the pain which follows it. But that this enumeration is complete, and that there are no other principles of association except these, may be difficult to prove to the satisfaction of the reader, or even to a man's own satisfaction. All we can do, in such cases, is to run over several instances, and examine carefully the principle which binds the different thoughts to each other, never stopping till we render the principle as general as possible. The more instances we examine, and the more care we employ, the more assurance shall we acquire, that the enumeration, which we form from the whole, is complete and entire.

SECTION IV

Sceptical Doubts Concerning the Operations of the Understanding

Part I

20 All the objects of human reason or enquiry may naturally be divided into two kinds, to wit, *Relations of Ideas,* and *Matters of Fact.* Of the first kind are the sciences of Geometry, Algebra, and Arithmetic; and in short, every affirmation which is either intuitively or demonstratively certain. *That the square of the hypothenuse is equal to the square of the two sides,* is a proposition which expresses a relation between these figures. *That three times five is equal to the half of thirty,* expresses a relation between these numbers. Propositions of this kind are discoverable by the mere operation of thought, without dependence on what is anywhere existent in the universe. Though there never were a circle or triangle in nature, the truths demonstrated by Euclid would for ever retain their certainty and evidence.

21 Matters of fact, which are the second objects of human reason, are not ascertained in the same manner; nor is our evidence of their truth, however great, of a like nature with the

foregoing. The contrary of every matter of fact is still possible; because it can never imply a contradiction, and is conceived by the mind with the same facility and distinctness, as if ever so conformable to reality. *That the sun will not rise to-morrow* is no less intelligible a proposition, and implies no more contradiction, than the affirmation, *that it will rise*. We should in vain, therefore, attempt to demonstrate its falsehood. Were it demonstratively false, it would imply a contradiction, and could never be distinctly conceived by the mind.

It may, therefore, be a subject worthy of curiosity, to enquire what is the nature of that evidence which assures us of any real existence and matter of fact, beyond the present testimony of our senses, or the records of our memory. This part of philosophy, it is observable, has been little cultivated, either by the ancients or moderns; and therefore our doubts and errors, in the prosecution of so important an enquiry, may be the more excusable; while we march through such difficult paths without any guide or direction. They may even prove useful, by exciting curiosity, and destroying that implicit faith and security, which is the bane of all reasoning and free enquiry. The discovery of defects in the common philosophy, if any such there be, will not, I presume, be a discouragement, but rather an incitement, as is usual, to attempt something more full and satisfactory than has yet been proposed to the public.

22   All reasonings concerning matter of fact seem to be founded on the relation of *Cause and Effect*. By means of that relation along we can go beyond the evidence of our memory and senses. If you were to ask a man, why he believes any matter of fact, which is absent; for instance, that his friend is in the country, or in France; he would give you a reason; and this reason would be some other fact; as a letter received from him, or the knowledge of his former resolutions and promises. A man finding a watch or any other machine in a desert island, would conclude that there had once been men in that island. All our reasonings concerning fact are of the same nature. And here it is constantly supposed that there is a connexion between the present fact

and that which is inferred from it. Were there nothing to bind them together, the inference would be entirely precarious. The hearing of an articulate voice and rational discourse in the dark assures us of the presence of some person: Why? because these are the effects of the human make and fabric, and closely connected with it. If we anatomize all the other reasonings of this nature, we shall find that they are founded on the relation of cause and effect, and that this relation is either near or remote, direct or collateral. Heat and light are collateral effects of fire, and the one effect may justly be inferred from the other.

23   If we would satisfy ourselves, therefore, concerning the nature of that evidence, which assures us of matters of fact, we must enquire how we arrive at the knowledge of cause and effect.

I shall venture to affirm, as a general proposition, which admits of no exception, that the knowledge of this relation is not, in any instance, attained by reasonings a *priori*; but arises entirely from experience, when we find that any particular objects are constantly conjoined with each other. Let an object be presented to a man of ever so strong natural reason and abilities; if that object be entirely new to him, he will not be able, by the most accurate examination of its sensible qualities, to discover any of its causes or effects. Adam, though his rational faculties be supposed, at the very first, entirely perfect, could not have inferred from the fluidity and transparency of water that it would suffocate him, or from the light and warmth of fire that it would consume him. No object ever discovers, by the qualities which appear to the senses, either the causes which produced it, or the effects which will arise from it; nor can our reason, unassisted by experience, ever draw any inference concerning real existence and matter of fact.

24   This proposition, *that causes and effects are discoverable, not by reason but by experience,* will readily be admitted with regard to such objects, as we remember to have once been altogether unknown to us; since we must be conscious of the utter inability, which we then lay under, of foretelling what would arise from them. Present two smooth pieces of marble to a man who has no tincture of natural philosophy; he will never

discover that they will adhere together in such a manner as to require great force to separate them in a direct line, while they make so small a resistance to a lateral pressure. Such events, as bear little analogy to the common course of nature, are also readily confessed to be known only by experience; nor does any man imagine that the explosion of gunpowder, or the attraction of a loadstone, could ever be discovered by arguments *a priori*. In like manner, when an effect is supposed to depend upon an intricate machinery or secret structure of parts, we make no difficulty in attributing all our knowledge of it to experience. Who will assert that he can give the ultimate reason, why milk or bread is proper nourishment for a man, not for a lion or a tiger?

But the same truth may not appear, at first sight, to have the same evidence with regard to events, which have become familiar to us from our first appearance in the world, which bear a close analogy to the whole course of nature, and which are supposed to depend on the simple qualities of objects, without any secret structure of parts. We are apt to imagine that we could discover these effects by the mere operation of our reason, without experience. We fancy, that were we brought on a sudden into this world, we could at first have inferred that one Billiard-ball would communicate motion to another upon impulse; and that we needed not to have waited for the event, in order to pronounce with certainty concerning it. Such is the influence of custom, that, where it is strongest, it not only covers our natural ignorance, but even conceals itself, and seems not to take place, merely because it is found in the highest degree.

25   But to convince us that all the laws of nature, and all the operations of bodies without exception, are known only by experience, the following reflections may, perhaps, suffice. Were any object presented to us, and were we required to pronounce concerning the effect, which will result from it, without consulting past observation; after what manner, I beseech you, must the mind proceed in this operation? It must invent or imagine some event, which it ascribes to the object as its effect; and it is plain that this invention must be entirely arbitrary. The mind can

never possibly find the effect in the supposed cause, by the most accurate scrutiny and examination. For the effect is totally different from the cause, and consequently can never be discovered in it. Motion in the second Billiard-ball is a quite distinct event from motion in the first; nor is there anything in the one to suggest the smallest hint of the other. A stone or piece of metal raised into the air, and left without any support, immediately falls: but to consider the matter *a priori*, is there anything we discover in this situation which can beget the idea of a downward, rather than an upward, or any other motion, in the stone or metal?

And as the first imagination or invention of a particular effect, in all natural operations, is arbitrary, where we consult not experience; so must we also esteem the supposed tie or connexion between the cause and effect, which binds them together, and renders it impossible that any other effect could result from the operation of that cause. When I see, for instance, a Billiard-ball moving in a straight line towards another; even suppose motion in the second ball should by accident be suggested to me, as the result of their contact or impulse; may I not conceive, that a hundred different events might as well follow from that cause? May not both these balls remain at absolute rest? May not the first ball return in a straight line, or leap off from the second in any line or direction? All these suppositions are consistent and conceivable. Why then should we give the preference to one, which is no more consistent or conceivable than the rest? All our reasonings *a priori* will never be able to show us any foundation for this preference.

In a word, then, every effect is a distinct event from its cause. It could not, therefore, be discovered in the cause, and the first invention or conception of it, *a priori*, must be entirely arbitrary. And even after it is suggested, the conjunction of it with the cause must appear equally arbitrary; since there are always many other effects, which, to reason, must seem fully as consistent and natural. In vain, therefore, should we pretend to determine any single event, or infer any cause or effect, without the assistance of observation and experience.

27   Nor is geometry, when taken into the assistance of natural philosophy, ever able to remedy this defect, or lead us into the knowledge of ultimate causes, by all that accuracy of reasoning for which it is so justly celebrated. Every part of mixed mathematics proceeds upon the supposition that certain laws are established by nature in her operations; and abstract reasonings are employed, either to assist experience in the discovery of these laws, or to determine their influence in particular instances, where it depends upon any precise degree of distance and quantity. Thus, it is a law of motion, discovered by experience, that the moment or force of any body in motion is in the compound ratio or proportion of its solid contents and its velocity; and consequently, that a small force may remove the greatest obstacle or raise the greatest weight, if, by any contrivance or machinery, we can increase the velocity of that force, so as to make it an overmatch for its antagonist. Geometry assists us in the application of this law, by giving us the just dimensions of all the parts and figures which can enter into any species of machine; but still the discovery of the law itself is owing merely to experience, and all the abstract reasonings in the world could never lead us one step towards the knowledge of it. When we reason *a priori*, and consider merely any object or cause, as it appears to the mind, independent of all observation, it never could suggest to us the notion of any distinct object, such as its effect; much less, show us the inseparable and inviolable connexion between them. A man must be very sagacious who could discover by reasoning that crystal is the effect of heat, and ice of cold, without being previously acquainted with the operation of these qualities.

Part II

28 But we have not yet attained any tolerable satisfaction with regard to the question first proposed. Each solution still gives rise to a new question as difficult as the foregoing, and leads us on to farther enquiries. When it is asked, *What is the nature of all our reasonings concerning matter of*

fact? the proper answer seems to be, that they are founded on the relation of cause and effect. When again it is asked, *What is the foundation of all our resonings and conclusions concerning that relation?* it may be replied in one word, Experience. But if we still carry on our sifting humour, and ask, *What is the foundation of all conclusions from experience?* this implies a new question, which may be of more difficult solution and explication. Philosophers, that give themselves airs of superior wisdom and sufficiency, have a hard task when they encounter persons of inquisitive dispositions, who push them from every corner to which they retreat, and who are sure at last to bring them to some dangerous dilemma. The best expedient to prevent this confusion, is to be modest in our pretensions; and even to discover the difficulty ourselves before it is objected to us. By this means, we may make a kind of merit of our very ignorance.

I shall content myself, in this section, with an easy task, and shall pretend only to give a negative answer to the question here proposed. I say then, that, even after we have experience of the operations of cause and effect, our conclusions from that experience are *not* founded on reasoning, or any process of the understanding. This answer we must endeavour both to explain and to defend.

29   It must certainly be allowed, that nature has kept us at a great distance from all her secrets, and has afforded us only the knowledge of a few superficial qualities of objects; while she conceals from us those powers and principles on which the influence of these objects entirely depends. Our senses inform us of the colour, weight, and consistence of bread; but neither sense nor reason can ever inform us of those qualities which fit it for the nourishment and support of a human body. Sight or feeling conveys an idea of the actual motion of bodies; but as to that wonderful force or power, which would carry on a moving body for ever in a continued change of place, and which bodies never lose but by communicating it to others; of this we cannot form the most distant conception. But notwithstanding this ignorance of natural powers and principles, we always pre-

sume, when we see like sensible qualities, that they have like secret powers, and expect that effects, similar to those which we have experienced, will follow from them. If a body of like colour and consistence with that bread, which we have formerly eat, be presented to us, we make no scruple of repeating the experiment, and foresee, with certainty, like nourishment and support. Now this is a process of the mind or thought, of which I would willingly know the foundation. It is allowed on all hands that there is no known connexion between the sensible qualities and the secret powers; and consequently, that the mind is not led to form such a conclusion concerning their constant and regular conjunction, by anything which it knows of their nature. As to past *Experience,* it can be allowed to give *direct* and *certain* information of those precise objects only, and that precise period of time, which fell under its cognizance: but why this experience should be extended to future times, and to other objects, which for aught we know, may be only in appearance similar; this is the main question on which I would insist. The bread, which I formerly eat, nourished me; that is, a body of such sensible qualities was, at that time, endued with such secret powers: but does it follow, that other bread must also nourish me at another time, and that like sensible qualities must always be attended with like secret powers? The consequence seems nowise necessary. At least, it must be acknowledge that there is here a consequence drawn by the mind; that there is a certain step taken; a process of thought, and an inference, which wants to be explained. These two propositions are far from being the same, *I have found that such an object has always been attended with such an effect,* and *I foresee, that other objects, which are, in appearance, similar, will be attended with similar effects.* I shall allow, if you please, that the one proposition may justly be inferred from the other: I know, in fact, that it always is inferred. But if you insist that the inference is made by a chain of reasoning, I desire you to produce that reasoning. The connexion between these propositions is not intuitive. There is required a medium, which may enable

the mind to draw such an inference, if indeed it be drawn by reasoning and argument. What that medium is, I must confess, passes my comprehension; and it is incumbent on those to produce it, who assert that it really exists, and is the origin of all our conclusions concerning matter of fact.

30   This negative argument must certainly, in process of time, become altogether convincing, if many penetrating and able philosophers shall turn their enquiries this way and no one be ever able to discover any connecting proposition or intermediate step, which supports the understanding in this conclusion. But as the question is yet new, every reader may not trust so far to his own penetration, as to conclude, because an argument escapes his enquiry, that therefore it does not really exist. For this reason it may be requisite to venture upon a more, difficult task; and enumerating all the branches of human knowledge, endeavour to show that none of them can afford such an argument.

All reasonings may be divided into two kinds, namely, demonstrative reasoning, or that concerning relations of ideas, and moral reasoning, or that concerning matter of fact and existence. That there, are no demonstrative arguments in the case seems evident; since it implies no contradiction that the course of nature may change, and that an object, seemingly like those which we have experienced, may be attended with different or contrary effects. May I not clearly and distinctly conceive that a body, falling from the clouds, and which, in all other respects, resembles snow, has yet the taste of salt or feeling of fire? Is there any more intelligible proposition than to affirm, that all the trees will flourish in December and January, and decay in May and June? Now whatever is intelligible, and can be distinctly conceived, implies no contradiction, and can never be proved false by any demonstrative argument or abstract reasoning *à priori.*

If we be, therefore, engaged by arguments to put trust in past experience, and make it the standard of our future judgment, these arguments must be probable only, or such as regard matter of fact and real existence, according to the division above mentioned. But that there is no argument of this kind, must appear, if our explication of that species of reasoning be admitted as solid and satisfactory. We have said that all arguments concerning existence are founded on the relation of cause and effect; that our knowledge of that relation is derived entirely from experience; and that all our experimental conclusions proceed upon the supposition that the future will be conformable to the past. To endeavour, therefore, the proof of this last supposition by probable arguments, or arguments regarding existence, must be evidently going in a circle, and taking that for granted, which is the very point in question.

31 In reality, all arguments from experience are founded on the similarity which we discover among natural objects, and by which we are induced to expect effects similar to those which we have found to follow from such objects. And though none but a fool or madman will ever pretend to dispute the authority of experience, or to reject that great guide of human life, it may surely be allowed a philosopher to have so much curiosity at least as to examine the principle of human nature, which gives this mighty authority to experience, and makes us draw advantage from that similarity which nature has placed among different objects. From causes which appear *similar* we expect similar effects. This is the sum of all our experimental conclusions. Now it seems evident that, if this conclusion were formed by reason, it would be as perfect at first, and upon one instance, as after ever so long a course of experience. But the case is far otherwise. Nothing so like as eggs; yet no one, on account of this appearing similarity, expects the same taste and relish in all of them. It is only after a long course of uniform experiments in any kind, that we attain a firm reliance and security with regard to a particular event. Now where is that process of reasoning which, from one instance, draws a conclusion, so different from that which it infers from a hundred instances that are nowise different from that single one? This question I propose as much for the sake of information, as with an intention of raising difficulties. I cannot find, I cannot imagine any such reasoning. But I keep my mind still open to instruction, if any one will vouchsafe to bestow it on me.

32 Should it be said that, from a number of uniform experiments, we *infer* a connexion between the sensible qualities and the secret powers; this, I must confess, seems the same difficulty, couched in different terms. The question still recurs, on what process of argument this *inference* is founded? Where is the medium, the interposing ideas, which join propositions so very wide of each other? It is confessed that the colour, consistence, and other sensible qualities of bread appear not, of themselves, to have any connexion with the secret powers of nourishment and support. For otherwise we could infer these secret powers from the first appearance of these sensible qualities, without the aid of experience; contrary to the sentiment of all philosophers, and contrary to plain matter of fact. Here, then, is our natural state of ignorance with regard to the powers and influence of all objects. How is this remedied by experience? It only shows us a number of uniform effects, resulting from certain objects, and teaches us that those particular objects, at that particular time, were endowed with such powers and forces. When a new object, endowed with similar sensible qualities, is produced, we expect similar powers and forces, and look for a like effect. From a body of like colour and consistence with bread we expect like nourishment and support. But this surely is a step or progress of the mind, which wants to be explained. When a man says, *I have found, in all past instances, such sensible qualities conjoined with such secret powers:* And when he says, *Similar sensible qualities will always be conjoined with similar secret powers,* he is not guilty of a tautology, nor are these propositions in any respect the same. You say that the one proposition is an inference from the other. But you must confess that the inference is not intuitive; neither is it demonstrative: Of what nature is it, then? To say it is experimental, is begging the question. For all inferences from experience suppose, as their foundation, that the future will resemble the past, and that similar powers will be conjoined

with similar sensible qualities. If there be any suspicion that the course of nature may change, and that the past may be no rule for the future, all experience becomes useless, and can give rise to no inference or conclusion. It is impossible, therefore, that any arguments from experience can prove this resemblance of the past to the future; since all these arguments are founded on the supposition of that resemblance. Let the course of things be allowed hitherto ever so regular; that alone, without some new argument or inference, proves not that, for the future, it will continue so. In vain do you pretend to have learned the nature of bodies from your past experience. Their secret nature, and consequently all their effects and influence, may change, without any change in their sensible qualities. This happens sometimes, and with regard to some objects: Why may it not happen always, and with regard to all objects? What logic, what process of argument secures you against this supposition? My practice, you say, refutes my doubts. But you mistake the purport of my question. As an agent, I am quite satisfied in the point; but as a philosopher, who has some share of curiosity, I will not say scepticism, I want to learn the foundation of this inference. No reading, no enquiry has yet been able to remove my difficulty, or give me satisfaction in a matter of such importance. Can I do better than propose the difficulty to the public, even though, perhaps, I have small hopes of obtaining a solution? We shall at least, by this means, be sensible of our ignorance, if we do not augment our knowledge.

33   I must confess that a man is guilty of unpardonable arrogance who concludes, because an argument has escaped his own investigation, that therefore it does not really exist. I must also confess that, though all the learned, for several ages, should have employed themselves in fruitless search upon any subject, it may still, perhaps, be rash to conclude positively that the subject must, therefore, pass all human comprehension. Even though we examine all the sources of our knowledge, and conclude them unfit for such a subject, there may still remain a suspicion, that the enumeration is not complete, or the examination

not accurate. But with regard to the present subject, there are some considerations which seem to remove all this accusation of arrogance or suspicion of mistake.

It is certain that the most ignorant and stupid peasants—nay infants, nay even brute beasts—improve by experience, and learn the qualities of natural objects, by observing the effects which result from them. When a child has felt the sensation of pain from touching the flame of a candle, he will be careful not to put his hand near any candle; but will expect a similar effect from a cause which is similar in its sensible qualities and appearance. If you assert, therefore, that the understanding of the child is led into this conclusion by any process of argument or ratiocination, I may justly require you to produce that argument; nor have you any pretence to refuse so equitable a demand. You cannot say that the argument is abstruse, and may possibly escape your enquiry; since you confess that it is obvious to the capacity of a mere infant. If you hesitate, therefore, a moment, or if, after reflection, you produce any intricate or profound argument, you, in a manner, give up the question, and confess that it is not reasoning which engages us to suppose the past resembling the future, and to expect similar effects from causes which are, to appearance, similar. This is the proposition which I intended to enforce in the present section. If I be right, I pretend not to have made any mighty discovery. And if I be wrong, I must acknowledge myself to be indeed a very backward scholar; since I cannot now discover an argument which, it seems, was perfectly familiar to me long before I was out of my cradle.

SECTION V

Sceptical Solution of These Doubts

Part I

34 The passion for philosophy, like that for religion, seems liable to this inconvenience, that, though it aims at the correction of our manners, and extirpation of our vices, it may only serve, by imprudent management, to foster a predominant inclination, and push the mind, with more

determined resolution, towards that side which already *draws* too much, by the bias and propensity of the natural temper. It is certain that, while we aspire to the magnanimous firmness of the philosophic sage, and endeavour to confine our pleasures altogether within our own minds, we may, at last, render our philosophy like that of Epictetus, and other *Stoics,* only a more refined system of selfishness, and reason ourselves out of all virtue as well as social enjoyment. While we study with attention the vanity of human life, and turn all our thoughts towards the empty and transitory nature of riches and honours, we are, perhaps, all the while flattering our natural indolence, which, hating the bustle of the world, and drudgery of business, seeks a pretence of reason to give itself a full and uncontrolled indulgence. There is, however, one species of philosophy which seems little liable to this inconvenience, and that because it strikes in with no disorderly passion of the human mind, nor can mingle itself with any natural affection or propensity; and that is the Academic or Sceptical philosophy. The academics always talk of doubt and suspense of judgement, of danger in hasty determinations, of confining to very narrow bounds the enquiries of the understanding, and of renouncing all speculations which lie not within the limits of common life and practice. Nothing, therefore, can be more contrary than such a philosophy to the supine indolence of the mind, its rash arrogance, its lofty pretensions, and its superstitious credulity. Every passion is mortified by it, except the love of truth; and that passion never is, nor can be, carried to too high a degree. It is surprising, therefore, that this philosophy, which, in almost every instance, must be harmless and innocent, should be the subject of so much groundless reproach and obloquy. But, perhaps, the very circumstance which renders it so innocent is what chiefly exposes it to the public hatred and resentment. By flattering no irregular passion, it gains few partizans: By opposing so many vices and follies, it raises to itself abundance of enemies, who stigmatize it as libertine, profane, and irreligious.

Nor need we fear that this philosophy, while it endeavours to limit our enquiries to common life, should ever undermine the reasonings of common life, and carry its doubts so far as to destroy all action, as well as speculation. Nature will always maintain her rights, and prevail in the end over any abstract reasoning whatsoever. Though we should conclude, for instance, as in the foregoing section, that, in all reasonings from experience, there is a step taken by the mind which is not supported by any argument or process of the understanding; there is no danger that these reasonings, on which almost all knowledge depends, will ever be affected by such a discovery. If the mind be not engaged by argument to make this step, it must be induced by some other principle of equal weight and authority; and that principle will preserve its influence as long as human nature remains the same. What that principle is may well be worth the pains of enquiry.

35   Suppose a person, though endowed with the strongest faculties of reason and reflection, to be brought on a sudden into this world; he would, indeed, immediately observe a continual succession of objects, and one event following another; but he would not be able to discover anything farther. He would not, at first, by any reasoning, be able to reach the idea of cause and effect; since the particular powers, by which all natural operations are performed, never appear to the senses; nor is it reasonable to conclude, merely because one event, in one instance, precedes another, that therefore the one is the cause, the other the effect. Their conjunction may be arbitrary and casual. There may be no reason to infer the existence of one from the appearance of the other. And in a word, such a person, without more experience, could never employ his conjecture or reasoning concerning any matter of fact, or be assured of anything beyond what was immediately present to his memory and senses.

Suppose, again, that he has acquired more experience, and has lived so long in the world as to have observed similar objects or events to be constantly conjoined together; what is the consequence of this experience? He immediately infers the existence of one object from the appearance of the other. Yet he has not, by all his experience, acquired any idea or knowledge of the secret power by which the one object produces the other; nor is it, by any process of reasoning, he is engaged to draw this inference. But still he finds himself determined to draw it: And though he should be convinced that his understanding has no part in the operation, he would nevertheless continue in the same course of thinking. There is some other principle which determines him to form such a conclusion.

36   This principle is Custom or Habit. For wherever the repetition of any particular act or operation produces a propensity to renew the same act or operation, without being impelled by any reasoning or process of the understanding, we always say, that this propensity is the effect of *Custom*. By employing that word, we pretend not to have given the ultimate reason of such a propensity. We only point out a principle of human nature, which is universally acknowledged, and which is well known by its effects. Perhaps we can push our enquiries no farther, or pretend to give the cause of this cause; but must rest contented with its as the ultimate principle, which we can assign, of all our conclusions from experience. It is sufficient satisfaction, that we can go so far, without repining at the narrowness of our faculties because they will carry us no farther. And it is certain we here advance a very intelligible proposition at least, if not a true one, when we assert that, after the constant conjunction of two objects—heat and flame, for instance, weight and solidity—we are determined by custom alone to expect the one from the appearance of the other. This hypothesis seems even the only one which explains the difficulty, why we draw from a thousand instances, an inference which we are not able to draw from one instance, that is, in no respect, different from them. Reason is incapable of any such variation. The conclusions which it draws from considering one circle are the same which it would form upon surveying all the circles in the universe. But no man, having seen only one body move after

being impelled by another, could infer that every other body will move after a like impulse. All inferences from experience, therefore, are effects of custom, not of reasoning.

Custom, then, is the great guide of human life. It is that principle alone which renders our experience useful to us, and makes us expect, for the future, a similar train of events with those which have appeared in the past. Without the influence of custom, we should be entirely ignorant of every matter of fact beyond what is immediately present to the memory and senses. We should never know how to adjust means to ends, or to employ our natural powers in the production of any effect. There would be an end at once of all action, as well as of the chief part of speculation.

37   But here it may be proper to remark, that though our conclusions from experience carry us beyond our memory and senses, and assure us of matters of fact which happened in the most distant places and most remote ages, yet some fact must always be present to the senses or memory, from which we may first proceed in drawing these conclusions. A man, who should find in a desert country the remains of pompous buildings, would conclude that the country had, in ancient times, been cultivated by civilized inhabitants; but did nothing of this nature occur to him, he could never form such an inference. We learn the events of former ages from history; but then we must peruse the volumes in which this instruction is contained, and thence carry up our inferences from one testimony to another, till we arrive at the eyewitnesses and spectators of these distant events. In a word, if we proceed not upon some fact, present to the memory or senses, our reasonings would be merely hypothetical; and however the particular links might be connected with each other, the whole chain of inferences would have nothing to support it, nor could we ever, by its means, arrive at the knowledge of any real existence. If I ask why you believe any particular matter of fact, which you relate, you must tell me some reason; and this reason will be some other fact, connected with it. But as you cannot

proceed after this manner, *in infinitum*, you must at last terminate in some fact, which is present to your memory or senses; or must allow that your belief is entirely without foundation.

38 What, then, is the conclusion of the whole matter? A simple one; though, it must be confessed, pretty remote from the common theories of philosophy. All belief of matter of fact or real existence is derived merely from some object, present to the memory or senses, and a customary conjunction between that and some other object. Or in other words; having found, in many instances, that any two kinds of objects—flame and heat, snow and cold—have always been conjoined together; if flame or snow be presented anew to the senses, the mind is carried by custom to expect heat or cold, and to *believe* that such a quality does exist, and will discover itself upon a nearer approach. This belief is the necessary result of placing the mind in such circumstances. It is an operation of the soul, when we are so situated, as unavoidable as to feel the passion of love, when we receive benefits; or hatred, when we meet with injuries. All these operations are a species of natural instincts, which no reasoning or process of the thought and understanding is able either to produce or to prevent.

At this point, it would be very allowable for us to stop our philosophical researches. In most questions we can never make a single step farther; and in all questions we must terminate here at last, after our most restless and curious enquiries. But still our curiosity will be pardonable, perhaps commendable, if it carry us on to still farther researches, and make us examine more accurately the nature of this *belief*, and of the *customary conjunction*, whence it is derived. By this means we may meet with some explications and analogies that will give satisfaction; at least to such as love the abstract sciences, and can be entertained with speculations, which, however accurate, may still retain a degree of doubt and uncertainty. As to readers of a different taste; the remaining part of this section is not calculated for them, and the following enquiries may well be understood, though it be neglected.

Part II

39 Nothing is more free than the imagination of man; and though it cannot exceed that original stock of ideas furnished by the internal and external senses, it has unlimited power of mixing, compounding, separating, and dividing these ideas, in all the varieties of fiction and vision. It can feign a train of events, with all the appearance of reality, ascribe to them a particular time and place, conceive them as existent, and paint them out to itself with every circumstance, that belongs to any historical fact, which it believes with the greatest certainty. Wherein, therefore, consists the difference between such a fiction and belief? It lies not merely in any peculiar idea, which is annexed to such a conception as commands our assent, and which is wanting to every known fiction. For as the mind has authority over all its ideas, it could voluntarily annex this particular idea to any fiction, and consequently be able to believe whatever it pleases; contrary to what we find by daily experience. We can, in our conception, join the head of a man to the body of a horse; but it is not in our power to believe that such an animal has ever really existed.

It follows, therefore, that the difference between *fiction* and *belief* lies in some sentiment or feeling, which is annexed to the latter, not to the former, and which depends not on the will, nor can be commanded at pleasure. It must be excited by nature, like all other sentiments; and must arise from the particular situation, in which the mind is placed at any particular juncture. Whenever any object is presented to the memory or senses, it immediately, by the force of custom, carries the imagination to conceive that object, which is usually conjoined to it; and this conception is attended with a feeling or sentiment, different from the loose reveries of the fancy. In this consists the whole nature of belief. For as there is no matter of fact which we believe so firmly that we cannot conceive the contrary, there would be no difference between the conception assented to and that which is rejected, were it not for some sentiment which distinguishes the one from the other. If I see a billiard-ball moving towards another, on a smooth table, I can easily conceive it to stop upon contact. This conception implies no contradiction; but still it feels very differently from that conception by which I represent to myself the impulse and the communication of motion from one ball to another.

40　Were we to attempt a *definition* of this sentiment, we should, perhaps, find it a very difficult, if not an impossible task; in the same manner as if we should endeavour to define the feeling of cold or passion of anger, to a creature who never had any experience of these sentiments. Belief is the true and proper name of this feeling; and no one is ever at a loss to know the meaning of that term; because every men is every moment conscious of the sentiment represented by it. It may not, however, be improper to attempt a *description* of this sentiment; in hopes we may, by that means, arrive at some analogies, which may afford a more perfect explication of it. I say, then, that belief is nothing but a more vivid, lively, forcible, firm, steady conception of an object, than what the imagination alone is ever able to attain. This variety of terms, which may seem so unphilosophical, is intended only to express that act of the mind, which renders realities, or what is taken for such, more present to us than fictions, causes them to weigh more in the thought, and gives them a superior influence on the passions and imagination. Provided we agree about the thing, it is needless to dispute about the terms. The imagination has the command over all its ideas, and can join and mix and vary them, in all the ways possible. It may conceive fictitious objects with all the circumstances of place and time. It may set them, in a manner, before our eyes, in their true colours, just as they might have existed. But as it is impossible that this faculty of imagination can ever, of itself, reach belief, it is evident that belief consists not in the peculiar nature or order of ideas, but in the *manner* of their conception, and in their *feeling* to the mind. I confess, that it is impossible perfectly to explain this feeling or manner of conception. We may make use of words which express something near it. But its true and proper name, as we observed before, is *belief*; which is a term that every one sufficiently understands in common life. And in

philosophy, we can go no farther than assert, that *belief* is something felt by the mind, which distinguishes the ideas of the judgement from the fictions of the imagination. It gives them more weight and influence; makes them appear of greater importance; enforces them in the mind; and renders them the governing principle of our actions. I hear at present, for instance, a person's voice, with whom I am acquainted; and the sound comes as from the next room. This impression of my senses immediately conveys my thought to the person, together with all the surrounding objects. I paint them out to myself as existing at present, with the same qualities and relations, of which I formerly knew them possessed. These ideas take faster hold of my mind, than ideas of an enchanted castle. They are very different to the feeling, and have a much greater influence of every kind, either to give pleasure or pain, joy or sorrow.

Let us, then, take in the whole compass of this doctrine, and allow, that the sentiment of belief is nothing but a conception more intense and steady than what attends the mere fictions of the imagination, and that this *manner* of conception arises from a customary conjunction of the object with something present to the memory or senses: I believe that it will not be difficult, upon these suppositions, to find other operations of the mind analogous to it, and to trace up these phenomena to principles still more general.

41　We have already observed that nature has established connexions among particular ideas, and that no sooner one idea occurs to our thoughts than it introduces its correlative, and carries our attention towards it, by a gentle and insensible movement. These principles of connexion or association we have reduced to three, namely, *Resemblance, Contiguity* and *Causation;* which are the only bonds that unite our thoughts together, and beget that regular train of reflection or discourse, which, in a greater or less degree, takes place among all mankind. Now here arises a question, on which the solution of the present difficulty will depend. Does it happen, in all these relations, that, when one of the objects is presented to the senses or memory, the mind is not only carried to the conception of the correlative, but reaches a steadier and stronger conception of it than what otherwise it would have been able to attain? This seems to be the case with that belief which arises from the relation of cause and effect. And if the case be the same with the other relations or principles of association, this may be established as a general law, which takes place in all the operations of the mind.

We may, therefore, observe, as the first experiment to our present purpose, that, upon the appearance of the picture of an absent friend, our idea of him is evidently enlivened by the *resemblance,* and that every passion, which that idea occasions, whether of joy or sorrow, acquires new force and vigour. In producing this effect, there concur both a relation and a present impression. Where the picture bears him no resemblance, at least was not intended for him, it never so much as conveys our thought to him: And where it is absent, as well as the person, though the mind may pass from the thought of the one to that of the other, it feels its idea to be rather weakened than enlivened by that transition. We take a pleasure in viewing the picture of a friend, when it is set before us; but when it is removed, rather choose to consider him directly than by reflection in an image, which is equally distant and obscure.

The ceremonies of the Roman Catholic religion may be considered as instances of the same nature. The devotees of that superstition usually plead in excuse for the mummeries, with which they are upbraided, that they feel the good effect of those external motions, and postures, and actions, in enlivening their devotion and quickening their fervour, which otherwise would decay, if directed entirely to distant and immaterial objects. We shadow out the objects of our faith, say they, in sensible types and images, and render them more present to us by the immediate presence of these types, than it is possible for us to do merely by an intellectual view and contemplation. Sensible objects have always a greater influence on the fancy than any other; and this influence they readily convey to those ideas to which they are related, and which they resemble.

I shall only infer from these practices, and this reasoning, that the effect of resemblance in enlivening the ideas is very common; and as in every case a resemblance and a present impression must concur, we are abundantly supplied with experiments to prove the reality of the foregoing principle.

42 We may add force to these experiments by others of a different kind, in considering the effect of *contiguity* as well as of *resemblance*. It is certain that distance diminishes the force of every idea, and that, upon our approach to any object; though it does not discover itself to our senses; it operates upon the mind with an influence, which imitates an immediate impression. The thinking on any object readily transports the mind to what is contiguous; but it is only the actual presence of an object, that transports it with a superior vivacity. When I am a few miles from home, whatever relates to it touches me more nearly than when I am two hundred leagues distant; though even at that distance the reflecting on any thing in the neighbourhood of my friends or family naturally produces an idea of them. But as in this latter case, both the objects of the mind are ideas; notwithstanding there is an easy transition between them; that transition alone is not able to give a superior vivacity to any of the ideas, for want of some immediate impression.

43 No one can doubt but causation has the same influence as the other relations of resemblance and contiguity. Superstitious people are fond of the reliques of saints and holy men, for the same reason, that they seek after types or images, in order to enliven their devotion and give them a more intimate and strong conception of those exemplary lives, which they desire to imitate. Now it is evident, that one of the best reliques, which a devotee could procure, would be the handwork of a saint; and if his cloaths and furniture are ever to be considered in this light, it is because they were once at his disposal, and were moved and affected by him; in which respect they are to be considered as imperfect effects, and as connected with him by a shorter chain of consequences than any of those, by which we learn the reality of his existence.

Suppose, that the son of a friend, who had been long dead or absent, were presented to us; it is evident, that this object would instantly revive its correlative idea, and recall to our thoughts all past intimacies and familiarities, in more lively colours than they would otherwise have appeared to us. This is another phaenomenon, which seems to prove the principle above mentioned.

44 We may observe, that, in these phaenomena, the belief of the correlative object is always presupposed; without which the relation could have no effect. The influence of the picture supposes, that we *believe* our friend to have once existed. Contiguity to home can never excite our ideas of home, unless we *believe* that it really exists. Now I assert, that this belief, where it reaches beyond the memory or senses, is of a similar nature, and arises from similar causes, with the transition of though and vivacity of conception here explained. When I throw a piece of dry wood into a fire, my mind is immediately carried to conceive, that it augments, not extinguishes the flame. This transition of thought from the cause to the effect proceeds not from reason. It derives its origin altogether from custom and experience. And as it first begins from an object, present to the senses, it renders the idea or conception of flame more strong and lively than any loose, floating reverie of the imagination. That idea arises immediately. The though moves instantly towards it, and conveys to it all that force of conception, which is derived from the impression present to the senses. When a sword is levelled at my breast, does not the idea of wound and pain strike me more strongly, than when a glass of wine is presented to me, even though by accident this idea should occur after the appearance of the latter object? But what is there in this whole matter to cause such a strong conception, except only a present object and a customary transition to the idea of another object, which we have been accustomed to conjoin with the former? This is the whole operation of the mind, in all our conclusions concerning matter of fact and existence; and it is a satisfaction to find some analogies, by which it may be explained. The transition from a present object

does in all cases give strength and solidity to the related idea.

Here, then, is a kind of pre-established harmony between the course of nature and the succession of our ideas; and though the powers and forces, by which the former is governed, be wholly unknown to us; yet our thoughts and conceptions have still, we find, gone on in the same train with the other works of nature. Custom is that principle, by which this correspondence has been effected; so necessary to the subsistence of our species, and the regulation of our conduct, in every circumstance and occurrence of human life. Had not the presence of an object instantly excited the idea of those objects, commonly conjoined with it, all our knowledge must have been limited to the narrow sphere of our memory and senses; and we should never have been able to adjust means to ends, or employ our natural powers, either to the producing of good, or avoiding of evil. Those, who delight in the discovery and contemplation of *final causes*, have here ample subject to employ their wonder and admiration.

45 I shall add, for a further confirmation of the foregoing theory, that, as this operation of the mind, by which we infer like effects from like causes, and *vice versa*, is so essential to the subsistence of all human creatures, it is not probable, that it could be trusted to the fallacious deductions of our reason, which is slow in its operations; appears not, in any degree, during the first years of infancy; and at best is, in every age and period of human life, extremely liable to error and mistake. It is more conformable to the ordinary wisdom of nature to secure so necessary an act of the mind, by some instinct or mechanical tendency, which may be infallible in its operations, may discover itself at the first appearance of life and thought, and may be independent of all the laboured deductions of the understanding. As nature has taught us the use of our limbs, without giving us the knowledge of the muscles and nerves, by which they are actuated; so has she implanted in us an instinct, which carries forward the thought in a correspondent course to that which she has established among external objects; though we are ignorant of those powers

and forces, on which this regular course and succession of objects totally depends.

SECTION VI

Of Probability

46 Though there be no such thing as *Chance* in the
world; our ignorance of the real cause of any
event has the same influence on the understanding, and begets a like species of belief or opinion.

There is certainly a probability, which arises
from a superiority of chances on any side; and
according as this superiority encreases, and surpasses the opposite chances, the probability
receives a proportionable encrease, and begets
still a higher degree of belief or assent to that
side, in which we discover the superiority. If a
dye were marked with one figure or number of
spots on four sides, and with another figure or
number of spots on the two remaining sides, it
would be more probable, that the former would
turn up than the latter; though, if it had a thousand sides marked in the same manner, and only
one side different, the probability would be
much higher, and our belief or expectation of the
event more steady and secure. This process of
the thought or reasoning may seem trivial and
obvious; but to those who consider it more narrowly, it may, perhaps, afford matter for curious
speculation.

It seems evident, that, when the mind looks
forward to discover the event, which may result
from the throw of such a dye, it considers the
turning up of each particular side as alike probable; and this is the very nature of chance, to render all the particular events, comprehended in it,
entirely equal. But finding a greater number of
sides concur in the one event than in the other,
the mind is carried more frequently to that
event, and meets it oftener, in revolving the various possibilities or chances, on which the ultimate result depends. This concurrence of several
views in one particular event begets immediately,
by an inexplicable contrivance of nature, the
sentiment of belief, and gives that event the
advantage over its antagonist, which is supported
by a smaller number of views, and recurs less frequently to the mind. If we allow, that belief is

nothing but a firmer and stronger conception of
an object than what attends the mere fictions of
the imagination, this operation may, perhaps, in
some measure, be accounted for. The concurrence of these several views or glimpses imprints
the idea more strongly on the imagination; gives
it superior force and vigour; renders its influence
on the passions and affections more sensible; and
in a word, begets that reliance or security, which
constitutes the nature of belief and opinion.

47 The case is the same with the probability of
causes, as with that of chance. There are some
causes, which are entirely uniform and constant
in producing a particular effect; and no instance
has ever yet been found of any failure or irregularity in their operation. Fire has always burned,
and water suffocated every human creature: The
production of motion by impulse and gravity is
an universal law, which has hitherto admitted of
no exception. But there are other causes, which
have been found more irregular and uncertain;
nor has rhubarb always proved a purge, or opium
a soporific to every one, who has taken these
medicines. It is true, when any cause fails of producing its usual effect, philosophers ascribe not
this to any irregularity in nature; but suppose,
that some secret causes, in the particular structure of parts, have prevented the operation. Our
reasonings, however, and conclusions concerning
the event are the same as if this principle had no
place. Being determined by custom to transfer
the past to the future, in all our inferences; where
the past has been entirely regular and uniform,
we expect the event with the greatest assurance,
and leave no room for any contrary supposition.
But where different effects have been found to
follow from causes, which are to *appearance*
exactly similar, all these various effects must
occur to the mind in transferring the past to the
future, and enter into our consideration, when
we determine the probability of the event.
Though we give the preference to that which has
been found most usual, and believe that this
effect will exist, we must not overlook the other
effects, but must assign to each of them a particular weight and authority, in proportion as we
have found it to be more or less frequent. It is
more probable, in almost every country of

Europe, that there will be frost sometime in January, than that the weather will continue open throughout that whole month; though this probability varies according to the different climates, and approaches to a certainty in the more northern kingdoms. Here then it seems evident, that, when we transfer the past to the future, in order to determine the effect, which will result from any cause, we transfer all the different events, in the same proportion as they have appeared in the past, and conceive one to have existed a hundred times, for instance, another ten times, and another once. As a great number of views do here concur in one event, they fortify and confirm it to the imagination, beget that sentiment which we call *belief*, and give its object the preference above the contrary event, which is not supported by an equal number of experiments, and recurs not so frequently to the thought in transferring the past to the future. Let any one try to account for this operation of the mind upon any of the received systems of philosophy, and he will be sensible of the difficulty. For my part, I shall think it sufficient, if the present hints excite the curiosity of philosophers, and make them sensible how defective all common theories are in treating of such curious and such sublime subjects.

SECTION VII

Of the Idea of Necessary Connexion

Part I

48 The great advantage of the mathematical sciences above the moral consists in this, that the ideas of the former, being sensible, are always clear and determinate, the smallest distinction between them is immediately perceptible, and the same terms are still expressive of the same ideas, without ambiguity or variation. An oval is never mistaken for a circle, nor an hyperbola for an ellipsis. The isosceles and scalenum are distinguished by boundaries more exact than vice and virtue, right and wrong. If any term be defined in geometry, the mind readily, of itself, substitutes, on all occasions, the definition for the term defined: Or even when no definition is employed, the object itself may be presented to the

senses, and by that means be steadily and clearly apprehended. But the finer sentiments of the mind, the operations of the understanding, the various agitations of the passions, though really in themselves distinct, easily escape us, when surveyed by reflection; nor is it in our power to recall the original object, as often as we have occasion to contemplate it. Ambiguity, by this means, is gradually introduced into our reasonings: Similar objects are readily taken to be the same: And the conclusion becomes at last very wide of the premises.

One may safely, however, affirm, that, if we consider these sciences in a proper light, their advantages and disadvantages nearly compensate each other, and reduce both of them to a state of equality. If the mind, with greater facility, retains the ideas of geometry clear and determinate, it must carry on a much longer and more intricate chain of reasoning, and compare ideas much wider of each other, in order to reach the abstruser truths of that science. And if moral ideas are apt, without extreme care, to fall into obscurity and confusion, the inferences are always much shorter in these disquisitions, and the intermediate steps, which lead to the conclusion, much fewer than in the sciences which treat of quantity and number. In reality, there is scarcely a proposition in Euclid so simple, as not to consist of more parts, than are to be found in any moral reasoning which runs not into chimera and conceit. Where we trace the principles of the human mind through a few steps, we may be very well satisfied with our progress; considering how soon nature throws a bar to all our enquiries concerning causes, and reduces us to an acknowledgment of our ignorance. The chief obstacle, therefore, to our improvement in the moral or metaphysical sciences is the obscurity of the ideas, and ambiguity of the terms. The principal difficulty in the mathematics is the length of inferences and compass of thought, requisite to the forming of any conclusion. And, perhaps, our progress in natural philosophy is chiefly retarded by the want of proper experiments and phaenomena, which are often discovered by chance, and cannot always be found, when requisite, even by the most diligent and prudent enquiry. As moral philosophy seems hitherto to have received less improvement than either geometry or physics, we may conclude, that, if there be any difference in this respect among these sciences, the difficulties, which obstruct the progress of the former, require superior care and capacity to be surmounted.

49   There are no ideas, which occur in metaphysics, more obscure and uncertain, than those of *power, force, energy* or *necessary connexion,* of which it is every moment necessary for us to treat in all our disquisitions. We shall, therefore, endeavour, in this section, to fix, if possible, the precise meaning of these terms, and thereby remove some part of that obscurity, which is so much complained of in this species of philosophy.

It seems a proposition, which will not admit of much dispute, that all our ideas are nothing but copies of our impressions, or, in other words, that it is impossible for us to *think* of any thing, which we have not antecedently *felt,* either by our external or internal senses. I have endeavoured to explain and prove this proposition, and have expressed my hopes, that, by a proper application of it, men may reach a greater clearness and precision in philosophical reasonings, than what they have hitherto been able to attain. Complex ideas may, perhaps, be well known by definition, which is nothing but an enumeration of those parts or simple ideas, that compose them. But when we have pushed up definitions to the most simple ideas, and find still some ambiguity and obscurity; what resource are we then possessed of? By what invention can we throw light upon these ideas, and render them altogether precise and determinate to our intellectual view? Produce the impressions or original sentiments, from which the ideas are copied. These impressions are all strong and sensible. They admit not of ambiguity. They are not only placed in a full light themselves, but may throw light on their correspondent ideas, which lie in obscurity. And by this means, we may, perhaps, attain a new microscope or species of optics, by which, in the moral sciences, the most minute, and most simple ideas may be so enlarged as to fall readily under our apprehension, and be equally known with the grossest and most sensible ideas, that can be the object of our enquiry.

50   To be fully acquainted, therefore, with the idea of power or necessary connexion, let us examine its impression; and in order to find the impression with greater certainty, let us search for it in all the sources, from which it may possibly be derived.

When we look about us towards external objects, and consider the operation of causes, we are never able, in a single instance, to discover any power or necessary connexion; any quality, which binds the effect to the cause, and renders the one an infallible consequence of the other. We only find, that the one does actually, in fact, follow the other. The impulse of one billiard-ball is attended with motion in the second. This is the whole that appears to the *outward* senses. The mind feels no sentiment or *inward* impression from this succession of objects: Consequently, there is not, in any single, particular instance of cause and effect, any thing which can suggest the idea of power or necessary connexion.

From the first appearance of an object, we never can conjecture what effect will result from it. But were the power or energy of any cause discoverable by the mind, we could foresee the effect, even without experience; and might, at first, pronounce with certainty concerning it, by the mere dint of thought and reasoning.

In reality, there is no part of matter, that does ever, by its sensible qualities, discover any power or energy, or give us ground to imagine, that it could produce any thing, or be followed by any other object, which we could denominate its effect. Solidity, extension, motion; these qualities are all complete in themselves, and never point out any other event which may result from them. The scenes of the universe are continually shifting, and one object follows another in an uninterrupted succession; but the power or force, which actuates the whole machine, is entirely concealed from us, and never discovers itself in any of the sensible qualities of body. We know, that, in fact, heat is a constant attendant of flame; but what is the connexion between them, we have no room so much as to conjecture or imagine. It is impossible, therefore, that the idea of power can be derived from the contemplation of bodies, in single instances of their operation; because no bodies ever discover any power, which can be the original of this idea.

51 Since, therefore, external objects as they appear to the senses, give us no idea of power or necessary connexion, by their operation in particular instances, let us see, whether this idea be derived from reflection on the operations of our own minds, and be copied from any internal impression. It may be said, that we are every moment conscious of internal power; while we feel, that, by the simple command of our will, we can move the organs of our body, or direct the faculties of our mind. An act of volition produces motion in our limbs, or raises a new idea in our imagination. This influence of the will we know by consciousness. Hence we acquire the idea of power or energy; and are certain, that we ourselves and all other intelligent beings are possessed of power. This idea, then, is an idea of reflection, since it arises from reflecting on the operations of our own mind, and on the command which is exercised by will, both over the organs of the body and faculties of the soul.

52 We shall proceed to examine this pretension; and first with regard to the influence of volition over the organs of the body. This influence, we may observe, is a fact, which, like all other natural events, can be known only by experience, and can never beforeseen from any apparent energy or power in the cause, which connects it with the effect, and renders the one an infallible consequence of the other. The motion of our body follows upon the command of our will. Of this we are every moment conscious. But the means, by which this is effected; the energy, by which the will performs so extraordinary an operation; of this we are so far from being immediately conscious, that it must for ever escape our most diligent enquiry.

For *first;* is there any principle in all nature more mysterious than the union of soul with body; by which a supposed spiritual substance acquires such an influence over a material one, that the most refined thought is able to actuate the grossest matter? Were we empowered, by a secret wish, to remove mountains, or control the planets in their orbit; this extensive authority would not be more extraordinary, nor more beyond our comprehension. But if by consciousness we perceived any power or energy in the will, we must know this power; we must know its connexion with the effect; we must know the secret union of soul and body, and the nature of both these substances; by which the one is able to operate, in so many instances, upon the other.

Secondly, We are not able to move all the organs of the body with a like authority; though we cannot assign any reason besides experience, for so remarkable a difference between one and the other. Why has the will an influence over the tongue and fingers, not over the heart or liver? This question would never embarrass us, were we conscious of a power in the former case, not in the latter. We should then perceive, independent of experience, why the authority of will over the organs of the body is circumscribed within such particular limits. Being in that case fully acquainted with the power or force, by which it operates, we should also know, why its influence reaches precisely to such boundaries, and no farther.

A man, suddenly struck with a palsy in the leg or arm, or who had newly lost those members, frequently endeavours, at first, to move them, and employ them in their usual offices. Here he is as much conscious of power to command such limbs, as a man in perfect health is conscious of power to actuate any member which remains in its natural state and condition. But consciousness never deceives. Consequently, neither in the one case nor in the other, are we ever conscious of any power. We learn the influence of our will from experience alone. And experience only teaches us, how one event constantly follows another; without instructing us in the secret connexion, which binds them together, and renders them inseparable.

Thirdly, We learn from anatomy, that the immediate object of power in voluntary motion, is not the member itself which is moved, but certain muscles, and nerves, and animal spirits, and, perhaps, something still more minute and more unknown, through which the motion is successively propagated, ere it reach the member itself whose motion is the immediate object of volition.

Can there be a more certain proof, that the power, by which this whole operation is performed, so far from being directly and fully known by an inward sentiment or consciousness, is, to the last degree, mysterious and unintelligible? Here the mind wills a certain event: Immediately another event, unknown to ourselves, and totally different from the one intended, is produced: This event produces another, equally unknown: Till at last, through a long succession, the desired event is produced. But if the original power were felt, it must be known: Were it known, its effect must also be known; since all power is relative to its effect. And *vice versa*, if the effect be not known, the power cannot be known nor felt. How indeed can we be conscious of a power to move our limbs, when we have no such power; but only that to move certain animal spirits, which, though they produce at last the motion of our limbs, yet operate in such a manner as is wholly beyond our comprehension?

We may, therefore, conclude from the whole, I hope, without any temerity, though with assurance; that our idea of power is not copied from any sentiment or consciousness of power within ourselves, when we give rise to animal motion, or apply our limbs to their proper use and office. That their motion follows the command of the will is a matter of common experience, like other natural events: But the power or energy by which this is effected, like that in other natural events, is unknown and inconceivable.

53   Shall we then assert, that we are conscious of a power or energy in our own minds, when, by an act or command of our will, we raise up a new idea, fix the mind to the contemplation of it, turn it on all sides, and at last dismiss it for some other idea, when we think that we have surveyed it with sufficient accuracy? I believe the same arguments will prove, that even this command of the will gives us no real idea of force or energy.

First, It must be allowed, that, when we know a power, we know that very circumstance in the cause, by which it is enabled to produce the effect: For these are supposed to be synonimous. We must, therefore, know both the cause and effect, and the relation between them. But do we pretend to be acquainted with the nature of the human soul and the nature of an idea, or the aptitude of the one to produce the other? This is a real creation; a production of something out of nothing: Which implies a power so great, that it may seem, at first sight, beyond the reach of any being, less than infinite. At least it must be owned, that such a power is not felt, nor known, nor even conceivable by the mind. We only feel the event, namely, the existence of an idea, consequent to a command of the will: But the manner, in which this operation is performed, the power by which it is produced, is entirely beyond our comprehension.

Secondly, The command of the mind over itself is limited, as well as its command over the body; and these limits are not known by reason, or any acquaintance with the nature of cause and effect, but only by experience and observation, as in all other natural events and in the operation of external objects. Our authority over our sentiments and passions is much weaker than that over our ideas; and even the latter authority is circumscribed within very narrow boundaries. Will any one pretend to assign the ultimate reason of these boundaries, or show why the power is deficient in one case, not in another.

Thirdly, This self-command is very different at different times. A man in health possesses more of it than one languishing with sickness. We are more master of our thoughts in the morning than in the evening: Fasting, than after a full meal. Can we give any reason for these variations, except experience? Where then is the power, of which we pretend to be conscious? Is there not here, either in a spiritual or material substance, or both, some secret mechanism or structure of parts, upon which the effect depends, and which, being entirely unknown to us, renders the power or energy of the will equally unknown and incomprehensible?

Volition is surely an act of the mind, with which we are sufficiently acquainted. Reflect upon it. Consider it on all sides. Do you find anything in it like this creative power, by which it raises from nothing a new idea, and with a kind of *Fiat*, imitates the omnipotence of its Maker, if I may be allowed so to speak, who called forth into existence all the various scenes of nature? So far from being conscious of this energy in the will, it requires as certain experience as that of which we are possessed, to convince us that such extraordinary effects do ever result from a simple act of volition.

54 The generality of mankind never find any difficulty in accounting for the more common and familiar operations of nature—such as the descent of heavy bodies, the growth of plants, the generation of animals, or the nourishment of bodies of food: But suppose that, in all these cases, they perceive the very force or energy of the cause, by which it is connected with its effect, and is for ever infallible in its operation. They acquire, by long habit, such a turn of mind, that, upon the appearance of the cause, they immediately expect with assurance its usual attendant, and hardly conceive it possible that any other event could result from it. It is only on the discovery of extraordinary phaenomena, such as earthquakes, pestilence, and prodigies of any kind, that they find themselves at a loss to assign a proper cause, and to explain the manner in which the effect is produced by it. It is usual for men, in such difficulties, to have recourse to some invisible intelligent principle as the imme-diate cause of that event which surprises them, and which, they think, cannot be accounted for from the common powers of nature. But philoso-phers, who carry their scrutiny a little farther, immediately perceive that, even in the most familiar events, the energy of the cause is as unin-telligible as in the most unusual, and that we only learn by experience the frequent *Conjunction* of objects, without being ever able to comprehend anything like *Connexion* between them.

55 Here, then, many philosophers think them-selves obliged by reason to have recourse, on all occasions, to the same principle, which the vul-gar never appeal to but in cases that appear mirac-ulous and supernatural. They acknowledge mind and intelligence to be, not only the ultimate and original cause of all things, but the immediate and sole cause of every event which appears in nature. They pretend that those objects which are commonly denominated *causes,* are in reality nothing but *occasions;* and that the true and

direct principle of every effect is not any power or force in nature, but a volition of the Supreme Being, who wills that such particular objects should for ever be conjoined with each other. Instead of saying that one billiard-ball moves another by a force which it has derived from the author of nature, it is the Deity himself, they say, who, by a particular volition, moves the second ball, being determined to this operation by the impulse of the first ball; in consequence of those general laws which he has laid down to himself in the government of the universe. But philoso-phers advancing still in their inquiries, discover that, as we are totally ignorant of the power on which depends the mutual operation of bodies, we are no less ignorant of that power on which depends the operation of mind on body, or of body on mind; nor are we able, either from our senses or consciousness, to assign the ultimate principle in one case more than in the other. The same ignorance, therefore, reduces them to the same conclusion. They assert that the Deity is the immediate cause of the union between soul and body; and that they are not the organs of sense, which, being agitated by external objects, produce sensations in the mind; but that it is a particular volition of our omnipotent Maker, which excites such a sensation, in consequence of such a motion in the organ. In like manner, it is not any energy in the will that produces local motion in our members: It is God himself, who is pleased to second our will, in itself impotent, and to command that motion which we erroneously attribute to our own power and efficacy. Nor do philosophers stop at this conclusion. They some-times extend the same inference to the mind itself, in its internal operations. Our mental vision or conception of ideas is nothing but a revelation made to us by our Maker. When we voluntarily turn our thoughts to any object, and raise up its image in the fancy, it is not the will which creates that idea: It is the universal Cre-ator, who discovers it to the mind, and renders it present to us.

56 Thus, according to these philosophers, every thing is full of God. Not content with the princi-ple, that nothing exists but by his will, that noth-ing possesses any power but by his concession:

They rob nature, and all created beings, of every power, in order to render their dependence on the Deity still more sensible and immediate. They consider not that, by this theory, they diminish, instead of magnifying, the grandeur of those attributes, which they affect so much to celebrate. It argues surely more power in the Deity to delegate a certain degree of power to inferior creatures than to produce every thing by his own immediate volition. It argues more wisdom to contrive at first the fabric of the world with such perfect foresight that, of itself, and by its proper operation, it may serve all the purposes of providence, than if the great Creator were obliged every moment to adjust its parts, and animate by his breath all the wheels of that stupendous machine.

But if we would have a more philosophical confutation of this theory, perhaps the two following reflections may suffice.

57   *First,* it seems to me that this theory of the universal energy and operation of the Supreme Being is too bold ever to carry conviction with it to a man, sufficiently apprized of the weakness of human reason, and the narrow limits to which it is confined in all its operations. Though the chain of arguments which conduct to it were ever so logical, there must arise a strong suspicion, if not an absolute assurance, that it has carried us quite beyond the reach of our faculties, when it leads to conclusions so extraordinary, and so remote from common life and experience. We are got into fairy land, long ere we have reached the last steps of our theory; and *there* we have no reason to trust our common methods of argument, or to think that our usual analogies and probabilities have any authority. Our line is too short to fathom such immense abysses. And however we may flatter ourselves that we are guided, in every step which we take, by a kind of verisimilitude and experience, we may be assured that this fancied experience has no authority when we thus apply it to subjects that lie entirely out of the sphere of experience. But on this we shall have occasion to touch afterwards.

Secondly, I cannot perceive any force in the arguments on which this theory is founded. We are ignorant, it is true, of the manner in which bodies operate on each other: Their force or energy is entirely incomprehensible: But are we not equally ignorant of the manner or force by which a mind, even the supreme mind, operates either on itself or on body? Whence, I beseech you, do we acquire any idea of it? We have no sentiment or consciousness of this power in ourselves. We have no idea of the Supreme Being but what we learn from reflection on our own faculties. Were our ignorance, therefore, a good reason for rejecting any thing, we should be led into that principle of denying all energy in the Supreme Being as much as in the grossest matter. We surely comprehend as little the operations of one as of the other. Is it more difficult to conceive that motion may arise from impulse than that it may arise from volition? All we know is our profound ignorance in both cases.

Part II

58 But to hasten to a conclusion of this argument, which is already drawn out to too great a length: We have sought in vain for an idea of power or necessary connexion in all the sources from which we could suppose it to be derived. It appears that, in single instances of the operation of bodies, we never can, by our utmost scrutiny, discover any thing but one event following another; without being able to comprehend any force or power by which the cause operates, or any connexion between it and its supposed effect. The same difficulty occurs in contemplating the operations of mind on body—where we observe the motion of the latter to follow upon the volition of the former, but are not able to observe or conceive the tie which binds together the motion and volition, or the energy by which the mind produces this effect. The authority of the will over its own faculties and ideas is not a whit more comprehensible: So that, upon the whole, there appears not, throughout all nature, any one instance of connexion which is conceivable by us. All events seem entirely loose and separate. One event follows another; but we never can observe any tie between them. They seem *conjoined,* but never *connected.* And as we can have no idea of any thing which never appeared to our outward sense or inward senti-

ment, the necessary conclusion *seems* to be that we have no idea of connexion or power at all, and that these words are absolutely without any meaning, when employed either in philosophical reasonings or common life.

59　But there still remains one method of avoiding this conclusion, and one source which we have not yet examined. When any natural object or event is presented, it is impossible for us, by any sagacity or penetration, to discover, or even conjecture, without experience, what event will result from it, or to carry our foresight beyond that object which is immediately present to the memory and senses. Even after one instance or experiment, where we have observed a particular event to follow upon another, we are not entitled to form a general rule, or foretell what will happen in like cases; it being justly esteemed an unpardonable temerity to judge of the whole course of nature from one single experiment, however accurate or certain. But when one particular species of event has always, in all instances, been conjoined with another, we make no longer any scruple of foretelling one upon the appearance of the other, and of employing that reasoning, which can alone assure us of any matter of fact or existence. We then call the one object, *Cause;* the other, *Effect.* We suppose that there is some connexion between them; some power in the one, by which it infallibly produces the other, and operates with the greatest certainty and strongest necessity.

It appears, then, that this idea of a necessary connexion among events arises from a number of similar instances which occur of the constant conjunction of these events; nor can that idea ever be suggested by any one of these instances, surveyed in all possible lights and positions. But there is nothing in a number of instances, different from every single instance, which is supposed to be exactly similar; except only, that after a repetition of similar instances, the mind is carried by habit, upon the appearance of one event, to expect its usual attendant, and to believe that it will exist. This connexion, therefore, which we *feel* in the mind, this customary transition of the imagination from one object to its usual attendant, is the sentiment or impression from which

we form the idea of power or necessary connexion. Nothing farther is in the case. Contemplate the subject on all sides; you will never find any other origin of that idea. This is the sole difference between one instance, from which we can never receive the idea of connexion, and a number of similar instances, by which it is suggested. The first time a man saw the communication of motion by impulse, as by the shock of two billiard balls, he could not pronounce that the one event was *connected:* but only that it was *conjoined* with the other. After he has observed several instances of this nature, he then pronounces them to be *connected.* What alteration has happened to give rise to this new idea of *connexion?* Nothing but that he now *feels* these events to be *connected* in his imagination, and can readily foretell the existence of one from the appearance of the other. When we say, therefore, that one object is connected with another, we mean only that they have acquired a connexion in our thought, and give rise to this inference, by which they become proofs of each other's existence: A conclusion which is somewhat extraordinary, but which seems founded on sufficient evidence. Nor will its evidence be weakened by any general diffidence of the understanding, or sceptical suspicion concerning every conclusion which is new and extraordinary. No conclusions can be more agreeable to scepticism than such as make discoveries concerning the weakness and narrow limits of human reason and capacity.

60　And what stronger instance can be produced of the surprising ignorance and weakness of the understanding than the present? For surely, if there by any relation among objects which it imports to us to know perfectly, it is that of cause and effect. On this are founded all our reasonings concerning matter of fact or existence. By means of it alone we attain any assurance concerning objects which are removed from the present testimony of our memory and senses. The only immediate utility of all sciences, is to teach us, how to control and regulate future events by their causes. Our thoughts and enquiries are, therefore, every moment, employed about this relation: Yet so imperfect are the ideas which we form concerning it, that it is impossible to give any just definition of cause, except what is drawn from something extraneous and foreign to it. Similar objects are always conjoined with similar. Of this we have experience. Suitably to this experience, therefore, we may define a cause to be *an object, followed by another, and where all the objects similar to the first are followed by objects similar to the second.* Or in other words *where, if the first object had not been, the second never had existed.* The appearance of a cause always conveys the mind, by a customary transition, to the idea of the effect. Of this also we have experience. We may, therefore, suitably to this experience, form another definition of cause, and call it, *an object followed by another, and whose appearance always conveys the thought to that other.* But though both these definitions be drawn from circumstances foreign to the cause, we cannot remedy this inconvenience, or attain any more perfect definition, which may point out that circumstance in the cause, which gives it a connexion with its effect. We have no idea of this connexion, nor even any distinct notion what it is we desire to know, when we endeavour at a conception of it. We say, for instance, that the vibration of this string is the cause of this particular sound. But what do we mean by that affirmation? We either mean *that this vibration is followed by this sound, and that all similar vibrations have been followed by similar sounds:* Or, *that this vibration is followed by this sound, and that upon the appearance of one the mind anticipates the senses, and forms immediately an idea of the other.* We may consider the relation of cause and effect in either of these two lights; but beyond these, we have no idea of it.

61   To recapitulate, therefore, the reasonings of this section: Every idea is copied from some preceding impression or sentiment; and where we cannot find any impression, we may be certain that there is no idea. In all single instances of the operation of bodies or minds, there is nothing that produces any impression, nor consequently can suggest any idea, of power or necessary connexion. But when many uniform instances appear, and the same object is always followed by the same event; we then begin to entertain the notion of cause and connexion. We then *feel* a new sentiment or impression, to wit, a customary connexion in the thought or imagination between one object and its usual attendant; and this sentiment is the original of that idea which we seek for. For as this idea arises from a number of similar instances, and not from any single instance, it must arise from that circumstance, in which the number of instances differ from every individual instance. But this customary connexion or transition of the imagination is the only circumstance in which they differ. In every other particular they are alike. The first instance which we saw of motion communicated by the shock of two billiard balls (to return to this obvious illustration) is exactly similar to any instance that may, at present, occur to us; except only, that we could not, at first, *infer* one event from the other; which we are enabled to do at present, after so long a course of uniform experience. I know not whether the reader will readily apprehend this reasoning. I am afraid that, should I multiply words about it, or throw it into a greater variety of lights, it would only become more obscure and intricate. In all abstract reasonings there is one point of view which, if we can happily hit, we shall go farther towards illustrating the subject than by all the eloquence and copious expression in the world. This point of view we should endeavour to reach, and reserve the flowers of rhetoric for subjects which are more adapted to them.

SECTION VIII

Of Liberty and Necessity

63 I hope, therefore, to make it appear that all men have ever agreed in the doctrine both of necessity and of liberty, according to any reasonable sense, which can be put on these terms; and that the whole controversy has hitherto turned merely upon words. We shall begin with examining the doctrine of necessity.

64   It is universally allowed that matter, in all its operations, is actuated by a necessary force, and that every natural effect is so precisely determined by the energy of its cause that no other effect, in such particular circumstances, could possibly have resulted from it. The degree and direction of every motion is, by the laws of

nature, prescribed with such exactness that a living creature may as soon arise from the shock of
two bodies, as motion, in any other degree or
direction than what is actually produced by it.
Would we, therefore, form a just and precise idea
of *necessity*, we must consider whence that idea
arises when we apply it to the operation of bodies.

It seems evident that, if all the scenes of
nature were continually shifted in such a manner
that no two events bore any resemblance to each
other, but every object was entirely new, without
any similitude to whatever had been seen before,
we should never, in that case, have attained the
least idea of necessity, or of a connexion among
these objects. We might say, upon such a supposition, that one object or event has followed
another; not that one was produced by the other.
The relation of cause and effect must be utterly
unknown to mankind. Inference and reasoning
concerning the operations of nature would, from
that moment, be at an end; and the memory and
senses remain the only canals, by which the
knowledge of any real existence could possibly
have access to the mind. Our idea, therefore, of
necessity and causation arises entirely from the
uniformity observable in the operations of nature,
where similar objects are constantly conjoined
together, and the mind is determined by custom
to infer the one from the appearance of the other.
These two circumstances form the whole of that
necessity, which we ascribe to matter. Beyond the
constant *conjunction* of similar objects, and the
consequent *inference* from one to the other, we
have no notion of any necessity or connexion.

If it appear, therefore, that all mankind have
ever allowed, without any doubt or hesitation,
that these two circumstances take place in the
voluntary actions of men, and in the operations
of mind; it must follow, that all mankind have
ever agreed in the doctrine of necessity, and that
they have hitherto disputed, merely for not
understanding each other.

65   As to the first circumstance, the constant
and regular conjunction of similar events, we
may possibly satisfy ourselves by the following
considerations. It is universally acknowledged
that there is a great uniformity among the
actions of men, in all nations and ages, and that

human nature remains still the same, in its principles and operations. The same motives always
produce the same actions: The same events follow from the same causes. Ambition, avarice,
self-love, vanity, friendship, generosity, public
spirit: these passions, mixed in various degrees,
and distributed through society, have been, from
the beginning of the world, and still are, the
source of all the actions and enterprises, which
have ever been observed among mankind.

66   We must not, however, expect that this uniformity of human actions should be carried to
such a length as that all men, in the same circumstances, will always act precisely in the same
manner, without making any allowance for the
diversity of characters, prejudices, and opinions.
Such a uniformity in every particular, is found in
no part of nature. On the contrary, from observing the variety of conduct in different men, we
are enabled to form a greater variety of maxims,
which still suppose a degree of uniformity and
regularity.

69 Thus it appears, not only that the conjunction
between motives and voluntary actions is as regular and uniform as that between the cause and
effect in any part of nature; but also that this regular conjunction has been universally acknowledged among mankind, and has never been the
subject of dispute, either in philosophy or common life. Now, as it is from past experience that
we draw all inferences concerning the future, and
as we conclude that objects will always be conjoined together which we find to have always
been conjoined; it may seem superfluous to prove
that this experienced uniformity in human
actions is a source whence we draw *inferences*
concerning them.

71 I have frequently considered, what could possibly be the reason why all mankind, though
they have ever, without hesitation, acknowledged the doctrine of necessity in their whole
practice and reasoning, have yet discovered such
a reluctance to acknowledge it in words, and
have rather shown a propensity, in all ages, to
profess the contrary opinion. The matter, I
think, may be accounted for after the following

manner. If we examine the operations of body, and the production of effects from their causes, we shall find that all our faculties can never carry us farther in our knowledge of this relation than barely to observe that particular objects are *constantly conjoined* together, and that the mind is carried, by a *customary transition*, from the appearance of one to the belief of the other. But though this conclusion concerning human ignorance be the result of the strictest scrutiny of this subject, men still entertain a strong propensity to believe that they penetrate farther into the powers of nature, and perceive something like a necessary connexion between the cause and the effect. When again they turn their reflections towards the operations of their own minds, and *feel* no such connexion of the motive and the action; they are thence apt to suppose, that there is a difference between the effects which result from material force, and those which arise from thought and intelligence. But being once convinced that we know nothing farther of causation of any kind than merely the *constant conjunction* of objects, and the consequent *inference* of the mind from one to another, and finding that these two circumstances are universally allowed to have place in voluntary actions; we may be more easily led to own the same necessity common to all causes. And though this reasoning may contradict the systems of many philosophers, in ascribing necessity to the determinations of the will, we shall find, upon reflection, that they dissent from it in words only, not in their real sentiment. Necessity, according to the sense in which it is here taken, has never yet been rejected, nor can ever, I think, be rejected by any philosopher. It may only, perhaps, be pretended that the mind can perceive, in the operations of matter, some farther connexion between the cause and effect; and a connexion that has not place in the voluntary actions of intelligent beings. Now whether it be so or not, can only appear upon examination; and it is incumbent on these philosophers to make good their assertion, by defining or describing that necessity, , and pointing it out to us in the operations of material causes.

72   It would seem, indeed, that men begin at the wrong end of this question concerning liberty and necessity, when they enter upon it by examining the faculties of the soul, the influence of the understanding, and the operations of the will. Let them first discuss a more simple question, namely, the operations of body and of brute unintelligent matter; and try whether they can there form any idea of causation and necessity, except that of a constant conjunction of objects, and subsequent inference of the mind from one to another. If these circumstances form, in reality, the whole of that necessity, which we conceive in matter, and if these circumstances be also universally acknowledged to take place in the operations of the mind, the dispute is at an end; at least, must be owned to be thenceforth merely verbal. But as long as we will rashly suppose, that we have some farther idea of necessity and causation in the operations of external objects; at the same time, that we can find nothing farther in the voluntary actions of the mind; there is no possibility of bringing the question to any determinate issue, while we proceed upon so erroneous a supposition. The only method of undeceiving us is to mount up higher; to examine the narrow extent of science when applied to material causes; and to convince ourselves that all we know of them is the constant conjunction and inference above mentioned. We may, perhaps, find that it is with difficulty we are induced to fix such narrow limits to human understanding: But we can afterwards find no difficulty when we come to apply this doctrine to the actions of the will. For as it is evident that these have a regular conjunction with motives and circumstances and characters, and as we always draw inferences from one to the other, we must be obliged to acknowledge in words that necessity, which we have already avowed, in every deliberation of our lives, and in every step of our conduct and behaviour.

73   But to proceed in this reconciling project with regard to the question of liberty and necessity; the most contentious question of metaphysics, the most contentious science; it will not require many words to prove, that all mankind

have ever agreed in the doctrine of liberty as well as in that of necessity, and that the whole dispute, in this respect also, has been hitherto merely verbal. For what is meant by liberty, when applied to voluntary actions? We cannot surely mean that actions have so little connexion with motives, inclinations, and circumstances, that one does not follow with a certain degree of uniformity from the other, and that one affords no inference by which we can conclude the existence of the other. For these are plain and acknowledged matters of fact. By liberty, them, we can only mean *a power of acting or not acting, according to the determinations of the will;* that is, if we choose to remain at rest, we may; if we choose to move, we also may. Now this hypothetical liberty is universally allowed to belong to every one who is not a prisoner and in chains. Here, then, is no subject of dispute.

74 　　Whatever definition we may give of liberty, we should be careful to observe two requisite circumstances; *first,* that it be consistent with plain matter of fact; *secondly,* that it be consistent with itself. If we observe these circumstances, and render our definition intelligible, I am persuaded that all mankind will be found of one opinion with regard to it.

　　It is universally allowed that nothing exists without a cause of its existence, and that chance, when strictly examined, is a mere negative word, and means not any real power which has anywhere a being in nature. But it is pretended that some causes are necessary, some not necessary. Here then is the advantage of definitions. Let any one *define* a cause, without comprehending, as a part of the definition, a *necessary connexion* with its effect; and let him show distinctly the origin of the idea, expressed by the definition; and I shall readily give up the whole controversy. But if the foregoing explication of the matter be received, this must be absolutely impracticable. Had not objects a regular conjunction with each other, we should never have entertained any notion of cause and effect; and this regular conjunction produces that inference of the understanding, which is the only connexion, that we can have any comprehension of. Whoever attempts a definition of cause, exclusive of these circumstances, will be obliged either to employ unintelligible terms or such as are synonymous to the term which he endeavours to define. And if the definition above mentioned be admitted; liberty, when opposed to necessity, not to constraint, is the same thing with chance; which is universally allowed to have no existence.

Part II

75 Necessity may be defined two ways, conformably to the two definitions of *cause,* of which it makes an essential part. It consists either in the constant conjunction of like objects, or in the inference of the understanding from one object to another. Now necessity, in both these senses, (which, indeed, are at bottom the same) has universally, though tacitly, in the schools, in the pulpit, and in common life, been allowed to belong to the will of man; and no one has ever pretended to deny that we can draw inferences concerning human actions, and that those inferences are founded on the experienced union of like actions, with like motives, inclinations, and circumstances. The only particular in which any one can differ, is, that either, perhaps, he will refuse to give the name of necessity to this property of human actions: But as long as the meaning is understood, I hope the word can do no harm: Or that he will maintain it possible to discover something farther in the operations of matter. But this, is must be acknowledged, can be of no consequence to morality or religion, whatever it may be to natural philosophy or metaphysics. We may here be mistaken in asserting that here is no idea of any other necessity or connexion in the actions of body: But surely we ascribe nothing to the actions of the mind, but what everyone does, and must readily allow of. We change no circumstance in the received orthodox system with regard to the will, but only in that with regard to material objects and causes. Nothing, therefore, can be more innocent, at least, than this doctrine.

76 　　All laws being founded on rewards and punishments, it is supposed as a fundamental principle, that these motives have a regular and uniform

influence on the mind, and both produce the good and prevent the evil actions. We may give to this influence what name we please; but, as it is usually conjoined with the action, it must be esteemed a *cause,* and be looked upon as a instance of that necessity, which we would here establish.

The only proper object of hatred or vengeance is a person or creature, endowed with thought and consciousness; and when any criminal or injurious actions excite that passion, it is only by their relation to the person, or connexion with him. Actions are, by their very nature, temporary and perishing; and where they proceed not from some *cause* in the character and disposition of the person who performed them, they can neither redound to his honour, if good; nor infamy, if evil. The actions themselves may be blameable; they may be contrary to all the rules of morality and religion: But the person is not answerable for them; and as they proceeded from nothing in him that is durable and constant, and leave nothing of that nature behind them, it is impossible he can, upon their account, become the object of punishment or vengeance. According to the principle, therefore, which denies necessity, and consequently causes, a man is as pure and untainted, after having committed the most horrid crime, as at the first moment of his birth, nor is his character anywise concerned in his actions, since they are not derived from it, and the wickedness of the one can never be used as a proof of the depravity of the other.

Men are not blamed for such actions as they perform ignorantly and casually, whatever may be the consequences. Why? but because the principles of these actions are only momentary, and terminate in them alone. Men are less blamed for such actions as they performed hastily and unpremeditately than for such as proceed from deliberation. For what reason? but because a hasty temper, though a constant cause or principle in the mind, operates only by intervals, and infects not the whole character. Again, repentance wipes off every crime, if attended with a reformation of life and manners. How is this to be accounted for? but by asserting that actions render a person criminal merely as they are proofs of criminal principles in the mind; and when, by an alteration of these principles, they cease to be just proofs, they likewise cease to be criminal. But, except upon the doctrine of necessity, they never were just proofs, and consequently never were criminal.

77   It will be equally easy to prove, and from the same arguments, that *liberty,* according to that definition above mentioned, in which all men agree, is also essential to morality, and that no human actions, where it is wanting, are susceptible of any moral qualities, or can be the objects either of approbation or dislike. For as actions are objects of our moral sentiment, so far only as they are indications of the internal character, passions, and affections; it is impossible that they can give rise either to praise or blame, where they proceed not from these principles, but are derived altogether from external violence.

SECTION XII

Of the Academic or Skeptical Philosophy

118 It seems evident, that men are carried, by a natural instinct or prepossession, to repose faith in their senses; and that, without any reasoning, or even almost before the use of reason, we always suppose an external universe, which depends not on our perception, but would exist, though we and every sensible creature were absent or annihilated. Even the animal creation are governed by a like opinion, and preserve this belief of external objects, in all their thoughts, designs, and actions.

It seems also evident, that, when men follow this blind and powerful instinct of nature, they always suppose the very images, presented by the senses, to be the external objects, and never entertain any suspicion, that the one are nothing but representations of the other. This very table, which we see white, and which we feel hard, is believed to exist, independent of our perception, and to be something external to our mind, which perceives it. Our presence bestows not being on it: our absence does not annihilate it. It preserves its existence uniform and entire, independent of the situation of intelligent beings, who perceive or contemplate it.

But this universal and primary opinion of all men is soon destroyed by the slightest philosophy, which teaches us, that nothing can ever be present to the mind but an image or perception, and that the senses are only the inlets, through which these images are conveyed, without being able to produce any immediate intercourse between the mind and the object. The table, which we see, seems to diminish, as we remove farther from it: but the real table, which exists independent of us, suffers no alteration: it was, therefore, nothing but its image, which was present to the mind. These are the obvious dictates of reason; and no man, who reflects, ever doubted, that the existences, which we consider, when we say, *this house* and *that tree*, are nothing but perceptions in the mind, and fleeting copies or representations of other existences, which remain uniform and independent.

119   So far, then, are we necessitated by reasoning to contradict or depart from the primary instincts of nature, and to embrace a new system with regard to the evidence of our senses. But here philosophy finds herself extremely embarrassed, when she would justify this new system, and obviate the cavils and objections of the sceptics. She can no longer plead the infallible and irresistible instinct of nature: for that led us to a quite different system, which is acknowledged fallible and even erroneous. And to justify this pretended philosophical system, by a chain of clear and convincing argument, or even any appearance of argument, exceeds the power of all human capacity.

By what argument can it be proved, that the perceptions of the mind must be caused by external objects, entirely different from them, though resembling them (if that be possible) and could not arise either from the energy of the mind itself, or from the 'suggestion of some invisible and unknown spirit, or from some other cause still more unknown to us? It is acknowledged, that, in fact, many of these perceptions arise not from anything external, as in dreams, madness, and other diseases. And nothing can be more inexplicable than the manner, in which body should so operate upon mind as ever to convey an image of itself to a substance, supposed of so different, and even contrary a nature.

It is a question of fact, whether the perceptions of the senses be produced by external objects, resembling them: how shall this question be determined? By experience surely; as all other questions of a like nature. But here experience is, and must be entirely silent. The mind has never anything present to it but the perceptions, and cannot possibly reach any experience of their connexion with objects. The supposition of such a connexion is, therefore, without any foundation in reasoning.

120   To have recourse to the veracity of the supreme Being, in order to prove the veracity of our senses, is surely making a very unexpected circuit. If his veracity were at all concerned in this matter, our senses would be entirely infallible; because it is not possible that he can ever deceive. Not to mention, that, if the external world be once called in question, we shall be at a loss to find arguments, by which we may prove the existence of that Being or any of his attributes.

121   This is a topic, therefore, in which the profounder and more philosophical sceptics will always triumph, when they endeavour to introduce an universal doubt into all subjects of human knowledge and enquiry. Do you follow the instincts and propensities of nature, may they say, in assenting to the veracity of sense? But these lead you to believe that the very perception or sensible image is the external object. Do you disclaim this principle, in order to embrace a more rational opinion, that the perceptions are only representations of something external? You here depart from your natural propensities and more obvious sentiments; and yet are not able to satisfy your reason, which can never find any convincing argument from experience to prove, that the perceptions are connected with any external objects.

122   There is another sceptical topic of a like nature, derived from the most profound philosophy; which might merit our attention, were it requisite to dive so deep, in order to discover arguments and reasonings, which can so little serve to any serious purpose. It is universally allowed by modern enquirers, that all the sensible qualities of objects, such as hard, soft, hot, cold, white, black, &c. are merely secondary, and exist not in the objects themselves, but are perceptions

of the mind, without any external archetype or model, which they represent. If this be allowed, with regard to secondary qualities, it must also follow, with regard to the supposed primary qualities of extension and solidity; nor can the latter be any more entitled to that denomination than the former. The idea of extension is entirely acquired from the senses of sight and feeling; and if all the qualities, perceived by the senses, be in the mind, not in the object, the same conclusion must reach the idea of extension, which is wholly dependent on the sensible ideas or the ideas of secondary qualities. Nothing can save us from this conclusion, but the asserting, that the ideas of those primary qualities are attained by *Abstraction,* an opinion, which, if we examine it accurately, we shall find to be unintelligible, and even absurd. An extension, that is neither tangible nor visible, cannot possibly be conceived: and a tangible or visible extension, which is neither hard nor soft, black nor white, is equally beyond the reach of human conception. Let any man try to conceive a triangle in general, which is neither *Isosceles* nor *Scalenum,* nor has any particular length or proportion of sides; and he will soon perceive the absurdity of all the scholastic notions with regard to abstraction and general ideas.

123   Thus the first philosophical objection to the evidence of sense or to the opinion of external existence consists in this, that such an opinion, if rested on natural instinct, is contrary to reason, and if referred to reason, is contrary to natural instinct, and at the same time carriers no rational evidence with it, to convince an impartial enquirer. The second objection goes farther, and represents this opinion as contrary to reason: at least, if it be a principle of reason, that all sensible qualities are in the mind, not in the object. Bereave matter of all its intelligible qualities, both primary and secondary, you in a manner annihilate it, and leave only a certain unknown, inexplicable *something,* as the cause of our perceptions; a notion so imperfect, that no sceptic will think it worth while to contend against it.

132 All other enquiries of men regard only matter of fact and existence; and these are evidently inca-

pable of demonstration. Whatever *is* may *not be.* No negation of a fact can involve a contradiction. The non-existence of any being, without exception, is as clear and distinct an idea as its existence. The proposition, which affirms it not to be, however false, is no less conceivable and intelligible, than that which affirms it to be. The case is different with the sciences, properly so called. Every proposition, which is not true, is there confused and unintelligible. That the cube root of 64 is equal to the half of 10, is a false proposition, and can never be distinctly conceived. But that Cæsar, or the angel Gabriel, or any being never existed, may be a false proposition, but still is perfectly conceivable, and implies no contradiction.

The existence, therefore, of any being can only be proved by arguments from its cause or its effect; and these arguments are founded entirely on experience. If we reason *a priori,* anything may appear able to produce anything. The falling of a pebble may, for aught we know, extinguish the sun; or the wish of a man control the planets in their orbits. It is only experience, which teaches us the nature and bounds of cause and effect, and enables us to infer the existence of one object from that of another. Such is the foundation of moral reasoning, which forms the greater part of human knowledge, and is the source of all human action and behaviour.

Moral reasonings are either concerning particular or general facts. All deliberations in life regard the former; as also all disquisitions in history, chronology, geography, and astronomy.

The sciences, which treat of general facts, are politics, natural philosophy, physic, chemistry, &c. where the qualities, causes and effects of a whole species of objects are enquired into.

Divinity or Theology, as it proves the existence of a Deity, and the immortality of souls, is composed partly of reasonings concerning particular, partly concerning general facts. It has a foundation in *reason,* so far as it is supported by experience. But its best and most solid foundations is *faith* and divine revelation.

Morals and criticism are not so properly objects of the understanding as of taste and sentiment. Beauty, whether moral or natural, is felt, more properly than perceived. Or if we reason concerning it, and endeavour to fix its standard, we regard a new fact, to wit, the general taste of mankind, or some such fact, which may be object of reasoning and enquiry.

When we run over libraries, persuaded of these principles, what havoc must we make? If we take in our hand any volume; of divinity or school metaphysics, for instance; let us ask, *Does it contain any abstract reasoning concerning quality or number? No. Does it contain any experimental reasoning concerning matter of fact and existence? No.* Commit it then to the flames: for it can contain nothing but sophistry and illusion.

STUDY QUESTIONS: HUME, AN ENQUIRY CONCERNING HUMAN UNDERSTANDING

1. Why does Hume say, 'Be a philosopher; but, amidst all your philosophy, be still a man'? Why is this point important for his philosophy?
2. Why does Hume propose to study the operations of the mind and human nature?
3. What is the difference between an impression and an idea? How does Hume define each?
4. How does Hume explain our capacity to form ideas of monsters that we have never seen?
5. When we suspect that a philosophical term is used without meaning, what question should we ask? Why should we ask that question?
6. Explain Hume's distinction between relations of ideas and matters of fact. What is the significance of this distinction?
7. Which type of judgment is discoverable by reason alone, and why?
8. What is the role and significance of the relation of cause and effect?
9. What are Hume's arguments for claiming that causes and effects are discoverable by experience and not reason? What role does this claim play in his philosophy?
10. What is the nature of all our reasoning concerning matters of fact? What is the foundation of that reasoning? What is the fundamental point that Hume wants to make with regard to such reasoning?
11. What was Hume's point concerning the bread that has nourished one in the past?
12. There is no contradiction that the course of nature may change. How does Hume support that claim?
13. What is the skeptical solution that Hume proposes to his doubts regarding inferences from experience?
14. What is the difference between belief and imagination (or fiction), according to Hume?
15. What are the three principles of connection or association? What role do these play in Hume's philosophy?
16. What are Hume's main conclusions about the idea of a necessary connection? How does he reach those conclusions?
17. What is a constant conjunction?
18. What are Hume's two definitions of a cause?
19. According to Hume, what is the meaning of 'liberty' when applied to voluntary actions?
20. What is the natural belief about tables that is destroyed by the slightest philosophy? What is the distinction that philosophers make? What does Hume say about this distinction?
21. What sort of book should one commit to the flames, and why?

A TREATISE OF HUMAN NATURE

There are some important aspects of Hume's philosophy that are not covered as deeply in the *Enquiry* as they were in the earlier *Treatise* of 1739. For example, the section on the origin of ideas is slightly more detailed in the *Treatise* (Part I, section I). In Part IV, section II of the *Treatise*, Hume applies his skepticism to the distinct and continued existence of bodies and also gives his naturalistic explanation of how we come to believe in their continued and distinct existence, despite the fact that we have no justification for such a belief. The corresponding parts of section XII of the *Enquiry*, that is, paragraphs 118–123, are less explicit. Finally, there is the famous section on personal identity in Part IV, section VI of the *Treatise*, in which Hume applies his skeptical principles to the notion of the self. There is nothing in the *Enquiry* that really corresponds to this discussion. In the Appendix to the *Treatise*, Hume reviews his own naturalistic explanation of the idea of personal identity and apparently expresses doubts about it.

BOOK I

OF THE UNDERSTANDING

Part I

Of Ideas, Their Origin, Composition, Connexion, Abstraction, &c.

Section I

Of the Origin of Our Ideas

All the perceptions of the human mind resolve themselves into two distinct kinds, which I shall call Impressions and Ideas. The difference betwixt these consists in the degrees of force and liveliness with which they strike upon the mind, and make their way into our thought or consciousness. Those perceptions, which enter with most force and violence, we may name *impressions*; and under this name I comprehend all our sensations, passions and emotions, as they make their first appearance in the soul. By *ideas* I mean the faint images of these in thinking and reasoning; such as, for instance, are all the perceptions excited by the present discourse, excepting only, those which arise from the sight and touch, and excepting the immediate pleasure or uneasiness it may occasion. I believe it will not be very necessary to employ many words in explaining this distinction. Every one of himself will readily perceive the difference betwixt feeling and thinking. The common

degrees of these are easily distinguished; tho' it is not impossible but in particular instances they may very nearly approach to each other. Thus in sleep, in a fever, in madness, or in any very violent emotions of soul, our ideas may approach to our impressions: As on the other hand it sometimes happens, that our impressions are so faint and low, that we cannot distinguish them from our ideas. But notwithstanding this near resemblance in a few instances, they are in general so very different, that no-one can make a scruple to rank them under distinct heads, and assign to each a peculiar name to mark the difference.

There is another division of our perceptions, which it will be convenient to observe, and which extends itself both to our impressions and ideas. This division is into Simple and Complex. Simple perceptions or impressions and ideas are such as admit of no distinction nor separation. The complex are the contrary to these, and may be distinguished into parts. Tho' a particular colour, taste, and smell are qualities all united together in this apple, 'tis easy to perceive they are not the same, but are at least distinguishable from each other.

Having by these divisions given an order and arrangement to our objects, we may now apply ourselves to consider with the more accuracy their qualities and relations. The first circumstance, that strikes my eyes, is the great resemblance betwixt our impres-

Hume, from *A Treatise of Human Nature*, ed. by L.A. Selby-Bigge. Part I: Sec. 1, 2; Part IV excerpts; Conclusion/Appendix, 1888.

sions and ideas in every other particular, except their degree of force and vivacity. The one seem to be in a manner the reflexion of the other; so that all the perceptions of the mind are double, and appear both as impressions and ideas. When I shut my eyes and think of my chamber, the ideas I form are exact representations of the impressions I felt; nor is there any circumstance of the one, which is not to be found in the other. In running over my other perceptions, I find still the same resemblance and representation. Ideas and impressions appear always to correspond to each other. This circumstance seems to me remarkable, and engages my attention for a moment.

Upon a more accurate survey I find I have been carried away too far by the first appearance, and that I must make use of the distinction of perceptions into *simple and complex,* to limit this general decision, *that all our ideas and impressions are resembling.* I observe, that many of our complex ideas never had impressions, that corresponded to them, and that many of our complex impressions never are exactly copied in ideas. I can imagine to myself such a city as the *New Jerusalem,* whose pavement is gold and walls are rubies, tho' I never saw any such. I have seen *Paris;* but shall I affirm I can form such an idea of that city, as will perfectly represent all its streets and houses in their real and just proportions?

I perceive, therefore, that tho' there is in general a great resemblance betwixt our *complex* impressions and ideas, yet the rule is not universally true, that they are exact copies of each other. We may next consider how the case stands with our *simple* perceptions. After the most accurate examination, of which I am capable, I venture to affirm, that the rule here holds without any exception, and that every simple idea has a simple impression, which resembles it; and every simple impression a correspondent idea. That idea of red, which we form in the dark, and that impression, which strikes our eyes in sun-shine, differ only in degree, not in nature. That the case is the same with all our simple impressions and ideas, tis impossible to prove by a particular enumeration of them. Every one may satisfy himself in this point by running over as many as he pleases. But if any one should deny this universal resemblance, I know no way of convincing him, but by desiring him to shew a simple impression, that has not a correspondent idea, or a simple idea, that has not a correspondent impression. If he does not answer this chal-

lenge, as 'tis certain he cannot, we may from his silence and our own observation establish our conclusion.

Thus we find, that all simple ideas and impressions resemble each other; and as the complex are formed from them, we may affirm in general, that these two species of perception are exactly correspondent. Having discover'd this relation, which requires no farther examination, I am curious to find some other of their qualities. Let us consider how they stand with regard to their existence, and which of the impressions and ideas are causes, and which effects.

The *full* examination of this question is the subject of the present treatise; and therefore we shall here content ourselves with establishing one general proposition, *That all our simple ideas in their first appearance are deriv'd from simple impressions, which are correspondent to them, and which they exactly represent.*

In seeking for phænomena to prove this proposition, I find only those of two kinds; but in each kind the phænomena are obvious, numerous, and conclusive. I first make myself certain, by a new review, of what I have already asserted, that every simple impression is attended with a correspondent idea, and every simple idea with a correspondent impression. From this constant conjunction or resembling perceptions I immediately conclude, that there is a great connexion betwixt our correspondent impressions and ideas, and that the existence of the one has a considerable influence upon that of the other. Such a constant conjunction, in such an infinite number of instances, can never arise from chance; but clearly proves a dependence of the impressions on the ideas, or of the ideas on the impressions. That I may know on which side this dependence lies, I consider the order of their *first appearance;* and find by constant experience, that the simple impressions always take the precedence of their correspondent ideas, but never appear in the contrary order. To give a child an idea of scarlet or orange, of sweet or bitter, I present the objects, or in other words, convey to him these impressions; but proceed not so absurdly, as to endeavour to produce the impressions by exciting the ideas. Our ideas upon their appearance produce not their correspondent impressions, nor do we perceive any colour, or feel any sensation merely upon thinking of them. On the other hand we find, that any impressions either of the mind or body is constantly followed by an idea, which resembles it, and is only different in the degrees of force and liveliness. The constant conjunction of our resembling perceptions, is a convincing proof, that the one are the causes of the other; and this priority of the impressions is an equal proof, that our impressions are the causes of our ideas, not our ideas of our impressions.

To confirm this I consider another plain and convincing phænomenon; which is, that where-ever by any accident the faculties, which give rise to any impressions, are obstructed in their operations, as when one is born blind or deaf; not only the impressions are lost, but also their correspondent ideas; so that there never appear in the mind the least traces of either of them. Nor is this only true, where the organs of sensation are entirely destroy'd, but likewise where they have never been put in action to produce a particular impression. We cannot form to ourselves a just idea of the taste of a pine-apple, without having actually tasted it.

There is however one contradictory phænomenon, which may prove, that 'tis not absolutely impossible for ideas to go before their correspondent impressions. I believe it will readily be allow'd, that the several distinct ideas of colours, which enter by the eyes, or those of sounds, which are convey'd by the hearing, are really different from each other, tho' at the same time resembling. Now if this be true of different colours, it must be no less so of the different shades of the same colour, that each of them produces a distinct idea, independent of the rest. For if this shou'd be deny'd, 'tis possible, by the continual gradation of shades, to run a colour insensibly into what is most remote from it; and if you will not allow any of the means to be different, you cannot without absurdity deny the extremes to be the same. Suppose therefore a person to have enjoyed his sight for thirty years, and to have become perfectly well acquainted with colours of all kinds, excepting one particular shade of blue, for instance, which it never has been his fortune to meet with. Let all the different shades of that colour, except that single one, be plac'd before him, descending gradually from the deepest to the lightest; 'tis plain, that he will perceive a blank, where that shade is wanting, and will be sensible, that there is a greater distance in that place betwixt the contiguous colours, than in any other. Now I ask, whether 'tis possible for him, from his own imagination, to supply this deficiency, and raise up to himself the idea of that particular shade, tho' it had never been conveyed to him by his senses? I believe there are few but will be of opinion that he can; and this may serve as a proof, that the simple ideas are not always derived from the correspondent impressions; tho' the instance is so particular and singular, that 'tis scarce worth our observing, and does not merit that for it alone we should alter our general maxim.

But besides this exception, it may not be amiss to remark on this head, that the principle of the priority of impressions to ideas must be understood with another limitation, *viz.* that as our ideas are images of our impressions, so we can form secondary ideas, which are images of the primary; as appears from this very reasoning concerning them. This is not, properly speaking, an exception to the rule so much as an explanation of it. Ideas produce the images of themselves in new ideas; but as the first ideas are supposed to be derived from impressions, it still remains true, that all our simple ideas proceed either mediately or immediately from their correspondent impressions.

This then is the first principle I establish in the science of human nature; nor ought we to despise it because of the simplicity of its appearance. For 'tis remarkable, that the present question concerning the precedency of our impressions or ideas, is the same with what has made so much noise in other terms, when it has been disputed whether there be any *innate ideas*, or whether all ideas be derived from sensation and reflexion. We may observe, that in order to prove the ideas of extension and colour not to be innate, philosophers do nothing but shew, that they are conveyed by our senses. To prove the ideas of passion and desire not to be innate, they observe that we have a preceding experience of these emotions in ourselves. Now if we carefully examine these arguments, we shall find that they prove nothing but that ideas are preceded by other more lively perceptions, from which they are derived, and which they represent. I hope this clear stating of the question will remove all disputes concerning it, and will render this principle of more use in our reasonings, than it seems hitherto to have been.

Section II

Division of the Subject

Since it appears, that our simple impressions are prior to their correspondent ideas, and that the exceptions are very rare, method seems to require we should examine our impressions, before we consider our ideas. Impressions may be divided into two kinds, those of SENSATION and those of REFLEXION. The first kind arises in the soul originally, from unknown causes. The second is derived in a great measure from our ideas, and that in the following order. An impression first strikes upon the senses, and makes us perceive heat or cold, thirst or hunger, pleasure or pain of some kind or other. Of this impression there is a copy taken by the mind, which remains after the impression ceases; and this we call an idea. This idea of pleasure or pain, when it returns upon the soul, produces the new impressions of desire and aversion, hope and fear, which may properly be called impressions of reflexion, because derived from it. These again are copied by the memory and imagination, and become ideas; which perhaps in their turn give rise to other impressions and ideas. So that the impressions of reflexion are only antecedent to their correspondent ideas; but posterior to those of sensation, and deriv'd from them. The examination of our sensations belongs more to anatomists and natural philosophers than to moral; and therefore shall not at present be enter'd upon. And as the impressions of reflexion, *viz.* passions, desires, and emotions, which principally deserve our attention, arise mostly from ideas, 'twill be necessary to reverse that method, which at first sight seems most natural; and in order to explain the nature and principles of the human mind, give a particular account of ideas, before we proceed to impressions. For this reason I have here chosen to begin with ideas.

Part IV

Of the Sceptical and Other Systems of Philosophy

Section II

Of Scepticism with Regard to the Senses

Thus the sceptic still continues to reason and believe, even tho' he asserts, that he cannot defend his reason by reason; and by the same rule he must assent to the principle concerning the existence of body, tho' he cannot pretend by any arguments of philosophy to maintain its veracity. Nature has not left this to his choice, and has doubtless esteem'd it an affair of too great importance to be trusted to our uncertain reasonings and speculations. We may well ask, *What causes induce us to believe in the existence of body?* but 'tis in vain to ask, *Whether there be body or not?* That is a point, which we must take for granted in all our reasonings.

The subject, then, of our present enquiry is concerning the *causes* which induce us to believe in the existence of body: And my reasonings on this head I shall begin with a distinction, which at first sight may seem superfluous, but which will contribute very much to the perfect understanding of what follows. We ought to examine apart those two questions, which are commonly confounded together, *viz.* Why we attribute a CONTINU'D existence to objects, even when they are not present to the senses; and why we suppose them to have an existence DISTINCT from the mind and perception. Under this last head I comprehend their situation as well as relations, their *external* position as well as the *independence* of their existence and operation. These two questions concerning the continu'd and distinct existence of body are intimately connected together. For if the objects of our senses continue to exist, even when they are not perceiv'd, their existence is of course independent of and distinct from the perception; and *vice versa*, if their existence be independent of the perception and distinct from it, they must continue to exist, even tho' they be not perceiv'd. But tho' the decision of the one question decides the other; yet that we may the more easily discover the principles of human nature, from whence the decision arises, we shall carry along with us this distinction, and shall consider whether it be the *senses*, *reason*, or the *imagination*, that produces the opinion of a *continu'd* or of a *distinct* existence. These are the only questions, that are intelligible on the present subject. For as to the notion of external existence, when taken for something specifically different from our perceptions, we have already shewn its absurdity.

To begin with the SENSES, 'tis evident these faculties are incapable of giving rise to the notion of the *continued* existence of their objects, after they no longer appear to the senses. For that is a contradiction in terms, and supposes that the senses continue to operate, even after they have ceas'd all manner of operation. These faculties, therefore, if they have any influence in the present case, must produce the opinion of a distinct, not of a continu'd existence; and in order to that, must present their impressions either as images and representations, or as these very distinct and external existences.

That our senses offer not their impressions as the images of something *distinct,* or *independent,* and *external,* is evident; because they convey to us nothing but a single perception, and never give us the least intimation of any thing beyond. A single perception can never produce the idea of a double existence, but by some inference either of the reason or imagination. When the mind looks farther than what immediately appears to it, its conclusions can never be put to the account of the senses; and it certainly looks farther, when from a single perception it infers a double existence, and supposes the relations of resemblance and causation betwixt them.

If our senses, therefore, suggest any idea of distinct existences, they must convey the impressions as those very existences, by a kind of fallacy and illusion. Upon this head we may observe, that all sensations are felt by the mind, such as they really are, and that when we doubt, whether they present themselves as distinct objects, or as mere impressions, the difficulty is not concerning their nature, but concerning their relations and situation. Now if the senses presented our impressions as external to, and independent of ourselves, both the objects and ourselves must be obvious to our senses, otherwise they cou'd not be compar'd by these faculties. The difficulty, then, is how far we are *ourselves* the objects of our senses.

To begin with the question concerning *external* existence, it may perhaps be said, that setting aside the metaphysics question of the identity of a thinking substance, our own body evidently belongs to us; and as several impressions appear exterior to the body, we suppose them also exterior to ourselves. The paper, on which I write at present, is beyond my hand. The table is beyond the paper. The walls of the chamber beyond the table. And in casting my eye towards the window, I perceive a great extent of fields and buildings beyond my chamber. From all this it may be infer'd, that no other faculty is requir'd, beside the senses, to convince us of the external existence of body. But to prevent this inference, we need only weigh the three following considerations. *First,* That, properly speaking, 'tis not our body we perceive, when we regard our limbs and members, but certain impressions, which enter by the senses; so that the ascribing a real and corporeal existence to these impressions, or to their objects, is an act of the mind as difficult to explain, as that which we examine at present. *Secondly,* Sounds, and tastes, and smells, tho' commonly regarded by the mind as continu'd independent qualities, appear not to have any existence in extension, and consequently cannot appear to the senses as situated externally to the body. The reason, why we ascribe a place to them, shall be consider'd afterwards. *Thirdly,* Even our sight informs us not of distance or outness (so to speak) immediately and without a certain reasoning and experience, as is acknowledg'd by the most rational philosophers.

As to the *independency* of our perceptions on ourselves, this can never be an object of the senses; but any opinion we form concerning it, must be deriv'd from experience and observation: And we shall see afterwards, that our conclusions from experience are far from being favourable to the doctrine of the independency of our perceptions. Mean while we may observe that when we talk of real distinct existences, we have commonly more in our eye their independency than external situation in place, and think an object has a sufficient reality, when its Being is uninterrupted, and independent of the incessant revolutions, which we are conscious of in ourselves.

Thus to resume what I have said concerning the senses; they give us no notion of continu'd existence, because they cannot operate beyond the extent, in which they really operate. They as little produce the opinion of a distinct existence, because they neither can offer it to the mind as represented, nor as original. To offer it as represented, they must present both an object and an image. To make it appear as original, they must convey a falshood; and this falshood must lie in the relations and situation: In order to which they must be able to compare the object with ourselves; and even in that case they do not, nor is it possible they shou'd, deceive us. We may, therefore, conclude with certainty, that the opinion of a continu'd and of a distinct existence never arises from the senses.

To confirm this we may observe, that there are three different kinds of impressions convey'd by the senses. The first are those of the figure, bulk, motion and solidity of bodies. The second those of colours, tastes, smells, sounds, heat and cold. The third are the pains and pleasures, that arise from the application of objects to our bodies, as by the cutting of our flesh with steel, and such like. Both philosophers and the vulgar suppose the first of these to have a distinct continu'd existence. The vulgar only regard the second as on the same footing. Both philosophers and the vulgar, again, esteem the third to be merely perceptions; and consequently interrupted and dependent beings.

Now 'tis evident, that, whatever may be our philosophical opinion, colours, sounds, heat and cold, as far as appears to the senses, exist after the same manner with motion and solidity, and that the difference we make betwixt them in this respect, arises not from the mere perception. So strong is the prejudice for the distinct continu'd existence of the former qualities, that when the contrary opinion is advanc'd by modern philosophers, people imagine they can almost refute it from their feeling and experience, and that their very senses contradict this philosophy. 'Tis also evident, that colours, sounds, &c. are originally on the same footing with the pain that arises from steel, and pleasure that proceeds from a fire; and that the difference betwixt them is founded neither on perception nor reason, but on the imagination. For as they are confest to be, both of them, nothing but perceptions arising from the particular configurations and motions of the parts of body, wherein possibly can their difference consist? Upon the whole, then, we may conclude, that as far as the senses are judges, all perceptions are the same in the manner of their existence.

We may also observe in this instance of sounds and colours, that we can attribute a distinct continu'd existence to objects without ever consulting REASON, or weighing our opinions by any philosophical principles. And indeed, whatever convincing arguments philosophers may fancy they can produce to establish the belief of objects independent of the mind, 'tis obvious these arguments are known but to very few, and that 'tis not by them, that children, peasants, and the greatest part of mankind are induc'd to attribute objects to some impressions, and deny them to others. Accordingly we find, that all the conclusions, which the vulgar form on this head, are directly contrary to those, which are confirm'd by philosophy. For philosophy informs us, that every thing, which

appears to the mind, is nothing but a perception, and is interrupted, and dependent on the mind; whereas the vulgar confound perceptions and objects, and attribute a distinct continu'd existence to the very things they feel or see. This sentiment, then, as it is entirely unreasonable, must proceed from some other faculty than the understanding. To which we may add, that as long as we take our perceptions and objects to be the same, we can never infer the existence of the one from that of the other, nor form any argument from the relation of cause and effect; which is the only one that can assure us of matter of fact. Even after we distinguish our perceptions from our objects, 'twill appear presently, that we are still incapable of reasoning from the existence of one to that of the other: So that upon the whole our reason neither does, nor is it possible it shou'd, upon any supposition, give us an assurance of the continu'd and distinct existence of body. That opinion must be entirely owing to the IMAGINATION: which must now be the subject of our enquiry.

Since all impressions are internal and perishing existences, and appear as such, the notion of their distinct and continu'd existence must arise from a concurrence of some of their qualities with the qualities of the imagination; and since this notion does not extend to all of them, it must arise from certain qualities peculiar to some impressions. 'Twill therefore be easy for us to discover these qualities by a comparison of the impressions, to which we attribute a distinct and continu'd existence, with those, which we regard as internal and perishing.

We may observe, then, that 'tis neither upon account of the involuntariness of certain impressions, as is commonly suppos'd, nor of their superior force and violence, that we attribute to them a reality, and continu'd existence, which we refuse to others, that are voluntary or feeble. For 'tis evident our pains and pleasures, our passions and affections, which we never suppose to have any existence beyond our perception, operate with greater violence, and are equally involuntary, as the impressions of figure and extension, colour and sound, which we suppose to be permanent beings. The heat of a fire, when moderate, is suppos'd to exist in the fire; but the pain, which it causes upon a near approach, is not taken to have any being except in the perception.

These vulgar opinions, then, being rejected, we must search for some other hypothesis, by which we may discover those peculiar qualities in our impressions, which makes us attribute to them a distinct and continu'd existence.

After a little examination, we shall find, that all those objects, to which we attribute a continu'd existence, have a peculiar *constancy,* which distinguishes them from the impressions, whose existence depends upon our perception. Those mountains, and houses, and trees, which lie at present under my eye, have always appear'd to me in the same order; and when I lose sight of them by shutting my eyes or turning my head, I soon after find them return upon me without the least alteration. My bed and table, my books and papers, present themselves in the same uniform manner, and change not upon account of any interruption in my seeing or perceiving them. This is the case with all the impressions, whose objects are suppos'd to have an external existence; and is the case with no other impressions, whether gentle or violent, voluntary or involuntary.

This constancy, however, is not so perfect as not to admit of very considerable exceptions. Bodies often change their position and qualities, and after a little absence or interruption may become hardly knowable. But here 'tis observable, that even in these changes they preserve a *coherence,* and have a regular dependence on each other; which is the foundation of a kind of reasoning from causation, and produces the opinion of their continu'd existence. When I return to my chamber after an hour's absence, I find not my fire in the same situation, in which I left it: But then I am accustom'd in other instances to see a like alteration produc'd in a like time, whether I am present or absent, near or remote. This coherence, therefore, in their changes is one of the characteristics of external objects, as well as their constancy.

Having found that the opinion of the continu'd existence of body depends on the COHERENCE and CONSTANCY of certain impressions, I now proceed to examine after what manner these qualities give rise to so extraordinary an opinion. . . .

Objects have a certain coherence even as they appear to our senses; but this coherence is must greater and more uniform, if we suppose the objects to have a continu'd existence; and as the mind is once in the train of observing an uniformity among objects, it naturally continues, till it renders the uniformity as compleat as possible. The simple supposition of their continu'd existence suffices for this purpose, and gives us a notion of a much greater regularity among objects, than what they have when we look no farther than our senses.

But whatever force we may ascribe to this principle, I am afraid 'tis too weak to support alone so vast an edifice, as is that of the continu'd existence of all external bodies; and that we must join the *constancy* of their appearance to the *coherence,* in order to give a satisfactory account of that opinion. As the explication of this will lead me into a considerable compass of very profound reasoning; I think it proper, in order to avoid confusion, to give a short sketch or abridgment of my system, and afterwards draw out all its parts in their full compass. This inference from the constancy of our perceptions, like the precedent from their coherence, gives rise to the opinion of the *continu'd* existence of body, which is prior to that of its *distinct* existence, and produces that latter principle.

When we have been accustom'd to observe a constancy in certain impressions, and have found, that the perception of the sun or ocean, for instance, returns upon us after an absence or annihilation with like parts and in a like order, as at its first appearance, we are not apt to regard these interrupted perceptions as different, (which they really are) but on the contrary consider them as individually the same, upon account of their resemblance. But as this interruption of their existence is contrary to their perfect identity, and make us regard the first impression as annihilated, and the second as newly created, we find ourselves somewhat at a loss, and are involv'd in a kind of contradiction. In order to free ourselves from this difficulty, we disguise, as much as possible, the interruption, or rather remove it entirely, by supposing that these interrupted perceptions are connected by a real existence, of which we are insensible. This supposition, or idea of continu'd existence, acquires a force and vivacity from the memory of these broken impressions, and from that propensity, which they give us, to suppose them the same; and according to the precedent reasoning, the very essence of belief consists in the force and vivacity of the conception. . . .

'Tis indeed evident, that as the vulgar *suppose* their perceptions to be their only objects, and at the same time *believe* the continu'd existence of matter, we must account for the origin of the belief upon that supposition. Now upon that supposition, 'tis a false opinion that any of our objects, or perceptions, are identically the same after an interruption; and consequently the opinion of their identity can never arise from reason, but must arise from the imagination. The imagination is seduc'd into such an opinion only by means of the resemblance of certain perceptions; since we find they are only our resembling perceptions, which we have a propension to suppose the same. This propension to bestow an identity on our resembling perceptions, produces the fiction of a continu'd existence; since that fiction, as well as the identity, is really false, as is acknowledg'd by all philosophers, and has no other effect than to remedy the interruption of our perceptions, which is the only circumstance that is contrary to their identity. . . .

The natural consequence of this reasoning shou'd be, that our perceptions have no more a continu'd than an independent existence; and indeed philosophers have so far run into this opinion, that they change their system, and distinguish, (as we shall do for the future) betwixt perceptions and objects, of which the former are suppos'd to be interrupted, and perishing, and different at every different return; the latter to be uninterrupted, and to preserve a continu'd existence and identity. But however philosophical this new system may be esteem'd, I assert that 'tis only a palliative remedy, and that it contains all the difficulties of the vulgar system, with some others, that are peculiar to itself. There are no principles either of the understanding or fancy, which lead us directly to embrace this opinion of the double existence of perceptions and objects, nor can we arrive at it but by passing thro' the common hypothesis of the identity and continuance of our interrupted perceptions. Were we not first persuaded, that our perceptions are our only objects, and continue to exist even when they no longer make their appearance to the senses, we shou'd never be led to think, that our perceptions and objects are different, and that our objects alone

preserve a continu'd existence. The latter hypothesis has no primary recommendation either to reason or the imagination, but acquires all its influence on the imagination from the former.

Section VI

Of Personal Identity

There are some philosophers, who imagine we are every moment intimately conscious of what we call our SELF; that we feel its existence and its continuance in existence; and are certain, beyond the evidence of a demonstration, both of its perfect identity and simplicity. The strongest sensation, the most violent passion, say they, instead of distracting us from this view, only fix it the more intensely, and make us consider their influence on *self* either by their pain or pleasure. To attempt a farther proof of this were to weaken its evidence; since no proof can be deriv'd from any fact, of which we are so intimately conscious; nor is there any thing, of which we can be certain, if we doubt of this.

Unluckily all these positive assertions are contrary to that very experience, which is pleaded for them, nor have we any idea of *self*, after the manner it is here explain'd. For from what impression cou'd this idea be deriv'd? This question 'tis impossible to answer without a manifest contradiction and absurdity; and yet 'tis a question, which must necessarily be answer'd, if we wou'd have the idea of self pass for clear and intelligible. It must be some one impression, that gives rise to every real idea. But self or person is not any one impression, but that to which our several impressions and ideas are suppos'd to have a reference. If any impression gives rise to the idea of self, that impression must continue invariably the same, thro' the whole course of our lives; since self is suppos'd to exist after that manner. But there is no impression constant and invariable . . . and pleasure, grief and joy, passions and sensations succeed each other, and never all exist at the same time. It cannot, therefore, be from any of these impressions, or from any other, that the idea of self is deriv'd; and consequently there is no such idea.

But farther, what must become of all our particular perceptions upon this hypothesis? All these are different, and distinguishable, and separable from each other, and may be separately consider'd, and may exist separately, and have no need of any thing to support their existence. After what manner, therefore, do they belong to self; and how are they connected with it? For my part, when I enter most intimately into what I call *myself*, I always stumble on some particular perception or other, of heat or cold, light or shade, love or hatred, pain or pleasure. I never can catch *myself* at any time without a perception, and never can observe any thing but the perception. When my perceptions are remov'd for any time, as by sound sleep; so long am I insensible of *myself*, and may truly be said not to exist. And were all my perceptions remov'd by death, and cou'd I neither think, nor feel, nor see, nor love, nor hate after the dissolution of my body, I shou'd be entirely annihilated, nor do I conceive what is farther requisite to make me a perfect non-entity. If any one upon serious and unprejudic'd reflexion, thinks he has a different notion of *himself*, I must confess I can reason no longer with him. All I can allow him is, that he may be in the right as well as well as I, and that we are essentially different in this particular. He may, perhaps, perceive something simple and continu'd, which he calls *himself*; tho' I am certain there is no such principle in me.

But setting aside some metaphysicians of this kind, I may venture to affirm of the rest of mankind, that they are nothing but a bundle or collection of different perceptions, which succeed each other with an inconceivable rapidity, and are in a perpetual flux and movement. Our eyes cannot turn in their sockets without varying our perceptions. Our thought is still more variable than our sight; and all our other senses and faculties contribute to this change; nor is there any single power of the soul, which remains unalterably the same, perhaps for one moment. The mind is a kind of theatre, where several perceptions successively make their appearance; pass, re-pass, glide away, and mingle in an infinite variety of postures and situations. There is properly no *simplicity* in it at one time, nor *identity* in different; whatever natural propension we may have to imagine that simplicity and identity. The comparison of the theatre must not mislead us. They are the successive perceptions only, that constitute the mind; nor have we the most distant notion of the place, where these scenes are represented, or of the materials, of which it is compos'd. . . .

The identity, which we ascribe to the mind of man, is only a fictitious one, and of a like kind with that which we ascribe to vegetables and animal bodies. It cannot, therefore, have a different origin, but must proceed from a like operation of the imagination upon like objects.

But lest this argument shou'd not convince the reader; tho' in my opinion perfectly decisive; let him weigh the following reasoning, which is still closer and more immediate. 'Tis evident, that the identity, which we attribute to the human mind, however perfect we may imagine it to be, is not able to run the several different perceptions into one, and make them lose their characters of distinction and difference, which are essential to them. 'Tis still true, that every distinct perception, which enters into the composition of the mind, is a distinct existence, and is different, and distinguishable, and separable from every other perception, either contemporary or successive. But, as, notwithstanding this distinction and separability, we suppose the whole train of perceptions to be united by identity, a question naturally arises concerning this relation of identity; whether it be something that really binds our several perceptions together, or only associates their ideas in the imagination. That is, in other words, whether in pronouncing concerning the identity of a person, we observe some real bond among his perceptions, or only feel one among the ideas we form of them. This question we might easily decide, if we wou'd recollect what has been already prov'd at large, that the understanding never observes any real connexion among objects, and that even the union of cause and effect, when strictly examin'd resolves itself into a customary association of ideas. For from thence it evidently follows, that identity is nothing really belonging to these different perceptions, and uniting them together; but is merely a quality, which we attribute to them, because of the union of their ideas in the imagination, when we reflect upon them. Now the only qualities, which can give ideas an union in the imagination, are these three relations abovemention'd. These are the uniting principles in the ideal world, and without them every distinct object is separable by the mind, and may be separately consider'd, and appears not to have any more connexion with any other object, than if disjoin'd by the greatest difference and remoteness. 'Tis, therefore, on some of these three relations of resemblance, contiguity and causation, that identity depends; and as the very essence of these relations consists in their producing an easy transition of ideas; it follows, that our notions of personal identity, proceed entirely from the smooth and uninterrupted progress of the thought along a train of connected ideas, according to the principles above-explain'd. . . .

Can I be sure, that in leaving all establish'd opinions I am following truth; and by what criterion shall I distinguish her, even if fortune shou'd at last guide me on her foot-steps? After the most accurate and exact of my reasonings, I can give no reason why I shou'd assent to it; and feel nothing but a *strong* propensity to consider objects *strongly* in that view, under which they appear to me. Experience is a principle, which instructs me in the several conjunctions of objects for the past. Habit is another principle, which determines me to expect the same for the future; and both of them conspiring to operate upon the imagination, make me form certain ideas in a more intense and lively manner, than others, which are not attended with the same advantages. Without this quality, by which the mind enlivens some ideas beyond others (which seemingly is so trivial, and so little founded on reason) we cou'd never assent to any argument, nor carry our view beyond those few objects which are present to our senses. Nay, even to these objects we cou'd never attribute any existence, but what was dependent on the senses; and must comprehend them entirely in that succession of perceptions, which constitutes our self or person. Nay father, even with relation to that succession, we cou'd only admit of those perceptions, which are immediately present to our consciousness, nor cou'd those lively images, with which the memory presents us, be ever receiv'd as true pictures of past perceptions. The memory, senses, and understanding are, therefore, all of them founded on the imagination, or the vivacity of our ideas. . . .

The *intense* view of these manifold contradictions and imperfections in human reason has so wrought upon me, and heated my brain, that I am ready to reject all belief and reasoning, and can look upon no opinion even as more probable or likely than another. Where am I, or what? From what causes do I derive my existence, and to what condition shall I return? Whose favour shall I court, and whose anger must I dread? What beings surround me? and on whom have I any influence, or who have any influence on me? I am confounded with all these questions, and begin to fancy myself in the most deplorable condition imaginable, inviron'd with the deepest darkness, and utterly depriv'd of the use of every member and faculty.

Most fortunately it happens, that since reason is incapable of dispelling these clouds, nature herself suffices to that purpose, and cures me of this philosophical melancholy and delirium, either by relaxing this bent of mind, or by some avocation, and lively impression of my senses, which obliterate all these chimeras. I dine, I play a game of back-gammon, I converse, and am merry with my friends; and when after three or four hours' amusement, I wou'd return to these speculations, they appear so cold, and strain'd, and ridiculous, that I cannot find in my heart to enter into them any farther.

APPENDIX

There is nothing I wou'd more willingly lay hold of, than an opportunity of confessing my errors; and shou'd esteem such a return to truth and reason to be more honourable than the most unerring judgment. A man, who is free from mistakes, can pretend to no praises, except from the justness of his understanding: But a man, who corrects his mistakes, shews at once the justness of his understanding, and the candour and ingenuity of his temper. I have not yet been so fortunate as to discover any very considerable mistakes in the reasonings deliver'd in the preceding volumes, except on one article: But I have found by experience, that some of my expressions have not been so well chosen, as to guard against all mistakes in the readers; and 'tis chiefly to remedy this defect, I have subjoin'd the following appendix. . . .

I had entertain'd some hopes, that however deficient our theory of the intellectual world might be, it wou'd be free from those contradictions, and absurdities, which seem to attend every explication, that human reason can give of the material world. But upon a more strict review of the section concerning *personal identity,* I find myself involv'd in such a labyrinth, that, I must confess, I neither know how to correct my former opinions, nor how to render them consistent. If this be not a good *general* reason for scepticism, 'tis at least a sufficient one (if I were not already abundantly supplied) for me to entertain a difference and modesty in all my decisions. I shall propose the arguments on both sides, beginning with those that induc'd me to deny the strict and proper identity and simplicity of a self or thinking being.

When we talk of *self* or *substance,* we must have an idea annex'd to these terms, otherwise they are altogether unintelligible. Every idea is deriv'd from preceding impressions; and we have no impression of self or substance, as something simple and individual. We have, therefore, no idea of them in that sense.

Whatever is distinct, is distinguishable; and whatever is distinguishable, is separable by the thought or imagination. All perceptions are distinct. They are, therefore, distinguishable, and separable, and may be conceiv'd as separately existent, and may exist separately, without any contradiction or absurdity.

When I view this table and that chimney, nothing is present to me but particular perceptions, which are of a like nature will all the other perceptions. This is the doctrine of philosophers. But this table, which is present to me, and that chimney, may and do exist separately. This is the doctrine of the vulgar, and implies no contradiction. There is no contradiction, therefore, in extending the same doctrine to all the perceptions.

In general, the following reasoning seems satisfactory. All ideas are borrow'd from preceding perceptions. Our ideas of objects, therefore, are deriv'd from that source. Consequently no proposition can be intelligible or consistent with regard to objects, which is not so with regard to perceptions. But 'tis intelligible and consistent to say, that objects exist distinct and independent, without any common *simple* substance or subject of inhesion. This proposition, therefore, can never be absurd with regard to perceptions.

When I turn my reflexion on *myself,* I never can perceive this *self* without some one or more perceptions; nor can I ever perceive any thing but the perceptions. 'Tis the composition of these, therefore, which forms the self.

We can conceive a thinking being to have either many or few perceptions. Suppose the mind to be reduc'd even below the life of an oyster. Suppose it to have only one perception, as of thirst or hunger. Consider it in that situation. Do you conceive any thing but merely that perception? Have you any notion of *self* or *substance?* If not, the addition of other perceptions can never give you that notion.

The annihilation, which some people suppose to follow upon death, and which entirely destroys this self, is nothing but an extinction of all particular perceptions; love and hatred, pain and pleasure, thought and sensation. These therefore must be the same with self; since the one cannot survive the other.

Is *self* the same with *substance?* If it be, how can that question have place, concerning the subsistence of self, under a change of substance? If they be distinct, what is the difference betwixt them? For my part, I have a notion of neither, when conceiv'd distinct from particular perceptions.

Philosophers begin to be reconcil'd to the principle, *that we have no idea of external substance, distinct from the ideas of particular qualities.* This must pave the way for a like principle with regard to the mind, *that we have no notion of it, distinct from the particular perceptions.*

So far I seem to be attended with sufficient evidence. But having thus loosen'd all our particular perceptions, when I proceed to explain the principle of connexion, which binds them together, and makes us attribute to them a real simplicity and identity; I am sensible, that my account is very defective, and that nothing but the seeming evidence of the precedent reasonings cou'd have induc'd me to receive it. If perceptions are distinct existences, they form a whole only by being connected together. But no connexions among distinct existences are ever discoverable by human understanding. We only *feel* a connexion or determination of the thought, to pass from one object to another. It follows, therefore, that the thought alone finds personal identity, when reflecting on the train of past perceptions, that compose a mind, the ideas of them are felt to be connected together, and naturally introduce each other. However extraordinary this conclusion may seem, it need not surprize us. Most philosophers seem inclin'd to think, that personal identity *arises* from consciousness; and consciousness is nothing but a reflected thought or perception. The present philosophy, therefore, has so far a promising aspect. But all my hopes vanish, when I come to explain the principles, that unite our successive perceptions in our thought or consciousness. I cannot discover any theory, which gives me satisfaction on this head.

In short there are two principles, which I cannot render consistent; nor is it in my power to renounce either of them, viz. *that all our distinct perceptions are distinct existences*, and *that the mind never perceives any real connexion among distinct existences*.

Did our perceptions either inhere in something simple and individual, or did the mind perceive some real connexion among them, there wou'd be no difficulty in the case. For my part, I must plead the privilege of a sceptic, and confess, that this difficulty is too hard for my understanding. I pretend not, however, to pronounce it absolutely insuperable. Others, perhaps, or myself, upon more mature reflexions, may discover some hypothesis, that will reconcile those contradictions.

STUDY QUESTIONS: HUME, A TREATISE OF HUMAN NATURE

1. What is the relationship between ideas and impressions?
2. How does Hume classify the perceptions of the mind?
3. Are we aware of anything else besides our own perceptions, according to Hume? Why?
4. How does Hume argue that our belief in the continued and distinct existence of external objects cannot be justified?
5. How does he explain the origin of that belief?
6. According to Hume's view, why would the idea of the self have to be derived from an impression?
7. What does Hume mean when he says he never catches himself without a perception? What is the importance of this?
8. What is the origin of our notion of personal identity, according to Hume?
9. When Hume is confounded by these questions, what does he do, and what is the result? Why does he mention this point?

Philosophical Bridges: Hume's Influence

We can discern at least four aspects of Hume's epistemological work: Empiricism, skepticism, naturalism, and noncognitivism. Each of these aspects has informed and inspired different philosophical traditions.

EMPIRICISM

The great British Empiricist of the nineteenth century, John Stuart Mill, knew surprisingly little of Hume's work. However, after 1874, when T. H. Green and T. H. Grose published a new edition of Hume's works, Hume became more widely known, and Green himself wrote *Introduction to Hume's Treatise* (1874). British philosophy at the time was largely Hegelian, and Hume's thinking appealed to the dominant idealistic strain. However, T. H. Huxley wrote a book, *Hume* (1879), in which he commends the Scottish thinker more for his skepticism.

Hume's thoroughgoing and radical Empiricism was a vital and direct influence on twentieth-century logical positivism, especially in the form advanced by A. J. Ayer in his work *Language, Truth and Logic*. What we now call Hume's fork, his division of judgments into those of ideas and those of matters of fact, foreshadows the logical positivist's claim that all statements are either analytic tautologies or based on observation. Like Hume himself, the positivists employed the distinction to argue against the apparently extravagant claims of metaphysics.

The early logical positivists, such as Carnap, also thought, like Hume, that we can be acquainted directly only with sense impressions, and, as a consequence, they attempted to show how the concept of an external object can be constructed out of simple sense impressions, much as Hume did.

SKEPTICISM

Hume's skeptical analysis of concepts has been most influential in the case of causation. How can we understand causation without appealing to the idea of a necessary connection between events or without the notion of natural necessity? Can we understand causation adequately in terms of mere regularities, as Hume suggests? These Hume-inspired questions have generated much debate in the twentieth century, some of which is summarized in J. L. Mackie's *Cement of the Universe* (1974). Furthermore, Hume's skepticism concerning induction has also generated a huge amount of literature in the twentieth century mostly dedicated to trying to answer Hume's argument that inductive reasoning cannot be justified. For example, in *Matters of Metaphysics* (1991), D. H. Mellor argues that induction is a reliable form of inference precisely because induction shows it to be so.

In the eighteenth century, Hume's skepticism was felt most immediately in the area of religion. He challenged vigorously British deism by showing that reason could not support even such a minimalist version of religious belief.

NATURALISM

In the case of Hume, 'naturalism' means roughly the thesis that beliefs that cannot be justified empirically or rationally nevertheless can be explained naturally. It is the attempt to replace justification with explanation. Hume's naturalism became a powerful philosophical strategy even before Darwin's theory of natural selection (1859). Hume tries to explain naturally our belief in external objects, causal connections, and the self, as well as religious and moral beliefs. This kind of program has appealed to radical Empiricists, who think that the request for the justification of basic beliefs is impossible to fulfill, and to pragmatists, who think that the request is theoretically redundant. Radical Empiricists, such as W. V. O. Quine (1908–2002), argue that our beliefs are underdetermined by sense experience and, hence, cannot be justified. Pragmatists, such as John Dewey (1859–1952), argue that the traditional conception of justification is redundant because it is divorced from practice. Both Dewey and Quine conclude that our beliefs should be explained rather than justified and that epistemological problems are really naturalistic. Like Hume, Dewey employs a similar analysis to morality.

NONCOGNITIVISM

During the nineteenth century, Hume's influence also spread in continental Europe. He had lived in France on two occasions, and his many friends in the country included the Enlightenment thinkers Diderot, d'Alembert, and the Romantic philosopher Rousseau. Hume's emphasis on the nonrational aspects of human nature and his arguments against Rationalism were an influence on Rousseau, who was briefly friends with Hume. Like Rousseau, Hume's anticognitivism was a forerunner to nineteenth-century Romanticism.

As an aside, it is worth noting that the Scottish Enlightenment, which Hume animated, was a conservative and skeptical movement, especially in comparison with prerevolutionary France. Other Scottish philosophers of the period include Francis Hutcheson (1694–1746), Adam Smith (1723–1790), Thomas Reid (1710–1796), and James Beattie (1735–1802).

Hume's naturalistic and noncognitive explanation of morality in terms of sentiments has been especially influential in the twentieth century. For instance, there are meta-ethical, noncognitivist theories of moral language, such as Stevenson's emotivism and R. M. Hare's prescriptivism, both of which rely on Hume's famous is/ought distinction. Hume has also inspired J. L. Mackie's error theory (in *Ethics: Inventing Right and Wrong*), which argues that all moral claims about the world are, strictly speaking, false.

However, in the final analysis, one of the most significant impacts of Hume's work was on Kant, who claimed that he had been awoken from his dogmatic slumbers by reading Hume, and who tried to take philosophy in a new direction in order to reply to Hume.

BIBLIOGRAPHY

GENERAL
Bennett, J., *Central Themes; Locke, Berkeley, Hume*, Oxford University Press, 1971
Woolhouse, R. S., *The Empiricists*, Oxford University Press, 1988

BACON
Primary
Bacon: Works, ed. Brian Vickers, Oxford University Press, 1996
The Great Instauration and *Novum Organum*, in *Francis Bacon: A Selection of His Works*, ed. Sidney Warhaft, Odyssey Press, 1965

Secondary
Anderson, F. H., *The Philosophy of Francis Bacon*, University of Chicago Press, 1948
Quinton, Anthony, *Francis Bacon*, Oxford University Press, 1980
Whitney, Charles, *Francis Bacon and Modernity*, Yale University Press, 1986

HOBBES
Primary
The Leviathan, ed. J. C. A. Gaskin, Oxford University Press, 1996
De Cive, in *Man and Citizen*, ed. B. Gert, Hackett, 1991

Secondary
Hampton, Jean, *Hobbes and the Social Contract Tradition*, Cambridge University Press, 1986

Martinich, A. P., *Thomas Hobbes*, St. Martin's, 1997
Peters, R. S., *Hobbes*, Penguin, 1967
Sorrel, Tom, *Hobbes, Arguments of the Philosophers*, Routledge & Kegan Paul, 1986
Sorrel, Tom, *The Cambridge Companion to Hobbes*, Cambridge University Press, 1996
Watkins, J. W. N., *Hobbes' System of Ideas*, London, 1973

LOCKE
Primary
An Essay Concerning Human Understanding, ed. P. H. Nidditch, Clarendon Press, 1975
A Treatise Concerning the True Original Extent and End of Civil Government, ed. Peter Laslett, Cambridge University Press, 1967

Secondary
Ayers, M., *Locke*, 2 vols., Routledge, 1991
Chappell, V., *The Cambridge Companion to Locke*, Cambridge University Press, 1994
Dunn, J., *Locke*, Oxford University Press, 1984
Jolley, N., *Locke: His Philosophical Thought*, Oxford University Press, 1999
Mackie, John, *Problems from Locke*, Oxford University Press, 1976
Rogers, G. A., *Locke's Philosophy: Content and Context*, Oxford University Press, 1994
Thomson, Garrett, *On Locke*, Wadsworth, 2001
Woolhouse, R. S., *Locke*, Brighton, 1983
Yolton, J., *Locke: An Introduction*, Oxford University Press, 1985

BERKELEY

Primary

Berkeley: Philosophical Works, ed. Michael Ayers, Dent, 1975

De Motu, The Works of George Berkeley, vol. 4, ed. A. A. Luce, T. E. Jessop, T. Nelson & Son Ltd., 1952

An Essay Towards a New Theory of Vision, Rowman & Littlefield, 1975

Three Dialogues Between Hylas and Philonous, ed. C. Turbayne, Liberal Arts Press, 1954

A Treatise Concerning the Principles of Human Knowledge, ed. Howard Robinson, Oxford University Press, 1996

Secondary

Dancy, Jonathan, *Berkeley: An Introduction*, Basil Blackwell, 1987

Foster, John, and Robinson, Howard, (eds.), *Essays on Berkeley*, Oxford University Press, 1985

Grayling, A. C., *Berkeley: The Central Arguments*, Duckworth, 1986

Pitcher, George, *Berkeley*, Routledge, 1977

Tipton, I. C., *Berkeley: The Philosophy of Immaterialism*, Methuen, 1974

Urmson, J. O., *Berkeley*, Oxford University Press, 1982

Warnock, G. J., *Berkeley*, Pelican, 1953

Winkler, K. P., *Berkeley: An Interpretation*, Oxford University Press, 1989

HUME

Primary

Dialogues Concerning Natural Religion, ed. H. D. Aiken, Hafner Publishing, 1972

An Enquiry Concerning Human Understanding, ed. Tom Beauchamp, Clarendon, 2000

The Natural History of Religion, ed. H. E. Root, Stanford University Press, 1967

A Treatise on Human Nature, ed. L. A. Selby-Bigge, Clarendon Press, 1973

Secondary

Baier, Annette, *A Progress of Sentiments: Reflections on Hume's Treatise*, Harvard University Press, 1991

Beauchamp, Tom, and Rosenburg R., *Hume and the Problem of Causation*, Oxford University Press, 1981

Fogelin, R., *Hume's Scepticism in the Treatise of Human Nature*, Routledge, 1985

Passmore, John, *Hume's Intentions*, Cambridge University Press, 1952

Pears, David, *Hume's System*, Oxford University Press, 1990

Penelhum, T., *Hume*, St Martin's, 1975

Quinton, A., *Hume*, Routledge, 1999

Strawson, G., *The Secret Connexion: Realism and David Hume*, Oxford University Press, 1989

Stroud, Barry, *Hume, Arguments of the Philosophers*, Routledge, 1977

SECTION IV

◇ THE ENLIGHTENMENT ◇
PHILOSOPHERS

◇ PROLOGUE

The Enlightenment of the late eighteenth century developed, primarily in France, from the attempt to extend the philosophical and scientific principles of the modern period to human social, political, and moral life. It derives its inspiration mostly from Locke and Newton. It is marked mainly by a belief in the ideals of progress, such as liberty of thought, social reform, and material betterment. These ideals fueled an interest in history as a story of cultural progress. The Enlightenment is also characterized by a rejection of authority, especially that of the Church, and by an attempt to understand human values in superstition and nontheological terms.

   These ideas inspired a generation of prolific French writers. For example, Montesquieu (1689–1755) studied different forms of government and legal systems, and argued that political liberty requires the separation of legislative, judicial, and executive powers. Condillac (1715–1780) adapted the Empiricist ideas of Locke to argue against the metaphysical systems of Spinoza and Leibniz. In *Man, a Machine*, La Mettrie (1709–1751) argued for a materialist view of the mind. One of the greatest works of the period was the *Encyclopedia*, edited by Diderot and d'Alembert which appeared between 1751 and 1780. The complete first edition consisted of 35 volumes. As well as functioning as a modern encyclopedia, the work contained social commentaries opposing the Church and the French establishment. However, the most eloquent and vociferous voice of the French Enlightenment was Voltaire, whose witty works defend the ideal of political liberty and advocate the idea of intellectual, scientific, and economic progress. Around 1751, after the suppression of the *Encyclopedia*, Voltaire began to openly attack the Catholic Church as an institution.

   In contrast, the thought of Rousseau points beyond the Enlightenment toward the Romanticism of the nineteenth century. Like Hume, Rousseau stressed the feeling side of human nature, and, unlike Voltaire, he saw civilization as the source of degeneration.

Rousseau praised nature and upheld a natural religion, even though he criticized religious dogmatism. His main work, the *Social Contract*, inspired the French Revolution.

In some ways, the work of Kant can be considered as the pinnacle of the modern period. In the *Critique of Pure Reason* (1781), Kant tries to identify and diagnose the conflicts between Rationalism and Empiricism, and produces a nonempiricist critique of rationalism. By defining the limits of theoretical reason, he opens the way for a moral and political theory based on the freedom of the will. He defines 'enlightenment' as 'man's release from his self-imposed tutelage. Tutelage is man's inability to make use of his understanding without direction from another.'

By this time, the long dramatic battle, pioneered by Galileo, Descartes, and Bacon, between modern science and medieval Scholastic philosophy was over. The Industrial age was beginning, and Kant's grand synthesis was itself to come under critical scrutiny.

François Voltaire (1694–1778)

Biographical History

Born François Marie Arouet, Voltaire was a very famous and prolific man of letters, whose literary and philosophical works epitomized the spirit of the Enlightenment. He composed many successful plays, poems, several works in history, and many essays. He was an astute businessman who became a millionaire, and he dabbled in science. As a young man, he visited England from 1726 to 1729, where he drew inspiration from the works of Locke and Newton and from the comparative liberty of English society. In 1738, he published the *Philosophy of Newton*, which was influential in replacing Descartes' physics with Newton's in France. After the great earthquake in Lisbon in 1755, Voltaire wrote his novel *Candide*, which, through the many misfortunes of the ever-optimistic Dr. Pangloss, satirizes Leibniz's claim that this is the best of all possible worlds. In his work of 1756, *Essay on the Manners and Spirit of Nations*, he describes the history of world civilizations. While exiled in Geneva, he published, in 1764, the popular *Dictionary of Philosophy*. In 1778, the dying Voltaire returned from exile to Paris, to great public acclaim.

Philosophical Overview

Voltaire was the leading spokesperson for the French Enlightenment in part because of the wide scope of his work. He was a poet, a playwright, an essayist, a historian, a political commentator, and many other things, as well as a philosopher. In many of these fields, he was preeminent.

As a philosopher, he wrote on Pascal, Descartes, Spinoza, Leibniz, Malebranche, and Newton, as well as Locke, whom he respected most. Voltaire believed in God and thought that his existence can be proved by the argument of design. However, he was a deist: the deity is infinite, and we cannot understand him. Nevertheless, Voltaire was a materialist. He did not believe in the existence of a soul distinct from matter. His view of physics was largely defined by Newton, whose system he supported against Descartes' physics.

Much of his philosophical work tends to focus on two themes: religion and politics. Regarding religion, he was strongly against standard religious belief and practice, which he regarded as superstitious, fanatic, and dogmatic. In contrast, Voltaire's conception of the ideal religion has two essential elements: the adoration of the Supreme Being and a simple, clear moral teaching that accords with reason.

Voltaire thought of good and bad primarily in social terms, even though he also believed that there is a natural moral law applicable to all persons that we can grasp through reason. The aim of politics is defined by the good and happiness of the whole community. Voltaire had two main concerns regarding this goal. First, it requires progress. Social and material progress can only come about through intellectual progress and freedom, primarily freedom of thought and cultural expression. Voltaire thought that an enlightened elite class would have a fundamental role in combating the superstition and fear that suppressed progress. At the same time, he was against all forms of political tyranny.

Second, Voltaire was concerned to define the type of social organization that would best promote such progress. Yet, it seems that he never settled on a definite answer. He never developed an overarching political theory as Rousseau did. Much of his political thought consisted in advocating reforms directed toward justice and liberty, but within existing political frameworks. He seemed willing to accept the kind of strong monarchy that existed in France at the time, as long as it was an enlightened rule. He also favored the radical republican constitution of Geneva, where he resided in exile.

DICTIONARY OF PHILOSOPHY

Voltaire's *Dictionary of Philosophy* consists of alphabetically organized subject headings. Many of the entries are hard-hitting commentaries that emphasize the absurdity of religious superstition. However, Voltaire was not an atheist. Like Rousseau, he believed in natural as opposed to revealed religion. For this reason, in his *Dictionary,* he says, 'Almost everything that goes beyond the adoration of a Supreme Being, and submitting one's heart to his eternal orders, is superstition.' Unlike Rousseau, Voltaire was a critic of the Church and orthodox dogma.

ÂME · SOUL

We call soul that which animates. Since our intelligence is limited, we know hardly anything more about the subject. Three-fourths of mankind go no further and don't worry about this thinking being; the other fourth look for it; no one has found it or will find it.

Poor pedant, you see a plant that vegetates, and you say *vegetation,* or even *vegetative soul.* You notice that bodies have and produce motion, and you say *force;* you see your hunting dog learn his craft from you, and you exclaim *instinct, sensitive soul;* you have complex ideas, and you say *spirit.*

But, please, what do you understand by these words? This flower vegetates, but is there any real being called *vegetation?* This body pushes another, but does it possess within itself a distinct being called *force?* This dog brings you a partridge, but is there a being called *instinct?* Wouldn't you laugh at a logician (had he been teacher to Alexander) who told you: "All animals live, therefore there is in them a being, a substantial form, which is life"?

If a tulip could talk and were to tell you: "My vegetation and I are two beings evidently joined together," wouldn't you laugh at the tulip?

Voltaire, from *Philosophical Dictionary* translated by Peter Gay, 1962.

Let's see first of all what you know and what you are sure of: that you walk with your feet, that you digest with your stomach, that you feel with your whole body, and that you think with your head. Let's see if your reason could have given you enough insight by itself to conclude, without supernatural aid, that you have a soul.

The opinion we should doubtless adopt is that the soul is an immaterial being; but certainly you can't imagine what that immaterial being is. "No," the scholars reply, "but we know that its nature is to think." And how do you know that? "We know it because it thinks." Oh, scholars! I'm afraid that you are as ignorant as Epicurus: the nature of the stone is to fall, because it falls; but I ask you what makes it fall.

BAPTÉME · BAPTISM

Another Addition

What a strange idea, that a pot of water should wash away all crimes—as though you were cleaning clothes! Today all children are baptized because an idea no less absurd supposes them all to be criminals; here they are, all saved until they reach the age of reason and can become guilty. Cut their throats, then, as quickly as possible to assure them paradise. This is so just a conclusion that there was once a devout sect that went about poisoning and killing all newly baptized infants. These pietists reasoned perfectly. They said: "We do these little innocents the greatest possible favor; we prevent them from being wicked and unhappy in this life, and we give them eternal life."

(From M. l'abbé Nicaise)

ÉGALITÉ · EQUALITY

On our miserable globe it is impossible for men living in society not to be divided into two classes, one the rich who command, the other the poor who serve; and these two subdivide themselves into a thousand, and these thousand have still several further divisions.

All the poor are not absolutely miserable. Most of them are born in that condition, and continual labor prevents them from feeling their situation too keenly; but when they do feel it, then you see wars, like that of the popular party against the senatorial party in Rome, or the peasant wars in Germany, England, and France. Sooner or later all these wars end with the enslavement of the people, because the powerful have money, and within a state money is the master of all: I say within a state, because the same is not true between nation and nation. The nation that puts the sword to the best use will always subjugate the one that has more gold and less courage.

Every man is born with a powerful urge toward domination, wealth, and pleasures, and with a strong taste for laziness; consequently every man would like the money and the women or the girls of others, to be their master, to subject them to all his caprices, and to do nothing, or at least to do only the very agreeable things. Obviously, with such benign dispositions it is just as impossible for men to be equal as it is impossible for two preachers or two professors of theology not to be jealous of one another.

Mankind, such as it is, cannot go on existing unless there is an infinite number of useful men who possess nothing at all; for surely a man who is well off will not leave his land to labor on yours; and if you need a pair of shoes, it won't be a *maître des requêtes* who'll make them for you. Thus, equality is at once the most natural and at the same time the most chimerical of things.

ENFER · HELL

Not long ago a good and honest Huguenot minister preached and wrote that the damned would one day be pardoned, that sin and suffering must be commensurate, and that the slip of a moment cannot deserve an infinite punishment. His colleagues, the preachers, dismissed this indulgent judge; one of them told him: "My friend, I no more believe in eternal hell than you do; but it is a good thing for your servant, your tailor, and even your lawyer to believe in it."

FANATISME · FANATICISM

Fanaticism is to superstition what delirium is to fever and rage to anger. The man visited by ecstasies and visions, who takes dreams for realities and his fancies for prophecies, is an enthusiast; the man who supports his madness with murder is a fanatic.

Once fanaticism has corrupted a mind, the malady is almost incurable.

The only remedy for this epidemic malady is the philosophical spirit which, spread gradually, at last tames men's habits and prevents the disease from starting; for, once the disease has made any progress, one must flee and wait for the air to clear itself. Laws and religion are not strong enough against the spiritual pest; religion, far from being healthy food for infected brains, turns to poison in them.

GUERRE · WAR

Famine, plague, and war are the three most precious ingredients of this vile world.

Under the classification of famine we may include all the unhealthy nourishment we are compelled to resort to in times of scarcity, abridging our life in the hope of sustaining it. In plague we include all the contagious illnesses, which number two or three thousand. These two gifts come to us from Providence.

But war, which unites all these gifts, comes to us from the imagination of three or four hundred people scattered over the surface of the globe under the name of princes or ministers; and it is perhaps for this reason that in dedications to some books they are called the living images of divinity.

Miserable physicians of souls, you shout for an hour and a quarter about some pin pricks, and you say nothing about the malady that tears us in a thousand pieces! Moral philosophers, burn all your books. As long as thousands of our brothers are honestly butchered for the caprice of some men, the part of mankind consecrated to heroism will be the most horrible thing in all nature.

What becomes of humanity, modesty, temperance, gentleness, wisdom, piety; and what do I care about them, while half a pound of lead, shot from six hundred feet away, shatters my body, and while I die at the age of twenty in inexpressible torments in the midst of five or six thousand dying men; while my eyes, opening for the last time, see the town in which I was born destroyed by iron and fire, and while the last sounds in my ears are the cries of women and children expiring under the ruins—all for the alleged interest of a man whom we don't know?

DU JUSTE ET DE L'INJUSTE

OF RIGHT AND WRONG

Who has given us our sense of right and wrong? God, who gave us a brain and a heart. But when does your reason teach you that there is vice and virtue? When it teaches you that two and two make four. There is no innate knowledge, for the same reason that there is no tree bearing leaves and fruit at the time it emerges from the ground. Nothing can be called innate; that is, needing no development; but let us say it once again, God creates us with organs which, as they grow, make us feel everything our species must feel in order to conserve that species.

How does this continual mystery work? Tell me, you yellow inhabitants of the Isles of Sunda, you black Africans, you beardless Canadians, and you, Plato, Cicero, Epictetus. All of you agree that it is better to give away your surplus bread, rice, or manioc to the poor man who humbly asks you for it than to kill him or to put out both his eyes. It is obvious to the whole world that a kindness is more decent than an injury, that gentleness is preferable to rage.

All we need do, then, is to use our reason to discriminate the nuances of honesty and dishonesty. Good and evil are often neighbors; our passions mix them up: who will enlighten us? We will, when we are calm. Whoever has written about our duties in every country in the world has written well, for he has written with his reason alone. They have all said the same thing: Socrates and Epicurus, Confucius and Cicero, Marcus Aurelius and Amurath II, had the same ethics.

Let us repeat it every day to all men: "Ethics is one, it comes from God; doctrines differ, they come from us."

Jesus taught no metaphysical doctrine whatever; he did not write theological books; he did not say: "I am consubstantial; I have two wills and two natures within one person." He left to the Franciscans and the Dominicans, who came twelve hundred years after him, the trouble of arguing whether his mother had been conceived in original sin; he never said that marriage is the visible sign of an invisible thing; he never said a word about concomitant grace; he appointed neither monks nor Inquisitors; he commanded nothing of what we see today.

God had given knowledge of right and wrong to all the ages that preceded Christianity. God has not changed and cannot change: the character of our soul, our principles of reason and ethics, will be the same for eternity. Theological distinctions, doctrines founded on these distinctions, persecutions founded on these doctrines—how do they aid virtue? Frightened and horrified by all these barbarous inventions, nature cries out to all men: "Be just, and not sophistical persecutors."

MORALE · MORALITY

There is no morality in superstition, it is not in ceremonies, it has nothing in common with dogmas. We cannot repeat too often that all dogmas are different, and that morality is the same among all men who make use of their reason. Hence, morality comes from God, like light. Our superstitions are nothing but darkness. Reader, reflect: work out this truth; draw your conclusions.

RELIGION

After our holy religion (which is doubtless the only good one) which would be the least bad?

Wouldn't it be the simplest one? Wouldn't it be the one that taught a good deal of morality and very little dogma? The one that tended to make men just, without making them absurd? The one that wouldn't command belief in impossible, contradictory things insulting to the Divinity and pernicious to mankind, and wouldn't dare to threaten with eternal punishment anyone who has common sense? Wouldn't it be the religion that didn't uphold its beliefs with executioners, and didn't inundate the world with blood for the sake of unintelligible sophisms? The one in which an ambiguity, a play on words, or two or three forged charters wouldn't make a sovereign and a god of a priest who is often a man who has committed incest, a murderer, and a poisoner? The one that wouldn't make kings subject to this priest? The one that taught nothing but the worship of a God, justice, tolerance, and humanity?

"What my sect teaches is obscure, I admit it," says a fanatic, "and it is by virtue of this obscurity that it must be believed; for it says itself that it is full of obscurities. My sect is absurd, therefore it is divine;

for how could what seems so mad be embraced by so many nations if it were not divine? It's precisely like the Koran, which, the Sunnites say, has the face of an angel and the face of a beast; don't be shocked by the snout of the beast, and revere the face of the angel." That's how this madman talks; but a fanatic of another sect replied to this fanatic: "You're the one who is the beast, and I'm the angel."

Now who will judge this contest? Who will decide between these two enthusiasts? The man who is reasonable, impartial, learned in a science which is not merely verbal, the man liberated from prejudices, and a lover of truth and justice; in a word, the man who is not a beast and doesn't think he is an angel.

SUPERSTITION

Chapter Taken from Cicero, Seneca, and Plutarch

Almost everything that goes beyond the worship of a supreme Being, and the submission of one's heart to his eternal commands, is superstition. A very dangerous superstition is the belief that certain ceremonies will win one pardon for one's crimes.

SUPERSTITION

Second Section

The superstitious man is to the rascal what the slave is to the tyrant. Indeed, more: the superstitious man is ruled by the fanatic, and turns into one. Superstition, born in paganism, adopted by Judaism, infected the Christian Church from the beginning. All the Fathers of the Church without exception believed in the power of magic. The Church always condemned magic, but it always believed in it: it didn't excommunicate sorcerers as madmen who were deceived, but as men who really had intercourse with devils.

TOLÉRANCE · TOLERATION

What is toleration? It is the endowment of humanity. We are all steeped in weaknesses and errors; let us forgive each other our follies; that is the first law of nature.

It is clear that every individual who persecutes a man, his brother, because he is not of his opinion, is a monster.

STUDY QUESTIONS: ROUSSEAU, *DICTIONARY OF PHILOSOPHY*

1. What is the point behind Voltaire's rhetorical question 'This flower vegetates, but is there any real being called *vegetation?*'
2. If a tulip could talk, what might it tell you, according to Voltaire, and how would you probably react?
3. Why does Voltaire want to say that the sect that poisoned newly baptized infants reasoned perfectly? Does this mean that he agrees with them?
4. Why does Voltaire say, 'Fanaticism is to superstition what delirium is to fever and rage to anger'?
5. What is the remedy for superstition?
6. What does Voltaire have to say about the causes of war?
7. What should we repeat everyday?
8. According to Voltaire, what is it that Jesus did not say?
9. What is toleration? What does Voltaire's answer mean?

Philosophical Bridges: The Influence of Voltaire

Voltaire was a leader in his own lifetime, which was the zenith of his influence. For example, his attempts to introduce Newton's physics into France and replace the Cartesian system were successful. His efforts to spread some of the main philosophical messages of Locke's work, such as tolerance and reasonableness, were also successful. His optimistic idea that history could be understood as the development of reason, culture, and industry became widely accepted. His criticisms of the Church were heard, as were his pleas for progress. As a result of all this, his voice almost defined the period. However, his work helped to create a culture that made the philosophy of Rousseau possible, and Rousseau's thought led to the French Revolution, which in its excesses meant the waning of Voltaire's influence. In 1783–1790, Pierre-Augustin Beaumarchais, the French playwright who also organized French military aid to the American War of Independence, financed the publication of the complete works of Voltaire in 70 volumes.

JEAN-JACQUES ROUSSEAU (1712–1778)

Biographical History

Jean-Jacques Rousseau was born in Geneva; his mother died a week later. In his early youth, he wandered around Europe, almost destitute. In 1742, he moved to Paris, where he became friends with the young Diderot. In 1749, his essay, the *Discourse on the Arts and Science*, an attack on the corrupting effects of civilization, won a literary prize. Rousseau composed music, and one of his operettas won acclaim. Tired of Paris, in 1754, he returned to Geneva and to the Protestant Church, having briefly been a Catholic. In his *Discourse on the Inequality Among Men* (1755), he argues that humans are naturally good, and that injustice is caused by civil society. In 1755, Rousseau and his common-law wife, Thérèse, moved to a cottage on the edge of the forest of Montmorency, where he wrote his popular and romantic novel *La Nouvelle Héloïs* (1761). In 1762, he published two of his best-known books, *The Social Contract* and *Emile*, his work on education. These works made Rousseau an outcast; his revolutionary works were banned, and he faced imprisonment for heresy. Furthermore, his Romantic naturalism and sensitive temperament brought him into conflict with the philosophers of the time, most notably Voltaire and his old friend, Diderot. Whereas Voltaire argued in favor of reason and progress, Rousseau praised spontaneous feeling and nature. For a while, the naturalist philosopher David Hume befriended Rousseau. However, they quarreled and, in 1767, after a 16-month stay in England, Rousseau and Thérèse returned illicitly to France, from which he was officially banned. His frank autobiography, the *Confessions*, was published posthumously in 1782.

Philosophical Overview

Much of Rousseau's philosophy is contained in a contrast between an optimistic view of human nature and a pessimistic view of social history. On the one hand, like Voltaire and other French Enlightenment philosophers, Rousseau rejects much of the teaching of the Church and especially the concept of original sin, claiming that humans are by nature fundamentally good. On the other hand, Rousseau subscribes to a pessimistic view of human social history, according to which human civilization has caused us to degenerate. He denies the standard Enlightenment view advanced by Voltaire that more civilization and learning bring progress to humankind. This contrast highlights how Rousseau's thought conflicted with both the conservative and the radical thinking of his day.

This very sharp contrast between nature and society also helps us to understand the central features of Rousseau's philosophy. Much of Rousseau's work praises nature and ways of life that are naturally simple. He idealizes the noble savage, who naturally loves the good and who lives freely. In contrast, Rousseau's writings condemn cosmopolitan civilization and corrupt commercial culture. We can find this contrast in Rousseau's views on education: children have a natural ability to learn and develop, but normally educational institutions thwart these natural tendencies by imposing adult expectations on children. We also find this general contrast in Rousseau's views on religion. Natural religion consists in a spontaneous love of the good. In contrast, the revealed religion of Scripture and the Church ends up being superstitious, dogmatic, and authoritarian.

This general contrast between nature and society defines the main problem of Rousseau's political theory. If humans are naturally good and free, then why are societies unjust, tyrannical, and corrupt? If a society were built on the right principles, then it ought to be possible for free persons to construct a social order in which they retain their freedom and natural goodness. What are the political principles that would govern such a society? The work *The Social Contract* (1762) attempts to answer this question.

THE SOCIAL CONTRACT

Rousseau's political theory is best understood as a contrast between three conditions of life: (1) the original state of nature, (2) society as it ought to be according to the social contract, and (3) society as it actually is. In their natural state, humans are different from the other animals not so much for their reasoning capacity, but rather for the soul's feeling of free will, which defies mechanical explanation. Humans are naturally free. In their natural state, they have self-love and natural compassion, but not egoism. There is no original sin. With this portrayal of human nature, Rousseau rejects rationalism, mechanistic philosophy, Hobbes, and the teaching of the Church.

For the sake of self-preservation, humans entered into a social contract, but, in order for this act of association to be justifiable, it must not diminish our natural freedom. Consequently, the social contract must consist in the formation of a collective body, or general will, which allows individual citizens to share power. Through this contract, a social morality of justice, rights, and duties replaces actions freely motivated by instinct, and, because of this, the individual citizen must be willing to follow the general will. However, this need not diminish freedom; the capacity to obey the law makes a person master of his or her own appetites, and thus freedom finds full expression in a civil society governed by the social contract. Rousseau wrote, 'Obedience to a law which we prescribe to ourselves is liberty.'

In sharp contrast to both of these states, actual society corrupts natural human goodness and destroys freedom. Thus, Rousseau's famous opening sentence of *The Social Contract*, 'Man is born free and everywhere he is in chains,' defines the problem of politics, which is the contrast between our fundamental nature and society as it actually is. The solution lies in the nature of the social contract, which defines how society should be.

In studying and thinking about Rousseau's social contract theory, there are three aspects to bear in mind. First, you might pay special attention to the summary of the essence of the social compact, which Rousseau provides in Chapter 6 of Book I. Second, according to Rousseau, humans are naturally free and, consequently, it is impossible for a person to renounce his or her liberty. Nevertheless, Rousseau claims that we are obliged to enter into a social contract. How and why does this not constitute an attempt to deny or reduce one's liberty? This is an important point to look out for in reading Rousseau because that is one of the main theoretical questions that his work should answer. Third, Rousseau constructs a concept of the general will, which requires the people to rule directly themselves through a citizens' assembly rather than indirectly through elected representatives. Rousseau lived for part of his life in Geneva, which was then a small city-state.

BOOK I

Chapter 1

Subject of the First Book

Man is born free; and everywhere he is in chains. One thinks himself the master of others, and still remains a greater slave than they. How did this change come about? I do not know. What can make it legitimate? That question I think I can answer.

If I took into account only force, and the effects derived from it, I should say: 'As long as a people is compelled to obey, and obeys, it does well; as soon as it can shake off the yoke, and shakes it off, it does still better; for, regaining its liberty by the same right as took it away, either it is justified in resuming it, or there was no justification for depriving them of it.'

But the social order is a sacred right which serves as a foundation for all others. This right, however, does not come from nature. It is therefore based on conventions. The question is to know what these conventions are. Before coming to that, I must establish what I have just laid down.

Chapter 2

The First Societies

The most ancient of all societies, and the only one that is natural, is the family: and even so the children remain attached to the father only so long as they need him for their preservation. As soon as this need ceases, the natural bond is dissolved. The children, released from the obedience they owed to the father, and the father, released from the care he owed his children, return equally to independence. If they remain united, they continue so no longer naturally, but voluntarily; and the family itself is then maintained only by convention.

This common liberty results from the nature of man. His first law is to provide for his own preservation, his first cares are those which he owes to himself; and, as soon as he reaches years of discretion, he is the sole judge of the proper means of preserving himself, and consequently becomes his own master.

The family then may be called the first model of political societies: the ruler corresponds to the father, and the people to the children; and all, being born free and equal, alienate their liberty only for their own advantage. The whole difference is that, in the family, the love of the father for his children repays him for the care he takes of them, while, in the State, the pleasure of commanding takes the place of the love which the chief cannot have for the peoples under him.

Chapter 3

The Right of the Strongest

The strongest is never strong enough to be always the master, unless he transforms strength into right, and obedience into duty. Hence the right of the strongest, which, though to all seeming meant ironically, is really laid down as a fundamental principle. But are we never to have an explanation of this phrase? Force is a physical power, and I fail to see what moral effect it can have. To yield to force is an act of necessity, not of will—at the most, an act of prudence. In what sense can it be a duty?

Suppose for a moment that this so-called 'right' exists. I maintain that the sole result is a mass of inexplicable nonsense. For, if force creates right, the effect changes with the cause: every force that is greater than the first succeeds to its right. As soon as it is possible to disobey with impunity, disobedience is legitimate; and, the strongest being always in the right, the only thing that matters is to act so as to become the strongest. But what kind of right is that which perishes when force fails? If we must obey perforce, there is no need to obey because we ought; and if we are not forced to obey, we are under no obligation to do so. Clearly, the word 'right' adds nothing to force: in this connection, it means absolutely nothing.

Let us then admit that force does not create right, and that we are obliged to obey only legitimate powers. In that case, my original question recurs.

Chapter 4

Slavery

Since no man has a natural authority over his fellow, and force creates no right, we must conclude that conventions form the basis of all legitimate authority among men.

If an individual, says Grotius, can alienate his liberty and make himself the slave of a master, why could not a whole people do the same and make itself subject to a king? There are in this passage plenty of ambiguous words which would need explaining; but let us confine ourselves to the word *alienate*. To alienate is to give or to sell. Now, a man who becomes the slave of another does not give himself; he sells himself, at the least for his subsistence: but for what does a people sell itself? A king is so far from furnishing his subjects with their subsistence that he gets his own only from them; and, as Rabelais says, kings do not live on nothing. Do subjects then give their persons on condition that the king takes their goods also? I fail to see what they have left to preserve.

To say that a man gives himself freely, is to say what is absurd and inconceivable; such an act is null and illegitimate, from the mere fact that he who does it is out of his mind. To say the same of a whole people is to suppose a people of madmen; and madness creates no right.

Even if each man could alienate himself, he could not alienate his children: they are born men and free; their liberty belongs to them, and no one but they has the right to dispose of it. Before they come to years of discretion, the father can, in their name, lay down conditions for their preservation and well-being, but he cannot give them irrevocably and without conditions: such a gift is contrary to the ends of nature, and exceeds the rights of paternity. It would therefore be necessary, in order to legitimize an arbitrary government, that in every generation the people should be in a position to accept or reject it; but, were this so, the government would be no longer arbitrary.

To renounce liberty is to renounce being a man, to surrender the rights of humanity and even its duties. For him who renounces everything no indemnity is possible. Such a renunciation is incompatible with man's nature; to remove all liberty from his will is to remove all morality from his acts. Finally, it is an empty and contradictory convention that sets up, on the one side, absolute authority, and, on the other, unlimited obedience.

So, from whatever aspect we regard the question, the right of slavery is null and void, not only as being illegitimate, but also because it is absurd and meaningless. The words *slave* and *right* contradict each other, and are mutually exclusive. It will always be equally foolish for a man to say to a man or to a people: 'I make with you a convention wholly at your expense and wholly to my advantage; I shall keep it as long as I like, and you will keep it as long as I like.'

Chapter 6

The Social Compact

I suppose men to have reached the point at which the obstacles in the way of their preservation in the state of nature show their power of resistance to be greater than the resources at the disposal of each individual for his maintenance in that state. That primitive condition can then subsist no longer; and the human race would perish unless it changed its manner of existence.

But, as men cannot engender new forces, but only unite and direct existing ones, they have no other means of preserving themselves than the formation, by aggregation, of a sum of forces great enough to overcome the resistance. These they have to bring into play by means of a single motive power, and cause to act in concert.

This sum of forces can arise only where several persons come together: but, as the force and liberty of each man are the chief instruments of his self-preservation, how can he pledge them without harming his own interests, and neglecting the care he owes to himself? This difficulty, in its bearing on my present subject, may be stated in the following terms:

'The problem is to find a form of association which will defend and protect with the whole common force the person and goods of each associate, and in which each, while uniting himself with all, may still obey himself alone, and remain as free as

before.' This is the fundamental problem of which the social contract provides the solution.

The clauses of this contract are so determined by the nature of the act that the slightest modification would make them vain and ineffective; so that, although they have perhaps never been formally set forth, they are everywhere the same and everywhere tacitly admitted and recognized, until, on the violation of the social compact, each regains his original rights and resumes his natural liberty, while losing the conventional liberty in favour of which he renounced it.

These clauses, properly understood, may be reduced to one—the total alienation of each associate, together with all his rights, to the whole community; for, in the first place, as each gives himself absolutely, the conditions are the same for all; and, this being so, no one has any interest in making them burdensome to others.

Moreover, the alienation being without reserve, the union is as perfect as it can be, and no associate has anything more to demand: for, if the individuals retained certain rights, as there would be no common superior to decide between them and the public, each, being on one point his own judge, would ask to be so on all; the state of nature would thus continue, and the association would necessarily become inoperative or tyrannical.

Finally, each man, in giving himself to all, gives himself to nobody; and as there is no associate over which he does not acquire the same right as he yields others over himself, he gains an equivalent for everything he loses, and an increase of force for the preservation of what he has.

If then we discard from the social compact what is not of its essence, we shall find that it reduces itself to the following terms:

'Each of us puts his person and all his power in common under the supreme direction of the general will, and, in our corporate capacity, we receive each member as an indivisible part of the whole.'

At once, in place of the individual personality of each contracting party, this act of association creates a corporate and collective body, composed of as many members as the assembly contains voters, and receiving from this act its unity, its common identity, its life, and its will. This public person, so formed by the union of all other persons, formerly took the name of city, and now takes that of *Republic* or *body politic*; it is called by its members *State* when passive, *Sovereign* when active, and *Power* when compared with others like itself. Those who associated in it take collectively the name of *people*, and severally are called *citizens*, as sharing in the sovereign authority, and *subjects*, as being under the laws of the State. But these terms are often confused and taken one for another: it is enough to know how to distinguish them when they are being used with precision.

Chapter 7

The Sovereign

This formula shows us that the act of association comprises a mutual undertaking between the public and the individuals, and that each individual, in making a contract, as we may say, with himself, is bound in a double relation; as a member of the Sovereign he is bound to the individuals, and as a member of the State to the Sovereign. But the maxim of civil right, that no one is bound by undertakings made to himself, does not apply in this case; for there is a great difference between incurring an obligation to yourself and incurring one to a whole of which you form a part.

In fact, each individual, as a man, may have a particular will contrary or dissimilar to the general will which he has as a citizen. His particular interest may speak to him quite differently from the common interest: his absolute and naturally independent existence may make him look upon what he owes to the common cause as a gratuitous contribution, the loss of which will do less harm to others than the payment of it is burdensome to himself; and, regarding the corporate person which constitutes the State as a *persona ficta*, because not a man, he may wish to enjoy the rights of citizenship without being ready to fulfil the duties of a subject. The continuance of such an injustice could not but prove the undoing of the body politic.

In order then that the social compact may not be an empty formula, it tacitly includes the undertaking, which alone can give force to the rest, that whoever refuses to obey the general will shall be compelled to do so by the whole body. This means nothing less than that he will be forced to be free; for this is the condition which, by giving each citizen to his country, secures him against all personal dependence. In this lies the key to the working of the political machine; this alone legitimizes civil undertakings, which, without it, would be absurd, tyrannical and liable to the most frightful abuses.

Chapter 8

The Civil State

The passage from the state of nature to the civil state produces a very remarkable change in man, by substituting justice for instinct in his conduct, and giving his actions the morality they had formerly lacked. Then only, when the voice of duty takes the place of physical impulses and right of appetite, does man, who so far had considered only himself, find that he is forced to act on different principles, and to consult his reason before listening to his inclinations. Although, in this state, he deprives himself of some advantages which he got from nature, he gains in return others so great, his faculties are so stimulated and developed, his ideas so extended, his feelings so ennobled, and his whole soul so uplifted, that, did not the abuses of this new condition often degrade him below that which he left, he would be bound to bless continually the happy moment which took him from it for ever, and, instead of a stupid and unimaginative animal, made him an intelligent being and a man.

Let us draw up the whole account in terms easily commensurable. What man loses by the social contract is his natural liberty and an unlimited right to everything he tries to get and succeeds in getting; what he gains is civil liberty and the proprietorship of all he possesses. If we are to avoid mistake in weighing one against the other, we must clearly distinguish natural liberty, which is bounded only by the strength of the individual, from civil liberty, which is limited by the general will; and possession, which is merely the effect of force or the right of the first occupier, from property, which can be founded only on a positive title.

We might, over and above all this, add, to what man acquires in the civil state, moral liberty, which alone makes him truly master of himself; for the mere impulse of appetite is slavery, while obedience to a law which we prescribe to ourselves is liberty. But I have already said too much on this head, and the philosophical meaning of the word liberty is not what concerns us here.

BOOK II

Chapter 1

That Sovereignty Is Inalienable

The first and most important deduction from the principles we have so far laid down is that the general will alone can direct the State according to the object for which it was instituted, i.e. the common good: for if the clashing of particular interests made the establishment of societies necessary, the agreement of these very interests made it possible. The common element in these different interests is what forms the social tie; and, were there no point of agreement between them all, no society could exist. It is solely on the basis of this common interest that every society should be governed.

I hold then that Sovereignty, being nothing less than the exercise of the general will, can never be alienated, and that the Sovereign, who is no less than a collective being, cannot be represented except by himself: the power indeed may be transmitted, but not the will.

In reality, if it is not impossible for a particular will to agree on some point with the general will, it is at least impossible for the agreement to be lasting and constant; for the particular will tends, by its very nature, to partiality, while the general will tends to equality. It is even more impossible to have any guarantee of this agreement; for even if it should always exist, it would be the effect not of art, but of chance. The Sovereign may indeed say: 'I now will actually what this man wills, or at least what he says he wills'; but it cannot say: 'What he wills tomorrow, I too shall will' because it is absurd for the will to bind itself for the future, nor is it incumbent on any will to consent to anything that is not for the good of the being who wills. If then the people promises simply to obey, by that very act it dissolves itself and loses what makes it a people; the moment a master exists, there is no longer a Sovereign, and from that moment the body politic has ceased to exist.

This does not mean that the commands of the rulers cannot pass for general wills, so long as the Sovereign, being free to oppose them, offers no opposition. In such a case, universal silence is taken to imply the consent of the people. This will be explained later on.

Chapter 2

That Sovereignty Is Indivisible

Sovereignty, for the same reason as makes it inalienable, is indivisible; for will either is, or is not, general; it is the will either of the body of the people, or only of a part of it. In the first case, the will, when declared, is an act of Sovereignty and constitutes law: in the second, it is merely a particular will, or act of magistracy—at the most a decree.

Chapter 3

Whether the General Will Is Fallible

It follows from what has gone before that the general will is always upright and always tends to the public advantage; but it does not follow that the deliberations of the people always have the same rectitude. Our will is always for our own good, but we do not always see what that is; the people is never corrupted, but it is often deceived, and on such occasions only does it seem to will what is bad.

There is often a great deal of difference between the will of all and the general will; the latter considers only the common interest, while the former takes private interest into account, and is no more than a sum of particular wills: but take away from these same wills the pluses and minuses that cancel one another, and the general will remains as the sum of the differences.

If, when the people, being furnished with adequate information, held its deliberations, the citizens had no communication one with another, the grand total of the small differences would always give the general will, and the decision would always be good.

Chapter 4

The Limits of the Sovereign Power

If the State is a corporate body whose life is in the union of its members, and if the most important of its cares is the care for its own preservation, it must have a universal and compelling force, in order to move and dispose each part as may be most advantageous to the whole. As nature gives each man absolute power over all his members, the social compact gives the body politic absolute power over all its members also; and it is this power which, under the direction of the general will, bears, as I have said, the name of Sovereignty.

But, besides the public person, we have to consider the private persons composing it, whose life and liberty are naturally independent of it. We are bound then to distinguish clearly between the respective rights of the citizens and the Sovereign, and between the duties the former have to fulfil as subjects, and the natural rights they should enjoy as men.

Each man alienates, I admit, by the social compact, only such part of his powers, goods, and liberty as it is important for the community to control; but it must also be granted that the Sovereign is sole judge of what is important.

Every service a citizen can render the State he ought to render as soon as the Sovereign demands it; but the Sovereign, for its part, cannot impose upon its subjects any fetters that are useless to the community, nor can it even wish to do so; for no more by the law of reason than by the law of nature can anything occur without a cause.

The undertakings which bind us to the social body are obligatory only because they are mutual; and their nature is such that in fulfilling them we cannot work for others without working for ourselves. Why is it that the general will is always upright, and that all continually will the happiness of each one, unless it is because there is not a man who does not think of 'each' as meaning him, and consider himself in voting for all? This proves that equality of rights and the idea of justice which such equality creates originate in the preference each man gives to himself, and accordingly in the very nature of man. It proves that the general will, to be really such, must be general in its object as well as its essence; that it must both come from all and apply to all; and that it loses its natural rectitude when it is directed to some particular and determinate object, because in such a case we are judging of something foreign to us, and have no true principle of equity to guide us. . . .

What, then, strictly speaking, is an act of Sovereignty? It is not a convention between a superior and an inferior, but a convention between the body and each of its members. It is legitimate, because based on the social contract, and equitable, because common to all; useful, because it can have no other object than the general good, and stable, because guaranteed by the public force and the supreme power. So long as

the subjects have to submit only to conventions of this sort, they obey no one but their own will; and to ask how far the respective rights of the Sovereign and the citizens extend, is to ask up to what point the latter can enter into undertakings with themselves, each with all, and all with each.

We can see from this that the sovereign power, absolute, sacred, and inviolable as it is, does not and cannot exceed the limits of general conventions, and that every man may dispose at will of such goods and liberty as these conventions leave him; so that the Sovereign never has a right to lay more charges on one subject than on another, because, in that case, the question becomes particular, and ceases to be within its competency.

Chapter 6

Law

By the social compact we have given the body politic existence and life; we have now by legislation to give it movement and will. For the original act by which the body is formed and united still in no respect determines what it ought to do for its preservation.

What is well and in conformity with order is so by the nature of things and independently of human conventions. All justice comes from God, who is its sole source; but if we knew how to receive so high an inspiration, we should need neither government nor laws. Doubtless, there is a universal justice emanating from reason alone; but this justice, to be admitted among us, must be mutual. Humanly speaking, in default of natural sanctions, the laws of justice are ineffective among men: they merely make for the good of the wicked and the undoing of the just, when the just man observes them towards everybody and nobody observes them towards him. Conventions and laws are therefore needed to join rights to duties and refer justice to its object. In the state of nature, where everything is common, I owe nothing to him whom I have promised nothing; I recognize as belonging to others only what is of no use to me. In the state of society all rights are fixed by law, and the case becomes different.

But when the whole people decrees for the whole people, it is considering only itself; and if a relation is then formed, it is between two aspects of the entire object, without there being any division of the whole. In that case the matter about which the decree is made is, like the decreeing will, general. This act is what I call a law.

When I say that the object of laws is always general, I mean that law considers subjects *en masse* and actions in the abstract, and never a particular person or action. Thus the law may indeed decree that there shall be privileges, but cannot confer them on anybody by name. It may set up several classes of citizens, and even lay down the qualifications for membership of these classes, but it cannot nominate such and such persons as belonging to them; it may establish a monarchical government and hereditary succession, but it cannot choose a king, or nominate a royal family. In a word, no function which has a particular object belongs to the legislative power.

On this view, we at once see that it can no longer be asked whose business it is to make laws, since they are acts of the general will; nor whether the prince is above the law, since he is a member of the State; nor whether the law can be unjust, since no one is unjust to himself; nor how we can be both free and subject to the laws, since they are but registers of our wills.

We see further that, as the law unites universality of will with universality of object, what a man, whoever he be, commands of his own motion cannot be a law; and even what the Sovereign commands with regard to a particular matter is no nearer being a law, but is a decree, an act, not of sovereignty, but of magistracy.

I therefore give the name 'Republic' to every State that is governed by laws, no matter what the form of its administration may be: for only in such a case does the public interest govern, and the *res publica* rank as a *reality*. Every legitimate government is republican; what government is I will explain later on.

Laws are, properly speaking, only the conditions of civil association. The people, being subject to the laws, ought to be their author: the conditions of the society ought to be regulated solely by those who come together to form it. But how are they to regulate them? Is it to be by common agreement, by a sudden inspiration? Has the body politic an organ to declare its will? Who can give it the foresight to formulate and announce its acts in advance? Or how is it to announce them in the hour of need? How can a blind multitude, which often does not know what it wills, because it rarely knows what is good for it, carry out for itself so great and difficult an enterprise as a system of legislation? Of itself the people wills always the good, but of itself it by no means always sees it. The general will is always upright, but the judgment which guides it is not always enlightened. It must be got to see objects as they are, and sometimes as they ought to appear to it; it must be shown the good road it is in search of, secured from the seductive influences of individual wills, taught to see the relationship of times and spaces, and made to weigh the attractions of present and sensible advantages against the danger of distant and hidden evils. The individuals see the good they reject; the public wills the good it does not see. All stand equally in need of guidance. The former must be compelled to bring their wills into conformity with their reason; the latter must be taught to know what it wills. If that is done, public enlightenment leads to the union of understanding and will in the social body: the parts are made to work exactly together, and the whole is raised to its highest power. This makes a legislator necessary.

STUDY QUESTIONS: ROUSSEAU, *THE SOCIAL CONTRACT*

1. Rousseau claims that man is born free but everywhere he is in chains. Explain what this means and why it is central to Rousseau's project.
2. Force does not create right. What reasoning does Rousseau give in favor of this proposition, and what impact does this point have on Rousseau's aims?
3. Why is it impossible to renounce one's liberty?
4. According to Rousseau, what is the essence of the social compact?
5. This compact shows that in the act of association, the individual binds him or herself in a double relation. What is this double relation?
6. What does Rousseau mean by 'the general will'?
7. Is the general will fallible?
8. Why is the legislator necessary?

Philosophical Bridges: Rousseau's Influence

The popularity of Rousseau's political philosophy first expressed itself in the French support for the American Revolution. Thomas Jefferson, who was the U.S. ambassador to France from 1785 to 1789, was influenced by Rousseau's views. Rousseau's doctrine of the sovereignty of the people became very popular in pre-Revolution France. For example, when Jean-Paul Marat read parts of *The Social Contract* in the street, he was met with enthusiastic applause. Rousseau's work gave tremendous impetus to the Revolution. According to the conservative English political thinker Edmund Burke, the French Revolutionary Constituent Assembly (1789–1791) almost worshiped Rousseau's thought.

When the revolution began, it was decidedly atheistic because of the influence of Voltaire and other Rationalist and antireligious Enlightenment thinkers. However, Robespierre was convinced by Rousseau's writings to support religious belief, and by 1793, as he rose to power, he persuaded the National Convention to adopt an article of faith based on Rousseau. Napoleon Bonaparte also agreed with Rousseau on the importance of religion. Ironically, the survival of the Church depended on Rousseau, who had been banished for heresy during his lifetime.

The German philosopher Kant was inspired by Rousseau's emphasis on human free will. Sometimes, Rousseau characterized liberty as obedience to a self-prescribed law, and Kant took this suggestion to heart by arguing that free will consists in the ability to follow the moral law. Furthermore, like Rousseau, Kant claims that, because the ability to obey the moral law requires that a person can master his or her own desires, freedom finds full expression only in a civil society where people are regarded equally as ends.

In a way, Rousseau was part of the French Enlightenment, but he was also very critical of its assumptions. He rejected its emphasis on rationality, scorned the assumption that civilization meant progress, and praised human life in the state of nature. These aspects of Rousseau's philosophy made him the darling of the Romantic movement that flourished in the nineteenth century. Moreover, his autobiography, the *Confessions*, became recognized almost as the founding document of the Romantic movement not only because it praised feeling and sentiments, but also because, apparently, it offered a way of understanding the human psyche that did not reduce a person to a machine.

Through the Romantic movement, Rousseau exercised an extraordinary influence on nineteenth century literature and thinking. In Germany, he inspired the poet Goethe and the philosopher Friedrich Schiller, in England the poets Wordsworth, Coleridge, Lord Byron, Shelly, and Keats; and in Russia Aleksandr Pushkin and Leo Tolstoy. Rousseau-inspired Romanticism also shaped art and popular tastes. There was a shift toward simpler clothing, love of the countryside, and the expression of romantic love.

In 1762, in *Emile*, Rousseau wrote, 'Nature provides for the child's growth in her own fashion, and this should never be thwarted.' According to this view, the development of a child occurs naturally, and the main job of a teacher is to facilitate this process and not to impede it by imposing rules and the preconception that children should know various facts. The Swiss educator Johann Pestalozzi (1746–1827) extended Rousseau's approach and put it into practice, as did John Dewey (1859–1952) and Maria Montessori (1870–1952). Another pioneer of Rousseau's progressive view of education was Friedrich Froebel (1782–1852), the founder of the kindergarten.

IMMANUEL KANT (1724–1804)

Biographical History

At the age of 31, Kant became a university instructor, lecturing on a wide variety of subjects, including logic, geography, natural history, anthropology, mathematics, and physics. His first published works were mainly scientific and his early philosophy was Rationalist, influenced by Leibniz. However, around 1770, his reading of Hume interrupted his 'dogmatic slumbers,' which led to his writing the *Critique of Pure Reason* and to a period of intense creativity. After 12 years' labor, the *Critique* was published in 1781, when Kant was 57. It is one of the greatest and most difficult works in philosophy. To explain his ideas more fully, Kant published the *Prolegomena* (1783) and a revised second edition of the *Critique* (1787). After 1781, Kant wrote several works that explain the implications of the *Critique* for ethics, science, religion, politics, and aesthetics: the *Groundwork of the Metaphysics of Morals*, 1785; the *Metaphysical Foundations of Natural Science*, 1786; the *Critique of Practical Reason*, 1788; and the *Critique of Judgment*, 1790. In 1793, he published *Religion Within the Limits of Reason Alone*, which earned censure from the king's minister and forced Kant to promise to refrain from publicly discussing religion.

Philosophical Overview

Kant rejects both the Rationalist and Empiricist traditions because they share certain fundamental assumptions. First, they assume that there is only one source of knowledge: either sense experience or reason. In contrast, Kant argues that sensation (or sensible intuition) and the understanding (or concepts) are both necessary for experience.

Second, they fail to separate the two distinctions, analytic/synthetic and a priori/empirical. Kant argues that not all a priori truths are analytic. Synthetic a priori truths are necessary truths that it would not be a contradiction to deny. Examples include 'every event must have a cause,' 'The three angles of a triangle equal 180 degrees,' and '$7 + 5 = 12$.' Such claims are necessary truths, but, because they are not analytic, they can give us knowledge of the world, and they form the basic principles of mathematics and science.

One major objective of the *Critique* is to explain how such truths are possible. In doing so, Kant develops a non-Empiricist theory of experience (in the Aesthetic and Analytic), which he employs to criticize Rationalist metaphysics (in the Dialectic). Kant argues, against Rationalism, that reason cannot yield theoretical knowledge that goes beyond what we could experience. Kant develops a non-Empiricist theory of experience to show how synthetic a priori truths about the world are possible. What makes such truths possible is precisely what makes Rationalist metaphysics impossible.

Kant's explanation of synthetic a priori truths about the world has two elements.

1. First, he argues that experience has certain structural necessary conditions, which he calls the a priori forms of experience. These consist in space and time and 12 categories.
2. Second, he argues that the world itself must conform to these a priori forms. This involves giving up the assumption that the world is totally independent of the character of experience. Transcendental idealism is the claim that the world of spatio-temporal objects is transcendentally ideal and empirically real. The world is empirically real because such objects are real in that they exist independently of us.

> The world is transcendentally ideal because such objects are, and must be, relative to the a priori forms of experience. In other words, although such objects are real, they are phenomena (relative to the a priori forms of experience) and not noumena (or things as they are absolutely in themselves). Transcendental idealism implies that spatio-temporal objects necessarily conform to the a priori conditions of experience and, thereby, explains how synthetic a priori truths about the world are possible.

In brief, that experience has a necessary or a priori structure refutes Empiricism, and that the world is transcendentally ideal shows that Rationalism is false. Both elements are needed to explain how the synthetic a priori claims of science and mathematics are possible.

Space and Time

Kant's main point is that space and time are necessary conditions of experience. One of his arguments for this claim is that it is required in order to explain how the synthetic a priori truths of geometry and arithmetic are possible.

The Categories

In the Transcendental Deduction, Kant presents an argument to show that the categories are also necessary conditions for any experience. The categories are the a priori concepts of the understanding. Kant's argument starts from the premise that any experience has to belong to a single, unified consciousness. He calls this formal condition of experience 'the transcendental unity of apperception' (or TUAP). The TUAP is not an awareness of a mental self because it is the unity of consciousness, which is necessary for all awareness, including self-consciousness. It is an a priori structural feature of experience and not an object of experience. The Transcendental Deduction argues that, because experience must be subject to the TUAP, it must consist in judgments that have the categories as their form.

Also in the Transcendental Deduction, Kant argues that the concept of objectivity is a necessary condition of experience. The objectivity of a judgment is expressed by the copula 'is.' For instance, the judgment that an object *is* heavy asserts that the object *is* heavy no matter what the state of the subject or the person making the judgment (B142). In this sense, the judgment is objective. Kant argues that this concept of objectivity is a necessary condition of experience. This is because the very thought 'I am having this experience' (i.e., the TUAP) requires the contrast between how things subjectively *seem* to be to me and how things *are* objectively. The thought of subjective experience itself requires the contrasting concept of something objective and distinct from experience.

Kant's Transcendental Deduction is an argument against Empiricism. Experience must have a unity and a structure, and, thus, Kant rejects the Empiricist idea of passively received sense impressions. Furthermore, because experience must have a structure, the categories cannot be derived from experience, as an Empiricist would claim. They must be a priori.

Principles

Kant also tries to show how each one of the 12 categories makes experience possible insofar as they determine the necessary structure of our consciousness of time. In the Analogies, Kant employs this idea with regard to the categories of substance and cause. For example, in the First Analogy, Kant tries to prove that all changes are alterations to the properties of substance and that the amount of substance cannot change; and in the Second Analogy, that all events must have a cause. Both of these principles are synthetic a priori. To show this, Kant argues that 'substance' and 'cause' are necessary conditions of experience because they alone enable us to distinguish the subjective time sequence of our perceptions from the objective sequence of events. This distinction cannot be made in relation to Newton's absolute time because it is not an object of possible experience. For this reason, the two categories are necessary for experience. Given this and given transcendental idealism, all events in the physical world must conform to the two principles regarding substance and cause.

The analogies are a reply to Hume's Skepticism. For example, Hume argues that the principle that every event must have a cause is unjustifiable on the grounds that it is not analytic or empirical. He appeals to his fork. In reply, Kant claims that this ignores the possibility that the causal principle is a synthetic a priori necessary condition of experience.

Transcendental Idealism

In the Refutation of Idealism, Kant tries to prove empirical realism. In other words, we can perceive directly external objects rather than just our own ideas. These external objects exist independently of being perceived. In this way, they are empirically real. At the same time, Kant tries to establish transcendental idealism, according to which these real objects in space and time are necessarily relative to the necessary conditions of experience. In that way, they do not have an absolute existence. For this reason, Kant calls them phenomena, as opposed to noumena. Kant needs transcendental idealism in order to explain how synthetic a priori truths about the world are possible. They are possible because the world necessarily conforms to the necessary conditions of experience.

The Critique of Metaphysics

Kant argues that it is impossible to have knowledge that transcends the bounds of possible experience because, beyond that, the categories have no sense. This is the basis of his critique of Rationalist metaphysics that claims a priori knowledge of the soul, God, and the universe. Reason is led to such transcendent ideas because it searches for a complete explanation of everything and, thus, searches for the unconditioned, which is not an object of possible experience. In this way, the Rationalists mistakenly try to apply the categories beyond the limits of possible experience.

To remedy this error, the Dialectic also describes the proper function of reason. Briefly, the Ideas of Reason lay down heuristic maxims that only guide investigation. The error is to suppose that these maxims provide a priori knowledge of the world. In other words, synthetic a priori truths are possible in science and mathematics precisely because they articulate the necessary conditions both of experience and of a transcendentally ideal world. In contrast, synthetic a priori truths in metaphysics are not possible because they do not do this.

Conclusion

In summary, Kant's main aim is to provide a non-Empiricist argument against Rationalism. Synthetic a priori judgments in science and mathematics are justified by two conditions: the necessary structure of experience and transcendental idealism. Traditional metaphysics fails to satisfy these two conditions. Metaphysics is impossible, not because it fails the two prongs of Hume's fork, but because it fails the third prong of Kant's trident: the synthetic a priori. Intuitions without concepts are blind, and, therefore, Empiricism is false. Concepts without intuitions are empty, and, therefore, Rationalism is false.

CRITIQUE OF PURE REASON

Kant published the first edition of the *Critique of Pure Reason* in 1781. Some of Kant's friends complained that the work was incomprehensible, and other readers clearly misunderstood crucial points such as Kant's transcendental idealism. As a remedy, Kant wrote the *Prolegomena* in 1783 and published a second edition of the *Critique* in 1787.

With a long and complex book like the *Critique*, it is important to have the overall aims, strategy, and structure clear. Kant's basic aim is to prove that theoretical transcendent metaphysics is impossible. He does this by first explaining how a priori knowledge of the world is possible, and then by showing that metaphysics fails to comply with the conditions that make such a priori knowledge possible. Mathematical principles and the basic laws of science can give us a priori knowledge of the world insofar as they articulate or specify the structures that any experience must have and given that the world necessarily conforms to those structures. A priori knowledge of the world is possible insofar as the world has the a priori structure that is necessary for experience. Metaphysics fails because its principles do not articulate the necessary conditions of experience and because it aims for knowledge of the world absolutely that is independent of those structures.

B vii. **PREFACE TO SECOND EDITION**

Whether the treatment of such knowledge as lies within the province of reason does or does not follow the secure path of a science, is easily to be determined from the outcome.

B viii.   That logic has already, from the earliest times, proceeded upon this sure path is evidenced by the fact that since Aristotle it has not required to retrace a single step, unless, indeed, we care to count as improvements the removal of certain needless subtleties or the clearer exposition of its recognised teaching, features which concern the elegance rather than the certainty of the science. It is remarkable also that to the present day this logic has not been able to advance a single step, and is thus to all appearance a closed and completed body of doctrine.

B ix.   The sphere of logic is quite precisely delimited; its sole concern is to give an exhaustive exposition and a strict proof of the formal rules of all thought, whether it be *a priori* or empirical, whatever be its origin or its object, and whatever hindrances, accidental or natural, it may encounter in our minds.

That logic should have been thus successful is an advantage which it owes entirely to its limitations, whereby it is justified in abstracting—indeed, it is under obligation to do so—from all objects of knowledge and their differences, leaving the understanding nothing to deal with save itself and its form. But for reason to enter on the sure path of science is, of course, much more difficult, since it has to deal not with itself alone but also with objects.

Mathematics and physics, the two sciences in which reason yields theoretical knowledge, have to determine their objects *a priori*, the former doing so quite purely, the latter having to reckon, at least partially, with sources of knowledge other than reason.

In the earliest times to which the history of human reason extends, *mathematics*, among that wonderful people, the Greeks, had already entered upon the sure path of science. . . .

A new light flashed upon the mind of the first man (be he Thales or some other) who demonstrated the properties of the isosceles triangle. The true method, so he found, was not to

From *Immanuel Kant's Critique of Pure Reason* translated by Norman-Kemp Smith, 1929. Reprinted by permission of Palgrave Macmillan.

B xii. inspect what he discerned either in the figure, or in the bare concept of it, and from this, as it were, to read off its properties; but to bring out what was necessarily implied in the concepts that he had himself formed *a priori,* and had put into the figure in the construction by which he presented it to himself. If he is to know anything with *a priori* certainty he must not ascribe to the figure anything save what necessarily follows from what he has himself set into it in accordance with his concept.

Natural science was very much longer in entering upon the highway of science. It is, indeed, only about a century and a half since Bacon, by his ingenious proposals, partly initiated this discovery, partly inspired fresh vigour in those who were already on the way to it. In this case also the discovery can be explained as being the sudden outcome of an intellectual revolution. In my present remarks I am referring to natural science only in so far as it is founded on *empirical* principles.

When Galileo caused balls, the weights of which he had himself previously determined, to roll down an inclined plane; when Torricelli made the air carry a weight which he had calculated beforehand to be equal to that of a definite volume of water; or in more recent times, when
B xiii. Stahl changed metals into oxides, and oxides back into metal, by withdrawing something and then restoring it, a light broke upon all students of nature. They learned that reason has insight only into that which it produces after a plan of its own, and that it must not allow itself to be kept, as it were, in nature's leading-strings, but must itself show the way with principles of judgment based upon fixed laws, constraining nature to give answer to questions of reason's own determining.

Metaphysics is a completely isolated speculative science of reason, which soars far above the teachings of experience, and in which reason is indeed meant to be its own pupil. Metaphysics rests on concepts alone—not, like mathematics, on their application to intuition. But though it is older than all other sciences, and would survive even if all the rest were swallowed up in the abyss of an all-destroying barbarism, it has not yet had

the good fortune to enter upon the secure path of a science. . . .

So far, too, are the students of metaphysics
B xv. from exhibiting any kind of unanimity in their contentions, that metaphysics has rather to be regarded as a battle-ground quite peculiarly suited for those who desire to exercise themselves in mock combats, and in which no participant has ever yet succeeded in gaining even so much as an inch of territory, not at least in such manner as to secure him in its permanent possession. This shows, beyond all questioning, that the procedure of metaphysics has hitherto been a merely random groping, and, what is worst of all, a groping among mere concepts.

What, then, is the reason why, in this field, the sure road to science has not hitherto been found? Is it, perhaps, impossible of discovery? Why, in that case, should nature have visited our reason with the restless endeavour whereby it is ever searching for such a path, as if this were one of its most important concerns?

The examples of mathematics and natural science, which by a single and sudden revolution
B xvi. have become what they now are, seem to me sufficiently remarkable to suggest our considering what may have been the essential features in the changed point of view by which they have so greatly benefited. Their success should incline us, at least by way of experiment, to imitate their procedure, so far as the analogy which, as species of rational knowledge, they bear to metaphysics may permit. Hitherto it has been assumed that all our knowledge must conform to objects. But all attempts to extend our knowledge of objects by establishing something in regard to them *a priori,* by means of concepts, have, on this assumption, ended in failure. We must therefore make trial whether we may not have more success in the tasks of metaphysics, if we suppose that objects must conform to our knowledge. This would agree better with what is desired, namely, that it should be possible to have knowledge of objects *a priori,* determining something in regard to them prior to their being given. We should then be proceeding precisely on the lines of Copernicus' primary hypothesis. Failing of satisfactory progress in explaining the movements of

the heavenly bodies on the supposition that they all revolved round the spectator, he tried whether he might not have better success if he B xvii. made the spectator to revolve and the stars to remain at rest. A similar experiment can be tried in metaphysics, as regards the *intuition* of objects. If intuition must conform to the constitution of the objects, I do not see how we could know anything of the latter *a priori*; but if the object (as object of the senses) must conform to the constitution of our faculty of intuition, I have no difficulty in conceiving such a possibility. Since I cannot rest in these intuitions if they are to become known, but must relate them as representations to something as their object, and determine this latter through them, either I must assume that the *concepts*, by means of which I obtain this determination, conform to the object, or else I assume that the objects, or what is the same thing, that the *experience* in which alone, as given objects, they can be known, conform to the concepts. In the former case, I am again in the same perplexity as to how I can know anything *a priori* in regard to the objects. In the latter case the outlook is more hopeful. For experience is itself a species of knowledge which involves understanding; and understanding has rules which I must presuppose as being in me prior to objects being given to me, and therefore as being *a priori*. They find expression in *a priori* concepts to which all objects of experience nec-B xviii. essarily conform, and with which they must agree. As regards objects which are thought solely through reason, and indeed as necessary, but which can never—at least not in the manner in which reason thinks them—be given in experience, the attempts at thinking them (for they must admit of being thought) will furnish an excellent touchstone of what we are adopting as our new method of thought, namely, that we can know *a priori* of things only what we ourselves put into them.

This experiment succeeds as well as could be desired, and promises to metaphysics, in its first part—the part that is occupied with those concepts *a priori* to which the corresponding objects, commensurate with them, can be given in experience—the secure path of a science. For

B xix. the new point of view enables us to explain how there can be knowledge *a priori*; and, in addition, to furnish satisfactory proofs of the laws which form the *a priori* basis of nature, regarded as the sum of the objects of experience—neither achievement being possible on the procedure hitherto followed. But this deduction of our power of knowing *a priori*, in the first part of metaphysics, has a consequence which is startling, and which has the appearance of being highly prejudicial to the whole purpose of metaphysics, as dealt with in the second part. For we are brought to the conclusion that we can never transcend the limits of possible experience, though that is precisely what this science is concerned, above all else, to achieve. This situation yields, however, just the very experiment by which, indirectly, we are enabled to prove the truth of this first estimate of our *a priori* knowledge of reason, namely, that such knowledge has to do only with appearances, and must leave the thing in itself as indeed real *per se*, but as not known by us. For what necessarily forces us to transcend the limits of experience and of all appearances is the *unconditioned*, which reason, by necessity and by right, demands in things in themselves, as required to complete the series of conditions. If, then, on the supposition that our empirical knowledge conforms to objects as things in themselves, we find that the unconditioned *cannot be thought without contradiction*, and that when, on the other hand, we suppose that our representation of things, as they are given to us, does not conform to these things as they are in themselves, but that these objects, as appearances, conform to our mode of representation, *the contradiction vanishes;* and if, therefore, we thus find that the unconditioned is not to be met with in things, so far as we know them, that is, so far as they are given to us, but only so far as we do not know them, that is, so far as they are things in themselves, we are justified in concluding that what we at first assumed for the purposes of experiment is now definitely confirmed. But when all progress in the field of the supersensible has thus been denied to speculative reason, it is still open to us to enquire whether, in the practical knowledge of reason, data may not be found sufficient to determine reason's transcendent concept of the unconditioned, and so to enable us, in accordance with the wish of metaphysics, and by means of knowledge that is possible *a priori*, though only from a practical point of view, to pass beyond the limits of all possible experience. Speculative reason has thus at least made room for such an extension; and if it must at the same time B xxii. leave it empty, yet none the less we are at liberty, indeed we are summoned, to take occupation of it, if we can, by practical data of reason.

But, it will be asked, what sort of a treasure is this that we propose to bequeath to posterity? What is the value of the metaphysics that is alleged to be thus purified by criticism and established once for all? On a cursory view of the present work it may seem that its results are merely *negative*, warning us that we must never venture with speculative reason beyond the limits of experience. Such is in fact its primary use. But such teaching at once acquires a *positive* value when we recognise that the principles with which speculative reason ventures out beyond its proper limits do not in effect *extend* the employment of reason, but, as we find on closer scrutiny, inevitably *narrow* it. These principles properly belong [not to reason but] to sensibility, and B xxv. when thus employed they threaten to make the bounds of sensibility coextensive with the real, and so to supplant reason in its pure (practical) employment. So far, therefore, as our Critique limits speculative reason, it is indeed *negative*; but since it thereby removes an obstacle which stands in the way of the employment of practical reason, nay threatens to destroy it, it has in reality a *positive* and very important use. At least this is so, immediately we are convinced that there is an absolutely necessary *practical* employment of pure reason—the *moral*—in which it inevitably goes beyond the limits of sensibility. Though [practical] reason, in thus proceeding, requires no assistance from speculative reason, it must yet be assured against its opposition, that reason may not be brought into conflict with itself. To deny that the service which the Critique renders is *positive* in character, would thus be like saying that the police are of no positive benefit, inasmuch as their main business is merely to prevent the violence of which citizens stand in mutual

fear, in order that each may pursue his vocation in peace and security. That space and time are only forms of sensible intuition, and so only conditions of the existence of things as appearances; that, moreover, we have no concepts of understanding, and consequently no elements for the knowledge of things, save in so far as intuition B xxvi. can be given corresponding to these concepts; and that we can therefore have no knowledge of any object as thing in itself, but only in so far as it is an object of sensible intuition, that is, an appearance—all this is proved in the analytical part of the Critique. Thus it does indeed follow that all possible speculative knowledge of reason is limited to mere objects of *experience*. But our further contention must also be duly borne in mind, namely, that though we cannot *know* these objects as things in themselves, we must yet be in position at least to *think* them as things in themselves; otherwise we should be landed in the absurd conclusion that there can be appearance B xxvii. without anything that appears. Now let us suppose that the distinction, which our Critique has shown to be necessary, between things as objects of experience and those same things as things in themselves, had not been made. In that case all things in general, as far as they are efficient causes, would be determined by the principle of causality, and consequently by the mechanism of nature. I could not, therefore, without palpable contradiction, say of one and the same being, for instance the human soul, that its will is free and yet is subject to natural necessity, that is, is not free. For I have taken the soul in both propositions *in one and the same sense*, namely as a thing in general, that is, as a thing in itself; and save by means of a preceding critique, could not have done otherwise. But if our Critique is not in error in teaching that the object is to be taken *in a twofold sense*, namely as appearance and as thing in itself; if the deduction of the concepts of understanding is valid, and the principle of causality therefore applies only to things taken in the former sense, namely, in so far as they are objects of experience—these same objects, taken in the other sense, not being subject to the principle—then there is no contradiction in B xxviii. supposing that one and the same will is, in the appearance, that is, in its visible acts, necessarily subject to the law of nature, and so far *not free,* while yet, as belonging to a thing in itself, it is not subject to that law, and is therefore *free.* My soul, viewed from the latter standpoint, cannot indeed be known by means of speculative reason (and still less through empirical observation); and freedom as a property of a being to which I attribute effects in the sensible world, is therefore also not knowable in any such fashion. For I should then have to know such a being as determined in its existence, and yet as not determined in time—which is impossible, since I cannot support my concept by any intuition. But though I cannot *know,* I can yet *think* freedom; that is to say, the representation of it is at least not self-contradictory, provided due account be taken of our critical distinction between the two modes of representation, the sensible and the intellectual, and of the resulting limitation of the pure concepts of understanding and of the principles which flow from them.

If we grant that morality necessarily presupposes freedom (in the strictest sense) as a property of our will; if, that is to say, we grant that it yields practical principles—original principles, proper to our reason—as *a priori data* of reason, B xxix. and that this would be absolutely impossible save on the assumption of freedom; and if at the same time we grant that speculative reason has proved that such freedom does not allow of being thought, then the former supposition—that made on behalf of morality—would have to give way to this other contention, the opposite of which involves a palpable contradiction. For since it is only on the assumption of freedom that the negation of morality contains any contradiction, freedom, and with it morality, would have to yield to the mechanism of nature.

Morality does not, indeed, require that freedom should be understood, but only that it should not contradict itself, and so should at least allow of being thought, and that as thus thought it should place no obstacle in the way of a free act (viewed in another relation) likewise conforming to the mechanism of nature. The doctrine of morality and the doctrine of nature may

each, therefore, make good its position. This, however, is only possible in so far as criticism has previously established our unavoidable ignorance of things in themselves, and has limited all that we can theoretically *know* to mere appearances.

This discussion as to the positive advantage of critical principles of pure reason can be similarly developed in regard to the concept of *God* and of the *simple nature* of our *soul;* but for the sake of brevity such further discussion may be omitted. [From what has already been said, it is evident that] even the *assumption*—as made on B xxx. behalf of the necessary practical employment of my reason—of *God, freedom,* and *immortality* is not permissible unless at the same time speculative reason be deprived of its pretensions to transcendent insight. For in order to arrive at such insight it must make use of principles which, in fact, extend only to objects of possible experience, and which, if also applied to what cannot be an object of experience, always really change this into an appearance, thus rendering all *practical extension* of pure reason impossible. I have therefore found it necessary to deny *knowledge,* in order to make room for *faith.* The dogmatism of metaphysics, that is, the preconception that it is possible to make headway in metaphysics without a previous criticism of pure reason, is the source of all that unbelief, always very dogmatic, which wars against morality.

Though it may not, then, be very difficult to leave to posterity the bequest of a systematic metaphysic, constructed in conformity with a critique of pure reason, yet such a gift is not to be valued lightly. For not only will reason be enabled to follow the secure path of a science, B xxxi. instead of, as hitherto, groping at random, without circumspection or self-criticism; our enquiring youth will also be in a position to spend their time more profitably than in the ordinary dogmatism by which they are so early and so greatly encouraged to indulge in easy speculation about things of which they understand nothing, and into which neither they nor anyone else will ever have any insight—encouraged, indeed, to invent new ideas and opinions, while neglecting the study of the better-established sciences. But, above all, there is the inestimable benefit, that all objections to morality and religion will be for ever silenced, and this in Socratic fashion, namely, by the clearest proof of the ignorance of the objectors. There has always existed in the world, and there will always continue to exist, some kind of metaphysics, and with it the dialectic that is natural to pure reason. It is therefore the first and most important task of philosophy to deprive metaphysics, once and for all, of its injurious influence, by attacking its errors at their very source.

B1 # INTRODUCTION

I. The Distinction Between Pure and Empirical Knowledge

There can be no doubt that all our knowledge begins with experience. For how should our faculty of knowledge be awakened into action did not objects affecting our senses partly of themselves produce representations, partly arouse the activity of our understanding to compare these representations, and, by combining or separating them, work up the raw material of the sensible impressions into that knowledge of objects which is entitled experience? In the order of time, therefore, we have no knowledge antecedent to experience, and with experience all our knowledge begins.

But though all our knowledge begins with experience, it does not follow that it all arises out of experience. For it may well be that even our empirical knowledge is made up of what we receive through impressions and of what our own faculty of knowledge (sensible impressions serving merely as the occasion) supplies from itself. If our faculty of knowledge makes any such addi- B2 tion, it may be that we are not in a position to distinguish it from the raw material, until with long practice of attention we have become skilled in separating it.

In what follows, therefore, we shall understand by *a priori* knowledge, not knowledge independent of this or that experience, but knowledge absolutely independent of all experi- B3 ence. Opposed to it is empirical knowledge,

which is knowledge possible only *a posteriori*, that is, through experience. A *priori* modes of knowledge are entitled pure when there is no admixture of anything empirical. Thus, for instance, the proposition, 'every alteration has its cause', while an *a priori* proposition, is not a pure proposition, because alteration is a concept which can be derived only from experience.

II. We are in Possession of Certain Modes of *a Priori* Knowledge, and Even the Common Understanding is Never Without Them

Now it is easy to show that there actually are in human knowledge judgments which are necessary and in the strictest sense universal, and which are therefore pure *a priori* judgments. If an example from the sciences be desired, we have only to look to any of the propositions of mathematics; if we seek an example from the under- B5 standing in its quite ordinary employment, the proposition, 'every alteration must have a cause', will serve our purpose. In the latter case, indeed, the very concept of a cause so manifestly contains the concept of a necessity of connection with an effect and of the strict universality of the rule, that the concept would be altogether lost if we attempted to derive it, as Hume has done, from a repeated association of that which happens with that which precedes, and from a custom of connecting representations, a custom originating in this repeated association, and constituting therefore a merely subjective necessity. Even without appealing to such examples, it is possible to show that pure *a priori* principles are indispensable for the possibility of experience, and so to prove their existence *a priori*. For whence could experience derive its certainty, if all the rules, according to which it proceeds, were always themselves empirical, and therefore contingent? Such rules could hardly be regarded as first principles. At present, however, we may be content to have established the fact that our faculty of knowledge does have a pure employment, and to have shown what are the criteria of such an employment.

Such *a priori* origin is manifest in certain concepts, no less than in judgments. If we remove from our empirical concept of a body, one by one, every feature in it which is [merely] empirical, the colour, the hardness or softness, the weight, even the impenetrability, there still remains the space which the body (now entirely vanished) occupied, and this cannot be B 6 removed. Again, if we remove from our empirical concept of any object, corporeal or incorporeal, all properties which experience has taught us, we yet cannot take away that property through which the object is thought as substance or as inhering in a substance (although this concept of substance is more determinate than that of an object in general). Owing, therefore, to the necessity with which this concept of substance forces itself upon us, we have no option save to admit that it has its seat in our faculty of *a priori* knowledge.

III. Philosophy Stands in Need of a Science Which Shall Determine the Possibility, the Principles, and the Extent of All *a Priori* Knowledge

But what is still more extraordinary than all the preceding is this, that certain modes of knowl-
A 3 edge leave the field of all possible experiences and have the appearance of extending the scope of our judgments beyond all limits of experience, and this by means of concepts to which no corresponding object can ever be given in experience. It is precisely by means of the latter modes of knowledge, in a realm beyond the world of the senses, where experience can yield neither guidance nor correction, that our reason carries
B 7 on those enquiries which owing to their importance we consider to be far more excellent, and in their purpose far more lofty, than all that the understanding can learn in the field of appearances. Indeed we prefer to run every risk of error rather than desist from such urgent enquiries, on the ground of their dubious character, or from disdain and indifference. These unavoidable problems set by pure reason itself are *God, freedom,* and *immortality.* The science which, with all its preparations, is in its final intention directed solely to their solution is metaphysics; and its procedure is at first dog-

matic, that is, it confidently sets itself to this task without any previous examination of the capacity or incapacity of reason for so great an undertaking.

IV. The Distinction Between Analytic and Synthetic Judgments

In all judgments in which the relation of a subject to the predicate is thought (I take into consideration affirmative judgments only, the subsequent application to negative judgments being easily made), this relation is possible in two different ways. Either the predicate B belongs to the subject A, as something which is (covertly) contained in this concept A; or B lies outside the concept A, although it does indeed stand in connection with it. In the one case I entitle the judg-
A 7 ment analytic, in the other synthetic. Analytic judgments (affirmative) are therefore those in which the connection of the predicate with the subject is thought through identity; those in which this connection is thought without identity should be entitled synthetic. The former, as
B 11 adding nothing through the predicate to the concept of the subject, but merely breaking it up into those constituent concepts that have all along been thought in it, although confusedly, can also be entitled explicative. The latter, on the other hand, add to the concept of the subject a predicate which has not been in any wise thought in it, and which no analysis could possibly extract from it; and they may therefore be entitled ampliative. If I say, for instance, 'All bodies are extended', this is an analytic judgment. For I do not require to go beyond the concept which I connect with 'body' in order to find extension as bound up with it. To meet with this predicate, I have merely to analyse the concept, that is, to become conscious to myself of the manifold which I always think in that concept. The judgment is therefore analytic. But when I say, 'All bodies are heavy', the predicate is something quite different from anything that I think in the mere concept of body in general; and the addition of such a predicate therefore yields a synthetic judgment.

Judgments of experience, as such, are one and all synthetic. For it would be absurd to found an analytic judgment on experience. Since, in framing the judgment, I must not go outside my concept, there is no need to appeal to the testimony of experience in its support. That a body is extended is a proposition that holds *a priori* and is B 12 not empirical. For, before appealing to experience, I have already in the concept of body all the conditions required for my judgment. I have only to extract from it, in accordance with the principle of contradiction, the required predicate, and in so doing can at the same time become conscious of the necessity of the judgment—and that is what experience could never have taught me. On the other hand, though I do not include in the concept of a body in general the predicate 'weight', none the less this concept indicates an object of experience through one of its parts, and I can add to that part other parts of this same experience, as in this way belonging together with the concept. From the start I can apprehend the concept of body analytically through the characters of extension, impenetrability, figure, etc., all of which are thought in the concept. Now, however, looking back on the experience from which I have derived this concept of body, and finding weight to be invariably connected with the above characters, I attach it as a predicate to the concept; and in doing so I attach it synthetically, and am therefore extending my knowledge. The possibility of the synthesis of the predicate 'weight' with the concept of 'body' thus rests upon experience. While the one concept is not contained in the other, they yet belong to one another, though only contingently, as parts of a whole, namely, of an experience which is itself a synthetic combination of intuitions.

A 9   But in *a priori* synthetic judgments this help
B 13 is entirely lacking: [I do not here have the advantage of looking around in the field of experience.] Upon what, then, am I to rely, when I seek to go beyond the concept A, and to know that another concept B is connected with it? Through what is the synthesis made possible? Let us take the proposition, 'Everything which happens has its cause.' In the concept of 'something which hap-

pens', I do indeed think an existence which is preceded by a time, etc., and from this concept analytic judgments may be obtained. But the concept of a 'cause' lies entirely outside the other concept, and signifies something different from 'that which happens', and is not therefore in any way contained in this latter representation. How come I then to predicate of that which happens something quite different, and to apprehend that the concept of cause, though not contained in it, yet belongs, and indeed necessarily belongs, to it? What is here the unknown = X which gives support to the understanding when it believes that it can discover outside the concept A a predicate B foreign to this concept, which it yet at the same time considers to be connected with it? It cannot be experience, because the suggested principle has connected the second representation with the first, not only with greater universality, but also with the character of necessity, and therefore completely *a priori* and on the basis of mere concepts. Upon such synthetic, that is, ampliative
A 10 principles, all our *a priori* speculative knowledge must ultimately rest; analytic judgments are very important, and indeed necessary, but only for
B 14 obtaining that clearness in the concepts which is requisite for such a sure and wide synthesis as will lead to a genuinely new addition to all previous knowledge.

V. In All Theoretical Sciences of Reason Synthetic *a Priori* Judgments are Contained as Principles

I. *All mathematical judgments, without exception, are synthetic.* This fact, though incontestably certain and in its consequences very important, has hitherto escaped the notice of those who are engaged in the analysis of human reason, and is, indeed, directly opposed to all their conjectures. For as it was found that all mathematical inferences proceed in accordance with the principle of contradiction (which the nature of all apodeictic certainty requires), it was supposed that the fundamental propositions of the science can themselves be known to be true through that principle. This is an erroneous view. For though a synthetic proposition can indeed be discerned in accordance with the principle of contradiction, this can only be if another synthetic proposition is presupposed, and if it can then be apprehended as following from this other proposition; it can never be so discerned in and by itself.

First of all, it has to be noted that mathematical propositions, strictly so called, are always judgments *a priori*, not empirical; because they B 15 carry with them necessity, which cannot be derived from experience. If this be demurred to, I am willing to limit my statement to *pure* mathematics, the very concept of which implies that it does not contain empirical, but only pure *a priori* knowledge.

We might, indeed, at first suppose that the proposition $7 + 5 = 12$ is a merely analytic proposition, and follows by the principle of contradiction from the concept of a sum of 7 and 5. But if we look more closely we find that the concept of the sum of 7 and 5 contains nothing save the union of the two numbers into one, and in this no thought is being taken as to what that single number may be which combines both. The concept of 12 is by no means already thought in merely thinking this union of 7 and 5; and I may analyse my concept of such a possible sum as long as I please, still I shall never find the 12 in it. We have to go outside these concepts, and call in the aid of the intuition which corresponds to one of them, our five fingers, for instance, or, as Segner does in his *Arithmetic*, five points, adding to the concept of 7, unit by unit, the five given in intuition. For starting with the number 7, and for the concept of 5 calling in the aid of the fingers of my hand as intuition, I now add one by one to the number 7 the units which I previously took B 16 together to form the number 5, and with the aid of that figure [the hand] see the number 12 come into being. That 5 should be added to 7, I have indeed already thought in the concept of a sum $= 7 + 5$, but not that this sum is equivalent to the number 12. Arithmetical propositions are therefore always synthetic. This is still more evident if we take larger numbers. For it is then obvious that, however we might turn and twist our concepts, we could never, by the mere analy-

sis of them, and without the aid of intuition, discover what [the number is that] is the sum.

Just as little is any fundamental proposition of pure geometry analytic. That the straight line between two points is the shortest, is a synthetic proposition. For my concept of *straight* contains nothing of quantity, but only of quality. The concept of the shortest is wholly an addition, and cannot be derived, through any process of analysis, from the concept of the straight line. Intuition, therefore, must here be called in; only by B 17 its aid is the synthesis possible. What here causes us commonly to believe that the predicate of such apodeictic judgments is already contained in our concept, and that the judgment is therefore analytic, is merely the ambiguous character of the terms used. We are required to join in thought a certain predicate to a given concept, and this necessity is inherent in the concepts themselves. But the question is not what we *ought* to join in thought to the given concept, but what we *actually* think in it, even if only obscurely; and it is then manifest that, while the predicate is indeed attached necessarily to the concept, it is so in virtue of an intuition which must be added to the concept, not as thought in the concept itself.

B 16   Some few fundamental propositions, presupposed by the geometrician, are, indeed, really analytic, and rest on the principle of contradic-B 17 tion. But, as identical propositions, they serve only as links in the chain of method and not as principles; for instance, $a = a$; the whole is equal to itself; or $(a + b) > a$, that is, the whole is greater than its part. And even these propositions, though they are valid according to pure concepts, are only admitted in mathematics because they can be exhibited in intuition.

2. *Natural science (physics) contains* a priori *synthetic judgments as principles*. I need cite only two such judgments: that in all changes of the material world the quantity of matter remains unchanged; and that in all communication of motion, action and reaction must always be equal. Both propositions, it is evident, are not B 18 only necessary, and therefore in their origin *a priori*, but also synthetic. For in the concept of matter I do not think its permanence, but only its presence in the space which it occupies. I go outside and beyond the concept of matter, joining to it *a priori* in thought something which I have not thought *in* it. The proposition is not, therefore, analytic, but synthetic, and yet is thought *a priori*; and so likewise are the other propositions of the pure part of natural science.

3. *Metaphysics,* even if we look upon it as having hitherto failed in all its endeavours, is yet, owing to the nature of human reason, a quite indispensable science, and *ought to contain* a priori *synthetic knowledge.* For its business is not merely to analyse concepts which we make for ourselves *a priori* of things, and thereby to clarify them analytically, but to extend our *a priori* knowledge. And for this purpose we must employ principles which add to the given concept something that was not contained in it, and through *a priori* synthetic judgments venture out so far that experience is quite unable to follow us, as, for instance, in the proposition, that the world must have a first beginning, and such like. Thus metaphysics consists, at least *in intention,* entirely of *a priori* synthetic propositions.

B 19 ## VI. The General Problem of Pure Reason

Much is already gained if we can bring a number of investigations under the formula of a single problem. For we not only lighten our own task, by defining it accurately, but make it easier for others, who would test our results, to judge whether or not we have succeeded in what we set out to do. Now the proper problem of pure reason is contained in the question: How are *a priori* synthetic judgments possible?

That metaphysics has hitherto remained in so vacillating a state of uncertainty and contradiction, is entirely due to the fact that this problem, and perhaps even the distinction between analytic and synthetic judgments, has never previously been considered. Upon the solution of this problem, or upon a sufficient proof that the possibility which it desires to have explained does in fact not exist at all, depends the success or failure of metaphysics. Among philosophers,

David Hume came nearest to envisaging this problem, but still was very far from conceiving it with sufficient definiteness and universality. He occupied himself exclusively with the synthetic proposition regarding the connection of an effect B 20 with its cause (*principium causalitatis*), and he believed himself to have shown that such an *a priori* proposition is entirely impossible. If we accept his conclusions, then all that we call metaphysics is a mere delusion whereby we fancy ourselves to have rational insight into what, in actual fact, is borrowed solely from experience, and under the influence of custom has taken the illusory semblance of necessity. If he had envisaged our problem in all its universality, he would never have been guilty of this statement, so destructive of all pure philosophy. For he would then have recognised that, according to his own argument, pure mathematics, as certainly containing *a priori* synthetic propositions, would also not be possible; and from such an assertion his good sense would have saved him.

In the solution of the above problem, we are at the same time deciding as to the possibility of the employment of pure reason in establishing and developing all those sciences which contain a theoretical *a priori* knowledge of objects, and have therefore to answer the questions:

How is pure mathematics possible?
How is pure science of nature possible?

Since these sciences actually exist, it is quite proper to ask *how* they are possible; for that they B 21 must be possible is proved by the fact that they exist. But the poor progress which has hitherto been made in metaphysics, and the fact that no system yet propounded can, in view of the essential purpose of metaphysics, be said really to exist, leaves everyone sufficient ground for doubting as to its possibility.

Yet, in a certain sense, this *kind of knowledge* is to be looked upon as given; that is to say, metaphysics actually exists, if not as a science, yet still as natural disposition (*metaphysica naturalis*). For human reason, without being moved merely by the idle desire for extent and variety of knowledge, proceeds impetuously, driven on by an inward need, to questions such as cannot be answered by any empirical employment of reason, or by principles thence derived. Thus in all men, as soon as their reason has become ripe for speculation, there has always existed and will always continue to exist some kind of. metaphysics. And so we have the question:

B 22 *How is metaphysics, as natural disposition, possible?*

that is, how from the nature of universal human reason do those questions arise which pure reason propounds to itself, and which it is impelled by its own need to answer as best it can?

But since all attempts which have hitherto been made to answer these natural questions—for instance, whether the world has a beginning or is from eternity—have always met with unavoidable contradictions, we cannot rest satisfied with the mere natural disposition to metaphysics, that is, with the pure faculty of reason itself, from which, indeed, some sort of metaphysics (be it what it may) always arises. It must be possible for reason to attain to certainty whether we know or do not know the objects of metaphysics, that is, to come to a decision either in regard to the objects of its enquiries or in regard to the capacity or incapacity of reason to pass any judgment upon them, so that we may either with confidence extend our pure reason or set to it sure and determinate limits. This last question, which arises out of the previous general problem, may, rightly stated, take the form:

How is metaphysics, as science, possible?

Thus the critique of reason, in the end, necessarily leads to scientific knowledge; while its dogmatic employment, on the other hand, lands us B 23 in dogmatic assertions to which other assertions, equally specious, can always be opposed—that is, in *scepticism*.

This science cannot be of any very formidable prolixity, since it has to deal not with the objects of reason, the variety of which is inexhaustible, but only with itself and the problems which arise entirely from within itself, and which are imposed upon it by its own nature, not by the nature of things which are distinct from it.

When once reason has learnt completely to understand its own power in respect of objects which can be presented to it in experience, it should easily be able to determine, with completeness and certainty, the extent and the limits of its attempted employment beyond the bounds of all experience.

We may, then, and indeed we must, regard as abortive all attempts, hitherto made, to establish a metaphysic *dogmatically*. For the analytic part in any such attempted system, namely, the mere analysis of the concepts that inhere in our reason *a priori*, is by no means the aim of, but only a preparation for, metaphysics proper, that is, the extension of its *a priori* synthetic knowledge. For such a purpose, the analysis of concepts is useless, since it merely shows what is contained in these concepts, not how we arrive at them *a priori*. A solution of this latter problem is required, that B 24 we may be able to determine the valid employment of such concepts in regard to the objects of all knowledge in general. Nor is much self-denial needed to give up these claims, seeing that the undeniable, and in the dogmatic procedure of reason also unavoidable, contradictions of reason with itself have long since undermined the authority of every metaphysical system yet propounded. Greater firmness will be required if we are not to be deterred by inward difficulties and outward opposition from endeavouring, through application of a method entirely different from any hitherto employed, at last to bring to a prosperous and fruitful growth a science indispensable to human reason—a science whose every branch may be cut away but whose root cannot be destroyed.

A 19 ## TRANSCENDENTAL DOCTRINE OF ELEMENTS

First Part

Transcendental Aesthetic

§ 1

In whatever manner and by whatever means a mode of knowledge may relate to objects, *intuition* is that through which it is in immediate relation to them, and to which all thought as a means is directed. But intuition takes place only in so far as the object is given to us. This again is only possible, to man at least, in so far as the mind is affected in a certain way. The capacity (receptivity) for receiving representations through the mode in which we are affected by objects, is entitled *sensibility*. Objects are *given* to us by means of sensibility, and it alone yields us *intuitions*; they are *thought* through the understanding, and from the understanding arise *concepts*. But all thought must, directly or indirectly, by way of certain characters, relate ultimately to intuitions, and therefore, with us, to sensibility, because in no other way can an object be given to us.

B 34 The effect of an object upon the faculty
A 20 of representation, so far as we are affected by it, is *sensation*. That intuition which is in relation to the object through sensation, is entitled *empirical*. The undetermined object of an empirical intuition is entitled *appearance*.

That in the appearance which corresponds to sensation I term its *matter*; but that which so determines the manifold of appearance that it allows of being ordered in certain relations, I term the *form* of appearance. That in which alone the sensations can be posited and ordered in a certain form, cannot itself be sensation; and therefore, while the matter of all appearance is given to us *a posteriori* only, its form must lie ready for the sensations *a priori* in the mind, and so must allow of being considered apart from all sensation.

I term all representations *pure* (in the transcendental sense) in which there is nothing that belongs to sensation. The pure form of sensible intuitions in general, in which all the manifold of intuition is intuited in certain relations, must be found in the mind *a priori*. This pure form of
B 35 sensibility may also itself be called *pure intuition*. Thus, if I take away from the representation of a body that which the understanding thinks in regard to it, substance, force, divisibility, etc., and
A 21 likewise what belongs to sensation, impenetrability, hardness, colour, etc., something still remains over from this empirical intuition, namely, exten-

sion and figure. These belong to pure intuition, which, even without any actual object of the senses or of sensation, exists in the mind *a priori* as a mere form of sensibility.

The science of all principles of *a priori* sensibility I call *transcendental aesthetic*. There must be such a science, forming the first part of the tran-
B 36 scendental doctrine of elements, in distinction from that part which deals with the principles of pure thought, and which is called transcendental logic.

A 22 In the transcendental aesthetic we shall, therefore, first *isolate* sensibility, by taking away from it everything which the understanding thinks through its concepts, so that nothing may be left save empirical intuition. Secondly, we shall also separate off from it everything which belongs to sensation, so that nothing may remain save pure intuition and the mere form of appearances, which is all that sensibility can supply *a priori*. In the course of this investigation it will be found that there are two pure forms of sensible intuition, serving as principles of *a priori* knowledge, namely, space and time. To the consideration of these we shall now proceed.

The Transcendental Aesthetic

B 37
Section I Space

§ 2

Metaphysical Exposition of this Concept

By means of outer sense, a property of our mind, we represent to ourselves objects as outside us, and all without exception in space. In space their shape, magnitude, and relation to one another are determined or determinable. Inner sense, by means of which the mind intuits itself or its inner state, yields indeed no intuition of the soul itself
A 23 as an object; but there is nevertheless a determinate form [namely, time] in which alone the intuition of inner states is possible, and everything which belongs to inner determinations is therefore represented in relations of time. Time cannot be outwardly intuited, any more than space can be intuited as something in us. What, then, are space and time? Are they real existences? Are they only determinations or relations

of things, yet such as would belong to things even if they were not intuited? Or are space and time such that they belong only to the form of intuition, and therefore to the subjective constitution of our mind, apart from which they could not be ascribed to anything whatsoever? In order to obtain light upon these questions, let us first give an exposition of the concept of space. By *exposition* (*expositio*) I mean the clear, though not necessarily exhaustive, representation of that which belongs to a concept: the exposition is *metaphysical* when it contains that which exhibits the concept *as given a priori*.

1. Space is not an empirical concept which has been derived from outer experiences. For in order that certain sensations be referred to something outside me (that is, to something in another region of space from that in which I find myself), and similarly in order that I may be able to represent them as outside and alongside one another, and accordingly as not only different but as in different places, the representation of space must be presupposed. The representation of space cannot, therefore, be empirically obtained from the relations of outer appearance. On the contrary, this outer experience is itself possible at all only through that representation.

2. Space is a necessary *a priori* representation, which underlies all outer intuitions. We can never represent to ourselves the absence of space, though we can quite well think it as empty of objects. It must therefore be regarded as the condition of the possibility of appearances, and not as a determination dependent upon them. It is an *a priori* representation, which necessarily underlies outer appearances.

3. Space is not a discursive or, as we say, general concept of relations of things in general, but a pure intuition. For, in the first place, we can represent to ourselves only one space; and if we speak of diverse spaces, we mean thereby only parts of one and the same unique space. Secondly, these parts cannot precede the one all-embracing space, as being, as it were, constituents out of which it can be composed; on the contrary, they can be thought only as *in* it. Space is essentially

one; the manifold in it, and therefore the general concept of spaces, depends solely on [the introduction of] limitations. Hence it follows that an *a priori*, and not an empirical, intuition underlies all concepts of space. For kindred reasons, geometrical propositions, that, for instance, in a triangle two sides together are greater than the third, can never be derived from the general concepts of line and triangle, but only from intuition, and this indeed *a priori*, with apodeictic certainty.

4. Space is represented as an infinite *given* magnitude. Now every concept must be thought as a representation which is contained in an infinite number of different possible representations (as their common character), and which therefore contains these *under* itself; but no concept, as such, can be thought as containing an infinite number of representations *within* itself. It is in this latter way, however, that space is thought; for all the parts of space coexist *ad infinitum*. Consequently, the original representation of space is an *a priori* intuition, not a concept.

§ 3

The Transcendental Exposition of the Concept of Space

I understand by a transcendental exposition the explanation of a concept, as a principle from which the possibility of other *a priori* synthetic knowledge can be understood. For this purpose it is required (1) that such knowledge does really flow from the given concept, (2) that this knowledge is possible only on the assumption of a given mode of explaining the concept.

Geometry is a science which determines the properties of space synthetically, and yet *a priori*. What, then, must be our representation of space, in order that such knowledge of it may be possible? It must in its origin be intuition; for from a mere concept no propositions can be obtained which go beyond the concept—as happens in geometry (Introduction, V). Further, this intuition must be *a priori*, that is, it must be found in us prior to any perception of an object, and must therefore be pure, not empirical, intuition. For geometrical propositions are one and all apodeictic, that is, are bound up with the consciousness of their necessity; for instance, that space has only three dimensions. Such propositions cannot be empirical or, in other words, judgments of experience, nor can they be derived from any such judgments (Introduction, II).

How, then, can there exist in the mind an outer intuition which precedes the objects themselves, and in which the concept of these objects can be determined *a priori?* Manifestly, not otherwise than in so far as the intuition has its seat in the subject only, as the formal character of the subject, in virtue of which, in being affected by objects, it obtains *immediate representation,* that is, *intuition,* of them; and only in so far, therefore, as it is merely the form of outer *sense* in general.

Our explanation is thus the only explanation that makes intelligible the *possibility* of geometry, as a body of *a priori* synthetic knowledge. Any mode of explanation which fails to do this, although it may otherwise seem to be somewhat similar, can by this criterion be distinguished from it with the greatest certainty.

Section II Time

§ 6

Conclusions from these Concepts

(*a*) Time is not something which exists of itself, or which inheres in things as an objective determination, and it does not, therefore, remain when abstraction is made of all subjective conditions of its intuition. Were it self-subsistent, it would be something which would be actual and yet not an actual object. Were it a determination or order inhering in things themselves, it could not precede the objects as their condition, and be known and intuited *a priori* by means of synthetic propositions. But this last is quite possible if time is nothing but the subjective condition under which alone intuition can take place in us. For that being so, this form of inner intuition can be represented prior to the objects, and therefore *a priori.*

A 33

(*b*) Time is nothing but the form of inner sense, that is, of the intuition of ourselves and of our inner state. It cannot be a determination of

outer appearances; it has to do neither with shape nor position, but with the relation of representations in our inner state. And just because this inner intuition yields no shape, we endeavour to make up for this want by analogies. We represent the time-sequence by a line progressing to infinity, in which the manifold constitutes a series of one dimension only; and we reason from the properties of this line to all the properties of time, with this one exception, that while the parts of the line are simultaneous the parts of time are always successive. From this fact also, that all the relations of time allow of being expressed in an outer intuition, it is evident that the representation is itself an intuition.

B 50

(*c*) Time is the formal *a priori* condition of all appearances whatsoever. Space, as the pure form of all *outer* intuition, is so far limited; it serves as the *a priori* condition only of outer appearances. But since all representations, whether they have for their objects outer things or not, belong, in themselves, as determinations of the mind, to our inner state; and since this inner state stands under the formal condition of inner intuition, and so belongs to time, time is an *a priori* condition of all appearance whatsoever. It is the immediate condition of inner appearances (of our souls), and thereby the mediate condition of outer appearances. Just as I can say *a priori* that all outer appearances are in space, and are determined *a priori* in conformity with the relations of space, I can also say, from the principle of inner sense, that all appearances whatsoever, that is, all objects of the senses, are in time, and necessarily stand in time-relations.

A 34

B 51

If we abstract from *our* mode of inwardly intuiting ourselves—the mode of intuition in terms of which we likewise take up into our faculty of representation all outer intuitions—and so take objects as they may be in themselves, then time is nothing. It has objective validity only in respect of appearances, these being things which we take *as objects of our senses.* It is no longer objective, if we abstract from the sensibility of our intuition, that is, from that mode of representation which is peculiar to us, and speak of *things in general.* Time is therefore a purely

A 35

subjective condition of our (human) intuition (which is always sensible, that is, so far as we are affected by objects), and in itself, apart from the subject, is nothing. Nevertheless, in respect of all appearances, and therefore of all the things which can enter into our experience, it is necessarily objective. We cannot say that all things are B 52 in time, because in this concept of things in general we are abstracting from every mode of their intuition and therefore from that condition under which alone objects can be represented as being in time. If, however, the condition be added to the concept, and we say that all things as appearances, that is, as objects of sensible intuition, are in time, then the proposition has legitimate objective validity and universality *a priori*.

What we are maintaining is, therefore, the *empirical reality* of time, that is, its objective validity in respect of all objects which allow of ever being given to our senses. And since our intuition is always sensible, no object can ever be given to us in experience which does not conform to the condition of time. On the other hand, we deny to time all claim to absolute real-A 36 ity; that is to say, we deny that it belongs to things absolutely, as their condition or property, independently of any reference to the form of our sensible intuition; properties that belong to things in themselves can never be given to us through the senses. This, then, is what constitutes the *transcendental ideality* of time. What we mean by this phrase is that if we abstract from the subjective conditions of sensible intuition, time is nothing, and cannot be ascribed to the objects in themselves (apart from their relation to our intuition) in the way either of subsistence B 53 or of inherence. This ideality, like that of space, must not, however, be illustrated by false analogies with sensation, because it is then assumed that the appearance, in which the sensible predicates inhere, itself has objective reality. In the case of time, such objective reality falls entirely away, save in so far as it is merely empirical, that is, save in so far as we regard the object itself merely as appearance. On this subject, the reader may refer to what has been said at the close of the preceding section.

Time and space are, therefore, two sources of knowledge, from which bodies of *a priori* synthetic A 39 knowledge can be derived. (Pure mathematics is a brilliant example of such knowledge, especially as B 56 regards space and its relations.) Time and space, taken together, are the pure forms of all sensible intuition, and so are what make *a priori* synthetic propositions possible. But these *a priori* sources of knowledge, being merely conditions of our sensibility, just by this very fact determine their own limits, namely, that they apply to objects only in so far as objects are viewed as appearances, and do not present things as they are in themselves. This is the sole field of their validity; should we pass beyond it, no objective use can be made of them. This ideality of space and time leaves, however, the certainty of empirical knowledge unaffected, for we are equally sure of it, whether these forms necessarily inhere in things in themselves or only in our intuition of them. Those, on the other hand, who maintain the absolute reality of space and time, whether as subsistent or only as inherent, must come into conflict with the principles of experience itself. For if they decide for the former alternative (which is generally the view taken by mathematical students of nature), they have to admit two eternal and infinite self-subsistent nonentities (space and time), which are there (yet without there being anything real) only in order to contain in themselves all that is real. If they A 40 adopt the latter alternative (as advocated by certain metaphysical students of nature), and regard space and time as relations of appearances, along-B 57 side or in succession to one another—relations abstracted from experience, and in this isolation confusedly represented—they are obliged to deny that *a priori* mathematical doctrines have any validity in respect of real things (for instance, in space), or at least to deny their apodeictic certainty. For such certainty is not to be found in the *a posteriori*. On this view, indeed, the *a priori* concepts of space and time are merely creatures of the imagination, whose source must really be sought in experience, the imagination framing out of the relations abstracted from experience something that does indeed contain what is general in these relations, but which cannot exist without the restrictions which nature has attached to them. The former thinkers obtain at least this advantage, that they keep the field of appearances open for mathematical propositions. On the other hand, they have greatly embarrassed themselves by those very conditions [space and time, eternal, infinite, and self-subsistent], when with the understanding they endeavour to go out beyond this field. The latter have indeed an advantage, in that the representations of space and time do not stand in their way if they seek to judge of objects, not as appearances but merely in their relation to the understanding. But since they are unable to appeal to a true and objectively valid *a priori* intuition, they can neither account for the possibility of *a priori* mathematical knowledge, nor bring the A 41 propositions of experience into necessary agree- B 58 ment with it. On our theory of the true character of these two original forms of sensibility, both difficulties are removed.

A 50 **TRANSCENDENTAL DOCTRINE OF** B 74 **ELEMENTS**

Second Part

Transcendental Logic

Introduction

Idea of a Transcendental Logic

I

Logic in General

Our knowledge springs from two fundamental sources of the mind; the first is the capacity of receiving representations (receptivity for impressions), the second is the power of knowing an object through these representations (spontaneity [in the production] of concepts).

If the *receptivity* of our mind, its power of receiving representations in so far as it is in any wise affected, is to be entitled sensibility, then the mind's power of producing representations from itself, the *spontaneity* of knowledge, should be called the understanding. Our nature is so constituted that our *intuition* can never be other than sensible; that is, it contains only the mode in which we are affected by objects. The faculty, on

the other hand, which enables us to *think* the object of sensible intuition is the understanding. To neither of these powers may a preference be given over the other. Without sensibility no object would be given to us, without understanding no object would be thought. Thoughts without content are empty, intuitions without concepts are blind. It is, therefore, just as necessary to make our concepts sensible, that is, to add the object to them in intuition, as to make our intuitions intelligible, that is, to bring them under concepts. These two powers or capacities cannot exchange their functions. The understanding can intuit nothing, the senses can think nothing. Only through their union can knowledge arise. B 76 But that is no reason for confounding the contribution of either with that of the other; rather is it a A 52 strong reason for carefully separating and distinguishing the one from the other. We therefore distinguish the science of the rules of sensibility in general, that is, aesthetic, from the science of the rules of the understanding in general, that is, logic.

ANALYTIC OF CONCEPTS

Chapter I

The Clue to the Discovery of All Pure Concepts of the Understanding

When we call a faculty of knowledge into play, then, as the occasioning circumstances differ, various concepts stand forth and make the faculty known, and allow of their being collected with more or less completeness, in proportion as observation has been made of them over a longer time or with greater acuteness. But when the enquiry is carried on in this mechanical fashion, we can never be sure whether it has been brought to com- A 67 pletion. Further, the concepts which we thus dis- B 92 cover only as opportunity offers, exhibit no order and systematic unity, but are in the end merely arranged in pairs according to similarities, and in series according to the amount of their contents, from the simple on to the more composite— an arrangement which is anything but systematic, although to a certain extent methodically instituted.

Transcendental philosophy, in seeking for its concepts, has the advantage and also the duty of proceeding according to a single principle. For these concepts spring, pure and unmixed, out of the understanding which is an absolute unity; and must therefore be connected with each other according to one concept or idea. Such a connection supplies us with a rule, by which we are enabled to assign its proper place to each pure concept of the understanding, and by which we can determine in an *a priori* manner their systematic completeness. Otherwise we should be dependent in these matters on our own discretionary judgment or merely on chance.

ANALYTIC OF CONCEPTS

The Transcendental Clue to the Discovery of All Pure Concepts of the Understanding

Section 1

The Logical Employment of the Understanding

The understanding has thus far been explained merely negatively, as a non-sensible faculty of knowledge. Now since without sensibility we A 68 cannot have any intuition, understanding cannot be a faculty of intuition. But besides intuition there is no other mode of knowledge except by B 93 means of concepts. The knowledge yielded by understanding, or at least by the human understanding, must therefore be by means of concepts, and so is not intuitive, but discursive. Whereas all intuitions, as sensible, rest on affections, concepts rest on functions. By 'function' I mean the unity of the act of bringing various representations under one common representation. Concepts are based on the spontaneity of thought, sensible intuitions on the receptivity of impressions. Now the only use which the understanding can make of these concepts is to judge by means of them. Since no representation, save when it is an intuition, is in immediate relation to an object, no concept is ever related to an object immediately, but to some other representation of it, be that other representation an intuition, or itself a concept. Judgment is therefore the mediate knowledge of an object, that is, the representation of a

representation of it. In every judgment there is a concept which holds of many representations, and among them of a given representation that is immediately related to an object. Thus in the judgment, 'all bodies are divisible', the concept of the divisible applies to various other concepts, but is here applied in particular to the concept A 69 of body, and this concept again to certain appearances that present themselves to us. These objects, therefore, are mediately represented through the concept of divisibility. Accordingly, all judgments are functions of unity among our representations; B 94 instead of an immediate representation, a *higher* representation, which comprises the immediate representation and various others, is used in knowing the object, and thereby much possible knowledge is collected into one. Now we can reduce all acts of the understanding to judgments, and the *understanding* may therefore be represented as a *faculty of judgment*. For, as stated above, the understanding is a faculty of thought. Thought is knowledge by means of concepts. But concepts, as predicates of possible judgments, relate to some representation of a not *yet* determined object. Thus the concept of body means something, for instance, metal, which can be known by means of that concept. It is therefore a concept solely in virtue of its comprehending other representations, by means of which it can relate to objects. It is therefore the predicate of a possible judgment, for instance, 'every metal is a body'. The functions of the understanding can, therefore, be discovered if we can give an exhaustive statement of the functions of unity in judgments. That this can quite easily be done will be shown in the next section.

A 70 ## The Clue to the Discovery of All Pure
B 95 ## Concepts of the Understanding

§ 9

The Logical Function of the Understanding in Judgments

If we abstract from all content of a judgment, and consider only the mere form of understanding, we find that the function of thought in judgment can be brought under four heads, each of which contains three moments. They may be conveniently represented in the following table:

TABLE OF JUDGMENTS

I

Quantity of Judgments

Universal
Particular
Singular

II
Quality

Affirmative
Negative
Infinite

III
Relation

Categorical
Hypothetical
Disjunctive

IV
Modality

Problematic
Assertoric
Apodeictic

As this division appears to depart in some, B 96 though not in any essential respects, from the technical distinctions ordinarily recognised by A 71 logicians, the following observations may serve to guard against any possible misunderstanding.

§ 10

The Pure Concepts of the Understanding, or Categories

General logic, as has been repeatedly said, abstracts from all content of knowledge, and looks to some other source, whatever that may be, for the representations which it is to transform into concepts by process of analysis. Transcendental logic, on the other hand, has lying before it a A 77 manifold of a priori sensibility, presented by transcendental aesthetic, as material for the concepts of pure understanding. In the absence of this material those concepts would be without any content, therefore entirely empty. Space and time contain a manifold of pure a priori intuition, but at the same time are conditions of the receptivity of our mind—conditions under which alone it can receive representations of objects, and which therefore must also always affect the concept of these objects. But if this manifold is to be known, the spontaneity of our thought requires that it be gone through in a certain way, taken up, and connected. This act I name synthesis.

B 103 By synthesis, in its most general sense, I understand the act of putting different representations together, and of grasping what is manifold in them in one [act of] knowledge. Such a synthesis is pure, if the manifold is not empirical but is given a priori, as is the manifold in space and time. Before we can analyse our representations, the representations must themselves be given, and therefore as regards content no concepts can first arise by way of analysis. Synthesis of a manifold (be it given empirically or a priori) is what first gives rise to knowledge. This knowledge may, indeed, at first, be crude and confused, and therefore in need of analysis. Still the synthesis is that which gathers the elements for knowledge, and unites them to [form] a certain content. It is A 78 to synthesis, therefore, that we must first direct our attention, if we would determine the first origin of our knowledge.

Synthesis in general, as we shall hereafter see, is the mere result of the power of imagination, a blind but indispensable function of the soul, without which we should have no knowledge whatsoever, but of which we are scarcely ever conscious. To bring this synthesis to concepts is a function which belongs to the understanding, and it is through this function of the understanding that we first obtain knowledge properly so called.

B 104 Pure synthesis, represented in its most general aspect, gives us the pure concept of the understanding. By this pure synthesis I understand that which rests upon a basis of a priori synthetic unity. Thus our counting, as is easily seen in the case of larger numbers, is a synthesis according to concepts, because it is executed according to a common ground of unity, as, for instance, the decade. In terms of this concept, the unity of the synthesis of the manifold is rendered necessary.

By means of analysis different representations are brought under one concept—a procedure treated of in general logic. What transcendental logic, on the other hand, teaches, is how we bring to concepts, not representations, but the pure synthesis of representations. What must first be given—with a view to the a priori knowledge A 79 of all objects—is the manifold of pure intuition; the second factor involved is the synthesis of this manifold by means of the imagination. But even this does not yet yield knowledge. The concepts which give *unity* to this pure synthesis, and which consist solely in the representation of this necessary synthetic unity, furnish the third requisite for the knowledge of an object; and they rest on the understanding.

The same function which gives unity to the various representations *in a judgment* also gives B 105 unity to the mere synthesis of various representations *in an intuition;* and this unity, in its most general expression, we entitle the pure concept of the understanding. The same understanding, through the same operations by which in concepts, by means of analytical unity, it produced the logical form of a judgment, also introduces a transcendental content into its representations, by means of the synthetic unity of the manifold in intuition in general. On this account we are entitled to call these representations pure concepts of the understanding, and to regard them as applying *a priori* to objects—a conclusion which general logic is not in a position to establish.

In this manner there arise precisely the same number of pure concepts of the understanding which apply *a priori* to objects of intuition in general, as, in the preceding table, there have been found to be logical functions in all possible judgments. For these functions specify the understanding completely, and yield an exhaustive inventory of its powers. These concepts we shall, A 80 with Aristotle, call *categories,* for our primary purpose is the same as his, although widely diverging from it in manner of execution.

B 106   TABLE OF CATEGORIES

I

Of Quantity
Unity
Plurality
Totality

II	III
Of Quality	*Of Relation*
Reality	Of Inherence and
Negation	Subsistence
Limitation	

(*substantia et accidens*)
Of Causality and
Dependence
(*cause and effect*)
Of Community
(reciprocity between
agent and patient)

IV

Of Modality

Possibility—Impossibility
Existence—Non-existence
Necessity—Contingency

This then is the list of all original pure concepts of synthesis that the understanding contains within itself *a priori*. Indeed, it is because it contains these concepts that it is called pure understanding; for by them alone can it *understand* anything in the manifold of intuition, that is, think an object of intuition. This division is A 81 developed systematically from a common principle, namely, the faculty of judgment (which is the same as the faculty of thought).

A 84 **ANALYTIC OF CONCEPTS**

Chapter II

The Deduction of the Pure Concepts of Understanding

Section I

§ 13

The Principles of any Transcendental Deduction

Jurists, when speaking of rights and claims, distinguish in a legal action the question of right (*quid juris*) from the question of fact (*quid facti*); and they demand that both be proved. Proof of the former, which has to state the right or the legal claim, they entitle the *deduction*. Many empirical concepts are employed without question from anyone. Since experience is always available for the proof of their objective reality, we believe ourselves, even without a deduction, to be justified in B 117 appropriating to them a meaning, an ascribed significance. But there are also usurpatory concepts, such as *fortune, fate,* which, though allowed to circulate by almost universal indulgence, are yet from time to time challenged by the question: *quid juris*. This demand for a deduction involves A 85 us in considerable perplexity, no clear legal title, sufficient to justify their employment, being obtainable either from experience or from reason.

Now among the manifold concepts which form the highly complicated web of human knowledge, there are some which are marked out for pure *a priori* employment, in complete independence of all experience; and their right to be so employed always demands a deduction. For since empirical proofs do not suffice to justify this kind of employment, we are faced by the problem how these concepts can relate to objects which they yet do not obtain from any experience. The explanation of the manner in which concepts can thus relate *a priori* to objects I entitle their transcendental deduction; and from it I distinguish empirical deduction, which shows the manner in which a concept is acquired through experience and through reflection upon experience, and which therefore concerns, not its legitimacy, but only its *de facto* mode of origination.

B 118 We are already in possession of concepts which are of two quite different kinds, and which yet agree in that they relate to objects in a completely *a priori* manner, namely, the concepts of space and time as forms of sensibility, and the categories as concepts of understanding. To seek an empirical deduction of either of these types of concept would be labour entirely lost. For their distinguishing feature consists just in this, that A 86 they relate to their objects without having borrowed from experience anything that can serve in the representation of these objects. If, therefore, a deduction of such concepts is indispensable, it must in any case be transcendental.

DEDUCTION OF THE PURE CONCEPTS OF THE UNDERSTANDING

[As restated in 2nd edition]

Section 2

Transcendental Deduction of the Pure Concepts of the Understanding

§ 15

The Possibility of Combination in General

The manifold of representations can be given in an intuition which is purely sensible, that is, nothing but receptivity; and the form of this intuition can lie *a priori* in our faculty of representation, without being anything more than the mode in which the subject is affected. But the combination (*conjunctio*) of a manifold in general can never come to us through the senses, and cannot, therefore, be already contained in the pure form of sensible intuition. For it is an act B 130 of spontaneity of the faculty of representation; and since this faculty, to distinguish it from sensibility, must be entitled understanding, all combination—be we conscious of it or not, be it a combination of the manifold of intuition, empirical or non-empirical, or of various concepts— is an act of the understanding. To this act the general title 'synthesis' may be assigned, as indicating that we cannot represent to ourselves anything as combined in the object which we have not ourselves previously combined, and that of all representations *combination* is the only one which cannot be given through objects. Being an act of the self-activity of the subject, it cannot be executed save by the subject itself. It will easily be observed that this action is originally one and is equipollent for all combination, and that its dissolution, namely, *analysis*, which appears to be its opposite, yet always presupposes it. For where the understanding has not previously combined, it cannot dissolve, since only as having been combined *by the understanding* can anything that allows of analysis be given to the faculty of representation.

But the concept of combination includes, besides the concept of the manifold and of its synthesis, also the concept of the unity of the manifold. Combination is representation of the B 131 *synthetic* unity of the manifold. The representation of this unity cannot, therefore, arise out of the combination. On the contrary, it is what, by adding itself to the representation of the manifold, first makes possible the concept of the combination. This unity, which precedes *a priori* all concepts of combination, is not the category of unity (§ 10); for all categories are grounded in logical functions of judgment, and in these functions combination, and therefore unity of given concepts, is already thought. Thus the category already presupposes combination. We must therefore look yet higher for this unity (as qualitative, § 12), namely in that which itself contains the ground of the unity of diverse concepts in judgment, and therefore of the possibility of the understanding, even as regards its logical employment.

§ 16

The Original Synthetic Unity of Apperception

It must be possible for the 'I think' to accompany all my representations; for otherwise something would be represented in me which could not be B 132 thought at all, and that is equivalent to saying that the representation would be impossible, or at least would be nothing to me. That representation which can be given prior to all thought is entitled intuition. All the manifold of intuition has, therefore, a necessary relation to the 'I think' in the same subject in which this manifold is found. But this representation is an act of *spontaneity*, that is, it cannot be regarded as belonging to sensibility. I call it *pure apperception*, to distinguish it from empirical apperception, or, again, *original apperception*, because it is that self-consciousness which, while generating the representation '*I think*' (a representation which must be capable of accompanying all other representations, and which in all consciousness is one and the same), cannot itself be accompanied by any further representation. The unity of this apperception I likewise entitle the *transcendental* unity of self-consciousness, in order to indicate the possibility of a *priori* knowledge arising from it. For the manifold representations, which are given in an intuition, would not be one and all *my* representations, if they did not all belong to one self-consciousness. As *my* representations (even if I am not conscious of them as such) they must conform to the condition under which alone they *can* stand together in one universal self-consciousness, because otherwise they B 133 would not all without exception belong to me. From this original combination many consequences follow.

This thoroughgoing identity of the apperception of a manifold which is given in intuition contains a synthesis of representations, and is possible only through the consciousness of this synthesis. For the empirical consciousness, which accompanies different representations, is in itself diverse and without relation to the identity of the subject. That relation comes about, not simply through my accompanying each representation with consciousness, but only in so far as I *conjoin* one representation with another, and am conscious of the synthesis of them. Only in so far, therefore, as I can unite a manifold of given representations in *one consciousness,* is it possible for me to represent to myself the *identity of the consciousness in [i.e. throughout] these representations.* In other words, the *analytic* unity of apperception is possible only under the presupposition of a certain *synthetic* unity.

B 134   The thought that the representations given in intuition one and all belong to me, is therefore equivalent to the thought that I unite them in one self-consciousness, or can at least so unite them; and although this thought is not itself the consciousness of the *synthesis* of the representations, it presupposes the possibility of that synthesis. In other words, only in so far as I can grasp the manifold of the representations in one consciousness, do I call them one and all *mine.* For otherwise I should have as many-coloured and diverse a self as I have representations of which I am conscious to myself. Synthetic unity of the manifold of intuitions, as generated *a priori,* is thus the ground of the identity of apperception itself, which precedes *a priori* all *my* determinate thought. Combination does not, however, lie in the objects, and cannot be borrowed from them, and so, through perception, first taken up into the understanding. On the contrary, it is an affair B 135 of the understanding alone, which itself is nothing but the faculty of combining *a priori,* and of bringing the manifold of given representations under the unity of apperception. The principle of apperception is the highest principle in the whole sphere of human knowledge.

This principle of the necessary unity of apperception is itself, indeed, an identical, and therefore analytic, proposition; nevertheless it reveals the necessity of a synthesis of the manifold given in intuition, without which the thoroughgoing identity of self-consciousness cannot be thought. For through the 'I', as simple representation, nothing manifold is given; only in intuition, which is distinct from the 'I', can a manifold be given; and only through *combination* in one consciousness can it be thought. An understanding in which through self-consciousness all the manifold would *eo ipso* be given, would be *intuitive;* our understanding can only *think,* and for intuition must look to the senses. I am conscious of the self as identical in respect of the manifold of representations that are given to me in an intuition, because I call them one and all *my* representations, and so apprehend them as constituting *one* intuition. This amounts to saying, that I am conscious to myself *a priori* of a necessary synthesis of representations— to be entitled the original synthetic unity of apperception—under which all representations that are given to me must stand, but under which they have also first to be brought by B 136 means of a synthesis.

§ 17

The Principle of the Synthetic Unity is the Supreme Principle of all Employment of the Understanding

The supreme principle of the possibility of all intuition in its relation to sensibility is, according to the Transcendental Aesthetic, that all the manifold of intuition should be subject to the formal conditions of space and time. The supreme principle of the same possibility, in its relation to understanding, is that all the manifold of intuition should be subject to conditions of the original synthetic unity of apperception. In so far as the manifold representations of intuition are *given* to us, they are subject to the former of these two principles; in so far as they must allow of being B 137 *combined* in one consciousness, they are subject to the latter. For without such combination nothing can be thought or known, since the given representations would not have in common the act of the apperception 'I think', and so could not be apprehended together in one self-consciousness. *Understanding* is, to use general terms, *the faculty of knowledge.* This knowledge consists in the determinate relation of given representations to an object; and an *object* is that in the concept

of which the manifold of a given intuition is *united.* Now all unification of representations demands unity of consciousness in the synthesis of them. Consequently it is the unity of consciousness that alone constitutes the relation of representations to an object, and therefore their objective validity and the fact that they are modes of knowledge; and upon it therefore rests the very possibility of the understanding.

The first pure knowledge of understanding, then, upon which all the rest of its employment is based, and which also at the same time is completely independent of all conditions of sensible intuition, is the principle of the original *synthetic* unity of apperception. Thus the mere form of outer sensible intuition, space, is not yet [by itself] knowledge; it supplies only the manifold of *a priori* intuition for a possible knowledge. To B 138 know anything in space (for instance, a line), I must *draw* it, and thus synthetically bring into being a determinate combination of the given manifold, so that the unity of this act is at the same time the unity of consciousness (as in the concept of a line); and it is through this unity of consciousness that an object (a determinate space) is first known. The synthetic unity of consciousness is, therefore, an objective condition of all knowledge. It is not merely a condition that I myself require in knowing an object, but is a condition under which every intuition must stand in order *to become an object for me.* For otherwise, in the absence of this synthesis, the manifold would *not* be united in one consciousness.

Although this proposition makes synthetic unity a condition of all thought, it is, as already stated, itself analytic. For it says no more than that all *my* representations in any given intuition must be subject to that condition under which alone I can ascribe them to the identical self as *my* representations, and so can comprehend them as synthetically combined in one apperception through the general expression, '*I think*'.

This principle is not, however, to be taken as applying to every possible understanding, but only to that understanding through whose pure apperception, in the representation 'I am', nothing manifold is given. An understanding which through its self-consciousness could supply to

B 139 itself the manifold of intuition—an understanding, that is to say, through whose representation the objects of the representation should at the same time exist—would not require, for the unity of consciousness, a special act of synthesis of the manifold. For the human understanding, however, which thinks only, and does not intuit, that act is necessary. It is indeed the first principle of the human understanding, and is so indispensable to it that we cannot form the least conception of any other possible understanding, either of such as is itself intuitive or of any that may possess an underlying mode of sensible intuition which is different in kind from that in space and time.

§ 18

The Objective Unity of Self-Consciousness

The transcendental unity of apperception is that unity through which all the manifold given in an intuition is united in a concept of the object. It is therefore entitled *objective,* and must be distinguished from the *subjective* unity of consciousness, which is a *determination* of *inner sense*—through which the manifold of intuition for such [objective] combination is empirically given. Whether I can become *empirically* conscious of the manifold as simultaneous or as successive depends on circumstances or empirical B 140 conditions. Therefore the empirical unity of consciousness, through association of representations, itself concerns an appearance, and is wholly contingent. But the pure form of intuition in time, merely as intuition in general, which contains a given manifold, is subject to the original unity of consciousness, simply through the necessary relation of the manifold of the intuition to the one 'I think', and so through the pure synthesis of understanding which is the *a priori* underlying ground of the empirical synthesis. Only the original unity is objectively valid; the empirical unity of apperception, upon which we are not here dwelling, and which besides is merely derived from the former under given conditions *in concreto,* has only subjective validity. To one man, for instance, a certain word suggests one thing, to another some other thing; the unity of consciousness in that which is

empirical is not, as regards what is given, necessarily and universally valid.

§ 19

The Logical Form of all Judgments consists in the Objective Unity of the Apperception of the Concepts which they contain

I have never been able to accept the interpretation which logicians give of judgment in general. It is, they declare, the representation of a B 141 relation between two concepts. I do not here dispute with them as to what is defective in this interpretation—that in any case it applies only to *categorical,* not to hypothetical and disjunctive judgments (the two latter containing a relation not of concepts but of judgments), an oversight from which many troublesome consequences have followed. I need only point out that the definition does not determine in what the asserted *relation* consists.

But if I investigate more precisely the relation of the given modes of knowledge in any judgment, and distinguish it, as belonging to the understanding, from the relation according to laws of the reproductive imagination, which has only subjective validity, I find that a judgment is nothing but the manner in which given modes of knowledge are brought to the objective unity of apperception. This is what is intended by B 142 the copula 'is'. It is employed to distinguish the objective unity of given representations from the subjective. It indicates their relation to original apperception, and its *necessary unity.* It holds good even if the judgment is itself empirical, and therefore contingent, as, for example, in the judgment, 'Bodies are heavy'. I do not here assert that these representations *necessarily* belong *to one another* in the empirical intuition, but that they belong to one another *in virtue of the necessary unity* of apperception in the synthesis of intuitions, that is, according to principles of the objective determination of all representations, in so far as knowledge can be acquired by means of these representations—principles which are all derived from the fundamental principles of the transcendental unity of apperception. Only in this way does there arise from this relation a *judgment,* that is, a relation which is *objectively valid,* and so can be adequately distinguished from a relation of the same representations that would have only subjective validity—as when they are connected according to laws of association. In the latter case, all that I could say would be, 'If I support a body, I feel an impression of weight'; I could not say, 'It, the body, is heavy'. Thus to say 'The body is heavy' is not merely to state that the two representations have always been conjoined in my perception, however often that perception be repeated; what we are asserting is that they are combined *in the object,* no matter what the state of the subject may be.

B 143 § 20

All Sensible Intuitions are subject to the Categories, as Conditions under which alone their Manifold can come together in one Consciousness

The manifold given in a sensible intuition is necessarily subject to the original synthetic unity of apperception, because in no other way is the *unity* of intuition possible (§ 17). But that act of understanding by which the manifold of given representations (be they intuitions or concepts) is brought under one apperception, is the logical function of judgment (cf. § 19). All the manifold, therefore, so far as it is given in a single empirical intuition, is *determined* in respect of one of the logical functions of judgment, and is thereby brought into one consciousness. Now the *categories* are just these functions of judgment, in so far as they are employed in determination of the manifold of a given intuition (cf. § 13). Consequently, the manifold in a given B 144 intuition is necessarily subject to the categories.

§ 21

Observation

A manifold, contained in an intuition which I call mine, is represented, by means of the synthesis of the understanding, as belonging to the *necessary* unity of self-consciousness; and this is effected by means of the category. This [requirement of a] category therefore shows that the empirical consciousness of a given manifold in a single intuition is subject to a pure self-consciousness *a priori,* just as is empirical intu-

ition to a pure sensible intuition, which likewise takes place *a priori.* Thus in the above proposition a beginning is made of a *deduction* of the pure concepts of understanding; and in this deduction, since the categories have their source in the understanding alone, *independently of sensibility,* I must abstract from the mode in which the manifold for an empirical intuition is given, and must direct attention solely to the unity which, in terms of the category, and by means of the understanding, enters into the intuition. In what follows (cf. § 26) it will be shown, from the mode in which the empirical intuition is given in sensi-
B 145 bility, that its unity is no other than that which the category (according to § 20) prescribes to the manifold of a given intuition in general. Only thus, by demonstration of the a priori validity of the categories in respect of all objects of our senses, will the purpose of the deduction be fully attained.

But in the above proof there is one feature from which I could not abstract, the feature, namely, that the manifold to be intuited must be given prior to the synthesis of understanding, and independently of it. How this takes place, remains here undetermined. For were I to think an understanding which is itself intuitive (as, for example, a divine understanding which should not represent to itself given objects, but through whose representation the objects should themselves be given or produced), the categories would have no meaning whatsoever in respect of such a mode of knowledge. They are merely rules for an understanding whose whole power consists in thought, consists, that is, in the act whereby it brings the synthesis of a manifold, given to it from elsewhere in intuition, to the unity of apperception—a faculty, therefore, which by itself knows nothing whatsoever, but merely combines and arranges the material of knowledge, that is, the intuition, which must be given to it by the object. This peculiarity of our understanding, that it can produce *a priori* unity of apperception
B 146 solely by means of the categories, and only by such and so many, is as little capable of further explanation as why we have just these and no other functions of judgment, or why space and time are the only forms of our possible intuition.

§ 22

The Category has no other Application in Knowledge than to Objects of Experience

To *think* an object and to *know* an object are thus by no means the same thing. Knowledge involves two factors: first, the concept, through which an object in general is thought (the category); and secondly, the intuition, through which it is given. For if no intuition could be given corresponding to the concept, the concept would still indeed be a thought, so far as its form is concerned, but would be without any object, and no knowledge of anything would be possible by means of it. So far as I could know, there would be nothing, and could be nothing, to which my thought could be applied. Now, as the Aesthetic has shown, the only intuition possible to us is sensible; consequently, the thought of an object in general, by means of a pure concept of understanding, can become knowledge for us only in so far as the

B 147 concept is related to objects of the senses. Sensible intuition is either pure intuition (space and time) or empirical intuition of that which is immediately represented, through sensation, as actual in space and time. Through the determination of pure intuition we can acquire *a priori* knowledge of objects, as in mathematics, but only in regard to their form, as appearances; whether there can be things which must be intuited in this form, is still left undecided. Mathematical concepts are not, therefore, by themselves knowledge, except on the supposition that there are things which allow of being presented to us only in accordance with the form of that pure sensible intuition. Now *things in space and .time* are given only in so far as they are perceptions (that is, representations accompanied by sensation)— therefore only through empirical representation. Consequently, the pure concepts of understanding, even when they are applied to *a priori* intuitions, as in mathematics, yield knowledge only in so far as these intuitions—and therefore indirectly by their means the pure concepts also— can be applied to empirical intuitions. Even, therefore, with the aid of [pure] intuition, the categories do not afford us any knowledge of things; they do so only through their possible application

to *empirical intuition*. In other words, they serve only for the possibility of *empirical knowledge;* and such knowledge is what we entitle experience. Our conclusion is therefore this: the categories, as yielding knowledge of *things*, have no kind of
B 148 application, save only in regard to things which may be objects of possible experience.

§ 24

The Application of the Categories to Objects of the Senses in General

The pure concepts of understanding relate, through the mere understanding, to objects of intuition in general, whether that intuition be our own or any other, provided only it be sensible. The concepts are, however, for this very reason, mere *forms of thought*, through which alone no determinate object is known. The synthesis or combination of the manifold in them relates only to the unity of apperception, and is thereby the ground of the possibility of *a priori* knowledge, so far as such knowledge rests on the understanding. This synthesis, therefore, is at once transcendental and also purely intellectual. But since there lies in us a certain form of *a priori* sensible intuition, which depends on the receptivity of the faculty of representation (sensibility), the understanding, as spontaneity, is able to determine inner sense through the manifold of given representations, in accordance with the synthetic unity of apperception, and so to think synthetic unity of the apperception of the manifold of *a priori sensible intuition*—that being the condition under which all objects of our human intuition must necessarily stand. In this way the categories, in themselves mere forms of thought, obtain objective reality,
B 151 that is, application to objects which can be given us in intuition. These objects, however, are only appearances, for it is solely of appearances that we can have *a priori* intuition.

§ 26

Transcendental Deduction of the Universally Possible Employment in Experience of the Pure Concepts of the Understanding

In the *metaphysical deduction* the *a priori* origin of the categories has been proved through their complete agreement with the general logical functions of thought; in the *transcendental deduction* we have shown their possibility as *a priori* modes of knowledge of objects of an intuition in general (cf. § § 20, 21). We have now to explain the possibility of knowing *a priori*, by means of *categories*, whatever objects may *present themselves to our senses*, not indeed in respect of the form of their intuition, but in respect of the laws of their combination, and so, as it were, of pre-

B 160 scribing laws to nature, and even of making nature possible. For unless the categories discharged this function, there could be no explaining why everything that can be presented to our senses must be subject to laws which have their origin *a priori* in the understanding alone.

First of all, I may draw attention to the fact that by *synthesis of apprehension* I understand that combination of the manifold in an empirical intuition, whereby perception, that is, empirical consciousness of the intuition (as appearance), is possible.

In the representations of space and time we have *a priori forms* of outer and inner sensible intuition; and to these the synthesis of apprehension of the manifold of appearance must always conform, because in no other way can the synthesis take place at all. But space and time are represented *a priori* not merely as *forms* of sensible intuition, but as themselves *intuitions* which contain a manifold [of their own], and therefore are represented with the determination of the unity of this manifold (*vide* the Transcendental Aesthetic).[1] Thus *unity of the synthesis* of the

B 161 manifold, without or within us, and consequently also a *combination* to which everything that is to be represented as determined in space or in time must conform, is given *a priori* as the condition of the synthesis of all *apprehension*—not indeed in, but with these intuitions. This synthetic unity can be no other than the unity of the combination of the manifold of a given *intuition in general* in an original consciousness, in accordance with the categories, in so far as the combination is applied to our *sensible intuition*. All synthesis, therefore, even that which renders perception possible, is subject to the categories; and since experience is knowledge by means of connected perceptions, the categories are conditions of the possibility of experience, and are therefore valid *a priori* for all objects of experience.

Categories are concepts which prescribe laws *a priori* to appearances, and therefore to nature, the sum of all appearances (*natura materialiter spectata*). The question therefore arises, how it can be conceivable that nature should have to proceed in accordance with categories which yet are not derived from it, and do not model themselves upon its pattern; that is, how they can determine *a priori* the combination of the manifold of nature, while yet they are not derived from it. The solution of this seeming enigma is as follows.

B 164 That the *laws* of appearances in nature must agree with the understanding and its *a priori* form, that is, with its faculty of *combining* the manifold in general, is no more surprising than that the appearances themselves must agree with the form of *a priori* sensible intuition. For just as appearances do not exist in themselves but only relatively to the subject in which, so far as it has senses, they inhere, so the laws do not exist in the appearances but only relatively to this same being, so far as it has understanding. Things in themselves would necessarily, apart from any understanding that knows them, conform to laws of their own. But appearances are only representations of things which are unknown as regards what they may be in themselves. As mere representations, they are subject to no law of connection save that which the connecting faculty prescribes.

A 137
B 176 # TRANSCENDENTAL DOCTRINE OF JUDGMENT (OR ANALYTIC OF PRINCIPLES)

Chapter I

The Schematism of the Pure Concepts of Understanding

In all subsumptions of an object under a concept the representation of the object must be *homogeneous* with the concept; in other words, the concept must contain something which is represented in the object that is to be subsumed under it. This, in fact, is what is meant by the expression, 'an object is contained under a concept'. Thus the empirical concept of a *plate* is homogeneous with the pure geometrical concept of a *circle*. The roundness which is thought in the latter can be intuited in the former.

But pure concepts of understanding being quite heterogeneous from empirical intuitions, and indeed from all sensible intuitions, can never be met with in any intuition. For no one will say B 177 that a category, such as that of causality, can be A 138 intuited through sense and is itself contained in appearance. How, then, is the *subsumption* of intuitions under pure concepts, the *application* of a category to appearances, possible? A transcendental doctrine of judgment is necessary just because of this natural and important question. We must be able to show how pure concepts can be applicable to appearances. In none of the other sciences is this necessary. For since in these sciences the concepts through which the object is thought in [its] general [aspects] are not so utterly distinct and heterogeneous from those which represent it *in concreto*, as given, no special discussion of the applicability of the former to the latter is required.

Obviously there must be some third thing, which is homogeneous on the one hand with the category, and on the other hand with the appearance, and which thus makes the application of the former to the latter possible. This mediating representation must be pure, that is, void of all empirical content, and yet at the same time, while it must in one respect be *intellectual,* it must in another be *sensible.* Such a representation is the *transcendental schema.*

The concept of understanding contains pure synthetic unity of the manifold in general. Time, as the formal condition of the manifold of inner sense, and therefore of the connection of all representations, contains an *a priori* manifold in pure intuition. Now a transcendental determination of time is so far homogeneous with the category, which constitutes its unity, in that it is B 178 universal and rests upon an *a priori* rule. But, on A 139 the other hand, it is so far homogeneous with appearance, in that time is contained in every empirical representation of the manifold. Thus an application of the category to appearances becomes possible by means of the transcendental

determination of time, which, as the schema of the concepts of understanding, mediates the subsumption of the appearances under the category.

The schema is in itself always a product of imagination. Since, however, the synthesis of imagination aims at no special intuition, but only at unity in the determination of sensibility, the schema has to be distinguished from the image. If five points be set alongside one another, thus, . . . , I have an image of the number five. But if, on the other hand, I think only a number in general, whether it be five or a hundred, this thought is rather the representation of a method whereby a multiplicity, for instance a thousand, may be represented in an image in conformity with a certain concept, than the image itself. For with such a number as a thousand the image can hardly be surveyed and compared with the concept. This representation of a universal proce- B 180 dure of imagination in providing an image for a concept, I entitle the schema of this concept.

Indeed it is schemata, not images of objects, A 141 which underlie our pure sensible concepts. No image could ever be adequate to the concept of a triangle in general. It would never attain that universality of the concept which renders it valid of all triangles, whether right-angled, obtuse-angled, or acute-angled; it would always be limited to a part only of this sphere. The schema of the triangle can exist nowhere but in thought. It is a rule of synthesis of the imagination, in respect to pure figures in space. Still less is an object of experience or its image ever adequate to the empirical concept; for this latter always stands in immediate relation to the schema of imagination, as a rule for the determination of our intuition, in accordance with some specific universal concept. The concept 'dog' signifies a rule according to which my imagination can delineate the figure of a four-footed animal in a general manner, without limitation to any single determinate figure such as experience, or any possible image that I can represent *in concreto,* actually presents. This schematism of our understanding, in its application to appearances and their mere form, is an art concealed in the depths of the human soul, whose real modes of activity

B 181 nature is hardly likely ever to allow us to discover, and to have open to our gaze. This much only we can assert: the *image* is a product of the empirical faculty of reproductive imagination; the *schema* of sensible concepts, such as of figures
A 142 in space, is a product and, as it were, a monogram, of pure *a priori* imagination, through which, and in accordance with which, images themselves first become possible. These images can be connected with the concept only by means of the schema to which they belong. In themselves they are never completely congruent with the concept. On the other hand, the schema of a *pure* concept of understanding can never be brought into any image whatsoever. It is simply the pure synthesis, determined by a rule of that unity, in accordance with concepts, to which the category gives expression. It is a transcendental product of imagination, a product which concerns the determination of inner sense in general according to conditions of its form (time), in respect of all representations, so far as these representations are to be connected *a priori* in one concept in conformity with the unity of apperception.

If knowledge is to have objective reality, that is, to relate to an object, and is to acquire meaning and significance in respect to it, the object must be capable of being in some manner given. Otherwise the concepts are empty; through them we have indeed thought, but in
B 195 this thinking we have really known nothing; we have merely played with representations. That
A 156 an object be given (if this expression be taken, not as referring to some merely mediate process, but as signifying immediate presentation in intuition), means simply that the representation through which the object is thought relates to actual or possible experience. Even space and time, however free their concepts are from everything empirical, and however certain it is that they are represented in the mind completely *a priori*, would yet be without objective validity, senseless and meaningless, if their necessary application to the objects of experience were not established. Their representation is a mere schema which always stands in relation to the

reproductive imagination that calls up and assembles the objects of experience. Apart from these objects of experience, they would be devoid of meaning. And so it is with concepts of every kind.

The *possibility of experience* is, then, what gives objective reality to all our *a priori* modes of knowledge. Experience, however, rests on the synthetic unity of appearances, that is, on a synthesis according to concepts of an object of appearances in general. Apart from such synthesis it would not be knowledge, but a rhapsody of perceptions that would not fit into any context according to rules of a completely interconnected (possible) consciousness, and so would not conform to the transcendental and necessary
B 196 unity of apperception. Experience depends, therefore, upon *a priori* principles of its form, that
A 157 is, upon universal rules of unity in the synthesis of appearances. Their objective reality, as necessary conditions of experience, and indeed of its very possibility, can always be shown in experience. Apart from this relation synthetic *a priori* principles are completely impossible. For they have then no third something, that is, no object, in which the synthetic unity can exhibit the objective reality of its concepts.

Accordingly, since experience, as empirical synthesis, is, in so far as such experience is possible, the one species of knowledge which is capable of imparting reality to any nonempirical synthesis, this latter [type of synthesis], as knowl-
B 197 edge *a priori*, can possess truth, that is, agreement with the object, only in so far as it contains noth-
A 158 ing save what is necessary to synthetic unity of experience in general.

The highest principle of all synthetic judgments is therefore this: every object stands under the necessary conditions of synthetic unity of the manifold of intuition in a possible experience.

Synthetic *a priori* judgments are thus possible when we relate the formal conditions of *a priori* intuition, the synthesis of imagination and the necessary unity of this synthesis in a transcendental apperception, to a possible empirical knowledge in general. We then assert that the conditions of the *possibility of experience* in general are likewise conditions of the *possibility of the objects of experience*, and that for this reason they have objective validity in a synthetic *a priori* judgment.

The System of the Principles of Pure Understanding

Section 3

Systematic Representation of all the Synthetic Principles of Pure Understanding

That there should be principles at all is entirely due to the pure understanding. Not only is it the faculty of rules in respect of that which happens, B 198 but is itself the source of principles according to A 159 which everything that can be presented to us as an object must conform to rules. For without such rules appearances would never yield knowledge of an object corresponding to them. Even natural laws, viewed as principles of the empirical employment of understanding, carry with them an expression of necessity, and so contain at least the suggestion of a determination from grounds which are valid *a priori* and antecedently to all experience. The laws of nature, indeed, one and all, without exception, stand under higher principles of understanding. They simply apply the latter to special cases [in the field] of appearance. These principles alone supply the concept which contains the condition, and as it were the exponent, of a rule in general. What experience gives is the instance which stands under the rule.

There can be no real danger of our regarding merely empirical principles as principles of pure understanding, or conversely. For the necessity according to concepts which distinguishes the principles of pure understanding, and the lack of which is evident in every empirical proposition, however general its application, suffices to make this confusion easily preventable. But there are pure *a priori* principles that we may not properly ascribe to the pure understanding, which is the faculty of concepts. For though they are medi-A 160 ated by the understanding, they are not derived B 199 from pure concepts but from pure intuitions. We find such principles in mathematics. The question, however, of their application to experience, that is, of their objective validity, nay, even the

deduction of the possibility of such synthetic *a priori* knowledge, must always carry us back to the pure understanding.

While, therefore, I leave aside the principles of mathematics, I shall none the less include those [more fundamental] principles upon which the possibility and *a priori* objective validity of mathematics are grounded. These latter must be regarded as the foundation of all mathematical principles. They proceed from concepts to intuition, not from intuition to concepts.

The table of categories is quite naturally our guide in the construction of the table of principles. For the latter are simply rules for the objective employment of the former. All principles of pure understanding are therefore—

1
Axioms
of intuition.

2   3
Anticipations   Analogies
of perception.   of experience.

4
Postulates
of empirical thought in general.

A

First Analogy

Principle of Permanence of Substance

In all change of appearances substance is permanent; its quantum in nature is neither increased nor diminished.

Proof

All appearances are in time; and in it alone, as substratum (as permanent form of inner intuition), can either coexistence or succession be represented. Thus the time in which all change of appearances has to be thought, remains and B 225 does not change. For it is that in which, and as determinations of which, succession or coexistence can alone be represented. Now time cannot by itself be perceived. Consequently there must be found in the objects of perception, that is, in the appearances, the substratum which represents time in general; and all change or coexistence must, in being apprehended, be perceived in this substratum, and through relation of the appearances to it. But the substratum of all that is real, that is, of all that belongs to the existence of things, is *substance;* and all that belongs to existence can be thought only as a determination of substance. Consequently the permanent, in relation to which alone all time-relations of appearances can be determined, is substance in the [field of] appearance, that is, the real in appearance, and as the substrate of all change remains ever the same. And as it is thus unchangeable in its existence, its quantity in nature can be neither increased nor diminished.

Our *apprehension* of the manifold of appearance is always successive, and is therefore always changing. Through it alone we can never determine whether this manifold, as object of experience, is coexistent or in sequence. For such determination we require an underlying ground which exists *at all times*, that is, something B 226 *abiding* and *permanent*, of which all change and coexistence are only so many ways (modes of time) in which the permanent exists. And simultaneity and succession being the only relations in A 183 time, it follows that only in the permanent are relations of time possible. In other words, the permanent is the *substratum* of the empirical representation of time itself; in it alone is any determination of time possible. Permanence, as the abiding correlate of all existence of appearances, of all change and of all concomitance, expresses time in general. For change does not affect time itself, but only appearances in time. (Coexistence is not a mode of time itself; for none of the parts of time coexist; they are all in succession to one another.) If we ascribe succession to time itself, we must think yet another time, in which the sequence would be possible. Only through the permanent does existence in different parts of the time-series acquire a magnitude which can be entitled duration. For in bare succession existence is always vanishing and recommencing, and never has the least magnitude. Without the permanent there is therefore no time-relation. Now time cannot be perceived in itself; the permanent in the appearances is therefore the substratum of all determination of time, and, as

likewise follows, is also the condition of the possibility of all synthetic unity of perceptions, that B 227 is, of experience. All existence and all change in time have thus to be viewed as simply a mode of the existence of that which remains and persists. In all appearances the permanent is the object itself, that is, substance as phenomenon; everyA 184 thing, on the other hand, which changes or can change belongs only to the way in which substance or substances exist, and therefore to their determinations.

I find that in all ages, not only philosophers, but even the common understanding, have recognised this permanence as a substratum of all change of appearances, and always assume it to be indubitable. The only difference in this matter between the common understanding and the philosopher is that the latter expresses himself somewhat more definitely, asserting that throughout all changes in the world *substance* remains, and that only the *accidents* change. But I nowhere find even the attempt at a proof of this obviously synthetic proposition. Indeed, it is very seldom placed, where it truly belongs, at the head of those laws of nature which are pure and completely *a priori*. Certainly the proposition, that substance is permanent, is tautological. For this permanence is our sole ground for applying the category of substance to appearance; and we ought first to have proved that in all appearances there is something permanent, and that the transitory is nothing but determination of its existence. But such a proof cannot be developed B 228 dogmatically, that is, from concepts, since it concerns a synthetic *a priori* proposition. Yet as it never occurred to anyone that such propositions are valid only in relation to possible experience, and can therefore be proved only through a A 185 deduction of the possibility of experience, we need not be surprised that though the above principle is always postulated as lying at the basis of experience (for in empirical knowledge the need of it is *felt*), it has never itself been proved.

A philosopher, on being asked how much smoke weighs, made reply: "Subtract from the weight of the wood burnt the weight of the ashes which are left over, and you have the weight of the smoke". He thus presupposed as undeniable that even in fire the matter (substance) does not vanish, but only suffers an alteration of form. The proposition, that nothing arises out of nothing, is still another consequence of the principle of permanence, or rather of the ever-abiding existence, in the appearances, of the subject proper. For if that in the [field of] appearance which we name substance is to be the substratum proper of all time-determination, it must follow that all existence, whether in past or in future time, can be determined solely in and by it. We can therefore give an appearance the title 'substance' just for the reason that we presuppose its existence through out all time, and that this is not adequately expressed by the word perma-

B 229 nence, a term which applies chiefly to future time. But since the inner necessity of persisting is inseparably bound up with the necessity of always having existed, the expression [principle of permanence] may be allowed to stand. *Gigni de*

A 186 *nihilo nihil, in nihilum nil posse reverti*, were two propositions which the ancients always connected together, but which are now sometimes mistakenly separated owing to the belief that they apply to things in themselves, and that the first would run counter to the dependence of the world—even in respect of its substance—upon a supreme cause. But such apprehension is unnecessary. For we have here to deal only with appearances in the field of experience; and the unity of experience would never be possible if we were willing to allow that new things, that is, new *substances*, could come into existence. For we should then lose that which alone can represent the unity of time, namely, the identity of the substratum, wherein alone all change has thoroughgoing unity. This permanence is, however, simply the mode in which we represent to ourselves the existence of things in the [field of] appearance.

The determinations of a substance, which are nothing but special ways in which it exists, are called *accidents*. They are always real, because they concern the existence of substance. (Negations are only determinations which assert the nonexistence of something in substance.) If we

B 230 ascribe a special [kind of] existence to this real

in substance (for instance, to motion, as an accident of matter), this existence is entitled inherence, in distinction from the existence of

A 187 substance which is entitled subsistence. But this occasions many misunderstandings; it is more exact and more correct to describe an accident as being simply the way in which the existence of a substance is positively determined. But since it is unavoidable, owing to the conditions of the logical employment of our understanding, to separate off, as it were, that which in the existence of a substance can change while the substance still remains, and to view this variable element in relation to the truly permanent and radical, this category has to be assigned a place among the categories of relation, but rather as the condition of relations than as itself containing a relation.

The correct understanding of the concept of *alteration* is also grounded upon [recognition of] this permanence. Coming to be and ceasing to be are not alterations of that which comes to be or ceases to be. Alteration is a way of existing which follows upon another way of existing of the same object. All that alters *persists*, and only its *state changes*. Since this change thus concerns only the determinations, which can cease to be or begin to be, we can say, using what may seem a somewhat paradoxical expression, that only the permanent (substance) is altered, and that the

B 231 transitory suffers no alteration but only a *change*, inasmuch as certain determinations cease to be and others begin to be.

A 188 Alteration can therefore be perceived only in substances. A coming to be or ceasing to be that is not simply a determination of the permanent but is absolute, can never be a possible perception. For this permanent is what alone makes possible the representation of the transition from one state to another, and from not-being to being. These transitions can be empirically known only as changing determinations of that which is permanent. If we assume that something absolutely begins to be, we must have a point of time in which it was not. But to what are we to attach this point, if not to that which already exists? For a preceding empty time is not an object of perception. But if we connect the coming to be with things which previously existed, and which persist in existence up to the moment of this coming to be, this latter must be simply a determination of what is permanent in that which precedes it. Similarly also with ceasing to be; it presupposes the empirical representation of a time in which an appearance no longer exists.

Substances, in the [field of] appearance, are the substrata of all determinations of time. If some of these substances could come into being and others cease to be, the one condition of the empirical unity of time would be removed. The appearances would then relate to two different B 232 times, and existence would flow in two parallel streams—which is absurd. There is only one time A 189 in which all different times must be located, not as coexistent but as in succession to one another.

Permanence is thus a necessary condition under which alone appearances are determinable as things or objects in a possible experience. We shall have occasion in what follows to make such observations as may seem necessary in regard to the empirical criterion of this necessary permanence—the criterion, consequently, of the substantiality of appearances.

B

Second Analogy

Principle of Succession in Time, in accordance with the Law of Causality

All alterations take place in conformity with the law of the connection of cause and effect.

Proof

(The preceding principle has shown that all appearances of succession in time are one and all only *alterations*, that is, a successive being and not-being of the determinations of substance which abides; and therefore that the being of substance as following on its not-being, or its B 233 not-being as following upon its being cannot be admitted—in other words, that there is no coming into being or passing away of substance itself. Still otherwise expressed the principle is, that *all change (succession) of appearances is merely alter-*ation. Coming into being and passing away of substance are not alterations of it, since the concept of alteration presupposes one and the same subject as existing with two opposite determinations, and therefore as abiding. With this preliminary reminder, we pass to the proof.)

I perceive that appearances follow one another, that is, that there is a state of things at one time the opposite of which was in the preceding time. Thus I am really connecting two perceptions in time. Now connection is not the work of mere sense and intuition, but is here the product of a synthetic faculty of imagination, which determines inner sense in respect of the time-relation. But imagination can connect these two states in two ways, so that either the one or the other precedes in time. For time cannot be perceived in itself, and what precedes and what follows cannot, therefore, by relation to it, be empirically determined in the object. I am conscious only that my imagination sets the one state before and the other after, not that the one state precedes the other in the object. In other words, the *objective relation* of appearances that B 234 follow upon one another is not to be determined through mere perception. In order that this relation be known as determined, the relation between the two states must be so thought that it is thereby determined as necessary which of them must be placed before, and which of them after, and that they cannot be placed in the reverse relation. But the concept which carries with it a necessity of synthetic unity can only be a pure concept that lies in the understanding, not in perception; and in this case it is the concept of the *relation of cause and effect,* the former of which determines the latter in time, as its consequence—not as in a sequence that may occur solely in the imagination (or that may not be perceived at all). Experience itself—in other words, empirical knowledge of appearances—is thus possible only in so far as we subject the succession of appearances, and therefore all alteration, to the law of causality; and, as likewise follows, the appearances, as objects of experience, are themselves possible only in conformity with the law.

The apprehension of the manifold of appearance is always successive. The representations of the parts follow upon one another. Whether they also follow one another in the object is a point which calls for further reflection, and which is not decided by the above statement. Everything, every representation even, in so far as we are conscious of it, may be entitled object. But it is a B 235 question for deeper enquiry what the word A 190 'object' ought to signify in respect of appearances when these are viewed not in so far as they are (as representations) objects, but only in so far as they stand for an object. The appearances, in so far as they are objects of consciousness simply in virtue of being representations, are not in any way distinct from their apprehension, that is, from their reception in the synthesis of imagination; and we must therefore agree that the manifold of appearances is always generated in the mind successively. Now if appearances were things in themselves, then since we have to deal solely with our representations, we could never determine from the succession of the representations how their manifold may be connected in the object. How things may be in themselves, apart from the representations through which they affect us, is entirely outside our sphere of knowledge. In spite, however, of the fact that the appearances are not things in themselves, and yet are what alone can be given to us to know, in spite also of the fact that their representation in apprehension is always successive, I have to show what sort of a connection in time belongs to the manifold in the appearances themselves. For instance, the apprehension of the manifold in the appearance of a house which stands before me is successive. The question then arises, whether the manifold of the house is also in itself successive. This, however, is what no one will B 236 grant. Now immediately I unfold the transcendental meaning of my concepts of an object, I A 191 realise that the house is not a thing in itself, but only an appearance, that is, a representation, the transcendental object of which is unknown. What, then, am I to understand by the question: how the manifold may be connected in the appearance itself, which yet is nothing in itself?

That which lies in the successive apprehension is here viewed as representation, while the appearance which is given to me, notwithstanding that it is nothing but the sum of these representations, is viewed as their object; and my concept, which I derive from the representations of apprehension, has to agree with it. Since truth consists in the agreement of knowledge with the object, it will at once be seen that we can here enquire only regarding the formal conditions of empirical truth, and that appearance, in contradistinction to the representations of apprehension, can be represented as an object distinct from them only if it stands under a rule which distinguishes it from every other apprehension and necessitates some one particular mode of connection of the manifold. The object is *that* in the appearance which contains the condition of this necessary rule of apprehension.

Let us now proceed to our problem. That something happens, *i.e.* that something, or some state which did not previously exist, comes to be, B 237 cannot be perceived unless it is preceded by an appearance which does not contain in itself this state. For an event which should follow upon an A 192 empty time, that is, a coming to be preceded by no state of things, is as little capable of being apprehended as empty time itself. Every apprehension of an event is therefore a perception that follows upon another perception. But since, as I have above illustrated by reference to the appearance of a house, this likewise happens in all synthesis of apprehension, the apprehension of an event is not yet thereby distinguished from other apprehensions. But, as I also note, in an appearance which contains a happening (the preceding state of the perception we may entitle A, and the succeeding B) B can be apprehended only as following upon A; the perception A cannot follow upon B but only precede it. For instance, I see a ship move down stream. My perception of its lower position follows upon the perception of its position higher up in the stream, and it is impossible that in the apprehension of this appearance the ship should first be perceived lower down in the stream and afterwards higher up. The order in which the perceptions succeed one another in apprehension is in this instance determined, and to this order apprehension is bound down. In the previous example of a house my perceptions could begin with the apprehension of the roof and end with the basement, or could begin from B 238 below and end above; and I could similarly apprehend the manifold of the empirical intuition either from right to left or from left to right. In the series of these perceptions there was thus A 193 no determinate order specifying at what point I must begin in order to connect the manifold empirically. But in the perception of an event there is always a rule that makes the order in which the perceptions (in the apprehension of this appearance) follow upon one another a *necessary* order.

In this case, therefore, we must derive the *subjective succession* of apprehension from the *objective succession* of appearances. Otherwise the order of apprehension is entirely undetermined, and does not distinguish one appearance from another. Since the subjective succession by itself is altogether arbitrary, it does not prove anything as to the manner in which the manifold is connected in the object. The objective succession will therefore consist in that order of the manifold of appearance according to which, *in conformity with a rule*, the apprehension of that which happens follows upon the apprehension of that which precedes. Thus only can I be justified in asserting, not merely of my apprehension, but of appearance itself, that a succession is to be met with in it. This is only another way of saying that I cannot arrange the apprehension otherwise than in this very succession.

In conformity with such a rule there must lie B 239 in that which precedes an event the condition of a rule according to which this event invariably A 194 and necessarily follows. I cannot reverse this order, proceeding back from the event to determine through apprehension that which precedes. For appearance never goes back from the succeeding to the preceding point of time, though it does indeed stand in relation to *some* preceding point of time. The advance, on the other hand, from a given time to the determinate time that follows is a necessary advance. Therefore, since

there certainly is something that follows [*i.e.* that is *apprehended* as following], I must refer it necessarily to something else which precedes it and upon which it follows in conformity with a rule, that is, of necessity. The event, as the conditioned, thus affords reliable evidence of some condition, and this condition is what determines the event.

Let us suppose that there is nothing antecedent to an event, upon which it must follow according to rule. All succession of perception would then be only in the apprehension, that is, would be merely subjective, and would never enable us to determine objectively which perceptions are those that really precede and which are those that follow. We should then have only a play of representations, relating to no object; that is to say, it would not be possible through our perception to distinguish one appearance from another as regards relations of time. For the succession in our apprehension would always be one and the same, and there B 240 would be nothing in the appearance which so determines it that a certain sequence is rendered A 195 objectively necessary. I could not then assert that two states follow upon one another in the [field of] appearance, but only that one apprehension follows upon the other. That is something merely subjective, determining no object; and may not, therefore, be regarded as knowledge of any object, not even of an object in the [field of] appearance.

If, then, we experience that something happens, we in so doing always presuppose that something precedes it, on which it follows according to a rule. Otherwise I should not say of the object that it follows. For mere succession in my apprehension, if there be no rule determining the succession in relation to something that precedes, does not justify me in assuming any succession in the object. I render my subjective synthesis of apprehension objective only by reference to a rule in accordance with which the appearances in their succession, that is, as they happen, are determined by the preceding state. The experience of an event [*i.e.* of anything as *happening*] is itself possible only on this assumption.

This may seem to contradict all that has hitherto been taught in regard to the procedure of our understanding. The accepted view is that only through the perception and comparison of events repeatedly following in a uniform manner upon preceding appearances are we enabled to discover a rule according to which certain events

B 241 always follow upon certain appearances, and that this is the way in which we are first led to construct for ourselves the concept of cause. Now

A 196 the concept, if thus formed, would be merely empirical, and the rule which it supplies, that everything which happens has a cause, would be as contingent as the experience upon which it is based. Since the universality and necessity of the rule would not be grounded *a priori*, but only on induction, they would be merely fictitious and without genuinely universal validity. It is with these, as with other pure *a priori* representations—for instance, space and time. We can extract clear concepts of them from experience, only because we have put them into experience, and because experience is thus itself brought about only by their means. Certainly, the logical clearness of this representation of a rule determining the series of events is possible only after we have employed it in experience. Nevertheless, recognition of the rule, as a condition of the synthetic unity of appearances in time, has been the ground of experience itself, and has therefore preceded it *a priori*.

We have, then, to show, in the case under consideration, that we never, even in experience, ascribe succession (that is, the happening of some event which previously did not exist) to the object, and so distinguish it from subjective

B 242 sequence in our apprehension, except when there is an underlying rule which compels us to

A 197 observe this order of perceptions rather than any other; nay, that this compulsion is really what first makes possible the representation of a succession in the object.

We have representations in us, and can become conscious of them. But however far this consciousness may extend, and however careful and accurate it may be, they still remain mere representations, that is, inner determinations of our mind in this or that relation of time. How, then, does it come about that we posit an object for these representations, and so, in addition to their subjective reality, as modifications, ascribe to them some mysterious kind of objective reality. Objective meaning cannot consist in the relation to another representation (of that which we desire to entitle object), for in that case the question again arises, how this latter representation goes out beyond itself, acquiring objective meaning in addition to the subjective meaning which belongs to it as determination of the mental state. If we enquire what new character *relation to an object* confers upon our representations, what dignity they thereby acquire, we find that it results only in subjecting the representations to a rule, and so in necessitating us to connect them in some one specific manner; and

B 243 conversely, that only in so far as our representations are necessitated in a certain order as regards their time-relations do they acquire objective meaning.

A 198 In the synthesis of appearances the manifold of representations is always successive. Now no object is hereby represented, since through this succession, which is common to all apprehensions, nothing is distinguished from anything else. But immediately I perceive or assume that in this succession there is a relation to the preceding state, from which the representation follows in conformity with a rule, I represent something as an event, as something that happens; that is to say, I apprehend an object to which I must ascribe a certain determinate position in time—a position which, in view of the preceding state, cannot be otherwise assigned. When, therefore, I perceive that something happens, this representation first of all contains [the consciousness] that there is something preceding, because only by reference to what precedes does the appearance acquire its time-relation, namely, that of existing after a preceding time in which it itself was not. But it can acquire this determinate position in this relation of time only in so far as something is presupposed in the preceding state upon which it follows invariably, that is, in accordance with a rule. From this there results a twofold consequence. In the first place, I cannot reverse the series, placing that which happens prior to that upon which it follows. And secondly, if the state which precedes is posited, this B 244 determinate event follows inevitably and necessarily. The situation, then, is this: there is an order in our representations in which the present, so far as it has come to be, refers us to some A 199 preceding state as a correlate of the event which is given; and though this correlate is, indeed, indeterminate, it none the less stands in a determining relation to the event as its consequence, connecting the event in necessary relation with itself in the time-series.

If, then, it is a necessary law of our sensibility, and therefore a *formal condition* of all perceptions, that the preceding time necessarily determines the succeeding (since I cannot advance to the succeeding time save through the preceding), it is also an indispensable law of *empirical representation* of the time-series that the appearances of past time determine all existences in the succeeding time, and that these latter, as events, can take place only in so far as the appearances of past time determine their existence in time, that is, determine them according to a rule. *For only in appearances can we empirically apprehend this continuity in the connection of times.*

Refutation of Idealism

Idealism—meaning thereby *material* idealism—is the theory which declares the existence of objects in space outside us either to be merely doubtful and indemonstrable or to be false and impossible. The former is the *problematic* idealism of Descartes, which holds that there is only one empirical assertion that is indubitably certain, namely, that 'I am'. The latter is the *dogmatic* idealism of Berkeley. He maintains that space, with all the things of which it is the inseparable condition, is something which is in itself impossible; and he therefore regards the things in space as merely imaginary entities. Dogmatic idealism is unavoidable, if space be interpreted as a property that must belong to things in themselves. For in that case space, and everything to which it serves as condition, is a non-entity. The ground on which this idealism rests has already been undermined by us in the Transcendental Aesthetic. Problematic idealism, which makes no such B 275 assertion, but merely pleads incapacity to prove, through immediate experience, any existence except our own, is, in so far as it allows of no decisive judgment until sufficient proof has been found, reasonable and in accordance with a thorough and philosophical mode of thought. The required proof must, therefore, show that we have *experience,* and not merely imagination of outer things; and this, it would seem, cannot be achieved save by proof that even our inner experience, which for Descartes is indubitable, is possible only on the assumption of outer experience.

Thesis

The mere, but empirically determined, consciousness of my own existence proves the existence of objects in space outside me.

Proof

I am conscious of my own existence as determined in time. All determination of time presupposes something *permanent* in perception. This permanent cannot, however, be something in me, since it is only through this permanent that my existence in time can itself be determined. Thus perception of this permanent is possible only through a *thing* outside me and not through the mere *representation* of a thing outside me; and consequently the determination of my existence in time is possible only through the existence of B 276 actual things which I perceive outside me. Now consciousness [of my existence] in time is necessarily bound up with consciousness of the [condition of the] possibility of this time-determination; and it is therefore necessarily bound up with the existence of things outside me, as the condition of the time-determination. In other words, the consciousness of my existence is at the same time an immediate consciousness of the existence of other things outside me.

Note 1. It will be observed that in the foregoing proof the game played by idealism has been turned against itself, and with greater justice. Idealism assumed that the only immediate experience is inner experience, and that from it we can only *infer* outer things—and this, moreover, only in an untrustworthy manner, as in all cases where we are inferring from given effects to determinate causes. In this particular case, the cause of the representations, which we ascribe, perhaps falsely, to outer things, may lie in ourselves. But in the above proof it has been shown B 277 that outer experience is really immediate,[2] and that only by means of it is inner experience—not indeed the consciousness of my own existence, but the determination of it in time—possible. Certainly, the representation 'I am', which expresses the consciousness that can accompany all thought, immediately includes in itself the existence of a subject; but it does not so include any *knowledge* of that subject, and therefore also no empirical knowledge, that is, no experience of it. For this we require, in addition to the thought of something existing, also intuition, and in this case inner intuition, in respect of which, that is, of time, the subject must be determined. But in order so to determine it, outer objects are quite indispensable; and it therefore follows that inner experience is itself possible only mediately, and only through outer experience.

Note 2. With this thesis all employment of our cognitive faculty in experience, in the determination of time, entirely agrees. Not only are we unable to perceive any determination of time save through change in outer relations (motion) relatively to the permanent in space (for instance, the motion of the sun relatively to B 278 objects on the earth), we have nothing permanent on which, as intuition, we can base the concept of a substance, save only *matter*; and even this permanence is not obtained from outer experience, but is presupposed *a priori* as a necessary condition of determination of time, and therefore also as a determination of inner sense in respect of [the determination of] our own existence through the existence of outer things. The consciousness of myself in the representation 'I' is not an intuition, but a merely *intellectual* representation of the spontaneity of a thinking subject. This 'I' has not, therefore, the least predicate of intuition, which, as permanent, might

serve as correlate for the determination of time in inner sense—in the manner in which, for instance, *impenetrability* serves in our *empirical* intuition of matter.

Note 3. From the fact that the existence of outer things is required for the possibility of a determinate consciousness of the self, it does not follow that every intuitive representation of outer things involves the existence of these things, for their representation can very well be the product merely of the imagination (as in dreams and delusions). Such representation is merely the reproduction of previous outer perceptions, which, as has been shown, are possible only through the reality of outer objects. All that we have here sought to prove is that inner experience in general is possible only through outer B 279 experience in general. Whether this or that supposed experience be not purely imaginary, must be ascertained from its special determinations, and through its congruence with the criteria of all real experience.

ANALYTIC OF PRINCIPLES

Chapter III
The Distinction of All Objects in General into Phenomena and Noumena

We have seen that everything which the understanding derives from itself is, though not borrowed from experience, at the disposal of the B 296 understanding solely for use in experience. The principles of pure understanding, whether constitutive *a priori*, like the mathematical principles, or merely regulative, like the dynamical, contain A 237 nothing but what may be called the pure schema of possible experience. For experience obtains its unity only from the synthetic unity which the understanding originally and of itself confers upon the synthesis of imagination in its relation to apperception; and the appearances, as data for a possible knowledge, must already stand *a priori* in relation to, and in agreement with, that synthetic unity. But although these rules of understanding are not only true *a priori*, but are indeed the source of all truth (that is, of the agreement of our knowledge with objects), inasmuch as they contain in themselves the ground of the possibility of experience viewed as the sum of all knowledge wherein objects can be given to us, we are not satisfied with the exposition merely of that which is true, but likewise demand that account be taken of that which we desire to know. . . .

If the assertion, that the understanding can employ its various principles and its various concepts solely in an empirical and never in a transcendental manner, is a proposition which can be B 298 known with certainty, it will yield important consequences. The transcendental employment of a concept in any principle is its application to things *in general and in themselves;* the empirical employment is its application *merely to appearances;* that is, to objects of a possible experience. A 239 That the latter application of concepts is alone feasible is evident from the following considerations. We demand in every concept, first, the logical form of a concept (of thought) in general, and secondly, the possibility of giving it an object to which it may be applied. In the absence of such object, it has no meaning and is completely lacking in content, though it may still contain the logical function which is required for making a concept out of any data that may be presented. Now the object cannot be given to a concept otherwise than in intuition; for though a pure intuition can indeed precede the object *a priori,* even this intuition can acquire its object, and therefore objective validity, only through the empirical intuition of which it is the mere form. Therefore all concepts, and with them all principles, even such as are possible *a priori,* relate to empirical intuitions, that is, to the data for a possible experience. Apart from this relation they have no objective validity, and in respect of their representations are a mere play of imagination or of understanding. Take, for instance, the concepts of B 299 mathematics, considering them first of all in their pure intuitions. Space has three dimensions; between two points there can be only one straight line, etc. Although all these principles, and the representation of the object with which this science occupies itself, are generated in the mind A 240 completely *a priori,* they would mean nothing, were we not always able to present their meaning

in appearances, that is, in empirical objects. We therefore demand that a bare concept be *made sensible,* that is, that an object corresponding to it be presented in intuition. Otherwise the concept would, as we say, be without *sense,* that is, without meaning. The mathematician meets this demand by the construction of a figure, which, although produced *a priori,* is an appearance present to the senses. In the same science the concept of magnitude seeks its support and sensible meaning in number, and this in turn in the fingers, in the beads of the abacus, or in strokes and points which can be placed before the eyes. The concept itself is always *a priori* in origin, and so likewise are the synthetic principles or formulas derived from such concepts; but their employment and their relation to their professed objects can in the end be sought nowhere but in experience, of whose possibility they contain the formal conditions.

B 300 That this is also the case with all categories and the principles derived from them, appears from the following consideration. We cannot define any one of them in any real fashion, that is, make the possibility of their object understandable, without at once descending to the conditions of sensibility, and so to the form of A 241 appearances—to which, as their sole objects, they must consequently be limited. For if this condition be removed, all meaning, that is, relation to the object, falls away; and we cannot through any example make comprehensible to ourselves what sort of a thing is to be meant by such a concept.

B 303 From all this it undeniably follows that the pure concepts of understanding can *never* admit of *transcendental* but *always* only of *empirical* employment, and that the principles of pure understanding can apply only to objects of the senses under the universal conditions of a possible experience, never to things in general without regard to the mode in which we are able to intuit them.

Accordingly the Transcendental Analytic leads to this important conclusion, that the most the understanding can achieve *a priori* is to anticipate the form of a possible experience in general. And since that which is not appearance

cannot be an object of experience, the under-standing can never transcend those limits of sen-
A 247 sibility within which alone objects can be given to us. Its principles are merely rules for the expo-sition of appearances; and the proud name of an Ontology that presumptuously claims to supply, in systematic doctrinal form, synthetic *a priori* knowledge of things in general (for instance, the principle of causality) must, therefore, give place to the modest title of a mere Analytic of pure understanding.

B 304   Thought is the act which relates given intu-ition to an object. If the mode of this intuition is not in any way given, the object is merely tran-scendental, and the concept of understanding has only transcendental employment, namely, as the unity of the thought of a manifold in general. Thus no object is determined through a pure cat-egory in which abstraction is made of every con-dition of sensible intuition—the only kind of intuition possible to us. It then expresses only the thought of an object in general, according to different modes. Now the employment of a concept involves a function of judgment whereby an object is subsumed under the concept, and so involves at least the formal condition under which something can be given in intuition. If this condition of judgment (the schema) is lack-ing, all subsumption becomes impossible. For in that case nothing is given that could be sub-sumed under the concept. The merely transcen-dental employment of the categories is, therefore, really no employment at all, and has no determi-nate object, not even one that is determinable in
A 248 its mere form. It therefore follows that the pure category does not suffice for a synthetic *a priori* principle, that the principles of pure understand-ing are only of empirical, never of transcendental employment, and that outside the field of possi-ble experience there can be no synthetic *a priori*
B 305 principles.

     It may be advisable, therefore, to express the situation as follows. The pure categories, apart from formal conditions of sensibility, have only
_ transcendental meaning; nevertheless they may not be employed transcendentally, such employ-ment being in itself impossible, inasmuch as all conditions of any employment in judgments are

lacking to them, namely, the formal conditions of the subsumption of any ostensible object under these concepts. Since, then, as pure cate-gories merely, they are not to be employed empir-ically, and cannot be employed transcendentally, they cannot, when separated from all sensibility, be employed in any manner whatsoever, that is, they cannot be applied to any ostensible object. They are the pure form of the employment of understanding in respect of objects in general, that is, of thought; but since they are merely its form, through them alone no object can be thought or determined.

     But we are here subject to an illusion from which it is difficult to escape. The categories are not, as regards their origin, grounded in sensibil-ity, like the *forms of intuition,* space and time; and they seem, therefore, to allow of an application extending beyond all objects of the senses. As a matter of fact they are nothing but *forms of thought,* which contain the merely logical faculty
B 306 of uniting *a priori* in one consciousness the mani-fold given in intuition; and apart, therefore, from the only intuition that is possible to us, they have even less meaning than the pure sensible forms. Through these forms an object is at least given, whereas a mode of combining the manifold—a mode peculiar to our understanding—by itself, in the absence of that intuition wherein the mani-fold can alone be given, signifies nothing at all. At the same time, if we entitle certain objects, as appearances, sensible entities (phenomena), then since we thus distinguish the mode in which we intuit them from the nature that belongs to them in themselves, it is implied in this distinction that we place the latter, consid-ered in their own nature, although we do not so intuit them, or that we place other possible things, which are not objects of our senses but are thought as objects merely through the under-standing, in opposition to the former, and that in so doing we entitle them intelligible entities (noumena). The question then arises, whether our pure concepts of understanding have mean-ing in respect of these latter, and so can be a way of knowing them.

     At the very outset, however, we come upon an ambiguity which may occasion serious misapprehension. The understanding, when it entitles an object in a [certain] relation mere phenomenon, at the same time forms, apart from that relation, a representation of an *object in itself,* and so comes to represent itself as also being able to B 307 form *concepts* of such objects. And since the understanding yields no concepts additional to the categories, it also supposes that the object in itself must at least be *thought* through these pure concepts, and so is misled into treating the entirely *indeterminate* concept of an intelligible entity, namely, of a something in general outside our sensibility, as being a *determinate* concept of an entity that allows of being known in a certain [purely intelligible] manner by means of the understanding.

If by 'noumenon' we mean a thing so far as it is *not an object of our sensible intuition,* and so abstract from our mode of intuiting it, this is a noumenon in the *negative* sense of the term. But if we understand by it an *object* of a *non-sensible intuition,* we thereby presuppose a special mode of intuition, namely, the intellectual, which is not that which we possess, and of which we cannot comprehend even the possibility. This would be 'noumenon' in the *positive* sense of the term.

The doctrine of sensibility is likewise the doctrine of the noumenon in the negative sense, that is, of things which the understanding must think without this reference to our mode of intuition, therefore not merely as appearances but as things in themselves. At the same time the understanding is well aware that in viewing things in this manner, as thus apart from our B 308 mode of intuition, it cannot make any use of the categories. For the categories have meaning only in relation to the unity of intuition in space and time; and even this unity they can determine, by means of general *a priori* connecting concepts, only because of the mere ideality of space and time. In cases where this unity of time is not to be found, and therefore in the case of the noumenon, all employment, and indeed the whole meaning of the categories, entirely vanishes; for we have then no means of determining whether things in harmony with the categories are even possible. On this point I need only refer the reader to what I have said in the opening

sentences of the *General Note* appended to the preceding chapter. The possibility of a thing can never be proved merely from the fact that its concept is not self-contradictory, but only through its being supported by some corresponding intuition. If, therefore, we should attempt to apply the categories to objects which are not viewed as being appearances, we should have to postulate an intuition other than the sensible, and the object would thus be a noumenon in the *positive sense.* Since, however, such a type of intuition, intellectual intuition, forms no part whatsoever of our faculty of knowledge, it follows that the employment of the categories can never extend further than to the objects of experience. Doubtless, indeed, there are intelligible entities B 309 corresponding to the sensible entities; there may also be intelligible entities to which our sensible faculty of intuition has no relation whatsoever; but our concepts of understanding, being mere forms of thought for our sensible intuition, could not in the least apply to them. That, therefore, which we entitle 'noumenon' must be understood as being such only in a *negative* sense.

If I remove from empirical knowledge all thought (through categories), no knowledge of any object remains. For through mere intuition nothing at all is thought, and the fact that this affection of sensibility is in me does not [by itself] amount to a relation of such representa- A 254 tion to any object. But if, on the other hand, I leave aside all intuition, the form of thought still remains—that is, the mode of determining an object for the manifold of a possible intuition. The categories accordingly extend further than sensible intuition, since they think objects in general, without regard to the special mode (the sensibility) in which they may be given. But they do not thereby determine a greater sphere of objects. For we cannot assume that such objects can be given, without presupposing the possibility of another kind of intuition than the sensible; and we are by no means justified in so doing. B 310 If the objective reality of a concept cannot be in any way known, while yet the concept contains no contradiction and also at the same time is connected with other modes of knowledge that involve given concepts which it serves to limit, I entitle that concept problematic. The concept of a *noumenon*—that is, of a thing which is not to be thought as object of the senses but as a thing in itself, solely through a pure understanding—is not in any way contradictory. For we cannot assert of sensibility that it is the sole possible kind of intuition. Further, the concept of a noumenon is necessary, to prevent sensible intuition from being extended to things in themselves, and thus to limit the objective validity of sensible knowledge. The remaining things, to which it does not apply, are entitled noumena, in order to show that this knowledge cannot extend its domain over everything which the understanding thinks. But none the less we are unable to comprehend how such noumena can be possible, and the domain that lies out beyond the sphere of appearances is for us empty. That is to say, we have an understanding which *problematically* extends further, but we have no intuition, indeed not even the concept of a possible intuition, through which objects outside the field of sensibility can be given, and through which the understanding can be employed *assertorically* beyond that field. The concept of a noumenon is thus a merely *limiting concept*, the function of which is to curb the pretensions of sensibility; and it is therefore only of negative employment. At the same time it is no arbitrary invention; it is bound up with the limitation of sensibility, though it cannot affirm anything positive beyond the field of sensibility.

A 255

B 311

The division of objects into phenomena and noumena, and the world into a world of the senses and a world of the understanding, is therefore quite inadmissible in the positive sense, although the distinction of concepts as sensible and intellectual is certainly legitimate. For no object can be determined for the latter concepts, and consequently they cannot be asserted to be objectively valid. If we abandon the senses, how shall we make it conceivable that our categories, which would be the sole remaining concepts for noumena, should still continue to signify something, since for their relation to any object more must be given than merely the unity of thought—namely, in addition, a possible intu-

A 256

ition, to which they may be applied. None the less, if the concept of a noumenon be taken in a merely problematic sense, it is not only admissible, but as setting limits to sensibility is likewise indispensable. But in that case a noumenon is not for our understanding a special [kind of] object, namely, an *intelligible object*; the [sort of] understanding to which it might belong is itself a problem. For we cannot in the least represent to ourselves the possibility of an understanding which should know its object, not discursively through categories, but intuitively in a non-sensible intuition. What our understanding acquires through this concept of a noumenon, is a negative extension; that is to say, understanding is not limited through sensibility; on the contrary, it itself limits sensibility by applying the term noumena to things in themselves (things not regarded as appearances). But in so doing it at the same time sets limits to itself, recognising that it cannot know these noumena through any of the categories, and that it must therefore think them only under the title of an unknown something.

B 312

THE TRANSCENDENTAL DIALECTIC

A 310

Book I

The Concepts of Pure Reason

The title 'concept of reason' already gives a preliminary indication that we are dealing with something which does not allow of being confined within experience, since it concerns a knowledge of which any empirical knowledge (perhaps even the whole of possible experience or of its empirical synthesis) is only a part. No actual experience has ever been completely adequate to it, yet to it every actual experience belongs. Concepts of reason enable us to *conceive*, concepts of understanding to *understand*—([as employed in reference to] perceptions). If the concepts of reason contain the unconditioned, they are concerned with something to which all experience is subordinate, but which is never itself an object of experience—something to which reason leads in its inferences from experience, and in accordance

A 311

with which it estimates and gauges the degree of its empirical employment, but which is never itself a member of the empirical synthesis. If, B 368 none the less, these concepts possess objective validity, they may be called *conceptus ratiocinati* (rightly inferred concepts); if, however, they have no such validity, they have surreptitiously obtained recognition through having at least an illusory appearance of being inferences, and may be called *conceptus ratiocinantes* (pseudo-rational concepts). But since this can be established only in the chapter on the dialectical inferences of pure reason, we are not yet in a position to deal with it. Meantime, just as we have entitled the pure concepts of understanding categories, so we shall give a new name to the concepts of pure reason, calling them transcendental ideas. This title we shall now explain and justify.

A 321 **First Book of the Transcendental Dialectic**

Section 2

The Transcendental Ideas

The Transcendental Analytic has shown us how the mere logical form of our knowledge may in itself contain original pure *a priori* concepts, which represent objects prior to all experience, or, speaking more correctly, indicate the synthetic unity which alone makes possible an B 378 empirical knowledge of objects. The form of judgments (converted into a concept of the synthesis of intuitions) yielded categories which direct all employment of understanding in experience. Similarly, we may presume that the form of syllogisms, when applied to the synthetic unity of intuitions under the direction of the categories, will contain the origin of special *a priori* concepts, which we may call pure concepts of reason, or *transcendental ideas,* and which will determine according to principles how understanding is to be employed in dealing with experience in its totality.

The function of reason in its inferences consists in the universality of knowledge [which it yields] according to concepts, the syllogism being itself a judgment which is determined *a priori* in the whole extent of its conditions. The proposi-

A 322 tion, 'Caius is mortal', I could indeed derive from experience by means of the understanding alone. But I am in pursuit of a concept (in this case, the concept 'man') that contains the condition under which the predicate (general term for what is asserted) of this judgment is given; and after I have subsumed the predicate under this condition taken in its whole extension ('All men are mortal'), I proceed, in accordance therewith, to determine the knowledge of my object ('Caius is mortal').

Accordingly, in the conclusion of a syllo-B 379 gism we restrict a predicate to a certain object, after having first thought it in the major premiss in its whole extension under a given condition. This complete quantity of the extension in relation to such a condition is called *universality* (*universalitas*). In the synthesis of intuitions we have corresponding to this the *allness* (*universitas*) or *totality* of the conditions. The transcendental concept of reason is, therefore, none other than the concept of the *totality* of the *conditions* for any given conditioned. Now since it is the *unconditioned* alone which makes possible the totality of conditions, and, conversely, the totality of conditions is always itself unconditioned, a pure concept of reason can in general be explained by the concept of the unconditioned, conceived as containing a ground of the synthesis of the conditioned.

A 323 The number of pure concepts of reason will be equal to the number of kinds of relation which the understanding represents to itself by means of the categories. We have therefore to seek for an *unconditioned,* first, of the *categorical* synthesis in a *subject*; secondly, of the *hypothetical* synthesis of the members of a *series*; thirdly, of the *disjunctive* synthesis of the parts in a *system.*

There is thus precisely the same number of kinds of syllogism, each of which advances through prosyllogisms to the unconditioned: first, to the subject which is never itself a predicate; B 380 secondly, to the presupposition which itself presupposes nothing further; thirdly, to such an aggregate of the members of the division of a concept as requires nothing further to complete the division. The pure concepts of reason—of totality in the synthesis of conditions—are thus at least necessary as setting us the task of extending the unity of understanding, where possible, up to the unconditioned, and are grounded in the nature of human reason. These transcendental concepts may, however, be without any suitable corresponding employment *in concreto,* and may therefore have no other utility than that of so directing the understanding that, while it is extended to the uttermost, it is also at the same time brought into complete consistency with itself.

Now the transcendental concept of reason is directed always solely towards absolute totality in the synthesis of conditions, and never terminates save in what is absolutely, that is, in all relations, unconditioned. For pure reason leaves everyB 383 thing to the understanding—the understanding [alone] applying immediately to the objects of intuition, or rather to their synthesis in the imagination. Reason concerns itself exclusively with absolute totality in the employment of the concepts of the understanding, and endeavours to carry the synthetic unity, which is thought in the category, up to the completely unconditioned. We may call this unity of appearances the *unity of reason,* and that expressed by the category the *unity of understanding.* Reason accordingly occupies itself solely with the employment of understanding, not indeed in so far as the latter contains the ground of possible experience (for the concept of the absolute totality of conditions is not applicable in any experience, since no experience is unconditioned), but solely in order to prescribe to the understanding its direction towards a certain unity of which it has itself no concept, and in such manner as to unite all the A 327 acts of the understanding, in respect of every object, into an *absolute* whole. The objective employment of the pure concepts of reason is, therefore, always *transcendent,* while that of the pure concepts of understanding must, in accordance with their nature, and inasmuch as their application is solely to possible experience, be always *immanent.*

I understand by idea a necessary concept of reason to which no corresponding object can be given in sense-experience. Thus the pure con-

cepts of reason, now under consideration, are B 384 *transcendental ideas.* They are concepts of pure reason, in that they view all knowledge gained in experience as being determined through an absolute totality of conditions. They are not arbitrarily invented; they are imposed by the very nature of reason itself, and therefore stand in necessary relation to the whole employment of understanding. Finally, they are transcendent and overstep the limits of all experience; no object adequate to the transcendental idea can ever be found within experience. If I speak of an idea, then as regards its object, viewed as an object of pure understanding, I am saying a *great deal,* but as regards its relation to the subject, that is, in respect of its actuality under empirical conditions, I am for the same reason saying *very little,* in that, as being the concept of a maximum, it can never be correspondingly given *in concreto.* Since in the merely speculative employment of reason the latter [namely, to determine the actu- A 328 ality of the idea under empirical conditions] is indeed our whole purpose, and since the approximation to a concept, which yet is never actually reached, puts us in no better position than if the concept were entirely abortive, we say of such a concept—it is *only* an idea. The absolute whole of all appearances—we might thus say—*is only an idea;* since we can never represent it in image, it remains a *problem* to which there is no solution.

Section 3

System of the Transcendental Ideas

All transcendental ideas can therefore be arranged in three classes, the *first* containing the absolute (unconditioned) *unity* of the *thinking subject,* the *second* the absolute *unity of the series of conditions of appearance,* the *third* the absolute *unity of the condition of all objects of thought in general.*

The thinking subject is the object of *psychology,* the sum-total of all appearances (the world) is the object of *cosmology,* and the thing which contains the highest condition of the possibility of all that can be thought (the being of all beings) the object of *theology.* Pure reason thus furnishes the idea for a transcendental doctrine of the soul (*psychologia rationalis*), for a transcen- B 392 dental science of the world (*cosmologia rationalis*),

A 335 and, finally, for a transcendental knowledge of God (*theologia transzendentalis*). The understanding is not in a position to yield even the mere project of any one of these sciences, not even though it be supported by the highest logical employment of reason, that is, by all the conceivable inferences through which we seek to advance from one of its objects (appearance) to all others, up to the most remote members of the empirical synthesis; each of these sciences is an altogether pure and genuine product, or problem, of pure reason.

A 341
B 399
Second Book of the Transcendental Dialectic

Chapter I

The Paralogisms of Pure Reason

A logical paralogism is a syllogism which is fallacious in form, be its content what it may. A transcendental paralogism is one in which there is a transcendental ground, constraining us to draw a formally invalid conclusion. Such a fallacy is therefore grounded in the nature of human reason, and gives rise to an illusion which cannot be avoided, although it may, indeed, be rendered harmless.

We now come to a concept which was not included in the general list of transcendental concepts but which must yet be counted as belonging to that list, without, however, in the least altering it or declaring it defective. This is the concept or, if the term be preferred, the judgment, 'I think'. As is easily seen, this is the vehicle of all concepts, and therefore also of transcendental concepts, and so is always included in the conceiving of these latter, and is itself transcendental. But it can have no special designation, because it serves only to introduce B 400 all our thought, as belonging to consciousness. Meanwhile, however free it be of empirical A 342 admixture (impressions of the senses), it yet enables us to distinguish, through the nature of our faculty of representation, two kinds of objects. 'I', as thinking, am an object of inner sense, and am called 'soul'. That which is an object of the outer senses is called 'body'. Accordingly the expression 'I', as a thinking

being, signifies the object of that psychology which may be entitled the 'rational doctrine of the soul', inasmuch as I am not here seeking to learn in regard to the soul anything more than can be inferred, independently of all experience (which determines me more specifically and *in concreto*), from this concept 'I', so far as it is present in all thought.

The *rational* doctrine of the soul is really an undertaking of this kind; for if in this science the least empirical element of my thought, or any special perception of my inner state, were intermingled with the grounds of knowledge, it would no longer be a rational but an *empirical* doctrine of the soul. Thus we have here what professes to be a science built upon the single proposition 'I *think*'. Whether this claim be well or ill grounded, we may, very fittingly, in accordance with the nature of a transcendental philosophy, proceed to investigate. The reader must not object that this proposition, which expresses the B 401 perception of the self, contains an inner experience, and that the rational doctrine of the soul founded upon it is never pure and is therefore to A 343 that extent based upon an empirical principle. For this inner perception is nothing more than the mere apperception 'I *think*', by which even transcendental concepts are made possible; what we assert in them is 'I think substance, cause', etc. For inner experience in general and its possibility, or perception in general and its relation to other perception, in which no special distinction or empirical determination is given, is not to be regarded as empirical knowledge but as knowledge of the empirical in general, and has to be reckoned with the investigation of the possibility of any and every experience, which is certainly a transcendental enquiry. The least object of perception (for example, even pleasure or displeasure), if added to the universal representation of self-consciousness, would at once transform rational psychology into empirical psychology.

'I *think*' is, therefore, the sole text of rational psychology, and from it the whole of its teaching has to be developed. Obviously, if this thought is to be related to an object (myself), it can contain none but transcendental predicates of that object, since the least empirical predicate would destroy the rational purity of the science and its independence of all experience.

THE PARALOGISMS OF PURE REASON [AS RESTATED IN SECOND EDITION]

Since the proposition 'I think' (taken problematically) contains the form of each and every judgment of understanding and accompanies all categories as their vehicle, it is evident that the inferences from it admit only of a transcendental employment of the understanding. And since this employment excludes any admixture of experience, we cannot, after what has been shown above, entertain any favourable anticipations in regard to its methods of procedure. We therefore propose to follow it, with a critical eye, through all the predicaments of pure psychology. But for the sake of brevity the examination had best proceed in an unbroken continuity.

The following general remark may, at the outset, aid us in our scrutiny of this kind of argument. I do not know an object merely in that I think, but only in so far as I determine a given intuition with respect to the unity of consciousness in which all thought consists. Consequently, I do not know myself through being conscious of myself as thinking, but only when I am conscious of the intuition of myself as determined with respect to the function of thought. *Modi* of self-consciousness in thought are not by themselves concepts of objects (categories), but are mere functions which do not give thought an object to be known, and accordingly do not give even myself as object. The object is not the consciousness of the *determining* self, but only that of the *determinable* self, that is, of my inner intuition (in so far as its manifold can be combined in accordance with the universal condition of the unity of apperception in thought).

B 407

(1) In all judgments I am the *determining* subject of that relation which constitutes the judgment. That the 'I', the 'I' that thinks, can be regarded always as *subject,* and as something which does not belong to thought as a mere predicate, must be granted. It is an apodeictic and indeed *identical* proposition; but it does not mean

that I, as *object,* am for myself a *self-subsistent* being or *substance.* The latter statement goes very far beyond the former, and demands for its proof data which are not to be met with in thought, and perhaps (in so far as I have regard to the thinking self merely as such) are more than I shall ever find in it.

(2) That the 'I' of apperception, and therefore the 'I' in every act of thought, is *one,* and cannot be resolved into a plurality of subjects, and consequently signifies a logically simple subject, is something already contained in the very concept of thought, and is therefore an analytic proposition. But this does not mean that the thinking 'I' is a simple *substance.* That proposition would be synthetic. The concept of substance always relates to intuitions which cannot in me be other than sensible, and which therefore lie entirely outside the field of the understanding and its thought. But it is of this thought that we are speaking when we say that the 'I' in thought is simple. It would, indeed, be surprising if what in other cases requires so much labour to determine—namely, what, of all that is presented in intuition, is substance, and further, whether this substance can be simple (*e.g.* in the parts of matter)—should be thus given me directly, as if by revelation, in the poorest of all representations.

B 408

(3) The proposition, that in all the manifold of which I am conscious I am identical with myself, is likewise implied in the concepts themselves, and is therefore an analytic proposition. But this identity of the subject, of which I can be conscious in all my representations, does not concern any intuition of the subject, whereby it is given as object, and cannot therefore signify the identity of the person, if by that is understood the consciousness of the identity of one's own substance, as a thinking being, in all change of its states. No mere analysis of the proposition 'I think' will suffice to prove such a proposition; for that we should require various synthetic judgments, based upon given intuition.

B 409

(4) That I distinguish my own existence as that of a thinking being, from other things outside me—among them my body—is likewise an analytic proposition; for *other* things are such as I

think to be *distinct* from myself. But I do not thereby learn whether this consciousness of myself would be even possible apart from things outside me through which representations are given to me, and whether, therefore, I could exist merely as thinking being (*i.e.* without existing in human form).

The analysis, then, of the consciousness of myself in thought in general, yields nothing whatsoever towards the knowledge of myself as object. The logical exposition of thought in general has been mistaken for a metaphysical determination of the object.

Indeed, it would be a great stumbling-block, or rather would be the one unanswerable objection, to our whole critique, if there were a possibility of proving *a priori* that all thinking beings are in themselves simple substances, and that consequently (as follows from this same mode of proof) personality is inseparable from them, and that they are conscious of their existence as separate and distinct from all matter. For by such procedure we should have taken a step beyond the world of sense, and have entered into the field of B 410 noumena; and no one could then deny our right of advancing yet further in this domain, indeed of settling in it, and, should our star prove auspicious, of establishing claims to permanent possession. The proposition, 'Every thinking being is, as such, a simple substance', is a synthetic *a priori* proposition; it is synthetic in that it goes beyond the concept from which it starts, and adds to the thought in general [*i.e.* to the concept of a thinking being] the mode of [its] existence: it is *a priori*, in that it adds to the concept a predicate (that of simplicity) which cannot be given in any experience. It would then follow that *a priori* synthetic propositions are possible and admissible, not only, as we have asserted, in relation to objects of possible experience, and indeed as principles of the possibility of this experience, but that they are applicable to things in general and to things in themselves—a result that would make an end of our whole critique, and would constrain us to acquiesce in the old-time procedure. Upon closer consideration we find, however, that there is no such serious danger.

The whole procedure of rational psychology is determined by a paralogism, which is exhibited in the following syllogism:

> *That which cannot be thought otherwise than as subject does not exist otherwise than as subject, and is therefore substance.*

B 411 *A thinking being, considered merely as such, cannot be thought otherwise than as subject. Therefore it exists also only as subject, that is, as substance.*

In the major premiss we speak of a being that can be thought in general, in every relation, and therefore also as it may be given in intuition. But in the minor premiss we speak of it only in so far as it regards itself, as subject, simply in relation to thought and the unity of consciousness, and not as likewise in relation to the intuition through which it is given as object to thought. Thus the conclusion is arrived at fallaciously, *per sophisma figurae dictionis.*[3]

B 412 That we are entirely right in resolving this famous argument into a paralogism will be clearly seen, if we call to mind what has been said in the General Note to the Systematic Representation of the Principles and in the Section on Noumena. For it has there been proved that the concept of a thing which can exist by itself as subject and never as mere predicate, carries with it no objective reality; in other words, that we cannot know whether there is any object to which the concept is applicable—as to the possibility of such a mode of existence we have no means of deciding—and that the concept therefore yields no knowledge whatsoever. If by the term 'substance' be meant an object which can be given, and if it is to yield knowledge, it must be made to rest on a permanent intuition, as being that through which alone the object of our concept can be given, and as being, therefore, B 413 the indispensable condition of the objective reality of the concept. Now in inner intuition there is nothing permanent, for the 'I' is merely the consciousness of my thought. So long, therefore, as we do not go beyond mere thinking, we are without the necessary condition for applying the concept of substance, that is, of a self-subsistent subject, to the self as a thinking being. And with the objective reality of the concept of substance, the allied concept of simplicity likewise vanishes; it is transformed into a merely logical qualitative unity of self-consciousness in thought in general, which has to be present whether the subject be composite or not.

Refutation of Mendelssohn's Proof of the Permanence of the Soul

This acute philosopher soon noticed that the usual argument by which it is sought to prove that the soul—if it be admitted to be a simple being—cannot cease to be through *dissolution*, is insufficient for its purpose, that of proving the necessary continuance of the soul, since it may be supposed to pass out of existence through simply *vanishing* In his *Phaedo* he endeavoured to prove that the soul cannot be subject to such a process of vanishing, which would be a true annihilation, by showing that a simple being cannot cease to exist. His argument is that since the soul cannot be diminished, and so gradually lose B 414 something of its existence, being by degrees changed into nothing (for since it has no parts, it has no multiplicity in itself), there would be no time between a moment in which it is and another in which it is not—which is impossible. He failed, however, to observe that even if we admit the simple nature of the soul, namely, that it contains no manifold of constituents external to one another, and therefore no extensive quantity, we yet cannot deny to it, any more than to any other existence, intensive quantity, that is, a degree of reality in respect of all its faculties, nay, in respect of all that constitutes its existence, and that this degree of reality may diminish through all the infinitely many smaller degrees. In this manner the supposed substance—the thing, the permanence of which has not yet been proved—may be changed into nothing, not indeed by dissolution, but by gradual loss (*remissio*) of its powers, and so, if I may be permitted the use of the term, by elanguescence. For consciousness itself has always a degree, which always allows of diminution, and the same must also hold of the faculty of being conscious of the self, and like-

B 415 wise of all the other faculties. Thus the permanence of the soul, regarded merely as object of inner sense, remains undemonstrated, and indeed indemonstrable. Its permanence during life is, of course, evident *per se*, since the thinking being (as man) is itself likewise an object of the outer senses. But this is very far from satisfying the rational psychologist who undertakes to prove from mere concepts its absolute permanence beyond this life.

B 416   If we take the above propositions in *synthetic* connection, as valid for all thinking beings, as indeed they must be taken in the system of rational psychology, and proceed from the category of relation, with the proposition, 'All think-B 417 ing beings are, as such, substances', backwards through the series of the propositions, until the circle is completed, we come at last to the *existence* of these thinking beings. Now in this system of rational psychology these beings are taken not only as being conscious of their existence independently of outer things, but as also being able, in and by themselves, to determine that existence in respect of the permanence B 418 which is a necessary characteristic of substance. This rationalist system is thus unavoidably committed to *idealism*, or at least to problematic idealism. For if the existence of outer things is not in any way required for determination of one's own existence in time, the assumption of their existence is a quite gratuitous assumption, of which no proof can ever be given.

If, on the other hand, we should proceed *analytically*, starting from the proposition 'I think', as a proposition that already in itself includes an existence as given, and therefore modality, and analysing it in order to ascertain its content, and so to discover whether and how this 'I' determines its existence in space or time solely through that content, then the propositions of the rational doctrine of the soul would not begin with the concept of a thinking being in general, but with a reality, and we should infer from the manner in which this reality is thought, after everything empirical in it has been removed, what it is that belongs to a thinking being in gen-B 419 eral. This is shown in the following table:

1. *I think,*

2. *as subject,*   3. *as simple subject,*

4. *as identical subject*
in every state of my thought.

In the second proposition it has not been determined whether I can exist and be thought as subject only, and not also as a predicate of another being, and accordingly the concept of a subject is here taken in a merely logical sense, and it remains undetermined whether or not we are to understand by it a substance. Similarly, the third proposition establishes nothing in regard to the constitution or subsistence of the subject; none the less in this proposition the absolute unity of apperception, the simple 'I' in the representation to which all combination or separation that constitutes thought relates, has its own importance. For apperception is something real, and its simplicity is already given in the mere fact of its possibility. Now in space there is nothing real which can be simple; points, which are the only simple things in space, are merely limits, not themselves anything that can as parts serve to constitute
B 420 space. From this follows the impossibility of any explanation in *materialist* terms of the constitution of the self as a merely thinking subject. But since my existence is taken in the first proposition as given—for it does not say that every thinking being exists, which would be to assert its absolute necessity and therefore to say too much, but only, *I exist* thinking'—the proposition is empirical, and can determine my existence only in relation to my representations in time. But since for this purpose I again require something permanent, which, so far as I think myself, is in no way given to me in inner intuition, it is quite impossible, by means of this simple self-consciousness, to determine the manner in which I exist, whether it be as substance or as accident. Thus, if materialism is disqualified from explaining my existence, spiritualism is equally incapable of doing so; and the conclusion is that in no way whatsoever can we know anything of the constitution of the soul, so far as the possibility of its separate existence is concerned.

How, indeed, should it be possible, by means of the unity of consciousness—which we only know because we cannot but make use of it, as indispensable for the possibility of experience— to pass out beyond experience (our existence in this life), and even to extend our knowledge to the nature of all thinking beings in general,
B 421 through the empirical, but in respect of every sort of intuition the quite indeterminate proposition, 'I think'?

Rational psychology exists not as *doctrine,* furnishing an addition to our knowledge of the self, but only as *discipline.* It sets impassable limits to speculative reason in this field, and thus keeps us, on the one hand, from throwing ourselves into the arms of a soulless materialism, or, on the other hand, from losing ourselves in a spiritualism which must be quite unfounded so long as we remain in this present life. But though it furnishes no positive doctrine, it reminds us that we should regard this refusal of reason to give satisfying response to our inquisitive probings into what is beyond the limits of this present life as reason's hint to divert our self-knowledge from fruitless and extravagant speculation to fruitful practical employment. Though in such practical employment it is directed always to objects of experience only, it derives its principles from a higher source, and determines us to regulate our actions as if our destiny reached infinitely far beyond experience, and therefore far beyond this present life.

From all this it is evident that rational psychology owes its origin simply to misunderstanding. The unity of consciousness, which underlies the categories, is here mistaken for an intuition of the subject as object, and the category of substance is then applied to it. But this unity is only unity
B 422 in *thought,* by which alone no object is given, and to which, therefore, the category of substance, which always presupposes a given *intuition,* cannot be applied. Consequently, this subject cannot be known. The subject of the categories cannot by thinking the categories acquire a concept of itself as an object of the categories. For in order to think them, its pure self-consciousness, which is what was to be explained, must itself be presupposed. Similarly, the subject, in which the representation of time has its original

ground, cannot thereby determine its own existence in time. And if this latter is impossible, the former, as a determination of the self (as a thinking being in general) by means of the categories, is equally so.

B 423   Thus the expectation of obtaining knowledge which while extending beyond the limits of possible experience is likewise to further the highest interests of humanity, is found, so far as speculative philosophy professes to satisfy it, to B 424 be grounded in deception, and to destroy itself in the attempt at fulfilment. Yet the severity of our criticism has rendered reason a not unimportant service in proving the impossibility of dogmatically determining, in regard to an object of experience, anything that lies beyond the limits of experience. For in so doing it has secured reason against all possible assertions of the opposite. That cannot be achieved save in one or other of two ways. Either we have to prove our proposition apodeictically; or, if we do not succeed in this, we have to seek out the sources of this inability, which, if they are traceable to the necessary limits of our reason, must constrain all opponents to submit to this same law of renunciation in respect of all claims to dogmatic assertion.

THE TRANSCENDENTAL DIALECTIC

Book II

Chapter II

The Antinomy of Pure Reason

We have shown in the introduction to this part of our work that all transcendental illusion of pure reason rests on dialectical inferences whose A 406 schema is supplied by logic in the three formal species of syllogisms—just as the categories find their logical schema in the four functions of all judgments. The first type of these pseudo-rational inferences deals with the unconditioned unity of the subjective conditions of all representations in general (of the subject or soul), in correspondence with the *categorical* syllogisms, the major premiss of which is a principle asserting B 433 the relation of a predicate to a subject. The sec-

ond type of dialectical argument follows the analogy of the *hypothetical* syllogisms. It has as its content the unconditioned unity of the objective conditions in the [field of] appearance. In similar fashion, the third type, which will be dealt with in the next chapter, has as its theme the unconditioned unity of the objective conditions of the possibility of objects in general.

But there is one point that calls for special notice. Transcendental paralogism produced a purely one-sided illusion in regard to the idea of the subject of our thought. No illusion which will even in the slightest degree support the opposing assertion is caused by the concepts of reason. Consequently, although transcendental paralogism, in spite of a favouring illusion, cannot disclaim the radical defect through which in the fiery ordeal of critical investigation it dwindles into mere semblance, such advantage as it offers is altogether on the side of pneumatism.

A completely different situation arises when reason is applied to the *objective* synthesis of A 407 appearances. For in this domain, however it may endeavour to establish its principle of unconditioned unity, and though it indeed does so with great though illusory appearance of success, it soon falls into such contradictions that it is constrained, in this cosmological field, to desist from any such pretensions.

We have here presented to us a new phenomenon of human reason—an entirely natural antithetic, in which there is no need of making subtle enquiries or of laying snares for the unwary, but into which reason of itself quite B 434 unavoidably falls. It certainly guards reason from the slumber of *fictitious* conviction such as is generated by a purely one-sided illusion, but at the same time subjects it to the temptation either of abandoning itself to a sceptical despair, or of assuming an obstinate attitude, dogmatically committing itself to certain assertions, and refusing to grant a fair hearing to the arguments for the counter-position. Either attitude is the death of sound philosophy, although the former might perhaps be entitled the *euthanasia* of pure reason.

Before considering the various forms of opposition and dissension to which this conflict or antinomy of the laws of pure reason gives rise, we may offer a few remarks in explanation and justification of the method which we propose to employ in the treatment of this subject. I entitle all transcendental ideas, in so far as they refer to absolute totality in the synthesis of appearances,

A 408 *cosmical concepts,* partly because this unconditioned totality also underlies the concept—itself only an idea—of the world-whole; partly because they concern only the synthesis of appearances, therefore only empirical synthesis. When, on the contrary, the absolute totality is that of the synthesis of the conditions of all possible things in

B 435 general, it gives rise to an *ideal* of pure reason which, though it may indeed stand in a certain relation to the cosmical concept, is quite distinct from it. Accordingly, just as the paralogisms of pure reason formed the basis of a dialectical psychology, so the antinomy of pure reason will exhibit to us the transcendental principles of a pretended pure rational cosmology. But it will not do so in order to show this science to be valid and to adopt it. As the title, conflict of reason, suffices to show, this pretended science can be exhibited only in its bedazzling but false illusoriness, as an idea which can never be reconciled with appearances.

The Antinomy of Pure Reason

Section I

System of Cosmological Ideas

A 409 . . . Reason does not really generate any concept. The most it can do is to *free* a concept of *understanding* from the unavoidable limitations of possible experience, and so to endeavour to extend it beyond the limits of the empirical,

B 436 though still, indeed, in terms of its relation to the empirical. This is achieved in the following manner. For a given conditioned, reason demands on the side of the conditions—to which as the conditions of synthetic unity the understanding subjects all appearances—absolute totality, and in so doing converts the category into a transcendental idea. For only by carrying the empirical synthesis as far as the unconditioned is it enabled to render it absolutely complete; and

the unconditioned is never to be met with in experience, but only in the idea. Reason makes this demand in accordance with the principle that if *the conditioned is given, the entire sum of conditions, and consequently the absolutely unconditioned* (through which alone the conditioned has been possible) *is also given.* The transcendental ideas are thus, in the *first* place, simply categories extended to the unconditioned, and can be reduced to a table arranged according to the [fourfold] headings of the latter.

A 416   There are several points which here call for notice. In the first place, the idea of absolute totality concerns only the exposition of *appearances,* and does not therefore refer to the pure concept, such as the understanding may form, of a totality of *things in general.* Appearances are here regarded as given; what reason demands is the absolute completeness of the conditions of their possibility, in so far as these conditions constitute a series. What reason prescribes is therefore an absolutely (that is to say, in every respect) complete synthesis, whereby the appearance may be exhibited in accordance with the laws of understanding.

Secondly, what reason is really seeking in this serial, regressively continued, synthesis of

B 444 conditions, is solely the unconditioned. What it aims at is, as it were, such a completeness in the series of premises as will dispense with the need of presupposing other premises. This *unconditioned* is always contained in the *absolute totality of the series* as represented in imagination. But this absolutely complete synthesis is again only an idea.

This unconditioned may be conceived in either of two ways. It may be viewed as consisting of the entire series in which all the members without exception are conditioned and only the totality of them is absolutely unconditioned. This regress is to be entitled infinite. Or alternatively, the absolutely unconditioned is only a part of the series—a part to which the other members are subordinated, and which does not itself stand under any other condition. On the first view, the

A 418 series *a parte priori* is without limits or beginning, *i.e.* is infinite, and at the same time is given in its entirety. But the regress in it is never completed, and can only be called potentially infinite. On the B 446 second view, there is a first member of the series which in respect of past time is entitled, *the beginning of the world*, in respect of space, *the limit of the world*, in respect of the parts of a given limited whole, the *simple*, in respect of causes, absolute *self-activity* (freedom), in respect of the existence of alterable things, absolute *natural necessity*.

Section 2

Antithetic of Pure Reason

A 426
B 454 The Antinomy of Pure Reason

A 427
B 455 First Conflict of the Transcendental Ideas

Thesis	*Antithesis*
The world has a beginning in time, and is also limited as regards space.	The world has no beginning, and no limits in space; it is infinite as regards both time and space.

Proof	*Proof*
If we assume that the world has no beginning in time, then up to every given moment an eternity has elapsed, and there has passed away in the world an infinite series of successive states of things. Now the infinity of a series consists in the fact that it can never be completed through successive synthesis. It thus follows that it is impossible for an infinite world-series to have passed away, and that a beginning of the world is therefore a necessary condition of the world's existence. This was the first point that called for proof. As regards the second	For let us assume that it has a beginning. Since the beginning is an existence which is preceded by a time in which the thing is not, there must have been a preceding time in which the world was not, *i.e.* an empty time. Now no coming to be of a thing is possible in an empty time, because no part of such a time possesses, as compared with any other, a distinguishing condition of existence rather than of non-existence; and this applies whether the thing is supposed to arise of itself or through some other cause. In the world many series of

point, let us again assume the opposite, namely, that the world is an infinite given whole of coexisting things. Now the magnitude of a quantum which is not given in intuition as within A 428 certain limits, can be B 456 thought only through a synthesis of its parts, and the totality of such a quantum only through a synthesis that is brought to completion through repeated addition of unit to unit. In order, therefore, to think, as a whole, the world which fills all spaces, the successive synthesis of the parts of an infinite world must be viewed as completed, that is, an infinite time must be viewed as having elapsed in the enumeration of all coexisting things. This, however, is impossible. An infinite aggregate of actual things cannot therefore be viewed as a given whole, nor consequently as simultaneously given. The world is, therefore, as regards extension in space, not infinite, but is enclosed within limits. This was the second point in dispute.

things can, indeed, begin; but the world itself cannot have a beginning, and is therefore infinite in respect of past time.

As regards the second point, let us start by assuming the opposite, namely, that the world in space is finite and limited, and consequently exists in an empty space which is unlimited. Things will therefore not only be related *in space* but also related *to space*. Now since the world is an absolute whole beyond which there is no object A 429 of intuition, and there- B 457 fore no correlate with which the world stands in relation, the relation of the world to empty space would be a relation of it to no *object*. But such a relation, and consequently the limitation of the world by empty space, is nothing. The world cannot, therefore, be limited in space; that is, it is infinite in respect of extension.

A 430
B 458 **Observation on the First Antinomy**

A 431
B 459 *I. On the Thesis* *II. On the Antithesis*
In stating these con- The proof of the in-
flicting arguments I have finitude of the given

not sought to elaborate sophisms. That is to say, I have not resorted to the method of the special pleader who attempts to take advantage of an opponent's carelessness—freely allowing the appeal to a misunderstood law, in order that he may be in a position to establish his own unrighteous claims by the refutation of that law. Each of the above proofs arises naturally out of the matter in dispute, and no advantage has been taken of the openings afforded by erroneous conclusions arrived at by dogmatists in either party.

I might have made a pretence of establishing the thesis in the usual manner of the dogmatists, by starting from a defective concept of the infinitude of a given magnitude. I might have argued that a magnitude is infinite if a greater than itself, as determined by the multiplicity of given units which it contains, is not possible. Now no multiplicity is the greatest, since one or more units can always be added to it. Consequently an infinite given magnitude, and therefore an infinite world (infinite as regards the world-series and of the world-whole, rests upon the fact that, on the contrary assumption, an empty time and an empty space, must constitute the limit of the world. I am aware that attempts have been made to evade this conclusion by arguing that a limit of the world in time and space is quite possible without our having to make the impossible assumption of an absolute time prior to the beginning of the world, or of an absolute space extending beyond the real world. With the latter part of this doctrine, as held by the philosophers of the Leibnizian school, I am entirely satisfied. Space is merely the form of outer intuition; it is not a real object which can be outwardly intuited; it is not a correlate of the appearances, but the form of the appearances themselves. And since space is thus no object but only the form of possible objects, it cannot be regarded as something absolute in itself that determines the existence of things. Things, as appearances, determine space, that is, of all its possible predicates of magnitude elapsed series or as regards extension) is impossible; it must be limited in both respects. Such is the line that my proof might have followed. But the above concept is not adequate to what we mean by an infinite whole. It does not represent *how great* it is, and consequently is not the concept of a A 432 *maximum.* Through it B 460 we think only its relation to any assignable unit in respect to which it is greater than all number. According as the unit chosen is greater or smaller, the infinite would be greater or smaller. Infinitude, however, as it consists solely in the relation to the given unit, would always remain the same. The absolute magnitude of the whole would not, therefore, be known in this way; indeed, the above concept does not really deal with it.

The true transcendental concept of infinitude is this, that the successive synthesis of units required for the enumeration of a quantum can never be completed. Hence it follows with complete certainty that an eternity of actual successive states leading up to a given (the and relation they determine this or that particular one to belong to the real. Space, on the other hand, viewed as a self-subsistent something, is nothing real in itself; and cannot, therefore, determine the magnitude or shape of real things. Space, it further follows, whether full or empty, may be limited by appearances, but appearances cannot be A 433 limited *by an empty* B 461 *space* outside them. This is likewise true of time. But while all this may be granted, it yet cannot be denied that these two non-entities, empty space outside the world and empty time prior to it, have to be assumed if we are to assume a limit to the world in space and in time.

The method of argument which professes to enable us to avoid the above consequence (that of having to assume that if the world has limits in time and space, the infinite void must determine the magnitude in which actual things are to exist) consists in surreptitiously substituting for the sensible world some intelligible world of which we know present) moment cannot have elapsed, and that the world must therefore have a beginning.

In the second part of the thesis the difficulty involved in a series that is infinite and yet has elapsed does not arise, since the manifold of a world which is infinite in respect of extension is given as *co-existing*. But if we are to think the totality of such a multiplicity, and yet cannot appeal to limits that of themselves constitute it a totality in intuition, we have to account for a concept which in this case cannot proceed from the whole to the determinate multiplicity of the parts, but which must demonstrate the possibility of a whole by means of the successive synthesis of the parts. Now since this synthesis must constitute a never to be completed series, I cannot think a totality either prior to the synthesis or by means of the synthesis. For the concept of totality is in this case itself the representation of a completed synthesis of the parts. And since this completion is impossible, so likewise is the concept of it.

nothing; for the first beginning (an existence preceded by a time of non-existence) an existence in general which presupposes no other condition whatsoever; and for the limits of extension boundaries of the world-whole—thus getting rid of time and space. But we are here treating only of the *mundus phaenomenon* and its magnitude, and cannot therefore abstract from the aforesaid conditions of sensibility without destroying the very being of that world. If the sensible world is limited, it must necessarily lie in the infinite void. If that void, and consequently space in general as *a priori* condition of the possibility of appearances, be set aside, the entire sensible world vanishes. This world is all that is given us in our problem. The *mundus intelligibilis* is nothing but the general concept of a world in general, in which abstraction is made from all conditions of its intuition, and in reference to which, therefore, no synthetic proposition, either affirmative or negative, can possibly be asserted.

A 434
B 462
A 435
B 463

The Antinomy of Pure Reason

Second Conflict of the Transcendental Ideas

Thesis	*Antithesis*
Every composite substance in the world is made up of simple parts, and nothing anywhere exists save the simple or what is composed of the simple.	No composite thing in the world is made up of simple parts, and there nowhere exists in the world anything simple.

Proof	*Proof*
Let us assume that composite substances are not made up of simple parts. If all composition be then removed in thought, no composite part, and (since we admit no simple parts) also no simple part, that is to say, nothing at all, will remain, and accordingly no substance will be given. Either, therefore, it is impossible to remove in thought all composition, or after its removal there must remain something which exists without composition, that is, the simple. In the former case the composite would not be made up of substances; composition, as applied to substances, is only an accidental relation in independence of which they must still persist as self-subsistent beings. Since this contradicts our supposition, there remains only the original supposition, that a	Assume that a composite thing (as substance) is made up of simple parts. Since all external relation, and therefore all composition of substances, is possible only in space, a space must be made up of as many parts as are contained in the composite which occupies it. Space, however, is not made up of simple parts, but of spaces. Every part of the composite must therefore occupy a space. But the absolutely first parts of every composite are simple. The simple therefore occupies a space. Now since everything real, which occupies a space, contains in itself a manifold of constituents external to one another, and is therefore composite; and since a real composite is not made up of accidents (for accidents could not

A 436
B 464

composite of substances in the world is made up of simple parts.

It follows, as an immediate consequence, that the things in the world are all, without exception, simple beings; that composition is merely an external state of these beings; and that although we can never so isolate these elementary substances as to take them out of this state of composition, reason must think them as the primary subjects of all composition, and therefore, as simple beings, prior to all composition.

exist outside one another, in the absence of substance) but of substances, it follows that the simple would be a composite of substances—which is self-contradictory.

The second proposition of the antithesis, that nowhere in the world does there exist anything simple, is intended to mean only A 437 this, that the existence B 465 of the absolutely simple cannot be established by any experience or perception, either outer or inner; and that the absolutely simple is therefore a mere idea, the objective reality of which can never be shown in any possible experience, and which, as being without an object, has no application in the explanation of the appearances. For if we assumed that in experience an object might be found for this transcendental idea, the empirical intuition of such an object would have to be known as one that contains no manifold [factors] external to one another and combined into unity. But since from the non-consciousness of such a manifold we cannot conclude to its complete impossibility in

every kind of intuition of an object; and since without such proof absolute simplicity can never be established, it follows that such simplicity cannot be inferred from any perception whatsoever. An absolutely simple object can never be given in any possible experience. And since by the world of sense we must mean the sum of all possible experiences, it follows that nothing simple is to be found anywhere in it.

This second proposition of the antithesis has a much wider application than the first. Whereas the first proposition banishes the simple only from the intuition of the composite, the second excludes it from the whole of nature. Accordingly it has not been possible to prove this second proposition by reference to the concept of a given object of outer intuition (of the composite), but only by reference to its relation to a possible experience in general.

A 438 **Observation on the Second Antinomy**
B 466
A 439
B 467

I. On the Thesis
When I speak of a whole as necessarily made up of simple parts,

II. On the Antithesis
Against the doctrine of the infinite divisibility of matter,

I am referring only to a substantial whole that is composite in the strict sense of the term 'composite', that is, to that accidental unity of the manifold which, given as *separate* (at least in thought), is brought into a mutual connection, and thereby constitutes a unity. Space should properly be called not *compositum* but *totum*, since its parts are possible only in the whole, not the whole through the parts. It might, indeed, be called a *compositum ideale*, but not *reale*. This, however, is a mere subtlety. Since space is not a composite made up of substances (nor even of real accidents), if I remove all compositeness from it, nothing remains, not even the point. For a point is possible only as the limit of a space, and so of a composite. A 440 Space and time do not, B 468 therefore, consist of simple parts. What belongs only to the state of a substance, even though it has a magnitude, *e.g.* alteration, does not consist of the simple; that is to say, a certain degree of alteration does not come about through the accretion of many simple alterations. Our inference from the composite

the proof of which is purely mathematical, objections have been raised by the monadists. These objections, however, at once lay the monadists open to suspicion. For however evident mathematical proofs may be, they decline to recognise that the proofs are based upon insight into the constitution of space, in so far as space is in actual fact the formal condition of the possibility of all matter. They regard them merely as inferences from abstract but arbitrary concepts, and so as not being applicable to real things. How can it be possible to invent a different kind of intuition from that given in the original intuition of space, and how can the *a priori* determinations of space fail to be directly applicable to what is only possible in so far as it fills this space! Were we to give heed to them, then beside the mathematical point, which, while simple, is not a part but only the limit of a space, we should have to conceive physical points as being likewise simple, and yet as having the distinguishing characteristic of

to the simple applies only to self-subsisting things. Accidents of the state [of a thing] are not self-subsisting. Thus the proof of the necessity of the simple, as the constitutive parts of the substantially composite, can easily be upset (and therewith the thesis as a whole), if it be extended too far and in the absence of a limiting qualification be made to apply to everything composite—as has frequently happened.

Moreover I am here speaking only of the simple in so far as it is necessarily given in the composite—the latter being resolvable into the simple, as its con- A 442 stituent parts. The word B 470 *monas*, in the strict sense in which it is employed by Leibniz, should refer only to the simple which is *immediately* given as simple substance (*e.g.* in self-consciousness), and not to an element of the composite. This latter is better entitled *atomus*. As I am seeking to prove the [existence of] simple substances only as elements in the composite, I might entitle the thesis of the second antinomy, transcendental *atomistic*. But as this word has long been appropriated

being able, as parts of space, to fill space through their mere aggregation. Without repeating the many familiar and conclusive refutations of this absurdity—it being quite futile to attempt to reason away by sophistical manipulation of purely discursive concepts the evident demonstrated truth of mathematics—I make only one observation, that when philosophy here plays tricks with A 441 mathematics, it does B 469 so because it forgets that in this discussion we are concerned only with *appearances* and their condition. Here it is not sufficient to find for the pure concept of the composite formed by the understanding the concept of the simple; what has to be found is an intuition of the simple for the intuition of the composite (matter). But by the laws of sensibility, and therefore in objects of the senses, this is quite impossible. Though it may be true that when a whole, made up of substances, is thought by the pure understanding alone, we must, prior to all composition of it, have the simple, this does to signify a particular mode of explaining bodily appearances (*moleculae*), and therefore presupposes empirical concepts, the thesis may more suitably be entitled the dialectical principle of *monadology*.

not hold of the *totum substantiale phaenomenon* which, as empirical intuition in space, carries with it the necessary characteristic that no part of it is simple, because no part of space is simple. The monadists have, indeed, been sufficiently acute to seek escape from this difficulty by refusing to treat space as a condition of the possibility of the objects of outer intuition (bodies), and by taking instead these and the dynamical relation of substances as the condition of the possibility of space. But we have a concept of bodies only as appearances; and as such they necessarily presuppose space as the condition of the possibility of all outer appearance. This evasion of the issue is therefore futile, and has already been sufficiently disposed of in the Transcendental Aesthetic. The argument of the monadists would indeed be valid if bodies were things in themselves.

The second dialectical assertion A 443 has this peculiarity, B 471 that over against it stands a dogmatic assertion which is the

only one of all the pseudo-rational assertions that undertakes to afford manifest evidence, in an empirical object, of the reality of that which we have been ascribing only to transcendental ideas, namely, the absolute simplicity of substance—I refer to the assertion that the object of inner sense, the 'I' which there thinks, is an absolutely simple substance. Without entering upon this question (it has been fully considered above), I need only remark, that if (as happens in the quite bare representation, 'I') anything is thought as object only, without the addition of any synthetic determination of its intuition, nothing manifold and no compositeness can be perceived in such a representation. Besides, since the predicates through which I think this object are merely intuitions of inner sense, nothing can there be found which shows a manifold [of elements] external to one another, and therefore real compositeness. Self-consciousness is of such a nature that since the subject which thinks is at the same time its own object, it cannot divide itself, though it can divide the determinations which inhere in it; for in regard to itself every object is absolute unity. Nevertheless, when this subject is viewed *outwardly*, as an object of intuition, it must exhibit [some sort of] compositeness in its appearance; and it must always be viewed in this way if we wish to know whether or not there be in it a manifold [of elements] *external* to one another.

A 444 **The Antinomy of Pure reason**
B 472
A 445 **Third Conflict of the Transcendental Ideas**
B 473

<table>
<tr><td>*Thesis*</td><td>*Antithesis*</td></tr>
<tr><td>Causality in accordance with laws of nature is not the only causality from which the appearances of the world can one and all be derived. To explain these appearances it is necessary to assume that there is also another causality, that of freedom.</td><td>There is no freedom; everything in the world takes place solely in accordance with laws of nature.</td></tr>
<tr><td>*Proof*</td><td>*Proof*</td></tr>
<tr><td>Let us assume that there is no other causality than that in accordance with laws of nature. This being so, everything which *takes place* presupposes a preceding state upon which it inevitably follows</td><td>Assume that there is freedom in the transcendental sense, as a special kind of causality in accordance with which the events in the world can have come about, namely, a power of absolutely beginning</td></tr>
</table>

according to a rule. But the preceding state must itself be something which has taken place (having come to be in a time in which it previously was not); for if it had always existed, its consequence also would have always existed, and would not have only just arisen. The causality of the cause through which something takes place is itself, therefore, something that has *taken place,* which again presupposes, in accordance with the law of nature, a preceding state and its causality, and this in similar manner a still earlier state, and so on. If, therefore, everything takes place solely in accordance with laws of nature, there will always be only a rela-
A 446 tive and never a first
B 474 beginning, and consequently no completeness of the series on the side of the causes that arise the one from the other. But the law of nature is just this, that nothing takes place without a cause *sufficiently* determined *a priori*. The proposition that no causality is possible save in accordance

a state, and therefore also of absolutely beginning a series of consequences of that state; it then follows that not only will a series have its absolute beginning in this spontaneity, but that the very determination of this spontaneity to originate the series, that is to say, the causality itself, will have an absolute beginning; there will be no antecedent through which this act, in taking place, is determined in accordance with fixed laws. But every beginning of action presupposes a state of the not yet acting cause; and a *dynamical* beginning of the action, if it is also a first beginning, presupposes a state which has no *causal* connection with the preceding state of the cause, that is to say, in nowise follows from it. Transcendental freedom thus stands opposed to the law of causality; and the kind of connection which it assumes as holding between the successive states A 447 of the active causes B 475 renders all unity of experience impossible. It is not to be met with laws of nature, when taken in unlimited universality, is therefore self-contradictory; and this cannot, therefore, be regarded as the sole kind of causality.

We must, then, assume a causality through which something takes place, the cause of which is not itself determined, in accordance with necessary laws, by another cause antecedent to it, that is to say, an *absolute spontaneity* of the cause, whereby a series of appearances, which proceeds in accordance with laws of nature, begins *of itself*. This is transcendental freedom, without which, even in the [ordinary] course of nature, the series of appearances on the side of the causes can never be complete.

with in any experience, and is therefore an empty thought-entity.

In nature alone, therefore, [not in freedom], must we seek for the connection and order of cosmical events. Freedom (independence) from the laws of nature is no doubt a liberation from compulsion, but also from the guidance of all rules. For it is not permissible to say that the *laws* of freedom enter into the causality exhibited in the course of nature, and so take the place of natural laws. If freedom were determined in accordance with laws, it would not be freedom; it would simply be nature under another name. Nature and transcendental freedom differ as do conformity to law and lawlessness. Nature does indeed impose upon the understanding the exacting task of always seeking the origin of events ever higher in the series of causes, their causality being always conditioned. But in compensation it holds out the promise of thoroughgoing unity of experience in accor-

dance with laws. The illusion of freedom, on the other hand, offers a point of rest to the enquiring understanding in the chain of causes, conducting it to an unconditioned causality which begins to act of itself. This causality is, however, blind, and abrogates those rules through which alone a completely coherent experience is possible.

A 448
B 476 ## Observation on the Third Antinomy

A 449
B 477

I. On the Thesis

The transcendental idea of freedom does not by any means constitute the whole content of the psychological concept of that name, which is mainly empirical. The transcendental idea stands only for the absolute spontaneity of an action, as the proper ground of its imputability. This, however, is, for philosophy, the real stumbling-block; for there are insurmountable difficulties in the way of admitting any such type of unconditioned causality. What has always so greatly embarrassed speculative reason in dealing with the question of the freedom of

II. On the Antithesis

The defender of an omnipotent nature (transcendental *physiocracy*), in maintaining his position against the pseudo-rational arguments offered in support of the counter-doctrine of freedom, would argue as follows. *If you do not, as regards time, admit anything as being mathematically first in the world, there is no necessity, as regards causality, for seeking something that is dynamically first.* What authority have you for inventing an absolutely first state of the world, and therefore an absolute beginning of the ever-flowing series of appearances, and so of the will, is its strictly transcendental aspect. The problem, properly viewed, is solely this: whether we must admit a power of *spontaneously* beginning a series of successive things or states. How such a power is possible is not a question which requires to be answered in this case, any more than in regard to causality in accordance with the laws of nature. For, [as we have found], we have to remain satisfied with the *a priori* knowledge that this latter type of causality must be presupposed; we are not in the least able to comprehend how it can be possible that through one existence the existence of another is determined, and for this reason must be guided by experience alone. The necessity of a first beginning, due to freedom, of a series of appearances we have demonstrated only in so far as it is required to make an origin of the world conceivable; for all the later following A 450 states can be taken as B 478 resulting according to purely natural laws. But since the power

procuring a resting-place for your imagination by setting bounds to limitless nature? Since the substances in the world have always existed— at least the unity of experience renders necessary such a supposition—there is no difficulty in assuming that change of their states, that is, a series of their alterations, has likewise always existed, and therefore that a first beginning, whether mathematical or dynamical, is not to be looked for. The possibility of such an infinite derivation, without a first member to which all the rest is merely a sequel, cannot indeed, in respect of its possibility, be rendered comprehensible. But if for this reason you refuse to recognise this enigma in nature, you will find yourself compelled to reject many fundamental synthetic properties and forces, which as little admit of comprehension. The possibility even of alteration A 451 itself would have to B 479 be denied. For were you not assured by experience that alteration actually occurs,

of spontaneously beginning a series in time is thereby proved (though not understood), it is now also permissible for us to admit within the course of the world different series as capable in their causality of beginning of themselves, and so to attribute to their substances a power of acting from freedom. And we must not allow ourselves to be prevented from drawing this conclusion by a misapprehension, namely that, as a series occurring in the world can have only a relatively first beginning, being always preceded in the world by some other state of things, no absolute first beginning of a series is possible during the course of the world. For the absolutely first beginning of which we are here speaking is not a beginning in time, but in causality. If, for instance, I at this moment arise from my chair, in complete freedom, without being necessarily determined thereto by the influence of natural causes, a new series, with all its natural consequences *in*

you would never be able to excogitate *a priori* the possibility of such a ceaseless sequence of being and not-being.

Even if a transcendental power of freedom be allowed, as supplying a beginning of happenings in the world, this power would in any case have to be outside the world (though any such assumption that over and above the sum of all possible intuitions there exists an object which cannot be given in any possible perception, is still a very bold one). But to ascribe to substances in the world itself such a power, can never be permissible; for, should this be done, that connection of appearances determining one another with necessity according to universal laws, which we entitle nature, and with it the criterion of empirical truth, whereby experience is distinguished from dreaming, would almost entirely disappear. Side by side with such a lawless faculty of freedom, nature [as an ordered system] is hardly thinkable; the influ-

infinitum, has its absolute beginning in this event, although as regards time this event is only the continuation of a preceding series. For this resolution and act of mine do not form part of the succession of purely natural effects, and are not a mere continuation of them. In respect of its happening, natural causes exercise over it no determining influence whatsoever. It does indeed follow upon them, but without arising out of them; and accordingly, in respect of causality though not of time, must be entitled an absolutely first beginning of a series of appearances.

This requirement of reason, that we appeal in the series of natural causes to a first beginning, due to freedom, is amply confirmed when we observe that all the philosophers of antiquity, with the sole exception of the Epicurean School, felt themselves obliged, when explaining cosmical movements, to assume a *prime mover,* that is, a freely acting cause, which first and of itself began this

ences of the former would so unceasingly alter the laws of the latter that the appearances which in their natural course are regular and uniform would be reduced to disorder and incoherence.

series of states. They made no attempt to render a first beginning conceivable through nature's own resources.

A 452
B 480
A 453
B 481

The Antinomy of Pure Reason

Fourth Conflict of the Transcendental Ideas

Thesis	*Antithesis*
There belongs to the world, either as its part or as its cause, a being that is absolutely necessary.	An absolutely necessary being nowhere exists in the world, nor does it exist outside the world as its cause.

Proof	*Proof*
The sensible world, as the sum-total of all appearances, contains a series of alterations. For without such a series even the representation of serial time, as a condition of the possibility of the sensible world, would not be given us. But every alteration stands under its condition, which precedes it in time and renders it necessary. Now every conditioned that is given presupposes, in respect of its existence, a complete series of conditions up to the unconditioned, which alone is absolutely necessary. Alteration thus existing as a consequence of the absolutely necessary, the existence of something	If we assume that the world itself is necessary, or that a necessary being exists in it, there are then two alternatives. Either there is a beginning in the series of alterations which is absolutely necessary, and therefore without a cause, or the series itself is without any beginning, and although contingent and conditioned in all its parts, none the less, as a whole, is absolutely necessary and unconditioned. The former alternative, however, conflicts with the dynamical law of the determination of all appearances in time; and the latter alternative contradicts itself, since the existence of a series cannot be

absolutely necessary must be granted. But this necessary existence itself belongs to the sensible world. For if it existed outside that world, the series of alterations in the world would derive its beginning from a necessary A 454 cause which would B 482 not itself belong to the sensible world. This, however, is impossible. For since the beginning of a series in time can be determined only by that which precedes it in time, the highest condition of the beginning of a series of changes must exist in the time when the series as yet was not (for a beginning is an existence preceded by a time in which the thing that begins did not yet exist). Accordingly the causality of the necessary cause of alterations, and therefore the cause itself, must belong to time and so to appearance—time being possible only as the form of appearance. Such causality cannot, therefore, be thought apart from that sum of all appearances which constitutes the world of sense. Something absolutely necessary is

necessary if no single member of it is necessary.

If, on the other hand, we assume that an absolutely necessary cause of the world exists outside the world, then this cause, as the highest member in the series of the A 455 causes of changes in B 483 the world, must begin the existence of the latter and their series. Now this cause must itself begin to act, and its causality would therefore be in time, and so would belong to the sum of appearances, that is, to the world. It follows that it itself, the cause, would not be outside the world—which contradicts our hypothesis. Therefore neither in the world, nor outside the world (though in causal connection with it), does there exist any absolutely necessary being.

therefore contained in the world itself, whether this something be the whole series of alterations in the world or a part of the series.

Section 6

Transcendental Idealism as the Key to the Solution of the Cosmological Dialectic

We have sufficiently proved in the Transcendental Aesthetic that everything intuited in space or time, and therefore all objects of any experience possible to us, are nothing but appearances, that A 491 is, mere representations, which, in the manner in B 519 which they are represented, as extended beings, or as series of alterations, have no independent existence outside our thoughts. This doctrine I entitle *transcendental idealism*. The realist in the transcendental meaning of this term, treats these modifications of our sensibility as self-subsistent things, that is, treats *mere representations* as things in themselves.

It would be unjust to ascribe to us that long-decried empirical idealism, which, while it admits the genuine reality of space, denies the existence of the extended beings in it, or at least considers their existence doubtful, and so does not in this regard allow of any properly demonstrable distinction between truth and dreams. As to the appearances of inner sense in time, empirical idealism finds no difficulty in regarding them as real things; indeed it even asserts that this inner experience is the sufficient as well as the only proof of the actual existence of its object (in itself, with all this time-determination).

B 520   Our transcendental idealism, on the contrary, admits the reality of the objects of outer intuition, as intuited in space, and of all changes in time, as represented by inner sense. For since space is a form of that intuition which we entitle A 492 outer, and since without objects in space there would be no empirical representation whatsoever, we can and must regard the extended beings in it as real; and the same is true of time. But this space and this time, and with them all appearances, are not in themselves *things*; they are nothing but representations, and cannot exist outside our mind. Even the inner and sensible intuition of our mind (as object of consciousness) which is represented as being determined by the succession of different states in time, is not the self proper, as it exists in itself—that is, is not the transcendental subject—but only an appearance that has been given to the sensibility of this, to us unknown, being. This inner appearance cannot be admitted to exist in any such manner in and by itself; for it is conditioned by time, and time cannot be a determination of a thing in itself. The empirical truth of appearances in space and time is, however, suf-

B 521 ficiently secured; it is adequately distinguished from dreams, if both dreams and genuine appearances cohere truly and completely in one experience, in accordance with empirical laws.

The objects of experience, then, are *never* given *in themselves,* but only in experience, and

A 493 have no existence outside it. That there may be inhabitants in the moon, although no one has ever perceived them, must certainly be admitted. This, however, only means that in the possible advance of experience we may encounter them. For everything is real which stands in connection with a perception in accordance with the laws of empirical advance. They are therefore real if they stand in an empirical connection with my actual consciousness, although they are not for that reason real in themselves, that is, outside this advance of experience. . . .

Only in another sort of relation, when these appearances would be used for the cosmological idea of an absolute whole, and when, therefore,

B 525 we are dealing with a question which oversteps the limits of possible experience, does distinction of the mode in which we view the reality of those objects of the senses become of importance, as

A 497 serving to guard us against a deceptive error which is bound to arise if we misinterpret our empirical concepts.

The Antinomy of Pure Reason

Section 7

Critical Solution of the Cosmological Conflict of Reason with itself

The whole antinomy of pure reason rests upon the dialectical argument: If the conditioned is given, the entire series of all its conditions is likewise given; objects of the senses are given as conditioned; therefore, etc. Through this syllogism, the major premiss of which appears so natural and evident, as many cosmological ideas are introduced as there are differences in the conditions (in the synthesis of appearances) that constitute a series. The ideas postulate absolute totality of these series; and thereby they set reason in unavoidable conflict with itself. We shall be in a better position to detect what is deceptive in this

B 526 pseudo-rational argument, if we first correct and define some of the concepts employed in it.

B 527 . . . If, however, what we are dealing with are appearances—as mere representations appear-

A 499 ances cannot be given save in so far as I attain knowledge of them, or rather attain them in themselves, for they are nothing but empirical modes of knowledge—I cannot say, in the same sense of the terms, that if the conditioned is given, all its conditions (as appearances) are likewise given, and therefore cannot in any way infer the absolute totality of the series of its conditions. The *appearances* are in their apprehension themselves nothing but an empirical synthesis in space and time, and are given only in *this synthesis.* It does not, therefore, follow, that if the conditioned, in the [field of] appearance, is given, the synthesis which constitutes its empirical condition is given therewith and is presupposed. This synthesis first occurs in the regress, and never exists without it. What we can say is that a *regress* to the conditions, that is, a continued empirical synthesis, on the side of the conditions, is enjoined or *set as a task,* and that *in this regress* there can be no lack of given conditions.

These considerations make it clear that the major premiss of the cosmological inference takes the conditioned in the transcendental sense of a pure category, while the minor premiss takes it in the empirical sense of a concept of the understanding applied to mere appearances. The

B 528 argument thus commits that dialectical fallacy which is entitled *sophisma figurae dictionis.*

A 506
B 534 Thus the antinomy of pure reason in its cosmological ideas vanishes when it is shown that it

is merely dialectical, and that it is a conflict due to an illusion which arises from our applying to appearances that exist only in our representations, and therefore, so far as they form a series, not otherwise than in a successive regress, that idea of absolute totality which holds only as a condition of things in themselves. From this antinomy we can, however, obtain, not indeed a dogmatic, but a critical and doctrinal advantage. It affords indirect proof of the transcendental ideality of appearances—a proof which ought to convince any who may not be satisfied by the direct proof given in the Transcendental Aesthetic. This proof would consist in the following dilemma. If the world is a whole existing in itself, it is either finite or infinite. But both alternatives are false (as shown in the proofs of the antithesis and thesis respectively). It is therefore also false that the world (the sum of all appearances) is a B 535 whole existing in itself. From this it then follows A 507 that appearances in general are nothing outside our representations—which is just what is meant by their transcendental ideality.

Section 9

III

Solution of the Cosmological Idea of Totality in the Derivation of Cosmical Events from their Causes

When we are dealing with what happens there are only two kinds of causality conceivable by us; the causality is either according to *nature* or arises from *freedom*. The former is the connection in the sensible world of one state with a preceding state on which it follows according to a rule.

A 533   By freedom, on the other hand, in its cosmo-
B 561 logical meaning, I understand the power of beginning a state *spontaneously*. Such causality will not, therefore, itself stand under another cause determining it in time, as required by the law of nature. Freedom, in this sense, is a pure transcendental idea, which, in the first place, contains nothing borrowed from experience, and which, secondly, refers to an object that cannot be determined or given in any experience. That everything which happens has a cause is a universal law, conditioning the very possibility of all experience.

A 538 **Possibility of Causality through Freedom, in Harmony**
B 566 **with the Universal Law of Natural Necessity**

Whatever in an object of the senses is not itself appearance, I entitle *intelligible*. If, therefore, that which in the sensible world must be regarded as appearance has in itself a faculty which is not an object of sensible intuition, but through which it can be the cause of appearances, the *causality* of this being can be regarded from two points of view. Regarded as the causality of a thing in itself, it is *intelligible* in its *action*; regarded as the causality of an appearance in the world of sense, it is *sensible* in its *effects*. We should therefore have to form both an empirical and an intellectual concept of the causality of the faculty of such a subject, and to regard both as referring to one and the same effect. This twofold manner of conceiving the faculty possessed by an object of the senses does not contradict any of the concepts which we have to form of appearances and of a possible experience. For since they are not things in themselves, they must rest upon a transcendental object which determines them as mere representations; and consequently there is nothing to pre-
A 539 vent us from ascribing to this transcendental
B 567 object, besides the quality in terms of which it appears, a *causality* which is not appearance, although its *effect* is to be met with in appearance. Every efficient cause must have a *character*, that is, a law of its causality, without which it would not be a cause. On the above supposition, we should, therefore, in a subject belonging to the sensible world have, first, an *empirical character*, whereby its actions, as appearances, stand in thoroughgoing connection with other appearances in accordance with unvarying laws of nature. And since these actions can be derived from the other appearances, they constitute together with them a single series in the order of nature. Secondly, we should also have to allow the subject an *intelligible character*, by which it is indeed the cause of those same actions [in their quality] as appearances, but which does not itself stand under any conditions of sensibility, and is not itself appearance. We can entitle the former the character of the thing in the [field of] appearance, and the latter its character as thing in itself.

In its intelligible character (though we can only have a general concept of that character) this same subject must be considered to be free from all influence of sensibility and from all determination through appearances. Inasmuch as it is *noumenon,* nothing *happens* in it; there can be no change requiring dynamical determination in time, and therefore no causal dependence upon appearances. And consequently, since natural necessity is to be met with only in the sensible world, this active being must in its actions be independent of, and free from all such necessity. No action begins *in* this active being itself; but we may yet quite correctly say that the active being *of itself* begins its effects in the sensible world. In so doing, we should not be asserting that the effects in the sensible world can begin of themselves; they are always predetermined through antecedent empirical conditions, though solely through their empirical character (which is no more than the appearance of the intelligible), and so are only possible as a continuation of the series of natural causes. In this way freedom and nature, in the full sense of these terms, can exist together, without any conflict, in the same actions, according as the actions are referred to their intelligible or to their sensible cause.

A 542
B 570 **Explanation of the Cosmological Idea of Freedom in its connection with Universal Natural Necessity**

That our reason has causality, or that we at least represent it to ourselves as having causality, is evident from the *imperatives* which in all matters of conduct we impose as rules upon our active powers. 'Ought' expresses a kind of necessity and of connection with grounds which is found nowhere else in the whole of nature. The understanding can know in nature only what is, what has been, or what will be. We cannot say that anything in nature *ought to be* other than what in all these time-relations it actually is. When we have the course of nature alone in view, 'ought' has no meaning whatsoever. It is just as absurd to ask what ought to happen in the natural world as to ask what properties a circle ought to have. All that we are justified in asking is: what happens in nature? what are the properties of the circle?

This 'ought' expresses a possible action the ground of which cannot be anything but a mere concept; whereas in the case of a merely natural action the ground must always be an appearance. The action to which the 'ought' applies must indeed be possible under natural conditions. These conditions, however, do not play any part in determining the will itself, but only in determining the effect and its consequences in the [field of] appearance. No matter how many natural grounds or how many sensuous impulses may impel me to *will,* they can never give rise to the 'ought', but only to a willing which, while very far from being necessary, is always conditioned; and the 'ought' pronounced by reason confronts such willing with a limit and an end—nay more, forbids or authorises it. Whether what is willed be an object of mere sensibility (the pleasant) or of pure reason (the good), reason will not give way to any ground which is empirically given. Reason does not here follow the order of things as they present themselves in appearance, but frames for itself with perfect spontaneity an order of its own according to ideas, to which it adapts the empirical conditions, and according to which it declares actions to be necessary, even although they have never taken place, and perhaps never will take place. And at the same time reason also presupposes that it can have causality in regard to all these actions, since otherwise no empirical effects could be expected from its ideas.

Chapter III
The Ideal of Pure Reason

Section 2

The Transcendental Ideal

(Prototypon Transcendentale)

Every concept is, in respect of what is not contained in it, undetermined, and is subject to the principle of *determinability.* According to this principle, of *every two* contradictorily opposed predicates only one can belong to a concept. This principle is based on the law of contradiction, and is therefore a purely logical principle. As such, it abstracts from the entire content of knowledge and is concerned solely with its logical form.

But every *thing*, as regards its possibility, is likewise subject to the principle of *complete* determination, according to which if *all the possible* predicates of *things* be taken together with their contradictory opposites, then one of each pair of contradictory opposites must belong to it. This principle does not rest merely on the law of contradiction; for, besides considering each thing in its relation to the two contradictory predicates, it also considers it in its relation to *the sum-total of all possibilities*, that is, to the sum-total of all predicates of things. Presupposing this sum as being an *a priori* condition, it proceeds to represent everything as deriving its own possibility from the share which it possesses in this sum of all possibilities. The principle of complete determination concerns, therefore, the content, and not merely the logical form. It is the principle of the synthesis of all predicates which are intended to constitute the complete concept of a thing, and not simply a principle of analytic representation in reference merely to one of two contradictory predicates. It contains a transcendental presupposition, namely, that of the material *for all possibility*, which in turn is regarded as containing *a priori* the data *for the particular possibility* of each and every thing.

The proposition, *everything which exists is completely determined*, does not mean only that one of every pair of *given* contradictory predicates, but that one of every [pair of] *possible* predicates, must always belong to it. In terms of this proposition the predicates are not merely compared with one another logically, but the thing itself is compared, in transcendental fashion, with the sum of all possible predicates. What the proposition therefore asserts is this: that to know a thing completely, we must know every possible [predicate], and must determine it thereby, either affirmatively or negatively. The complete determination is thus a concept, which, in its totality, can never be exhibited *in concreto*. It is based upon an idea, which has its seat solely in the faculty of reason— the faculty which prescribes to the understanding the rule of its complete employment.

Although this idea of the *sum-total of all possibility*, in so far as it serves as the condition of the complete determination of each and every thing, is itself undetermined in respect of the predicates which may constitute it, and is thought by us as being nothing more than the sum-total of all possible predicates, we yet find, on closer scrutiny, that this idea, as a primordial concept, excludes a number of predicates which as derivative are already given through other predicates or which are incompatible with others; and that it does, indeed, define itself as a concept that is completely determinate *a priori*. It thus becomes the concept of an individual object which is completely determined through the mere idea, and must therefore be entitled an *ideal* of pure reason. . . .

If, therefore, reason employs in the complete determination of things a transcendental substrate that contains, as it were, the whole store of material from which all possible predicates of things must be taken, this substrate cannot be anything else than the idea of an *omnitudo realitatis*. All true negations are nothing but limitations—a title which would be inapplicable, were they not thus based upon the unlimited, that is, upon "the All."

But the concept of what thus possesses all reality is just the concept of a *thing in itself* as completely determined; and since in all possible [pairs of] contradictory predicates one predicate, namely, that which belongs to being absolutely, is to be found in its determination, the concept of an *ens realissimum* is the concept of an individual being. It is therefore a transcendental *ideal* which serves as basis for the complete determination that necessarily belongs to all that exists. This ideal is the supreme and complete material condition of the possibility of all that exists—the condition to which all thought of objects, so far as their content is concerned, has to be traced back. It is also the only true ideal of which human reason is capable. For only in this one case is a concept of a thing—a concept which is in itself universal—completely determined in and through itself, and known as the representation of an individual.

Section 3

The Arguments of Speculative Reason in Proof of the Existence of a . . .

If we admit something as existing, no matter what this something may be, we must also admit that

Marginal references:
A 572
B 600

A 573
B 601

A 574
B 602

A 576
B 604

there is something which exists *necessarily*. For the contingent exists only under the condition of some other contingent existence as its cause, and from this again we must infer yet another cause, until we are brought to a cause which is not contingent, and which is therefore unconditionally necessary. This is the argument upon which reason bases its advance to the primordial being.

A 585 Now reason looks around for a concept that B 613 squares with so supreme a mode of existence as that of unconditioned necessity—not for the purpose of inferring *a priori* from the concept the existence of that for which it stands (for if that were what it claimed to do, it ought to limit its enquiries to mere concepts, and would not then require a given existence as its basis), but solely in order to find among its various concepts that concept which is in no respect incompatible with absolute necessity. For that there must be something that exists with absolute necessity, is regarded as having been established by the first step in the argument. If, then, in removing everything which is not compatible with this necessity, only one existence remains, this existence must be the absolutely necessary being, whether or not its necessity be comprehensible, that is to say, deducible from its concept alone.

Now that which in its concept contains a therefore for every wherefore, that which is in no respect defective, that which is in every way suf- ficient as a condition, seems to be precisely the being to which absolute necessity can fittingly be ascribed. For while it contains the conditions of all that is possible, it itself does not require and indeed does not allow of any condition, and therefore satisfies, at least in this one feature, the concept of unconditioned necessity. In this A 586 respect all other concepts must fall short of it; for B 614 since they are deficient and in need of completion, they cannot have as their characteristic this independence of all further conditions. We are not indeed justified in arguing that what does not contain the highest and in all respects complete condition is therefore itself conditioned in its existence. But we are justified in saying that it does not possess that one feature through which alone reason is in a position, by means of an *a pri-*

ori concept, to know, in regard to any being, that it is unconditioned.

The concept of an *ens realissimum* is therefore, of all concepts of possible things, that which best squares with the concept of an unconditionally necessary being; and though it may not be completely adequate to it, we have no choice in the matter, but find ourselves constrained to hold to it. For we cannot afford to dispense with the existence of a necessary being; and once its existence is granted, we cannot, in the whole field of possibility, find anything that can make a better grounded claim [than the *ens realissimum*] to such pre-eminence in the mode of its existence.

Such, then, is the natural procedure of human reason. It begins by persuading itself of the existence of *some* necessary being. This being it apprehends as having an existence that is unconditioned. It then looks around for the concept of that which is independent of any condition, and finds it in that which is itself the A 587 sufficient condition of all else, that is, in that B 615 which contains all reality. But that which is all-containing and without limits is absolute unity, and involves the concept of a single being that is likewise the supreme being. Accordingly, we conclude that the supreme being, as primordial ground of all things, must exist by absolute necessity.

A 592 B 620

Chapter III

Section 4

The Impossibility of an Ontological Proof of the Existence of God

It is evident, from what has been said, that the concept of an absolutely necessary being is a concept of pure reason, that is, a mere idea the objective reality of which is very far from being proved by the fact that reason requires it. For the idea instructs us only in regard to a certain unattainable completeness, and so serves rather to limit the understanding than to extend it to new objects. But we are here faced by what is indeed strange and perplexing, namely, that while the inference from a given existence in general to some absolutely necessary being seems to be both imperative and legitimate, all those conditions under which alone the understanding can form a concept of such a necessity are so many obstacles in the way of our doing so.

In all ages men have spoken of an *absolutely necessary* being, and in so doing have endeavoured, not so much to understand whether and how a thing of this kind allows even of being thought, but rather to prove its existence. There is, of course, no difficulty in giving a verbal definition of the concept, namely, that it is something the non-existence of which is impossible. A 593 But this yields no insight into the conditions B 621 which make it necessary to regard the non-existence of a thing as absolutely unthinkable. It is precisely these conditions that we desire to know, in order that we may determine whether or not, in resorting to this concept, we are thinking anything at all. The expedient of removing all those conditions which the understanding indispensably requires in order to regard something as necessary, simply through the introduction of the word *unconditioned*, is very far from sufficing to show whether I am still thinking anything in the concept of the unconditionally necessary, or perhaps rather nothing at all.

Nay more, this concept, at first ventured upon blindly, and now become so completely familiar, has been supposed to have its meaning exhibited in a number of examples; and on this account all further enquiry into its intelligibility has seemed to be quite needless. Thus the fact that every geometrical proposition, as, for instance, that a triangle has three angles, is absolutely necessary, has been taken as justifying us in speaking of an object which lies entirely outside the sphere of our understanding as if we understood perfectly what it is that we intend to convey by the concept of that object.

All the alleged examples are, without exception, taken from *judgments*, not from *things* and their existence. But the unconditioned necessity of judgments is not the same as an absolute necessity of things. The absolute necessity of the judgment is only a conditioned necessity of the thing, or of the predicate in the judgment. A 594 The above proposition does not declare that B 622 three angles are absolutely necessary, but that, under the condition that there is a triangle (that

is, that a triangle is given), three angles will necessarily be found in it. So great, indeed, is the deluding influence exercised by this logical necessity that, by the simple device of forming an *a priori* concept of a thing in such a manner as to include existence within the scope of its meaning, we have supposed ourselves to have justified the conclusion that because existence necessarily belongs to the object of this concept—always under the condition that we posit the thing as given (as existing)—we are also of necessity, in accordance with the law of identity, required to posit the existence of its object, and that this being is therefore itself absolutely necessary—and this, to repeat, for the reason that the existence of this being has already been thought in a concept which is assumed arbitrarily and on condition that we posit its object.

If, in an identical proposition, I reject the predicate while retaining the subject, contradiction results; and I therefore say that the former belongs necessarily to the latter. But if we reject subject and predicate alike, there is no contradiction; for nothing is then left that can be contradicted. To posit a triangle, and yet to reject its three angles, is self-contradictory; but there is no contradiction in rejecting the triangle together with its three angles. The same holds true of the A 595 concept of an absolutely necessary being. If its B 623 existence is rejected, we reject the thing itself with all its predicates; and no question of contradiction can then arise. There is nothing outside it that would then be contradicted, since the necessity of the thing is not supposed to be derived from anything external; nor is there anything internal that would be contradicted, since in rejecting the thing itself we have at the same time rejected all its internal properties. 'God is omnipotent' is a necessary judgment. The omnipotence cannot be rejected if we posit a Deity, that is, an infinite being; for the two concepts are identical. But if we say, 'There is no God', neither the omnipotence nor any other of its predicates is given; they are one and all rejected together with the subject, and there is therefore not the least contradiction in such a judgment.

We have thus seen that if the predicate of a judgment is rejected together with the subject, no internal contradiction can result, and that this holds no matter what the predicate may be. The only way of evading this conclusion is to argue that there are subjects which cannot be removed, and must always remain. That, however, would only be another way of saying that there are absolutely necessary subjects; and that is the very assumption which I have called in question, and the possibility of which the above argument professes to establish. For I cannot form the least concept of a thing which, should it be rejected with all its predicates, leaves behind a

A 596 contradiction; and in the absence of contradic-
B 624 tion I have, through pure *a priori* concepts alone, no criterion of impossibility.

Notwithstanding all these general considerations, in which every one must concur, we may be challenged with a case which is brought forward as proof that in actual fact the contrary holds, namely, that there is one concept, and indeed only one, in reference to which the not-being or rejection of its object is in itself contradictory, namely, the concept of the *ens realissimum*. It is declared that it possesses all reality, and that we are justified in assuming that such a being is possible (the fact that a concept does not contradict itself by no means proves the possibility of its object: but the contrary assertion I am for the moment willing to allow). Now [the argument proceeds] 'all reality' includes existence; existence is therefore contained in the concept of a thing that is possible. If, then, this thing is rejected, the internal possibility of the

A 597 thing is rejected—which is self-contradictory.
B 625 My answer is as follows. There is already a contradiction in introducing the concept of existence—no matter under what title it may be disguised—into the concept of a thing which we profess to be thinking solely in reference to its possibility. If that be allowed as legitimate, a seeming victory has been won; but in actual fact nothing at all is said: the assertion is a mere tautology. We must ask: Is the proposition that *this or that thing* (which, whatever it may be, is allowed as possible) *exists*, an analytic or a synthetic proposition? If it is analytic, the assertion of the existence of the thing adds nothing to the thought of the thing; but in that case either the

thought, which is in us, is the thing itself, or we have presupposed an existence as belonging to the realm of the possible, and have then, on that pretext, inferred its existence from its internal possibility—which is nothing but a miserable tautology. The word 'reality', which in the concept of the thing sounds other than the word 'existence' in the concept of the predicate, is of no avail in meeting this objection. For if all positing (no matter what it may be that is posited) is entitled reality, the thing with all its predicates is already posited in the concept of the subject, and is assumed as actual; and in the predicate this is

A 598 merely repeated. But if, on the other hand, we
B 626 admit, as every reasonable person must, that all existential propositions are synthetic, how can we profess to maintain that the predicate of existence cannot be rejected without contradiction? This is a feature which is found only in analytic propositions, and is indeed precisely what constitutes their analytic character.

I should have hoped to put an end to these idle and fruitless disputations in a direct manner, by an accurate determination of the concept of existence, had I not found that the illusion which is caused by the confusion of a logical with a real predicate (that is, with a predicate which determines a thing) is almost beyond correction. Anything we please can be made to serve as a logical predicate; the subject can even be predicated of itself; for logic abstracts from all content. But a *determining* predicate is a predicate which is added to the concept of the subject and enlarges it. Consequently, it must not be already contained in the concept.

'*Being*' is obviously not a real predicate; that is, it is not a concept of something which could be added to the concept of a thing. It is merely the positing of a thing, or of certain determinations, as existing in themselves. Logically, it is merely the copula of a judgment. The proposition, 'God is omnipotent', contains two concepts, each of which has its object—God and omnipotence. The small word 'is' adds no new predicate, but only serves to posit the predicate

A 599 *in its relation* to the subject. If, now, we take the
B 627 subject (God) with all its predicates (among which is omnipotence), and say 'God is', or

'There is a God', we attach no new predicate to the concept of God, but only posit the subject in itself with all its predicates, and indeed posit it as being an *object* that stands in relation to my *concept*. The content of both must be one and the same; nothing can have been added to the concept, which expresses merely what is possible, by my thinking its object (through the expression 'it is') as given absolutely. Otherwise stated, the real contains no more than the merely possible. A hundred real thalers do not contain the least coin more than a hundred possible thalers. For as the latter signify the concept, and the former the object and the positing of the object, should the former contain more than the latter, my concept would not, in that case, express the whole object, and would not therefore be an adequate concept of it. My financial position is, however, affected very differently by a hundred real thalers than it is by the mere concept of them (that is, of their possibility). For the object, as it actually exists, is not analytically contained in my concept, but is added to my concept (which is a determination of my state) synthetically; and yet the conceived hundred thalers are not themselves in the least increased through thus acquiring existence outside my concept.

A 600
B 628
By whatever and by however many predicates we may think a thing—even if we completely determine it—we do not make the least addition to the thing when we further declare that this thing *is*. Otherwise, it would not be exactly the same thing that exists, but something more than we had thought in the concept; and we could not, therefore, say that the exact object of my concept exists. If we think in a thing every feature of reality except one, the missing reality is not added by my saying that this defective thing exists. On the contrary, it exists with the same defect with which I have thought it, since otherwise what exists would be something different from what I thought. When, therefore, I think a being as the supreme reality, without any defect, the question still remains whether it exists or not. For though, in my concept, nothing may be lacking of the possible real content of a thing in general, something is still lacking in its relation to my whole state of thought, namely,

[in so far as I am unable to assert] that knowledge of this object is also possible *a posteriori*. And here we find the source of our present difficulty. Were we dealing with an object of the senses, we could not confound the existence of the thing with the mere concept of it. For through the concept the object is thought only as conforming to the *universal conditions* of possible empirical

A 601
B 629
knowledge in general, whereas through its existence it is thought as belonging to the context of experience as a whole. In being thus connected with the *content* of experience as a whole, the concept of the object is not, however, in the least enlarged; all that has happened is that our thought has thereby obtained an additional possible perception. It is not, therefore, surprising that, if we attempt to think existence through the pure category alone, we cannot specify a single mark distinguishing it from mere possibility.

Whatever, therefore, and however much, our concept of an object may contain, we must go outside it, if we are to ascribe existence to the object. In the case of objects of the senses, this takes place through their connection with some one of our perceptions, in accordance with empirical laws. But in dealing with objects of pure thought, we have no means whatsoever of knowing their existence, since it would have to be known in a completely *a priori* manner. Our consciousness of all existence (whether immediately through perception, or mediately through inferences which connect something with perception) belongs exclusively to the unity of experience; any [alleged] existence outside this field, while not indeed such as we can declare to be absolutely impossible, is of the nature of an assumption which we can never be in a position to justify.

The concept of a supreme being is in many respects a very useful idea; but just because it is a mere idea, it is altogether incapable, by itself

A 602
B 630
alone, of enlarging our knowledge in regard to what exists. It is not even competent to enlighten us as to the *possibility* of any existence beyond that which is known in and through experience. The analytic criterion of possibility, as consisting in the principle that bare positives (realities) give rise to no contradiction, cannot be denied to it. But since the realities are not

given to us in their specific characters; since even if they were, we should still not be in a position to pass judgment; since the criterion of the possibility of synthetic knowledge is never to be looked for save in experience, to which the object of an idea cannot belong, the connection of all real properties in a thing is a synthesis, the possibility of which we are unable to determine *a priori*. And thus the celebrated Leibniz is far from having succeeded in what he plumed himself on achieving—the comprehension *a priori* of the possibility of this sublime ideal being.

The attempt to establish the existence of a supreme being by means of the famous ontological argument of Descartes is therefore merely so much labour and effort lost; we can no more extend our stock of [theoretical] insight by mere ideas, than a merchant can better his position by adding a few noughts to his cash account.

APPENDIX TO THE TRANSCENDENTAL DIALECTIC

The Regulative Employment of the Ideas of Pure Reason

The outcome of all dialectical attempts of pure reason does not merely confirm what we have already proved in the Transcendental Analytic, namely, that all those conclusions of ours which profess to lead us beyond the field of possible experience are deceptive and without foundation; it likewise teaches us this further lesson, that human reason has a natural tendency to transgress these limits, and that transcendental ideas are just as natural to it as the categories are to understanding—though with this difference, that while the categories lead to truth, that is, to the conformity of our concepts with the object, the ideas produce what, though a mere illusion, is none the less irresistible, and the harmful influence of which we can barely succeed in neutralising even by means of the severest criticism.

Reason is never in immediate relation to an object, but only to the understanding; and it is only through the understanding that it has its own [specific] empirical employment. It does not, therefore, *create* concepts (of objects) but only *orders* them, and gives them that unity which

they can have only if they be employed in their widest possible application, that is, with a view to obtaining totality in the various series. The understanding does not concern itself with this totality, but only with that connection through which, in accordance with *concepts*, such *series* of conditions *come into being*. Reason has, therefore, A 644 as its sole object, the understanding and its effec- B 672 tive application. Just as the understanding unifies the manifold in the object by means of concepts, so reason unifies the manifold of concepts by means of ideas, positing a certain collective unity as the goal of the activities of the understanding, which otherwise are concerned solely with distributive unity.

I accordingly maintain that transcendental ideas never allow of any constitutive employment. When regarded in that mistaken manner, and therefore as supplying concepts of certain objects, they are but pseudo-rational, merely dialectical concepts. On the other hand, they have an excellent, and indeed indispensably necessary, regulative employment, namely, that of directing the understanding towards a certain goal upon which the routes marked out by all its rules converge, as upon their point of intersection.

When merely regulative principles are treated B 694 as constitutive, and are therefore employed as A 666 objective principles, they may come into conflict with one another. But when they are treated merely as *maxims*, there is no real conflict, but merely those differences in the interest of reason that give rise to differing modes of thought. In actual fact, reason has only one single interest, and the conflict of its maxims is only a difference in, and a mutual limitation of, the methods whereby this interest endeavours to obtain satisfaction.

Thus pure reason, which at first seemed to promise nothing less than the extension of knowledge beyond all limits of experience, contains, if properly understood, nothing but regulative principles, which, while indeed prescribing greater unity than the empirical employment of understanding can achieve, yet still, by the very fact that they place the goal of its endeavours at A 702 so great a distance, carry its agreement with it- B 730 self, by means of systematic unity, to the highest possible degree. But if, on the other hand, they be misunderstood, and be treated as constitutive principles of transcendent knowledge, they give rise, by a dazzling and deceptive illusion, to persuasion and a merely fictitious knowledge, and therewith to contradictions and eternal disputes.

Thus all human knowledge begins with intuitions, proceeds from thence to concepts, and ends with ideas. Although in respect of all three elements it possesses a priori sources of knowledge, which on first consideration seem to scorn the limits of all experience, a thoroughgoing critique convinces us that reason, in its speculative employment, can never with these elements transcend the field of possible experience, and that the proper vocation of this supreme faculty of knowledge is to use all methods, and the principles of these methods, solely for the purpose of penetrating to the innermost secrets of nature, in accordance with every possible principle of unity—that of ends being the most important—but never to soar beyond its limits, outside which there is for us nothing but empty space. The critical examination, as carried out in the Transcendental Analytic, of all propositions which may A 703 seem to extend our knowledge beyond actual B 731 experience, has doubtless sufficed to convince us that they can never lead to anything more than a possible experience. Were it not that we are suspicious of abstract and general doctrines, how-

ever clear, and were it not that specious and alluring prospects tempt us to escape from the compulsion which these doctrines impose, we might have been able to spare ourselves the laborious interrogation of all those dialectical witnesses that a transcendent reason brings forward in support of its pretensions. For we should from the start have known with complete certainty that all such pretensions, while perhaps honestly meant, must be absolutely groundless, inasmuch as they relate to a kind of knowledge to which man can never attain. But there is no end to such discussions, unless we can penetrate to the true cause of the illusion by which even the wisest are deceived. Moreover, the resolution of all our transcendent knowledge into its elements (as a study of our inner nature) is in itself of no slight value, and to the philosopher is indeed a matter of duty. Accordingly, fruitless as are all these endeavours of speculative reason, we have none the less found it necessary to follow them up to their primary sources. And since the dialectical illusion does not merely deceive us in our judge-
B 732 ments, but also, because of the interest which we
A 704 take in these judgments, has a certain natural attraction which it will always continue to possess, we have thought it advisable, with a view to the prevention of such errors in the future, to draw up in full detail what we may describe as being the records of this lawsuit, and to deposit them in the archives of human reason.

NOTES

[1]Space, represented as object (as we are required to do in geometry), contains more than mere form of intuition; it also contains combination of the manifold, given according to the form of sensibility, in an intuitive representation, so that the form of intuition gives only a manifold, the formal intuition gives unity of representation. In the Aesthetic I have treated this unity as belonging merely to sensibility, simply in order to emphasise that it precedes any concept, although, as a matter of fact, it presupposes a synthesis which does not belong to the senses but through which all concepts of space and time first become possible. For since by its means (in that the understanding determines the sensibility) space and time are first given as intuitions, the unity of this a priori intuition belongs to space and time, and not to the concept of the understanding (cf. § 24).

[2]The immediate consciousness of the existence of outer things is, in the preceding thesis, not presupposed, but proved, be the possibility of this consciousness understood by us or not. The question as to its possibility would be this: whether we have an inner sense only, and no outer sense, but merely an outer imagination. It is clear, however, that in order even only to imagine

something as outer, that is, to present it to sense in intuition, we must already have an outer sense, and must thereby immediately distinguish the mere receptivity of an outer intuition from the spontaneity which characterises every act of imagination. For should we merely be imagining an outer sense, the faculty of intuition, which is to be determined by the faculty of imagination, would itself be annulled.

[3]The fallacy of equivocation or having an ambiguous middle term in the two premises of a syllogism. (editors' footnote)

STUDY QUESTIONS: KANT, *CRITIQUE OF PURE REASON*

1. What are Kant's main aims as outlined in the Preface?
2. What does Kant mean by a priori knowledge? How does such knowledge relate to the aims of the *Critique?*
3. How does Kant distinguish between analytic and synthetic judgments?
4. How does Kant distinguish a priori and empirical or a posteriori judgments?
5. What does Kant mean by synthetic a priori judgments? What examples does he give of such judgments? How do these judgments relate to the main aim of the *Critique?*
6. Why does Kant ask, 'How are a priori synthetic judgments possible?'
7. Do we obtain our intuitions of space and time from any experience?
8. What does Kant mean when he says that space is the a priori form of intuition?
9. What is an a priori intuition?
10. What conclusion does Kant draw from the claim that geometry consists in synthetic a priori judgments?
11. What does Kant mean by 'The empirical reality of time'? What is empirical idealism?
12. What Kant mean by 'The transcendental ideality of time'? What is transcendental idealism?
13. What does Kant mean by the 'logical forms of judgment'? What are these forms?
14. What is synthesis? Why is it important?
15. At A79, Kant says, 'The same function which gives unity to the various representations *in a judgment* also gives unity to the mere synthesis of various representations *in an intuition*.' What does this mean? Why is this an important point?
16. What are the categories? How many are there? Please name each one. Why does Kant have to give a transcendental deduction of them?
17. What does Kant mean by the manifold of sensible intuitions?
18. What is Kant's main point about the combination of the manifold of sensible intuitions?
19. Why *must* it be possible for the 'I think' to accompany all of one's representations?
20. What is the transcendental unity of apperception?
21. The thought that all the representations given in intuition belong to oneself is equivalent to what other thought? Why is this point important?
22. The synthetic unity of apperception is an objective condition of all knowledge, says Kant. What does this mean? What reasons does he provide for thinking that this is true?
23. What does it mean to say that a judgment is objectively valid? What is it that makes such judgments possible, according to Kant?
24. Summarize the argument given in section 20 for the conclusion that the manifold of intuitions is necessarily subject to the categories.

25. For what reason does Kant say that the categories have no other application in knowledge than to objects of experience?
26. 'Categories are concepts which prescribe laws a priori to . . . nature.' Please explain this point. How would Kant defend it?
27. What is a schematism, and why is it necessary?
28. What gives objective reality to our a priori modes of knowledge?
29. How are synthetic a priori judgments possible?
30. List the principles of understanding.
31. What is the First Analogy? How does Kant try to prove it?
32. What is the Second Analogy? How does Kant try to prove that?
33. How does Kant's position regarding causation try to answer Hume's Skepticism?
34. What is the argument of the Refutation of Idealism? How does Kant's view differ from Descartes'?
35. Why does Kant say that 'noumenon' must be understood in a negative sense only? Why is the concept necessary?
36. What is a pure idea of reason?
37. What does Kant mean by 'metaphysics'?
38. Why is it an error to conceive of the 'I' as an absolute subject?
39. What does pure reason demand?
40. What are the thesis and antithesis of the four antinomies?
41. What are the antinomies supposed to prove?
42. When Kant says that the ideas of reason are purely regulative and are not constitutive, what does he mean? What is his argument for this claim?
43. What is the critique of pure reason?

GROUNDWORK OF THE METAPHYSICS OF MORALS

The main aim of Kant's *Groundwork* is to explain and justify the claim that moral demands are inescapable. He distinguishes hypothetical and categorical imperatives. Hypothetical imperatives specify the means to some end. Because they are conditional on an end, they are escapable. In contrast, moral demands are inescapable and, thus, consist in a Categorical Imperative of the unconditional form: you ought to do Y. Kant's main aim is to explain how the Categorical Imperative is possible. Empirical factors cannot explain the inescapable nature of morality. Therefore, the Categorical Imperative must constitute the a priori form of morality. In brief, Kant argues that the categorical demand of morality is inherent in our being persons with free will.

    In the first chapter of the work, Kant tries to show that the Categorical Imperative is already part of our everyday morality. The basis of popular morality is the will. He argues that the moral worth of an action does not depend on its consequences. In part, this is because the will, by definition, is under our own control, whereas the effects of our actions depend on factors beyond our control. Furthermore, a morally right action must be done

Immanuel Kant, from *Groundwork of the Metaphysics of Morals,* translated by H. J. Paton. Copyright © 1948. Reprinted by permission of Routledge, an imprint of Taylor & Francis Books.

for the sake of duty. Actions that happen to accord with duty are different from those that are actually motivated by it. By 'duty,' Kant means 'the necessity of acting out of reverence for the (moral) law.'

In the second chapter, Kant tries to demonstrate different versions of the Categorical Imperative. The four main versions are as follows:

1. Universal law: *Act on that maxim through which you can at the same time will that it should become a universal law.* The Categorical Imperative cannot prescribe action for the sake of any specific empirical ends because that would convert it into a hypothetical imperative. Consequently, the only end that the Categorical Imperative can recommend is the universality of law as such. Initially, the only thing reason can recommend is rationality itself. This abstract principle rules out inconsistent willing. I cannot will that other people should not lie to me, and will that I lie to them. There are two kinds of inconsistent willing ruled out in this way. First, some maxims strictly cannot be universalized. For example, it is impossible to universalize the following maxim: I will borrow money, but not repay it. If everyone had that maxim, money-lending institutions could not exist. This kind of maxim generates perfect duties—acts that one must not perform at any time. Second, some universalized maxims are not strictly self-contradictory, but they are inconsistent with natural ends that a rational person would will, such as the development of one's talents. These maxims generate imperfect duties—acts that, in general, one should perform.

2. Respect for persons: *Act in such a way that you always treat humanity, whether in your own person or that of another, never simply as a means but always at the same time as an end.* In other words, we must respect persons by never using them merely as instruments for some goal, for example by manipulating them. We should respect the fact that persons are beings with free will. This version of the Imperative follows from the first, because the will must be determined by an end, that must be valid for all rational beings as such and, therefore, is not based on any desire. This end must be rational nature itself, which cannot be merely a means.

3. Autonomy: *So act that your will can regard itself at the same time as making universal law through its maxims.* This formulation introduces the idea of a person as a lawmaker, or as an autonomous being. The earlier second version postulated rational nature as an end in itself, but rational nature is the capability to will freely, which is the capacity to act according to self-made laws. Thus, if a being is rational, then he or she is a lawmaker. The third version of the Categorical Imperative enjoins us to will maxims that are consistent with our status as lawmakers.

4. Kingdom of ends: *Act on the maxim of a member who makes universal law for a merely possible kingdom of ends.* The idea is that each member of a potential community of persons should regard his or her maxims as making a law that would govern the actions of all the other members too. Only in this way can a possible community of rational beings treat one another as ends.

The basis of Kant's moral theory is the thesis that if we are beings with a free will, then the Categorical Imperative applies to us without exception. Kant's argument for this fundamental claim comes in three steps. The first step is that beings with a free will must also have practical reason such that their actions can be guided by reasons or principles. Second, that we are capable of being moved by reason implies that we are capable of acting in accord with the Categorical Imperative. The third step is to show that if the Categorical Imperative is possible, then it is necessarily binding on us. This is because the only end that could be recommended by the Categorical Imperative is rationality itself.

In summary, Kant's moral philosophy involves free will in three ways. First, we are under an inescapable moral obligation because this is inherent in our being free. Second, morality requires that we will in accordance with its demand. Third, this demand requires that we respect the freedom of persons. In other words, morality directs our will to respect the will, because we have a will.

387] i PREFACE

[The Different Branches of Philosophy.]

Ancient Greek philosophy was divided into three sciences: *physics, ethics,* and *logic.*

All philosophy so far as it rests on the basis of experience can be called *empirical* philosophy. If it sets forth its doctrines as depending entirely on *a priori* principles, it can be called *pure* philosophy. The latter when wholly formal is called *logic;* but if it is confined to determinate objects of the understanding, it is then called *metaphysics.*

In this way there arises the Idea of a two-fold metaphysic—*a metaphysic of nature* and *a metaphysic of morals.* Thus physics will have its empirical part, but it will also have a rational one; and likewise ethics—although here the empirical part might be called specifically *practical anthropology,* while the rational part might properly be called *morals.*

Since my aim here is directed strictly to moral philosophy, I limit my proposed question to this point only—Do we not think it a matter of the utmost necessity to work out for once a pure moral philosophy completely cleansed of vi everything that can only be empirical and appropriate to anthropology? That there must be such a philosophy is already obvious from the common Idea of duty and from the laws of morality. Every one must admit that a law has to carry with it absolute necessity if it is to be valid morally—valid, that is, as a ground of obligation; that the command 'Thou shalt not lie' could not hold merely for men, other rational beings having no obligation to abide by it—and similarly with all other genuine moral laws; that here consequently the ground of obligation must be looked for, not in the nature of man nor in the circumstances of the world in which he is placed, but

solely *a priori* in the concepts of pure reason; and that every other precept based on principles of mere experience—and even a precept that may in a certain sense be considered universal, so far as it rests in its slightest part, perhaps only in its motive, on empirical grounds—can indeed be called a practical rule, but never a moral law.

vii Thus in practical knowledge as a whole, not only are moral laws, together with their principles, essentially different from all the rest in which there is some empirical element, but the whole of moral philosophy is based entirely on the part of it that is pure. When applied to man it does not borrow in the slightest from acquaintance with him (in anthropology), but gives him laws *a priori* as a rational being. These laws admittedly require in addition a power of judgement sharpened by experience, partly in order to distinguish the cases to which they apply, partly to procure for them admittance to the will of man and influence over practice; for man, affected as he is by so many inclinations, is capable of the Idea of a pure practical reason, but he has not so easily the power to realize the Idea *in concreto* in his conduct of life.

A metaphysic of morals is thus indispensably necessary, not merely in order to investigate, from motives of speculation, the source of practical 390] viii principles which are present *a priori* in our reason, but because morals themselves remain exposed to corruption of all sorts as long as this guiding thread is lacking, this ultimate norm for correct moral judgement. For if any action is to be morally good, it is not enough that it should *conform* to the moral law—it must also be done *for the sake of the moral law:* where this is not so, the conformity is only too contingent and precarious, since the non-moral ground at work will now and then produce actions which accord with the law, but very often actions which transgress it.

392] xiii   The sole aim of the present Groundwork is to seek out and establish *the supreme principle of morality*. This by itself is a business which by its very purpose constitutes a whole and has to be separated off from every other enquiry. The application of the principle to the whole system would no doubt throw much light on my answers to this central question, so important and yet hitherto so far from being satisfactorily discussed; and the adequacy it manifests throughout would afford it strong confirmation. All the same, I had to forego this advantage, which in any case would be more flattering to myself than helpful to others, since the convenience of a principle in use and its seeming adequacy afford no completely safe proof of its correctness. They rather awaken a certain bias against examining and weighing it in all strictness for itself without any regard to its consequences.

[The Method of the Groundwork.]

xiv The method I have adopted in this book is, I believe, one which will work best if we proceed analytically from common knowledge to the formulation of its supreme principle and then back again synthetically from an examination of this principle and its origins to the common knowledge in which we find its application. Hence the division turns out to be as follows:—

1. *Chapter I:* Passage from ordinary rational knowledge of morality to philosophical.
2. *Chapter II:* Passage from popular moral philosophy to a metaphysic of morals.
3. *Chapter III:* Final step from a metaphysic of morals to a critique of pure practical reason.

393] 1 CHAPTER I

PASSAGE FROM ORDINARY RATIONAL KNOWLEDGE OF MORALITY TO PHILOSOPHICAL

[The Good Will.]

It is impossible to conceive anything at all in the world, or even out of it, which can be taken as good without qualification, except a *good will*. Intelligence, wit, judgement, and any other

talents of the mind we may care to name, or courage, resolution, and constancy of purpose, as qualities of *temperament*, are without doubt good and desirable in many respects; but they can also be extremely bad and hurtful when the will is not good which has to make use of these gifts of nature, and which for this reason has the term '*character*' applied to its peculiar quality. It is exactly the same with *gifts of fortune*. Power, wealth, honour, even health and that complete well-being and contentment with one's state which goes by the name of '*happiness*', pro-
2 duce boldness, and as a consequence often overboldness as well, unless a good will is present by which their influence on the mind—and so too the whole principle of action—may be corrected and adjusted to universal ends; not to mention that a rational and impartial spectator can never feel approval in contemplating the uninterrupted prosperity of a being graced by no touch of a pure and good will, and that consequently a good will seems to constitute the indispensable condition of our very worthiness to be happy.

Some qualities are even helpful to this good will itself and can make its task very much easier. They have none the less no inner unconditioned
394 worth, but rather presuppose a good will which sets a limit to the esteem in which they are rightly held and does not permit us to regard them as absolutely good. Moderation in affections and passions, self-control, and sober reflexion are not only good in many respects: they may even seem to constitute part of the *inner* worth of a person. Yet they are far from being properly described as good without qualification (however unconditionally they have been commended by the ancients). For without the principles of a
3 good will they may become exceedingly bad; and the very coolness of a scoundrel makes him, not merely more dangerous, but also immediately more abominable in our eyes than we should have taken him to be without it.

[The Good Will and Its Results.]

A good will is not good because of what it effects or accomplishes—because of its fitness for attaining some proposed end: it is good through its willing alone—that is, good in itself. Considered in itself it is to be esteemed beyond comparison as far higher than anything it could ever bring about merely in order to favour some inclination or, if you like, the sum total of inclinations. Even if, by some special disfavour of destiny or by the niggardly endowment of stepmotherly nature, this will is entirely lacking in power to carry out its intentions; if by its utmost effort it still accomplishes nothing, and only good will is left (not, admittedly, as a mere wish, but as the straining of every means so far as they are in our control); even then it would still shine like a jewel for its own sake as something which has its full value in itself. Its usefulness or fruitlessness can neither add to, nor subtract from, this value. Its usefulness would be merely, as it were, the setting which enables us to handle it better in our 4 ordinary dealings or to attract the attention of those not yet sufficiently expert, but not to commend it to experts or to determine its value.

[The Function of Reason.]

Yet in this Idea of the absolute value of a mere will, all useful results being left out of account in its assessment, there is something so strange that, in spite of all the agreement it receives even from ordinary reason, there must arise the suspicion that perhaps its secret basis is merely some high-flown fantasticality, and that we may have misunderstood the purpose of nature in attaching 395 reason to our will as its governor. We will therefore submit our Idea to an examination from this point of view.

In the natural constitution of an organic being—that is, of one contrived for the purpose of life—let us take it as a principle that in it no organ is to be found for any end unless it is also the most appropriate to that end and the best fitted for it. Suppose now that for a being possessed of reason and a will the real purpose of nature were his *preservation*, his *welfare*, or in a word his *happiness*. In that case nature would have hit on a very bad arrangement by choosing reason in the creature to carry out this purpose. For all the actions he has to perform with this end in view,

5 and the whole rule of his behaviour, would have been mapped out for him far more accurately by instinct; and the end in question could have been maintained far more surely by instinct than it ever can be by reason. . . .

In actual fact too we find that the more a cultivated reason concerns itself with the aim of enjoying life and happiness, the farther does man get away from true contentment. This is why there arises in many, and that too in those who have made most trial of this use of reason, if they 6 are only candid enough to admit it, a certain degree of *misology*—that is, a hatred of reason; for when they balance all the advantage they draw, I will not say from thinking out all the arts of ordinary indulgence, but even from science (which in the last resort seems to them to be also an indulgence of the mind), they discover that they have in fact only brought more trouble on their 396 heads than they have gained in the way of happiness. On this account they come to envy, rather than to despise, the more common run of men, who are closer to the guidance of mere natural instinct, and who do not allow their reason to have much influence on their conduct.

For since reason is not sufficiently serviceable 7 for guiding the will safely as regarded its objects and the satisfaction of all our needs (which it in part even multiplies)—a purpose for which an implanted natural instinct would have led us much more surely; and since none the less reason has been imparted to us as practical power—that is, as one which is to have influence on the *will*; its true function must be to produce a *will* which is *good*, not as a *means* to some further end, but *in itself*; and for this function reason was absolutely necessary in a world where nature, in distributing her aptitudes, has everywhere else gone to work in a purposive manner. Such a will need not on this account be the sole and complete good, but it must be the highest good and the condition of all the rest, even of all our demands for happiness. In that case we can easily reconcile with the wisdom of nature our observation that the cultivation of reason which is required for the first and unconditioned purpose may in many ways, at least in this life, restrict the attainment of the second purpose—namely, happiness—which is always conditioned; and indeed that it can even reduce happiness to less than zero without nature proceeding contrary to its purpose; for reason, which recognizes as its highest practical function the establishment of a good will, in attaining this end is capable only of its own peculiar kind of contentment—contentment in fulfilling a pur-

8 pose which in turn is determined by reason alone, even if this fulfillment should often involve interference with the purposes of inclination.

[The Good Will and Duty.]

397 We have now to elucidate the concept of a will estimable in itself and good apart from any further end. This concept, which is already present in a sound natural understanding and requires not so much to be taught as merely to be clarified, always holds the highest place in estimating the ·total worth of our actions and constitutes the condition of all the rest. We will therefore take up the concept of *duty*, which includes that of a good will, exposed, however, to certain subjective limitations and obstacles. These, so far from hiding a good will or disguising it, rather bring it out by contrast and make it shine forth more brightly.

[The Motive of Duty.]

I will here pass over all actions already recognized as contrary to duty, however useful they may be with a view to this or that end; for about these the question does not even arise whether they could have been done *for the sake of duty* inasmuch as they are directly opposed to it. I will also set aside actions which in fact accord with duty, yet for which men have *no immediate inclination*, but perform them because impelled to do so by some other inclination. For there it is easy to

9 decide whether the action which accords with duty has been done *from duty* or from some purpose of self-interest. This distinction is far more difficult to perceive when the action accords with duty and the subject has in addition an *immediate* inclination to the action. For example, it certainly accords with duty that a grocer should not overcharge his inexperienced customer; and where there is much competition a sensible shopkeeper refrains from so doing and keeps to a fixed

and general price for everybody so that a child can buy from him just as well as anyone else. Thus people are served *honestly*; but this is not nearly enough to justify us in believing that the shopkeeper has acted in this way from duty or from principles of fair dealing; his interests required him to do so. We cannot assume him to have in addition an immediate inclination towards his customers, leading him, as it were out of love, to give no man preference over another in the matter of price. Thus the action was done neither from duty nor from immediate inclination, but solely from purposes of self-interest.

On the other hand, to preserve one's life is a duty, and besides this every one has also an immediate inclination to do so. But on account of this the often anxious precautions taken by the greater part of mankind for this purpose have no inner worth, and the maxim of their action is

398 without moral content. They do protect their lives *in conformity with duty*, but not *from the*

10 *motive of duty*. When on the contrary, disappointments and hopeless misery have quite taken away the taste for life; when a wretched man, strong in soul and more angered at his fate than faint-hearted or cast down, longs for death and still preserves his life without loving it—not from inclination or fear but from duty; then indeed his maxim has a moral content.

To help others where one can is a duty, and besides this there are many spirits of so sympathetic a temper that, without any further motive of vanity or self-interest, they find an inner pleasure in spreading happiness around them and can take delight in the contentment of others as their own work. Yet I maintain that in such a case an action of this kind, however right and however amiable it may be, has still no genuinely moral worth. It stands on the same footing as other inclinations—for example, the inclination for honour, which if fortunate enough to hit on something beneficial and right and consequently honourable, deserves praise and encouragement, but not esteem; for its maxim lacks moral content, namely, the performance of such actions, not from inclination, but *from duty*.

To assure one's own happiness is a duty (at least indirectly); for discontent with one's state,

12 in a press of cares and amidst unsatisfied wants, might easily become a great *temptation to the transgression of duty*. But here also apart from regard to duty, all men have already of themselves the strongest and deepest inclination towards happiness, because precisely in this Idea of happiness all inclinations are combined into a sum total. The prescription for happiness is, however, often so constituted as greatly to interfere with some inclinations, and yet men cannot form under the name of 'happiness' any determinate and assured conception of the satisfaction of all inclinations as a sum.

[The Formal Principle of Duty.]

Our second proposition is this: An action done from duty has its moral worth, *not in the purpose* to be attained by it, but in the maxim in accordance with which it is decided upon; it depends
400 therefore, not on the realization of the object of the action, but solely on the *principle* of *volition* in accordance with which, irrespective of all objects of the faculty of desire, the action has been performed. That the purposes we may have in our actions, and also their effects considered as ends and motives of the will, can give to actions no unconditioned and moral worth is clear from what has gone before. Where then can his worth be
14 found if we are not to find it in the will's relation to the effect hoped for from the action? It can be found nowhere but *in the principle of the will*, irrespective of the ends which can be brought about by such an action; for between its *a priori* principle, which is formal, and its *a posteriori* motive, which is material, the will stands, so to speak, at a parting of the ways; and since it must be determined by some principle, it will have to be determined by the formal principle of volition when an action is done from duty, where, as we have seen, every material principle is taken away from it.

[Reverence for the Law.]

Our third proposition, as an inference from the two preceding, I would express thus: *Duty is the necessity to act out of reverence for the law*. For an

object as the effect of my proposed action I can have an *inclination*, but *never reverence*, precisely because it is merely the effect, and not the activity, of a will. Similarly for inclination as such, whether my own or that of another, I cannot have reverence: I can at most in the first case approve, and in the second case sometimes even love—that is, regard it as favorable to my own advantage. Only something which is conjoined with my will solely as a ground and never as an effect—something which does not serve my
15 inclination, but outweighs it or at least leaves it entirely out of account in my choice—and therefore only bare law for its own sake, can be an object of reverence and therewith a command. Now an action done from duty has to set aside altogether the influence of inclination, and along with inclination every object of the will; so there is nothing left able to determine the will except objectively the *law* and subjectively *pure reverence* for this practical law, and therefore the maxim of obeying this law even to the detriment
401 of all my inclinations.

Thus the moral worth of an action does not depend on the result expected from it, and so too does not depend on any principle of action that needs to borrow its motive from this expected result. For all these results (agreeable states and even the promotion of happiness in others) could have been brought about by other causes as well, and consequently their production did not require the will of a rational being, in which, however, the highest and unconditioned good can alone be found. Therefore nothing but the *idea of the law* in itself, *which admittedly is present only in a rational being*—so far as it, and not
16 an expected result, is the ground determining the will—can constitute that pre-eminent good which we call moral, a good which is already present in the person acting on this idea and has not to be awaited merely from the result.

[The Categorical Imperative.]

402] 17 But what kind of law can this be the thought of which, even without regard to the results expected from it, has to determine the will if this is to be called good absolutely and without qualification? Since I have robbed the will of every inducement that might arise for it as a consequence of obeying any particular law, nothing is left but the conformity of actions to universal law as such, and this alone must serve the will as its principle. That is to say, I ought never to act except in such a way *that I can also will that my maxim should become a universal law*. Here bare conformity to universal law as such (without having as its base any law prescribing particular actions) is what serves the will as its principle, and must so serve it if duty is not to be everywhere an empty delusion and a chimerical concept. The ordinary reason of mankind also agrees with this completely in its practical judgements and always has the aforesaid principle before its eyes.

18   Take this question, for example. May I not, when I am hard pressed, make a promise with the intention of not keeping it? Here I readily distinguish the two senses which the question can have—Is it prudent, or is it right, to make a false promise? The first no doubt can often be the case. I do indeed see that it is not enough for me to extricate myself from present embarrassment by this subterfuge: I have to consider whether from this lie there may not subsequently accrue to me much greater inconvenience than that from which I now escape, and also—since, with all my supposed *astuteness,* to foresee the consequences is not so easy that I can be sure there is no chance, once confidence in me is lost, of this proving far more disadvantageous than all the ills I now think to avoid—whether it may not be a *more prudent* action to proceed here on a general maxim and make it my habit not to give a promise except with the intention of keeping it. Yet it becomes clear to me at once that such a maxim is always founded solely on fear of consequences. To tell the truth for the sake of duty is something entirely different from doing so out of concern for inconvenient results; for in the first case the concept of the action already contains in itself a law for me, while in the second case I have first of all to look around
19 elsewhere in order to see what effects may be

bound up with it for me. When I deviate from
403 the principle of duty, this is quite certainly bad; but if I desert my prudential maxim, this can often be greatly to my advantage, though it is admittedly safer to stick to it. Suppose I seek, however, to learn in the quickest way and yet unerringly how to solve the problem 'Does a lying promise accord with duty?' I have then to ask myself 'Should I really be content that my maxim (the maxim of getting out of a difficulty by a false promise) should hold as a universal law (one valid both for myself and others)? And could I really say to myself that every one may make a false promise if he finds himself in a difficulty from which he can extricate himself in no other way?' I then become aware at once that I can indeed will to lie, but I can by no means will a universal law of lying; for by such a law there could properly be no promises at all, since it would be futile to profess a will for future action to others who would not believe my profession or who, if they did so over-hastily, would pay me back in like coin; and consequently my maxim, as soon as it was made a universal law, would be bound to annul itself.

Thus I need no far-reaching ingenuity to find out what I have to do in order to possess a
20 good will. Inexperienced in the course of world affairs and incapable of being prepared for all the chances that happen in it, I ask myself only 'Can you also will that your maxim should become a universal law?' Where you cannot, it is to be rejected, and that not because of a prospective loss to you or even to others, but because it cannot fit as a principle into a possible enactment of universal law. For such an enactment reason compels my immediate reverence, into whose grounds (which the philosopher may investigate) I have as yet no *insight,* although I do at least understand this much: reverence is the assessment of a worth which far outweighs all the worth of what is commended by inclination, and the necessity for me to act out of *pure reverence* for the practical law is what constitutes duty, to which every other motive must give way because it is the condition of a will good *in itself,* whose value is above all else.

406] 25 CHAPTER II

PASSAGE FROM POPULAR MORAL PHILOSOPHY TO A METAPHYSIC OF MORALS

If so far we have drawn our concept of duty from the ordinary use of our practical reason, it must by no means be inferred that we have treated it as a concept of experience.

All moral concepts have their seat and origin in reason completely *a priori*, and indeed in the most ordinary human reason just as much as in the most highly speculative: they cannot be abstracted from any empirical, and therefore merely contingent, knowledge. In this purity of their origin is to be found their very worthiness to serve as supreme practical principles, and everything empirical added to them is just so much taken away from their genuine influence and from the absolute value of the corresponding actions. It is not only a requirement of the utmost necessity in respect of theory, where our 35 concern is solely with speculation, but is also of the utmost practical importance, to draw these concepts and laws from pure reason, to set them forth pure and unmixed, and indeed to determine the extent of this whole practical, but pure, rational knowledge—that is, to determine the whole power of pure practical reason. We ought never—as speculative philosophy does allow and even at times finds necessary—to make principles depend on the special nature of human rea-412 son. Since moral laws have to hold for every rational being as such, we ought rather to derive our principles from the general concept of a rational being as such, and on this basis to expound the whole of ethics—which requires anthropology for its *application* to man—at first independently as pure philosophy, that is, entirely as metaphysics (which we can very well do in this wholly abstract kind of knowledge).

36   In this task of ours we have to progress by natural stages, not merely from ordinary moral judgement (which is here worthy of great respect) to philosophical judgement, as we have already done, but from popular philosophy, which goes no further than it can get by fumbling about with the aid of examples, to metaphysics. (This no longer lets itself be held back by anything empirical, and indeed—since it must survey the complete totality of this kind of knowledge—goes right to Ideas, where examples themselves fail.) For this purpose we must follow—and must portray in detail—the power of practical reason from the general rules determining it right up to the point where there springs from it the concept of duty.

Everything in nature works in accordance with laws. Only a rational being has the power to act *in accordance with his idea* of laws—that is, in accordance with principles—and only so has he a *will*. Since *reason* is required in order to derive actions from laws, the will is nothing but practical reason. If reason infallibly determines the will, then in a being of this kind the actions which are recognized to be objectively necessary are also subjectively necessary—that is to say, the will is then a power to choose *only that* which reason independently of inclination recognizes to 37 be practically necessary, that is, to be good. But if reason solely by itself is not sufficient to determine the will; if the will is exposed also to subjective conditions (certain impulsions) which do not always harmonize with the objective ones; if, 413 in a word, the will is not *in itself* completely in accord with reason (as actually happens in the case of men); then actions which are recognized to be objectively necessary are subjectively contingent, and the determining of such a will in accordance with objective laws is *necessitation*. That is to say, the relation of objective laws to a will not good through and through is conceived as one in which the will of a rational being, although it is determined by principles of reason, does not necessarily follow these principles in virtue of its own nature.

The conception of an objective principle so far as this principle is necessitating for a will is called a command (of reason), and the formula of this command is called an *Imperative*.

All imperatives are expressed by an 'ought' (*Sollen*). By this they mark the relation of an objective law of reason to a will which is not necessarily determined by this law in virtue of its subjective constitution (the relation of necessitation). They say that something would be good to do or to leave undone; only they say it to a will 38 which does not always do a thing because it has been informed that this is a good thing to do. The practically *good* is that which determines the will by concepts of reason, and therefore not by subjective causes, but objectively—that is, on grounds valid for every rational being as such. It is distinguished from the *pleasant* as that which influences the will, not as a principle of reason valid for every one, but solely through the medium of sensation by purely subjective causes valid only for the senses of this person or that.

414] 39   A perfectly good will would thus stand quite as much under objective laws (laws of the good), but it could not on this account be conceived as *necessitated* to act in conformity with law, since of itself, in accordance with its subjective constitution, it can be determined only by the concept of the good. Hence for the *divine* will, and in general for a *holy* will, there are no imperatives: 'I *ought*' is here out of place, because 'I *will*' is already of itself necessarily in harmony with the law. Imperatives are in consequence only formulae for expressing the relation of objective laws of willing to the subjective imperfection of the will of this or that rational being—for example, of the human will.

All *imperative* command either *hypothetically* or *categorically*. Hypothetical imperatives declare a possible action to be practically necessary as a means to the attainment of something else that one wills (or that one may will). A categorical imperative would be one which represented an action as objectively necessary in itself apart from its relation to a further end.

Every practical law represents a possible action as good and therefore as necessary for a 40 subject whose actions are determined by reason. Hence all imperatives are formulae for determining an action which is necessary in accordance with the principle of a will in some sense good. If the action would be good solely as a means *to something else*, the imperative is *hypothetical*; if the action is represented as good *in itself* and

therefore as necessary, in virtue of its principle, for a will which of itself accords with reason, then the imperative is *categorical*.

An imperative therefore tells me which of my possible actions would be good; and it formulates a practical rule for a will that does not perform an action straight away because the action is good—whether because the subject does not always know that it is good or because, even if he did know this, he might still act on maxims contrary to the objective principles of practical reason.

A hypothetical imperative thus says only that an action is good for some purpose or 415 other, either *possible* or *actual*. In the first case it is a *problematic* practical principle; in the second case an *assertoric* practical principle. A categorical imperative, which declares an action to be objectively necessary in itself without reference to some purpose—that is, even without any further end—ranks as an *apodeictic* practical principle. . . .

It is concerned, not with the matter of the action and its presumed results, but with its form and with the principle from which it follows; and what is essentially good in the action consists in the mental disposition, let the consequences be what they may. This imperative may be called the imperative of *morality*.

[How Are Imperatives Possible?]

The question now arises 'How are all these imperatives possible?' This question does not ask how we can conceive the execution of an action commanded by the imperative, but merely how we can conceive the necessitation of the will expressed by the imperative in setting us a task. How an imperative of skill is possible requires no 45 special discussion. Who wills the end, wills (so far as reason has decisive influence on his actions) also the means which are indispensably necessary and in his power. So far as willing is concerned, this proposition is analytic: for in my willing of an object as an effect there is already conceived the causality of myself as an acting cause—that is, the use of means; and from the concept of willing an end the imperative merely extracts the concept of actions necessary to this end. (Synthetic propositions are required in order to determine the means to a proposed end, but these are concerned, not with the reason for performing the act of will, but with the cause which produces the object.)

If it were only as easy to find a determinate concept of happiness, the imperatives of pru-
46 dence would agree entirely with those of skill and would be equally analytic. For here as there it could alike be said 'Who wills the end, wills also (necessarily, if he accords with reason) the sole
418 means which are in his power'. Unfortunately, however, the concept of happiness is so indeterminate a concept that although every man wants to attain happiness, he can never say definitely and in unison with himself what it really is that he wants and wills. The reason for this is that all the elements which belong to the concept of happiness are without exception empirical—that is, they must be borrowed from experience; but that none the less there is required for the Idea of happiness an absolute whole, a maximum of well-being in my present, and in every future, state. Now it is impossible for the most intelligent, and at the same time most powerful, but nevertheless finite, being to form here a determinate concept of what he really wills. Is it riches that he wants?

Beyond all doubt, the question 'How is the imperative of *morality* possible?' is the only one in need of a solution; for it is in no way hypothetical, and consequently we cannot base the objective necessity which it affirms on any presupposition, as we can with hypothetical imperatives. Only we must never forget here that it is impossible to settle *by an example*, and so empirically, whether there is any imperative of this kind at all: we must rather suspect that all imperatives which seem to be categorical may none the less be covertly hypothetical. Take, for example, the saying 'Thou shalt make no false promises'. Let us assume that the necessity for this abstention is no mere advice
49 for the avoidance of some further evil—as it might be said 'You ought not to make a lying promise lest, when this comes to light, you destroy your credit'. Let us hold, on the contrary,

that an action of this kind must be considered as bad in itself, and that the imperative of prohibition is therefore categorical.

We shall thus have to investigate the possibility of a *categorical* imperative entirely *a priori*,
420 since here we do not enjoy the advantage of having its reality given in experience and so of being obliged merely to explain, and not to establish its possibility. So much, however, can be seen provisionally—that the categorical imperative alone purports to be a practical *law*, while all the
50 rest may be called *principles* of the will but not laws; for an action necessary merely in order to achieve an arbitrary purpose can be considered as in itself contingent, and we can always escape from the precept if we abandon the purpose; whereas an unconditioned command does not leave it open to the will to do the opposite at its discretion and therefore alone carries with it that necessity which we demand from a law.

In the second place, with this categorical imperative or law of morality the reason for our difficulty (in comprehending its possibility) is a very serious one. We have here a synthetic *a priori* practical proposition; and since in theoretical knowledge there is so much difficulty in comprehending the possibility of propositions of this kind, it may readily be gathered that in practical knowledge the difficulty will be no less.

[The Formula of Universal Law.]

51 In this task we wish first to enquire whether perhaps the mere concept of a categorical imperative may not also provide us with the formula containing the only proposition that can be a categorical imperative; for even when we know the purport of such an absolute command, the question of its possibility will still require a special and troublesome effort, which we postpone to the final chapter.

When I conceive a *hypothetical* imperative in general, I do not know beforehand what it will contain—until its condition is given. But if I conceive a *categorical* imperative, I know at once what it contains. For since besides the law this
421 imperative contains only the necessity that our

maxim should conform to this law, while the law, as we have seen, contains no condition to limit it, there remains nothing over to which the maxim has to conform except the universality of a law as such; and it is this conformity alone that the imperative properly asserts to be necessary.

There is therefore only a single categorical imperative and it is this: '*Act only on that maxim through which you can at the same time will that it should become a universal law*'.

Now if all imperatives of duty can be derived from this one imperative as their principle, then even although we leave it unsettled whether what we call duty may not be an empty concept, we shall still be able to show at least what we understand by it and what the concept means.

Since the universality of the law governing the production of effects constitutes what is properly called *nature* in its most general sense (nature as regards its form)—that is, the existence of things so far as determined by universal laws—the universal imperative of duty may also run as follows: '*Act as if the maxim of your action were to become through your will a universal law of nature.*'

[Illustrations.]

We will now enumerate a few duties, following their customary division into duties towards self and duties towards others and into perfect and imperfect duties.

1. A man feels sick of life as the result of a series of misfortunes that has mounted to the point of despair, but he is still so far in possession of his reason as to ask himself whether taking his own life may not be contrary to his duty to himself. He now applies the test 'Can the maxim of my action really become a universal law of nature?' His maxim is 'From self-love I make it my principle to shorten my life if its continuance threatens more evil than it promises pleasure'. The only further question to ask is whether this principle of self-love can become a universal law of nature. It is then seen at once that a system of nature by whose law the very same feeling whose function (*Bestimmung*) is to stimulate the fur-

therance of life should actually destroy life would contradict itself and consequently could not subsist as a system of nature. Hence this maxim cannot possibly hold as a universal law of nature and is therefore entirely opposed to the supreme principle of all duty.

2. Another finds himself driven to borrowing money because of need. He well knows that he will not be able to pay it back; but he sees too that he will get no loan unless he gives a firm promise to pay it back within a fixed time. He is inclined to make such a promise; but he has still enough conscience to ask 'Is it not unlawful and contrary to duty to get out of difficulties in this way?' Supposing, however, he did resolve to do so, the maxim of his action would run thus: 'Whenever I believe myself short of money, I will borrow money and promise to pay it back, though I know that this will never be done'. Now this principle of self-love or personal advantage is perhaps quite compatible with my own entire future welfare; only there remains the question 'Is it right?' I therefore transform the demand of self-love into a universal law and frame my question thus: 'How would things stand if my maxim became a universal law?' I then see straight away that this maxim can never rank as a universal law of nature and be self-consistent, but must necessarily contradict itself. For the universality of a law that every one believing himself to be in need can make any promise he pleases with the intention not to keep it would make promising, and the very purpose of promising, itself impossible, since no one would believe he was being promised anything, but would laugh at utterances of this kind as empty shams.

3. A third finds in himself a talent whose cultivation would make him a useful man for all sorts of purposes. But he sees himself in comfortable circumstances, and he prefers to give himself up to pleasure rather than to bother about increasing and improving his fortunate natural aptitudes. Yet he asks himself further 'Does my maxim of neglecting my natural gifts, besides agreeing in itself with my tendency to indulgence, agree also with what is called duty?' He then sees that a system of nature could

indeed always subsist under such a universal law, although (like the South Sea Islanders) every man should let his talents rust and should be bent on devoting his life solely to idleness, indulgence, procreation, and, in a word, to enjoyment. Only he cannot possibly *will* that this should become a universal law of nature or should be 56 implanted in us as such a law by a natural instinct. For as a rational being he necessarily wills that all his powers should be developed, since they serve him, and are given him, for all sorts of possible ends.

4. Yet a *fourth* is himself flourishing, but he sees others who have to struggle with great hardships (and whom he could easily help); and he thinks 'What does it matter to me? Let every one be as happy as Heaven wills or as he can make himself; I won't deprive him of anything; I won't even envy him; only I have no wish to contribute anything to his well-being or to his support in distress!' Now admittedly if such an attitude were a universal law of nature, mankind could get on perfectly well—better no doubt than if everybody prates about sympathy and goodwill, and even takes pains, on occasion, to practise them, but on the other hand cheats where he can, traffics in human rights, or violates them in other ways. But although it is possible that a universal law of nature could subsist in harmony with this maxim, yet it is impossible to *will* that such a principle should hold everywhere as a law of nature. For a will which decided in this way would be in conflict with itself, since many a situation might arise in which the man needed love and sympathy from others, and in which, by such a law of nature sprung from his own will, he 57 would rob himself of all hope of the help he wants for himself.

These are some of the many actual duties—or at least of what we take to be such—whose derivation from the single principle cited above leaps to the eye. We must *be able to will* that a 424 maxim of our action should become a universal law—this is the general canon for all moral judgment of action. Some actions are so constituted that their maxim cannot even be *conceived* as a

universal law of nature without contradiction, let alone be *willed* as what *ought* to become one. In the case of others we do not find this inner impossibility, but it is still impossible to *will* that their maxim should be raised to the universality of a law of nature, because such a will would contradict itself. It is easily seen that the first kind of action is opposed to strict or narrow (rigorous) duty, the second only to wider (meritorious) duty; and thus that by these examples all duties—so far as the type of obligation is concerned (not the object of dutiful action)—are fully set out in their dependence on our single principle.

If we now attend to ourselves whenever we transgress a duty, we find that we in fact do not 58 will that our maxim should become a universal law—since this is impossible for us—but rather that its opposite should remain a law universally: we only take the liberty of making an *exception* to it for ourselves (or even just for this once) to the advantage of our inclination. Consequently if we weighed it all up from one and the same point of view—that of reason—we should find a contradiction in our own will, the contradiction that a certain principle should be objectively necessary as a universal law and yet subjectively should not hold universally but should admit of exceptions. Since, however, we first consider our action from the point of view of a will wholly in accord with reason, and then consider precisely the same action from the point of view of a will affected by inclination, there is here actually no contradiction, but rather an opposition of inclination to the precept of reason (*antagonismus*), whereby the universality of the principle (*universalitas*) is turned into a mere generality (*generalitas*) so that the practical principle of reason may meet our maxim half-way. This procedure, though in our own impartial judgment it cannot be justified, proves none the less that we in fact recognize the validity of the categorical imperative and (with 59 all respect for it) merely permit ourselves a few exceptions which are, as we pretend, inconsiderable and apparently forced upon us.

425 We have thus at least shown this much—that if duty is a concept which is to have meaning and real legislative authority for our actions,

this can be expressed only in categorical imperatives and by no means in hypothetical ones. At the same time—and this is already a great deal—we have set forth distinctly, and determinately for every type of application, the content of the categorical imperative, which must contain the principle of all duty (if there is to be such a thing at all). But we are still not so far advanced as to prove a priori that there actually is an imperative of this kind—that there is a practical law which by itself commands absolutely and without any further motives, and that the following of this law is duty.

The will is conceived as a power of determining oneself to action *in accordance with the idea of certain laws*. And such a power can be found only in rational beings. Now what serves the will as a subjective ground of its self-determination is an *end*; and this, if it is given by reason alone, must be equally valid for all rational beings. What, on the other hand, contains merely the ground of the possibility of an action whose effect is an end is called a *means*. The subjective ground of a desire is an *impulsion (Triebfeder)*; the objective ground of a volition is a *motive (Bewegungsgrund)*. Hence the difference between subjective ends, which are based on impulsions, and objective 64 ends, which depend on motives valid for every rational being. Practical principles are *formal* if they abstract from all subjective ends; they are *material,* on the other hand, if they are based on such ends and consequently on certain impulsions. Ends that a rational being adopts arbitrarily as *effects* of his action (material ends) are in every case only relative; for it is solely their relation to special characteristics in the subject's power of appetition which gives them their value. Hence this value can provide no universal principles, no principles valid and necessary for all rational beings and also for every volition—that is, no practical laws. Consequently all these 428 relative ends can be the ground only of hypothetical imperatives.

Suppose, however, there were something *whose existence* has *in itself* an absolute value, something which as *an end in itself* could be a ground of determinate laws; then in it, and in it

alone, would there be the ground of a possible categorical imperative—that is, of a practical law.

Now I say that man, and in general every rational being, *exists* as an end in himself, *not merely as a means* for arbitrary use by this or that will: he must in all his actions, whether they are directed to himself or to other rational beings, always be viewed *at the same time as an end.* All 65 the objects of inclination have only a conditioned value; for if there were not these inclinations and the needs grounded on them, their object would be valueless. Inclinations themselves, as sources of needs, are so far from having an absolute value to make them desirable for their own sake that it must rather be the universal wish of every rational being to be wholly free from them. Thus the value of all objects that can *be produced* by our action is always conditioned. Beings whose existence depends, not on our will, but on nature, have none the less, if they are non-rational beings, only a relative value as means and are consequently called *things*. Rational beings, on the other hand, are called *persons* because their nature already marks them out as ends in themselves—that is, as something which ought not to be used merely as a means—and consequently imposes to that extent a limit on all arbitrary treatment of them (and is an object of reverence). Persons, therefore, are not merely subjective ends whose existence as an object of our actions has a value *for us:* they are *objective ends*—that is, things whose existence is in itself an end, and indeed an end such that in its place we can put no other end to which they should serve *simply* as means; for unless this is so, nothing at all of *absolute* value would be found any-66 where. But if all value were conditioned—that is, contingent—then no supreme principle could be found for reason at all.

If then there is to be a supreme practical principle and—so far as the human will is concerned—a categorical imperative, it must be such that from the idea of something which is necessarily an end for every one because it is an 429 *end in itself* it forms an *objective* principle of the will and consequently can serve as a practical law. The ground of this principle is: *Rational nature*

exists as an end in itself. This is the way in which a man necessarily conceives his own existence: it is therefore so far a *subjective* principle of human actions. But it is also the way in which every other rational being conceives his existence on the same rational ground which is valid also for me; hence it is at the same time an *objective* principle, from which, as a supreme practical ground, it must be possible to derive all laws for the will. The practical imperative will therefore be as follows: *Act in such a way that you always treat humanity, whether in your own person or in the per-*
67 *son of any other, never simply as a means, but always at the same time as an end.* We will now consider whether this can be carried out in practice.

[Illustrations.]

Let us keep to our previous examples.
66   *First,* as regards the concept of necessary duty to oneself, the man who contemplates suicide will ask 'Can my action be compatible with the Idea of humanity *as an end in itself?*' If he does away with himself in order to escape from a painful situation, he is making use of a person merely as *a means* to maintain a tolerable state of affairs till the end of his life. But man is not a thing—not something to be used *merely* as a means: he must always in all his actions be regarded as an end in himself. Hence I cannot dispose of man in my person by maiming, spoiling, or killing. (A more precise determination of this principle in order to avoid all misunderstanding— for example, about having limbs amputated to save myself or about exposing my life to danger in order to preserve it, and so on—I must here forego: this question belongs to morals proper.)
     Secondly, so far as necessary or strict duty to others is concerned, the man who has a mind to make a false promise to others will see at once that he is intending to make use of another man *merely as a means* to an end he does not share. For
68 the man whom I seek to use for my own purposes by such a promise cannot possibly agree with my way of behaving to him, and so cannot himself share the end of the action. This incompatibility
430 with the principle of duty to others leaps to the

eye more obviously when we bring in examples of attempts on the freedom and property of others. For then it is manifest that a violator of the rights of man intends to use the person of others merely as a means without taking into consideration that, as rational beings, they ought always at the same time to be rated as ends—that is, only as beings who must themselves be able to share in the end of the very same action.

     Thirdly, in regard to contingent (meritorious) duty to oneself, it is not enough that an action
69 should refrain from conflicting with humanity in our own person as an end in itself: it must also *harmonize with this end.* Now there are in humanity capacities for greater perfection which form part of nature's purpose for humanity in our person. To neglect these can admittedly be compatible with the *maintenance* of humanity as an end in itself, but not with the *promotion* of this end.

     Fourthly, as regards meritorious duties to others, the natural end which all men seek is their own happiness. Now humanity could no doubt subsist if everybody contributed nothing to the happiness of others but at the same time refrained from deliberately impairing their happiness. This is, however, merely to agree negatively and not positively with *humanity as an end in itself* unless every one endeavours also, so far as in him lies, to further the ends of others. For the ends of a subject who is an end in himself must, if this conception is to have its *full* effect in me, be also, as far as possible, *my* ends.

[The Formula of Autonomy.]

This principle of humanity, and in general of every rational agent, *as an end in itself* (a principle
431] 70 which is the supreme limiting condition of every man's freedom of action) is not borrowed from experience; firstly, because it is universal, applying as it does to all rational beings as such, and no experience is adequate to determine universality; secondly, because in it humanity is conceived, not as an end of man (subjectively)—that is; as an object which, as a matter of fact, happens to be made an end—but as an objective end—one which, be our ends what they may, must, as a law,

constitute the supreme limiting condition of all subjective ends and so must spring from pure reason. That is to say, the ground for every enactment of practical law lies *objectively in the rule* and · in the form of universality which (according to our first principle) makes the rule capable of being a law (and indeed a law of nature); *subjectively,* however, it lies in the *end;* but (according to our second principle) the subject of all ends is to be found in every rational being as an end in himself. From this there now follows our third practical principle for the will—as the supreme condition of the will's conformity with universal practical reason—namely, the Idea *of the will of every rational being as a will which makes universal law.*

By this principle all maxims are repudiated which cannot accord with the will's own enact-
71 ment of universal law. The will is therefore not merely subject to the law, but is so subject that it must be considered as also *making the law* for itself and precisely on this account as first of all subject to the law (of which it can regard itself as the author).

[The Exclusion of Interest.]

Imperatives as formulated above—namely, the imperative enjoining conformity of actions to universal law on the analogy of *a natural order* and that enjoining the universal *supremacy* of rational beings in themselves *as ends*—did, by the mere fact that they were represented as categorical, exclude from their sovereign authority every admixture of interest as a motive. They were, however, merely *assumed* to be a categorical because we were bound to make this assumption if we wished to explain the concept of duty. That there were practical propositions which commanded categorically could not itself be proved, any more than it can be proved in this chapter generally; but one thing could have been done—namely, to show that in willing for the sake of duty renunciation of all interest, as the specific mark distinguishing a categorical from a hypothetical imperative, was expressed in the very imperative itself by means of some determi-

432 nation inherent in it. This is what is done in the present third formulation of the principle—namely, in the Idea of the will of every rational being as *a will which makes universal law.*

72   Once we conceive a will of this kind, it becomes clear that while a will *which is subject to law* may be bound to this law by some interest, nevertheless a will which is itself a supreme lawgiver cannot possibly as such depend on any interest; for a will which is dependent in this way would itself require yet a further law in order to restrict the interest of self-love to the condition that this interest should itself be valid as a universal law.

Thus the *principle* that every human will is *a will which by all its maxims enacts universal law*— provided only that it were right in other ways— would be *well suited* to be categorical imperative in this respect: that precisely because of the Idea of making universal law it is *based on no interest* and consequently can alone among all possible imperatives be *unconditioned.* Or better still—to convert the proposition—if there is a categorical imperative (that is, a law for the will of every rational being), it can command us only to act
73 always on the maxim of such a will in us as can at the same time look upon itself as making universal law; for only then is the practical principle and the imperative which we obey unconditioned, since it is wholly impossible for it to be based on any interest.

We need not now wonder, when we look back upon all the previous efforts that have been made to discover the principle of morality, why they have one and all been bound to fail. Their authors saw man as tied to laws by his duty, but it never occurred to them that he is subject only to *laws which are made by himself* and yet are *universal,* and that he is bound only to act in conformity with a will which *is his own* but has as nature's purpose for it the function of making universal law. For when they thought of man merely as subject to a law (whatever it might be),
433 the law had to carry with it some interest in order to attract or compel, because it did not spring as a law from *his own* will: in order to conform with the law his will had to be necessitated by

something else to act in a certain way. This absolutely inevitable conclusion meant that all the labour spent in trying to find a supreme principle of duty was lost beyond recall; for what they discovered was never duty, but only the necessity of acting from a certain interest. This interest might be one's own or another's; but on such a view the imperative was bound to be always a 74 conditioned one and could not possibly serve as a moral law. I will therefore call my principle the principle of the *Autonomy* of the will in contrast with all others, which I consequently class under *Heteronomy*.

[The Formula of the Kingdom of Ends.]

The concept of every rational being as one who must regard himself as making universal law by all the maxims of his will, and must seek to judge himself and his actions from this point of view, leads to a closely connected and very fruitful concept—namely, that of *a kingdom of ends*.

I understand by a 'kingdom' a systematic union of different rational beings under common laws. Now since laws determine ends as regards their universal validity, we shall be able—if we abstract from the personal differences between rational beings, and also from all the content of their private ends—to conceive a whole of all ends in systematic conjunction (a whole both of rational beings as ends in themselves and also of the personal ends which each may set before himself); that is, we shall be able to conceive a kingdom of ends which is possible in accordance with the above principles.

For rational beings all stand under the *law* that each of them should treat himself and all 75 others, *never merely as a means*, but always *at the same time as an end in himself*. But by so doing there arises a systematic union of rational beings under common objective laws—that is, a kingdom. Since these laws are directed precisely to the relation of such beings to one another as ends and means, this kingdom can be called a kingdom of ends (which is admittedly only an Ideal).

A rational being belongs to the kingdom of ends as a *member*, when, although he makes its universal laws, he is also himself subject to these laws. He belongs to it as its *head*, when as the maker of laws he is himself subject to the will of no other.

434   A rational being must always regard himself as making laws in a kingdom of ends which is possible through freedom of the will—whether it be as member or as head. The position of the latter he can maintain, not in virtue of the maxim of his will alone, but only if he is a completely independent being, without needs and with an unlimited power adequate to his will.

Thus morality consists in the relation of all action to the making of laws whereby alone a kingdom of ends is possible. This making of laws must be found in every rational being himself 76 and must be able to spring from his will. The principle of his will is therefore never to perform an action except on a maxim such as can also be a universal law, and consequently such *that the will can regard itself as at the same time making universal law by means of its maxim*. Where maxims are not already by their very nature in harmony with this objective principle of rational beings as makers of universal law, the necessity of acting on this principle is practical necessitation—that is, *duty*. Duty does not apply to the head in a kingdom of ends, but it does apply to every member and to all members in equal measure.

The practical necessity of acting on this principle—that is, duty—is in no way based on feelings, impulses, and inclinations, but only on the relation of rational beings to one another, a relation in which the will of a rational being must always be regarded as *making universal law*, because otherwise he could not be conceived as *an end in himself*. Reason thus relates every maxim of the will, considered as making universal law, to every other will and also to every action towards oneself: it does so, not because of any further motive or future advantage, but from 77 the Idea of the *dignity* of a rational being who obeys no law other than that which he at the same time enacts himself.

[The Dignity of Virtue.]

In the kingdom of ends everything has either a *price* or a *dignity*. If it has a price, something else can be put in its place as an *equivalent*; if it is exalted above all price and so admits of no equivalent, then it has a dignity.

What is relative to universal human inclinations and needs has a *market price*; what, even without presupposing a need, accords with a certain taste—that is, with satisfaction in the mere 435 purposeless play of our mental powers—has a *fancy price* (*Affektionspreis*); but that which constitutes the sole condition under which anything can be an end in itself has not merely a relative value—that is, a price—but has an intrinsic value—that is, *dignity*.

Now morality is the only condition under which a rational being can be an end in himself; for only through this is it possible to be a law-making member in a kingdom of ends. Therefore morality, and humanity so far as it is capable of morality, is the only thing which has dignity. 78 Skill and diligence in work have a market price; wit, lively imagination, and humour have a fancy price; but fidelity to promises and kindness based on principle (not on instinct) have an intrinsic worth. In default of these, nature and art alike contain nothing to put in their place; for their worth consists, not in the effects which result from them, not in the advantage or profit they produce, but in the attitudes of mind—that is, in the maxims of the will—which are ready in this way to manifest themselves in action even if they are not favoured by success. Such actions too need no recommendation from any subjective disposition or taste in order to meet with immediate favour and approval; they need no immediate propensity or feeling for themselves; they exhibit the will which performs them as an object of immediate reverence; nor is anything other than reason required to *impose* them upon the will, not to *coax* them from the will—which last would anyhow be a contradiction in the case of duties. This assessment reveals as dignity the value of such a mental attitude and puts it infinitely above all price, with which it cannot be brought into reckoning or comparison without, as it were, a profanation of its sanctity.

What is it then that entitles a morally good attitude of mind—or virtue—to make claims so

79 high? It is nothing less than the *share* which it affords to a rational being *in the making of universal law*, and which therefore fits him to be a member in a possible kingdom of ends. For this he was already marked out in virtue of his own proper nature as an end in himself and consequently as a maker of laws in the kingdom of ends—as free in respect of all laws of nature, obeying only those laws which he makes himself and in virtue of which his maxims can have their part in the making of universal law (to which he at the same 436 time subjects himself). For nothing can have a value other than that determined for it by the law. But the law-making which determines all value must for this reason have a dignity—that is, an unconditioned and incomparable worth—for the appreciation of which, as necessarily given by a rational being, the word *'reverence'* is the only becoming expression. *Autonomy* is therefore the ground of the dignity of human nature and of every rational nature.

[Review of the Formulae.]

The aforesaid three ways of representing the principle of morality are at bottom merely so many formulations of precisely the same law, one of them by itself containing a combination of the other two. . . .

[Review of the Whole Argument.]

We can now end at the point from which we started out at the beginning—namely, the concept of an unconditionally good will. The *will is absolutely good* if it cannot be evil—that is, if its maxim, when made into a universal law, can never be in conflict with itself. This principle is therefore also its supreme law: 'Act always on that maxim whose universality as a law you can at the same time will'. This is the one principle on which a will can never be in conflict with itself, and such an imperative is categorical. Because the validity of the will as a universal law for possible actions is analogous to the universal interconnexion of existent things in accordance with universal laws—which constitutes the formal aspect of nature as such—we can also express the categorical imperative as follows: '*Act on that maxim which can at the same time have for its object itself as a universal law of nature*'. In this way we provide the formula for an absolutely good will.

Rational nature separates itself out from all other things by the fact that it sets itself an end. An end would thus be the matter of every good will. But in the Idea of a will which is absolutely good—good without any qualifying condition (namely, that it should attain this or that end)— there must be complete abstraction from every end that has to be *produced* (as something which would make every will only relatively good). Hence the end must here be conceived, not as an end to be produced, *but as a self-existent* end. It must therefore be conceived only negatively— that is, as an end against which we should never act, and consequently as one which in all our willing we must never rate *merely* as a means, but always at the same time as an end. Now this end can be nothing other than the subject of all possible ends himself, because this subject is also the subject of a will that may be absolutely good; for such a will cannot without contradiction be subordinated to any other object. The principle 'So act in relation to every rational being (both to yourself and to others) that he may at the same time count in your maxim as an end in himself' is thus at bottom the same as the principle 'Act on a maxim which at the same time contains in itself its own universal validity for every rational being'. For to say that in using means to every end I ought to restrict my maxim by the condition that it should also be universally valid as a law for every subject is just the same as to say this—that a subject of ends, namely, a rational being himself, must be made the ground for all maxims of action, never *merely* as a means, but as a supreme condition restricting the use of every means—that is, always also as an end.

Now from this it unquestionably follows that every rational being, as an end in himself, must be able to regard himself, as also the maker of universal law in respect of any law whatever to which he may be subjected; for it is precisely the fitness of his maxims to make universal law that marks him out as an end in himself. . . .

Thus *morality* lies in the relation of actions to the autonomy of the will—that is, to a possible making of universal law by means of its maxims. An action which is compatible with the autonomy of the will is *permitted*; one which does not harmonize with it is *forbidden*. A will whose maxims necessarily accord with the laws of autonomy is a *holy*, or absolutely good, will. The dependence of a will not absolutely good on the principle of autonomy (that is, moral necessitation) is *obligation*. Obligation can thus have no reference to a holy being. The objective necessity to act from obligation is called *duty*.

STUDY QUESTIONS: KANT, GROUNDWORK OF THE METAPHYSICS OF MORALS

1. What is Kant's main aim in the *Groundwork?* How does this relate to the idea that morals should not remain exposed to corruption?
2. What is the objective of Chapter 1 of the *Groundwork?*
3. According to Kant, what is the only thing that is good without qualification? What arguments does Kant offer for this conclusion?
4. What is the purpose of Kant's example of a grocer?
5. What does Kant mean by 'the maxim of their action,' and how does this enter into his second proposition?
6. How does the third proposition define duty? What does his answer mean?
7. What are the objectives of the second chapter of the *Groundwork?*
8. What is the relationship between the will and practical reason?
9. What is the difference between the Categorical Imperative and a hypothetical imperative?
10. Why does Kant have to investigate the possibility of the Categorical Imperative entirely a priori?
11. What is the formula of the universal law?

12. How does Kant distinguish between perfect and imperfect duties?
13. What is the practical imperative regarding the treatment of persons? How does Kant derive this principle?
14. What is the formula of autonomy, and how does Kant derive this version of the Categorical Imperative?
15. What is the formula of the kingdom of ends?
16. How does Kant answer his question, 'How is the categorical imperative possible?'

AN ANSWER TO THE QUESTION: 'WHAT IS ENLIGHTENMENT?'

Kant composed this famous essay in 1784. By way of background, let us examine very briefly Kant's view of politics and history. For Kant, politics is the application of the Categorical Imperative to society. The function and justification of the state are to preserve individual autonomy. Ideally, it should reconcile each person's freedom with that of others in accordance with a universal law. The aim of politics should not be to make people happy, and benevolent despotism cannot be justified on such grounds. The fundamental principle of politics is that the constitution of a state should enable the greatest possible human freedom and that its laws should ensure that the freedom of each citizen is compatible with that of everyone else. This principle requires that there be enforced laws, which are concerned with the outer and enforceable aspect of perfect moral duties to others.

Kant defines a political ideal, which internationally is a just order of perpetual peace. He argues that this ideal requires an international peaceful confederation of republics. He also contends that this ideal is required in order to make sense of history. History is ideally a process of progressing toward greater freedom, but this does not mean that all change is progress.

Enlightenment is man's emergence from his self-incurred immaturity. Immaturity is the inability to use one's own understanding without the guidance of another. This immaturity is *self-incurred* if its cause is not lack of understanding, but lack of resolution and courage to use it without the guidance of another. The motto of enlightenment is therefore: *Sapere aude!* Have courage to use your *own* understanding!

Laziness and cowardice are the reasons why such a large proportion of men, even when nature has long emancipated them from alien guidance (*naturaliter maiorennes*), nevertheless gladly remain immature for life. For the same reasons, it is all too easy for others to set themselves up as their guardians. It is so convenient to be immature! If I have a book to have understanding in place of me, a spiritual adviser to have a conscience for me, a doctor to judge my diet for me, and so on, I need not make any efforts at all. I need not think, so long as I can pay; others will soon enough take the tiresome job over for me. The guardians who have kindly taken upon themselves the work of supervision will soon see to it that by far the largest part of mankind (including the entire fair sex) should consider the step forward to maturity not

Immanuel Kant, from *Kant: Political Writings*, 2nd Edition, edited by Hans Reis, translated by H. B. Nisbet. Copyright © Cambridge University Press, 1970, 1991. Reprinted with the permission of Cambridge University Press.

only as difficult but also as highly dangerous. Having first infatuated their domesticated animals, and carefully prevented the docile creatures from daring to take a single step without the leading-strings to which they are tied, they next show them the danger which threatens them if they try to walk unaided. Now this danger is not in fact so very great, for they would certainly learn to walk eventually after a few falls. But an example of this kind is intimidating, and usually frightens them off from further attempts.

Thus it is difficult for each separate individual to work his way out of the immaturity which has become almost second nature to him. He has even grown fond of it and is really incapable for the time being of using his own understanding, because he was never allowed to make the attempt. Dogmas and formulas, those mechanical instruments for rational use (or rather misuse) of his natural endowments, are the ball and chain of his permanent immaturity. And if anyone did throw them off, he would still be uncertain about jumping over even the narrowest of trenches, for he would be unaccustomed to free movement of this kind. Thus only a few, by cultivating their own minds, have succeeded in freeing themselves from immaturity and in continuing boldly on their way.

There is more chance of an entire public enlightening itself. This is indeed almost inevitable, if only the public concerned is left in freedom. For there will always be a few who think for themselves, even among those appointed as guardians of the common mass. Such guardians, once they have themselves thrown off the yoke of immaturity, will disseminate the spirit of rational respect for personal value and for the duty of all men to think for themselves. The remarkable thing about this is that if the public, which was previously put under this yoke by the guardians, is suitably stirred up by some of the latter who are incapable of enlightenment, it may subsequently compel the guardians themselves to remain under the yoke. For it is very harmful to propagate prejudices, because they finally avenge themselves on the very people who first encouraged them (or whose predecessors did so). Thus a public can only achieve enlightenment slowly. A revolution may well put an end to autocratic despotism and to rapacious or power-seeking oppression, but it will never produce a true reform in ways of thinking. Instead, new preju-

dices, like the ones they replaced, will serve as a leash to control the great unthinking mass.

For enlightenment of this kind, all that is needed is *freedom*. And the freedom in question is the most innocuous form of all—freedom to make *public use* of one's reason in all matters. But I hear on all sides the cry: *Don't argue!* The officer says: Don't argue, get on parade! The tax-official: Don't argue, pay! The clergyman: Don't argue, believe! (Only one ruler in the world says: *Argue* as much as you like and about whatever you like, *but obey!*) All this means restrictions on freedom everywhere. But which sort of restriction prevents enlightenment, and which, instead of hindering it, can actually promote it? I reply: The *public* use of man's reason must always be free, and it alone can bring about enlightenment among men; the *private use* of reason may quite often be very narrowly restricted, however, without undue hindrance to the progress of enlightenment. But by the public use of one's own reason I mean that use which anyone may make of it *as a man of learning* addressing the entire *reading public*. What I term the private use of reason is that which a person may make of it in a particular *civil* post or office with which he is entrusted.

Now in some affairs which affect the interests of the commonwealth, we require a certain mechanism whereby some members of the commonwealth must behave purely passively, so that they may, by an artificial common agreement, be employed by the government for public ends (or at least deterred from vitiating them). It is, of course, impermissible to argue in such cases; obedience is imperative. But in so far as this or that individual who acts as part of the machine also considers himself as a member of a complete commonwealth or even of cosmopolitan society, and thence as a man of learning who may through his writings address a public in the truest sense of the word, he may indeed argue without harming the affairs in which he is employed for some of the time in a passive capacity. Thus it would be very harmful if an officer receiving an order from his superiors were to quibble openly, while on duty, about the appropriateness or usefulness of the order in question. He must simply obey. But he cannot reasonably be banned from making observations as a man of learning on the errors in the military service, and from submitting these to his public for judgement. The citizen cannot refuse to pay the taxes imposed upon him; presumptuous criticisms of such taxes, where someone is called upon to pay them, may be punished as an outrage which could lead to general insubordination. Nonetheless, the same citizen does not contravene his civil obligations if, as a learned individual, he publicly voices his thoughts on the impropriety or even injustice of such fiscal measures. In the same way, a clergyman is bound to instruct his pupils and his congregation in accordance with the doctrines of the church he serves, for he was employed by it on that condition. But as a scholar, he is completely free as well as obliged to impart to the public all his carefully considered, well-intentioned thoughts on the mistaken aspects of those doctrines, and to offer suggestions for a better arrangement of religious and ecclesiastical affairs. And there is nothing in this which need trouble the conscience. For what he teaches in pursuit of his duties as an active servant of the church is presented by him as something which he is not empowered to teach at his own discretion, but which he is employed to expound in a prescribed manner and in someone else's name. He will say: Our church teaches this or that, and these are the arguments it uses. He then extracts as much practical value as possible for his congregation from precepts to which he would not himself subscribe with full conviction, but which he can nevertheless undertake to expound, since it is not in fact wholly impossible that they may contain truth. At all events, nothing opposed to the essence of religion is present in such doctrines. For if the clergyman thought he could find anything of this sort in them, he would not be able to carry out his official duties in good conscience, and would have to resign. Thus the use which someone employed as a teacher makes of his reason in the presence of his congregation is purely *private*, since a congregation, however large it is, is never any more than a domestic gathering. In view of this, he is not and cannot be free as a priest, since he is acting on a commission imposed from outside. Conversely, as a scholar addressing the real public (i.e. the world at large) through his writings, the clergyman making *public use* of his reason enjoys unlimited freedom to use his own reason and to speak in his own person. For to maintain that the guardians of the people in spiritual matters should themselves be immature, is an absurdity which amounts to making absurdities permanent.

But should not a society of clergymen, for example an ecclesiastical synod or a venerable presbytery (as the Dutch call it), be entitled to commit itself by oath to a certain unalterable set of doctrines, in order to secure for all time a constant guardianship over each of its members, and through them over the people? I reply that this is quite impossible. A contract of this kind, concluded with a view to preventing all further enlightenment of mankind for ever, is absolutely null and void, even if it is ratified by the supreme power, by Imperial Diets and the most solemn peace treaties. One age cannot enter into an alliance on oath to put the next age in a position where it would be impossible for it to extend and correct its knowledge, particularly on such important matters, or to make any progress whatsoever in enlightenment. This would be a crime against human nature, whose original destiny lies precisely in such progress. Later generations are thus perfectly entitled to dismiss these agreements as unauthorised and criminal. To test whether any particular measure can be agreed upon as a law for a people, we need only ask whether a people could well impose such a law upon itself. This might well be possible for a specified short period as a means of introducing a certain order, pending, as it were, a better solution. This would also mean that each citizen, particularly the clergyman, would be given a free hand as a scholar to comment publicly, i.e. in his writings, on the inadequacies of current institutions. Meanwhile, the newly established order would continue to exist, until public insight into the nature of such matters had progressed and proved itself to the point where, by general consent (if not unanimously), a proposal could be submitted to the crown. This would seek to protect the congregations who had, for instance, agreed to alter their religious establishment in accordance with their own notions of what higher insight is, but it would not try to obstruct those who wanted to let things remain as before. But it is absolutely impermissible to agree, even for a single lifetime, to a permanent religious constitution which no-one might publicly question. For this would virtually nullify a phase in man's upward progress, thus making it fruitless and even detrimental to subsequent generations. A man may for his own person, and even then only for a limited period, postpone enlightening himself in matters he ought to know about. But to renounce such enlightenment completely, whether for his own person or even more so for later generations, means violating and trampling underfoot the sacred rights of mankind. But something which a people may not even impose upon itself can still less be imposed on it by a monarch; for his legislative authority depends precisely upon his uniting the collective will of the people in his own. So long as he sees to it that all true or imagined improvements are compatible with the civil order, he can otherwise leave his subjects to do whatever they find necessary for their salvation, which is none of his business. But it is his business to stop anyone forcibly hindering others from working as best they can to define and promote their salvation. It indeed detracts from his majesty if he interferes in these affairs by subjecting the writings in which his subjects attempt to clarify their religious ideas to governmental supervision. This applies if he does so acting upon his own exalted opinions—in which case he exposes himself to the reproach: *Caesar non est supra Grammaticos*—but much more so if he demeans his high authority so far as to support the spiritual despotism of a few tyrants within his state against the rest of his subjects.

If it is now asked whether we at present live in an *enlightened* age, the answer is: No, but we do live in an age of *enlightenment*. As things are at present, we still have a long way to go before men as a whole can be in a position (or can even be put into a position) of using their own understanding confidently and well in religious matters, without outside guidance. But we do have distinct indications that the way is now being cleared for them to work freely in this direction, and that the obstacles to universal enlightenment, to man's emergence from his self-incurred immaturity, are gradually becoming fewer. In this respect our age is the age of enlightenment, the century of *Frederick*.

A prince who does not regard it as beneath him to say that he considers it his duty, in religious matters, not to prescribe anything to his people, but to allow them complete freedom, a prince who thus even declines to accept the presumptuous title of *tolerant*, is himself enlightened. He deserves to be praised by a grateful present and posterity as the man who first liberated mankind from immaturity (as far as government is concerned), and who left all men free to use their own reason in all matters of conscience.

Under his rule, ecclesiastical dignitaries, notwithstanding their official duties, may in their capacity as scholars freely and publicly submit to the judgement of the world their verdicts and opinions, even if these deviate here and there from orthodox doctrine. This applies even more to all others who are not restricted by any official duties. This spirit of freedom is also spreading abroad, even where it has to struggle with outward obstacles imposed by governments which misunderstand their own function. For such governments can now witness a shining example of how freedom may exist without in the least jeopardising public concord and the unity of the commonwealth. Men will of their own accord gradually work their way out of barbarism so long as artificial measures are not deliberately adopted to keep them in it.

I have portrayed *matters of religion* as the focal point of enlightenment, i.e. of man's emergence from his self-incurred immaturity. This is firstly because our rulers have no interest in assuming the role of guardians over their subjects so far as the arts and sciences are concerned, and secondly, because religious immaturity is the most pernicious and dishonourable variety of all. But the attitude of mind of a head of state who favours freedom in the arts and sciences extends even further, for he realises that there is no danger even to his *legislation* if he allows his subjects to make *public* use of their own reason and to put before the public their thoughts on better ways of drawing up laws, even if this entails forthright criticism of the current legislation. We have before us a brilliant example of this kind, in which no monarch has yet surpassed the one to whom we now pay tribute.

But only a ruler who is himself enlightened and has no fear of phantoms, yet who likewise has at hand a well-disciplined and numerous army to guarantee public security, may say what no republic would dare to say: *Argue as much as you like and about whatever you like, but obey!* This reveals to us a strange and unexpected pattern in human affairs (such as we shall always find if we consider them in the widest sense, in which nearly everything is paradoxical). A high degree of civil freedom seems advantageous to a people's *intellectual* freedom, yet it also sets up insuperable barriers to it. Conversely, a lesser degree of civil freedom gives intellectual freedom enough room to expand to its fullest extent. Thus once the germ on which nature has lavished most care—man's inclination and vocation to *think freely*—has developed within this hard shell, it gradually reacts upon the mentality of the people, who thus gradually become increasingly able to *act freely*.

Eventually, it even influences the principles of governments, which find that they can themselves profit by treating man, who is *more than a machine*, in a manner appropriate to his dignity.

Königsberg in Prussia, 30th September, 1784.

STUDY QUESTIONS: KANT, 'WHAT IS ENLIGHTENMENT?'

1. How does Kant define 'enlightenment'?
2. What are the main causes of immaturity?
3. Why can the public achieve enlightenment only slowly?
4. What is the main requirement for general enlightenment to occur?
5. Why is it important for members of a commonwealth to voice their thoughts publicly? What are the exceptions?
6. How does Kant's idea apply to clergymen and to a church?
7. Why has Kant portrayed matters of religion as the focal point of enlightenment?
8. How does Kant's analysis of enlightenment differ from the relevant views of both Rousseau and Voltaire?

Philosophical Bridges: Kant's Influence

Kant had a huge influence on the history of philosophy, which, for the sake of simplicity, we can divide into seven parts.

First, his transcendental idealism inspired many nineteenth-century German idealists, such as Johann Fichte, Schelling, and Hegel. In broad terms, these thinkers accepted Kant's idea of phenomena but rejected his notion of noumena, which they considered to be the major inconsistency in his idealism. They regarded the ideal world of objects in space and time as constituted by the thinking of the Absolute, thereby avoiding the solipsism inherent in the personal idealism of Berkeley. (As an aside, the work of Schopenhauer can be seen in part as an attempt to rescue Kant's transcendental idealism from this interpretation; instead of jettisoning the notion of noumena, Schopenhauer transformed it into the Will.) In the second half of the nineteenth century, Hegel's philosophy took root in Britain and the United States, even though its influenced had waned in Germany. Kant was swept in with this Hegelian wave of interest as the first systematic studies of Kant in English appeared, such as H. Cohen's *Kant's Theory of Experience* (1861) and Edward Caird's 1877 commentary on Kant.

Second, in sharp contrast to the German idealists, Kant's work was also part of a realist reaction against the idealism of the late nineteenth century. For example, Kant influenced, among others, H. A. Pritchard at the University of Oxford in England, who, in his book *Kant's Theory of Knowledge* (1909), argues that knowledge presupposes that the reality known exists independently of the knowledge of it. It may seem surprising that Kant's work has stimulated both idealism and the realist reaction against it; however, he was an empirical realist as well as a transcendental idealist. Since the 1960s, many commentators have understood Kant's transcendental idealism in a way that stresses more explicitly his empirical realism (i.e., the claim that objects in space and time are empirically real, meaning that they can exist unperceived). In this manner, Kant has been perceived as a thinker who opposes hard realism but avoids simple idealism. He opposes the claim that objects in space and time exist independently of all concepts (namely, the categories) and yet, at the same time, avoids the thesis that they cannot exist unperceived. This aspect of Kant's voice has found sympathetic ears in recent philosophers, such as Hilary Putnam.

Third, Kant's non-Empiricism has initiated whole traditions of non-Rationalist philosophers who reject Empiricism. Within continental philosophy, for example, after 1900 the phenomenologist Edmund Husserl rejected the Empiricist tradition exemplified in Mill's claim that logical and mathematical claims are psychological; he does so for the Kantian reason that such claims are a priori as opposed to empirical. Husserl's phenomenology employs Kant's notion of the a priori forms of perception in the study of consciousness, and, from there, Heidegger develops the notion of a priori structures as lived by a person. Heidegger's existentials are a priori characteristics of our mode of being; this idea in turn influenced the existentialist Jean-Paul Sartre. In analytic philosophy, Peter Strawson's publications *Individuals* (1959) and the *Bounds of Sense* (1966) helped to reanimate Kant's notion of the a priori conditions of experience as a set of conceptual as opposed to psychological requirements that reality and any experience of it must meet. For example, in *Individuals*, Strawson supports Kant's claim that any experience must be of spatio-temporal particulars.

Fourth, in the philosophy of science, some of Kant's ideas were essential to the historical development of contemporary physics. For example, Kant claimed that non-Euclidean geometries are logically possible, and, in the nineteenth century, such geometries were indeed developed and subsequently became integral to Einstein's theory of gravity, his general theory of relativity. Kant's theory of causation has influenced writers such as the physicist Hans Reichenbach to develop a so-called causal theory of time, which aims to specify a physical basis for time relations through causality without presupposing temporal notions. Kant influenced the great French mathematician Henri Poincaré, who came close to developing the theory of special relativity. Among the important insights that Kant had was the idea that space and time are not absolute entities in the way that Newton supposed, and that they must be constituted through the interactions in the physical world. Distance cannot be conceived in terms of absolute space; it must be thought of in terms of the possible motion of a body. In short, Kant required that spatial and temporal concepts be operationalized in a way that anticipates Einstein's ideas about simultaneity.

Fifth, Kant's claims that mathematical statements are synthetic a priori, and that their proof requires a construction in pure intuition, have given rise to a view in the philosophy of mathematics called Intuitionism, first developed by L. E. J. Brouwer (1881–1966). According to this analysis, mathematical objects are only mental constructions, and the truth of a mathematical statement is equivalent to its having been proved. In other words, there are no Platonic mathematical objects.

Sixth, Kant invented various powerful new ways of doing philosophy. For example, the notion of a transcendental argument is Kantian: it is the idea of arguing against a position on the grounds that it undermines its own possibility (e.g., Empiricism makes experience impossible). Other philosophers have sought transcendental arguments, for example, against Skepticism. Kant asks the question 'How is knowledge possible?' and his answer involves articulating the necessary conditions for knowledge. Recent philosophers have asked similar questions such as 'How is language possible?' For instance, in his early work the *Tractatus*, Wittgenstein seeks the necessary conditions of logic.

Seventh, Kant's moral philosophy has become one of the major positions in ethics, which continues to attract generally sympathetic commentaries from important recent figures, such as Onora O'Neil, Thomas Hill, and Christine Koorsgard. For instance, the latter's work *The Sources of Normativity* tries to explain the source of our moral obligations in generally Kantian terms. Kant's ethics has been influential because it stresses autonomy as a fundamental value and also because of his claim that moral judgments have a categorical form. Kant's thesis that we should never treat persons merely as means has influenced many writers, including Karl Marx in his theory of labor alienation, and the existential psychoanalyst Martin Buber in his views on I and Thou. Additionally, Kant's notion of autonomy influenced deeply the existentialist Jean-Paul Sartre in his formulation of bad faith and authenticity, the thinking of Jürgen Habermas, and the work of John Rawls, authors who are all represented in Volume 5.

The influence of Kant's thought extends beyond the *Critique of Pure Reason* and his work in ethics. For example, his theory of natural beauty had a profound effect on Friedrich Schiller (1759–1805) and on his friend, the great poet Goethe, as well as Schopenhauer and, thus, on the nineteenth-century Romantic movement as a whole.

Philosophical Bridges: The Influence of the Modern Philosophers

The modern philosophers set the agenda of much twentieth-century thinking. Their problems, and to some extent their solutions, direct some recent philosophy. This is because they invented two fundamental concepts that are still important: (1) the notion of inert matter that is governed by mechanical and mathematically describable causal laws, and (2) the idea that knowledge must be based on the systematic observation of nature and on rational principles. In short, they instigated the natural sciences and wrestled with some of the philosophical problems that arise from their invention, such as whether the claim that the universe is composed of inert matter can be reconciled with the description of a person as a self-conscious being with an autonomous free will. In a rather similar vein, some contemporary thought is concerned with the question of how the natural sciences seem to threaten morality and other meaningful ways of understanding ourselves. Today these kinds of issues are addressed often in the philosophy of language and mind. In contrast, for the modern thinkers, these issues were focused often around religion and metaphysics.

These points indicate that some of the metaphysical problems that concern some philosophers today, such as freedom versus determinism, the mind-body relation, and the nature of perception, were shaped by modern thinkers. It also means that modern themes underlie many other contemporary discussions, such as the relationship between the natural and social sciences and the nature of linguistic meaning.

However, at the same time, much twentieth-century philosophy is explicitly antimodern. Today, many philosophers reject the core theses of, for instance, Descartes, Locke, and Hume, such as the claim that we can perceive only our own private mental ideas. In sharp contrast, many philosophers today stress the public nature of knowledge and the social nature of meaning. Furthermore, there are critiques of the Enlightenment ideas of the autonomous individual, historical progress, objectivity, and reason. These critiques seem to suggest a new postmodern age. Nevertheless, when contemporary thinkers try to define their own positions in opposition to modern conceptions, this attests to the continuing significance of modern philosophy. In other words, often, modern thought is so close to us that we still need to reject it explicitly. The process of rethinking modern philosophy is a work in progress.

Bibliography

GENERAL

Cassirer, E., *The Philosophy of the Enlightenment*, Princeton University Press, 1951

Gay, P., *The Enlightenment: An Interpretation*, Knopf, 1966

Gilmour, Peter, ed., *Philosophers of the Enlightenment*, Barnes & Noble Books, 1990

VOLTAIRE
Primary

Candide, trans. Roger Pearson, Knopf, 1992

Letters Concerning the English Nation, ed. N. Cronk, Oxford University Press, 1994

Philosophical Dictionary, trans. Peter Gay, Basic Books, 1962

Voltaire: Political Writings, ed. David William, Cambridge University Press, 1934

Secondary

Aldridge, A. Owen, *Voltaire and the Century of Light*, Princeton University Press, 1975

Ayer, A. J., *Voltaire*, Random House, 1986

Wade, Ira, *The Intellectual Development of Voltaire*, Princeton University Press, 1969

ROUSSEAU
Primary

Emile, ed. Allan Bloom, Basic Books, 1979

Political Writings, ed. Victor Gourevitch, Cambridge University Press, 1997

Secondary

Cooper, Laurence D., *Rousseau, Nature, and the Problem of the Good Life*, Pennsylvania State University Press, 1999

Grimsley, Ronald, *The Philosophy of Rousseau*, Oxford University Press, 1973

Melzer, Arthur M., *The Natural Goodness of Man: On the System of Rousseau's Thought*, University of Chicago Press, 1990

Wokler, Robert, *Rousseau*, Oxford University Press, 1995

KANT
Primary

Critique of Judgment, trans. W. S. Pluhar, Hackett, 1987

Critique of Practical Reason, trans. L. W. Beck, MacMillan, 1993

Critique of Pure Reason, trans. Norman Kemp-Smith, MacMillan, 1975

Groundwork of the Metaphysics of Morals, trans. H. J. Paton, Harper & Row, 1956

Metaphysical Foundations of Natural Science, trans. J. W. Ellington, Hackett, 1985

Prolegomena to Any Future Metaphysics, ed. P. Gray-Lucas, Manchester University Press, 1978

Secondary

Allison, Henry, *Kant's Transcendental Idealism*, Yale University Press, 1983

Americks, Karl, *Kant's Theory of the Mind*, Oxford University Press, 1982

Bennett J., *Kant's Analytic*, Cambridge University Press, 1966

———, *Kant's Dialectic*, Cambridge University Press, 1974

Brittain, G., *Kant's Theory of Science*, Princeton University Press, 1975

Guyer, P., *The Cambridge Companion to Kant*, Cambridge University Press, 1992

———, *Kant and the Claims of Knowledge*, Cambridge University Press, 1987

Kitcher, Patricia, *Kant's Critique of Pure Reason: Critical Essays*, Rowman & Littlefield, 1998

Scruton, Roger, *Kant*, Oxford University Press, 1982

Strawson, Sir Peter, *The Bounds of Sense*, Methuen 1966

Thomson, Garrett, *On Kant*, Wadsworth, 2000

Walker, Ralph, *Kant*, Routledge, 1979

Wood, Allen, *Kant's Moral Religion*, Cornell University Press, 1970

◆ SOURCES ◆

SECTION I: SCIENTIFIC THINKERS

Page 6: Copernicus, Nicholas, *On the Revolutions,* complete works, vol. 2, trans. Edward Rosen, John Hopkins University Press, 1992. Selections from the preface, and Book I: Introduction, and chs. 10 and 11.

Page 13: Kepler, *New Astronomy,* trans. W. H. Donahue, Cambridge University Press, 1992, selections from the introduction.

Page 17: Galilei, Galileo:
1. *Sidereus Nuncius, (The Sidereal Messenger),* trans. Albert Van Helden, University of Chicago Press, 1989.
2. *Dialogue on the Great World Systems,* selection from Day 2, trans. G. de Santillana, University of Chicago Press, 1953.

Page 29: Newton, Isaac, *The Principia,* trans. Bernard Cohen and Anne Whitman, University of California Press, 1999; selections from *The Definitions, Scholium and Axioms* or *Laws of Motion,* and *Rules for the Study of Natural Philosophy* from Book 3.

SECTION II: RATIONALISM

Page 39: Descartes, René, from *The Philosophical Works of Descartes,* trans. E. Haldare and G. Ross, Cambridge University Press, 1911:
1. *Meditations,* complete.
2. *Objections and Replies:* Second Set of Objections and Author's Replies, selections from 30–35, 38–41, 47–48, 52–59; Third Set of Objections and Author's Replies, complete; Fourth Set of Objections and Author's Replies, selections from 79–86, 96–104.
3. *Rules for the Direction of Our Native Intelligence: Rules One to Thirteen.*

Page 101: Pascal, Blaise, *Pensées,* trans. A. J. Krailsheimer, Penguin Classics, 1966, secs. 167, 173, 174, 175, 182, 183, 185, 188, 190, 193, 418, 419, 420, 423, and 424.

Page 106: Spinoza, Baruch de, *The Ethics,* trans. R. H. M. Elwes, *The Works of Benedict de Spinoza,* Dover, 1955: Part I, 1–14, 15–16, 18, 28–29, and 32–34; Part II, 1–29, 32–36, 40–44, and 48–49; Part III, 1–7 and 28; Part IV, appendix; and Part V, 1–4, 6–7, 10, 14–16, 18, and 23–41.

Page 144: Leibniz, Gottfried, *Leibniz: Philosophical Writings,* trans. Mary Morris and G. H. R. Parkinson, Rowman & Littlefield, 1973:

1. Letters to Arnauld, 12 April 1686, 51; and 30 April 1687, 67–69.
2. *Primary Truths,* 87–92.
3. *Necessary and Contingent Truths,* 96–99.
4. *Discourse on Metaphysics.*
5. *Monadology,* 1–15, 19–21, 29–45, 53–58, 60–66, 70–73, and 78–84.
6. Letters to Clarke: Third Letter, 210–12; and Fourth Letter, 215–17.

SECTION III: EMPIRICISM

Page 180: Bacon, Francis, *The Great Instauration* and *Novum Organum,* in *Francis Bacon: A Selection of His Works,* ed. Sidney Warhaft, Odyssey Press, 1965. Selections from *The Great Instauration:* Preface and Plan of the work; from *Novum Organum:* Preface; Aphorisms Book I, 1–4; 7–14; 19–22, 38–48, 50; 52–55, 58–62, 68–70, 95, 98–99, 103–8, and 130; and Book II, 1–7, 10–16, 18–21, and 52.

Page 203: Hobbes, Thomas, *The Leviathan,* from Hobbes selections, ed. F. Woodbridge, Charles Scribrer's Sons, 1930, selections: Part 1: chs. 1, 2, 3, 5, 6, 9, 13, 14, 15, and 16. Book II: chs. 17, 18, 19, and 21.

Page 222: Locke, John:
1. *An Essay Concerning Human Understanding,* ed. John Yolton, Everyman, 1961:
   Book I: ch. 1, 1–4, 7–8; ch. 2, 1–5.
   Book II: ch. 1: 1–9; ch. 2: 1–2; ch. 3: 1; ch. 5: 1; ch. 6: 1–2; ch. 7: 1–2 and 7–10; ch. 8: 7–25; ch. 9, 1–4 and 8; ch. 11: 4, 6, and 9; ch. 12: 1–8; ch. 21: 1–5, 7–17, 19, 21, and 27; ch. 22: 1–3; ch. 23: 1–1 and 14; ch. 27: 1–7, 9–10, 13–17, 19–20, 22–23, and 25–26.
   Book III: ch. 2: 1–2; ch. 3: 1–4, 6, 9, 11, and 15–18; ch 6: 2, 26, and 28; ch. 9: 5; and ch. 10: 4.
   Book IV: ch. 1: 1–7; ch. 2: 1–4 and 14; ch. 3: 1–2, 6, 16, and 18; ch. 4: 3–5, 7, and 12; ch. 9: 1 and 3; ch.10: 2, 4, 8, and 11; ch. 11: 1 and 3–10; ch. 12: 7, 9, and 11.
2. *A Treatise Concerning the True Original Extent and End of Civil Government,* ed. Peter Laslett, Cambridge University Press, 1967. Selections from the Second Treatise: ch. 1: 3; ch. 2: 4, 6, 7, 8, 11, and 14; ch. 3: 16, 17, 19, and 21; ch. 5: 27, 34, 36, and 51; ch. 7: 87, 88, 89, 90, and 91;

ch. 8: 95, 96, 97, 98, and 99; and ch. 9: 123, 124, 125, 126, and 127.

Page 278: Berkeley, George, *A Treatise Concerning the Principles of Human Knowledge,* ed. Howard Robinson, Oxford University Press, 1996. Selections from the Introduction and secs. 1–72 and 97–156.

Page 321: Hume, David:

1. *An Enquiry Concerning Human Understanding,* ed. Tom Beauchamp, Clarendon, 2000:
   Book 1: Sec. 1, 1–3, 4, 8, and 10:
   Sec. II: 11–17 (complete); Sec. III: 18–19 (complete); and Sec. IV: 20–25 and 27–33; Sec. V: 34–45 (complete); Sec. VI: 46–47 (complete); Sec. VII: 48–61 (complete); Sec. VIII: 63–66, 69, and 71–77; and Sec. XI: 118–23 and 132.
2. *A Treatise of Human Nature,* ed. L. A. Selby-Bigge, Clarendon Press, 1973: Part 1, sec. 1, sec. 2; Part IV, 187–95, 198–99, 209, 211, 251–53, and 259–60; Conclusion: 265, 268–69; Appendix: 633–36.

SECTION IV:
ENLIGHTENMENT PHILOSOPHERS

Page 374: Voltaire, François, *Philosophical Dictionary,* trans. Peter Gay, Basic Books, 1962; selections from the entries: Ame (Soul), Baptism, Equality, Enfer (Hell), Fanaticism, Guerre (War), Du Juste et de L'Injuste (of Right and Wrong), Morality, Religion, Superstition, and Tolerance.

Page 379: Rousseau, Jean-Jacques, *The Social Contract,* ed. G. D. H. Cole, J. M. Dent and Sons, London, 1973, selections from Book I, chs. 1, 2, 3, 4, 6, 7, and 8; and Book II, chs. 1, 2, 3, 4, and 6.

Page 389: Kant, Immanuel:

1. *Critique of Pure Reason,* trans. Norman Kemp-Smith, MacMillan Press, 1975: Selections from Preface to the Second Edition; Introduction; Transcendental Aesthetic: secs. §1–3 and §6–7; Transcendental Logic: I; Analytic of Concepts, ch. 1 and secs. §9 and 10; Transcendental Deduction B edition §13, §15–22; §24 and §26; Analytic of Principles, ch. 1: the Schematism; System of the Principles of Pure Understanding, sec. 3; First Analogy; Second Analogy; Refutation of Idealism; Analytic of Principles ch. 3 (Phenomena and Noumena); Transcendental Dialectic: Book 1 ch. 1, Secs. 1–3; Book 2, ch. 1: Paralogisms of Pure Reason (B edition); Book II ch. 2 Antinomy of Pure Reason: Secs. 1, 2, 6, 7, and 9; Book II ch. 3, The Transcendental Ideal, Secs. 2 and 3; and Appendix to the Transcendental Dialectic.
2. *Groundwork of the Metaphysic of Morals,* trans. H. J. Paton, Harper & Row, 1956 from chs. 1 and 2.
3. 'What Is Enlightenment?' from *Kant: Political Writings,* ed. Hans Reis, trans. H. B. Nisbet, Cambridge University Press, 1991.

.